Social Prob

A Down-to-Earth Approach

THIRTEENTH EDITION

James M. Henslin
Southern Illinois University, Edwardsville

Executive Portfolio Manager: Jeff Marshall
Content Producer: Mary Donovan
Content Developer: Jennifer Auvil
Portfolio Manager Assistant: Heather Torres
Product Marketing Manager: Candice Madden
Sr. Field Marketing Manager: Kelly Ross
Content Producer Manager: Amber Mackey
Content Development Manager: Brooke Wilson
Art/Designer: Integra Software Services, Pvt Ltd.

Digital Studio Course Producer: Elissa Senra-Sargent
Full-Service Project Manager:
   Integra Software Services, Pvt Ltd.
Compositor: Integra Software Services, Pvt Ltd.
Printer/Binder: LSC Communications, Inc.
Cover Printer: Phoenix Color/Hagerstown
Cover Design: Jennifer Hart Design
Cover Credit: Chipstudio/ Digital Vision Vectors/
   Getty images

Acknowledgements of third party content appear on pages within the text.

Library of Congress Cataloging-in-Publication Data

Names: Henslin, James M., author.
Title: Social problems : a down-to-earth approach / James M. Henslin,
   Southern Illinois University, Edwardsville.
Description: Thirteenth edition. | New York, NY : Pearson, [2018] | Includes
   bibliographical references and index.
Identifiers: LCCN 2018058892 (print) | LCCN 2019001305 (ebook) | ISBN
   9780135257104 (ebook) | ISBN 9780135164709 (alk. paper)
Subjects: LCSH: Social problems. | Deviant behavior. | Equality. | Social
   change. | Symbolic interactionism. | United States—Social
   conditions—1980–
Classification: LCC HM585 (ebook) | LCC HM585 .H45 2018 (print) | DDC
   303.4—dc23
LC record available at https://lccn.loc.gov/2018058892

4 2022

Access Code Card
ISBN-10:   0-13-521539-0
ISBN-13: 978-0-13-521539-5

Revel Combo Card
ISBN-10:   0-13-525710-7
ISBN-13: 978-0-13-525710-4

Rental Edition
ISBN-10:   0-13-516470-2
ISBN-13: 978-0-13-516470-9

Loose-Leaf Edition
ISBN-10:   0-13-528620-4
ISBN-13: 978-0-13-528620-3

Instructor's Review Copy
ISBN-10:   0-13-525705-0
ISBN-13: 978-0-13-525705-0

Brief Contents

Contents

9 Inequalities of Gender and Sexual Orientation **251**

10 Medical Care: Physical and Mental Illness **289**

Boxed Features

The boxed inserts are one of my favorite features of the text. I especially enjoyed writing them because many focus on provocative ideas. These boxed features, which take students to the cutting edge of social problems, can be a source of stimulating class discussions.

Spotlight on Social Research

Guide to Social Maps

Social maps illustrate the old Chinese saying, "A picture is worth 10,000 words." They allow you to see at a glance how social characteristics are distributed among the 50 U.S. states or among the nations of the world. The U.S. Social Maps are a concise way of illustrating how our states compare on such factors as divorce, voting, safety, or women in the workforce. The global Social Maps show how the world's nations compare on such characteristics as income, the percentage of the elderly, and the number of large cities.

These Social Maps are unique to this text. I have produced them for you from original data. At a glance, you can see how your state compares with your region and the other states—or you can see how the United States compares with other countries. If you have suggestions for other Social Maps that you would like to see in the next edition, please let me know.

Jim Henslin

henslin@aol.com

The Social Maps

Preface

The Exciting Potential of Social Problems

Social Problems is perhaps the most exciting, enticing course in the sociological curriculum. In this course, you will focus on events of life that rivet your students' attention. You will touch on matters that elicit not only fears, but also the hope for constructing a better society. The scope of the problems reviewed in this text is equally as broad, focusing on such intensely individual topics as abortion and rape as well as on such global problems as poverty and war. You can expect emotional reactions, probing questions about causation, and discussions on how we can change our current situation. This text is designed to stimulate critical thinking and guide students in evaluating current social problems and their potential solutions.

The goal of this book is to make the study of social problems down to earth, that is, to present the analysis of social problems clearly and to show how social problems relate to the student's own life. Instructors and students alike have responded positively to this text. Instructors have commented on how the clear presentation of the sociological perspective helps their teaching, and students have written to say that this text stimulates their thinking and learning. A primary reason for this positive response is that I have personalized social problems—an approach that continues in this pleasant milestone of the 13th edition.

You can expect that this text will enliven your classroom. It will elicit emotional reactions, probing questions about causation, and discussions on how we can change our current situation. You can also expect the text to be a source of provocative discussions about major issues facing our society. The potential is that from the ideas presented in the fascinating topics of this text, your students will learn a perspective from which they can view social life and their place in it.

Here are some of the major features of this text.

Spotlight on Social Research

The thirteenth edition enhances the popular and unique feature called *Spotlight on Social Research,* in which sociologists share their personal research experiences with students. Writing specifically for *Social Problems: A Down-to-Earth Approach,* these researchers explain how they became interested in a particular social problem and how they collected their data. As they do this, they take students "into the field" with them, offering an over-the-shoulder look as they recount how they confronted and solved difficulties in their real-world study of social problems.

The authors who share their research experiences are

Chapter 2: Phyllis Moen, Discovering that the elderly are "young people who got old"

Chapter 3: Edward Laumann, Studying human sexuality—and the stigma that comes from doing this research

Chapter 5: Ruth Horowitz, Getting an insider's perspective on Chicano gangs

Chapter 5: Jim Henslin, Doing research on a serial killer

Chapter 6: William Chambliss, A personal journey into the study of crime

Chapter 7: Herbert Gans, Doing research on the exploitation of people in poverty

Chapter 8: Nazli Kibria, Studying identity problems of Asian Americans

Chapter 8: Rafael Ezekiel, How a Jew entered the world of Neo-Nazis and Klans

Chapter 9: Donna Eder, Sitting in on adolescent conversations

Chapter 9: Kirsten Dellinger, Discovering how the meaning of sexual harassment changes with work settings

Chapter 10: William Cockerham, Solving the medical mystery of unexpected deaths in Russia

Chapter 11: Cynthia and Robert Reed, Choosing not to have children

Chapter 11: Kathleen Ferraro, Gaining an unwelcome insider's view of intimate violence

Chapter 13: Robert Gottlieb, Discovering changing meanings of the environment

Chapter 14: Morten Ender, What I do as an "embedded" sociologist in the military

Scope and Coverage of the 13th Edition

Social Problems is a pleasure to teach. The fascinating and often controversial matters you will review with your students range from prostitution and pornography to inequalities of social class, race–ethnicity, and gender. Part of the pleasure of teaching this course is to experience with your students the broad range of vision these social problems encompass. At times, your students will focus on the comparative safety or danger of their own neighborhoods, while at other times their eyes will be on the changing relationships of power among the nation-states of the world. All of the problems are significant, whether they are as intensely personal as suicide and individual victimization or as broad as global stratification and capitalism.

In this text, your students will explore the vital social issues that face our nation and the world and events and conditions that influence their present and their future. Not only will your students gain a sociological understanding of these problems, but also they will be able to explore—and evaluate—their own ideas and opinions about specific social problems. As the course progresses, your students will attain greater awareness of the social forces that shape not only their orientations to social problems but also their perspectives on social life. The ideas in this book, then, can penetrate students' thinking, giving shape to a lasting sociological perspective, one they will take out of the classroom and into their everyday lives.

The Sociological Task: The Goal of Objectivity

This process of insight and self-discovery—so essential to sociology and good teaching—is one of the most rewarding aspects of teaching *Social Problems*. But teaching a class in social problems presents a special challenge because it requires objectivity in the middle of deep controversy, objectivity while examining emotion-producing topics, some of which may threaten your own values. In this text, I attempt to present both sides of controversial topics objectively. I know, of course, that it is impossible to achieve total objectivity, no matter how ardently we may desire or pursue it, but objectivity should be the hallmark of *Social Problems*. I have tried to attain it in this text.

When you turn to Chapter 1, you will immediately see this purposed attempt to bring objectivity to the text. In this opening chapter, I use abortion as a substantive issue to illustrate basic sociological principles. Beginning the text with this topic helps jump-start your course, as it places your students squarely in the middle of one of the most controversial and heated issues in the United States. This topic also brings deep-seated attitudes to the surface. Used creatively, this approach allows us to illustrate the social origin of ideas, which is essential to the objective understanding of social problems.

To determine whether I had achieved objectivity on this sensitive issue, I sent the first chapter to national officers of both pro-choice and right-to-life organizations for review. I was elated when *both sides* responded with practically the same words—that their side was represented accurately but that the text seemed "too fair" to the other side.

Within this framework of objectivity, the goal of this text is to present the major research findings on social problems, explain their theoretical interpretations, and describe clearly the underlying assumptions and implications of competing points of view. In endeavoring to reach this goal, I strive to present the most recent research on the sociology of social problems and to introduce competing views fairly. If I have been successful, your students should not only find themselves content when they read views with which they agree, but they should also attain a clear understanding of views with which they disagree. This should hold true for students of all persuasions, whether "radical," "liberal," "conservative," or anywhere in between. In short, this text can serve as a strong foundation for an exciting class.

Incorporating Theory into Your Teaching

Students often find the word *theory* to be frightening. Many expect to land squarely in the center of vague, abstract ideas, where they wander blindly in a foggy marsh. But theories don't have to be like this. Students can find theories clear and easy to understand—even enjoyable—*if* they are presented clearly and creatively. I have been pleased with how students and instructors have reacted favorably to how sociological theories are presented in this text. One of the main reasons for this favorable reaction is that I embed the theories in clarifying contexts. For example, when I first introduce the theories in Chapter 2—symbolic interactionism theory, functional theory, conflict theory, and feminist theory—I make them concrete. The topical focus of this chapter is aging, so I apply each theory to problems that the elderly confront. This makes the theories much easier to understand.

In the following chapters, I consistently apply most of the theories to *each* social problem. This approach helps give students a cohesive understanding of what otherwise might appear to be a disparate collection of events and issues. The effect is cumulative, for each new chapter allows students to broaden their understanding of these perspectives. As one reviewer said, some texts in social problems mention theory in an initial chapter and then dispense with it thereafter, but this text follows through with the "theoretical promise" of its introductory chapters.

Chapter Organization and Features

To help your students do well in this course, I use a consistent structure within each chapter. This gives your students a "road map" to guide them through each social problem, letting them know what to expect as they read the chapters. Except for the first two introductory chapters that orient students to social problems and the sociological perspective, I use the following framework to analyze each social problem:

Opening Vignette This brief opening story presents essential elements of the social problem, arousing student interest in the social problem and stimulating the desire to read more about it.

The Problem in Sociological Perspective This broad sociological background sets the stage for understanding the particular social problem.

The Scope of the Problem Presenting basic data on the extent or severity of the problem helps students grasp the problem's wider ramifications.

Looking at the Problem Theoretically These theoretical analyses of the problem or some major aspect of it generally begin on the more personal level, with symbolic interactionism theory, moving from there to functional theory and concluding with conflict theory. Feminist theory is usually presented as part of conflict theory.

Research Findings The current and classic sociological studies presented in this section, supplemented by studies from other academic disciplines, introduce students to primary research. In addition, the feature written by researchers themselves, *Spotlight on Research*, helps students understand how a researcher's personal background leads to interest in a social problem and how research on social problems is actually done.

Social Policy This focus on actions that have been taken or could be taken to try to solve the social problem highlights the assumptions on which social policies are based and the dilemmas that social policies create.

The Future of the Problem As we look at the direction a social problem is likely to take, given what we know about the problem's dimensions and trends, students get a glimpse into what lies ahead and its possible effects on their lives.

Summary and Review This succinct point-by-point summary of the main ideas in the chapter reinforces what the students are learning. Your students may find this summary helpful for review purposes, especially for refreshing their memory before a test. Some students also find it useful as a preview of the chapter, reading the summary *before* they read the chapter.

Key Terms When a term first appears in the text, it is set in bold and is defined in context.

Thinking Critically about the Chapter The questions that follow each chapter help students evaluate what they have read. Many of these questions lend themselves to stimulating class discussions.

New in This Edition

*You can assume that I have updated the topics, figures, and tables from the previous edition, so in the following list of changes I won't include these numerous updates. Instead, I will list just the *new* tables, figures, and boxes and the many *new* topics.*

Chapter 1 The number of abortions performed each year has dropped to the lowest since abortion became legal • 26 states require that a woman who seeks an abortion have a sonogram

Chapter 2 Residents of nursing homes who are given psychotropic drugs die sooner than those who do not receive them • New examples of inhumane treatment in nursing homes • About 5 million elderly in Japan suffer from dementia • Only 1 of 6,000 reaches age 100, but for every man who is a centenarian, there are *five and one half* women centenarians • About 1 of 5 million Americans becomes a supercentenarian (age 110) • The dependency ratio (workers to retired) has dropped to 3.6 to 1

Chapter 3 *Issues in Social Problems:* What Happened When Prostitution Became Legal? Problems in Knowing • *Technology and Social Problems:* Cyborg Sex Partners • Figure 3.1 Spurious Correlations • Table 3.3 Rhode Island's Rape Rates since Indoor Prostitution became Illegal • Table 3.4 Rhode Island's Gonorrhea Rates since Indoor Prostitution became Illegal • Apps connect prostitutes and customers, allowing them to negotiate prices and services • Nevada's brothels ("ranches") are ranked on the Internet • Women in their 30s and 40s are the typical customer for men selling sex to women • Adult websites have more monthly visitors than Amazon, Netflix, and Twitter combined • Under a new federal law, victims of child pornography have the right to restitution for their sexual exploitation • Chinese officials are using optical character recognition to censor the Internet

Chapter 4 *Thinking Critically about Social Problems*: Unexpected Death, The Opioid Crisis • *Thinking Critically about Social Problems:* Vaping: Cool, Fun–and Dangerous? • Figure 4.1 Opioid Crisis-Intervention Stages • Racism in Congressional hearings regarding the Chinese and opium in the late 19th century • Juuls and vaping among high school students • Most states permit the sale of marijuana for medical purposes, and others allow smoking marijuana for pleasure • Marijuana is being used to relieve chronic pain and various medical conditions, including multiple sclerosis and Parkinson's disease, but we don't know marijuana's effects on health • Continued drug violence in Mexico, including corruption of local governments by drug dealers • Profits by pharmaceutical companies are at the basis of the opioid crisis

Chapter 5 *A Global Glimpse:* When Gangs Triumph • *Thinking Critically about Social Problems:* Enough is Enough, The Social Movement to Limit Gun Ownership • Figure 5.6 Arrests for Rape, by Age • New examples of the revenge rapist • Rape victims continue to be disbelieved by the legal system • Only 28% of rape victims report their rape to the police • About 10 percent of U.S. rape victims are males • The high school shooting in Parkland, Florida • The federal government appropriated $80 million to test stored rape kits

Chapter 6 Table 6.4 U.S. Prisoners, by Race-Ethnicity • New research on in-group bias by judges in sentencing white and African American juvenile offenders • The criminogenic subculture of Wells Fargo • The public and sociologists continue to debate incapacitation and electronic monitoring of offenders • The future: implants in an offender's brain that send pain if the individual deviates from scheduled activities

Chapter 7 Figure 7.4 Income of Families by Race–Ethnicity • What happens when workers are replaced by robots and automation • How a universal basic income might work • Attacks on the Gilens-Page research that supports the power elite thesis of U.S. policy making • A revolving door between Wall Street and the White House: whether an Obama or a Trump is in the White House, you see representatives of Goldman Sachs

Chapter 8 Proposals to build a wall along the Mexican border as a divisive political issue • Data on individuals claiming two or more race-ethnicities added to Table 8.3 • One in four Native Americans dies before the age of 25, compared with the national average of one in seven • The rate of alcoholism for Native Americans is higher than the national average • Casinos continue to cause division among Native American tribes • The wealthiest tribe (the Mdewakanton Sioux of Minnesota) distributes $1 million to each adult member of the tribe each year, which erodes the incentive to go to college or to work

Chapter 9 Figure 9.2 The Five Countries with the Least Literacy • To reduce female circumcision, WHO declared an International Day of Zero Tolerance on Female Genital

Mutilation/Cutting • Female circumcision has dropped 25 percent globally • Janelle Monáe illustrates greater fluidity in gender images in music • An indicator of fundamental change: some children's books feature transgender children • In advertising, women are still more likely to be shown in the kitchen and men are twice as likely to be shown with paid work • In video games, only 8 percent of the main characters are female • Between 8 and 9 million more women than men are of voting age • The #MeToo Social Movement reveals how far reaching sexual harassment is • The case against Harvey Weinstein as a catalyst of the #MeToo movement

Chapter 10 The birth of a baby now costs 100 times more than it did in 1962 • Slight declines in life expectancy of Americans are likely linked to deaths from the country's opioid crisis • With an increase in U.S. suicide rates, experts are trying to get people to think of suicide as a social problem instead of a personal problem • The Internet, especially online discussion groups for rare diseases, has helped patients gain some control over their medical care • That people's emotional well-being is worse the lower they are on the social class ladder continues to be supported by research • Health experts fear a global outbreak of drug-resistant typhoid • Forty percent of Americans are now obese

Chapter 11 Figure 11.13 Living Arrangements of the Elderly in Old Age • The U.S. divorce rate continues to be high, but lower than its peak of 20 years ago • Cohabitation continues to increase, reaching the highest levels in our history • Couples who are comfortable financially depend less on adult children for emotional support; couples who are financially squeezed get more satisfaction from adult children • Middle-aged adults are likely to help their parents and receive satisfaction from doing so • Many adult children create *virtual intimacy* with remote elderly parents, using digital devices and technology to share pictures and maintain communication • Critics of the Middletown research point out that the researchers missed the experience of minorities

Chapter 12 54 percent of the world's people live in cities • Publicity campaigns during gentrification focus on rehabbed buildings and renewal, but more areas of the city are deteriorating than are gentrifying and property values there are declining • With African women averaging 4.7 children each, 41 percent of Africans are under the age of 15 • In 30 years, Africa' population will double from today's 1.2 billion people to 2.5 billion

Chapter 13 *Thinking Critically about Social Problems:* Social Policy and Moral Dilemmas in a Global Age • The ozone layer is repairing itself, but won't be fully healed until 2065 • As a result of the Clean Air Act of 1970, acid rain is no longer an environmental threat • Water contaminated from cooling the nuclear fuel at the Fukushima Nuclear Disaster leaks into the ocean • New outbreaks of salmonella from contaminated turkey, dried coconut, raw sprouts, chicken salad, and Kellogg's Honey Smacks cereal • Contaminated Romaine lettuce sickened 210 people and killed five from listeria • Artificial flavors used in baked goods, candy, and ice cream may contain cancer-causing chemicals • In 35 states, 160 million pounds of radioactive wastes that last thousands of years are stored in temporary containers • The United States withdrew from the Paris Climate Agreement • Brazil is building roads in the rain forest • Today's average car gets 77 percent better fuel mileage than cars did 45 years ago • Electric cars contribute to pollution from the manufacturing process and production of electricity

Chapter 14 Figure 14.1 The World's Top Ten Military Spenders • Russia's risk of war by annexing the Crimean Peninsula added to the chapter opening vignette • The United States spends $610 billion a year on national defense • The verification process for the reduction of nuclear arms, including SLBMs (submarine launched ballistic missiles), in Russia and the United States has gone well • Iran suspended its nuclear program • 19 nations have terminated their nuclear programs • 90 percent of the world's stockpiles of chemical weapons have been destroyed • The New Cold War • South Korea and the United States threatened to annihilate one another in a nuclear storm • Russian agents poisoned a former colonel in the Russian intelligence who was living in England

Suggestions for Using This Text

An author of a social problems text, as well as those who teach this course, must decide whether to begin with a more "micro" or "macro" approach to social problems. Each approach has much to recommend it. The choice in this text is to introduce the micro level and go from there to the macro level. I begin by focusing on problems of personal concern to students—issues about which they are already curious and have questions they want answered. In my teaching experience, this approach provides a compelling context for helping students become familiar with the sociological perspective and sociological theory. From there, we examine broader social problems—those whose more apparent connections to global events often make them seem more remote to students.

This is nothing more than a preference, and it is equally as logical to begin with problems that involve large-scale social change and then to wrap up the course with a focus on more individualistic problems. Instructors who wish to begin with the more macro problems can simply move Part II of this text to the end of their course. Nothing else will be affected.

Invitation for You to Respond

This text flows from years of teaching social problems, with students from diverse backgrounds. The reactions of students to my teaching have been a powerful factor in writing this text. Similarly formative has been the feedback that instructors have graciously shared. I have designed this text to help make your course more successful—so it would both challenge students' thinking and make the sociological perspective clear and readily understandable. What matters, of course, is how this text works in *your* classroom. I would appreciate your feedback—whether positive or negative—as this is one of the ways I continue to be a lifelong student of social problems and develop more effective ways of teaching students. If you would, please let me know about your classroom experience with this text. You can reach me at *henslin@aol.com*

Acknowledgments

A successful textbook depends not only on an author having the right background and skills, but also on a team of people who have the right background and skills—and who wholeheartedly support the project through its many phases. I want to acknowledge the contributions of the people I have worked with on this edition. Thanks go to Jennifer Plum Auvil for coordinating the many related items that must coalesce if a text is to appear; to Kate Cebik for looking for just the "right" photos; and to Jeff Marshall for fielding problems in the production of the text.

I am also grateful to the many instructors who have offered valuable comments during the development of *Social Problems: A Down-to-Earth Approach*. I would like to acknowledge these reviewers, too.

Reviewers

Sharon Arnold, *Lebanon Valley College*
Gary Burbridge, *Grand Rapids Community College*
Allison Camelot, *Saddleback College*
Carole A. Campbell, *California State University–Long Beach*
Cheryl Childers, *Washburn University*
Susan Claxton, *Floyd College*
Shawna Cleary, *University of Central Oklahoma*
Al Cook, *Trinity Valley Community College*
Sandra Emory, *Pensacola Junior College*
David Fasenfest, *Wayne State University*
Wayne Flake, *Eastern Arizona University*
Michael W. Flota, *Daytona Beach Community College*
David O. Friedrichs, *University of Scranton*
Michele Gigliotti, *Broward Community College*
Rosalind Gottfried, *San Joaquin Delta College*
Charles Hall, *Purdue University*
Daniel Hall, *South Puget Sound Community College*
Carl M. Hand, *Valdosta State University*
Rosa Haritos, *University of North Carolina at Chapel Hill*
Rachel Ivie, *South Plains College*
Sharon Jackson, *Fontbonne University*
Cardell Jacobson, *Brigham Young University*

Joseph F. Jones, *Portland State University*
Victor M. Kogan, *Saint Martin's College*
Rosalind Kopfstein, *Western Connecticut State University*
Wilbrod Madzura, *Normandale Community College*
Paul Magee, *North Lake College*
Marguerite Marin, *Gonzaga University*
Daniel Martorella, *Quinnipiac College*
Stephanie Medley-Rath, *Lake Land College*
Amanda Miller, *University of Central Oklahoma*
Mark Miller, *East Texas Baptist University*
John Mitrano, *Central Connecticut State University*
Sharon Erickson Nepstad, *University of Colorado–Boulder*
Kevin R. Ousley, *East Carolina University*
Lesli Overstreet, *Bridgewater State College*
Dennis L. Peck, *The University of Alabama*
Carla Pfeffer, *Purdue University North Central*
Bonni Raab, *Dominican College*
Adrian Rapp, *Lonestar College*
Richard P. Rettig, *University of Central Oklahoma*
Barbara L. Richardson, *Eastern Michigan University*
Daniel M. Roddick, *Rio Hondo College*
Edwin Rosenberg, *Appalachian State University*
Annette M. Schwabe, *Florida State University*
James P. Sikora, *Illinois Wesleyan University*
Sheryl Skaggs, *University of Texas, Dallas*
Stephen Soreff, *Boston University*
K. S. Thompson, *Northern Michigan University*
Melodie Toby, *Kean University*
Richard T. Vick, *Idaho State University*
Brian Ward, *University of Maryland*
Linda Whitman, *Johnson County Community College*
Gary Wyatt, *Emporia State University*

Authors of Supplements

I want to also thank those who have written the supplements, which help incorporate other components into the teaching experience.

I hope this text provides understanding and insight into the major problems facing our country, many of which have global ramifications—and all of which have an impact on our own lives.

Jim Henslin

James M. Henslin
Professor Emeritus
Department of Sociology
Southern Illinois University, Edwardsville

Revel™

Revel is an interactive learning environment that deeply engages students and prepares them for class. Media and assessment integrated directly within the authors' narrative lets students read, explore interactive content, and practice in one continuous learning path. Thanks to the dynamic reading experience in Revel, students come to class prepared to discuss, apply, and learn from instructors and from each other.

Revel for Social Problems: A Down-to-Earth Approach

Revel offers a fully interactive digital experience that allows students to investigate and understand social problems while using various types of interactives and assessment. These activities are directly related to the author's narrative and enhance the learning experience.

- **Hearing from the Author Audio Clips** are a new Revel feature in which Jim Henslin personalizes the content and engages the students by commenting on personal photos, graphs, and other, and topics. He also reads the opening vignettes. This feature gives students additional context for understanding more difficult topics, while the interweaving of observations and personal experiences reinforces how social problems affect us on a personal and global level. This is a hallmark of the instructional design, as Jim's goal is to make sociology "down to earth." To help students grasp the fascination of sociology, he continuously stresses sociology's relevance to their lives. As both instructors and students have commented, this helps make sociology "come alive."

- The *Pearson Original* **docuseries videos** highlight stories that exemplify and humanize the concepts covered in Sociology courses. These videos illustrate a variety of social issues and current events, bringing key topics to life for students while creating opportunities to further develop their understanding of sociology. Therefore, students not only connect with the people and stories on a personal level, but also view these stories and individuals with greater empathy all while contextualizing core course concepts. These videos are incorporated into the chapters and can also be easily accessed from the instructor's Resources folder within Revel.

- **Interactive figures and tables** feature Social Explorer technology to show data in interactive graphs with rollover information to support the data and show movement over time. Some figures utilize Social Explorer's predictive graphing, which allows students to see trends in social life and to make predictions on how these trends might continue. PowerPoint presentations with every Social Explorer Visualization can be accessed from the instructor's Resources folder within Revel.

Table 6.6 Prisoners Executed, by Race–Ethnicity

Scroll to see the rest of the table.

Year	White		African American		Native American/Asian American		Latinos		Total
	Number	Percentage	Number	Percentage	Number	Percentage	Number	Percentage	
Before the death penalty was abolished									
1930–39	827	50%	816	49%	24	1%			1,667
1940–49	490	38%	781	61%	13	1%			1,284
1950–59	336	47%	376	52%	5	1%			717
1960–69	98	51%	93	49%	0	0%			191
Totals	1,751	45%	2,066	54%	42	1%			3,859
Since the death penalty was reinstated	Number	Percentage	Number	Percentage	Number	Percentage	Number	Percentage	

Source: Based on *Sourcebook of Criminal Justice Statistics* 1998: Table 6.88; 2004: Table 6.86; 2012: Table 8.86; Death Penalty Information Center 2018.

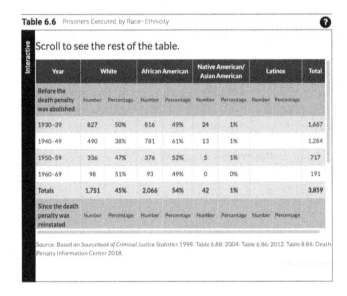

Watch: America's Opioid Crisis: Portraits of an Epidemic

AMERICA'S OPIOID CRISIS:
Portraits of an Epidemic

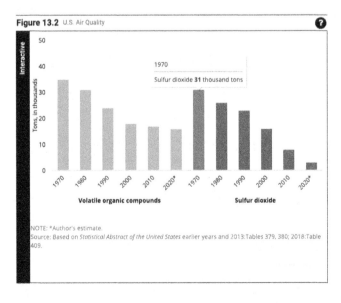

Figure 13.2 U.S. Air Quality

1970
Sulfur dioxide **31** thousand tons

Tons, in thousands

Volatile organic compounds   Sulfur dioxide

NOTE: *Author's estimate.
Source: Based on *Statistical Abstract of the United States* earlier years and 2013: Tables 379, 380; 2018: Table 409.

- **Surveys** consider their own opinions on a variety of social problems and see how their responses compare to those of other students who have taken the survey.

- **Interactive Maps** are based on the Social Maps Jim has created for *Social Problems: A Down-to-Earth Approach.* These Social Maps illustrate how social problems vary among the states and by regions of the country. Using Social Explorer, students can click through these maps. They can hover over their own state, if they want to, and consider how it compares with the rest of the country.

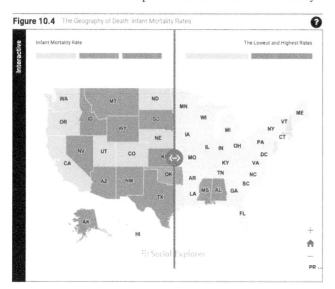

Figure 10.4 The Geography of Death: Infant Mortality Rates

- Interactive **Review the Chapter** summaries utilize flashcards that feature key terms and definitions to allow students to review and reinforce the chapter's content.

- **Assessments**, which are tied to each chapter's major sections, allow instructors and students to track progress and get immediate feedback. It is the same with the full chapter tests.

Question 1 / 5

Worth 3 points

_____ involves making judgments about others based on preexisting notions.

○ Misogyny

○ Discrimination

✕ ◉ Superiority ⟩ Consider This: These are feelings that people have about others, usually including assumptions about them even before meeting them. 8.1 Distinguish between minority and dominant groups, know the origin and goals of minority groups and the policies of dominant groups, and explain why race is a social category.

○ Prejudice

2 attempts remaining

Submit

✕ **Incorrect.** Try again.

- **Integrated Writing Opportunities** help students reason and write more clearly. Each chapter offers the following writing prompts:

- **Journal prompts** invite students to reflect on a chapter's content and to consider how social problems affect their country, communities, and personal lives.

- **Shared writing** prompts invite students to sharpen their critical thinking skills while sharing their own views and responding to each other's reactions and opinions. Students reflect on and consider issues related to the social problems highlighted in each chapter.

- **Essay prompts** are from Pearson's Writing Space, where instructors can assign both automatically graded and instructor-graded prompts. Writing Space is the best way to develop and assess concept mastery and critical thinking through writing. Writing Space provides a single place within Revel to create, track, and grade writing assignments, access writing resources, and exchange meaningful, personalized feedback quickly and easily to improve results. For students, Writing Space provides everything they need to keep up with writing assignments, access assignment guides and checklists, write or upload completed assignments, and receive grades and feedback—all in one convenient place. For educators, Writing Space makes assigning, receiving, and evaluating writing assignments easier. It's simple to create new assignments and upload relevant materials, see student progress, and receive alerts when students submit work. Writing Space helps students be more focused and effective. They also are able to express themselves with personalized feedback. Writing Space can also check students' work for improper citation or plagiarism by comparing it against the world's most accurate text comparison database available from Turnitin.

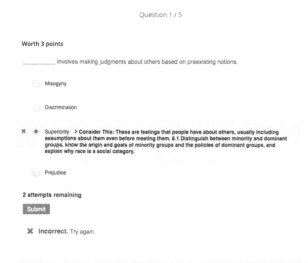

Journal 8.1: Racial-Ethnic Classifications

How do you think our racial–ethnic classifications will change in the future?

The response entered here will appear in the performance dashboard and can be viewed by your instructor.

Submit

Question

Worth 20 points

Minority groups share five characteristics: unequal treatment, distinctive traits, solidarity, membership by birth, and marriage within their own group. Pick any minority group in the United States and give examples of how these five characteristics apply to that group.

A minimum number of characters is required to post and earn points. After posting, your response can be viewed by your class and instructor, and you can participate in the class discussion.

Post   0 characters | 140 minimum

About the Author

I was born in a rented room in a little town on the bitterly cold Canadian border in Minnesota. My mother was a teenager who hadn't completed high school, and my father hadn't even made it beyond the seventh grade. Our next home, a converted garage, didn't have indoor plumbing. One of my colder memories goes back to age 10 or 11, when I froze my nose while delivering newspapers in my little northern village. I was elated at age 16 when my parents packed up the car and moved to sunny California, where I graduated from high school and junior college. During the summer following high school graduation, while working as a laborer on construction projects, I took a correspondence course in Greek from the University of California at Berkeley. Indiana was where I graduated from college. I was awarded scholarships at Washington University in St. Louis, Missouri, where I earned my master's and doctorate in sociology. After winning a competitive postdoctoral fellowship from the National Institute of Mental Health, I spent a year studying how people adjust to the suicide of a family member.

My primary interests in sociology are the sociology of everyday life, deviance, and international relations. One of my main goals in sociology is to make sociological concepts and research findings down to earth. Among my books are *Sociology: A Down-to-Earth Approach* (Allyn and Bacon), in its 14th edition, and *Essentials of Sociology: A Down-to-Earth Approach* (Allyn and Bacon), in its 12th edition. There is also *Mastering Sociology* (Allyn and Bacon), in its first edition. I have published widely in sociology journals, including *Social Problems* and *American Journal of Sociology*. The topics range from the esoteric ethnomethodological locationalities to the everyday nitty-gritty of cab drivers shooting midnight craps in St. Louis alleys.

While a graduate student, I taught at the University of Missouri at St. Louis. After completing my doctorate, I joined the faculty at Southern Illinois University, Edwardsville, where I am Professor Emeritus of Sociology. With its fascinating variety and its focus on the major issues facing the nation, Social Problems has always been a joy to teach.

What a pleasure to introduce students to the sociological context of issues that have such far-reaching effects on both their current lives and their future experiences!

I enjoy research and reading (obviously), but also fishing, kayaking, and a little weight lifting. My two favorite activities are writing and traveling. I especially enjoy visiting other cultures, even living in them. This brings me face to face with behaviors and ways of thinking that challenge my perspectives, begging me to explore why they and I view the world so differently. These cultural excursions take me beyond the standard research and make sociological principles come alive. They provide a more global context for interpreting social problems, which I am able to share with you in this text.

I am grateful to be able to live in such exciting social, technological, and geopolitical times—and to have access to portable broadband Internet while I pursue my sociological imagination.

A Note from the Publisher on Supplements

Supplements

Make more time for your students with instructor resources that offer effective learning assessments and classroom engagement. Pearson's partnership with educators does not end with the delivery of course materials; Pearson is there with you on the first day of class and beyond. A dedicated team of local Pearson representatives will work with you to not only choose course materials but also integrate them into your class and assess their effectiveness. Our goal is your goal—to improve instruction with each semester.

Pearson is pleased to offer the following resources to qualified adopters of *Social Problems: A Down-to-Earth Approach*. Several of these supplements are available to instantly download from Revel or on the Instructor Resource Center (IRC); please visit the IRC at **www.pearson-highered.com/irc** to register for access.

- **TEST BANK** Evaluate learning at every level. Reviewed for clarity and accuracy by author, James M. Henslin, the Test Bank measures this material's learning objectives with multiple-choice and essay questions. You can easily customize the assessment to work in any major learning management system and to match what is covered in your course. Word, BlackBoard, and WebCT versions are available on the IRC, and Respondus versions are available on request from **www.respondus.com**.

- **PEARSON MYTEST** This powerful assessment generation program includes all of the questions in the Test Bank. Quizzes and exams can be easily authored and saved online, and then printed for classroom use, giving you ultimate flexibility to manage assessments anytime and anywhere. To learn more, visit **www.pearsonhighered.com/mytest**.

- **INSTRUCTOR'S RESOURCE MANUAL** Create a comprehensive road map for teaching classroom, online, or hybrid courses. Designed for new and experienced instructors, the Instructor's Resource Manual includes a chapter overview, learning objectives, chapter outline, lecture suggestions, activities for in or out of class, discussion questions, suggested short and long assignments, suggested films/TV shows, readings, and websites, as well as a Revel features section. Available within Revel and on the IRC.

- **POWERPOINTS** in order to support varied teaching styles while making it easy to incorporate dynamic Revel features in class, two sets of PowerPoint presentations are available for this edition: (1) A set of accessible lecture PowerPoint slides outlines each chapter of the text. (2) An additional set of the lecture PowerPoint slides includes LiveSlides, which link to each Social Explorer data visualization and interactive map within the Revel product. These presentations are available to adopters in electronic formats at the Instructor's Resource Center (www.pearsonhighered.com/irc) or in the Instructor's Resources folder within the Revel product.

Chapter 1
How Sociologists View Social Problems: The Abortion Dilemma

Alex Milan Tracy/SIPA/AP Images

Learning Objectives

After reading this chapter, you should be able to:

1.1 Understand the sociological imagination (sociological perspective) and explain the difference between personal and social problems.

1.2 Explain the significance of social location and explain why sociologists can use social location to predict *group* behavior but not *individual* behavior.

1.3 Explain why a social problem consists of both objective conditions and subjective concerns and why social problems are relative.

1.4 Identify the four stages through which social problems evolve.

1.5 Describe the contributions that sociologists can make in studying social problems.

1.6 Explain why common sense is not adequate to understand social problems.

1.7 Understand the four basic research designs and research methods that sociologists use to study social problems.

1.8 Summarize the disagreement in sociology regarding whether or not sociologists should choose sides.

Lisa felt desperate. The argument with her grandmother seemed to have gone on forever, and they both were now at their wits' end.

"You don't know what you're doing, Lisa. You're taking the life of an innocent baby!" her grandmother said once again.

"You're wrong! There's only one life involved here—mine!" said Lisa. "I told you. It's my body and my life. I've worked too hard for that manager's job to let a pregnancy ruin everything."

"But Lisa, you have a new responsibility—to the baby."

"But you don't understand! It's not a baby!"

"Of course, you're carrying a baby. What do you think it is, a puppy?"

"You're being ridiculous! You're trying to judge my life by your standards. You never wanted a career. All you ever wanted was to raise a family."

"That's not the point," her grandmother pressed. "You're carrying a baby, and now you want to kill it."

"How can you talk like that? This is just a medical procedure—like when you had your appendix taken out."

"I can't believe my own granddaughter is saying that killing a baby is like taking out an appendix!"

Lisa and her grandmother look at each other, knowing they are worlds apart. They both begin to cry inside.

> ## "But you don't understand! It's not a baby!"

The Sociological Imagination

1.1   Understand the sociological imagination (sociological perspective) and explain the difference between personal and social problems.

Like Lisa and her grandmother, when we are confronted with problems, we usually view them in highly personal—and often emotional—terms. Our perspective is usually limited to our immediate surroundings. With our eyes focused on things that are close to us, the larger social forces recede from view. Yet it is these broader social patterns that shape the problems we experience. In this text, you will learn how to connect your personal life with the larger social context. You will also understand how social problems develop and how we might be able to solve them.

What Is the Sociological Imagination?

One of the goals of this text is to help you develop your **sociological imagination** (also called the *sociological perspective*). This term, coined by sociologist C. Wright Mills, refers to looking at people's actions and attitudes in the context of the social forces that shape them. As Mills (1959b) said, to understand our experiences in life, we must understand our historical period and the social forces that are sweeping the time in which we live.

Another way of saying this is that we want to understand how our **personal troubles** (the problems we experience) are connected to the broader conditions of our society. As with Lisa and her grandmother, for example, attitudes toward abortion don't "come out of nowhere." These attitudes arise from conditions in society: in this case, technology (birth control and surgical techniques), gender (ideas about how women and men should relate to one another), and the law (abortion being legal or illegal). Change these conditions, and ideas about abortion will change.

As we apply the sociological imagination in this text, you will discover how forces greater than yourself set the stage for the personal troubles that you experience.

Applying the Sociological Imagination to Personal Troubles

To better understand the connection between personal troubles and historical change, let's apply the sociological imagination to Lisa and her grandmother. This means that we want to examine the larger context that shaped their views about abortion. When

Lisa's grandmother was growing up, marriage and motherhood were considered a woman's destiny, her purpose in life. Without them, a woman was considered incomplete. At this time, careers for women were an interlude between completing education and marriage. Abortion was illegal, and almost everyone agreed that abortion was murder. Some women who had abortions were taken to their destination blindfolded in a taxi. They endured unsanitary surgery, risking postoperative infection and death.

Lisa grew up in a different society. To be sure, it was the same society geographically, but not socially. Lisa learned different ideas about herself and her place in life. The women's movement had transformed ideas about women's education, career, marriage, and motherhood. It had also changed women's ideas about the choices they could make about their bodies, including the right to terminate a pregnancy. Some say that a woman's right in this area is absolute: She can choose to have an abortion at any point in her pregnancy, even if she is 9 months along. If married, she does not even have to let her husband know about it.

Neither Lisa nor her grandmother saw this finely woven net that had been cast over them, one that was turning their lives upside down, making them confront one another like opponents instead of the close friends they are.

You and I are like Lisa and her grandmother. Although the winds of social change affect what we think and feel and what we do, we tend to see life from a close-up perspective—the immediate things that are affecting us. In contrast, the sociological imagination (also called the **sociological perspective**) invites us to place our focus on the social context, to see how broader forces shape or influence our ideas and actions, even our attitudes and emotions.

Our social context, which has such remarkable influence on us, has three levels: the broad, the narrow, and the intimate. The *broad* social context includes historical and current events such as war and peace, economic booms and busts, depression and prosperity. The *narrow* social context includes our gender, race–ethnicity, religion, and social class. The *intimate* social context refers to our relationships with family, friends, or coworkers. These are not just abstract ideas, things irrelevant to your life. Rather, these three levels merge into a powerful force that shapes the way you look at life.

Social Location

1.2   **Explain the significance of social location and explain why sociologists can use social location to predict *group* behavior but not *individual* behavior.**

The term **social location** refers to where you are located in society. It includes, of course, physical places, such as your neighborhood and city and where you go to school. But social location also refers to what your family and friends are like and to your personal characteristics, such as your education, age, sex, race–ethnicity, and marital status.

The Significance of Social Location

Few of us know how significant our social location is. We are aware that we have a social location and that it has an impact on our lives, of course, but our awareness is foggy. We are so caught up in the immediate present—the things that we have to do to get through everyday life—that the impact of our social location becomes practically invisible. Yet our social location influences almost all aspects of our lives. For example, if you are a woman, social location even influences whether or not you will have an abortion.

You might think that I am exaggerating to make a sociological point, but I'm not. Look at Table 1.1, and you will see the differences in abortion by age, race–ethnicity, marital status, and length of pregnancy. Look at age: Women in their early 20s are the most likely to have abortions. You can see how much lower the rate of abortion is before the early 20s and how sharply it drops after this age. Now look at the influence of race–ethnicity. As you can see, African American women are by far the most likely to have abortions. Their rate is more than three times that of white women, more than double that of Latinas. Another striking difference—one that cuts across both age and race–ethnicity—is marital status: You can see that almost all women who have abortions are unmarried. You can also see that most abortions take place before the 9th week of pregnancy, and that close to half of the women who have an abortion have had one, or more, before.

Table 1.1 Who Has Abortions?

Abortions	Number of Abortions	Percentage of All Abortions	Abortion Rate per 1,000 Women[1]
Total Abortions	**653,000**	**100%**	**16**
Age			
Under 15	1,600	0.3%	0.5
15–19	54,100	10.4%	7.5
20–24	166,400	32.2%	21.3
25–29	138,100	26.7%	18.4
30–34	88,600	17.1%	11.9
35–39	50,000	9.7%	7.2
40 and over	18,700	3.6%	2.6
Race–Ethnicity			
Whites	149,400	38.0%	7.5
African Americans	141,800	36.0%	26.6
Latinas	72,100	18.3%	12.3
Others[2]	30,200	7.7%	13.5
Marital Status			
Married	48,200	15%	NA[3]
Unmarried	280,600	85%	NA
Length of Gestation			
Less than 9 weeks	295,200	67%	NA
9 to 13 weeks	108,000	24.6%	NA
14 to 15 weeks	14,600	3.3%	NA
16 to 17 weeks	8,800	1.9%	NA
18 to 20 weeks	8,200	1.9%	NA
21 weeks or more	5,600	1.3%	NA
Number of Prior Abortions			
None	251,100	55%	NA
1	112,300	25%	NA
2	52,800	12%	NA
3 or more	39,100	9%	NA

[1]Based on the number of women in the category.

[2]The source uses this general category to include everyone other than African Americans, Latinas, and whites.

[3]Not Available or Not Applicable.

Note: The totals in the source vary from category to category.

Source: By the author. Based on Jatlaoui et al. 2017:Tables 3,7,12,15,17,19.

Now apply this to the women on your campus who become pregnant. Can you see how much more likely they are to have an abortion if they are single than if they are married? During the first two months of pregnancy than after this point?

Predictions from Social Location: The Group, Not the Individual

It is important to emphasize that social location does *not* determine our actions. Rather, it means that people in each corner of life are surrounded by a bundle of ideas, beliefs, and expectations. As each of us grows up in our particular social location, we are exposed to influences that help shape our ideas and actions.

For example, you are of a certain race–ethnicity and age. You are also either married or single. But this does *not* mean that because of these characteristics you will do some particular thing, such as, if you are a woman and pregnant, having or not having an abortion. Social location makes a profound difference in your attitudes and actions, but in any individual case, including your own, it is impossible to know in advance the result of those influences. We can't predict that any particular woman will have an abortion. But—and this is important—as Table 1.1 makes apparent, sociologists can make predictions about *groups* because groups do follow well-traveled social avenues.

In Sum   Sociologists stress the need to use the sociological imagination (or perspective) to understand how personal troubles are related to conditions in society and to people's social location. The sociological perspective helps make us aware of how the social context—from our historical era to our smaller social locations—influences our ideas, actions, and personal troubles.

I would like to stress that the social context also shapes our views of what is or is not a social problem and of our ideas about how to solve social problems. Let's look more closely at how this shaping takes place.

What Is a Social Problem?

1.3   Explain why a social problem consists of both objective conditions and subjective concerns and why social problems are relative.

Because **social problems**—conditions in a society that a large number of people are concerned about and would like changed—are the focus of this text, it is important to understand clearly what social problems are. We might think that social problems are natural things, like hurricanes and earthquakes. But they are not. Social problems are *socially constructed*. This means that people decide if some condition of society is or is not a social problem. This will become clearer as we examine this process.

The Characteristics of Social Problems

For a social problem to exist, two characteristics *must* be present: objective conditions and subjective concerns. After reviewing these essential conditions, we will see how social problems evolve and why they are relative.

Social Problems: Objective Conditions and Subjective Concerns   Social problems have two essential components. The first is **objective conditions**, conditions of society that can be measured or experienced. With abortion, objective conditions include whether abortions are legal, who obtains them, and under what circumstances. The second essential component is **subjective concerns**, the concerns that a significant number of people (or a number of significant people) have about the objective conditions. For abortion, subjective concerns go in two directions: Some people are concerned that some women give birth to unwanted children, while others are concerned that some women terminate their pregnancies.

Because people around the world live in different cultures, they develop different ideas about life, including social problems. The differences in subjective concerns from one culture to another can be extreme, as you will see in the following *Global Glimpse.*

Social Problems Are Dynamic, Evolving   As societies change, so do people's concerns. Because social problems are built around people's concerns, this means that social problems are always evolving. Let's see how this applies to abortion. Until 1973, abortion was illegal in the United States, and any doctor who performed an abortion could be arrested and put in prison. But in that year, a significant event transformed this social problem: The U.S. Supreme Court made a landmark ruling in a case known as *Roe v. Wade.*

Here is how the Court's ruling affected the two essential elements of this social problem—its objective conditions and subjective concerns. Before 1973, the *objective conditions* were based on abortion being illegal, especially the dangerous conditions in

A Global Glimpse

Only Females Eligible: Sex-Selection Abortion in India—and the United States

"May you be the mother of a hundred sons" is the toast made to brides in India. Indians rejoice at the birth of a son, but the birth of a daughter brings them tears of sadness.

Why such a toast? In India, a son continues the family name, keeps wealth and property in the family, takes care of aged parents (the elderly have no social security), and performs the parents' funeral rites. Hinduism even teaches that a man without a son cannot achieve salvation.

A daughter, in contrast, is a liability. Men want to marry only virgins, and the parents of a daughter bear the burden of having to be on guard constantly to protect her virginity. For their daughter to marry, the parents must also pay a dowry to her husband. A common saying in India reflects the female's low status: "To bring up a daughter is like watering a neighbor's plant."

This cultural context sets the stage for female infanticide, the killing of newborn baby girls, a practice that has been common in India for thousands of years. Today, much female infanticide has been replaced by sex-selection abortion. No longer must prospective parents wait until birth to see whether their newborn baby will be a boy or girl. Prenatal tests give them an immediate answer, letting them decide now if they will abort the fetus.

And if women are reluctant to abort their female fetuses? Medical personnel have developed techniques to nudge them in the right direction. In one clinic, nurses reach under the counter where they keep the preserved fetuses of twin girls. When a woman sees these bottled fetuses, the horror of double vigilance and two dowries is often sufficient to convince her to have an abortion.

The national legislature passed a law forbidding doctors to tell would-be parents the sex of their fetuses. Physicians who violate the law can be sent to prison. One ingenious way doctors get around the law is to use a code. "Come back to see me on **M**onday" means the child will be a male, while "I'll see you this coming **F**riday" means it will be a female. The anti-daughter social context is so strong in India that an eminent physician made this public statement: "The need for a male child is an economic need in our society, and our feminists who are raising such hue and cry

Sons are greatly preferred in India, for the reasons explained in this box. You can see the joy this son is bringing his mother. In my travels in India, I have seen daughters just as loved by their mothers.

about female feticide should realize that it is better to get rid of an unwanted child than to make it suffer all its life."

How extensive is the assault on females in India? Around the world for each 100 baby girls, there are 105 baby boys. In India, for every 100 baby girls, there are 112 baby boys. Between sex-selection abortion and female infanticide, *India has 10 to 15 million fewer girls and women than it would have if these practices didn't exist*.

In an interesting twist, sex-selection abortion is coming to the United States. As U.S. demographers pored over their data, they found that immigrants from India have fewer female children than they would by chance.

Based on Wheeler 2009; Jha 2011; Nelson 2014; Gupta 2017; "Illegal Abortions..." 2018.

For Your Consideration

→ Granted the cultural situation that Indians face, do you think that Indians in poverty should practice sex-selection abortion? Why or why not?

→ Do you think that the U.S. Congress should pass a law against sex-selection abortion for Americans?

---

which most abortions took place. And the *subjective concerns?* People were upset about two main things—that women who wanted abortions could not get them and that women faced dangers from botched underground abortions.

As concerns grew that women could not have legal abortions, some people began to work to change the law. Their success turned the problem on its head: The *Roe v. Wade* decision, which made abortion legal, upset large numbers of people. Convinced that abortion is murder, these people began their own campaigns to change the law, in this case to repeal *Roe v. Wade*. Activists who favor legal abortion opposed each step these people took. We'll look more closely at this process in a moment, but at this point I simply want you to see that social problems evolve, *that they take shape as groups react to one another.*

Social Problems Are Relative   *What some view as a social problem, others see as a solution.* As you can see from how people line up on either side of the abortion issue, what people consider to be a social problem depends on their values. A **value** is a belief about whether something is good or bad. People's values contrast so sharply that some view the *Roe v. Wade* decision of 1973 as a moral victory, while others see it as a moral disaster. It is the same with other social problems. Mugging, for example, is not a social problem for muggers. Nor do Boeing and other corporations that profit from arming the world consider the billions of dollars spent on weapons to be a social problem. In the same way, nuclear power is not a social problem for the corporations that use it to generate electricity.

In the following *Issues in Social Problems*, we explore the relativity of social problems.

Issues in Social Problems

A Problem for Some Is a Solution for Others: The Relativity of Social Problems

Here is a basic sociological principle: As we interact with others—from our family and friends to people at school and work—their perspectives tend to become part of how we view life. Among these perspectives are ways we view social problems.

Our views might be firm, but they are not written in stone. Many of us think the subjective concerns we have about some social problem are the only right and reasonable way of viewing some objective condition. But from where did our views originate except from our experiences with particular groups and our exposure to certain ideas?

Just as our social locations are the source of our subjective concerns, so our views can change if our journey in life takes us to different social locations. Going to college is an example. There, we experience new groups and encounter different ideas, attitudes, and information. These experiences tug and pull at our own ideas and attitudes, reshaping them. On rare occasions, these experiences even transform our ideas and attitudes.

Keep in mind that we do not have to go to a different physical location, such as from home to college, for our subjective concerns to change. This process occurs when we are exposed to competing views and values, which can happen at home while we are reading a book, watching television, or talking to a friend.

And changes in our subjective concerns do not have to occur. When confronted with different views, we can dig in all the deeper to hold onto what we consider to be the absolute truth of reality. Or we might consider the contrasting view ridiculous and not worth considering.

This relativity of subjective concerns is central to the social problem of abortion. How do you define the status of the unborn? Is the fetus a human being, as some believe, or only a potential human, as others believe?

Let's look at the two main opposing views.

Sebastian Kaulitzki/Fotolia

How people define the unborn is the essence of how they view abortion. Look at the photo. That which is pictured here is about eleven weeks' gestation. What is it? Those on one side of the abortion controversy use terms such as "fetus" and "product of conception," while those on the other side call it a "baby."

The Fetus Is *Not* a Human Being

This is the position of most people who believe that abortion is a woman's right. "The fetus is a potential person that looks increasingly human as it develops" (NARAL Pro-Choice America). It follows, then, that abortion is not killing, but rather, a medical procedure that removes a potential person, with the emphasis on *potential*. Women should have the right to have an abortion for *any* reason. The reason might include health problems or financial pressures, but it also might be to attain goals, to limit family size, to finish school, or simply to win a promotion at work. The reason should be solely up to the woman. The state has no business limiting women's rights and should permit abortion on demand.

What Do You Think?

The Fetus *Is* a Human Being

This is the position of most people who oppose abortion. It follows, then, that abortion is murder—the killing of unborn babies, the most defenseless of all humans. How can anyone justify murdering a baby? We need to protect and nourish babies, not kill them. To say that women have a right to abortion is the equivalent of saying that women have the right to murder their children. It is not just the woman's body that is involved in a pregnancy: There are two bodies, and the other one is a baby. The exception to this concept of abortion is that rare situation when another human life, the mother's, lies in the balance. The state has no business legalizing murder, and abortion should be illegal.

What Do You Think?

Subjective concerns, although relative and evolving, are extremely important in determining how we view social problems. Look at Table 1.2. You can see that whether people view abortion as favorable or unfavorable colors the way they view everything connected with abortion. Subjective concerns about social problems, then, can sort people into such contrasting worlds that, like Lisa and her grandmother, it becomes difficult for people to communicate with one another.

Table 1.2 How People's Definitions of Abortion Affect Their Views

	THE VIEWS (DEFINITIONS) OF		
	People Who Favor Abortion	People Who Oppose Abortion	People Who Do Abortions
What Is Abortion?	A woman's right	Murder	Part of my work
What Is Aborted?	A fetus	A baby	A fetus
Who Is the Woman?	An individual exercising her rights	A mother	A client
What Is the Act of Abortion?	A service to women	Killing a baby	A medical procedure
Who Is the One Who Does the Abortion?	A skilled technician	A killer	A professional

Source: By the author. Modified from Roe, Kathleen M. "Private Troubles and Public Issues: Providing Abortion Amid Competing Definitions." *Social Science and Medicine*, 29, 10, 1989:1191–1198.

Competing Views As you know, our pluralistic society is filled with competing, contrasting, and conflicting groups. This variety certainly makes life interesting, as it means that we are exposed to competing, contrasting, and conflicting views of life. But in our dynamic world where some groups fiercely promote their particular ideas and values, whose definition of a social problem wins? The answer centers on **power**, the ability to get your way despite resistance.

After abortion became legal, most observers assumed that because the opponents of abortion had lost, they would quietly fade away. What a naïve assumption this turned out to be. Feelings were so strong that groups that had been hostile to one another for centuries, such as Roman Catholics and Baptists, began to work together to try to stop abortion. Shocked at what they considered the killing of babies, they took to the streets and to the courts, fighting battle after battle over this issue.

These, then, are central characteristics of social problems: objective conditions, subjective concerns, change, relativity, and competing views. Let's see how these fascinating characteristics of social problems help us to understand how abortion became a social problem.

The Natural History of Social Problems: Four Stages

1.4 Identify the four stages through which social problems evolve.

Social problems go through four stages, called *the natural history of social problems*. To illustrate this process, we will look at abortion in the United States. To do so, we need to stress again that abortion used to be illegal in all fifty states. Abortion was allowed only under special circumstances, such as when pregnancy endangered the mother's life.

To see how this changed, we need to go back to an outbreak of German measles that hit Hawaii in 1964 and 1965. During this time, many obstetricians aborted fetuses to prevent them from being born with deformities. This was a turning point for Hawaii's physicians. They began to change their views on abortion, and the rate of abortion in Hawaii never fell back to its pre-1964 level. In 1970, Hawaii changed its law, making abortion a private, noncriminal act.

Now that we've set this brief background, we can trace the natural history of abortion as a social problem in the United States. For a summary of the four stages of social problems, look at Table 1.3.

Table 1.3 The Four Stages of Social Problems

1. The Beginning: Pressures for Change
Defining the problem
Emergence of leaders
Initial organization
2. The Official Response
Reactions to the growing pressure
Reprisal, condemnation, accommodation, cooptation
3. Reacting to the Official Response
Taking sides
Acts of approval and disapproval
Further divisions of dissident elements
4. Alternative Strategies
Continuing controversy
New strategies to overcome the opposition

Source: By the author.

Before we look at these four stages in detail, it is important to note that our society is marked by unrest and agitation about numerous matters, but very few of these issues turn into social problems. Most remain diffuse matters of discontent. Around some social issues, however, social movements develop. The trigger that sometimes launches a social movement is a dramatic event that captures the imagination, desires, or discontent of large numbers of people. Following a precipitating incident, decades of simmering discontent can erupt in sudden and violent acts of rage, which burn out, with no social movement. Or a simmering discontent that goes back decades can lead to an ongoing social movement, as with abortion in the United States. What often transforms these emotions into a dynamic force for change is organizing of some sort.

Let's look at these stages:

The First Stage: Defining the Problem, the Emergence of Leaders, and Beginning to Organize

As we begin with the earliest stage of a social problem, we'll pick up events in Hawaii, and go from there.

Defining the Problem As you have just seen, for a social problem to come into being, people have to become upset about some objective condition in society. This concern involves a shift in outlook, a questioning of something that people had taken for granted. This change in perspective often comes about when values change, making an old, established pattern no longer look the same. This is what happened with abortion. The 1960s were a period of turmoil that brought wrenching social change to the United States. Young people—primarily teenagers and those in their 20s—began to challenge long-established values. The women's movement was especially significant, encouraging women to speak out and demand equality. Within this agitational and supportive context, many women decided that they should not have to break the law to terminate a pregnancy—that they had the right to safe, legal abortions.

The Emergence of Leaders As people discussed their concerns about abortion being illegal, leaders emerged who helped to crystallize the issues. In Hawaii, Vincent Yano, a Roman Catholic state senator and the father of 10, took the public stage. He argued that if abortion were a sin, it would be better to have no abortion law than to have one that allowed it under certain circumstances (Steinhoff and Diamond 1977). This reasoning allowed Yano to maintain his religious opposition to abortion while favoring the repeal of Hawaii's law against abortion.

Organizing around the Issue Another leader emerged: Joan Hayes, a former Washington lobbyist. She went even further, arguing that the major issue was the right of pregnant women to choose whether or not to have a baby. Hayes used the media effectively. Concentrating on influential people, she organized leaders in medicine, business, labor, politics, religion, education, and the media. Focusing on women's choice, she aroused public support for her position.

The Second Stage: Crafting an Official Response

It is important to stress that the stages of a social problem don't have neat boundaries. The edges are blurry, and the stages overlap. In the years before Hawaii changed its law, legislators had introduced several bills to soften the state's abortion law. These bills were not passed, but since their purpose was to broaden the circumstances under which abortion would be permitted, they were attempts to redefine abortion. You can see that the first stage of defining the social problem and the second stage of developing an official response to it were intertwined.

The turning point in Hawaii came when Senator Yano announced that he would support the repeal of the abortion law. This stimulated other official responses from organizations such as the Chamber of Commerce and the Roman Catholic Church. Public forums and legislative hearings were then held, which generated huge amounts of publicity. This publicity served as a vital bridge between the passive public at large and the leaders who were advocating repeal of Hawaii's abortion law. As Hawaiians became keenly aware of the abortion issue, polls showed that most favored repealing the law. In 1970, Hawaii did just that.

The Third Stage: Reacting to the Official Response

An official response to a social problem certainly does not mean the end of a social problem. Some will be disappointed and angry at the official response, giving them new reason to continue their struggle.

Invigorating Activists and Stimulating Change Official responses can invigorate activists, and this is just what happened with abortion. In 1973, the U.S. Supreme Court agreed with the Hawaiian legislation and struck down all state laws that prohibited abortion. Incensed by what they saw as legalized murder, antiabortion groups held protests, trying to swing public opinion to their side.

Besides inspiring new opposition, an official response can also stimulate efforts to bring about even more change. In this case, those who had fought to strike down the abortion laws were also dissatisfied: Their Supreme Court victory fell short of what they wanted. It was still difficult for women to obtain abortions, as most U.S. counties did not have facilities to perform them. To solve this, proabortion groups began to promote the development of abortion clinics around the country.

Figure 1.1 shows the success of their efforts. In 1973, the first year of legal abortion, 745,000 abortions were performed. This number climbed quickly to one million, then to a

Figure 1.1 Number of Abortions and Live Births

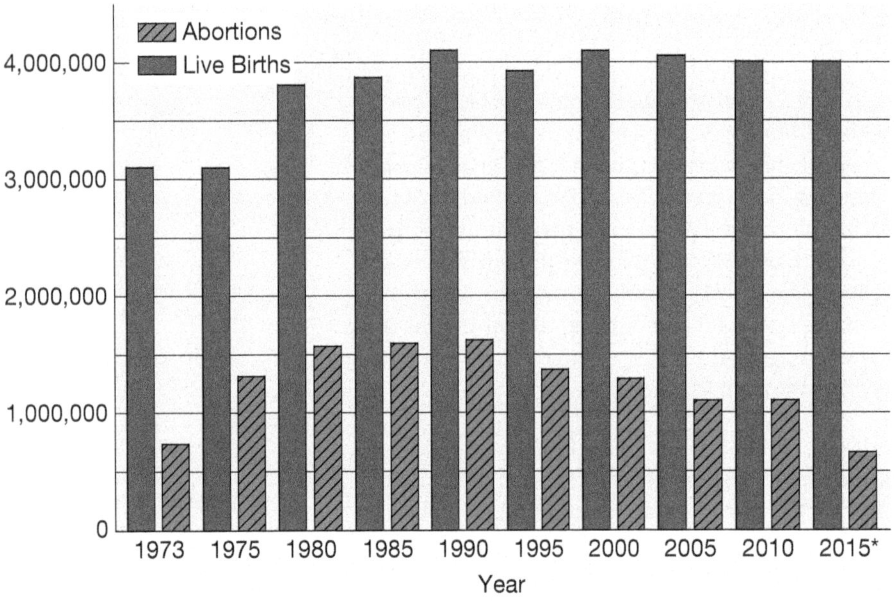

*The latest year available.

Sources: By the author. Based on Jatlaoui et al. 2017 (see Above); Jones and Jerman 2017 (Jones, Rachel K., and Jenna Jerman. "Abortion Incidence and Service Availability in the United States, 2014." *Perspectives on Sexual and Reproductive Health*, 49 (1), 2017.); *Statistical Abstract of the United States* 2003:Tables 83,95,104; 2014:Table 109; 2018:Table 81; CDC 2018j.

million and a half, where it reached a plateau. In 1995, the total began to drop, and now, at 638,000, it is the lowest since abortion became legal.

Figure 1.2 gives us another overview of abortion. From this figure, you can see that the number of abortions per live births climbed sharply after abortion was legalized. After plateauing for about 10 years, the number of abortions then began to drop, which it has done steadily since then. Today, for every 100 live births there are 19 abortions, the lowest ratio since data were collected on abortion.

A Note on Terms Before we look at the fourth stage of social problems, it is good for us to pause and consider terms. Terms are always significant, but especially so when we deal with sensitive matters. You probably noticed that I just used the term *proabortion* to refer to those who favor the legal right to abortion and *antiabortion* to refer to those who

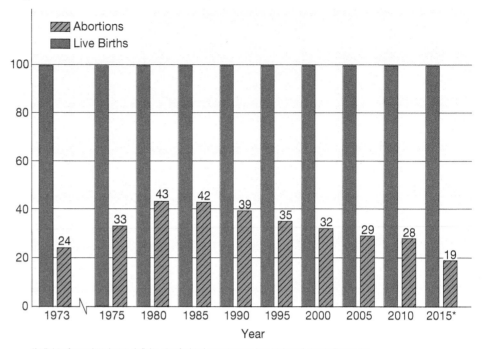

Figure 1.2 Number of Abortions per 100 Live Births

*In light of growing, huge deficits, the federal government has reduced expenditures on gathering, analyzing, and reporting statistics. I regret that 2015 is currently the latest year available.

Sources: By the author. *Statistical Abstract of the United States* 1988: Tables 81,103; 2014:Table 98; 2016: Table 86, 110; Centres for Disease Prevention and control, 2016d; Based on *Statistical Abstract of the United States* 1988:Tables 81,103; 2014:Table 98; 2018:Table 85; CDC 2018j.

oppose this legal right. (The longer terms would be *pro-legal-abortion* and *anti-legal-abortion*.) I am going to avoid the terms *pro-choice* and *pro-life,* which are used by advocates on each side of this social problem, because they represent one-sided, hardened attitudes and positions. (As discussed in the Preface, neither side involved in the abortion issue prefers the terms I have chosen.) If I have succeeded in my intentions, even if you do not like the terms I have chosen, whether you favor the legal right to abortion or oppose it, you will feel that I am providing a balanced presentation of your view.

The Fourth Stage:
Developing Alternative Strategies

The millions of legal abortions that took place after the Supreme Court's landmark 1973 ruling led to pitched battles in a controversy that is still with us today, especially evident when a vacancy occurs in the U.S. Supreme court. Let's look at some of the alternative strategies that the pro- and antiabortion groups use to promote their positions.

Alternative Strategies of the Antiabortionists After the Supreme Court made its *Roe v. Wade* decision in 1973, antiabortion groups began to try to persuade Congress to restrict abortion. They first succeeded in eliminating federal funding of abortions for military personnel and their dependents, federal prisoners, and workers with the Peace Corps. Their major victory on the federal level also took place early: In 1976, they persuaded Congress to pass the Hyde Amendment, which prohibits Medicaid funding for abortions unless the woman's life is in imminent danger. A more recent victory is on the state level, getting 26 states to require that a woman who seeks an abortion have a sonogram (Talbot 2017). The goal is for women to change their minds when they see the fetus moving.

The antiabortion groups also established "crisis pregnancy centers." Women who call "pregnancy hotlines" (sometimes called life lines or birth lines) are offered free pregnancy testing. If the test shows that a woman is pregnant, she is directed to counselors who encourage her to give birth. The counselors inform her about fetal development and point her to sources of financial aid and social support during pregnancy. They also advise women on how to find adoptive parents or how to obtain financial support after the birth. Some activists also operate maternity homes and provide adoption services.

Strategies of Moderates   We can classify antiabortionists as moderates or radicals, depending on the techniques they use to support their views. The strategies that moderates choose are mild, such as forwarding e-mail to their friends, running newspaper ads, writing their representatives, posting blogs, and operating Internet sites. As speakers at conferences, the moderates feature women who have had abortions, but who regret their decision. Taking their cue from the civil rights movement of the 1950s, in the years after *Roe v. Wade* many practiced passive resistance to laws they considered unjust. Lying immobile in front of abortion clinics, they would go limp as the police carried them to jail. The battle grew fierce, and arrests of abortion protesters became a regular part of the nightly news. After the U.S. Supreme Court ruled that it was legal to restrict demonstrations at clinics and the homes of clinic staff, however, this tactic practically disappeared. Although the Supreme Court ruled in 2014 that some restrictions violate the right of free speech, confrontations have been few.

Strategies of Radicals   To try to stop abortions, radical activists choose more extreme methods. Some have thrown blood on the walls of abortion clinics, unplugged abortion equipment, jammed clinic doors with superglue, and set off stink bombs. Others have called women who had abortions and played recordings of babies screaming. Radical activists have burned and bombed abortion clinics and killed eleven people, including abortion doctors (Cruz 2018). In the town in which I taught, Edwardsville, Illinois, radicals kidnapped a physician and threatened his life if he did not shut down his abortion clinics. These extreme acts have been condemned by both proabortionists and antiabortionists alike.

Alternative Strategies of the Proabortionists   Proabortion groups see the right to choose abortion as central to women's freedom from the dominance of men. One of their alternative strategies is to stress how dangerous it used to be for women to have abortions. They use the stories of women who had abortions when it was back-alley business—blindfolded in taxis, taken to unknown destinations, and kitchen table abortions with unclean instruments–to warn the public about what it would be like if the courts take away women's legal right to abortion. Their ultimate message is that thousands of women will die from underground abortions if it does not remain legal.

Like Lisa and her grandmother in the chapter's opening vignette, why might this grandmother and granddaughter have different opinions about abortion? Both were born and raised in the United States. What does it mean to say they grew up in different societies?

Central to the efforts of the proabortionists is protecting *Roe v. Wade*. They work tirelessly to prevent the antiabortionists from chipping away at the ruling. They fear that *Roe* might be overturned, and one counterattack, so far unsuccessful, is to try to get the right to abortion written into state constitutions.

Making Mutual Accusations Each side follows the same key strategy: pointing a finger at the other. As each side promotes its own point of view, it paints the other as grotesque, uncaring, even evil. Proabortionists accuse antiabortionists of being concerned about fetuses but not about pregnant women. They also point to the killing of physicians as evidence of hypocrisy—people who say they stand for life killing others. For their part, anti-abortionists accuse proabortionists of suppressing information about the health risks of abortion—and of murdering unborn children.

The Controversy Continues: The Supreme Court after *Roe v. Wade*. In the abortion debate, the U.S. Supreme Court remains the final arbiter. If either side on this issue succeeds in getting a law passed, the Supreme Court decides whether that law is constitutional. Consequently, each side uses the same key alternative strategy, trying to influence whom the president nominates to fill vacancies on the Supreme Court and how the Senate votes on them. For the past four decades, U.S. presidents have taken strong positions on abortion and have proposed nominees for the Supreme Court who reflect their position. We can expect this stacking of the Court to continue.

Three Supreme Court rulings since the 1973 *Roe v. Wade* decision are especially significant. The first is *Webster v. Reproductive Services* (1989). In this ruling, the Court concluded that the states have no obligation to finance abortion. Individual states can ban abortions at state hospitals and refuse to fund counseling services for women who are considering abortion.

The second significant decision is *Casey v. Planned Parenthood* (1992). In this ruling, hailed as a victory by the antiabortionists, the Supreme Court ruled that to get an abortion, women under the age of 18 must first obtain the consent of at least one parent. This ruling also requires a waiting period of 24 hours before an abortion can be performed. During this waiting period, the woman must be given materials on fetal development, as well as a list of adoption agencies in the area. In a nod to the proabortionists, the Court ruled in this same decision that a wife has no obligation to inform her husband before she has an abortion.

The third major Supreme Court decision came in 2007. In *Gonzales v. Carhart*, the Court upheld the Partial-Birth Abortion Ban that Congress had passed in 2003. This law bans a procedure in which the doctor dilates the woman's cervix, then pulls the fetus through the birth canal feet first until only the head remains inside. Using scissors or another sharp instrument, the doctor then punctures the head and compresses the skull, so it, too, can fit through the dilated cervix (Rovner 2006).

This ruling highlights the significance of terms. The proabortionists call this procedure intact dilation and extraction, a dry-sounding medical term, while the antiabortionists call it partial birth abortion, an emotionally evocative term. That Congress called its law the Partial-Birth Abortion Ban indicates the success that the antiabortion groups had in formulating this law and in this Supreme Court ruling.

The Controversy Continues: More Supreme Court Decisions As you have seen, both sides use alternative strategies, and both sides have been successful in getting laws passed that favor their position. The antiabortionists managed a stunning victory when the Supreme Court ruled on a Massachusetts law that required protestors to stay 35 feet away from women who are entering an abortion clinic. The Court said the law was unconstitutional because it infringed on the right of free speech (Kendall et al. 2014). The proabortionists also managed a stunning victory when they succeeded in getting abortion covered by the Affordable Care Act. This aroused intense opposition from several religious groups, including Baptists and Roman Catholics, as it violates their religious beliefs and conscience. So far, the Supreme Court has avoided making a ruling on this matter by sending cases back to lower courts (Feldman 2016). In coming years, the Supreme Court will continue to rule on law after law that states pass regarding abortion.

No Middle Ground The depth of feelings and convictions on *both* sides of this issue run so deeply that alternative strategies pursued by proabortionists and antiabortionists are merely skirmishes in a drawn-out war. Each side is seeking total victory, and neither is satisfied with strategies that bring anything less. What the antiabortionists want is a *Federal Right to Life Law,* a constitutional amendment that would assert that human life begins at conception. Abortion would then be officially classified as a type of murder. For their part, what the proabortionists want is a *Federal Freedom of Choice Law* that would remove all state and federal restrictions on abortion. You can see that the views and goals of abortion activists are totally incompatible.

The final results of this struggle for and against legal abortion are still unclear. On *each* side of this issue are highly motivated people who consider their view the *only* "right" way of looking at the world. Each views the other as misinformed and unreasonable. Each is rationally and emotionally dedicated to their own view of morality: One argues that the only moral course of action is to outlaw abortion because it kills babies. The other argues that the only moral course of action is to keep abortion legal because it is part of women's freedom to make decisions about their own bodies. With no middle ground to bridge this chasm, there is no end in sight to this bitter, determined struggle, and the groups are likely to continue to confront one another for some time.

The Role of Sociology in Social Problems

1.5 Describe the contributions that sociologists can make in studying social problems.

As you have seen with the example of abortion, social problems are filled with conflicting emotions, views, and values. In the midst of such turmoil, how can sociology help?

A basic human characteristic is to think of our world in personal and moral terms. In the chapter's opening vignette, for example, Lisa may think that her grandmother is narrow-minded, and her grandmother may wonder how Lisa acquired such casual morals. Most of us are convinced that our views on moral issues are right, and that people who hold contrary views are ignorant, short-sighted, and wrong. Our defenses go up when anyone questions our moral positions.

It is difficult to penetrate such self-protective attitudes and defenses, especially since they go beyond the rational and are clad in emotions. Let's see how **sociology**, the systematic and objective study of human groups, can help us see past the emotions that surround social problems.

Sociology as a Tool for Gaining an Objective Understanding of Social Problems

So how can sociology penetrate emotions and provide an objective understanding of social problems? This is a tall order, but sociology is in a unique position to do this. Let's look at five ways.

Five Contributions That Sociologists Can Make

1. *Sociologists can measure objective conditions.* In the case of abortion, sociologists can gather information on the number of abortions performed in clinics and hospitals, trends in the number of abortions and who has them, and how the states differ on making abortion accessible. They also can determine how women make their decisions to have or to not have an abortion, how women adjust to their decisions, and how their decisions affect their relationships with their husbands, boyfriends, or significant others.

2. *Sociologists can measure subjective concerns.* To determine social policies about a social problem, it is useful to know people's attitudes and views. Sociologists can also measure these. Establishing sound social policy involves more than measuring public opinion, of course, but accurate measurements can guide policy makers.

For an example, look at Table 1.4, which summarizes Americans' attitudes about the legality of abortion. I stressed earlier how significant *social location* is for people's attitudes, and here you can see how attitudes toward abortion are related to people's sex, race–ethnicity, age, education, and politics.

Table 1.4 Should Abortion Be Legal or Illegal?

A representative sample of Americans was asked if they thought abortion should be legal in all cases or in most cases, or illegal in all cases or most cases.

	Legal in All or Most Cases	Illegal in All or Most Cases
Overall Average	**57%**	**40%**
Sex		
Male	55%	42%
Female	59%	38%
Race–Ethnicity		
White	58%	40%
Black	62%	34%
Latino	50%	49%
Age		
18–29	65%	33%
30–49	59%	40%
50–64	53%	43%
65+	53%	44%
Education		
High School or Less	49%	48%
Some College	57%	40%
College Grad or More	69%	29%
Politics		
Republican	34%	65%
Democrat	75%	22%
Independent	60%	38%

Source: By the author. Based on "Public Opinion on Abortion." PEW Research Center, July 7, 2017.

3. *Sociologists can apply the sociological imagination.* Sociologists can place social problems in their broad social context. For example, people's ideas about abortion are related to their views of individual freedom and privacy, sexuality and sex roles, and when life begins. They are also related to their views of parenting, wife-husband relationships, morality, and even their ideas about God and an afterlife.
4. *Sociologists can identify possible social policies.* To address a social problem, sociologists can suggest potential courses of action for public and private agencies, educational programs, public awareness campaigns, and legal changes.
5. *Sociologists can evaluate likely consequences of social policies.* Sociologists can suggest which consequences are likely to result if some particular social policy is followed (Becker 1966). With abortion, for example, sociologists can estimate how a social policy might affect the birthrate, population growth, crime rate, and expenditures for welfare and education.

Sociology and Values That sociologists can do objective research does not mean that sociology has all the answers. Far from it. Although sociologists can identify consequences that are likely to result from social policy, we sociologists have no expertise for determining which social policy *should* be followed. Social policy is based on values, on the outcomes that people want. *Because sociology cannot dictate that one set of values is superior to another, it provides no basis for making value decisions.* We'll come back to this in a moment, but first let's consider using common sense to solve social problems.

Sociology and Common Sense

1.6 Explain why common sense is not adequate to understand social problems.

Do we really need sociological research? We use **common sense**, the ideas common to our society (or to some group within our society), to get through daily life, so why don't we just use common sense to solve social problems?

The short answer is that common sense is not adequate, as some of our ideas are built on faulty assumptions. For example, a commonsense idea is that abortion is a last resort. For some women, it is, of course, but this is not always the case. Soviet Russia provides a remarkable example. In the Soviet Union, abortion was a *major means* of birth control, and the *average* Russian woman used to have six abortions in her lifetime (Yablonsky 1981; Eberstadt 1988). The abortion rate has plummeted since the collapse of the Soviet Union, but abortion became part of the culture, and even today for every 1,000 live births Russian women have 480 abortions (Ferris-Rotman 2017).

You know, of course, from personal experience how common sense falls short. Haven't we all made assumptions about something, only to discover to our dismay or embarrassment that we were in error? We continue to learn from our failures and our successes, refining our common sense, but we know how easy it is to be mistaken in our assumptions.

Since it is easy for commonsense ideas to be wrong, we need solid research. To see how sociologists produce objective findings, let's turn to how they do their research.

Methods for Studying Social Problems

1.7 Understand the four basic research designs and research methods that sociologists use to study social problems.

When sociologists study social problems, they choose from several **research methods** (ways of doing research). Which method they select depends on three factors. The first is the question they want to investigate. Suppose, for example, that you want to find out how people form their ideas about abortion. To answer this question, you would use a different method of research than if you want to compare the abortion rates of high school dropouts and college-educated women. A second factor is the matter of practicality. You might want to do face-to-face interviews with people across the country, but you can't because you have neither enough money nor enough time. A third factor is ethics. Some methods that might yield good data are unethical. They might cause emotional harm, violate people's privacy, or be illegal.

Let's look at the methods that sociologists use to study social problems. We shall first consider how sociologists design their studies, then describe how they gather their data.

Four Basic Research Designs

Most research falls into one of four **research designs**: case studies, surveys, experiments, and field studies. Let's look at each.

Case Studies The **case study** is used to gather in-depth information on a specific situation. As the name implies, the researcher focuses on one case—an individual, an event, or even an organization such as an abortion clinic or a crisis pregnancy center. Let's suppose that you want in-depth information about how women experience abortion. You might want to learn how the women wrestle with the decision of whether to give birth or to have an abortion. Or you might want to know how women adjust after an abortion. A case study could provide this type of depth of understanding.

Surveys While case studies provide rich detail, you cannot generalize from them. They can provide remarkable insight, but if you focus on just one woman, how can you know whether her experiences are similar to those of other women? To overcome this limitation, sociologists use **surveys**. In a survey, you focus on a **sample** of the group you want to study. (Sociologists use the term **population** to refer to the target group.) Samples are intended to represent the entire group that you are studying. Done correctly, surveys allow you to **generalize** what you find—that is, you are able to apply your findings to people who belong to the group but who are not in your sample.

The best sample is a **random sample**. This is a sample in which everyone in your population has an equal chance of being included in your research. When researchers do national surveys, whether on attitudes toward abortion or anything else, they need to get information from only about 2,000 people. Yet random samples are so powerful that these surveys can accurately represent the opinions of 330 million Americans.

Experiments   Another research method is the **experiment**. If you were to use this method, you would divide people who have certain characteristics (such as Latinas between the ages of 18 and 21 who have had an abortion) into two groups. You would expose half of them to some experience (such as a video of a woman giving birth). These people are called the **experimental group**. You would do this to see how their reactions differ from those of the other half, the **control group**, those who do not view the video. How the experimental group responds is thought to be generalizable to people who share their characteristics (in this case, Latinas who have had an abortion).

Experiments are rare in the study of social problems, partly because ethics do not allow us to create problems for people. (Having a woman who has recently had an abortion watch a video of a birth is likely to cause stress.) However, you can use experiments in more limited ways. For example, you could measure attitudes toward abortion before and after listening to a lecture on abortion.

Field Studies   In **field studies** (or **participant observation**), researchers go into a setting that they want to learn more about. (This is called "going into the field.") For example, sociologists did participant observation in a hospital in Salvador, Brazil. They found that some medical personnel expressed negative attitudes toward women who were having abortions. As one young woman was being admitted to the hospital, a doctor said to her, "Who wants to see a dead fetus?" They also found that some of the women referred to their aborted fetus as "my child." The researchers conclude that the women used this term because during their pregnancy they anticipated a relationship with a future child (McCallum et al. 2016).

No other research method produces such rich detail on people's experiences.

Four Methods for Gathering Information

After selecting a research design, sociologists decide how to gather their information. They choose from four basic techniques: interviews, questionnaires, documents, and observations. Let's look at each.

Interviews   If you use an **interview**, you ask people questions on the topics that you want to explore. You can choose from two types of interviews. If you use a **structured interview**, you ask everyone the same questions (for example, "What is your relationship to the man who made you pregnant?"). If you use an **unstructured interview**, you let people talk in depth about their experiences; however, you must make certain that everyone covers certain topics (such as contraceptive history, family relations, and the reasons for the abortion).

Questionnaires   If you use the second technique, **questionnaires**, you ask people to answer a list of written questions. These can be in paper/pencil form or they can be questions on a computer program. Your questions can be either *open-ended* (people answer in their own words) or *closed-ended* (people choose from a list of prepared answers). An open-ended question might be "What is your relationship to the man who made you pregnant?" The woman would put the relationship in her own words. A closed-ended form of this question would ask the woman to check an item on a list, such as husband, life partner, boyfriend, casual acquaintance, other. It is easier to compare answers to closed-ended questions, but open-ended questions tap a richer world, eliciting comments, attitudes, and even topics that you might not anticipate.

If sociologists were to analyze what you see in this photo that I took at the Bulguksa Temple in Kyung Joo City, South Korea, they would want to know what the Buddha and the other four figures represent to the worshippers, why the people prostrate themselves in this form, and, especially, how their religious beliefs influence their lives.

Henslin, James M.

Analysis of Documents   Written sources or records, called **documents**, can also provide valuable data about social problems. You might examine official records like census data or hospital records. Or you might look at more informal records, such as journals, blogs, e-mail, and Internet discussion groups. These documents can reveal people's attitudes, opinions, and actions. They also can provide insight into how people cope with troubles.

Observation   The fourth technique, **observation**, is just what the term implies: To use it, you observe what is occurring in some setting. You watch and listen to what is taking place and record or take field notes on people's actions or what they say. You might use an audio or video recorder, but if recording will interfere with what people are doing or saying, you take notes instead, either while something occurs or afterward. If you use *overt observation*, you will identify yourself as a researcher, but if you use *covert observation*, the people in the setting will not be aware that you are studying them.

Combining Methods   As you do research, you are not limited to a single method. A common combination of methods for sociologists is participant observation, interviews, and the analysis of documents.

Striving for Accuracy and Objectivity

As sociologists strive for accuracy and objectivity, they are aware that *questions can shape answers*. Look at Table 1.5, in which we compare biased and neutral questions. The bias of the questions on the left should be obvious to you. But what is biased about number two on the antiabortion side?

Did you spot the bias in number two on the antiabortion side? To make the bias more obvious, think about the terms *father* and *baby*. These terms contain assumptions that bias the question in an antiabortion direction.

Like everyone else, those of us who are sociologists get our views of life from the groups with which we associate and the ideas to which we are exposed. This gives us opinions about what is desirable and undesirable in life, from politics to morality. These views provide ways to interpret or understand life. When they creep into our research, they are called *biases*. They can contaminate our research even without our being aware of it. Fortunately, we have a safeguard, the publication of our findings. In our articles and

Table 1.5 Bias and Objectivity in Research Questions

Biased Questions	Neutral Questions
The Antiabortion Bias	
1. What is your opinion about killing babies by abortion?	**1.** What is your opinion about abortion?
2. What is your opinion about women not having to inform the father of the baby before they have an abortion?	**2.** If a husband or boyfriend gets a woman pregnant, do you think he should be informed before the woman has an abortion?
The Proabortion Bias	
3. What is your opinion about forcing a woman to have a baby when she wants an abortion?	**3.** What is your opinion about abortion?
4. Why do you think that any man who gets a woman pregnant should have a say in the woman's choice of what to do with her own body?	**4.** If a husband or boyfriend gets a woman pregnant, do you think he should be informed before the woman has an abortion?
5. By the author.	

books, we include details on the methods we use. Other sociologists comb over our publications in detail, eager to point out any flaws they can find, including biases.

To help you better understand how sociologists do research, I asked several sociologists to share their experiences with you. The result is a feature that runs through this text called *Spotlight on Social Research*. Here is an overview of this feature:

Spotlight on Social Research

An Overview of This Feature

Sociologists do a lot of research on social problems. In fact, this is one of their favorite areas of study. As we review social problems in this text, you will be introduced to both classic and current research.

To acquaint you with researchers in social problems, 10 chapters have a boxed feature titled *Spotlight on Social Research*. Each box features a researcher who has studied a particular social problem. These boxes are unique, for the researchers themselves have written them.

The research that you will read about in *Spotlight on Social Research* is incredibly varied. With these researchers, you will visit a youth gang in Chicago, a bar in Chicago's inner city where gangsters hang out, and neo-Nazis in Detroit. You'll even be present at a Klan rally. In a study of workers at two magazines, you will learn how views of sexual harassment differ from one work setting to another. You will also learn how one sociologist became so interested in military matters that he went to Iraq. One researcher recounts how his picking beans in the fields of Washington led to a lifetime of doing research on crime. Another researcher shares how her own abuse at the hands of her husband while she was a student motivated her to do research on intimate partner violence.

"That's the worst set of opinions I've heard in my entire life."

To attain their goal of objectivity and accuracy in their research, sociologists must put away their personal opinions or biases.

© Robert Weber/The New Yorker Collection/ www.cartoonbank.com

As these researchers reflect on their studies, they pull back the curtains to let you look behind the scenes to see how research is done. To help provide a broader context for appreciating their research, I open each box by sharing a little about the researcher's background and how the researcher became interested in a particular social problem.

I think that you'll enjoy *Spotlight on Social Research*. The "inside" information that these researchers share gives a unique flavor to this text. From these reports, you will learn things about research that are not available anywhere else. I am grateful to these researchers for taking time out of their research and teaching to share their experiences with me. It was a pleasure corresponding with them and gaining insight into their work.

Should Sociologists Take Sides?

1.8 Summarize the disagreement in sociology regarding whether or not sociologists should choose sides.

Whether or not sociologists should take sides in social problems can ignite fierce debate. Let's see why.

The Issues Involved in Taking Sides

Within simple matters often lurk complex issues. This is how it is with taking sides on social problems. Let's begin with the problem of determining morality.

Sociology and Determining Morality   As I mentioned earlier, sociologists can do objective research but sociology does not provide a basis for making value judgments. Our four research methods allow us to gather objective information on social problems, but they do not reveal what attitude or social policy is "correct." Abortion, for example, is interwoven with thorny philosophical and religious issues concerning the "great questions" of life, death, morality, freedom, responsibility, and ultimate existence. Sociologists can study people's ideas about such topics, but sociology has no basis to judge whether one person's ideas are right and someone else's ideas are wrong, much less determine the ultimate meaning that may underlie their ideas.

To take a position on a social problem is to take sides—and because sociology does not equip us to make judgments about values and morality, sociology cannot tell us which side to take. Even so, the question of taking sides on social problems is debated hotly among sociologists, for, like other thoughtful people, sociologists have their own subjective concerns about social problems. Let's look at this debate.

Taking the Side of the Oppressed   Many sociologists are convinced that they have a moral obligation to take a stand on social issues. "If sociology is not useful for helping to reform society," they ask, "of what value is it?" They stress that although sociology does not provide a basis for making moral choices, it does provide sociologists the ability to relate the surface manifestations of a social problem (such as poverty) to deeper social causes (such as the control of a country's resources by the wealthy and powerful). They say that sociologists have the obligation to do their research objectively—but that they should side with those who are being hurt and exploited. Some go further than this and say that sociologists have a moral obligation to make the oppressed aware of their condition and to organize them to do battle against those who oppress them.

This view that we should take the side of the oppressed—a popular view running through sociology—does not give us a direction for taking sides in the abortion dilemma. Those who take the proabortion view would argue that they are siding with women who are hurt and exploited. But those who take the antiabortion view would argue that they are siding with the hurt and exploited unborn. We end up full circle to where we started. Again, sociology cannot provide the basis for choosing values.

Uncovering Values   To better bring these views into focus, let's assume that some sociologists have studied unmarried pregnant teenagers. After analyzing the problems that these young women face and the consequences for their children, they conclude that unmarried pregnant teenagers should have abortions. Arguments can be made for and against this position, of course, but the question is: Should sociologists promote such a point of view?

To make this issue clearer, let's consider an even more extreme case. Suppose that sociologists analyze the soaring costs of Social Security and Medicare. They become convinced that these programs are bankrupting the nation and that the solution is to euthanize the physically and mentally handicapped. Let's also assume that one of their conclusions is that all people, after celebrating their 80th birthday, should be "put to sleep" by means of painless drugs. Arguments can be made for and against this position, of course, but the question is: Should sociologists promote such a point of view?

I doubt that any sociologist would ever support any of these proposals, but I think you get the point. *Whenever someone takes any position on a social problem, values of some sort underlie that person's views.* We sociologists are no exception to this principle. We develop our values just like everyone else does. Like others, our positions are located in historically-rooted values and changing ideas of ideal reality. And like others, we, too, feel that our values, though relative and changing, somehow represent bedrock, ultimate reality.

A problem sociologists grapple with when they analyze social problems is objectivity (dispassionate analysis) versus partisanship (taking sides). When it comes to poverty, as in this photo I took in India, taking sides wins hands down.

Taking Sides: Divisions and Agreement   Besides taking sides as individuals, sociological associations such as the Society for the Study of Social Problems and the American Sociological Association sometimes take sides. Because sociologists do not all think alike, this creates divisions among the association's members. When these associations pass resolutions favoring or opposing some social action program or for or against some position of the president, the result is heated debates, usually not about the particular issue but whether or not our professional groups should take a public stand on the matter.

As mentioned, the most popular view among sociologists is that we should work toward changing society in order to help the less powerful. But this is not the only view. In contrast, some are convinced that sociology's proper role is only to investigate and to report research findings objectively. They say that if sociologists want to take sides on any issue, they should do so as private citizens, not as sociologists.

This ongoing debate keeps sociologists sensitive to the boundaries between objectivity and partisanship. Although there is little room for middle ground, most sociologists attempt to resolve this dilemma by separating research findings from their own values and opinions. What they observe and measure, they attempt to report dispassionately and to analyze as accurately as possible.

Despite their disagreements about taking sides on social problems, sociologists agree that they are in a unique position to study social problems and that they should produce thorough and objective studies. Sociologists do possess the tools to do such research, and their studies can be valuable for both the public and policy makers.

A Personal Note   I sincerely hope that this text helps you to acquire a sociological perspective that will allow you to work toward creative solutions for the pressing social problems we face. We sociologists can provide facts on objective conditions, sensitize you to the broader context that nourishes social problems, and suggest the likely consequences of particular actions. Your decisions about what should be done, however, will have to be made according to *your* values.

Summary and Review

1. Sociologists use what is called the *sociological imagination* (or perspective) to view the social problems that affect people's lives. This means that they look at how *social locations* shape people's behavior and attitudes.

2. A *social problem* is some aspect of society that large numbers of people are concerned about and would like changed. It consists of *objective conditions* (things that are measurable) and *subjective concerns* (the ideas, feelings, and attitudes that people have about those conditions). Social problems are relative—one group's solution may be another group's problem.

3. Social problems go through a natural history of four stages that often overlap: defining the problem, crafting an official response, reacting to the official response, and pursuing alternative strategies.

4. The sociological understanding of a social problem differs from a commonsense understanding because the sociological perspective (or imagination) is not based on emotions or personal values. Instead, sociologists examine how social problems affect people, view the causes of social problems as located in society rather than in individuals, and use objective methods to gather information about social problems.

5. Sociologists are able to make five contributions to the study of social problems: They can help determine the extent of a social problem, clarify people's attitudes toward social problems, apply the sociological imagination to social problems, identify potential social policies for dealing with social problems, and evaluate likely consequences of those policies.

6. To study social problems, sociologists use four major research designs: *surveys, case studies, experiments,* and *field studies*. Sociologists gather information in four basic ways: *interviews, questionnaires, analysis of documents,* and *observation*. These methods are often used in combination.

7. Because social problems can be viewed from so many vantage points, sociologists disagree on whether they should choose sides as professionals. They do agree, however, that sociological research must provide objective, accurate, and verifiable data.

Thinking Critically about Chapter 1

1. What are the differences between personal problems and social problems? Apply this distinction to abortion; to robbery.

2. If you were a sociologist and you wanted to study abortion, which research design would you use? Why?

3. Do you agree with the author's statement that science, including sociology, cannot answer questions of morality? Why or why not?

4. Do you think that sociologists have a responsibility to take sides on social problems? Why or why not?

Key Terms

case study, 16
common sense, 16
control group, 17
documents, 18
experiment, 17
experimental group, 17
field studies (or participant observation), 17
generalize, 17
interview, 17
objective conditions, 5
observation, 18
personal troubles, 2
population, 17
power, 8
questionnaires, 17

random sample, 17
research designs, 16
research methods, 16
sample, 17
social location, 3
social problems, 5
sociological imagination, 2
sociological perspective, 3
sociology, p. 14
structured interview, 17
subjective concerns, 5
surveys, 17
unstructured interview, 17
value, 7

Chapter 2
Interpreting Social Problems: Aging

Monkey Business Images/Shutterstock

Learning Objectives

After reading this chapter, you should be able to:

2.1 Explain why we need theory—how theory is related to "facts."

2.2 Explain functionalism and apply it to social problems.

2.3 Explain conflict theory and apply it to social problems.

2.4 Explain feminist theory and apply it to social problems.

2.5 Explain symbolic interactionism and apply it to social problems.

2.6 Discuss the possible generational struggle regarding the elderly.

In 1928, Charles Hart, an anthropologist working on his Ph.D., did fieldwork among the Tiwi, a pre-literate people living on an island off the northern coast of Australia. Every Tiwi belongs to a clan, and to help Hart fit in they assigned him to the bird (Jabijabui) clan. They even assigned Hart an adoptive mother, a woman Hart described as "toothless and almost blind." Hart also said that this woman was "physically revolting and mentally senile."

Toward the end of Hart's time with the Tiwi, several of the senior men of the Jabijabui clan reminded him that it was Tiwi custom to "cover up" old women who became too feeble to look after themselves. They told Hart that they had decided it was time to follow this custom for the old woman who now called Hart son and whom he now called mother. They said to prevent feuds among the clans, all the sons and brothers of an old woman had to agree to cover her up. Hart said that the woman he called "mother" was now so blind that she fell over logs, even into fires. The men said that the woman's senior clansmen agreed that she would be better out of the way. They wanted to know if Hart agreed.

> ... the men would dig a hole in the ground... put the old woman in the hole, and fill it with dirt until only the woman's head was showing

Hart already knew about the Tiwi custom of "covering up," that the men would dig a hole in the ground in some remote place, put the old woman in the hole, and fill it with dirt until only the woman's head was showing. Everyone would then leave the place. In a couple of days, when they went back to the hole, to their surprise they would discover that the old woman was dead. In Tiwi's eyes, no one had killed her. The woman had died a natural death. She simply had been too weak to lift her hands from the dirt and climb out of the hole.

Hart asked if he, as the woman's "son," would have to be present at the "covering up."

The men said that he did not have to attend the "covering up," and Hart agreed that it should be done. A week or two later, the report went around camp that his "mother" was dead. Hart put on the customary mourning accouterments and joined the other men in wailing the death of his "mother."

—Adapted from Charles William Merton Hart, Arnold R. Pilling, *The Tiwi of North Australia*, Holt McDougal, 1979, used with permission.

I don't know about you, but I was shocked when I read Hart say that he did not hesitate to agree that the old woman should be "covered up." His only concern was whether he would have to watch the woman die. In our society, too, we have people who would like to find ways to "cover up" the elderly who seem to have outlived their social usefulness. "Why spend all that money for medical care on people who have only a few years—or just a few months—more to live?" goes their reasoning. "Wouldn't we be better off ushering them off the stage of life—with dignity, of course?"

This kind of thinking sends chills down the spine of most of us. But let's suppose that programs of euthanasia were put into effect. Who would decide which old people were "socially valuable," and which were not? Would the frail elderly turn out to be just the first targets? Might others follow, those whom some officials decide are "useless"—or at least of "less value"—and for the good of the general society need to be "covered up"?

Suggesting that something like this is even possible might sound ridiculous. But, then, we must recall that the Nazis under *der Führer* developed such programs. Few human groups choose "covering up" as their solution, but every society must deal with the problem of people who grow old and frail. If you read closely, you may have noted that the Tiwi "covered up" only old women. This is an extreme example of the discrimination against females that is common throughout the world. We will return to this topic in Chapter 9. In this present chapter, we want to consider how theories help us to understand social life. As we do this, we will explore the social problem of the elderly.

Sociological Theories and Social Problems

2.1   Explain why we need theory—how theory is related to "facts."

As sociologists do research on social problems, they uncover a lot of "facts." If you have just a jumble of "facts," however, how can you understand anything? To make sense of those "facts," you have to put them in some order, so you can see how they are related to one another. To do this, sociologists use theories. A **theory** explains how two or more concepts (or "facts"), such as age and suicide, are related. A *theory*, then, gives us a framework for organizing "facts." As it does so, it provides a way of interpreting those "facts" of social life.

In this chapter, we look at three main theories that sociologists use—functionalism, conflict theory, and symbolic interactionism. Before we begin, you may want to look at an overview of these theories, which are summarized in Table 2.1. Because each theory focuses on some particular "slice" of a social problem, each provides a different perspective on the problem. As you study these theories, keep in mind that each theory is like a spotlight shining into a dark room: It illuminates only a particular part of that room. Taken together, these theories throw more light on a social problem than any one theory alone.

Table 2.1 A Summary of Sociological Theories

	Functionalism	Conflict Theory	Symbolic Interactionism
What is society?	A social system composed of parts that work together to benefit the whole	Groups competing with one another within the same social system	People's patterns of behavior; always changing
What are the key terms?	Structure Function System Equilibrium Goals	Competition Conflict Special interests Power Exploitation	Symbols Interaction Communication Meanings Definitions
What is a social problem?	The failure of some part to fulfill its function, which interferes with the smooth functioning of the system	The inevitable outcome of interest groups competing for limited resources	Whatever a group decides is a social problem is a social problem for that group
How does something become a social problem?	Some part of the system fails, usually because of rapid social change	Authority and power are used by the powerful to exploit weaker groups	One set of definitions becomes accepted; competing views are rejected

Source: By the author.

Functionalism and Social Problems

2.2   Explain functionalism and apply it to social problems.

A major theory that sociologists use to interpret social problems is **functionalism** (or *functional analysis*). Functionalists compare society to a self-adjusting machine. Each part of the machine has a **function**. When a part is working properly, it fulfills that function, and the machine hums along. Some functionalists use the analogy of the human body: A human has many organs, and when an organ is working properly, it contributes to the well-being of the person. Like the parts of a machine or the organs of a human body, society's parts also have functions. When a part is working properly, it contributes to the well-being (stability or equilibrium) of the other parts.

To see why functionalists stress that the parts of society contribute to the well-being of one another, consider health care and Social Security. Of the vast sums spent on health care for the elderly, some goes into medical research. The discoveries of medical researchers help not only the elderly but also children and adults of all ages. In the same way, Social Security brings benefits not only to the 53 million retired and disabled workers who get monthly checks, but also to the 65,000 people who work for this federal agency (*Statistical Abstract* 2018:Tables 521, 566). Their families also benefit. So do businesses across the nation, as the billions of dollars paid by Social Security work their way through the economy.

As you know, the parts of society don't always work properly. Functionalists call these failures **dysfunctions**. Dysfunctions can be minor, and soon resolved. But if dysfunctions linger, they can create problems for other parts of society. *And this is what a social problem is from the functionalist perspective—the failure of some part of society, which then interferes with society's smooth functioning.* Many dysfunctions show up when we examine the agencies that serve the elderly. Among these dysfunctions is "red tape," a term that refers to the strict regulations that make it difficult for an agency to accomplish its purposes. For example, an agency's rules can delay the benefits that people need or prevent elderly people with medical problems from receiving health care.

The Development of Functionalism

Let's turn to three people significant in the development of functionalism: Comte, Durkheim, and Merton.

Auguste Comte: Organs Working Together Functionalism has its roots in the origins of sociology. Auguste Comte (1798–1857) (called the founder of sociology because he coined the term) regarded society as similar to an animal: Just as an animal has tissues and organs that are interrelated and function together, so does society. For a society to function smoothly, its parts must be in balance.

Emile Durkheim: Normal and Abnormal States Sociologist Emile Durkheim (1858–1917) built on this idea that a society is composed of parts that perform functions. When society's parts perform the functions they are supposed to, Durkheim said, that society is in a "normal" state. When society's parts fail to perform their functions, that society is in an "abnormal" or "pathological" state. To understand society, Durkheim stressed that we must look not only at function—how each part contributes to society—but also at **structure**—how the parts of a society are related to one another.

Robert Merton: Functions and Dysfunctions In the 20th century, sociologist Robert Merton (1910–2003) dropped the idea that society is like an animal but refined functionalism's concepts. He defined functions as the beneficial consequences of people's actions. Functions can be either manifest or latent. A **manifest function** is an action *intended* to help some part of the system. For example, Social Security is intended to make life better for the elderly. Improving the quality of life of the elderly, then, is a *manifest function* of Social Security. As Merton emphasized, our actions can also have **latent functions**, consequences that help some part of the social system but were not intended for that purpose. For example, the salaries paid to the 65,000 federal employees of the Social Security Administration help to stabilize our economy. Because this beneficial consequence of Social Security was not intended, however, it is a *latent function*.

Merton (1968) stressed that human actions also have dysfunctions. These are consequences that disrupt a system's stability, making it more difficult to survive. If a part fails to meet its functions, it contributes to society's maladjustment and is part of a social problem.

Because the consequences of people's actions that disrupt a system's equilibrium usually are unintended, Merton called them **latent dysfunctions**. For example, the Social Security Administration has thousands of rules, written in incredible detail, designed to anticipate every potential situation. If the 65,000 employees of this agency were to follow each procedure exactly, the resulting red tape would interfere with their ability to serve the elderly. Because these rules are not intended to have this effect, they are latent dysfunctions.

In Sum   Functionalists sensitize us to think in terms of systems. Instead of seeing something in isolation, we need to see how it is related to other parts of the same system. As we do so, we look for both functions and dysfunctions. Let's apply these terms of functionalism to the social problem of aging.

Applying Functionalism to Social Problems

From the functionalist perspective, *society* is a social system composed of interconnected parts that function together. Each of those parts, if it is working well, contributes to the equilibrium of society. *Equilibrium* simply means that society's parts are balanced, that they are adjusted to one another. A *social problem*, then, is a condition in which some part of a society is not working well.

To explore functions and dysfunctions of our growing numbers of elderly, let's look at nursing homes.

Functions of Nursing Homes   With all the negative news and views about nursing homes, it might surprise you that we are going to look at their *functions*. Let's consider how these homes have helped society adjust to social change.

Care of the elderly used to fall primarily on women's shoulders. Because almost all women worked at home and there were few non-home settings for the elderly, the daughters, sisters, and aunts cared for the elderly at home. Then came two changes that upset this arrangement among these "parts" of society: Life expectancy increased, and more women began to work outside the home. Just as the numbers of frail elderly who needed care grew, there were fewer women available to care for them. To replace these women who would have been caretakers of family members, nursing homes were developed. Each year, 2.8 percent of Americans age 65 and over live in nursing homes (*Statistical Abstract* 2018:Tables 17, 178). Over the years, these annual totals add up, and eventually about 40 percent of all people who reach age 65 or over enter nursing homes. The elderly in nursing homes, though, are not typical of older people: Most are ill or disabled, unable to take care of themselves, and have no family. About half are age 85 and older. As you can see, nursing homes are a way that society adjusted to social change.

No stereotype does justice to the variety of the elderly. The two lifestyles represented here are likely a reflection of lifestyles followed in earlier stages of the life course. These choices also have a major impact on health, as we discuss in Chapter 10.

Africa Studio/Shutterstock

Rawpixel.com/Shutterstock

Lighthunter/Shutterstock

A common fear is that old age will bring dementia, dependence, even the lack of control over body functions.

Dysfunctions of Nursing Homes   As you know, nursing homes also have dysfunctions. Few nursing homes are pleasant places. Some people refer to them as "houses of death" or "human junkyards." Every time I have visited a nursing home, I have found it to be a depressing experience. Some stink of urine, and it is sad to see old lonely people clustered together, most of them waiting to die. After being admitted to a nursing home, most elderly people decline physically and mentally. One reason is the dehumanized way they are treated—segregated from the outside world, denied privacy, placed under rigid controls, and treated like children.

Neglect and abuse are common dysfunctions of nursing homes, but most incidents are not reported (NCEA 2018). Most neglect is minor, such as giving medications late. On a more serious level is ignoring residents who request medical attention or who need assistance in going to the bathroom. Then there is atrocious neglect:

> *A nursing home patient was sent to the hospital for the treatment of a bedsore. The hospital staff treated the condition and gave the nursing home instructions on how to keep the wound clean and dressed. Several days later, family members noticed an odor and seepage from the wound and asked that the patient be returned to the hospital. The hospital staff looked at the bandage and saw that it had not been changed as they had instructed. When the bandage was removed, insects crawled and flew out of the wound (Harris and Benson 2006:87).*

Less common is abuse, such as shouting at patients, pinching or hitting them, or sexually abusing them—or this case:

> *The daughter of an 86-year old brain-damaged woman installed a hidden camera in her mother's room. This is what the woman's caretaker told the woman before she went to sleep: "Die, die you bitch. You've got to die now" (Pedersen et al. 2018).*

Another dysfunction of nursing homes is using demeaning ways to control patients. Nursing home personnel used to tie unruly patients to chairs or to beds, where they would stay restrained all day. After investigations revealed this abuse, there was a public outcry, and nursing homes turned to "chemical straitjackets" instead, drugs such as Prozac, Risperdal, Seroquel, and Thorazine (Human Rights Watch 2018). These drugs keep patients quiet, but they can reduce people to empty shells of their former selves. Their personality disappears, and they become zombies sitting and staring into space.

Psychotropic drugs also kill, but slowly. Residents of nursing homes who are given these drugs die sooner than those who do not receive them (Human Rights Watch 2018). If the estimate that chemical restraints kill about 15,000 elderly nursing home patients a year (Hendren 2010) is anywhere near accurate, do you think that using "chemical restraints" might be a modern form of the "covering up" that the Tiwi used to practice?

Overcoming the Dysfunctions   With the public painfully aware of neglect and abuse in nursing homes, the decision to place an elderly family member in a nursing home can be agonizing. Even though an aged parent has become too sick to be cared for at home, when the adult children place a parent in a nursing home, they can feel that they are betraying love and duty. However, nursing homes don't have to be abusive places. With adequate finances, nursing homes can have well-paid, well-trained staff and be more pleasant places to live. They can be redesigned, with a kitchen and bedrooms that open onto an inviting, well furnished, shared living room.

Around the world, a major concern is what to do about the growing numbers of elderly, especially those who are frail, dependent, and sick. In the following *Global Glimpse*, we look at the severe problem that Japan is facing.

A Global Glimpse

Japan's Tidal Wave of Elderly

"Old people are tax burdens who should hurry up and die."
Taro Aso, Former Minister of Finance of Japan

A tidal wave of elderly is hitting Japan. Japan has a larger percentage of its population age 65 and over than any other country. One of every three to four Japanese is an elderly person, almost double the rate in the United States. As you can see from Table 2.2, in another generation, two of every five Japanese will be elderly.

Table 2.2 Japan's Population Age 65 and Older

1950	1975	2000	2025	2050
5%	8%	17%	30%	40%

In 1950, only 66 Japanese turned 100. Now, each year, more than 1,700 become centenarians. This kind of change, unprecedented in the history of the world, presents incredible challenges.

Think about what a deluge of elderly means for a society. How can a country's health care services handle so many old people? Already about 5 million elderly Japanese suffer from dementia, some unable to dress or feed themselves or even to go to the bathroom by themselves. Who will care for all these people? Who will pay the cost of their medical care? With more deaths than births, Japan's population is declining and its workforce is shrinking.

Let's place this question in the context of Japanese culture. As you probably know, the Japanese are taught that they owe high respect and obligations to the elderly. The Japanese believe that because parents took care of their children, the children are obligated to care for their parents. Unlike in the United States,

when Japanese get old, most of them live with their adult children. As the number of elderly mushrooms, many Japanese families are not able to carry on their traditional caregiving and protective roles.

Japan's low birthrate amidst a surging older population has led to a search for alternative workers to care for the elderly. The Japanese do not want a lot of immigrants, and in an Orwellian twist, Japanese companies are coming up with an unusual answer: Humanoids. These robots can carry and talk to patients. To keep residents of nursing homes mentally active, the robots ask riddles and quiz residents on math problems. They also can chat with residents and ask about their health.

It sounds as though the Japanese are taking innovative steps to solve its tidal wave of elderly. But beyond these solutions lies a grim reality. For three decades, Japan has been in the midst of a depression that won't let loose. Japan's federal deficits are huge and growing rapidly. While Japan's elderly population is growing, its youth population is shrinking. With the country mired in a depression and less able to compete in world markets, where will the money come from to pay for the care of the elderly?

Based on Fukue 2017; *Statistical Handbook of Japan* 2017; *Statistical Abstract of the United States* 2018:Table 1355.

For Your Consideration

→ Besides throwing up their collective hands in desperation, what do you think the Japanese can do to solve their growing problem of elderly dependence?

→ Japan is today's extreme, but many countries are destined to follow this same gerontological path of increasing numbers of elderly and a shrinking workforce. Do you think any will consider a required (but dignified, of course) death for its people at some specified age? Why or why not?

Functionalism and Social Problems: A Summary

Table 2.3 presents an overview of functionalism. As you look at this table, begin with the column marked *Action*. This column refers to actions that have taken place. The examples in this table refer to business, government, the family, and medicine, but we could include other social institutions. The column titled *Manifest Function* refers to a beneficial consequence that was intended by the action. The column titled *Latent Function* refers to a beneficial consequence of the action that was not intended. The last column, *Latent Dysfunction,* refers to an unintended harmful consequence of the action.

Remember that functionalists assume that society is like a self-adjusting machine. Functionalists examine how the parts of that machine (society or some other social system) are interrelated and how they adjust to one another. As society undergoes change, a social problem arises when some parts of society do not adjust to the change and are not functioning properly.

Table 2.3 Old Age: A Functionalist Overview

Related Parts of the Social System[1]	Action	Manifest Function	Latent Function	Latent Dysfunction
Economic (business)	Pension and retirement benefits	Provide income and leisure time for the aged	Jobs for younger workers	Displacement of the elderly; loss of self-esteem; loss of purpose
Political (government)	Social Security payments	Stable income for the aged; dignity in old age	Employment for 65,000 people by the Social Security Administration	Inadequate income; many recipients live in poverty
Family	Adult children live apart from their parents	Independence of both younger and older generations	Institutionalized care for the elderly; greater mobility of younger workers	Isolation of elderly parents; loneliness, despair, and resentment
Medical	Technological developments; gerontological specialties	People live longer and healthier lives	The elderly become more independent	The Social Security system becomes costly
	Medicare and Medicaid	Provide good health care for the elderly	Financing bonanza for the medical profession	High cost; "rip-off" nursing homes

[1]As used here, "parts" of the social system are social institutions.
Source: By the author.

Conflict Theory and Social Problems

2.3   Explain conflict theory and apply it to social problems.

"We couldn't disagree more," reply conflict theorists to the functionalist position. The parts of society do not work together harmoniously. If you look below the surface, you will see that society's parts are competing with one another for limited resources. There are only so many resources to go around, and the competition for them is so severe that conflict is barely kept in check. Whether they recognize it or not, the elderly are competing with younger people for money and health care. If the competition heats up, open conflict between the youth and the elderly could erupt, throwing society into turmoil. In short, the functionalists are wrong: The guiding principle of social life is disequilibrium and conflict, not equilibrium and harmony.

From the conflict perspective, social problems are the natural and inevitable outcome of struggle over limited resources. No matter what a social problem may look like on its surface, at its essence is conflict between groups. As the more powerful exploit society's resources, they oppress the less powerful, creating such social problems as poverty, discrimination, and war. As those who are exploited react to their oppression, other social problems emerge: street crime, escapist drug abuse, suicide, homicide, riots, revolution, and terrorism. To understand a social problem, we need to penetrate the problem's surface and expose the basic, underlying conflict.

The Development of Conflict Theory

We'll look at three people significant in the development of the conflict perspective: Marx, Simmel, and Coser.

Karl Marx: Capitalism and Conflict Karl Marx (1818–1883), the founder of **conflict theory**, witnessed the Industrial Revolution that transformed Europe. Dirty, crowded cities grew even dirtier and more crowded as farmers and laborers in poverty fled rural areas to seek work in factories. With men hungry for work, competing for the few jobs available, the new factory owners were able to pay near-starvation wages. Poverty and exploitation grew, political unrest followed, and upheaval swept across Europe.

Shocked by the suffering and inhumanity that he saw, Marx concluded that the hallmark of history is a struggle for power. In this struggle, some group always gains the top position, and, inevitably, that group oppresses the groups beneath it. Marx also concluded that a major turning point in this historical struggle occurred when **capitalism** became dominant in the Western world—that is, when a small group of people gained control over the means of production and made profit their goal. As machinery replaced workers' tools, the **capitalists** (owners of the capital, factories, and equipment) gained the power to exploit workers.

Because tens of thousands of families from farms and villages had crowded into the cities in a desperate search for work, the capitalists, who owned the means of production, were able to impose miserable working conditions. They paid workers little—sometimes only enough to buy a loaf of bread for 12 hours of work—and fired them at will. Through their money, the capitalists also controlled politicians. When workers rebelled, the capitalists could count on the police to use violence to bring the workers under control. "This misery," said Marx, "is going to lead to a bloody day of reckoning when the workers overthrow their oppressors. The workers will establish a classless society in which the goal will be not profits for the few but, rather, the good of the many."

In Marx's time, workers were at the mercy of their bosses. They lacked what some workers today take for granted—a minimum wage, eight-hour workdays, five-day work-weeks, coffee breaks, paid vacations, medical benefits, sick leave, unemployment compensation, pensions, Social Security, even the right to strike. Conflict theorists remind us that the workers who enjoy such benefits today have them not because of the generous hearts of the rich but because workers at an earlier period fought for them—sometimes to the death.

Georg Simmel: Subordinates and Superordinates Some sociologists have extended conflict theory well beyond the relations between workers and capitalists. Sociologist Georg Simmel (1858–1918), for example, compared the relationships of superordinates (people who occupy higher positions) with subordinates (those who are in lower positions). Simmel noted that a main concern of superordinates is to protect their positions of privilege. Because subordinates possess some power, however, the more powerful must take them into consideration as they make their decisions (Coser 1977). Consequently, superordinate–subordinate relationships are marked not by one-way naked power but by exchange. If employers want to reduce the benefits of a pension plan, for example, they must get unions to agree. In return, the workers will insist on a trade-off, such as increased job security.

Simmel argued that conflict also has benefits. For example, when the members of a group confront an external threat, they tend to pull together (Ellemers and Jetten 2013). War is a good example. Even some antagonistic groups shelve their differences and work together for the good of the nation. During World War II, U.S. workers gave up their right to strike, and the U.S. Justice Department asked the head of the Mafia, Lucky Luciano, to spy on dock workers. When the Russians invaded Afghanistan in 1979, clans that hated each other worked together for 10 years to repel them. The U.S. experienced the same thing in its invasion of Afghanistan.

Lewis Coser: Conflict in Social Networks Sociologist Lewis Coser (1913–2003) analyzed why conflict is likely to develop among people who have close relationships with one another. A group of friends or the members of a family, for example, are parts of a little social network in which the members have worked out expectations about their relative power, responsibilities, and rewards. These expectations are easily upset, especially when one member of the family wants a change, or even as he or she fails to do what others expect. Even here, conflict lies uneasily below the surface.

Applying Conflict Theory to Social Problems

Let's consider how conflict theory helps us to understand social problems.

Social Conflict and Social Security As we apply the conflict perspective to the elderly, let's see how Social Security came about. In this drama, the three major players are elderly workers, younger workers, and employers. A fourth, Congress, also appears. From this perspective, Congress represents the interests of the employers.

Let's start with the historical background. Because of their experience, older workers used to be prized. Before machines were at the center of production, work took a lot of skill, and it took years to develop these skills. Then came the Industrial Revolution, which turned things upside down. To make things by machinery rather than by hand didn't take much experience or skill. With young workers learning to run the machines quickly—and willing to work for less—the owners fired many of the elderly. This pushed the elderly into poverty, because in those days there was neither unemployment compensation nor Social Security. By the 1920s, *most* Americans over 65 could not support themselves (SSA 2018). In short, industrialization transformed the elderly from a productive and respected group to a deprived and humiliated group.

Then the Great Depression struck, bringing suffering to millions of elderly. In 1930, in the midst of national despair, Francis Everett Townsend, a dentist in Long Beach, California, launched and directed a huge social movement. He rallied the elderly into a political force, enrolling one-third of all Americans over 65 in his Townsend Clubs. From their new base of power, the elderly demanded "old-age pensions" (Russell 2014). Townsend's ultimate goal was for the federal government to levy a national sales tax of 2 percent to provide $200 a month for every unemployed person over 60. This is the equivalent of about $3,600 a month today. The elderly would have to spend the $200 in the month they received it, which, Townsend said, would lift the nation out of the depression.

In 1934, the Townsend Plan went before Congress. This was an election year, and Congress felt vulnerable to a grassroots revolt by older people. But Congress was caught in a bind: About 25 percent of workers were unemployed, and the country was strapped for money. Congress looked for a way out. But how could it reject the Townsend Plan without angering the clamoring crowds of elderly? Seizing the opportunity to take center stage, President Franklin Roosevelt announced his own, more modest Social Security plan in June 1934—with the first payment starting eight years later. Relieved at this way out of its bind, Congress embraced Roosevelt's proposal.

Although the Townsend Clubs did not get their plan passed, they did pressure Congress to pass Social Security. The clubs then turned to the goal of improving Social Security. Benefits were not scheduled to begin until 1942, which would leave millions of workers without support. As the Great Depression lingered, dragging even more old people into poverty, the clubs stepped up their pressure. As a result, Congress voted to begin paying Social Security benefits in 1940 and to increase the amounts paid to the destitute elderly (called old-age assistance grants).

The U.S. elderly are a potent political force today. They were not considered so until Dr. Francis Everett Townsend (pictured here) organized them as a political force in the 1930s. Townsend proposed a radical $200 per month pension plan for the elderly in the midst of the Great Depression. His plan and campaign frightened Congress.

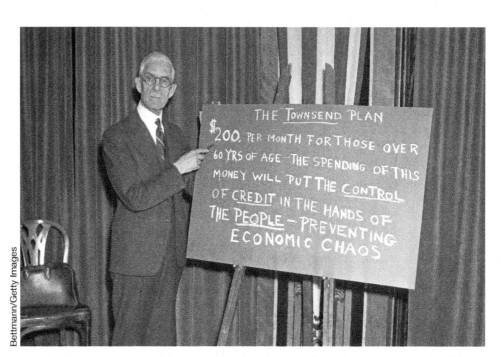

Bettmann/Getty Images

In Sum   When conflict theorists analyze a social problem, they look for how interest groups compete for scarce resources. In this example, they emphasize that today's Social Security benefits did not come from generous hearts in Congress, but from the political power of the elderly, who had banded together to push their own interests. To appease the elderly and avoid a political crisis, Congress gave in, but granted as little as it thought it could get by with. Only when the elderly stepped up the pressure did Congress increase benefits—and this but reluctantly. The elderly, however, paid dearly for their benefits: They were removed from the workforce when Congress set a mandatory retirement age of 65 (which was revoked in 1978). This, in turn, gave employers the goal they wanted: a younger, less costly workforce.

Conflict Theory and Social Problems: A Summary

It is important to understand that from the conflict perspective, there are two types of social problems.

Who Experiences the Problem?   One type of social problem is the trouble experienced by people who are exploited by the powerful. The other type is the trouble experienced by the powerful when the exploited resist, rebel, or even appeal to higher values. Although their resources are limited, the exploited do find ways to resist. Some join protest marches, go on hunger strikes, or campaign for political office. Others take up arms against those in power. As we saw with the Townsend movement, the elderly—a group weak in and of itself—were able to unite and seize the initiative during a troubled period, forcing a change to improve their circumstances.

Conflict and Social Problems   At the root of each social problem lies competition over the distribution of power and privilege. This means that social problems are inevitable, for power and privilege are limited and groups are always competing for them. Most conflict, though, is limited to political struggle, not a battle to the death. Retired Americans, for example, have not fought bloody battles in the streets, but they have formed political lobbies to compete for resources with other groups. Understanding that power and privilege lie at the root of social problems helps analysts to penetrate the surface and pinpoint what any particular social problem is all about.

Introducing Feminist Theory

2.4   **Explain feminist theory and apply it to social problems.**

In the 1970s, sociologists started to apply the conflict perspective to the relationships of women and men. From their analyses came **feminist theory**, which examines male–female relationships from the perspective of the powerful oppressing the powerless and the reactions to that oppression. Feminists go beyond studying these relationships: They also want to change them and, in so doing, to transform society. They argue, as Marx did, that the first step in bringing about fundamental change is for the oppressed to become aware of the source of their oppression. In this application of conflict theory, women must become aware of how their oppression is rooted in their relationships with men.

Just as Marx took a broad historical view as he examined the relationship of workers and employers and the control of resources, so feminist theorists have taken a broad historical view. As they examine historical relationships between women and men, they place their analytical lens on **patriarchy**, the dominance of men-as-a-group over women-as-a-group. They stress that throughout history men have had greater power than women in both public and private spheres and that men have exercised this power to control women. Feminist theorists analyze how men maintain and create boundaries and obstacles to prevent women from gaining or exercising power.

The Development of Feminist Theory

In the 1970s, *feminist theory* was an umbrella term that referred to the application of conflict theory to the relationships of women and men. The emphasis was on how men oppressed women and the need to bring about fundamental change. After severe disagreements, feminist theorists split into several branches (Bronstein 2011). Here are five of them (Code 2000; Gaard 2018).

- **Radical feminism.** The central thesis of radical feminists is that we must dismantle society in order to get rid of patriarchy. The goal of radical feminists is to free both men and women of rigid gender roles by waging war against patriarchy. This type of feminism attracts much publicity, and many people assume that this is the only kind of feminism there is.
- **Liberal feminism.** The central argument of liberal feminists is that all people deserve equal rights. Liberal feminists argue that patriarchy and oppression exist because our institutions socialize men and women into believing oppressive ideology. The ideology must be changed to emphasize equality, and any structures that foster inequality must be dismantled.
- **Socialist feminism.** Socialist feminists, the closest kin to Marx, stress that there is a direct link between capitalism and the oppression of women. The main rewards go to those who perform in the workplace, not in the home. Women's traditional work in the home is not respected because it often produces nothing tangible.
- **Cultural feminism.** Cultural feminists argue that we need to appreciate the biological differences between men and women. They claim that women are inherently kinder and gentler than men. If women ruled the world, patriarchy, oppression, and capitalism would not exist, and the world would be a better place.
- **Ecofeminism.** Ecofeminists stress that patriarchy is oppressive not only for women but also for the environment. They point out that men want to dominate not only women but also nature. Women need to free themselves from the dominance of men and take the lead in protecting the natural environment.

I don't want you to get the idea from this list that there are just five branches of feminist theory. These are five of its many divisions. One variety after another has evolved, and today there are such branches as indigenous feminism, postcolonial feminism, spiritual feminism, radical-cultural feminism, eco-socialist feminism, and even anarchist and cyborg feminism (Code 2000; Brown 2018). *Regardless of the particular branching, the central point that unites feminists is their focus on unequal power relations between men and women.* Let's take a quick look at how feminist theory applies to social problems.

Applying Feminist Theory to Social Problems: Focusing on Gender

To apply feminist theory to social problems, we examine relations between women and men. To continue with our example of the elderly, we can begin by focusing on *the sexual division of labor,* how men and women are sorted into different types of work. "Work" in this context refers not only to jobs but also to types of activities. Caring for elderly parents, for example, is usually defined as "women's work." This places the burden for the care of the elderly mainly on daughters, not sons. Ideas about paid work also come into play, especially the assumption that a husband's wages are more important than the wife's housework and child care. This assumption encourages men to focus on their work and to neglect family relations, including the care of elderly parents.

The increasing numbers of elderly leads to a major question: Who will take care of the frail elderly? Will we simply multiply our nursing homes, those places perceived by the elderly as vile places to go to die? This isn't what the elderly want, and here is where the gender issue I just mentioned comes into play. Elderly parents tend to expect their *daughters* to take care of them, regardless of whether their daughters have the money or the time to do so (Mascio 2007; Burby 2017).

This is just one aspect of the social problem of the elderly that we could look at through the lens of feminist theory. The point to remember is that feminist theorists, regardless of their specific orientation, view the root of social problems as a struggle over power and privilege among men and women.

Symbolic Interactionism and Social Problems

2.5   Explain symbolic interactionism and apply it to social problems.

The sociological theory that focuses on how we make sense out of life is called **symbolic interactionism**. The essence of this perspective is that we see the world through **symbols**, things to which we attach meaning and that we use to communicate with one another. Let's see how this perspective applies to social problems—and to your own life.

The Significance of Symbols in Social Life

Symbolic interactionists study how symbols, such as the terms we use to classify people, give us our view of the world. As we use the symbols that our culture provides for us to communicate with one another, we share and reinforce the ways we look at life. The images on television, movies and videos, the printed and spoken word, our gestures, tone of voice, clothing, even hairstyles—all are symbols by which we communicate ideas, even views of life. And our views include what we consider to be social problems.

This might seem vague, so let's go back to our example of the elderly. What does "old age" mean? When we first see a person who is advanced in years, we tend to classify him or her as an "old man" or "old woman." As we look at this person, we tend to see the characteristics that our culture packs into the symbol "old." In our culture, this symbol often includes being weak, unattractive, unstylish, and over the hill. Because everyone internalizes the symbols that dominate their culture, many elderly also see themselves in such terms. "Old person," however, doesn't mean the same thing in all cultures. In some cultures, old age brings images of wisdom. In others, old age is associated with power or privilege. Someone from such a culture, then, tends to perceive an old person in ways quite different than we do—and so does that elderly person.

When Symbols Change, Perceptions Change

Biologically, old age creeps up on us all. As the years pass, we feel and see our bodies gradually age. Sociologically, however, old age comes suddenly—perhaps at retirement, with the first Social Security check, or with a heart attack or some other unexpected health problem. Our images of old age are largely negative. We use phrases such as old and sick, old and crabby, old and dependent, old and useless. Take your pick. None is pleasant.

It might surprise you that during an earlier period of the United States "old" summoned positive images. Back then—and strange to our ears— "old" was associated with wisdom, ability, generosity, even graciousness and beauty.

Why did earlier generations have ideas of old age so startlingly different from ours? The reason is that social life itself was different back then. Two hundred years ago, most people died young. With few people reaching old age, those who did manage to survive to old age were admired for their accomplishment (Fischer 1977; Achenbaum 1978). There were also different ideas about work. At that time, people placed a high value on being actively involved in work, no matter what your age. To quit working simply because of old age was considered foolish. And work itself was different back

Prior to machine production, the elderly were given high respect because of their skills. Respect for the elderly dropped as machines replaced human skills. Exceptions remain, such as this artisan.

Jamie Hooper/Shutterstock

then. This was before machinery displaced individual skills, when it took years to be able to do fine work. With the elderly more skilled at their jobs, younger workers looked up to them. They perceived elderly workers as having accumulated valuable knowledge during their lives.

How did such a fundamental shift occur in how people perceive old age? We can trace this change back to the late 1800s, an era that saw major advances in public health, especially improvements in sanitation. These changes allowed many people to reach old age, which made being elderly no longer a unique distinction. Ideas about work were also changing. Machinery and mass production were "deskilling" work. No longer did it take years of apprenticeship under highly skilled workers to learn how to do a job. The new machines were social levelers; they made the younger workers just as knowledgeable and productive as the older workers. As the elderly lost the uniqueness that had brought them respect, the meaning of "old person" was turned upside down. Old age began to suggest uselessness rather than usefulness, foolishness rather than wisdom.

From Personal Problem to Social Problem

Don't miss this central aspect of symbolic interactionism and social problems: *Because symbols change, so do the matters considered to be social problems.* Earlier in our history, when most people died young, some people survived the odds and reached old age. At that time, if they had problems because of their age, those problems were matters for them or their family to handle. They were no one else's responsibility. Old age was a *personal* problem, not a *social* problem. Today, in contrast, with so many people reaching old age, we think of elderly people as a group. We tend to lump them together, and we consider social action (laws and policies) to be appropriate for solving their problems. A major transition has occurred: *What was once a personal problem has become a social problem.*

In Sum   From our brief review of what it meant to be elderly during an earlier period in the United States, we can see that as society changes, so do its symbols. Because the term *social problem* is also a symbol, what people consider to be a social problem also changes from one historical period to another. What we now take for granted, we may later see as a problem, and what we now see as a problem, we may later take for granted. *From the perspective of symbolic interactionism, then, social problems are whatever people in a society define as social problems.*

For more on how changing symbols change perception and how different social locations lead to different views of the social problem of old age, read the following *Spotlight on Social Research.*

Spotlight on Social Research

Studying Young People Who Became Old

PHYLLIS MOEN, *professor of sociology at the University of Minnesota, does research on the problems and challenges people face as they advance through the life course. Much of her research focuses on the careers and working lives of people who are approaching retirement age. Here is what she wrote for you.*

Courtesy of Phyllis Moen

Gerontologists are scholars who study older people. I became a gerontologist by the back door. I started out (and continue to be) a life-course sociologist, interested in people's pathways through work and family roles and relationships, and how our pathways are shaped by gender and social policy.

When I was a young professor at Cornell University, I found out that one of my colleagues (Robin M. Williams, Jr.) had, many years previously (in the 1950s), interviewed a random sample of young women in Elmira, New York. This is the only project he had never completed, and Robin regretted over the years never having followed through on it. One of my graduate students, Donna

Dempster-McClain, and I got together to study his 1950s data and were fascinated by the differences in women's lives then from our own. Donna and I got the bright idea of re-interviewing these women 30 years later and re-interviewing their (now adult) daughters as well. We thought this a wonderful opportunity to document the ways tremendous social changes in gender roles touched women's lives across the generations. With the help of graduate students, other committed researchers, and a grant from the National Institute on Aging, we found almost all of these women and re-interviewed them and their daughters, capturing their remarkable life histories from the 1950s through the 1980s. What we knew cognitively but hadn't counted on emotionally was that these young mothers in the 1950s had, three decades later, aged. And that is how I got into studying older people!

Because my focus has been on lives and not any one age group, my perspective is not on people as being "old." I always encourage students to capture the life histories of older people, to see the remarkable ways they have come to be the people they are today. Students who do so often find that interviewing earlier cohorts (and especially their own grandparents, great–grandparents, aunts, and uncles) offers a window on history and time. If you ask them, you may find that these people born in a different time and into a different world have defined social problems very differently when they were in their teens and twenties. They certainly have had distinctive experiences, opportunities, and challenges, and as a consequence, continue to have distinctive viewpoints about contemporary social issues.

Asking about the timing of people's trajectories and transitions in education, paid work, and family life helps to reveal the "person" behind the stereotypes and myths about older people. The interviewees may be in their 60s, 70s, or 80s, but still see themselves as the same person they were years ago—the kid attending school, the employee starting a job, part of a couple buying the first house and raising a family—in what seems to them like only yesterday. I continue to study differences in life pathways by cohort and gender, especially as people move from their career jobs to what are traditionally thought of as the retirement years.

My research breaks the myths and stereotypes about retirement as the gateway to being "old." I find that most older workers and retirees in their 60s and early 70s want to work—whether for pay or as a volunteer—but not full-time! Boomers can look forward to unparalleled health and longevity as they age, along with potential "second acts": opportunities for flexible new careers, whether as paid employees or as unpaid volunteers. The large baby boom cohort confronts this transition in a climate of uncertainty and ambiguity, where career jobs and pensions often disappear in the face of globalization, mergers, and downsizing.

And, for the first time in history, women are also retiring in unprecedented numbers. Couples often face two retirements: his and hers. My research shows that couples may live together longer "retired" than they did prior to retirement. But they seldom plan for retirement, beyond thinking about the age or date they will retire. It is the same way many young people plan for the wedding but not the years of married life. And yet the retirees I interview typically say they should have planned for life in retirement: how they will spend the 10, 20, or 30 years of healthy, "youthful" living they can now look forward to.

The Development of Symbolic Interactionism

Symbols are so essential for what we become that we could call them the element that separates us from the rest of life on this planet. Symbols allow us to think about other people and objects, even when they are not present. We also symbolize our own self, that is, we think about our self in certain ways, such as young, attractive, and personable.

How we symbolize our self is vital for the choices we make. To match our self-images, we choose the clothing we wear and the type of car we drive, as well as the music we listen to, the type of career we aspire to, and for some, even the shampoo we use. Symbols are central to our lives and relationships.

Let's look at two of the theorists who developed symbolic interactionism.

Mead and Taking the Role of the Other   George Herbert Mead (1863–1931) taught at the University of Chicago, where symbolic interactionism flourished. At one point, from the 1920s to the 1940s, this department of sociology and this perspective were so intertwined that the term **Chicago School of Sociology** was used to refer to both.

Mead focused on the significance of symbols. He said that symbols are so important that without them we couldn't have social life. What he meant is that symbols allow us to have goals, to plan, to evaluate, even to have words to say that something is "true love." Mead concluded that even our self-concept, which evolves during childhood, is based on symbols. One of the major means by which we develop our self-concept is learning to **take the role of the other**. That is, as children we gradually become capable of putting ourselves in someone else's shoes, able to understand how that person feels and thinks and to anticipate how he or she will act. After learning to understand the perspective of a few individuals, we learn to take the role of people in general—which Mead called the **generalized other**.

One of Mead's favorite examples was baseball. Let's use it.

> *Suppose that you are a high school senior. After an exhausting, but exhilarating, season, your team has made it to the playoffs for the state championship. Now, in the final game of the series, it is the bottom of the ninth inning. The score is tied, there are two outs, and the bases are loaded. You are up to bat. Everything depends on you. You can imagine the intense pressure you would feel, unlike anything you've experienced before. This could be your moment of glory—or of bitter defeat and humiliation. In a moment, you will either be carried on the shoulders of shouting teammates or walking dejectedly, head down, to the dugout.*

At this climactic moment, you probably would sense a heightened awareness of what Mead called the *generalized other*. In this instance, the term would refer to your teammates, your coach, the opposing team, your family, and the fans. You sense how they will feel if you strike out or get a hit.

Cooley and the Looking-Glass Self   Charles Horton Cooley (1864–1929), who taught at the University of Michigan, was also a central figure in the development of symbolic interactionism. He analyzed how the self develops through interaction with others. He said that *people come to view themselves as they think others perceive them.*

Cooley said that our interactions with others create a **looking-glass self**, which he summarized in the following couplet

Each to each a looking-glass
Reflects the other that doth pass.

By *looking-glass self*, Cooley meant that our self has three elements: (1) how we imagine we appear to others, (2) how we think others feel about what they perceive in us, and (3) how we feel about this reflected image. An essential aspect of our looking-glass self is that it produces the way we feel about our self. We can apply this principle to the elderly: If a society reflects negative images to its old people, the elderly tend to think of themselves negatively.

Berger and Luckmann and the Social Construction of Reality   Sociologists Peter Berger (1929–2017) and Thomas Luckmann (1927–2016) are key figures in the development of one of symbolic interactionism's major concepts, the **social construction of reality**. Let's take a brief look at this strange-sounding term and see if we can bring it down to earth.

The idea is simple enough. Things happen to you, and when they do you have to figure out what they mean. For example, if a stranger makes an unexpected contact with you, you have to decide whether it is a "shove," an "accidental touch," or even a "groping." Since these three are significantly different, you can see how your reaction will depend on how you interpret the contact.

This principle of constantly needing to interpret people's actions and intentions applies to your entire life. As you live your life, you continuously try to make sense out of what happens to you. A more formal way of saying this is that as you go through life, you are involved in the social construction of reality.

Applying the Social Construction of Reality: When Does Old Age Begin?   The concept is simple, but its implications are profound. *It means that reality does not come with built-in meanings,* but rather you construct your realities as you apply symbols to your experiences in life. Let's apply this idea to the question of when "old age" begins.

Did you know that "old age" is rooted more in social experiences than in biology? Certainly, there is nothing magical about turning 65—or any other age—that automatically makes someone "old." Yet the 65th birthday has become a standard marker of old age. Why? Strangely, it is rooted in 19th-century German politics. At that time, Otto von Bismarck (1815–1898), the architect of the German empire, was fighting against a political movement known as socialism. In order to weaken the appeal of socialism to Germans, Bismarck pioneered the idea of social security payments to older people. But at what age should such payments begin? To force some of his generals out of power, Bismarck chose 65 as the mandatory retirement age. Bismarck's arbitrary decision stuck, becoming a symbol that affects how we perceive age today.

Applying the Social Construction of Reality: What Does Suicide Mean?   Not all cultures have the same symbols, so the social construction of reality changes from culture to culture. This yields remarkably different views of life. Consider the family of a Japanese military officer who has purposely fallen on his sword after losing a battle. To understand why he took his life, their culture provides the symbols of honor and duty, and Japanese interpret the individual's death in those terms. ("He did his duty and died an honorable death.") Now think about Americans who have just learned that their sister has committed suicide: They don't have symbols like this to help them figure out why she took her life. Their symbols include the responsibility of friends and family in preventing suicide, which leads them to such questions as: "Am I to blame for not picking up on her hints of suicide?" "Should I feel guilty?" "What could I have done differently?"

Although the answers that the Japanese and the Americans come up with (that is, socially construct) regarding the suicide are different, the principle is the same. Both the Japanese and the Americans are using the symbols their culture provides to socially construct reality. They come up with different answers because they use different symbols. To catch a glimpse of Americans as they work out answers to the "why" of suicide, see the following *Thinking Critically about Social Problems*.

Thinking Critically about Social Problems

Making Sense of Suicide: Socially Constructing Reality

Some of the most difficult research I have done was to interview the friends and family of people who had committed suicide. Their wrenching emotional turmoil created similar feelings within me. The interviews yielded rich data, however, and here are some things I found concerning suicide and the social construction of reality.

After someone commits suicide, people who were close to that person try to make sense out of what happened. As their shock wears off, they mentally relive events associated with the dead person. They begin to interpret these events in light of the suicide. As they do so, the events take on new meaning. Survivors ask why the individual took his or her life. As they explore this "why," some confront the horrifying possibility that they themselves could have been part of the reason. They then face this burning issue: "If I had done something different, maybe he (she) would still be alive."

This search for meaning and for cause leads survivors to reconstruct the past, which can be a torturous process. Listen to this father of a 25-year-old who shot himself with a handgun. You can hear the questions that plague him as he reconstructs events in his search for answers regarding his son's death:

When Anthony Bourdain, celebrity chef and television personality, committed suicide in 2018, millions of people around the world were left wondering why such a talented, personable, and rich person would do such a thing. The process of developing an answer to such questions is known as the social construction of reality.

Clinton Wallace/Globe Photos/Zuma Wire/Zuma Press, Inc. /Alamy Live News/Alamy Stock Photo

I've wondered where it began if it was suicide. Was it in grade school? Or college? Or was it all this girl? Could I have done something different? Or wouldn't it have helped? Wondering which is right and which is wrong.... I think this thing or that thing could have been done to change the course of events. But you just don't know. I even thought, "If we hadn't moved from St. Louis to Crestview years ago."

As part of our everyday life, we all use the symbols our culture provides to interpret what happens to us, that is, to socially construct our reality. When it comes to death by suicide, however, our culture does not offer satisfactory symbols. This leaves people confused as they search for meaning. Consider how different it is when someone dies from a disease. That person's family members don't face this type of challenge to the self. Seldom does the symbol *disease* trigger the question "Could I have done something different?" Instead, the symbol of disease points to causes beyond us—to germs and chances in life and other factors usually beyond a person's control. The symbol *suicide,* in contrast, denies us this more comfortable interpretation of causation.

Our culture offers many symbols to help people adjust to the death of loved ones. Among them is "God's will." This symbol, if it can be used, moves causation clearly beyond the survivors of the deceased, allowing easier acceptance of the event. If God called the individual home, the survivors certainly bear no responsibility for the death. The family members of a suicide, however, are denied this category. Listen to this woman as she struggles with the meaning of her husband's death:

> *Well, I would have felt in my own mind that God had called him from the earth and that he had a reason for calling him, and that we could have accepted it as Christians that it was the will of God, and that we could feel in our hearts that God, in his tenderness, had taken him up with him. I can't feel that this was the will of God.*

From these examples, you can see that culture provides symbols (labels, categories, concepts, words, and terms) that people use to interpret the events of their lives. By looking at how the survivors of suicide search for meaning, we can observe the social construction of reality as it occurs. We can see that the usual symbols our culture offers at someone's death are denied these people, plunging them into uncertainty, a search for meaning that often ends in confusion and sometimes in despair.

Knowing why family members react to suicide as they do can make us more aware of how we use our culture's symbols to provide meaning for our experiences. You can see that if our culture provided different symbols, we would interpret our experiences differently. The social construction of reality, a concept sometimes difficult to understand, is an ordinary part of our everyday lives.

For Your Consideration

→ Why do the suicide of a Japanese general after a failed battle and the suicide of a lonely U.S. woman in her 80s have different meanings? Where do those meanings come from?

→ What is meant by the social construction of reality, and how is suicide an example of it?

In Sum   The social construction of reality is part of everyday life. We all try to make sense of what happens to us—whether this means figuring out why we received an A or an F on a test, why we were promoted or fired at work, or even why we like or dislike some television program or video game. In short, the events of life do not come with built-in meanings, and we all use the symbols provided by our culture to make sense out of life. Symbolic interactionists call this process *the social construction of reality.*

Applying Symbolic Interactionism to Social Problems

Sociologists use a phrase that sounds like a foreign language to most people: The social construction of social problems. Let's see what it means.

The Social Construction of Social Problems   What does it mean to say that social problems are socially constructed? This means that social problems don't have an independent existence. They are not like grapefruit that you pick out at the grocery store. *Social problems don't exist until some condition of society is called a social problem.* Until then, that condition is simply a characteristic of society, like so many other things.

To make this point clearer, let's go back to the elderly. That there are old people in a society does not mean that there is a social problem in that society. The status of the elderly depends on how the elderly are viewed or labeled. We saw how the elderly once were admired and respected in the United States and how their status dropped sharply as machinery deskilled work. At this point in our history, the poverty rate of the elderly is lower than the national average, and their status is improving. If this continues, more and more positive characteristics will be associated with old age, and the elderly will receive greater respect. In short, because social problems are socially constructed, what is considered a social problem changes over time.

Symbolic Interactionism and Social Problems: A Summary

Symbolic interactionists stress that social problems are socially constructed. This means that a social problem is an objective condition of society that people have labeled a "social problem." If people don't place this label on that objective condition, it is not a social problem. If they do, it is. To understand a social problem, then, we need to understand how some objective condition was turned into a social problem. We must also take into account what that problem means to the people who are involved in it.

In the coming chapters, we will apply these theoretical perspectives to the social problems that we analyze. To conclude this chapter, let's look at the probable future of "old age" as a social problem.

The Future of the Problem: The Pendulum Swings

2.6   Discuss the possible generational struggle regarding the elderly.

From what we have reviewed in this chapter, it should be apparent that what a social problem is depends on how people view some condition in their society. Let's look at this essential aspect of social problems again, and then consider a major shift in the relationship of younger and older people.

Changing Objective Conditions and Subjective Concerns

Objective conditions of elderly Americans have undergone major change. One hundred years ago, most elderly Americans lived in poverty. By 1970, the poverty rate had dropped to 1 of 4 elderly persons. Today, with economic growth and state and federal programs, the elderly's rate of poverty has dropped to 1 of 11, *less* than the 15 percent overall rate of poverty in the United States (*Statistical Abstract* 1990:Table 746; 2018:Table 737).

Will the poverty rate of the elderly remain low? No one knows what the future will bring, but we do have some ominous trends. The United States has changed from a nation with a large trade surplus to a nation whose trade deficit is so huge that we now are the world's largest debtor nation. Our sea of debt is so gigantic—and growing—that it numbers in the trillions of dollars. This debt, which we are leaving for future generations to pay, cannot continue to grow forever. At some point, the nation must either tighten its belt or declare bankruptcy. If federal spending is reduced, and if it includes a reduction of programs for the elderly, their poverty rate will increase. With the political clout of today's elderly accompanied by our elected officials' ardent desire to remain in office, we can be certain that such reductions will be postponed until there is no alternative.

A major concern of the public and of politicians is the costs of health care for the elderly. Look at Figure 2.1. You can see how the costs of Medicare and Medicaid have soared. These costs have exceeded the wildest projections of earlier years.

As you know, concerns about Social Security are also growing. In 1950, Social Security paid out $784 *million*, but now the payout is $911 *billion* a year. Analysts are alarmed when they see that today's payment is 1,160 times larger than the amount paid in 1950 (*Statistical Abstract* 1997:Table 518; 2018:Table 566).

If we project the escalating costs of Social Security, Medicare, and Medicaid into the indefinite future, they eventually would be larger than the entire production (gross domestic product) of the United States. This is impossible. So, when and how will this change? No one has the answer, but you can see that a crisis is in the making. Could this crisis even pit the young against the elderly? Let's turn to this possibility.

Poverty of the aged is a global problem. I took the photo of the woman searching through garbage in Riga, Latvia, and the photo of the man begging on the street corner in Rome, Italy. In all societies, people who have more money have fewer physical and mental health problems and an easier time adjusting to old age.

Henslin, James M.

Henslin, James M.

Figure 2.1 Health Care Costs for the Elderly and Disabled

Legend:
- Cost of Medicare
- Cost of Medicaid

Data labels (Medicare): $7, $15, $36, $66, $107, $180, $215, $334, $551, $672

Data labels (Medicaid): $5, $13, $21, $23, $41, $79, $118, $182, $318, $411, $475, $566

Y-axis: $1 trillion

X-axis: Year — 1970, 1975, 1980, 1985, 1990, 1995, 2000, 2005, 2010, 2015, 2020*, 2025*

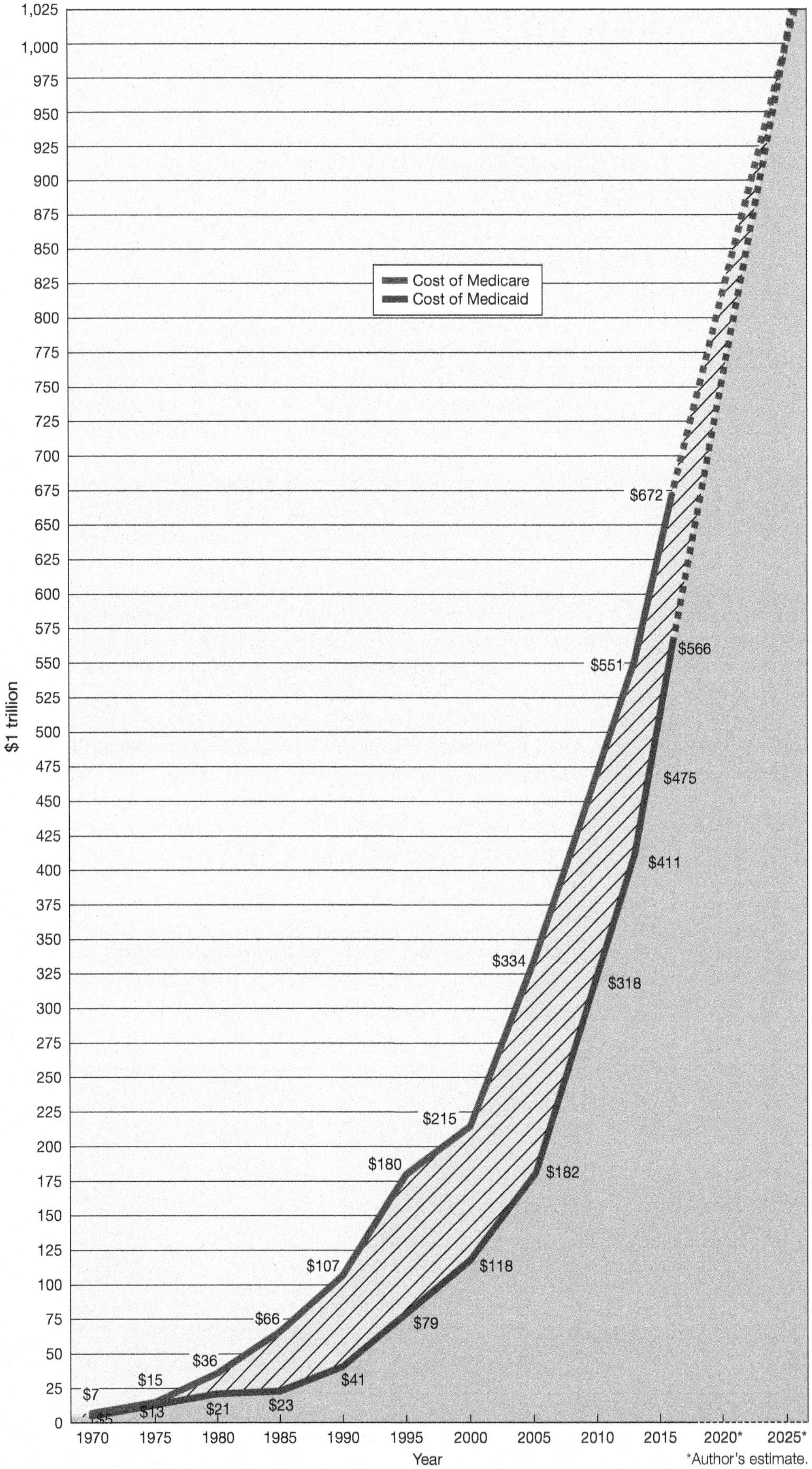

*Author's estimate.

Note: Medicare is intended for the elderly and disabled, Medicaid for the poor. About 2 percent of Medicaid payments ($11 billion) go for medical care for the elderly (*Statistical Abstract of the United States* 2017:Table 161).

Source: By the author. Based on *Statistical Abstract of the United States*, various years, and CMMS 2018.

The Emerging Struggle

The objective conditions of this social problem are likely to get worse. As you can see from Figure 2.2, about 1 in 6 Americans is age 65 or over and that in about 10 years this total will increase to 1 in 5. This rapid increase of the elderly means that the costs of Social Security and health care, already bursting at the seams, will escalate.

Figure 2.2 The Graying of America

The percentage of Americans in these age groups

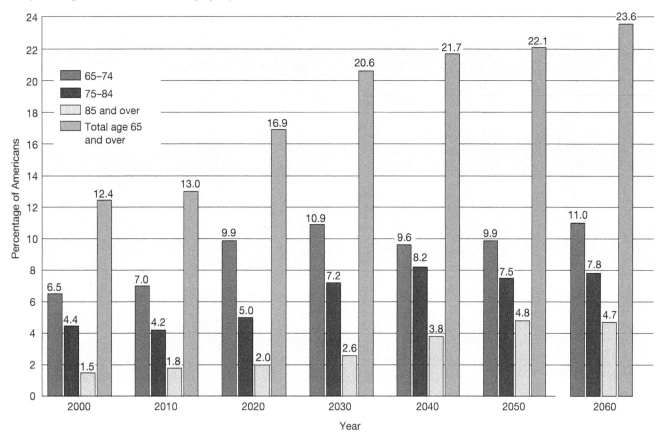

Source: By the author. Based on *Statistical Abstract of the United States* 2002:Table 12; 2018:Tables 6, 8.

As discussed in the following *Issues in Social Problems*, one of the fastest-growing groups of the elderly is those who are age 100 or more, most of whom need extensive medical care.

Issues in Social Problems

The Genetic Lottery and the New Centenarians

Because centenarian refers to someone who has reached age 100 or more, *new centenarians* may seem to be an oxymoron. Until recently, though, hardly anyone made it to age 100 or beyond. Why have the "new" centenarians appeared at this point in world history? The reasons seem to be our improved public health, advanced medicines, and ample food supply.

While reaching 100 isn't exactly common today, it is frequent. About 89,000 Americans report that they are age 100 or more (*Statistical Abstract* 2018:Table 8). Census officials think that people fudge a bit about their age when they get to be very old. They become proud about making it that far, and they tend to tack on a few years. Even if we lop off 9,000 people, this still leaves us with 80,000 Americans who have managed to reach age 100 or more.

As you probably expect, more women than men reach 100, but the difference might surprise you. For every man who is a centenarian, there are between *5 and 6* women centenarians. And there is this surprising statistic: About 15 percent of centenarians have no disease. They are still healthy and feeling good. About 15 percent (but not necessarily the same individuals) have no change in their ability to think. This is encouraging. It means that dementia is not inevitable with extreme aging (Boston University 2018).

Centenarians are both poor and rich, are of different race-ethnicities, and are both vegetarians and carnivores. They do handle stress well, but the key seems to be lucky genetics. Only 1 of 6,000 wins this genetic lottery (Boston University 2018).

On the individual level—why Dick and Jane make it to 100 while Bill and Mary do not—there appear to be two main reasons besides genetics: lifestyle and just plain luck. For lifestyle, some people take better care of their bodies, while others like to ride motorcycles and jump out of airplanes. Then there is luck—or the lack of it. You can be in the wrong place at the wrong time,

New to the world scene are the centenarians, most of whom are women. Shown here is a centenarian, surrounded by family and friends, blowing out the candles on her cake during her 100th birthday party at a nursing home.

Marmaduke St. John/Alamy Stock Photo

such as driving on an interstate highway when in the incoming lane a boat unhooks from a trailer and smashes into your car, taking your head with it, as happened to two friends of mine.

Our trend toward longer life has brought with it a new term, the *supercentenarians,* those who live to 110 or beyond. About 1 of 5 million people makes it to 110. If the genetics researchers learn more about manipulating our genes, one day we may be talking about the new centenarians-and-a-half or even the double centenarians.

For Your Consideration

→ If centenarians become more common, what do you think the consequences will be for society?

→ If you could be one of the 15 percent who have a healthy body and mind, would you like to become a centenarian? Why or why not?

A battle between the generations may be shaping up. To protect the resources they have and to demand more, older Americans have organized a powerful political lobby. This group, AARP (formerly called the American Association of Retired Persons), boasts 40 million members, a staff of 1,800, and 160,000 volunteers. Politicians find it difficult to ignore such numbers. If they try to reduce benefits for the elderly, they are flooded with letters, e-mails, and telephone calls. On blogs, they are accused of being stingy and threatened with being voted out of office.

Another group, the Gray Panthers, is featured in the following *Issues in Social Problems.*

Issues in Social Problems

What Do You Mean, Gray Panthers?

Gray Panthers. Such a strange name. What does it mean? Back in the 1960s, a black liberation group sprang onto the national scene, spawning sensationalistic news reports. Blacks were arming themselves! The images frightened local police, the FBI, and other authorities across the nation. This group called itself the Black Panthers, and they carried rifles to show that they meant business. Maggie Kuhn, who was forced to retire at age 65, the law back in 1970, wanted to change this law and improve the

welfare of the elderly. She seized the unique opportunity that the appearance of the Black Panthers presented. Hers would be a group of old, grey-haired people that the authorities would have to listen to. And so, the *Gray* Panthers was born.

In contrast to the Black Panthers, armed blacks who seemed to pose a threat to the nation itself—yes, such were the alarms that went off during the fabled 1960s—the police didn't bat an eye at a few old people who wanted more respect and a better retirement.

But Maggie's little group did grow from a bunch of disgruntled old people who wrote "manifestos" and letters to the editor and congressmen (basically no women in high government office back then) to a nationally organized group that employs professional lobbyists to work to improve the lives of elderly Americans. The Gray Panthers remain a much quieter group than Maggie seemed to have in mind. She was a feisty lady who wanted to disrupt the status quo, or at least create a few waves.

The elderly have become such a powerful political force that it is perilous for politicians to ignore their demands.

Cultura RF/Seb Oliver/Getty Images

of children organizing for their own welfare, or of groups of adults effectively advocating for the welfare of children, which we reviewed earlier, might be an indicator of future conflict between the generations—and of the greediness of the elderly.

To ward off such dire accusations, which would harm the organization's image, the Gray Panthers' literature declares that it is a group of old and young people who work together for "common concerns for human liberation and social change for the old and the young."

Like social movement organizations everywhere that grow elderly, this one, too, is largely focused on making sure the money keeps flowing in, protecting the positions of its leaders, and maintaining publicity for the organization. Each time Congress holds a hearing regarding the elderly, and they have to call somebody to testify, with its effective self-promotion, this is about the only organization that comes to mind.

The Gray Panthers might be a quiet behind-the-scenes organization that works to obtain more benefits and resources for the elderly, but gains by the elderly sometimes means less for children and youth. The impact of this statement, accompanied by the lack

Uh Huh. Sure. The name *Gray* Panthers says it all.

For Your Consideration

→ Who is going to advocate for the children? Actually, there are many organizations that do this, some called simply Advocates for Children. But in keeping with this theme, what would you think about forming a group called The Baby Panthers? (Cute little kids dressed in panther costumes might go a long way to loosen the purse strings of Congress.) And perhaps another called The Teenaged Panthers?

The interests of the younger and older groups are running on a collision course. Consider Social Security again. The money a worker pays to Social Security is not put into that worker's own account. Instead, the money collected from current workers is given to retired workers—an arrangement by which the younger support the older. But the number of people collecting Social Security benefits is growing faster than the number of people entering the workforce. This creates a major shift in the **dependency ratio**, the number of workers compared with the number of people who receive Social Security. Until recently, four workers were paying Social Security taxes to support each person who was collecting Social Security. This ratio has now dropped to 3.6 to 1. In about a generation, it will hit 3 to 1 (*Statistical Abstract* 2018:Tables 565, 566).

In the United States, a land of wealth and bountiful resources, we can ask why millions of children continue to live in poverty.

Shestock/Blend Images/Getty Images

Here is another indicator of the potential conflict: The U.S. government has collected almost $3 trillion more in Social Security taxes than it has paid to retirees (*Statistical Abstract* 2018:Table 568). Supposedly, officials have placed this huge excess in a trust fund, reserved for future generations. The "fund," however, does not exist, It has been looted by the U.S. government. In a fraud perpetrated on the elderly, this excess money disappears just as fast as it comes in. The federal government "borrows" it, spending it on whatever it desires (Henslin 2018). The Social Security Trust Fund is supposed to prevent an intergenerational showdown, but as some have pointed out, there is no fund, and you can't trust it. A day of reckoning between generations can't be far off.

Summary and Review

1. The frameworks sociologists use to interpret their research findings are called *theories.* To interpret social problems, sociologists use three major theories: *functionalism, conflict theory,* and *symbolic interactionism.* In this chapter, we look at *feminist theory* as part of conflict theory. Each theory provides a different interpretation of society and of social problems. No theory is *the* right one. Rather, taken together, these perspectives give us a more complete picture of the whole.

2. *Functionalists* see society as a self-correcting, orderly system, much like a well-oiled machine. Its parts work in harmony to bring the whole into equilibrium. Each part performs a *function* (hence, the term *functional analysis*) that contributes to the system's well-being. When a part is functioning inadequately, however, it creates problems for the system. These *dysfunctions* are called social problems.

3. *Conflict theorists* view social problems as an outcome of unequal power. Those in power try to preserve the social order and their own privileged position within it. They take the needs of other groups into consideration only when it is in their own interest to do so. As they exploit others, the powerful create social problems, such as poverty, discrimination, and war. Other social problems, such as revolution, crime, suicide, and drug abuse, represent reactions of the oppressed to their exploitation. *Feminist theorists* also focus on the exploitation of the powerless by the powerful, looking at *patriarchy* or male dominance as the primary cause.

4. *Symbolic interactionists* view social problems not as objective conditions but as broadly held views, as a perspective that is applied to an objective condition. In short, if people view something as a social problem, it is a social problem. If they do not, it is not. As people's views (or definitions or symbols) change, so do their ideas about social problems.

Thinking Critically about Chapter 2

1. Of the theories identified in this chapter, which one do you think does the best job of explaining social problems? Why?

2. Select a social problem other than aging:
   - How would functionalists explain the problem?
   - How would conflict theorists explain the problem?
   - How would symbolic interactionists explain the problem?
   - How would feminist theorists explain the problem?

3. What main problems do you think we are likely to face in coming years regarding the "graying of America" (the aging of the U.S. population)? Propose solutions to these problems.
   - Why do you think your solutions might work?
   - What might prevent your solutions from working?

Key Terms

capitalism, 31
capitalists, 31
Chicago School of Sociology, 37
conflict theory, 30
dependency ratio, 45
dysfunctions, 26
feminist theory, 33
functions, 25
functionalism, 25
generalized other, 38
latent dysfunctions, 27

latent functions, 26
looking-glass self, 38
manifest functions, 26
patriarchy, 33
social construction of reality, 38
structure, 26
symbolic interactionism, 35
symbols, 35
taking the role of the other, 38
theory, 25

Chapter 3
Social Problems Related to Sexual Behavior

Scott Warren/Alamy Stock Photo

 ## Learning Objectives

After reading this chapter, you should be able to:

3.1 Explain the role of sociology in determining morality and studying social problems.

3.2 Contrast various attitudes toward prostitution.

3.3 Explain the functionalist perspective on prostitution.

3.4 Explain the conflict/feminist perspective on prostitution.

3.5 Summarize the research findings on types of prostitutes, becoming a prostitute, pimps, and male prostitutes.

3.6 Explain why pornography is a social problem and how symbolic interactionism (establishing meaning) applies to pornography.

3.7 Explain the controversy over pornography and understand the major research findings on pornography.

3.8 Discuss the issue of making consensual behavior illegal—and its alternatives.

3.9 Explain the likely future of prostitution and pornography.

Jack Helmer (a pseudonym) has been attracted to little girls since he can't remember when. Even as a little boy, he liked to spend time with them. Now at 45, Jack still enjoys their imaginations and finds their conversations delightful. It used to be that whenever he had the opportunity, he would babysit for them.

The problem is that Jack's interest in little girls is also sexual.

Fifteen years ago, Jack was arrested for molesting a minor and put on probation for 3 years. During his probation, he was charged with molesting his girlfriend's 10-year-old daughter. For this offense, he served 5 years in prison.

Every cab driver knew where the kiddie brothels were located.

Jack was especially displeased when his name, address, and photo appeared on an Internet sexual offenders' website. Knowing that both the police and the neighbors were watching him, Jack kept away from children. One day, he read about an area in Phnom Penh, the capital of Cambodia, with brothels that feature children. Jack decided to travel to Cambodia, far from the prying eyes of the police and neighbors.

It took Jack quite a while to save the money for the trip, but by cutting down expenses, he managed to put together what he needed for the flight and hotel. When he arrived in Phnom Penh, Jack found that what he had read was correct. Children were available for sexual purposes, and the price was low. Every cab driver knew where the kiddie brothels were located.

Jack should have read a little more closely. What he missed was that the United States had passed laws to prosecute predatory crimes against children outside the U.S. borders.

When Jack returned from Cambodia, federal officials were waiting at the airport. Jack is now serving a 20-year prison sentence.

Sexual Behavior: Objective Conditions and Subjective Concerns

3.1   Explain the role of sociology in determining morality and studying social problems.

You will recall from our discussion in the first chapter that objective conditions alone are not adequate to make something a social problem. Also essential are subjective concerns: A lot of people must dislike or be upset about some objective condition and want to see it changed. The events in our opening vignette easily meet this definition of a social problem.

We will come back to discuss the sexual abuse of children, but before we move into the topics of this chapter, it is important to lay a little groundwork. First, what do we mean by sex? Let's define **sex** in a fairly standard way as those activities associated with sexual arousal and intercourse. Second, it is important to stress a sociological principle that is fundamental to this chapter: As much as we may prefer it to be otherwise, *sex is never only a personal matter.* All societies control or channel human sexual behavior, primarily through the social institution of marriage and family. We learn our first ideas of morality, including sexual morality, in the family, and we don't take challenges to our opinions of what is right and wrong about sexual behavior lightly.

Because many people view the topics of this chapter in moral terms, it is also important to stress another point made in the first chapter: *Sociology does not make moral judgments.* Sociologists take positions on social issues, of course, because they are members of society and share many of the ideas common in their society. I don't know of a single sociologist, for example, who would defend the prostitution of children or their use in pornography. When it comes to adult prostitution and pornography, however, there is a wide variety of opinions among sociologists, just as there is among the general public.

As stressed in Chapter 1, although sociology has no basis for taking a moral stand on human behavior, even though sociologists do, sociology is well-equipped to study the two essential conditions of social problems, their objective conditions and their subjective concerns, the controversies that make contemporary life so interesting. To learn more about how sociologists study sex, look at the following *Spotlight on Social Research*.

Spotlight on Social Research

Studying Sex in America

EDWARD LAUMANN, *Professor of Sociology and the College at the University of Chicago, has done research on health, politics, power, status, and sex. Although he has a long history of theoretical work in how people form, maintain, and dissolve relationships, it is his research on sex that has received the most attention. Here is what he wrote for your text.*

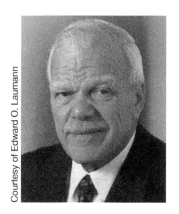

Courtesy of Edward O. Laumann

In the 1980s, when we were in the midst of an AIDS epidemic so vicious that the number of people with this disease was doubling every 10 months, I organized a workshop on AIDS and Society. As I listened to the presentations, I became convinced that there would be no magic bullet to stop this epidemic through immunization. To contain the spread of AIDS, people would have to change their behavior. Robert Michael, an economic demographer, and I concluded that we needed a national sex survey to document the sex practices of Americans. With this information, we could design ways to persuade people to take defensive measures.

Research into human sexual behavior is often considered "illegitimate," even by many social scientists. Despite this disapproval, we wanted the University of Chicago to pool its strengths in survey and sample design to conduct this national survey. John Gagnon, a sexologist, joined our research team. When the National Institutes of Health announced a search for research proposals to combat AIDS, we submitted our design for a national sex survey. We won that competition.

When *Science* magazine reported that our proposal was under review at the White House's Office of Management and the Budget, the *Washington Times* picked the story up with screaming headlines. Within a few days, a white paper was circulating to every member of the House and Senate. One objection was that sex reports normalize immoral sexual behavior, such as masturbation and anal and oral sex. Another was that the government has no business invading people's private lives, even if it is for reasons of the public's health. Michael and I were accused of being fronts for a cabal of homophiles who were attempting to legitimize gay sex.

Although the Senate Appropriations Committee recommended that our survey be funded, the House Appropriations Committee disagreed. For two years, we lobbied congressional staffers, senators, and representatives for their support in funding the research, but with few results. Then Senator Jesse Helms submitted an amendment to an appropriations bill that transferred the funding that had been intended for our sex survey to a "say no to sex" campaign. The Senate voted 66 to 34 in favor of the amendment, giving me the dubious distinction of having Congress trying to stop my research.

With government funding cut off, we turned to private foundations. The Robert Wood Johnson, Henry Kaiser, Rockefeller, and MacArthur foundations, amongst others, agreed to fund our research. To share the results of our survey with the scientific community, we wrote *The Social Organization of Sexuality.* This is a technical book, and as some have noted, it took the University of Chicago to take the fun out of sex.

We felt strongly that the public needed to know what we had discovered, and we wanted to have a hand in framing the public's understanding, not leave it to others. To do this, we arranged for Gina Kolata, a *New York Times* reporter who specializes in science and health news, to write a companion volume, *Sex in America.*

Prostitution

3.2 Contrast various attitudes toward prostitution.

With this short background on objective conditions, subjective concerns, and sociological research, let's turn to an overview of prostitution, one of the areas of human behavior that upsets a lot of people.

Getting the Larger Picture

It is no accident that **prostitution**, the renting of one's body for sexual purposes, has been called "the world's oldest profession." Accounts of prostitution by both females and males reach back to the beginning of recorded history, and prostitution exists in one form or another almost everywhere. Let's take quick look at how attitudes about prostitution differ.

Attitudes toward Prostitution You might be surprised to learn that prostitution used to be part of some religions. In Canaan, Greece, Phoenicia, and Sumeria, prostitution was viewed as a service to their gods (Sanderson 2018). Some groups practiced **temple prostitution**, dedicating some women to the gods as *sacred prostitutes*—either for a specific time or for life. Other groups required every woman to perform an act of prostitution before she was allowed to marry (Henriques 1966). On a visit to India, I was surprised to find that in some villages temple prostitution still exists.

In some countries, prostitution is viewed as a necessary evil—something for which there is a demand that will be satisfied whether the activity is legal or illegal. In Germany and New Zealand, for example, prostitutes, called sex workers, are licensed to work in brothels. Some prostitutes insist on working the streets, however, where they create problems for residents (Drury 2018). In Amsterdam, Holland, licensed prostitutes sell sex at stated prices in approved locations. They have legal labor rights, pay taxes on their sales, and collect state pensions.

In the United States, attitudes toward legalizing prostitution vary greatly. Although it is illegal in all parts of the United States except in parts of Nevada, prostitution flourishes. Let's look at this aspect of prostitution.

This 1902 painting depicts a poet, Peter Altenberg, with three elegantly dressed prostitutes in Vienna's Stephansplatz. He is paying one while another is stealing from him.

Erich Lessing/Art Resource

Prostitution Today

Eliot Spitzer, the then governor of New York, arranged for a 22-year-old prostitute to take a train from New York and meet him at a Washington, D.C., hotel, where he paid her $5,500. What he didn't know was that the police were recording his telephone calls. During an outburst of national publicity and indignation, Spitzer resigned as governor.

Although attitudes toward prostitution are mixed, few people will tolerate a governor with a wife and three children who visits prostitutes—especially a governor who has taken a public stance for "family values," a crusading former prosecutor who had his eye on the White House (Bone 2008).

Because of where and how she works, this woman has more control over her choice of clients. Her income is higher than that of most prostitutes, and she faces little threat to her personal safety.

If prostitution flourishes in the United States, and it does, you might wonder how many prostitutes there are. Wondering the same thing, researchers set out to find the answer. Using sampling techniques, they estimate that there are 69,000 prostitutes in the United States, about 23 prostitutes per 100,000 Americans (Pottêrat et al. 1990; Brewer et al. 2000). With the increase in the U.S. population since this research, if the ratio still holds, today there are about 75,000 prostitutes. Apparently, the average prostitute has 694 customers a year. The range, however, is huge. Some prostitutes have just one or two customers a week, while those who work in crack houses might have 5,000 a year.

The only place in the United States where prostitution is legal is Nevada. But women are not licensed to sell sex in Reno, Las Vegas, and Lake Tahoe. Officials in these counties have banned prostitution for fear that it would drive away family vacationers. From the photo of the man advertising "girls in 20 minutes," however, you can see that prostitution, although illegal, is practiced almost openly in Las Vegas.

Prostitutes try to keep up with the times. The "whorehouses" of yesterday have been replaced by massage parlors, escort services, corporate prostitution, and sex tourism. Under cover of a legitimate service, "massage parlors" offer sex for sale. Escort services use the Internet to arrange dates for a fee, which is not illegal, and the client privately negotiates the sex. Prostitutes, both men and women, advertise online. Prostitutes take credit cards, listing their sexual services as consulting. Apps connect prostitutes and customers, allowing them to negotiate both prices and the specific services to be purchased ("More Bang..." 2014).

Some corporations offer prostitutes as sexual perks for their employees and customers. A Wall Street firm paid $250,000 to rent a Miami mansion for a Super Bowl weekend, its executives lounging around the pool with rent-a-dates (Pulliam and Bray 2011). Top salesmen are sometimes rewarded with prostitutes (Iwersen 2016).

Our opening vignette is about **sex tourism**, traveling to some location in order to purchase sexual experiences. We explore this topic further in the following *Global Glimpse*.

From this photo that I shot in Las Vegas, would you know that prostitution is illegal in this city?

A Global Glimpse

Sex Tourism

With prostitution legal in Brazil and with the country hosting international sporting events, Brazilian television featured "I'm a happy prostitute" ads. The smiling prostitutes did look happy—and appealing. When criticized that tourists were getting the wrong message, officials jerked the ads ("Brazil Drops..." 2013).

This chapter's opening vignette featured sex tourism for the purpose of child prostitution. Most sex tourism, though, is more garden variety, typically that of men visiting a country in order to have sex with young women of a background they perceive as exotic. Some women are also sex tourists, with Jamaica a common destination for sex with young men. Sex tourism also appeals to some homosexuals, who, like some heterosexuals, enjoy "sexual holidays" with either children or adults.

Sex tourism is often related to *global stratification,* the layering of countries according to their relative power, wealth, and prestige in global affairs. In the least industrialized nations, poverty is high, and often prostitution is high there as well. The authorities of at least one country, Thailand, view many of its women in poverty as a cash crop, encouraging prostitution as a way to accumulate wealth for some (not the women, but those behind the sex trade) and perhaps capital for national investment. Of Thailand's 30 million females, between a half million and a million are prostitutes. About 20,000 are under the age of 15.

Sex slavery is often part of sex tourism. Some of the prostitutes were sold as children. Others are held in bondage while they pay off their families' debts. Some are even locked up to keep them from running away.

There is also the matter of AIDS. In Nairobi, about 10,000 prostitutes serve this thriving industry. About half are infected with AIDS. Sex tourism also facilitates the destruction of children. Customers

PE Forsberg/Alamy Stock Photo

This photo of a museum of prostitution is in the De Wallen area of Amsterdam, Holland. As customers stroll along the canalside streets of this legal red light district, they window shop for prostitutes, who sit behind lighted windows next to an entrance door.

often demand young girls and boys, paying more for those who are said to be virgins or "clean." Children are vulnerable to infection from lesions and injuries during intercourse as well as AIDS and other sexually transmitted diseases. When the children become too sick to service clients—or their diseases grow too noticeable—they are discarded on the streets like so much rubbish.

Based on Adams 2013; Ridley 2016; Schifter 2017.

For Your Consideration

→ What is your opinion about sex tourism?
→ If prostitution is legal in a country, to help balance its budget why shouldn't it promote sex tourism?

Prostitution Viewed Theoretically: Applying Functionalism

3.3 **Explain the functionalist perspective on prostitution.**

Let's look at the social functions of prostitution.

The Social Functions of Prostitution

Let's start with prostitution's most obvious function—it satisfies sexual desires that are not met elsewhere. This, of course, is precisely why prostitution will never be eliminated, for there always will be people with such desires and others who will satisfy them for a fee. In a classic article that goes back about 85 years, sociologist Kingsley Davis (1937) concluded that prostitutes provide a sexual outlet for men who

1. have difficulty establishing sexual relationships (such as disfigured or shy men or those with handicaps)
2. lack long-term partners (such as travelers and sailors)

3. have a broken relationship (such as the separated or divorced)
4. want sexual acts they can't get from their wives or girlfriends.

Other researchers (Weitzer 2009; Schifter 2017) note that prostitutes also provide a sexual outlet for men who want sex

5. without attachment
6. with someone of a preferred age, race–ethnicity, or body type
7. with someone who makes them feel they are special.

For some men, prostitution is not a fleeting, detached arrangement (Huff 2011; Schifter 2017). Instead, they seek intimacy by having sex with the same prostitute repeatedly. They develop emotional bonds, sharing feelings and thoughts with her that they aren't comfortable sharing with others. Some of these men are convinced that the woman from whom they are buying sex has special feelings for them. Some escort services cater to this need of intimacy, offering women who specialize in "the girlfriend experience." Some men also pay for "the boyfriend experience" (Tewksbury and Lapsey 2017).

The Functionalist Conclusion: Prostitution as a Way of Controlling Sexual Behavior
Most of these findings may seem obvious, but from them functionalists draw a surprising conclusion. Prostitution, they stress, is *a way of controlling men's sexual behavior.* By this, they mean that by meeting such needs as those I just described, prostitution channels men's sexual desires away from unwilling women to women who, for a price, are willing to satisfy the men. For example, some people (whom prostitutes call "kinkies," "weirdos," and "freaks") achieve sexual gratification by inflicting pain on others (**sadists**) or by having someone inflict pain on them (**masochists**). Some customers receive sexual satisfaction from humiliating women. Others enjoy being humiliated: They pay prostitutes to tell them they have been naughty and should be punished, to have women spank them or urinate or defecate on them. Others combine sex with fantasy role playing. Some wear diapers, while others enjoy sex in coffins. Some wear costumes, pretending they are some historical character. Such desires are difficult to satisfy in traditional relationships, but for a fee prostitutes satisfy them. After their fantasy sex, the clients return to their regular lives. As functionalists stress, prostitution redirects these men to willing outlets.

The typical customers of prostitutes, however, are not like these men. Most customers (called "johns") are "regular" married, middle-aged men (Sawyer and Metz 2009; Milrod and Monto 2016). Why do married men patronize prostitutes? Apparently, some find their wives sexually unreceptive, while others desire sexual variety that their wives are unwilling to provide.

Functionalists stress that when people demand a service that is not supplied by legitimate sources, a **black market** will develop. This illegitimate channeling of services is *symbiotic,* that is, it is a mutually beneficial relationship: Those who purchase the service, those who provide it, and those who suppress it all benefit from the illegal activity. The clients of prostitutes purchase the sex they want; prostitutes work with a minimum of legal hassles (even calling their occasional fines the cost of "licensing"); pimps and criminal organizations earn untaxed income; and for a price, police who are "on the take" look the other way.

In Sum   Functionalists view prostitution as a means of controlling or channeling sexual behavior. In what is usually a fleeting relationship, prostitutes meet the needs of the sexually unattached and of those who want sexual acts that are not readily available to them. Also, prostitutes do not threaten the male ego—few "johns" are turned down.

The Conflict/Feminist Perspective

3.4   Explain the conflict/feminist perspective on prostitution.

The feminist perspective contrasts sharply with that of the functionalists. The feminist perspective diverges into two points of view. In the first, where the exchange of sex for money is between willing, consenting adults, they view prostitution as a form of female empowerment. Their view is that because the women are choosing to sell sex, no one should make laws to tell women what they can or cannot do with their bodies. The women, called *sex workers*, should organize, unionize, and demand higher wages and better working conditions.

In the second point of view, feminists—who call prostitution "sexual slavery" and "paid rape"—see prostitution as another of the many ways that men exploit and degrade women. They point out that some men exploit prostitutes for their own pleasure, while other men (pimps and police "on the take") exploit prostitutes for profit.

Research on Prostitution

3.5 Summarize the research findings on types of prostitutes, becoming a prostitute, pimps, and male prostitutes.

Let's look at some of the major findings on prostitutes, both female and male.

Types of Prostitutes

Besides escort prostitutes, what are other kinds of prostitutes? Let's do a quick overview.

Call girls, the elite of the prostitutes, can be selective in choosing their customers. Building a repeat business, they usually meet their customers at their own places or at the client's chosen location. To keep up with appointments, they use cell phones, pagers, tablets, e-mail, and apps.

Convention prostitutes, as the name implies, are women who specialize in conventions. Posing as secretaries or sales agents, they roam hotel lobbies, display rooms, and cocktail parties. Sometimes organizers of conventions make arrangements for prostitutes to be available.

Apartment prostitutes rent apartments outside of their own homes and set up businesses at which they work set hours. Some apartment prostitutes are married women who match their apartment hours with the husbands' working hours. Some husbands are ignorant of the wife's activities and think that she has a regular job.

Hotel prostitutes work out of a hotel and share their fees with the bell captain, desk clerk, or bellboys who steer johns to them. Because this "added service" attracts guests, some hotels provide the prostitutes a free or discounted room.

House prostitutes work in a brothel or "whorehouse." During the 1800s and early 1900s, almost all large U.S. cities and many small ones had brothels, which were located in an area of the city known as a "red light district." A red bulb shining from a window or house informed outsiders of what went on behind those closed doors.

Brothels are now unusual in the United States, but some still exist. The most well known are those in Nevada, where they are legal. The john usually has a drink or two while he makes his selection from the women sitting in the living room or bar area. From there, they go into a private bedroom. These "ranches" are listed and ranked on the Internet.

Bar girls, also known as "B-girls," wait in bars for customers. Some pay or "tip" the bartender for using the bar. Others hustle drinks (get johns to buy overpriced drinks), receiving a fee for each drink they sell.

Parking lot lizards frequent truck stops, moving from one truck to another in search of clients.

Streetwalkers have the lowest status among prostitutes. Visible to the public and police as they "work the street," they are the most frequently arrested. In some U.S. cities, streetwalkers are aggressive, hailing passing cars and opening the doors of cars that have stopped at traffic lights. Many are drug addicts involved in other criminal behaviors.

As you can see, prostitutes are often classified by the place where they work, a list that could be extended. For a different form of prostitution, see the following *Technology and Social Problems.*

Technology and Social Problems

"Female College Student Available: Wants Sugar Daddy"

I AM CURRENTLY ATTENDING COLLEGE. MY GOAL IS TO BECOME A CORRECTIONAL COUNCELER AND EVENTUALLY A LAWYER SO I CAN FIGHT THE DOJ (Department of Justice) TO CHANGE THE WAY THE CORRECTIONAL SYSTEM IS RUN.

And I am very playful. Am I what you're looking for?

I found this Internet ad (with the caps and misspelling) especially amusing because of its unusual juxtaposition of the serious (change the DOJ) and the kittenish feminine (playful). The image of a sexually playful lawyer whose goal is to reform the Department of Justice and make society a better place is almost mind boggling.

This ad reminds me of the young women who, paraded on stage in swimsuits, their bodies ogled as they are judged by officials on a 1 to 10 system, are asked to show their "talents." After twirling flaming batons, when asked about their goals in life, they recite something about ending war and eliminating global poverty.

There is something ludicrous about it all.

But let's get back to this form of prostitution, women who are offering their bodies for long-term rental fees on the Internet.

Here is one who wants $5,000 to $10,000 a month to be "made happy":

I'm a petite 18-year old from France. I'm looking for a mentor who can provide me with the finer things in life and make me happy.

Some women let their potential sugar daddies know that they are sincere sugar babies. This woman is looking for a real emotional connection with a man she can trust:

I'm just a young model still trying to decide which direction i want to take in this crazy world. I know i want to start a business one day. But haven't quite decided on anything. I'd love to meet an older wiser man that lets me pick his brain and feel like i can look up to him. Someone that will help me choose the right path for me and truly does care about my well-being. I want someone who makes me feel like a woman and treats me like a lady should be treated!

But just so the man doesn't start thinking that such a relationship will be without cost, she adds:

*People always ask "well How do we get started?" A good way to get started is start the allowance ! *hint* If you're a real SD, i wont have to worry about any of my own expenses and i shouldn't have to bring up an allowance.*

Sugar Daddies advertise, too.

Some are actually Sugar Granddaddies. A 73-year-old heads his ad: "Play with Daddy in his Paradise"

This man is looking for a woman who is "funny, lazy, whose idea of the 'good life' is playing with her Silver haired Papi at Pepes Hideaway, my popular boutique hotel, in tropical Mexico."

"Will you be my Sugar Daddy? I want to be your Sugar Baby."

Buena Vista Images/Stockbyte/Getty Images

Unfortunately, if you read Pepe's ad all the way through, you will find that Viagra hasn't been able to work its magic on him. At least he's up front about this.

Maybe a younger sugar daddy is preferable, one in his 40s who doesn't need Viagra. This one, who describes himself as Generous Gentleman, says he is athletic and a sports fan. He likes volleyball, basketball, and football.

Or if you are looking for someone a little more intellectual who likes to travel, this sugar daddy says he is "Well read and avid film buff. Love to cook and dine at the finest restaurants. I have traveled the world on business and there are dozens of places i would like to revisit for pure pleasure."

Each potential sugar daddy lists his budget. Hardly any offers to spend less than $5,000 a month on the "ONE sweet, outgoing, young girl who wants to have a great time and enjoy life to the fullest," the one they "want to spoil me and I will spoil you in return."

There also are sites that focus on gay sugar daddies/sugar babies.

The sugar daddy/sugar baby relationship has been around as long as older men have had the money to buy themselves young women—and that point is lost in history. What is new is this technological twist—the Internet allowing the interested parties to make contact with each other and to discuss their arrangements before they get involved.

This form of prostitution comes so close to the boyfriend-helping-his-girlfriend that neither party is likely to feel like a prostitute or john. It is also so close to the girlfriend/boyfriend relationship that the participants are safe from the law.

For Your Consideration

→ Do you think sugar babies are prostitutes and sugar daddies are johns? Why or why not?

→ Other than the frankness about their intentions, what is the difference between these individuals and a woman whose boyfriend helps pay her rent—or her college tuition?

Becoming a Prostitute

Researchers typically study streetwalkers, as they are visible and easily accessible. This means that most of the research on prostitution comes from poor women who have been arrested. Other prostitutes are less accessible to the police—and to sociologists. Keep this biased sampling in mind as we review the research on how women become prostitutes.

Why does someone become a prostitute? The simplest reason is money—to make as much of it as easily as possible. This is an oversimplification, however, for running through the accounts that prostitutes give of their early home life are themes of poverty, emotional deprivation, and sexual abuse (Farley 2018). For streetwalkers, this conclusion does seem to apply: Abused as children, most often by men, these women become locked into a way of life in which they continue to be victimized by men—by pimps who exploit their bodies for profit and by johns who exploit them for sexual pleasure.

But bad childhoods do not apply to all prostitutes. When we turn our focus on more privileged prostitutes, the themes of abuse and emotional deprivation are less likely to appear. Call girls often become prostitutes much like anyone chooses any occupation (Sales 2016; Siegel 2018). In a study of call girls in Australia, seven out of 10 said they would "choose this work" if they had it to do over again (Weitzer 2007).

In the following *Issues in Social Problems*, a call girl who was in a course I was teaching explains how she became a prostitute.

Issues in Social Problems

Me, a Prostitute?

Many women learn to be prostitutes gradually, going through a process similar to the one recounted here. This account, written by one of my students, who wishes to remain anonymous, has been reproduced as it was originally written (including typos and misspellings). To keep the impact of what she wrote, I have adjusted the dollar totals to account for inflation.

I am a average looking blond with blue eyes. I am a female of twenty years of age. My mother is a elementary school teacher with a doctorit degree. My father is the head of instramentation for a large oil company. He write books, makes movies and teaches around the world. I have one sibbling. She is 10 years old. My parents are very old fashioned. they are strickt with both my sister and I. We are Hard-Shell-Baptist, and attend church no-matter-what. They've instilled wonderful values in me. We live in the country on a farm (pleasure, we don't grow things). Our home is large and because both of my parents work we have a maid that comes three days a week to clean. I've always had to work around the house. Cooking meals, cleaning and doing farm chores such as, feeding the horses and cows, have always been a part of my dayly routine. Yet, there's never been anything I've ever done without. Anything that could be bought was automatically mine, just for the asking. Our entire family is close. We visit one another frequently and have get-togethers regularly.

I am from a family with an average annual income of over $100,000.00. My parents have never neglected me. No one has ever abused me. I've caused my share of trouble, but it was all jouvenile, never anything against the law of the state. I've never been a

There was nothing about the looks of the student who wrote this box to set her apart from other students.

Gaudilab/Shutterstock

misfit. I was one of the "cool" kids. I was in with the "popular" crowd. I was in Student Government and Peer Leadership in High School. I was elected Snow Queen my junior year. I never had any problems with guys. There was always plenty around my house. I just could never get attached to guys my age, they came and they went…no big deal! I had a taste for older men even then.

When I was seventeen, I met a guy who was twenty-two. He was exciting and fun. He was my first love. He was also the first guy I'd ever had sex with. Kinky wouldn't even begin to explain him. We went out for about a year and a half. Through him I met Jesse. A gorgeous Spaniard, queer as a three dollar bill, but one of the nicest people you'll ever meet. Jesse is a "BIG" record promoter for a famous record corporation. We've been friends since the day we met. We call each other all the time and "dish" on guys.

I called Jesse up one day and asked if he'd get me tickets to go to a concert I wanted to see. He said sure as he had a million times before. Only this time he too had a request. He said, "I'm in a bit of a bind. I need someone to pick up a client and show him around town Friday!" "Cool!" I said. Jesse went on to explain, "You'll be given $400.00 to buy him dinner, go dancing, or whatever else he may want to do...what's left is yours to keep." "Wow, thats great," I exclaimed! I thought to myself, what could be better, a date in which we can do anything, the sky's the limit...you get payed for playing!!! What could possibly be better than that?

I made about $140. I had a wonderful time and so did the client. I told Jesse I loved being a escort and to fix me up as often as he liked. I was assigned many men after that. I'd say a good 75 percent wanted to finish off their evenings with sex. Some even would get quite insistent. I asked Jesse what to do. Jesse said do what you want to do, guys will offer you their own money (as a write off to their own company as entertainment). To sleep with me, I thought. He said, "Do what you want to do, if you want the money, go for it! If you don't keep standing firm!" I told Jesse I couldn't do it. So, he began to filter my dates more so and more so. He was always careful not to set me up with the weirdo's or the real wild party hardy guys. I mostly got the married with three kids and a dog type from then on.

I worked at the pace of picking up $40–$200 per date, for about three months; about 60 guys total. Then I met with a client from Europe for the second time. He was a very attractive man of 40. His black hair was salted with a whitened silver. He was a family man. Though, as was the story with many of the men I escorted, he was having alot of problems with his wife. While sitting at a bar he whispered in my ear, "Would you please consider being with me tonight?" Knowing I'd turned him down the last time he was in town, he reached into his pocket for inspiration. $1,000.00 in crisp $100.00 bills he waved out like a fan and placed on the table. I looked at him and shook my head "No" I said. He put his hand on my arm and said, "How much do I have to offer you, $1,200, $1,400?" At this point I was getting pissed! In order to control my temper I flew off to the restroom in a rage. I remember standing at

the sink, looking into the mirror, and thinking who in the hell does this man think he is!! I don't need his money! But still that much money, for sex?!...how could it be? I went back to the table with thousands of thoughts running through my mind. He looked at me and said, "I'm sorry if I upset you, but, I'm willing to give you all the money I have with me, $2,000 dollars. Hows that sound?" My initial thought was to slap the crap out of him, however, the things I could do with $2,000 cash. I agreed and it wasn't hard. No commitments, no future to worry about, and no love to get in the way of habitions. I went home that night with 20 crisp $100 dollar bills and four $20's left over from the date, in my coat pocket. There's nothing to it. I can spend $200 on myself and stick the rest in a savings account. It's no biggy!

I told Jesse about it. I told him I couldn't believe how easy or how much money I made. He laughed and asked me if I had plans of ever doing this again. I said sure, it's no problem. I made over $20,000 in the 4 months to follow. Enough to buy me a new car. I never have made $2,000 in a evening again but, it became a game to me. How high can you raise the bid? How much will it take to make this man make an offer straight up? How much teasing can you get buy with, without having him drop his attention?

I've worked more than 2 yrs. I've totally mellowed out of the games. If it looks good to me, and if I find the man attractive I'll do it. I've become very secure financially. I have multiple CD's, bonds and ect. I have three savings accounts and alot of money tied up in the stock market. My only regrets are I have to keep it a complete secret from everyone. My parents, who mean more to me than the world, my family, and even my dearest friends. I miss out on the average everyday social life of a college student. I have to lie to practically everyone I meet. But, nowhere will I find a job in which I can save as much money for my future. Or for that matter when I get out of college and get a respectable job in advertising, make that kind of money. But, my life will be back to a "normal" one. One in which I can be proud of, one which I can share with my friends and family, one in which I can make a "honest" living.

Three Stages in Becoming a Prostitute As you just read, becoming a prostitute can be a gradual process. In a classic symbolic interactionist study, sociologist Nanette Davis (1978) studied this process. After interviewing prostitutes in three correctional institutions in Minnesota, Davis identified three stages in becoming a prostitute:

1. In the first stage, women *drift* from casual sex to their first act of prostitution. During this "drift," they face a series of forks in the road, and the choices they make channel them toward or away from prostitution. Circumstances that lead to drifting toward prostitution include broken homes, dropping out of school, pregnancy, drug use, a juvenile record, and having sex at a young age. On average, these women first had sexual intercourse at age 13 (the youngest was age 7, the oldest 18). The girls engaged in casual sex for an average of 4 years before they drifted into prostitution. One prostitute described it this way:

   I was going to school and I wanted to go to this dance the night after. I needed new clothes. I went out at ten o'clock and home at twelve. I had three tricks the first time, and fifteen dollars (about $50 in today's money) for every trick.

2. During the second stage, *transitional deviance* (which lasts an average of 6 months), girls experience **role ambivalence**—that is, they are not sure they want to be prostitutes.

They feel both attracted to and repulsed by prostitution. To help overcome their ambivalence, many girls tell themselves that what they are doing is normal. As one girl said,

> *I'm a person who likes to walk. There's nothing wrong with picking somebody up while you're walking. I always like walking around at night, and girls will be tempted. Girls like the offer. They like to see what a guy is going to say.*

3. During the third stage, *professionalization,* the girls identify themselves as prostitutes. They begin to build their lives around this identity and defend the selling of sex. Some sound as though they have read the functionalist perspective—they claim they reduce marital tension by giving unsatisfied men a sexual outlet. Others say that prostitution helps prevent rape.

Age of Prostitutes To see how young and how old some prostitutes are, look at Table 3.1. That there are children in the sex industry angers most people. We shall return to this topic in the section on child pornography.

Table 3.1 Arrests for Prostitution and Commercialized Sex, by Age

Age	Percent	Number
Under 10	—	1
10–12	—	4
13–14	0.1%	43
15–17	1.1%	348
18–24	27.9%	8,515
25–34	33.9%	10,332
35–44	18.8%	5,730
45–54	12.3%	3,746
55–64	4.6%	1,416
65 and older	1.2%	377
Total arrested:		30,509

Note: This category in the source includes not only the arrests of prostitutes but also those arrested for "assisting or promoting prostitution."

Source: By the author. Based on *FBI Uniform Crime Reports* 2014: Table 38, U.S. Department of Commerce.

The Pimp and the Prostitute

Why would a woman rent her body to strangers, knowing she might be hurt by sadists and risk her health through exposure to AIDS and other sexually transmitted diseases—and then turn the money she makes over to a man? Let's use the sociological perspectives to explain this.

Functionalists would emphasize the services that pimps provide: They locate customers, screen out sadistic johns, and bail prostitutes out of jail. Some pimps do these things, but researchers have found that pimps are more likely to make the women they control find their own customers, to remain unconcerned if they are beaten, and to be unavailable when they are arrested (Hodgson 1997; Weitzer 2009). For this reason, we have to move beyond functionalism for an explanation.

Conflict–feminist theorists would claim that the answer lies in the pimp's power. Pimps, not the prostitutes, rule the streets. To control women, the pimps use their greater physical strength, and they are ruthless in using it (Luthern 2018).

Symbolic interactionists would stress that there is more to the story than the pimps' power or the services they provide. Symbolic interactionists look for an answer in what pimps mean to prostitutes. The typical young street prostitute is likely to have run away from an intolerable home life. Pimps play on her insecurities and fears, some offering a sense of belonging, affection, and tenderness. Some pimps hold out the hope of marriage, children, even a home in the suburbs after they save enough money from the woman's earnings. Pimps, however, are exploiters, and they may be making the same promises to several women. The pimp tells each that she is the special woman in his life, cautioning her not to tell the others so the two of them can use the earnings of the other women to fulfill their plans.

Changes in Pimping   The idea of the pimp as controlling, powerful, and exploitive is being challenged by researchers. Sociologists who did research on prostitution in New York City and Atlantic City were surprised at the absence of pimps (Marcus et al. 2014; Horning and Marcus 2017). Going out on the streets, they had no difficulty in locating prostitutes. But the pimps—where were they? At first, they thought the pimps were staying out of sight. As they dug deeper, however, they discovered that there weren't many pimps. For reasons that are not entirely clear, women now seem to have more control (called agency) over selling sex, and few prostitutes have pimps.

For many women who are not street prostitutes, technology has made pimps irrelevant by giving sex workers greater agency over their work. The women advertise their services, make their own appointments, negotiate their prices, and keep all the money. What effects the crackdowns on Internet sites that advertise sexual services will bring are unknown at present.

Male Prostitutes

Male prostitution also reaches far back in history. Written about 3,000 years ago, the Old Testament book of 1 Kings (14:24) refers to male religious prostitutes. Whether their customers were men or women is not stated. As we look at what researchers have found about male prostitution today, we will consider men who sell sex to both women and men.

Men Selling Sex to Women   Men who sell sex to women are sometimes known as *gigolos*. With so many men willing to have sex, it is difficult for some to believe that there would be any market for men to sell sex to women. It is apparent from the "beach boys" of Bali to the "rent boys" of the Internet, however, that a fair number of women do pay men for sex. These women are seeking the same things as men who buy sex from women: convenience, pleasure, variety, youth, and companionship. The typical woman customer is in her 30s and 40s (Kingston et al. 2018).

Some Internet sites even have a customer satisfaction section. One woman wrote:

> Now I'm not the type of lady to kiss and tell so I'll just leave it up to the reader's imagination, but this I will say: he's no amateur when it comes to romance and taking good care of a woman's needs. I will definitely call upon this fine gentleman's services again in the near future (Lee-Gonyea et al. 2009:339–340).

A few years ago in Nevada, a brothel was opened where women could buy sex from men (Powers 2010). Few women wanted the "prostidudes," though, and the endeavor was short-lived.

Males Selling Sex to Men   Most male prostitutes who sell sex to men are teenagers. Sociologist have studied them since the 1960s, focusing on how they maintain a heterosexual identity (if they do), and how they find clients, negotiate prices, and protect themselves from violence. The male prostitutes often gather in urban areas they call "meat racks," public settings such as parks or certain street corners. They have a hierarchy that parallels that of female prostitutes: At the top in terms of money and prestige are escort prostitutes who work for dating agencies, in the middle are bar hustlers, and at the bottom are street hustlers. The Internet is making itself felt here, too, with "rent boys" advertising their availability (Reiss 1961; Luckenbill 1986; Ellison 2017; Ellison and Weitzer 2017).

Many see the apparent increase in male prostitution as a social problem. As with heterosexual prostitution, a related problem is sexually transmitted diseases.

Some teenagers who end up "on the streets" turn to prostitution to survive. As they age, they become less appealing to men, who seek younger entrants to street prostitution.

AJR_photo/Shutterstock

Prostitution as a Social Problem: A Summary of Subjective Concerns

Why does prostitution arouse so much subjective concern? Here are major points of view that I have culled from the extensive literature on prostitution:

1. *Morality:* Prostitution involves sexual relations that are bought and sold, not freely given in a loving relationship.
2. *Exploitation:* Prostitution of women exploits their bodies, degrades their spirits, and subjugates them to men.
3. *Property:* Prostitution ruins "good" neighborhoods. It depresses property values by bringing in unsavory characters and illegal activities such as drug dealing.
4. *Crime:* Victimless or not, prostitution is illegal.
5. *Corruption:* Profits from prostitution corrupt police and judges, uniting these "enforcers of morality" with pimps, madams, and organized criminals.
6. *Diseases:* Prostitutes spread AIDS and other sexually transmitted diseases.
7. *Aesthetics:* People feel disgusted when they see used condoms and tissues discarded in public places, including schoolyards.

Another sexual behavior that arouses intense subjective concern is pornography. Let's see what sociological issues are involved in pornography.

Pornography

3.6 Explain why pornography is a social problem and how symbolic interactionism (establishing meaning) applies to pornography.

Originally, *pornography* referred to erotic writings by prostitutes or to descriptions of the life of prostitutes. (*Porna* is Greek for "prostitute.") There are always problems with definitions, but for our purposes we can define **pornography** as writings, pictures, or objects of a sexual nature that people object to as being filthy or immoral.

As discussed in the following *Thinking Critically about Social Problems*, why pornography is a social problem is not decided easily.

Thinking Critically about Social Problems

Just What Is Pornography? And What Makes It a Social Problem?

Materials intended to cause sexual excitement have existed since early history. Pornography abounded in the Roman Empire, as shown by excavations of the Mediterranean resort city of Pompeii, which was destroyed by an eruption of Mount Vesuvius in 79 A.D. There, archeologists uncovered brothels decorated with mosaic murals of men and women engaging in a variety of sexual acts. The *Kamasutra*, an Indian religious book that goes back 1,300 years, describes sexual acts in explicit detail. It includes not only illustrations of 64 sexual positions, some of which seem to require a contortionist, but also instructions on how prostitutes can please their customers (Pawar 2014). Our own society is filled with representations of almost every sort intended to cause sexual excitement—from movies and videos to comic books and novels. We even license stores that specialize in selling sex toys and other objects whose purpose is sexual arousal.

But what makes representations designed to arouse people sexually a social problem? Remember that we need both objective conditions and subjective concerns. The wall decorations of Pompeii were intended to arouse

Hubert Boesl/picture-alliance/dpa/AP Images

Although pornography is detested by some, deplored by others, and lamented by many, if not yet in the mainstream it is getting close. Shown here are two porn stars, now called adult film actors, attending an annual awards night for porn performances.

people sexually, but it is most unlikely that either prostitutes or clients objected to them. Similarly, the illustrations of the *Kamasutra* did not arouse concern by the priests, their followers, or the prostitutes of the time. These objects were *not* part of a social problem.

As time passes, ideas of life change, including what is good and bad, the stuff that goes into morality. So it is today, and many object to the sexual illustrations of Pompeii and the *Kamasutra*—and similar depictions of sexual acts wherever they may occur—whether in movies, writing, or objects. This is the subjective concern that we need in order to have a social problem. And we have it in abundance.

Not everyone has these objections or concerns, of course, which takes us to the heart of the relativity of social problems.

For Your Consideration

→ In your eyes, what makes something pornographic?

→ Do you think pornography is a social problem? Why or why not?

Background: Getting the Larger Picture

From the boxed feature you just read, you can see that deciding if something is pornographic is like deciding whether something is beautiful or ugly. The decision lies in the eye of the beholder. Some people think nude statues are pornographic, but for others, those same statues are works of art. Are movies that show sexual intercourse pornographic? More would probably say they are. How about movies or photos that depict oral sex? A larger number would probably say yes. How about those that depict anal intercourse? The number would probably increase. How about movies that show sex between humans and animals? Or those that show adults having sex with children? At this point, the rate of agreement that these are pornographic would jump sharply.

The Pornifying of America—and the World   From its beginnings as an underground cottage industry, pornography has grown into an open and aggressive multibillion-dollar-a-year business. Behind today's pornography lies an extensive network of people who profit from it: writers, publishers, actors, and filmmakers; owners of bookstores, theaters, Internet sites, and streaming services; supermarket chains, banks, cable and credit card companies. Internet service providers and HBO and Time Warner also grab profits from pornographic movies, as do Holiday Inn, Marriott, Hyatt, Hilton, Sheraton, and other international hotel chains that offer pay-per-view pornography. Like politics, pornography makes strange bedfellows.

Pornography has become so common that we can say the United States has been *pornified*. With its 4 million plus porn sites, the Internet—sometimes called "the global pornography factory"—allows anyone to peruse pornography in private. About 12 percent of all Internet traffic are for adult websites, which have more monthly visitors than

Netflix, Twitter, and Amazon combined (Ahmed et al. 2016). One adult site has 64 million visitors a day (Kelly 2017). Although some Internet sites target women, the vast majority are directed by men for men—with men dominant, bending both resisting and nonresisting women to their will.

Pornography Viewed Theoretically: Applying Symbolic Interactionism

Legislation from the 1900s seems quaint today, but as we apply symbolic interactionism, let's look at issues that bedeviled U.S. legislators. The first is the thorny matter of determining what pornography is?

Trying to Determine Meaning   As background, keep this essential element of symbolic interactionism in mind: Until people attach meaning to something, words are merely sounds or scratch marks on paper or on a computer screen, and human acts are merely behavior. If two people look at the same photo or watch the same movie, video, or stage play, one might see the portrayal of sexual intercourse as an expression of beauty, art, or love, while the other might perceive it as filth and depravity.

This helps us understand what went wrong when the U.S. Supreme Court took upon itself the job of defining pornography for the nation. In *Roth v. United States,* its famous 1957 decision, the Court ruled that materials are pornographic or obscene when:

1. *Taken as a whole,* the *dominant theme* appeals to *prurient interest* in sex.
2. The material affronts *contemporary community standards.*
3. The material is *utterly without redeeming social value.*

If you look at the Court's major terms, which I have placed in italics, you can see why the *Roth* decision didn't settle anything. *Prurient,* for example, means "lewd or impure," but this word simply takes us back to the initial question of what pornography is. What is lewd or impure to me might be humorous or delightful to you. And *redeeming social value*? Who decides that there is some "social value" that "redeems" anything? Where does this leave us if I decide that the sexual content of a book or movie has "redeeming social value" but you do not?

And *contemporary community standards.* What community? What standards? Our society is broken into so many groups that few standards unite people into a community. Instead, there are many "communities," with vastly different views. And *contemporary*? Our society is changing so fast that what is acceptable today can be controversial tomorrow and discarded the day after that. An exaggeration, but not far off.

At this time in our history, prosecutors were trying to jail people for pornography. Instead of clearing up matters for the police and courts, the *Roth* decision only muddied the waters, and in 1973 the Court tried again. In *California v. Miller,* the Court kept the dominant "prurient" theme, and said that "contemporary community standards" meant the local community. The Court simply gave up on trying to figure out what it had meant by "redeeming social value" and dropped the term (Collins 2012).

And the reaction to this confusing decision? With what is or is not pornographic remaining in the eye of the beholder, some cities allowed live performances of sexual acts while others banned even the sale of such images. With such glaring inconsistencies, pornography again landed in the lap of the Supreme Court. Rubbing its collective head in despair, this time the Court didn't even try to define pornography. It simply ruled that it is constitutional to restrict the location of adult movie theaters (Adler 2007).

Child Pornography

It is easier to define child pornography because it contains the word *child,* which is defined by age. You can skip the confusing word pornography and simply say sex. It might surprise you, but in the 1970s, child pornography was not illegal. Adult bookstores sold magazines that featured photos of children in sexual acts. In magazines that bore such titles as *Lollitots* and *Moppets,* some of the children were as young as 3 or 4, but more popular were prepubescents between the ages of 8 and 10 (Dubar 1980).

As the states passed laws against child pornography, and judges sent people to prison for possessing these materials, magazines and movies featuring children practically disappeared. Child pornography, of course, did not disappear. It just went underground, resurfacing on the Internet. There, people who are stimulated by sex with children "meet" in chat rooms, where they share stories of their exploits, real or imagined. They also disseminate child pornography via e-mail, instant messaging, websites, newsgroups, bulletin boards, and peer-to-peer networks. Possessing photos, movies, or videos of children who have been bribed, tricked, or forced into sex acts carries severe prison sentences, but the use of passwords and encryption makes it difficult to track down those responsible for child pornography. Sting operations occasionally net dozens of offenders (Burns 2018).

Who is aroused sexually by watching children in sex acts? You might think it is the scum of the earth, but the arrests show something quite different. While we have no random samples of people who view child pornography, the person is likely to be your neighbor. What do I mean by this? Simply that many ordinary, "good" people view child pornography. This is a logical conclusion to draw from those who are caught in sting operations, who offer to swap files, or who have images of child porn on their computers: Teachers, doctors, police, and FBI agents are among them ("Former FBI Agent..." 2012; Banks 2016).

Virtual Child Pornography Computer-generated images of children in sex acts are called virtual child pornography. In a 2002 decision, *Ashcroft v. Free Speech Coalition*, the U.S. Supreme Court ruled that because no real child is involved, there is no victim, and it is legal to possess virtual child pornography. Congress didn't like this ruling, and the next year Congress passed the PROTECT Act, specifying that it is illegal to produce, distribute, or possess "a visual depiction of any kind of a minor engaging in sexually explicit conduct." This includes drawings, cartoons, sculptures, and paintings—unless, Congress added, it has "serious literary, artistic, political, or scientific value." By now, these words should alert you to a recurring problem of establishing meaning. How do we determine "serious," "artistic," and "value"?

Although the Court has not overthrown its 2002 *Free Speech* decision, possessing computer-generated images of children having sex *seems* to be illegal. This seems to also apply to drawings and paintings, perhaps even to four-fingered comic characters on the Internet. "These are just lines on paper," claim those who think the law preposterous. It will take more decisions by the Court to clarify what is legal and illegal. The rulings have become less ambiguous, and people are being arrested and sent to prison for possession of cartoons that officials view as obscene or pornographic (Masuchika 2015).

As you can see, these are thorny issues. With no easy answers, they must be sorted out by lawmakers, lawyers, and judges—and all within a rapidly changing society where ideas of morality are continuously evolving. In the next *Thinking Critically about Social Problems*, we examine another issue that is being sorted out.

Thinking Critically about Social Problems

Restitution for Child Pornography?

It is hard to describe what it feels like to know that at any moment, anywhere, someone is looking at pictures of me as a little girl being abused by my uncle and is getting some kind of sick enjoyment from it. It's like I am being abused over and over again.

Amy was just a little girl when her uncle (now in prison) began to molest her—and to take pictures and videos of himself having sex with her. He also posted these photographs and videos on the Internet, where they have been circulating for a dozen years. The images of Amy sometimes show up in the pornographic collections of men who have been arrested for possessing child pornography.

Now an adult, Amy decided to fight back: "Those men who are looking at my pictures and watching those videos aren't innocent. They are guilty of exploiting me, just like my uncle did."

Amy went to an attorney, who agreed with her. He said that these men should have to pay restitution for the harm that was done to her. Amy and her attorney decided that she was owed $3.5 million for damages.

Amy gets notices from the courts whenever prosecutors identify her images in the pornography collections of people who are arrested. She has received more than 1,500 notices and has collected $1 million. Amy and her lawyer plan to keep these lawsuits going until Amy receives the full $3.5 million.

Not all judges agree with the law, and a little judicial rebellion appeared. Some judges ordered payments of just $100. Others refused to order any restitution. They said, in legal language, that "the link between possession and the harm done is too tenuous to reach the level of proximate harm." In plain terms, this means that those who made and distributed the images have harmed Amy, but not those who possess or view the images.

Congress disagreed and passed the Amy, Vicky, and Andy

In pornography involving children, the children are victims. Some are tricked into participating, while others are forced into the pornography. The abuse of children is an issue that unites Americans.

Child Pornography Victim Assistance Act. This federal law gives victims of child pornography the right to restitution for their sexual exploitation. Eventually, the Supreme Court will decide if this law is constitutional.

Based on Forliti 2010; Schwartz 2010; "Possession of..." 2014; Riley et al. 2018.

For Your Consideration

→ Do you think that someone who views photos of a child being abused sexually owes restitution to the child?
→ How has a person who viewed photos of a child being abused harmed the child?

Controversy and Research on Pornography

3.7 Explain the controversy over pornography and understand the major research findings on pornography.

When photography was invented in the 1800s, some of the first photographs were of nude women and sex acts. This was controversial then and remains controversial today. Let's look at some of the research.

A National Response to Pornography

Strong opinions and emotions, sometimes even fear, are a hallmark of social problems. Pornography is no exception. A common fear concerning pornography is that it destroys people's morals, perverts their sense of sexuality, and even encourages men to rape. Does it? While we can't measure whether pornography corrupts morals or perverts sexuality, as these are personal judgments—people's sense of right and wrong—we can report on the relationship of pornography and rape.

The National Commission on Obscenity and Pornography How times have changed. In the 1960s, pornography was seen as such a serious problem that the president of the United States appointed a national commission to study pornography. In 1970, Lyndon Johnson's National Commission on Obscenity and Pornography reported its findings. As Table 3.2 shows, one of its conclusions was that pornography affects some people more than others.

Interesting findings, perhaps, but they certainly didn't address what was on a lot of people's minds—their concerns that viewing pornography was harmful.

Table 3.2 Pornography's Effects

More Sexual Stimulation	Less Sexual Stimulation
Younger	Older
More educated	Less educated
Not actively involved in a religion	Actively involved in a religion
More sexual experience	Less sexual experience

Source: Schmidt and Sigusch 1970.

The Meese Commission Pornography continued to proliferate, increasing concerns that it was harming people and society. The mild conclusions of Johnson's national commission did not satisfy those who saw pornography as evil and were convinced that pornography was viciously harmful. Facing pressure from people with these views, President Ronald Reagan asked the attorney general to appoint another commission to study the effects of pornography. This group, the Meese Commission, came to markedly different conclusions, ones that matched the views of those who wanted the new commission. One of the conclusions of the Meese Commission (1986:39) was that pornography is a threat to women. The commission stated: "There is a causal relationship between exposure to sexually violent materials and an increase in aggressive behavior directed towards women." The commission also said that because pornography makes rape seem "legitimate," an increase in pornography "will cause an increase in the level of sexual violence directed at women."

Cause, Effect, and Concerns about Morality

You might be wondering how these two national commissions could come to such contradictory conclusions—one that pornography causes no harm and the other that it causes rape. People at the time wondered, too.

I have already hinted at the answer. For members of the Meese Commission, that pornography causes rape was "common sense." You might recall from Chapter 1 that I stressed that "common sense" can be quite wrong. If all we need is common sense, we wouldn't need science, and science requires verifiable evidence. Critics said that the Meese Commission was predisposed to see pornography as evil and as the cause of crime. This colored the members' views, becoming a lens through with they viewed the research. They amplified anything that fit their ideas and minimized anything that contradicted them (Baron 1987; Brannigan 1987; Linz et al. 1987).

This fundamental error led the Meese Commission astray. The members confused **correlation** (two or more things occurring together) with **causation** (one thing producing an effect on something else). The commission found that rapists had viewed substantial amounts of pornography. This is *correlation*, two items that occur together. From this correlation, the members of the commission jumped to the conclusion that pornography *causes* men to rape.

To make it clearer why correlation is not causation, consider this: If the commission had found that the men who raped loved cheeseburgers and read comic books, this would be a correlation. But this finding would not prove that either eating cheeseburgers or reading comics causes men to rape. I'm trying to use a ludicrous example to get the point across, but it is no less inaccurate to draw this conclusion than to conclude that because rapists viewed pornography the pornography caused them to rape.

Because a picture is worth a thousand words, look at the spurious correlation in Figure 3.1.

Many people have the fear that pornography, especially pornography that shows violence against women, stimulates men to rape. Even though the Meese Commission confused correlation with causation, its conclusion could have been right. Maybe pornography does cause rape, but the Meese Commission just didn't have the evidence.

How could the Meese Commission have tested its

Figure 3.1 Spurious Correlations

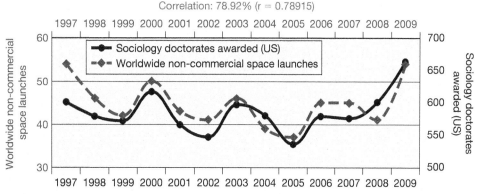

Source: Tyler Vigen, *Spurious Correlations*, Hachette Books, 2015.

conclusion? If they could have increased pornography in society, then we could have seen if rape increased. This would still be a correlation, but it would be in the right direction, suggesting that the Meese Commission was right. By contrast, if the unthinkable happened—if the Meese Commission had been able to increase pornography and rape dropped—we would know that the Meese Commission was wrong.

A Natural Experiment The Meese Commission could not experiment with people, but then two surprising things happened. After the commission finished its report, the United States and other countries did their own *natural experiment*, and we were able to measure the results.

Pornography laws loosened, and the Internet was invented. As the use of personal computers began, a few sites on the Internet appeared that featured explicit sex. Then as computers became common, such sites multiplied, becoming popular with both men and women, the young and the old. From being an under-the-counter, furtive backroom purchase in special stores, pornography moved into America's living rooms and bedrooms. Major hotel chains began to offer pornography on demand, the names of their XXX-rated movies conveniently not listed on their guests' hotel bills. No longer lurking in back alleys, pornographers began to hold annual trade shows in Las Vegas, promoting the stars of their latest hits.

Quite a change. This *natural experiment* includes *millions* of pornographic sites on the Internet offering access to photographs and streaming videos of people in sexual activities. Some sites feature professional actors, others highlight amateurs. Sites are indexed, from A to Z, anal to zoo. Viewers can choose from teenagers to grannies; whites, blacks, Asians, Latinos; country of origin; skinny, heavy; little breasts, big breasts; heterosexual, gay; the old and young together. If someone likes to watch men or women having sex with animals, that is available, too. If there is a market for any type of sexual preference, some Internet entrepreneur somewhere is more than eager to meet it.

So, what is the result of this natural experiment? How much did rape increase, as the Meese Commission said it would if pornography increased? Look at Figure 3.2. You can see that since the Meese Commission's 1986 report, rape increased, but only to 1992, when the rate started to drop. And it kept dropping, although pornography kept increasing. The rape rate hit a low in 2015. Since then it has increased, and now is the same as it was in 2008.

Figure 3.2 Forcible Rape in the United States

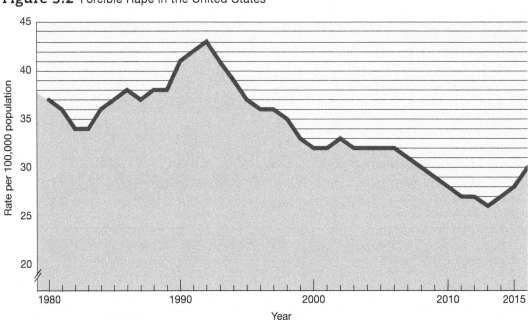

Source: By the author. Based on *Statistical Abstract of the United States* 1990:Table 283; *Crime in the United States* 2016:Table 1.

What Can We Conclude?   As you can see, the results do *not* support the "commonsense" idea that pornography causes rape. You can also see that the evidence points in the opposite direction, that pornography *reduces* rape. In general, the more that pornography has increased, the more that rape has decreased. The members of the Meese Commission would roll over in their graves at such a suggestion, but we need to look at evidence with open minds, not try to make the evidence fit our commonsense ideas.

But is this evidence that pornography reduces rape? It might be, but we don't know because this is still correlation, not causation. This unexpected finding also shows up in other countries, especially when it comes to sexual attacks against children. When Denmark made hard-core pornography legal in the 1960s, that country's sex crimes against children dropped (Kutchinsky 1973). This also happened in Japan in the 1980s when that country began to allow the sale of hard-core pornography. Then 20 years later when the Czech Republic decriminalized the possession of child pornography, what do you think happened? Common sense might predict that offenses against children would increase. But they didn't. Instead, sexual abuse against children dropped there, too (Diamond 2009).

How can this possibly be? If pornography does reduce sex crimes, there has to be a reason. The answer probably goes something like this: Some men who are sexually attracted to children find it better to masturbate to pornographic images of children than to face the threat of shame and prison if they carry out their fantasies with real children. For men who are attracted to rape, it likely is the same. Pornographic images provide a much safer substitute.

One thing is clear: As pornography in the United States—including that depicting violence against women—has become more common, rape has become less common. It is difficult to determine cause and effect in human behavior, but one thing seems certain: If an increase in pornography were accompanied by an *increase* in sexual attacks, you would have to put your hands over your ears to shut out the outcry. With the evidence going in the opposite direction, listen carefully: Do you hear an outcry that to protect women, we should increase pornography?

In the three countries that legalized child pornography, sex crimes against children dropped. As outrageous as it might seem to our common sense, it is possible that child pornography might be a way to *protect* children. But if so, can you imagine any group in the United States demanding that child pornography be legalized "for the sake of the children"?

Science versus Social Action

This is science at work. When research is published, it enters what we might call the "courtroom of science," where it is judged by a jury of critical scientific peers. When researchers report their findings, other researchers meticulously comb the research for errors. They challenge the research in scientific papers, or repeat the research, or reanalyze the original data and publish their own conclusions. This critical process exposes biases and errors that might be present. In this way, knowledge builds, which either replaces or confirms our commonsense ideas about social problems.

Determining cause and effect is difficult because of the amazing variety of people who make up our world. Human action, of whatever type, has different effects on different people. This includes pornography. Some researchers have found that pornography that shows violence against women can trigger sexual aggression in men who are angry and aggressive, but the same pornography does not have these effects on more relaxed, "laid back" men (Malamuth et al. 2012). This still does not settle anything, and we need considerable more research.

Some people find the rigorous and exacting process of science too slow. Convinced that severe consequences are at stake, they feel a pressing need to take a stand now. And based on their commonsense ideas about what is right and wrong—and what they find offensive—they often do take a stand.

For example, many people are upset about how pornography portrays women. They are convinced that pornography teaches men to view women as "pieces of meat" and that it teaches women to devalue their own bodies. Whether pornography causes sex crimes is not the point, they insist. Even if it does not, the portrayal of women in pornography debases and victimizes women. This is reason enough to ban pornography—at least the type that shows violence against females. From the following *Thinking Critically about Social Problems,* you can see that resistance to pornography was once strong and how the porn industry won.

Thinking Critically about Social Problems

The Pornifying of America: Crushing Resistance and Co-Opting Feminists

Pornography flourishes in the United States and many countries, but these business interests had an uphill struggle. To be able to sell zillions of magazines, photographs, and videos and movies required an amazing turnabout in attitude. With Americans overwhelmingly opposed to pornography, considering it immoral, how did porn manage to prosper in the midst of attitudes that would destroy it?

Religious conservatives view pornography as a moral issue. For them, pornography is sin. They see the growing pornography industry as a sign of the growing depravity of U.S. culture. Conservatives continue to put up occasional resistance, but as pornography has become common, they have mostly come to view resistance as labor wasted on a lost cause. Religious leaders will occasionally bemoan pornography, but they realize they are preaching to the choir—and that some in their choirs devour pornography at home. So do some religious leaders.

During the struggle against pornography, feminists split on this issue. Some were appalled at pornography, but they didn't want to be aligned with people they considered religious fanatics (Bronstein 2011; Whittier 2014). Their objection was not that pornography is sinful but that pornography degrades and exploits women. Not only are women shown as a bunch of body parts to be used for the pleasure of men, they stressed, but also women who work in the porn industry suffer sexual and emotional abuse. On the other side are feminists who say that pornography liberates women sexually, that it frees them from culturally imposed prudishness. For these feminists, pornography is seen as a way for women to explore and express their sexuality. They support better working conditions and health standards for women who work in pornography.

One issue that divides feminists is pornography, especially the portrayal of women. This protester is concerned about possible changes in the laws regarding pornography.

John Stillwell/PA Images/Alamy Stock Photo

As you can imagine, this division among feminists delighted the porn industry. The feminists who were opposed to pornography found themselves opposing other feminists and seemingly aligned with conservative religious folk, a disaster as they saw it. They quickly backed off the porn issue.

How great is the victory of the porn industry? While we haven't yet come to the point that pornography is a family activity, we can note that women's magazines that used to suggest how to decorate the house for holidays now lay out suggestions for how to use pornography to enhance or to help women get "in touch" with their sexuality. To oppose pornography has become retrograde, old-fashioned, and especially threatening, "uncool."

Some feminists are producing what they call "feminist porn," pornography that emphasizes women's sexual pleasure and challenges dominant images of gender, sexuality, and body types (Potter 2016). They want porn to depict women exploring their erotic freedom and sexual identity, not women being dominated by men. They also are opposed to only certain types of women—primarily skinny women with big breasts—being portrayed as sexually desirable.

The question seems to have abruptly changed from pornography as evil to pornography as a means of transforming images of women and rechanneling men's sexual desires. Now this is quite a change.

For Your Consideration

→ Do you think the United States has been "pornified"? Why or why not?
→ What effects do you think pornography is having on society?

Social Policy

3.8   Discuss the issue of making consensual behavior illegal—and its alternatives.

Earlier in this chapter, I made the point that sex is not merely a personal matter. Rather, the social group with a stake in our sexuality sets up ways to channel or control our sexuality. Even consensual acts behind closed doors can be public issues. Notable examples are purchasing a prostitute's services and watching child pornography in one's own home. This takes us to the issues of privacy, consent, and legality, central issues that surround human sexual behavior as a social problem.

The Question of Making Consensual Behavior Illegal

Sociologists use the term **victimless crime** to refer to illegal acts between consenting adults. The crime has no victim because the people agree to do something with, to, or for one another. Someone pays a woman or a man for sex; someone else sells or buys pictures of adults involved in some unusual sexual act—both activities may be illegal, but they occur with the consent of the people involved.

In most crimes, someone acts *against* another person. There is a victim and a perpetrator (a "perp," as the cops say). When a victim reports a crime, the police know where and when it happened and who the victim is. Without a victim, however, the police spend limited public resources attempting to determine that a crime occurred, and then prosecutors have difficulty in obtaining convictions because the people involved consented to what took place. Unless there is a public outcry, both the public and the police prefer that law enforcement agents pursue criminals who have victims—thieves, muggers, rapists, and murderers.

Not all prostitution and pornography are victimless crimes, however. These activities can involve force, threats, drugging, deception, or less than informed consent. If there is force, it is rape, a different matter entirely. If there is less than informed consent, there is also a victim. Slipping cameras surreptitiously under women's skirts in public, for example, does not involve consent. Neither is child pornography a victimless crime. The children are not of age to give their consent, and child pornography often involves the abuse of adult authority. To deal adequately with social policy, we must separate such instances from those that involve full consent.

Alternatives to Making Consensual Behavior Illegal

Let's explore alternatives to making consensual behavior illegal.

Legalizing Prostitution   Because prostitution is a commercial transaction—a business—some argue that it should be legal. We license and tax businesses, so why not do the same with prostitution? Those who favor legalization point out that prostitution is not going away, no matter what anyone thinks, and they suggest it is time for the state to regulate it. We discuss this in the following *Thinking Critically about Social Problems.*

Thinking Critically about Social Problems

Should We Legalize Prostitution?

Yes

1. Prostitutes perform a service for society. They provide sex for people who can't find other sexual partners. They even help marriages by providing an outlet for sexual desires that the spouse doesn't want to be a part of.

2. Keeping prostitution illegal stigmatizes and marginalizes women who want to work as prostitutes. It also corrupts police officers, who accept bribes to allow prostitutes to work. Pimps often control prostitutes by force, and some prostitution is run by organized crime, with women held in bondage. Legalizing prostitution will eliminate these problems.

3. If prostitution is legal, the government can regulate it like other businesses. Prostitutes will be licensed and taxed. The licensing will ensure that prostitutes have regular medical check-ups, and the taxes will bring in revenue. The prostitutes will be required to display a dated and signed medical certificate confirming that they are free of sexually transmitted diseases.

No

1. Prostitution is immoral, and we should not legalize immoral activities. The foundation of society is the family, and we should take steps to strengthen the family, not tear it apart by approving sex as a commercial transaction outside the family.

2. Prostitution degrades and exploits women. To legalize prostitution is to give the state's approval to women's degradation. Legalization would also affirm class oppression: Most prostitutes come from the marginal working class and serve as objects to satisfy the sexual desires of men from the more privileged classes.

3. The legalization of prostitution will not stop prostitutes from infecting their clients with sexually transmitted diseases (STDs). A prostitute can receive and transmit STDs, including HIV, before the disease shows up in blood tests. Even though prostitutes are licensed, they will spread STDs during this interval.

For Your Consideration

→ Do you think we should legalize prostitution? Why or why not?

→ What are the sources of your attitudes about the legalization of prostitution?

Giovanni Mereghetti/ MARKA/Alamy Stock Photo

Like gambling, selling and buying marijuana, and many other activities that involve only consenting adults, should we legalize prostitution?

Without intending to, lawmakers in the state of Rhode Island once made prostitution legal. In the following *Issues in Social Problems,* you can see what happened.

Issues in Social Problems

What Happened When Prostitution Became Legal? Problems in Knowing

Lawmakers in the state of Rhode Island were bombarded with complaints about prostitutes in the streets. In 1980, they responded as lawmakers do, by passing another law. In their haste, they accidently deleted the law against prostitution. What they did was make it illegal to solicit on the streets but not indoors.

Ads for sex in my apartment, your apartment, your motel room, and so on proliferated. No one complained about all the "indoor sex" that was going on, but the lawmakers corrected their mistake in 2009 when they again made indoor prostitution illegal.

So, what happened between 1980 and 2009—besides whatever went on behind closed doors? Sociologists Scott Cunningham and Manisha Shah (2014) decided to find out. Their findings are fascinating. The rape rate dropped. So did the rate of gonorrhea. The researchers ran different kinds of statistical tests, and they found no other explanation except the accidental decriminalization of indoor prostitution. They suggest that prostitutes who work indoors practice safer sex and that some men will pay prostitutes rather than rape someone else.

Fascinating. This would mean that laws against prostitution actually increase sexually transmitted diseases and rape.

I checked Rhode Island's rape rates since indoor prostitution was again made illegal, and I was quite surprised at what I found. As you can see from Table 3.3, since 2009, rape increased by 10 percent.

These rape rates are in the predicted direction, but you can also see that they have bounced around a bit. The most I would be comfortable in concluding is that they indicate the possibility that these laws have latent dysfunctions, unanticipated negative consequences for women.

How about Rhode Island's rates of gonorrhea since 2009? Take a look at Figure 3.3.

That's right. Rhode Island's rate of gonorrhea has more than doubled!

So, with the rates of both rape and gonorrhea dropping after indoor prostitution became legal and then both increasing after it became illegal, can we conclude that laws that permit indoor prostitution would decreases rape and gonorrhea? It would

Table 3.3 Rhode Island's Rape Rates Since Indoor Prostitution became Illegal

Year	Rate
2009	28.1
2010	28.1
2011	30.4
2012	27.4
2013	31.6
2014	24.0
2015	32.4
2016	31.0

Source: By the author. Based on *Crime in the United States* 2010:Table 4; 2012:Table 4; 2014:Table 4; 2016:Table 2.

Figure 3.3

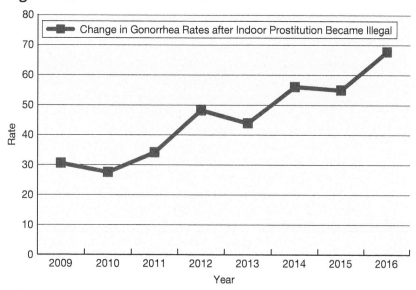

Source: By the author. Based on *Crime in the United States* 2010:Table 4; 2012:Table 4; 2014:Table 4; 2016:Table 2; CDC "Sexually Transmitted Diseases Surveillance," years 2009–2016.

certainly seem so, and, if this were true, I would suggest that we start a social movement to legalize indoor prostitution. But—and there is a big one—we can't draw this conclusion.

Do you recall what I wrote about spurious correlations? We certainly have correlations in Figure 3.3, but we cannot be certain that we have causation. Perhaps the changed rates are due to something else, to what sociologists call underlying third variables. That this is likely the case here as evident in the changed rates of gonorrhea. At the same time that Rhode Island's rates of gonorrhea increased, the same thing was happening across the United States. What was going on? The Internet, dating sites, and dating apps—and people hooking up and being extremely careless about protecting themselves from sexually transmitted diseases.

In fact, if you look at the bigger picture, Rhode Island came out quite well. As you can see from Figure 3.4, during our epidemic

of STDs, Rhode Island's rate of gonorrhea dropped from 39th to 44th in the nation (CDC, various years).

If you get the idea that tracing causation in human affairs is difficult, you would be right. From this, you might also better understand why sociologists are cautious when they talk about causation. What seems obvious often is not.

For Your Consideration

→ Why is it difficult to prove causation in human behavior?

→ What arguments other than morality can you make against legalizing prostitution?

→ How can we legislate morality when our society is pluralistic, with many competing ideas about what is moral?

Figure 3.4 Where Rhode Island Ranks in U.S. Gonorrhea Rates

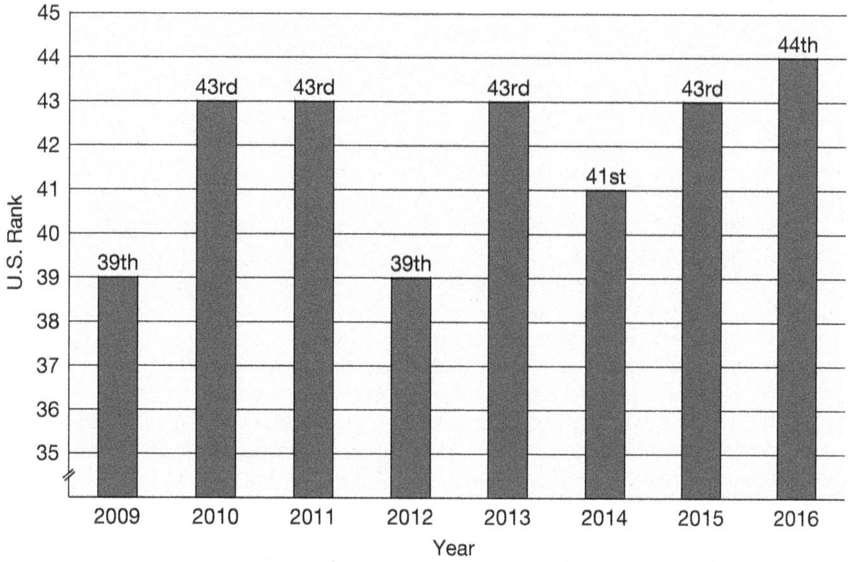

Source: By the author. Based on CDC "Sexually Transmitted Diseases Surveillance," years 2009–2016.

The Matter of Privacy   Central to deciding social policy is the issue of privacy. The argument is that if adults want to have sex in private, why should it concern the state? It may be a sin to some, but should those people's attitudes make it a crime?

There is yet another side to the privacy argument—the right of *privacy from* people who are involved in sexual acts. Even if these behaviors are or become legal, those who find those sexual behaviors repugnant should not have to see them. Following this, the law should prohibit street solicitation by prostitutes, sex in public places, and nudity and/or sexual acts on the covers of magazines in supermarkets.

This argument also stresses that there is such a thing as public decorum or decency. Even if a sexual act is seen as good and desirable, such as sex between a husband and wife, this does not provide reason for husbands and wives to have sex in public. This can offend both adults and children. According to this view, some things belong in the intimacy of the bedroom.

To allow people to pay for sex *and* ensure that others don't have to see it if they don't want to, some suggest **segregation**—limiting these activities to specified areas. This is the solution chosen in Nevada, where counties decide whether or not to license houses of prostitution. If they allow prostitution, they also determine how many brothels to allow and specify where they will be located. Segregating prostitution to specified areas helps the *freedom from* issue. To this end, blatant advertising can be banned even in those areas. Prostitutes could advertise for customers in newspapers, on the Internet, or even by a red light in an apartment window, but they could not solicit on the streets. Nor could pornographic theaters show sexually explicit marquees or posters. This would allow the patrons of prostitutes and the consumers of pornography to carry out their consensual activities in private, while respecting the rights of others to avoid seeing their activities.

The Matter of Children

The use of children in prostitution and pornography is an entirely different matter. Almost everyone agrees that children should be protected from sexual exploitation. Their basic position is this: If the purpose of the law is not to protect the defenseless of our society, then what is its purpose? In the following *Issues in Social Problems*, you can see how private citizens are protecting children from sexual victimization.

Lois Lee

Lois Lee, the sociologist who founded Children of the Night.

Issues in Social Problems

Applying Sociology: Taking Back Children from the Night

Lois Lee isn't afraid to apply her sociological training to social problems. Lee did her master's thesis on the pimp–prostitute relationship and her doctoral dissertation on the social world of the prostitute. During Lee's research, adult prostitutes told her, "You know, it's too late for you to help us, Lois. You've got to do something about these kids. We made a choice to be out here … a conscious decision. But these kids don't stand a chance."

While still in graduate school, Lee found children as young as eleven working as prostitutes on the street. She founded Children of the Night in 1979, and between 1979 and 1981 over 250 children came through her home. Her home telephone became the first Children of the Night hotline.

After receiving her Ph.D. in sociology from United States International University in 1981, Lee opened the first drop-in center in Hollywood for children she found prostituting on the streets for food and a place to sleep. She provided these children with crisis intervention for medical or life-threatening situations, family counseling, job placement, and foster home or group placement. Soon she developed street teams to travel the western region of the United States providing services for street prostitutes in cities and truck stops.

In 1989 Lee opened a world-class shelter home for child sex trafficking victims offering 24 beds, on-site schooling, case management, counseling, and recreation. From 1992 to 2017 there were 3,048 children who called Children of the Night home.

Lee closed the shelter on December 31st, 2017 when state and federal policies determined that every child sex trafficking victim fell under the jurisdiction of Children's Services or federal policies, allowing the police to hold children in solitary confinement or witness protection until they testified against a pimp/trafficker (often a family member or someone they loved). Lee had fought for more involvement of Children's Services and law enforcement in the lives of children victimized by prostitution, but she had mixed feelings about the inability of these agencies to perform and some of the cruel tactics of law enforcement.

Lee created new, relevant programs for child sex trafficking victims on the run from social services and police. She offered them 24/7 case management and stabilization programs and, because she was privately funded, she did not report the children to the police or other officials.

Lee also developed an innovative educational plan where U.S. children could receive one-on-one tutoring to prepare for the high school equivalency exam. She wanted to make sure child sex trafficking victims were not going to be illiterate because of new policies and their rejection of government aid.

Lee's work has brought her national publicity, most notably the prestigious President's Volunteer Action Award in 1984. She also received the 1994 National Caring Award, and her portrait hangs in the Frederick Douglass Museum and Hall of Fame for Caring Americans in Washington, D.C.

Lee's life was depicted in the 1985 TV Movie *Children of the Night*. In 1987, she was profiled on *60 Minutes*, and lauded by Richard Marx in a song *Children of the Night*, which raised over $500,000 to build the Children of the Night home.

Lee credits her success to her sociological training, especially the sensitivities it gave her "to understand and move safely through intersecting deviant worlds, to relate positively to police and caretaking agencies while retaining a critical perspective, to know which game to play in which situation."

As Lee said during a CBS interview, "I know what the street rules are, I know what the pimp game is, I know what *the* con games are, and it's up to me to play that game correctly. It's all sociology. That's why when people call me a social worker, I always correct them."

Decades of films, news, talk shows, and print media on the Children of the Night and Lee's work are currently being archived for permanent placement in museums and other sites.

Based on Buff 1987; Markman 2009; Rosenthal 2012; "Professor for a Day" 2016; Lee 2019.

For Your Consideration

→ Do you think that teen prostitution is a social problem? Why or why not?

→ Do you think that teen prostitution is a different kind of problem than that of women and men in their 20s who rent their bodies? Why or why not?

→ If you think that teen prostitution is a social problem, how do you think we should solve it?

The Future of the Problem

3.9   Explain the likely future of prostitution and pornography.

With such rapid social change engulfing us, it is difficult to peer far into the future. Assuming that the United States does not devolve into a dictatorship, which could drive prostitution and pornography underground, I foresee the following.

Prostitution and the Future

Perhaps the easiest forecast in the entire book is this one: The demand for the services of prostitutes will continue. There will always be sexually deprived, frustrated, or adventuresome people who want to patronize prostitutes, as well as those who want to pay for specialized sexual services. And there will always be poor people who need the money.

Although prostitution will continue to flourish, it will remain illegal in almost all areas of the United States. The police will overlook all but the most blatant acts, both because they feel that they have better things to do and because many of them are convinced that sexual acts between consenting adults should be legal. The prostitution of children is an entirely different matter. There is strong agreement that this is a loathsome act, so we can expect harsher laws and severe punishments. For teenage prostitutes, we are likely to see more emphasis on these children as victims, rather than as lawbreakers. If so, more efforts should go into their treatment, rather than simply locking them up in juvenile facilities. Whether the public wants to see their tax dollars spent in this way, however, is another matter.

Just as technology is changing almost all of life, as discussed in the following *Technology and Social Problems,* it might have a new impact on prostitution.

Technology and Social Problems

Cyborg Sex Partners

The marriage of silicone, engineered parts, and artificial intelligence (AI) is bringing cyborg sex partners. These life-like machines can not only wiggle, but they can also hold conversations. The talk is simple at the moment, but advances in AI hold the promise of quite real-life conversations in the future.

And speaking of almost real life, these silicon sweeties have all that it takes, from beautiful faces and figures to parts that move when touched. Always willing. No excuses.

The robot moves her eyes, blinks her eyelids, turns her head, dips her chin, and changes her facial expressions.

Get tired of the same face? No problem. They come removable and replaceable.

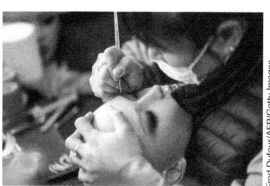

Fred Dufour/AFP/Getty Images

This worker in China is painting the face of a silicone "smart" sex robot, which is available not only for sex but also can talk, play music, and turn on the dishwasher.

Get bored with the same personality? No problem. Do you want sultry or shy? Talkative with a British accent? All available.

Life-like sex robots are available for both men and women. Apparently, however, most of the male sex robots are bought by gay men. It seems that women have much less interest than men in these machines.

Just an interesting innovation? Or are we peering into a future where people increasingly withdraw from the demands of human interaction into more solitary human-machine interaction?

Proponents of sex robots point to less prostitution, but already brothels featuring sex robots have opened in London and Paris.

Based on Kragen 2017; Braun 2018; Devlin and Lake 2018.

For Your Consideration

→ What is your opinion of cyborg sex partners?

Pornography and the Future

Changes in pornography are likely to be driven by two forces: technology and profits. As each new communication technology appears, pornography will be adapted to fit it. With today's technology making it easy to produce and view moving images, even more pornography will flood the market, much of it produced by amateurs. With profits beckoning, it is also likely that the mainstream media will embrace pornography even more. Cable television is likely to offer more explicit programs than its current XXX-rated options, perhaps broadcasting live sex programs. The line between pornography and art will continue to blur, making it difficult to distinguish between pornography and regular films. In the following *Technology and Social Problems,* we focus on electronic pornography.

Technology and Social Problems

Pornography on the Internet

Why is electronic pornography a problem? Why can't people exchange nude photos on the Internet with one another if they want to? If this were the issue, there would be no problem. The real issue, however, is quite different. What disturbs many people are the photos that show bondage, torture, rape, and bestiality (humans having sex with animals). Judging from the number of such sites on the Internet, apparently many people derive sexual excitement from such photos and videos.

The Internet abounds with "chat rooms." No one is bothered about the chat rooms that center on Roman architecture or rap music or turtle racing. But chat rooms where the focus is on how to torture women are another matter. So are those where the participants talk about seducing grade-school children—or that extol the delights of having sex with 4-year-olds.

Any call for censorship raises the hackles of civil libertarians, who see all censorship as an attack on basic freedoms. Censorship, they say, is just the first step toward a totalitarian society. If we let the government censor the Internet an inch, it will stretch that inch into a mile and censor other things it doesn't like—such as criticisms of government officials. They point to how Chinese officials are using optical character recognition to censor the Internet, even removing words they dislike from personal blogs.

Most civil libertarians in the United States do accept a limit on free speech, drawing the line at child pornography, but only reluctantly—and they don't want the line drawn any further.

Based on Foley 2008; Boden 2012; Pham 2018.

OpenAperture/Alamy Stock Photo

Violence against women, a subtheme of much pornography, elicits little protest and no outrage, unlike what would occur if violence were directed against members of a particular racial-ethnic group. Why do you think this is?

For Your Consideration

→ Do you think it should be legal to exchange photos of women being abused sexually or tortured? Why or why not?

→ Should it be legal to discuss ways to seduce children? Why or why not?

→ If we make the exchange of photos of women being abused or a discussion about ways to seduce children illegal, then what other communications should we prohibit? On what basis?

→ If we don't censor, how do we protect young children from pornography?

Some continuing clash between the pro- and anti-pornography forces seems inevitable, for the values of these groups are contrary, and each desires to control the media. But U.S. society is now so pornified that those who oppose pornography seem to have given up. It is likely that those who oppose pornography will limit themselves to an occasional statement decrying the fall of American values and then retreat quietly into enclaves of people who agree with their views.

Summary and Review

1. All societies attempt to channel sexual behavior in ways they consider proper or acceptable. When the violation of sexual norms is felt to be a threat to society, especially to the family, people get upset. Their subjective concerns turn the objective conditions into a social problem.

2. Through the lens of functionalism, we saw that prostitution persists because it serves social functions. From a functionalist perspective, as prostitutes service customers who are sexually dissatisfied or whose sexual desires are deviant, they relieve pressures that these individuals might place on people who are unwilling to participate. The three stages in becoming a prostitute are drift (drifting from casual sex into selling sex), ambivalence, and professionalization. Some young men who sell sex to men manipulate symbols to maintain heterosexual identities.

3. Deciding what is and is not pornographic has confused many, including the U.S. Supreme Court. In the tradition of symbolic interactionism, the Court has ruled that what a community decides is pornographic is pornographic—for them.

4. Social scientists have been unable to determine the social effects of pornography; but where hard-core pornography has become legal, violent sex crimes have decreased. Feminists are split on the issue of pornography, from those who say it dehumanizes women and encourages men to see women as sexual objects to those who say that pornography liberates women to explore their sexuality. Some feminists are producing what they call "feminist porn." Social activists take action on the basis of their convictions, not on the basis of proof about causation.

5. *Victimless crimes* are illegal acts to which the participants consent. Prostitution and pornography are classified as victimless crimes by sociologists when adults participate, but not when children are involved, since children cannot give full consent. The suggestion that the government legalize prostitution runs into firm opposition.

6. Prostitutes will continue to adjust to changing technology. With society now pornified, opponents of pornography seem to have given up their struggle.

Thinking Critically about Chapter 3

1. This chapter began by stating that all societies control human sexual behavior. Why do you think this is true? What is it about sex that makes us inclined to control the sexual behavior of others? Be sure to base your answer on group aspects of society—not on personality or individuals.

2. What is your opinion about pornography? On what do you base your opinion?

3. What is your opinion of the following? Child pornography is illegal, and people are arrested and put in prison for possessing it. Pictures of tortured and sexually abused women are legal.

Key Terms

black market, 53
causation, 65
correlation, 65
masochists, 53
pornography, 60
prostitution, 50
role ambivalence, 57

sadists, 53
segregation, 72
sex, 48
sex tourism, 51
temple prostitution, 50
victimless crime, 68

Chapter 4
Alcohol and Other Drugs

Tom Briglia/National Geographic Image Collection/Getty Images

Learning Objectives

After reading this chapter, you should be able to:

4.1 Illustrate how subjective concerns change and how they make a drug part of a social problem.

4.2 Explain why drug use or abuse is a personal or a social problem.

4.3 Contrast the symbolic interactionist, functionalist, and conflict perspectives on drugs.

4.4 Explain what medicalizing human problems means and how it is related to the abuse of prescription drugs.

4.5 Give a brief overview of the drug use of college students.

4.6 Summarize research findings on nicotine, alcohol, marijuana, and cocaine.

4.7 Summarize research findings on LSD, peyote and mescaline, PCP, and ecstasy.

4.8 Summarize research findings on amphetamines and barbiturates.

4.9 Summarize research findings on steroids.

4.10 Summarize research findings on heroin and morphine.

4.11 Explain why it is difficult to establish social policy on drug use and abuse.

4.12 Explain the likely future of the social problem of drug abuse.

"Debbie! What's this?"

Seeing the familiar plastic bag, Debbie felt her face redden. Why hadn't she put it away as she always did? She swallowed, then burst out defiantly:

"My purse! You've got no business snooping in my purse!"

"I was just looking for a match—but I found a lot more! I never expected a daughter of mine to be a drug addict."

"Drug addict? That's funny! Just because someone smokes grass doesn't mean she's a drug addict."

"Everybody knows marijuana is the first step to the hard stuff, like heroin–and I don't care that some states are so stupid they are making it legal."

At this, Debbie shook her head in disbelief at her mother's thinking. Then she said, "Mom, it's you who's hooked. The first thing you do in the morning is light up a cigarette and have a cup of coffee. And after that you start popping Prozac."

"Don't you compare my medicine to your drugs. My doctor prescribes Prozac for my nerves."

"Okay, then what do you call your martinis? And I know why you dug in my purse for a match—it's because you're hooked on cigarettes."

"Don't you talk back to me, young lady. Ever since you started college, you think you know it all. Just wait' til your dad gets home."

"Yeah, sure. Then you'll do the same thing you do every night—talk about it over a drink."

> **"Mom, it's you who's hooked."**

The Problem in Sociological Perspective

4.1 **Illustrate how subjective concerns change and how they make a drug part of a social problem.**

Just as Debbie's mother was shocked to discover that her daughter smokes marijuana, hundreds of thousands of other parents have had similar rude awakenings. The use of marijuana has become so common that it shows up among presidential candidates. Presidents Bill Clinton and Barack Obama have smoked marijuana, although Clinton said, "But I didn't inhale." Everyone needs a good laugh now and then. Obama was more open as he discussed his use of marijuana as a young man. President Trump denied that he has ever smoked marijuana—or even a cigarette.

A Quick Historical Background

The use of drugs such as marijuana and cocaine goes far back in history. More than 4,000 years ago, a Chinese emperor recommended what we today call medical marijuana– using marijuana to help rheumatism, malaria, constipation, and absent-mindedness. And cocaine? About 600 years ago, the Spanish *Conquistadores* found that the natives of Peru chewed coca leaves for the stimulating effects of cocaine (Hart and Ksir 2018).

Using drugs, however, can elicit strong negative reactions. Let's look at some extremes.

Tobacco When Christopher Columbus landed in North America, he found that Native Americans smoked tobacco. This plant wasn't native to Europe, and he took some back with him. Europeans tried it and liked it, and smoking tobacco became common. King James I of England was sure that smoking causes health problems, and in 1604 he wrote a pamphlet warning his subjects that tobacco was "harmful to the brain and dangerous to the lungs" (Hart and Ksir 2018). Other rulers went somewhat beyond issuing warnings. In 1634, the czar of Russia ordered his officials to slit the noses of tobacco smokers. The rulers of China went further—they had smokers' heads cut off (Goode 1989). All of these anti-tobacco campaigns failed.

Caffeine Today, Starbucks franchises dot the landscape, and almost every home and office has a coffee machine. But how different it used to be. After coffee was introduced to the Arab world during the 1500s, Islamic religious leaders became upset when people drank coffee to help them stay awake during long vigils. Stating that coffee was intoxicating and prohibited by the Koran, religious leaders ordered coffee dealers to be beaten across the soles of their feet (Brecher et al. 1972). A century later, in 1674, a group of English women wrote a pamphlet titled "The Women's Petition Against Coffee." They complained that their men were leaving "good old ale" in order to drink "base, black, thick, nasty, bitter, stinking, nauseous" coffee. Even worse, the coffee, they said, was making their men less sexually active (Meyer 1954; Ellis 2006).

Opium in the United States   For opium, the acceptable-unacceptable route goes in the opposite direction. As you know, using opium is illegal today, but in the 1800s, you could buy opium across the United States—in drugstores, grocery stores, and general stores. You could even order opium by mail. Opium was advertised as a cure for diarrhea, colds, fever, teething, pelvic disorders, and even athlete's foot and baldness. To soothe their babies, mothers fed their babies opium-laced syrup. To smoke cigarettes or drink alcohol was more offensive than to use opium (Brecher et al. 1972; Inciardi 1986; Hart and Ksir 2018).

Top athletes used to recommend cigarettes. After all, Chesterfield was "The best Cigarette for *You* to Smoke." Can you imagine athletes today sponsoring a brand of cigarettes and encouraging youth to smoke?

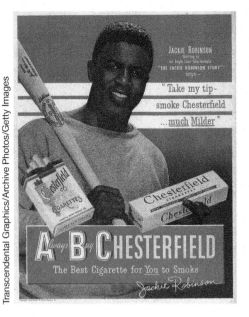

Transcendental Graphics/Archive Photos/Getty Images

Why This Brief History of Drugs?   It is important for you to see how people at different times define *the same drug* as good and as bad. This is because—and this is an essential point for this chapter—*No drug is good or bad in and of itself.*

Consider tobacco again. You are familiar with today's anti-smoking climate and the health warnings on cigarette packages. In the 1940s and 1950s, the situation was somewhat different. As you can see from the ad for Chesterfield, even top athletes used to recommend cigarettes.

This drives home the point that I made in Chapter 1 about objective conditions and subjective concerns. *Objective conditions* can be important—such as the harm connected with some drug—but without *subjective concerns*, that drug will never be part of a social problem. As with abortion and prostitution, which we discussed in earlier chapters, people acquire different views of drugs and line up on opposing sides of the issue.

In Sum   Whether a drug is considered good or bad, and therefore acceptable or unacceptable, does not depend on the drug's objective conditions. Rather, this depends on people's subjective concerns, which change over time. Subjective concerns are the central sociological principle of drug use and abuse, and I shall stress them over and over in this chapter.

The Scope of the Problem

4.2   **Explain why drug use or abuse is a personal or a social problem.**

Debbie, in our opening vignette, is just one of the 7 million 18- to 25-year-old Americans who smoked marijuana during the past month (NIH 2017; *Statistical Abstract* 2018:Table 10). To her, marijuana is no big deal. It makes her feel good, and she likes to smoke with her friends. Debbie's mother is also like a lot of other Americans—she drinks coffee, alcohol, and sodas; smokes cigarettes; and ingests a variety of substances that she does not think of as drugs.

But these substances are drugs—so what makes their use a social problem, not just a personal matter or even a personal problem?

A Personal Problem or a Social Problem?

Marijuana, alcohol, nicotine, and caffeine are all drugs. Drugs are not just substances that are sold in alleys or exchanged furtively for money in an SUV someplace. A **drug** is a substance that people take to produce a change in their thinking, consciousness, emotions, bodily functions, or behavior. We can define **drug abuse** as using drugs in such a way that they harm one's health, impair one's physical or mental functioning, or interfere with one's social life. Once again—the reason that a drug is part of a social problem is not because the drug is harmful but *because the substance is socially disapproved.* Approval and disapproval takes us to clashing perspectives, such as those of Debbie and her mother.

We live in a pro-drug society. We are born with the aid of drugs, and drugs help ease our departure from this life. In between, we use drugs for sickness and for pleasure, to relieve anxiety, queasy stomachs, headaches, and all sorts of other pains and discomforts. As with alcohol, we take drugs to help us be sociable. As with coffee, tea, and colas, we take drugs routinely, unthinkingly, and habitually. You know that cigarettes are addictive, but so are coffee, tea, Coke, and Pepsi. Some people "just can't get going" in the morning without their "fixes" of caffeine.

Most of us take the use of drugs for granted, but when drug use interferes with someone's health or how that person gets along in life, we begin to question it. This we consider a *personal problem.* But if large numbers of people become upset about a drug and want to see something done about it, then that drug becomes part of a *social problem.*

Addiction to Drugs

Using some drugs leads to **drug addiction**, or *drug dependence.* Someone who is addicted to a drug comes to depend on its consumption to make it through the day. When people think of drug addicts, they are likely to think of people huddled in slum doorways, the dregs of society who steal to support their habits. Let's look at drug addiction a little more closely.

> *A guest speaker came into sociologist Lori Fowler's class. As he stood at the front of the class, he reached into a pocket and pulled out a vibrating voice machine. He lowered the high collar covering his tracheotomy and set the vibrating machine onto his throat. He talked through the machine and told the students how, even after losing his voice, he still smoked cigarettes through his tracheotomy hole.*

Whether the addiction is to nicotine or to heroin, why don't drug addicts just quit—especially when they know it is ruining their lives or hurting their loved ones? The reason is to avoid **withdrawal**, the intense distress—nausea, vomiting, aches and pains, nervousness, anxiety, and depression—people feel when they abstain from a drug. Withdrawal creates **craving**, intense desire for the missed drug. Even after someone has kicked the habit, the craving can last for years. And even after the craving is over, people may still experience an occasional desire for the drug. This is referred to as **psychological dependence**.

> *On a personal note, I used to be a drug addict. I never thought of myself as one, but I began smoking at age 13 and quit 26 years later. The physical withdrawal was severe for six weeks, and then tapered off. The psychological dependence continued much longer. Even three years after quitting, I would dream that I was smoking cigarettes. These dreams were so vivid and disturbing that I would awaken abruptly—feeling guilty for having fallen back into the habit.*

Looking at the Problem Theoretically

4.3   Contrast the symbolic interactionist, functionalist, and conflict perspectives on drugs.

It is legal to use drugs as lethal as nicotine and alcohol, and yet people are sent to prison for using milder drugs. Why such inconsistency? As we go back in history a bit to unveil the reasons, keep in mind that *subjective concerns outweigh objective conditions.* Let's see what pictures emerge when we look at drugs through our three theoretical lenses.

Symbolic Interactionism

From previous chapters, you know that symbolic interactionists stress that objects and events have no meaning by themselves, that an object or event takes on whatever meanings people give it. Let's look at how this principle applies to alcohol.

What Does a Drug Mean? The Temperance Movement   Alcohol has been part of U.S. culture since the arrival of the Pilgrims, who brought beer with them (Keller 2018). Yet in 1919, the 18th Amendment to the U.S. Constitution was ratified, making it illegal to produce, sell, or consume alcohol. The following 14 years are known as Prohibition.

Why such a remarkable change? Sociologist Joseph Gusfield (1963) traced the law to culture conflict. Anglo-Saxon Protestants had settled New England, and their customs and religion dominated the region. Then in the 1820s, uneducated, poor immigrants poured into this area from Italy, Germany, and Ireland. The newcomers drank a lot, which offended the educated and well-to-do New Englanders. Many of the immigrants were also Roman Catholics, which also offended the established Protestants. They held up their noses and called them ignorant, Catholic drunks.

As more immigrants poured in, political power began to shift. Feeling their power slipping away, the members of the old establishment began a campaign (called temperance) to transform the new immigrants into clean, sober, godly people who would reflect the values of New England's traditional moral leadership. Abstinence came to symbolize hardworking people with good reputations, while drinking was associated with unreliable, uneducated immigrants of questionable background. Anyone who wanted higher social standing had to abstain from alcohol.

As the United States grew more urban and secular, the culture conflict continued. Seeing their power and values slipping even further, Protestants intensified their efforts to uphold temperance. Their victory came in 1919 when the Eighteenth Amendment to the Constitution was passed. Overnight, it became illegal for Americans to buy even a glass of beer. Prohibition, Gusfield said, marked the victory of middle-class, Protestant, rural values over working-class, Roman Catholic, urban values.

Prohibition, of course, did not stop people from making and drinking alcohol, and gradually the forces behind temperance weakened. Fourteen years later, in 1933, this grand experiment in drug control was repealed, and again Americans could drink alcohol legally.

Making a drug illegal—or keeping one legal—can certainly differ from common sense. Let's consider this in the following *Issues in Social Problems*.

This photo, taken during Prohibition (1920–1933), shows one of the many failed attempts to eradicate alcohol from American life.

"Bootlegged"(illegal) whiskey, highly profitable during Prohibition, was an impetus to organized crime. The bloody violence between gangs competing for control of bootlegged alcohol was one reason Prohibition was repealed. Shown here is the body of Frankie Yale, gunned down on a Brooklyn street in retaliation for the killing of a rival, Big Ed Murphy.

Issues in Social Problems

Sociology and Common Sense: Legal and Illegal Drugs

Common Sense

1. Illegal drugs are harmful, and legal drugs are not harmful.

2. If a legal drug is discovered to be addictive and is abused, it will be made illegal.

3. If a non-narcotic drug has been classified mistakenly in the law as a narcotic, it will be reclassified.

Sociology

1. The harm that a drug causes is not the reason that the drug becomes illegal. Making a drug illegal is a political process. If a drug is classified as illegal, some interest groups have managed to get their points of view translated into law.

2. Some addictive drugs (alcohol, nicotine, Prozac, Valium, OxyContin, and fentanyl) are backed by well-financed interest groups and remain legal.

3. Marijuana was classified incorrectly as a narcotic in the 1937 Marijuana Tax Act. Although knowledge of this error is common, no interest group has been powerful enough to get this misclassification corrected.

For Your Consideration

→ Why do you think sociological findings sometimes, as here, differ so greatly from common sense?

Functionalism

When functionalists study drugs, whether they are legal or illegal, they examine their functions and dysfunctions. In this short section, we will place the focus on prescription drugs.

The Social Functions and Dysfunctions of Drugs While *functions* are the intended positive effects of a drug, *dysfunctions* are its unintended negative effects. A function of recreational drug use is to "loosen" people up, or otherwise help remove tensions that interfere with sociability. These drugs are also functional for those who make money from growing, processing, distributing, and selling them. These same drugs are dysfunctional for those who abuse them and for their family members.

Prescription drugs are functional both for medical professionals and their patients. A striking example is the prescription drugs used to treat mental health patients. In the 1950s, more than 500,000 Americans were locked up in mental hospitals. Today, the number of beds in psychiatric hospitals has plummeted to just 68,000 (*Statistical Abstract* 2018:Table 190). This huge decline is due in large part to the discovery of mood-altering drugs, or psychopharmaceuticals. These drugs allow several hundred thousand people to remain at their jobs and with their families.

Prescription drugs also have dysfunctions. Some drugs are not tested adequately before they are approved. They turn out to have severe side effects, including disabilities and deaths. Others bring harm when doctors prescribe them for purposes for which they were not intended. Instead of trying to find out what is wrong with a patient, some physicians take the easier route and prescribe mood-altering drugs. "Doped-up" patients become befuddled and lethargic, and some suffer permanent neurological damage. As sociologist Donald Light (2011) says, the harmful side effects of prescription drugs are an overlooked epidemic, leading to over a million hospitalizations a year.

The dysfunctions of drug use—not just prescription drugs but also nicotine, alcohol, heroin, and others—extend far beyond the individual. They include crimes that are committed to support addiction, the spread of AIDS among addicts who share needles, deaths and injuries from automobile accidents, and the loss to society of a reservoir of human potential. The following *Personal Account* illustrates how drug addiction is devastating not only for addicts but also for their families.

Personal Account

Addiction: Not Just the Individual

While I was working on an earlier draft of this chapter, Jenn, who was helping with research, mentioned that her brother had died a few months before, "after a long struggle with an addiction to alcohol and OxyContin." She stressed how addiction is not just a "street" experience and how devastating it is to families. I asked if she would share her experience with us. This is what she wrote.

Hi Jim,

I am writing to tell you about my brother, Matt. He died this summer while receiving treatment for alcohol and OxyContin addiction. Matt was 37 and left a wife and four young children behind.

Alcohol was always an issue with Matt. He belonged to a partying crowd in high school and had occasional run-ins with the police for underage drinking. As he moved into adulthood, the partying continued, but he became a union carpenter and worked 50–60 hours a week. So, we worried, but assured ourselves that if he never missed a day of work because of drinking, then he had it under control. He didn't, though, and a DUI arrest initiated what would be a ten-year on-and-off participation in Alcoholics Anonymous, with on-and-off success.

Matt married, and this seemed to help. Then two months after his first child was born, she died of SIDS. I can't possibly describe what this was like; it was beyond words. Around the same time, Matt had hernia surgery for a work injury and received his first prescription for Percocet. This chain of events was his undoing, and his addiction to alcohol made it increasingly difficult to resist using pills. It was not a quick decline; it was a multi-year pattern of six months of sobriety and hard work until union work would dry up, and his alcohol and pill use would increase, followed by a week in rehab. What always shocked me about rehab was the hours he would have to spend on the phone trying to find a rehab with an open bed, and the ridiculous requirement that he arrive intoxicated. So, we would take turns waiting for a clearheaded and determined Matt to make his calls; then we would buy a bunch of nips so he could drink them on the way.

He would clear his body of toxins, and after five or six days of rehab would be making calls to find work. He never stayed very long, always anxious to return to work and to not incur charges after his insurance was used up. He and his wife had gone on to have three more children, and he had a lot of demands on his income and time. Things grew worse. His sober periods became shorter and shorter, he lived through one overdose, he lost his driver's license for eight years, his marriage became strained, and he lived more and more at my parents' house so they could drive him to work.

Drug abuse can ravage the individual's body, employment, and social standing. As this box stresses, the individual's family also suffers.

A year and a half ago, Matt called me for what I had started to call a "rehab drive." This time he was determined to do a long rehab stint. He ended up doing six months in a sober house in Nantucket and was able to work construction there. We felt glimmers of hope. But he missed his children terribly and came home for Christmas. Once home, he underwent a quick decline. He was drinking and using pills. He was starting to have big memory gaps. So much of his personality disappeared. It didn't seem like there was much of "him" left in him. My parents were afraid to go away for the weekend and leave him alone. I am ashamed that I avoided some of his calls because he was asking me for money.

Last summer, he was back in the hospital, so we felt like we could go on vacation while he was in a safe place. We took his kids and went up to Maine with my parents. We felt sad on Father's Day because his kids were without their father. We were right to feel that way because he died in the hospital on Father's Day morning. He was on "dry out" medication, but he obtained alcohol inside the hospital and died from a toxic reaction of the alcohol and anti-anxiety medication. Nurses checked on him as he slept, and he was alive at 7:30 A.M. but was dead by 10:30. Two days later, his wife received a letter from him saying how dedicated he was to getting better and returning to his family.

Addiction consumes all the energy in a family. Could I have done more for Matt? Probably, but taking care of his kids, taking care of my kids, being a bright spot for my parents, supporting my younger brother, reacting to emergencies, all felt like a lot.

Thanks for the opportunity to tell this story,

Jenn

For Your Consideration

→ From this case, what costs of drug addiction do you see to the individual?

→ From this case, what costs of drug addiction do you see to the family?

→ Does drug addiction bring costs to society? If so, what might they be?

→ Suggest changes to improve the way we deal with drug addiction.

Conflict Theory

Let's turn to the conflict perspective, which gives us an entirely different picture.

Drug Laws as a Political Tool   Conflict theorists point out how drug laws are sometimes used as political tools. If a particular drug (such as crack cocaine) is common among some group, to make that drug illegal allows authorities to unleash the police against this group. Does this really happen? U.S. history is littered with examples.

One of the most notable examples might surprise you, how drug laws once targeted Chinese immigrants. In the 1800s, the transcontinental railroad was being built to connect the east and west coasts of the United States. Short of labor to complete this gigantic project, the railroads sent agents to China, where they recruited thousands of men. When the railroad was completed, these men were not needed—and not wanted. Tensions grew when the Chinese men competed for jobs with whites, offering to work for lower wages.

Tensions boiled over when a national financial panic and depression hit in 1873. In some areas, the whites rioted, beating and killing the Chinese. Many of these Chinese men smoked opium, a legal drug at the time (de Oliveira 2018). To target men who threatened the jobs of whites, San Francisco and other West Coast cities passed laws that made smoking opium illegal. The target was not the opium, but the Chinese.

The racism of this period drenches the mind. Here is "testimony" given at a Congressional hearing on laws to regulate opium:

> In the Chinatown of the city of Philadelphia there are enormous quantities of opium consumed, and it is quite common, gentlemen, for these Chinese or "Chinks," as they are called, to have a concubine as a white woman. There is one particular house where I would say there are 20 white women living with Chinamen as their common-law wives. The Chinamen require these women to do no work, and they do nothing but smoke opium all day and night. A great many of the girls are girls of family, and the history of them is very pathetic. You will find those girls in their younger days out with sporty boys, and they got to drinking. The next step was cigarettes. Then they go to Chinese restaurants, and after they go there a couple of times and get a drink in them they want to "hit the pipe." They do it out of curiosity or pure devilishness (Cited in Chin and Ormond 2018).

Our history is strewn with examples of how those in power use drugs to arouse sentiment against disfavored groups. Consider the series of "evil forces" behind the narcotics trade. During World War I, German anarchists were supposedly smuggling heroin into this country. With the outbreak of World War II, Japan was identified as the evil smuggler. Then during the Cold War of the 1950s, the Soviet secret police were fingered as the sinister heroin supplier. During the Korean War, China became the culprit. During the Vietnam War, North Vietnam was named as the mastermind of the narcotics trade (Karmen 1980). With our war on terror, the Taliban and al Qaeda were fingered as the new vile suppliers (Perl 2001). Now it has become China's turn again—the head of a global network that fuels the fentanyl crisis in the United States (Whalen and Spegele 2016). This accusation has occurred just as China's modernized navy has begun to challenge the United States over control of the South China Sea.

In Sum   Each theory contributes to the understanding of drugs as a social problem. Symbolic interactionists stress how drugs become powerful symbols that affect social life, as was the case with alcohol and the great drug experiment known as Prohibition. Functionalists examine the functions and dysfunctions of drug use—how, for example, some psychiatric patients benefit from legal mood-altering drugs, while those same drugs impair the physical or social functioning of other patients. Conflict theorists analyze how drug laws are used to arouse sentiment against groups that pose a threat to power arrangements.

Among the many performers who have died from drug abuse is Prince Rogers Nelson. He was found dead in his home, his life cut short by drug abuse.

■ Research Findings: The Use and Abuse of Drugs

After considering what it means to medicalize human problems, we'll look at the abuse of prescription drugs and then drug use and abuse by students.

Medicalizing Human Problems

4.4 Explain what medicalizing human problems means and how it is related to the abuse of prescription drugs.

Prince, a musician who had sold more than 100 million records and had won 7 Grammys, was found dead at age 57. The coroner ruled that Prince, who was addicted to painkillers, died from an accidental overdose of fentanyl, a synthetic drug 50 times more powerful than heroin (Coscarelli and Eldred 2018).

Though extreme, celebrity deaths like those of Elvis Presley, Michael Jackson, and Amy Winehouse pinpoint one of today's major drug problems: the abuse of legal prescription drugs. Let's get a quick overview of what has led to this type of abuse.

Expanding the Medical Model

Physicians have always taken care of people's bodies, and, often, of their personal problems as well. However, until the 1930s, they lacked medicines to treat personal problems. At that time, the pharmaceutical industry began to produce psychoactive drugs, and physicians began to prescribe antidepressants and antianxiety drugs for conditions that people used to assume were a normal part of life. Anxiety, distress, irritability, inability to concentrate, feeling "down," even feelings of "not fitting in"—all became "medical conditions" for physicians to treat. This change, called the **medicalization of human problems**, was an amazing transition: from ordinary personal problems of everyday life to medical conditions, from personal coping to the need to see a doctor for prescription drugs.

The same thing has happened again with kids who give their parents and teachers a hard time. For a one-sided presentation that is likely to either make you smile or make you angry, read the following *Thinking Critically about Social Problems*.

Thinking Critically about Social Problems

Doping Problem Kids: ADHD and the Ritalin Riddle

Children have always driven parents and teachers wild. All kids "act up" sometimes, and some seem to do it all the time. From kids who won't sit quietly at their desks to kids who talk back or hit other kids, there is no end to the problems.

If only you could just give these kids a drug to settle them down, like the drugs they give to all those unruly old folks in the nursing homes (which you read about in Chapter 2). And this is exactly what happened. Parents and teachers kept complaining about problem kids. The doctors listened—and they came up with a special kid medicine. Give that problem kid some Ritalin, and smooth out your life.

Developing a Medical Solution

Of course, you can't dope kids because they are rambunctious. You have to have an illness to justify giving drugs to kids to settle them down. Illnesses require names, and the medical profession needed one to turn those problem behaviors into an illness. At first, all they could come up with was hyperactivity, which simply means that a kid is highly active. Not too good. The limitations of that name are obvious. The doctors needed something better, maybe more frightening and certainly official-sounding. Their new name, **attention-deficit hyperactivity disorder (ADHD)**, did the trick. Now any kid who has *that* must really be sick.

An Ambiguous "Epidemic"

No one knows what this term means—although you can get a list of symptoms: The child is forgetful, the child doesn't pay attention, the child daydreams, and on and on. Sounds like they might be future poets. If a doctor applies the term ADHD to the child, though, you know the child has an illness. And as everyone in our medicalized society knows, an illness calls for medicine. Evidently, an epidemic of ADHD has swept through our schools, for *3 million* U.S. schoolchildren receive ADHD drugs, including Ritalin and Adderall (Danielson 2018).

Expanding the Medical Solution

If you think I'm being unduly severe in my criticism, listen to child psychiatrist Carl Kline. He phrased his objection even more strongly. Ritalin, he said, is "nothing more than a street drug being administered to cover the fact that we don't know what's going on with these children" (Livingston 1997). Child psychologist Alan Sroufe (2012) adds that "no study has found any long-term benefit of attention-deficit medication on academic performance, peer relationships or behavior problems, the very things we would most want to improve."

If you've got a good thing going, why not expand it? Incredibly—at least to me—doctors now prescribe drugs for toddlers who are going through their "terrible twos" (Schultz 2014). No special name here—not yet, but I'm sure one is on the way. I suggest that these little ones probably have "two terribilus."

There are times when I think that with physicians giving our kids so much Ritalin, there must be a good reason for it. Then I read something that convinces me otherwise. It probably doesn't

Although there is increasing awareness of the burden that Ritalin places on schoolchildren, the problem continues.

Andy Shell/Shutterstock

surprise you if someone says that some teenagers are angry, irritable, argumentative, defiant, or vindictive toward authority figures. It might surprise you to learn, however, that this pattern of behavior is now being called a psychiatric illness, one that needs Ritalin to subdue and make life easier for us.

Whether or not you are surprised at any of this, the name given to this illness will likely surprise you. It is being called ODD. No, I didn't make this up. ODD is an acronym for Oppositional Defiant Disorder (Schoorl et al. 2018). At least someone has a sense of humor in calling the kids ODD. But isn't it time to say that the emperor has no clothes?

Culture and Genetics

What does culture have to do with ADHD? Some analysts say that genetics and brain function underlie ADHD (Hinshaw and Scheffler 2014). They point out that the ability to concentrate, to sit still and focus for long periods of time, is not an either-or thing. Instead, all of us are located somewhere on a continuum, from those most capable of these behaviors to those least capable of them. Only when societies demand more formal education of their youth, increasing the need for intense focusing for prolonged periods, do those with the lesser abilities to do so become upset and act out, becoming a problem for themselves and others.

For Your Consideration

→ How would you evaluate the arguments made in this *Thinking Critically about Social Problems?*

Profits provide a strong motivation to expand the medical model to every possible problem of life. The drug companies flood television and magazines with ads for medications that you *cannot* buy over the counter. People see the ads and imagine themselves living happy, carefree lives—running across sunlit fields of wild flowers—if only they could just get their hands on Xanax, Prozac, or some other drug. They tell their doctors what they want, and the doctors (who make money from writing prescriptions) comply. Drug companies make obscene amounts marketing these drugs, while pharmacists joyfully go to the bank after counting the little pills and putting them in little plastic tubes.

Abusing Prescription Drugs

Prescription drugs are necessary to treat a variety of medical problems, and some of us would not be alive without them. The abuse of prescription drugs, however, has become a major problem. As you just read, the pharmaceutical companies and the medical profession are sometimes a central part of this abuse. This is the focus of the following *Thinking Critically about Social Problems.*

Thinking Critically about Social Problems

Unexpected Death: The Opioid Crisis

You get 15 people hooked on opioids, and you're a thug who deserves to rot in hell; you get 150,000 people hooked, and you're a marketing genius who deserves a huge bonus (Kristof 2017).

As I write this, the situation is so extreme that this past year 70,000 Americans died from drug overdoses—more than all the Americans (58,000) who died during the entire war in Vietnam. With more Americans dying from drug overdoses than AIDS killed at the peak of the HIV epidemic, drug overdoses are now the leading cause of death for Americans under 50.

What happened? We always have some deaths from heroin and other drugs, but then the synthetic opioids—fentanyl and its analogues—entered the drug scene. Fentanyl, 50 times more powerful than heroin and often prescribed for pain, is powerfully addictive.

At the root of this crisis are doctors and pharmaceutical companies. When the synthetic opioids were developed, the pharmaceutical companies found themselves

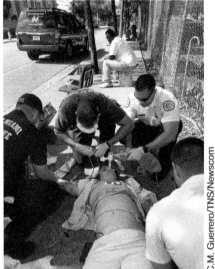

Deaths from opioids have become a national emergency. Some communities have run out of refrigerated coolers to place bodies while they await autopsy.

with a bonanza of wealth—as long as they could keep the demand flowing. These companies misled doctors by overstating fentanyl's pain-relieving benefits and understating its addictive powers. They sponsored conferences for doctors all over the country at which they touted fentanyl as a magic drug that doctors couldn't do without.

Like sheep, the doctors prescribed the opiate painkillers. They now write about *230 million* opioid prescriptions a year—about one bottle of opioids for every adult American.

As you can expect, these prescriptions let the drug companies rake in billions of dollars in obscene profits. And at what a cost in human lives and suffering. The 70,000 deaths a year—465 a day—are more than all the Americans who die by guns or accidents.

Look again at the quote that opened this *Thinking Critically*. The drug companies purposely hooked people who were suffering from pain. And when these people became addicted, they needed more fentanyl to ward off the withdrawals of fentanyl. Many went doctor shopping, getting more and more prescriptions for more and

Figure 4.1 Stages of Intervening in the Opioid Crisis

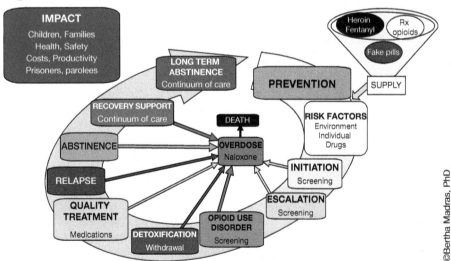

more fentanyl from multiple sources. When this failed to meet their growing addiction, they turned to street drugs, a cycle that is ending in death for so many.

What can be done? After studying this problem, a commission appointed by the president came up with multiple solutions. As you can see from Figure 4.1, the proposed solutions begin with reducing the supply, including fewer prescriptions, and move on to prevention and care.

For Your Consideration

→ Has your life been touched in some way by the opioid problem? How?

→ Suppose you have just been appointed by the president of the United States to head a well-funded new agency to solve the opioid problem. Based on Figure 4.1, where would you focus your resources? Why?

(Based on President's Commission 2017. https://www.whitehouse.gov/sites/whitehouse.gov/files/images/Final_Report_Draft_11-15-2017.pdf)

Drug Use by College Students

4.5 Give a brief overview of the drug use of college students.

For an overview of the drug use of college students, look at Table 4.1. The sample on which this table is based is so good that we can generalize these findings to *all* college students across the nation. Don't try to generalize these findings to all colleges, however. They apply to college students in general, but not to specific colleges. At some colleges, for example, hardly anyone binge drinks, while for good reason others have national reputations as party schools.

As you can see, alcohol is by far the favorite drug of college students, followed by marijuana. All other drugs shrink in comparison with these two. Nicotine in the form of cigarettes used to be the second most popular drug, but over the past 25 years cigarette smoking has plummeted, while marijuana smoking has stayed about the same. This change in the popularity of cigarettes has dropped tobacco to third place and raised marijuana to second place.

Despite the similarities in how men and women college students use their two most popular drugs, this table also reveals differences. There are minor distinctions, such as slightly more women than men have drunk alcohol and smoked marijuana during the past month. You can see, too, that men are more likely to get drunk and to binge drink. If you look at the *daily use* of alcohol and marijuana, you will see a fundamental difference—that, men are much more likely than women to smoke marijuana daily and about *twice* as likely to drink alcohol every day of the month.

A major concern of college officials is **binge drinking**—five or more drinks in a row for men or four or more drinks for women on a single occasion. From this table, you can see why binge drinking is a concern. During the past month, about one-third of all college students have binge drunk. To say the least, this is a lot of hangovers. But there is much more. Students who binge drink are more likely to experience a wide range of problems, from academic difficulties to risky sexual behavior (Wechsler and Nelson 2008; Lewis et al. 2015). Then there is alcohol poisoning, a life-threatening

Table 4.1 What Drugs Do Full-Time College Students Use?

	Men	Women
In the Past 30 Days		
Alcohol	62.4%	63.7%
Been Drunk	45.4%	38.1%
Marijuana	21.6%	22.5%
Cigarettes	10.8%	7.7%
Amphetamines	6.0%	2.5%
Tranquilizers	3.0%	1.1%
Cocaine	2.6%	0.7%
Ecstasy (MDMA)	1.1%	0.9%
Sedatives (Barbiturates)	0.8%	1.0%
LSD	0.7%	0.2%
Heroin	0.5%	0.0%[*]
Daily Use		
Marijuana	6.6%	3.9%
Alcohol	6.1%	3.2%
Cigarettes	2.9%	2.4%
Binge Drinking[1]	35.4%	30.5%

[1]Five or more drinks in a row in the past two weeks

[*]So few that the total is less than 0.05%.

Source: By the author. Based on Schulenberg, John E., Lloyd D. Johnston, Patrick M. O'Malley, Jerald G. Bachman, Richard A. Miech, and Megan E. Patrick. Monitoring the Future, National Survey Results on Drug Use, 1975-2016. Volume II: College Students and Adults Ages 19-55. Ann Arbor: Institute for Social Research, University of Michigan, 2017.

consequence of binge drinking. Too much alcohol interferes with the body's involuntary reflexes—including the gag reflex. If someone's gag reflex isn't working properly, that person can choke to death on vomit. (On a personal note, one of my former students was tried for manslaughter when his hook-up suffocated from swallowing her vomit. It certainly was not a pretty death, and it made for sensational headlines in our local newspaper.)

Research Findings:
The Recreational Mood Elevators

4.6 Summarize research findings on nicotine, alcohol, marijuana, and cocaine.

Nicotine, alcohol, marijuana, and cocaine are called recreational mood elevators because people often use them to increase feelings of well-being or confidence. Let's look at research findings on these drugs.

Nicotine

What a major social problem smoking is. The following example should get the point across in alarming detail.

Nicotine as a Social Problem

> *Let's suppose you are on your way to the airport, leaving for a long-awaited vacation. You are listening to the radio and anticipating your arrival in sunny Hawaii. Suddenly, an announcer breaks into your reverie with a flash bulletin: Terrorists have hidden bombs aboard six U.S. jumbo jets scheduled for takeoff today. Each jet will carry 200 passengers and crew.*
>
> *The announcer pauses, then adds: "The authorities have not been able to locate the bombs. Because no one knows which flights will crash, all flights will depart on schedule."*
>
> *In your mind's eye, you can see the planes plummeting from the skies, leaving a trail of agonizing screams as the passengers and crew meet their pitiful destiny. One of these planes might be yours.*
>
> *What would you do? My guess is that you would turn your car around and go home. Adios to Hawaii's beaches, and hello to your own backyard.*

If six fully loaded U.S. jets, each carrying 200 passengers and 20 crew members, crashed each and every day, what would the death toll be in a year? If you answered about 480,000, you would be right. And each year, about 480,000 Americans die from cigarette smoking (CDC 2017a). It is mind numbing, but these "crashes" continue without letup, day after day, year after year. The passengers *know* that these "jets" will crash that day; yet they climb aboard anyway, hoping that it won't be *their* plane that crashes.

Obviously, no one would get on a jet if they crashed like this. Who in their right mind would take the risk that their plane would not be among the six that crashed that day? Yet smokers do. They know that nicotine is lethal. They also know that smoking-related deaths are lingering and painful, a burden to both the victims and their families. Although smoking cuts the average smoker's life by at least 10 years, one of seven (15 percent) Americans age 18 and over continues to smoke (*Statistical Abstract* 2018:Table 211). They put this deadly poison to their lips, hoping it won't be their plane that goes down.

The Decline of Nicotine Addiction
You might be surprised to learn how common smoking used to be. Professors and students even smoked in class. I used to smoke cigars as I lectured, and students would put their cigarettes out by squishing them underfoot.

Look at Table 4.2, which shows national statistics. You can see that at the height of addiction, most men smoked. So did one of three women. Men's cigarette smoking is now just a third of what it was, and close to this for women. Today, about one in six men and one in seven women smokes.

Table 4.2 Cigarette Smoking by Sex and Age

	1965	1975	1985	1995	2005	2015*
By Sex						
Male	52%	43%	33%	27%	24%	17%
Female	34%	32%	28%	23%	18%	14%
By Sex and Age						
Males						
18–24 years	54%	42%	28%	28%	28%	15%
25–34 years	61%	51%	38%	30%	28%	21%
35–44 years	58%	51%	38%	32%	26%	18%
45–64 years	52%	43%	33%	27%	25%	18%
65 and over	29%	25%	20%	15%	9%	10%
Females						
18–24 years	38%	34%	30%	22%	21%	11%
25–34 years	44%	39%	32%	26%	22%	15%
35–44 years	44%	40%	32%	27%	21%	17%
45–64 years	32%	33%	30%	24%	19%	16%
65 and over	10%	12%	14%	12%	8%	7%

*Latest year available

Sources: By the author. Based on National Center for Health Statistics, National Health Interview Survey, 2015:Table A-12; *Statistical Abstract of the United States* 1994:Table 212; 1998:Table 238; 2018:Table 211.

What brought about such a remarkable change? The answer is a social movement, one that followed the pattern described in Chapter 1. As awareness grew of how smoking ravages the body, leaders emerged, officials responded, and smokers and nonsmokers confronted one another. One battled to limit smoking, the other to preserve the right to smoke anywhere. One fought under the banner of freedom from harm, the other under the banner of freedom of choice. The nonsmokers, as you know, won the battle. Legislation outlawed smoking on commercial flights and in airports, workplaces, and public buildings. Even bars became "smoke free." Smokers are forced to smoke outside, even in the cold of winter, where others stare at them as outcasts.

Figure 4.2 gives you a picture of this sharp decline. This change in smoking is preventing hundreds of thousands of early deaths as well as the avoidance of untold suffering. It also shows what citizens can accomplish when they unite for a cause—even when they face well-financed campaigns from big business to prevent their success.

Recruiting More Addicts With cigarettes known as cancer sticks, the tobacco industry faces a shrinking market. Its solution? Spend *$1 million an hour* ($9 billion a year) to convince young people that smoking is sexy and a sign of maturity (CDC 2018a). But fewer of today's youth are buying their message, one that seduced an earlier generation.

With a shrinking market, tobacco companies have turned to the least industrialized nations. As they target these countries, they place youth at the center of their bull's eye (Drope and Schluger 2018). The inevitable result of their enticing ads is to increase the globe's tobacco deaths. The following *Thinking Critically about Social Problems* features another attempt by the tobacco industry to recruit new smokers.

Figure 4.2 Number of Cigarettes That Americans Age 18 and Older Smoke Each Year

Sources: By the author. Based on Economic Research Service, U.S. Department of Agriculture, *Statistical Abstract of the United States* 2009:Table 981, and "The Tax Burden on Tobacco" 2017. Projections are by the author.

Thinking Critically about Social Problems

"Vaping: Cool, Fun—and Dangerous?"

If you're cool, then you Juul with other people, and you post about it, so everyone will see that you're social and ironic and funny. But, if you're addicted, you go off by yourself and Juul because you need it, and everyone knows.

—said by a high school girl to a reporter

To many, e-cigarettes are cool and fun. Their popularity among youth has soared. In the past 30 days, 14 percent of high school students have vaped with nicotine-laced liquids (Johnston et al. 2018).

But to be cool, you need to Juul—that is, use the highly popular vaporizer that you can recharge by plugging it into your computer (Tolentino 2018b).

With vaping sweeping our high schools, the unresolved question is "Are e-cigarettes harmful to health?"

Vaping has become popular as a supposed safe alternative to cigarettes, but its own health consequences are yet to be determined.

Sunshine Pics/Alamy Stock Photo

Enough people think so that the U.S. Surgeon General ordered a national study on e-cigarettes (Surgeon General 2016). The report was highly negative, with an emphasis on harmful chemicals and the targeting of kids by the tobacco companies by using "kid flavors" such as chocolate and fruit in the nicotine liquid.

The report has been criticized as a scary exaggeration of the dangers of e-cigarettes. Critics say that as of now, there is no good research on the effects of e-cigarettes on human health (Polosa et al. 2017). In defense of e-cigarettes, they add that the huge decline of high school youth who smoke cigarettes is at least partially the result of vaping.

We can expect this controversy to continue for years, until better data are available. Based on current subjective concerns and objective conditions, I anticipate that after years of research the results will go something like this:

1. Cigarettes are toxic. They kill.
2. E-cigarettes are harmful, perhaps just one tenth or less of the harm that comes from smoking tobacco cigarettes.
3. We should limit and discourage the use of e-cigarettes.

4. E-cigarettes, though not good, are preferable to tobacco cigarettes.

For Your Consideration

→ Do you think e-cigarettes should be regulated? Why or why not?
→ If so, do you think the sale of e-cigarettes should be limited to people age 18 and over?

Alcohol

Smokers aren't the only passengers on crashing jets. Let's look at some of their seatmates.

Alcohol as a Social Problem Alcohol is more dangerous than its broad social acceptance would imply. Alcohol-related motor vehicle accidents kill 10,000 Americans each year. That's about 27 each and every day (*Statistical Abstract* 2018:Table 1129). To go back to the analogy I used for nicotine, this is the equivalent of a passenger plane loaded with 190 passengers and crew crashing each week of the year. Drunk-driving deaths, though, occur mostly one at a time. Being much less spectacular, although just as final, these deaths seldom make anything but the local news.

Then there are those who are addicted to alcohol. About 10 million Americans are considered **alcoholics**, people who have severe alcohol-related problems. Relatively few of them wind up in homeless shelters or sitting on a corner unwashed and muttering nonsense. Almost all—whether working or middle class—continue with their routines but have impaired social relationships. Their work and loved ones suffer the most. Their organs ravaged from long-term abuse, alcoholics become a burden to themselves and to their families.

Each year, about 700,000 Americans are treated for alcohol problems (*Statistical Abstract* 2018:Table 213). Two hundred thousand are treated for alcohol problems alone, and another half million for a combination of alcohol and other drug problems. The cost of treatment runs several billion dollars a year, which everyone, including abstainers, must pay. Then, too, there are the costs of reduced productivity, alcohol-related crime and accidents, and social welfare. *These combined costs make alcohol the most expensive of all drug abuse problems.* Alcohol abuse also brings costs that cannot be measured in dollars—the sufferings of the spouse, family, and children, as well as shattered marriages.

Drinking and Sex Roles Of those 10,000 Americans who die in alcohol-related car and truck wrecks each year, most are men. Why are men more likely than women to drive drunk? A good part of the reason is that risk-taking behavior is one of the ways that young (and older) men prove to themselves and others that they are *real* men. This makes driving after heavy drinking a symbol of male potency. ("Did you see what John did last night? He was so wasted he could barely see, and he drove through the rain and made it to the dorm. Look where he parked!" [Car is next to the main entrance, hanging over the curb, half on the street and half on the sidewalk.] "What a guy!")

I've been through this stuff myself. And so have my friends. And, frankly, not all of us made it alive through this period of proving our budding masculinity.

Gender Transitions Gender change swirls around us. Many of the changes go unnoticed, as they are gradual. An example is women adopting so many traditionally masculine behaviors and characteristics that "feminine" is being redefined.

A classic ad in Great Britain to encourage drinking.

Picture Post/Stringer/Hulton Archive/Getty Images

Getting drunk and blowing off steam, for example, was previously almost exclusively a masculine activity. Now one-fourth of those arrested for drunk driving are women (*Statistical Abstract* 2018:Table 357).

Look back at Table 4.1 to see another indication of how women are adopting gender patterns that had been associated almost exclusively with men. In just the past month, about 30 percent of college women have binge drunk. Binge drinking often brings its own problems. Women, for example, report that when they binge drink, they not only take more chances when they drive but they also have riskier sex (Carpenter et al. 2008; Lewis et al. 2015).

Health Consequences of Alcohol   To understand any social problem, we need solid research—whether the findings match anyone's preconceived notions or not. Research on alcohol, for example, shows both negative and positive consequences for health. Let's continue with the negative consequences.

Because binge drinking is prevalent among college students, as you saw in Table 4.1, I want to stress this significant finding: Heavy drinking hurts the drinker's health. Heavy drinkers are more likely to die from strokes and heart attacks. They also are more likely to have problems with their endocrine, immune, metabolic, and reproductive systems and to suffer from depression and diabetes. Heavy drinking also brings several types of cancer—cancers of the tongue, mouth, throat, larynx, stomach, liver, esophagus, colon, and rectum. For women, heavy drinking can disrupt their menstrual cycle and bring breast diseases, including cancer (O'Keefe et al. 2014; CDC 2016a; 2018b). And for reasons I am sure you understand, excessive drinking sometimes also brings unexpected and unwanted pregnancy.

Although some researchers disagree, it seems that in contrast to heavy drinking, light to moderate drinking of alcoholic beverages brings *health benefits* (Haseeb 2017). Light to moderate is defined as one to two drinks a day, five or six days a week. This type of drinking relaxes people and reduces their anxieties, but it does more than this. Compared to people who drink no alcohol, light to moderate drinkers have fewer heart attacks. Red wine is especially good for the heart, but it seems to make no difference whether someone drinks red wine, white wine, beer, whiskey, or vodka (Midling 2016). Whatever its source, alcohol apparently stimulates production of HDL—the "good" cholesterol.

Do You Have a Problem with Alcohol?   If you find yourself dead drunk and covered with vomit hanging over a toilet bowel, you should know you have a problem with alcohol. But apart from such an extreme situation, how can you tell? Are there early signs that might alert you, so you can take steps to get help before you have a severe problem? Take a look at the next *Thinking Critically about Social Problems.*

Thinking Critically about Social Problems

How Can You Tell If You Have a Drinking Problem?

Here are 11 questions that can help anyone decide if they have a drinking problem. These are my version of questions developed by the American Psychiatric Association (APA). If you drink alcohol, apply these questions to yourself.

During the past year, have you:

1. Drunk more alcohol or drunk longer than you intended?
2. Felt a strong need or urge to drink?
3. Tried to cut down or stop drinking, but couldn't?
4. Drunk more than you once did in order to get the effects you want?
5. Been sick from drinking?
6. Had a memory blackout because of drinking?
7. Felt anxious, depressed, irritable, nauseous, or shaky when the effects of alcohol were wearing off?
8. Driven a vehicle, swam, or had unsafe sex when you were drinking?

9. Cut back or stopped activities that you find important or interesting in order to drink?
10. Found that your drinking interfered with taking care of your home or family—or with your work or school?
11. Continued to drink even though it caused trouble with your friends or family?

For Your Consideration

To anyone who answers yes to two or three of these questions, I would say that you need to do a quick evaluation of your life and stop drinking now. To anyone who answers yes to four or five, I would say that you should get help soon. To anyone who answers yes to six or more, I would say, "Severe problem? Very severe. Run to the nearest place you can get help. Do not delay. You are cutting your life short."

→ Do you agree with me? Why or why not?

Want to Give Your Baby a Beer? How about a Whiskey? Embedded within this social problem is another problem: Pregnant women who drink. ("If she drinks, the baby drinks.") The alcohol enters not just the pregnant woman's circulatory system but also that of her fetus. Unlike the woman, the fetus cannot metabolize alcohol. The alcohol becomes concentrated in the fetus' blood, raising its blood alcohol level as high as that of the woman's (Lange et al. 2018).

The consequences of drinking while pregnant are anything but pleasant. Each year about 5,000 babies are born in the United States with a cluster of problems called **fetal alcohol spectrum disorders (FASD)**. The most serious is **fetal alcohol syndrome (FAS)**. Born addicted to alcohol, these children suffer painful withdrawal for a week to six months. They are irritable, their little hearts beat irregularly, and some go into convulsions. Others suffer brain damage, making learning, memory, speech, and coordination difficult. Some die from malformed hearts (Lange et al. 2018).

Significance of How People Learn to Drink *How* people learn to drink can set the stage for having or not having alcohol-related problems. Groups with low rates of alcoholism have five behaviors and attitudes that are key to low-problem drinking (Hanson 1995; Schipper et al. 2013):

- Drinking is a regular part of life.
- Drinking alcohol starts early in the home, with the parents providing examples of moderate drinking.
- Drinking alcohol is neutral—neither bad nor good.
- Drinking alcohol is not a sign of adulthood or virility.
- Abusive drinking is not tolerated.

Apparently, people who learn to drink in these contexts are much less likely to have problems related to alcohol. To appreciate why, reverse these five points. Perhaps you can see why these conditions would lead to alcohol-related problems:

- Drinking alcohol is considered something special.
- Learning to drink is a sneaky activity, taking place outside the home.
- Alcohol is viewed as either sinful or as a substance that makes the world more pleasant.
- Drinking is considered a sign of adulthood.
- Getting drunk is tolerated, even approved, perhaps viewed as humorous.

Now look at Figure 4.3. About one of every 11 tenth-graders and one of every five high school students have been drunk in just the past month. A large number of teenagers are learning to drink in ways that maximize future problems with alcohol, not minimize them.

Marijuana

As a social drug, marijuana is in the midst of fundamental change. But why was marijuana made illegal? This takes us to an interesting part of our history, recounted in the next *Issues in Social Problems*.

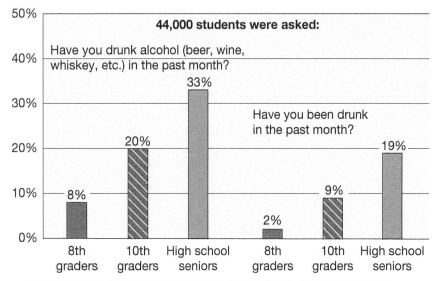

Figure 4.3 High School Students and Alcohol

44,000 students were asked:

Have you drunk alcohol (beer, wine, whiskey, etc.) in the past month?
- 8th graders: 8%
- 10th graders: 20%
- High school seniors: 33%

Have you been drunk in the past month?
- 8th graders: 2%
- 10th graders: 9%
- High school seniors: 19%

Source: By the author. Johnston, Lloyd D., Richard A. Miech, Patrick M. O'Malley, Jerald G. Bachman, John E. Schulenberg, and Megan E. Patrick. Monitoring the Future: National Survey Results on Drug Use, 1975–2017. Overview, Key Findings on Adolescent Drug Use. Ann Arbor: Institute for Social Research, the University of Michigan, 2018.

Issues in Social Problems

"It Drives You Crazy and Makes You Kill": The Crusade against Marijuana

How does something become illegal? Sometimes people get upset about some matter and demand that a law be passed. At other times, special-interest groups put pressure on lawmakers. Then there are **moral entrepreneurs**, crusading reformers who battle to enforce their ideas of morality. In making marijuana illegal, Harry Anslinger was that moral entrepreneur (Newton 2017).

It was the 1930s, and the country was in the midst of the Great Depression. Anslinger was the head of the Treasury Department's Bureau of Narcotics, and Congress had cut his budget. Anslinger saw marijuana as an opportunity to strengthen his faltering organization. He chose wisely, for marijuana was associated with Mexican immigrants who were seen as taking jobs away from citizens (Galliher and Walker 1977). Anslinger also had a strong ally: Fearing that marijuana might compete with alcohol, the liquor industry backed him (Rockwell 1972).

Anslinger launched a campaign that seems bizarre today, but back then people took him seriously. He got his message across by telling frightening stories. Here is one he published in a popular magazine:

> There was this young girl.... Her story is typical...a friend produced a few cigarettes of the loosely rolled "homemade" type. They were passed from one to another of the young people, each taking a few puffs.
>
> The results were weird. Some of the party went into paroxysms of laughter; every remark, no matter how silly, seemed excruciatingly funny. Others of mediocre musical ability became almost expert.... The girl danced without fatigue, and the night of unexplainable exhilaration seemed to stretch out as though it were a year long.... With every puff of the smoke the feeling of despondency lessened. Everything was going to be all right—at last. The girl was "floating" now, a term given to marijuana intoxication. Suddenly, in the midst of laughter and dancing, she thought of her school problems. Instantly

Poster for a 1936 movie that depicts people who smoke marijuana going wild sexually, becoming insane, and killing themselves.

George A. Hirliman Productions, Inc./20th Century Fox/Photofest

they were solved. Without hesitancy, she walked to a window and leaped to her death (in Swartz 2012).

Here's another story that Anslinger told to scare people:

> An entire family was murdered by a youthful addict in Florida. When officers arrived at the home they found the youth staggering about in a human slaughterhouse. With an ax he had killed his father, his mother, two brothers, and a sister. He seemed to be in a daze... The officers knew him as a sane, rather quiet young man; now he was pitifully crazed. They sought the reason. The boy said he had been in the habit of smoking something which youthful friends called "muggles," a childish name for marijuana (in Torgoff 2016).

Anslinger also used racism to drum up support. Here is one of his infamous statements:

> Marihuana influences Negroes to look at white people in the eyes, step on white men's shadows and look at white women twice (in Newton 2017:183).

Swearing that this killer weed drove girls to suicide, transformed boys into killers, and threatened white supremacy, this moral entrepreneur traveled the country and testified before Congress. He was the "expert," the public was upset, and without the testimony of even a single person who had done research on marijuana, Congress passed the Marihuana Tax Act of 1937 (Staples 2014). This law made marijuana illegal across the nation.

For Your Consideration

→ What do you think has changed in U.S. society so that what was once taken seriously seems ludicrous today?

→ If Congress holds future hearings on marijuana, do you think scientific evidence will be used? Why or why not?

Today, marijuana is in the midst of being legalized. As I write this, marijuana possession still violates federal law, but the federal government does not enforce it. Ten states and Washington, D.C. have passed laws that permit smoking marijuana for pleasure (recreational smoking) and another 23 states permit the sale of marijuana for medical purposes (Berke and Gould 2019). It seems inevitable that the federal law against marijuana will be rescinded.

Look at Figure 4.4 to see how popular marijuana is among high school and college students. These totals might not surprise you, but this might: *Marijuana is much less popular today than it was in the 1970s* (when today's law-abiding grandparents were in their rebellious phase). In 1979, one in three Americans ages 18 to 25 smoked marijuana at least once a month. Today, one in five (20 percent) of this age group smokes marijuana this often (*Statistical Abstract* 1998:Table 237; 2018:Table 214). The percentage of Americans over the age of 12 who have *ever* smoked marijuana is much higher, of course—close to half (44 percent), about 120 million people (*Statistical Abstract* 2018:Tables 10, 214).

Health Consequences of Smoking Marijuana How does marijuana affect health? On the negative side, reports indicate that marijuana smoking is related to smaller babies (Brown et al. 2016), more miscarriages (Lee et al. 2006; Wang et al. 2006), testicular cancer (Li et al. 2015), reduced sperm count, sperm motility, estrogen, and ovulation, and possibly lowered intelligence (WHO 2016). The negative effects on health are higher among those who start smoking before the age of 18 and those who smoke marijuana more than once a week.

On the positive side, marijuana relieves chronic pain, even the pain of multiple sclerosis (Grinspoon 2018). It also lessens the tremors of Parkinson's disease; reduces glaucoma, migraine headaches, anxiety, depression, fatigue, nausea, vomiting, and the pain of withdrawal from alcohol and narcotics (Grant et al. 2010). Not surprisingly, marijuana also produces pleasant side effects.

But the most accurate statement we can make at this point is that we really don't know how marijuana affects health. There are serious problems with samples and in separating cause and effect (WHO 2016). More rigorous research is on the way.

For a surprising health effect of marijuana, read *Thinking Critically about Social Problems.*

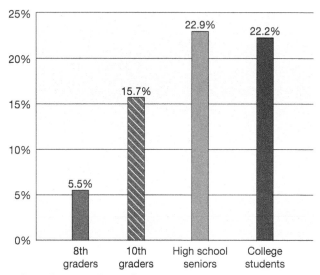

Figure 4.4 Who Has Smoked Marijuana during the Past 30 Days?

Source: By the author. Based on Schulenberg et al, Monitoring the Future, National Survey Results on Drug Use, 1975–2016. Volume II: College Students and Adults Ages 19–55. Ann Arbor: Institute for Social Research, University of Michigan, 2017; Johnston et al, Monitoring the Future: National Survey Results on Drug Use, 1975–2017. Overview, Key Findings on Adolescent Drug Use. Ann Arbor: Institute for Social Research, the University of Michigan, 2018.

Thinking Critically about Social Problems

Driving High

Smoking marijuana reduces a person's distance perception, reaction time, and ability to pay attention (Kelly et al. 2004; Sewell et al. 2009; Mikulskaya and Martin 2018). It isn't surprising, then, that legalizing marijuana is going to lead to more car wrecks and greater highway fatalities.

If social life were only this simple! But research casts doubt on even something this obvious.

Most states now allow medical marijuana and several permit recreational smoking—so has this increased highway fatalities? All the answers are not in, but the first reports are. Researchers examined traffic deaths in the first 16 states where using marijuana for medical purposes became legal. Comparing these states' fatalities before and after the medical marijuana laws, they found something rather surprising (Anderson and Rees 2011). After medical marijuana became legal, traffic deaths in these states *dropped* by a stunning 12 percent per 100,000 licensed drivers. After three years, when more medical marijuana patients had registered, the death total dropped even further, to 15 percent less.

How could this possibly be? These researchers also analyzed alcohol and traffic deaths, and they came to two main conclusions:

1. Marijuana and alcohol are substitutes. This is not an either-or situation, as many people combine the use of marijuana and alcohol. Marijuana smokers, however, drink less alcohol.

Behind marijuana becoming a legal drug in some states has been a continuous effort for 60 years to change laws. This photo is from Portland, Maine. Although marijuana remains a drug prohibited by federal law, its medical effects, positive and negative, are now being researched.

This is especially true for younger smokers, the drivers who are more likely to have car wrecks.

OK, less alcohol. But what about the marijuana, which we know impairs driving? This is where the researchers' second conclusion comes in.

2. The marijuana smokers compensated. They knew their reactions were not as sharp as usual, so they drove slower and kept more distance from cars ahead of them. People drinking alcohol, it seems, are not likely to do this; instead, they are likely to increase their risk-taking.

Follow-up research in states that have medical marijuana laws has confirmed these initial findings (Santaella-Tenorio et al. 2017). Research in Colorado and Washington after these states passed laws permitting recreational smoking of marijuana, however, showed neither a decrease nor an increase in traffic fatalities (Aydelotte et al. 2017).

For Your Consideration

→ If smoking marijuana leads to fewer traffic deaths, do you think we should encourage people to smoke marijuana? Why or why not?

Addiction and Marijuana   When marijuana smoking reached the height of its popularity a generation or so ago, alarmed parents and officials warned youth that marijuana was addictive. Marijuana smokers scoffed, saying that they could quit at any time. And they were right—or at least most of them were.

But there is more to the picture than this. Recent research shows that between 3 percent and 9 percent of marijuana smokers become addicted to cannabis, or THC. They become preoccupied with making certain that they are able to smoke every day, and they suffer symptoms of withdrawal when they try to stop smoking (Volkow et al. 2014; Davis et al. 2016).

Social Consequences of Smoking Marijuana   Researchers have found that adolescents who smoke marijuana tend to receive lower grades than those who don't smoke marijuana. They also are more likely to drop out of school and to never complete high school or college (Silins et al. 2014). Can we then say that smoking marijuana causes low grades, dropping out of school, and attaining less education?

These are "facts," but as we reviewed in Chapter 1, "facts" must be interpreted. But what can there be besides this obvious interpretation? Here is an alternative explanation: Marijuana smokers, especially those who smoke weekly or daily, tend to be involved in a subculture that places less value on academic achievement. In other words, we don't know that doing poorly in school comes from smoking marijuana or from the smokers' associations (Kleinman et al. 1987; Ingraham 2014). We need more research, and with marijuana now legal in many states, we can be sure that this research will be on the way.

Subjective Concerns   Marijuana is an excellent example of the lively nature of social problems, of how competing meanings vie for dominance. Reactions range from perceiving marijuana as a threat to society to viewing it as a treatment for medical problems. Until 1937, when the Marihuana Tax Act was passed, marijuana was an ingredient in about 30 medicines that physicians prescribed for their patients (Carroll 2000). This law ushered in a startling change—from marijuana being legal for anyone to the federal government punishing anyone of any age for possessing it. Although most states now allow people to possess marijuana, federal agents make thousands of arrests, each year, seizing *4 million pounds* of marijuana (*Statistical Abstract* 2018:Table 355).

As you saw with alcohol, a drug's social reputation can change. A drug can even be vilified and then be rehabilitated. The following *Issues in Social Problems* looks at marijuana's changing subjective concerns.

Issues in Social Problems

Medical Marijuana Dispensaries and Legalizing Marijuana

For years, arguments have been made for and against legalizing marijuana. The arguments for legalizing marijuana have ranged from its medicinal benefits to its misclassification in federal law as a narcotic. Some have presented a simple argument: Marijuana is fun, and its use or nonuse should be a matter of individual choice. The message, repeated over and over, is that the government has no business dictating to a free people what they can and cannot smoke.

The contrary argument is also simple: Marijuana is evil, and people need to be protected from it.

Investor money is now behind the many state campaigns to legalize marijuana. As with alcohol and nicotine, the legalization of marijuana can bring vast profits. This photo was taken in Union Square in New York City.

Luiz Rampelotto/Sipa USA/Newscom

To repeat, whether a drug is legal or illegal does not depend on the harm that the drug does, but rather on its social reputation. Marijuana has a lot of negative associations—law breaking, dropping out of school, and a gateway to hard drugs. With the many millions of Americans who have smoked marijuana, these subjective concerns have eased. Just as previous generations of youth were bewildered that anyone would have been jailed for drinking a beer or a cocktail, so many of today's youth wonder why their predecessors would have put anyone in jail for smoking this plant.

The national legalization of marijuana seems to be getting closer. As medical dispensaries of marijuana have increased, so the medical reasons for being able to purchase marijuana have expanded. From extremes of having to be in chemotherapy or suffering horrible pain during one's last days on earth have come backaches, trouble going to sleep, or even just feeling a little anxious. (Maybe anxious that the dispensary might close?)

As of this writing, nine states have dispensed with the pretense of marijuana for medical purposes and are saying, "Light up, if you want to (but pay your marijuana taxes)." Does this mean that we have taken the first steps to making marijuana legal on a national level? It is possible. But it seems more likely that some marijuana issue will be brought before the U.S. Supreme Court, and that the Court will decide that each state has the right to criminalize or legalize the use of marijuana.

For Your Consideration

→ Do you think marijuana will be legalized nationally?

→ Are you for or against the legalization of marijuana? Why?

→ As individual states decide whether to legalize marijuana, how influential do you think this argument will be?: If we legalize marijuana, we can tax it and raise billions of dollars to create jobs, help the poor, and improve schools.

Cocaine

Another popular drug for "getting high" is cocaine. This drug has an even more fascinating social history.

The Social History of Cocaine As mentioned, in the 1500s the Spanish invaders reported that the people of Peru chewed coca leaves. The Spaniards attributed the drug's effects to the devil and said that cocaine was evil.

This didn't stop the Spaniards from taking the coca plant back home with them, though. By the 1800s in Europe, cocaine was being used in medicines. Cocaine also became a popular recreational drug—and far beyond Spain. By the late 1800s, Sigmund Freud, the founder of psychoanalysis, and Sir Arthur Conan Doyle, the creator of Sherlock Holmes, swore that cocaine got their creative juices going. When Angelo Mariani, a French chemist, introduced a wine that contained the coca leaf extract, the pope enjoyed the wine so much that he presented Mariani with a medal (Hart and Ksir 2015). By this time, hundreds of thousands of Americans were sipping cocaine as a "pick-me-up," for cocaine had become an ingredient in Coca-Cola, a drink that is named after the coca leaf.

By 1910, though, cocaine had been transformed from a medicine and a "pick-me-up" into a dangerous drug, much as Dr. Jekyll became Mr. Hyde—a story, by the way, that Robert Louis Stevenson wrote in three days while he was high on cocaine (Ashley 1975). What led to this abrupt, profound change and the drug's social downfall?

In the late 1800s, reporters had begun to link cocaine with poverty and crime. They reported that gunmen used cocaine to get up their nerve to commit robberies (Ashley 1975). These news stories led to a public outcry, and in 1903 the Coca-Cola Company found it prudent to eliminate cocaine from its drink. Even today, however, Coca-Cola contains an extract from the coca leaf (Miller 1994; Edwards 2015). In the early 1900s, it was still legal to use cocaine in products, as long as the cocaine was listed as an ingredient. Although cocaine is a stimulant, in 1914 the Harrison Act mistakenly classified cocaine as a narcotic, making it illegal to sell or purchase the drug.

The Black Market in Cocaine The Harrison Act paved the way for a black market in cocaine. This black market is so profitable that some cocaine is even delivered by submarines (Woody 2016). So much cocaine comes into the United States that each year federal agents seize more than 100 *tons* of cocaine. About 15 percent of Americans age 12 and over—about 40 million people—have used cocaine. About 2 million use this drug at least once a month (*Statistical Abstract* 2018:Tables 10, 214). As you saw in Table 4.1, of full-time college students, in just the past month 2.6 percent of the men and 0.7 percent of the women used cocaine. This comes to about 300,000 students (*Statistical Abstract* 2018:Table 289). Although most users prefer to snort cocaine, smoking cocaine base, called *freebasing,* is also popular.

Uses of Cocaine Cocaine has a variety of uses. The most common is recreational, to get high. The cocaine high brings a sense of euphoria, with feelings of energy, confidence, and optimism. Cocaine also has a reputation—deserved or undeserved—as an aphrodisiac, of increasing or heightening sexual desires, pleasure, and endurance.

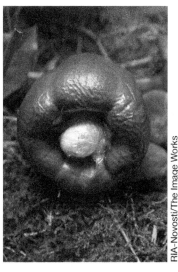

"More to fruit than meets the eye." One of the many ways cocaine has been smuggled into the United States.

RIA-Novosti/The Image Works

To many, the most surprising use of cocaine is in medicine. Surgeons apply cocaine as a local anesthetic and as a substance to reduce blood flow to the area they are operating on. The drug is so effective that cocaine is the medical profession's anesthetic of choice for surgery involving the nose, throat, larynx, and lower respiratory passages.

And from the coca plant comes an abundance of legal products: soft drinks, cosmetics, medicines, soaps, shampoos, toothpaste, flour, and tea (Forero 2006; Delgado 2016). Before he became president of Bolivia, Evo Morales was a farmer who used to grow coca. Morales argues that farmers should be able to grow coca and that its legal products should be accepted internationally. Against U.S. opposition, he permits the cultivation of the coca plant.

Dysfunctions of Cocaine The primary dysfunction of cocaine is addiction. The cocaine high—whether from the powder or crystal ("crack") form—is intense. Those who become addicted to cocaine desire the high, but they also want to avoid the crash that comes when the high is over. Their intense craving is difficult for nonaddicts to grasp, but it is so strong that some sell their possessions and steal from friends. Some women rent their bodies for crack, giving us the term "crack whore."

Racial injustice is also part of crack cocaine's social history. In 1986, Congress made possessing or selling crack cocaine a federal offense, with penalties more severe than those for powder cocaine. It turned out that whites are more likely to use powder cocaine and African Americans to use crack cocaine. The result was that, on average, African Americans received longer sentences (Riley 1998; Moore 2009). After charges of racial discrimination, the U.S. District Court in Georgia declared in 1994 that crack cocaine and powder cocaine are one and the same drug. Despite this, the disparity in sentencing continued. In 2010, Congress passed a law that narrowed the penalty for crack and powder cocaine violations (Palamar et al. 2015).

Principles Underlying a Drug's Social Reputation From this brief social history of cocaine, we can see the principles that help to determine a drug's social reputation and public acceptance:

1. Like humans, drugs gain their reputation and acceptance or nonacceptance not primarily because of objective conditions but through the people and events with which they are associated. If objective conditions were the primary factor in determining a drug's legality, alcohol and tobacco would be illegal.
2. Drugs associated with higher-status (or "respectable") people are likely to be defined as good and desirable, while drugs associated with lower-status (disreputable, poor) people are likely to be defined as bad and undesirable.
3. The reputation or social acceptability of a drug can change over time.

Research Findings: Hallucinogens

4.7 Summarize research findings on LSD, peyote and mescaline, PCP, and ecstasy.

The hallucinogens have intrigued researchers who explore the human mind. They have also attracted people who in cult-like fashion want to explore altered states of consciousness (Pollan 2018). As we review this fascinating journey, let's begin with LSD.

LSD

Perhaps the most famous of the hallucinogens is LSD (lysergic acid diethylamide). This drug was first synthesized in 1938 by Albert Hoffman, a Swiss chemist. Hoffman discovered that LSD was psychoactive when he accidentally inhaled a minute dose of the drug. Here is what he says happened to him:

> *Last Friday, April 16, 1943, I was forced to stop my work in the laboratory in the middle of the afternoon and to go home, as I was seized by a peculiar restlessness associated with*

a sensation of mild dizziness. Having reached home, I lay down and sank in a kind of drunkenness which was not unpleasant and which was characterized by extreme activity of imagination. As I lay in a dazed condition with my eyes closed (I experienced daylight as disagreeably bright) there surged upon me an uninterrupted stream of fantastic images of extraordinary plasticity and vividness and accompanied by an intense, kaleidoscope-like play of colors. This condition gradually passed off after about two hours (Hoffman 1968:184–185).

LSD is so powerful that an ounce of this tasteless, odorless substance contains 300,000 doses. It produces intense, mind-altering effects (Pollan 2018). If one does not know what to expect, the result can be psychotic reactions, even suicide.

When LSD first came to the public's attention during the social and mind altering 1960s, it was followed by headlines across the nation. At that time, sociologist Howard S. Becker (1967) studied how people were using LSD. He found that the initial panic surrounding LSD occurred because people did not know what to expect. As a subculture grew up around the drug, people who had already experienced LSD introduced the drug to their friends, explaining what they could expect. As novices saw strange colors, observed walls breathing, or felt a unity with plants, their "trip guides" assured them that this was normal, that it was temporary, and that they should relax and enjoy the sensations. As negative LSD experiences were replaced with positive ones, the panics and suicides disappeared from the news.

Today, LSD lacks the media frenzy that surrounded its use in the 1960s hippie culture, but LSD remains a vibrant part of the college scene. The United States has about 20 million college students (*Statistical Abstract* 2018:Table 289). As you saw in Table 4.1, about 0.7 percent of the men and 0.2 percent of the women took LSD during the past month. These small percentages add up, translating to about 80,000 students.

Peyote and Mescaline

Peyote, a small cactus that produces intense visual effects, was being used by some Native Americans when the Spanish *Conquistadores* arrived in North America (Pollan 2018). Mescaline, which is synthesized from peyote, produces similar hallucinatory experiences. Both peyote and mescaline have had famous proponents: Havelock Ellis (1897, 1902) was enthusiastic about peyote, and Aldous Huxley (1954) sang the praises of mescaline. Members of the Native American Church, who use peyote for religious purposes, claim constitutional protection under freedom of religion. The U.S. Supreme Court ruled, however, that Oregon could arrest these users (Hart and Ksir 2018).

Psilocybin

In the 1500s, the *Conquistadores* found that Native Americans in Mexico were using another substance, the mushroom *Psilocybe mexicana*, for its hallucinatory experiences. Because this mushroom was associated with pagan rituals, the Roman Catholic Spanish launched campaigns against it, and its use seemed to disappear. In the 1930s, it was discovered that some natives of southern Mexico were still using this mushroom, whose active ingredient is psilocybin. As with peyote, reports about the effects of this drug often contain a spiritual or religious emphasis (Hart and Ksir 2018).

PCP

In 1957, scientists at Parke-Davis, a pharmaceutical company, synthesized PCP (phencyclidine hydrochloride), which the company sold as a painkiller. As people soon discovered, this drug produced hallucinations, and because PCP requires little equipment to manufacture, it often is made in home laboratories. Known as *angel dust*, PCP alters body images and produces a variety of feelings, from unreality, euphoria, and a sense of power to loneliness and isolation. Some people experience feelings of dying, which is why some users refer to PCP as "embalming fluid." PCP affects the central nervous system, producing numbness and making it difficult to speak. Higher dosages can result in loss of inhibition, disorientation, rage, convulsions, or coma (Crider 1986; Hart and Ksir 2018).

Ecstasy

As you saw in Table 4.1, about 200,000 college students used Ecstasy in just the past month (1.1 percent of male college students and 0.9 percent of female college students). Ecstasy (MDMA, methylenedioxyamphetamine) produces a euphoric rush like that of cocaine combined with some of the mind-altering effects of the psychedelics. This popular party drug increases empathy and feelings of intimacy. Ecstasy is sometimes called "the love drug" because it enhances sensual experiences, making touching and other physical contact more intense and pleasurable. Negative side effects for some users are mental confusion and anxiety. The main concern about this drug is that it may act as a toxic substance and cause permanent brain damage (Carroll 2000; Hart and Ksir 2018).

Research Findings: Amphetamines and Barbiturates

4.8   Summarize research findings on amphetamines and barbiturates.

Let's turn our lens on amphetamines and barbiturates.

Amphetamines

For decades, people have bought Sudafed, a cold medicine, and extracted pseudoephedrine in order to produce a methamphetamine high. The meth leads to severe problems such as addiction and ruined health. To reduce meth addiction, laws were passed that limit the sale of Sudafed and similar medicines. The result? Once again, the black market. In this case, drug cartels from Mexico have made it easier than ever to get meth (Balko 2014).

"Meth," "crystal," and "ice" are street terms for amphetamines—Benzedrine, Dexedrine, Methedrine, Desoxyn, Biphetamine, and Dexamyl. The amphetamines are also called "uppers," "pep pills," "bennies," "dexies," and "speed." Discovered in 1887, Benzedrine became popular in the 1920s in over-the-counter inhalers intended to dilate the bronchial tubes. In the 1930s, Benzedrine was used for hyperkinesis and as an appetite suppressant. During World War II, the military gave amphetamines to soldiers to help them stay awake. Amphetamine abuse began at this time, as people began to soak the amphetamines from Benzedrine inhalers.

"Speed" (methamphetamine dissolved in liquid) is used by "speed freaks." Some inject the drug every two or three hours, for "runs" of three or four days. Each injection produces a "rush" or "flash," a sudden feeling of intense pleasure, followed by moderate feelings of euphoria. Some users hallucinate, while others develop feelings of paranoia, or become hostile and aggressive—symptoms called the *amphetamine psychosis* (Mullen and Crawford 2018). Heavy amphetamine use is sometimes accompanied by behavioral fixations, such as repeatedly cleaning the same room or counting the corn flakes in a box of cereal over and over again. Amphetamine withdrawal can bring outbursts of aggression, feelings of terror, and thoughts of suicide or homicide. Meth addiction can cause brain damage, leading to permanent psychosis.

To see one reason that methamphetamine ("meth") addiction has become a major concern, look at the photos that follow.

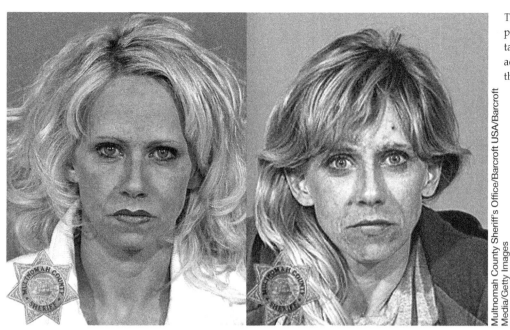

These two photos are of the same person. The one on the left was taken at the start of this woman's addiction to meth, and the one on the right just four years later.

Multnomah County Sheriff's Office/Barcroft USA/Barcroft Media/Getty Images

From the little vignette that opens this section, you can see how attempts to control the amphetamines have backfired. Inevitably, laws or no laws, where there is a demand, there are suppliers. With meth produced easily at home from chemicals readily available, the supply extends from "meth labs" at home, in motel rooms, and in vans and cars to highly organized distribution networks from Mexico that have spread throughout the United States.

Barbiturates

In 1862, Dr. A. Bayer (the Bayer of aspirin fame from Munich, Germany) combined urea with malonic acid and made a new compound, barbituric acid. Of the 2,500 drugs that have been derived from barbituric acid, the best known are phenobarbital (Luminal), amobarbital (Amytal), pentobarbital (Nembutal), and secobarbital (Seconal). Physicians prescribe barbiturates to treat anxiety, insomnia, and epilepsy. Barbiturates provide an experience similar to that of alcohol. Regular barbiturate use leads to addiction, whose withdrawal is severe—nausea, anxiety, sweating, dizziness, trembling, muscular twitching, and sometimes convulsions, coma, and death. Because the risk of death is higher for those who stop "cold turkey" (abruptly), physicians usually substitute a long-lasting barbiturate and then withdraw it slowly (Hart and Ksir 2018).

Research Findings: Steroids

4.9   Summarize research findings on steroids.

Anabolic steroids have a wide variety of medical uses. They are used to treat such health problems as hormone deficiency, kidney failure, and breast and prostate cancer; to regulate the development of muscles and testicles; and to counteract the effects of radiation therapy (Ganesan and Pellegrini 2018). Readily available on the black market, especially from diverted prescriptions, the steroids are in high demand from body builders and from individuals who want to "beef up." Soviet trainers have used steroids to build the muscles of their Olympic athletes. They succeeded, but the cost was high, not only in harmed Olympic reputations but also in the heart disease and strokes that struck Russian athletes in the prime of life. Other side effects are depression, liver cysts, and shrinking testes, not a nice cluster of characteristics. To avoid steroids' feminizing side effects, men who use steroids also take anti-estrogen drugs.

The side effects of steroids are striking, but what has really caught the attention of the public is the illegal use of steroids by athletes to build body mass and muscle. Let's look at this in the following *Thinking Critically about Social Problems*.

Thinking Critically about Social Problems

Steroids and Athletes

Anabolic steroids are so common at gyms that body builders call them "gym candy." No one seems to be much bothered that these muscular hulks, in competition with one another for the largest this or that, use steroids to "beef up." The attitude seems to be, "So what? How else can they look like *that* in body-building competition?"

You hulks can pose proudly. No one really cares how you got to look like that, just that you do.

But athletes who use steroids in competitive sports arouse subjective concerns. The essence of the concerns is that steroids enhance performance, giving athletes who use them an unfair advantage.

Marion Jones was a star athlete who became a role model for girls. She even won a gold medal at the Olympics. She denied under oath that she had used steroids. She was stripped of her medal and put in prison for perjury.

Roger Clemens, one of baseball's fabled pitchers, also denied under oath that he had used steroids. Clemens was tried for perjury and found not guilty.

Barry Bonds, who broke the all-time home run record, left the San Francisco Giants under a cloud of accusations of steroid use. After an investigation that took eight years and a lengthy trial for perjury, Bonds was found guilty of one count of obstruction of justice. He was given a $4,000 fine and sentenced to remain at home for a month. Bonds lives in a 50,000-square-foot home in Beverly Hills ("Barry Bonds..." 2011). The conviction was overturned on appeal (Masisak 2018).

Mark McGwire broke Roger Maris' record for the most home runs in a season. Maris' record of 61 homers had stood since 1961. In 1998, the year that McGwire broke what had become

Ron Antonelli/NY Daily News Archive/Getty Images

Alex Rodriguez, one of the most famous baseball players, was suspended for the entire 2014 season for the use of steroids.

almost a mythical record, it was apparent that McGwire was beefing up. Fans were even commenting on his chest and biceps, wondering whether he was using steroids.

As concerns about athletes using steroids grew, in 2005 Congress held an investigation. Called to testify, McGwire refused to say whether he had used steroids. Finally, to the dismay of his fans, in 2010 McGwire admitted steroid use in the 1990s (Kepner 2010). He said that he was sorry he had taken steroids, but in a backhanded justification for doing so, McGwire also said that he had taken them only to overcome sports injuries. He added that he was certain that he would have beaten Maris' home run record even without steroids. Then, to cover all bases, McGwire called Maris' widow and told her he was sorry. Apparently, this was adequate because the St. Louis Cardinals hired McGwire as a hitting coach. The Cards also honored McGwire's steroid-enhanced achievement of home run king by giving a Mark McGwire Bobblehead to all fans who attended one of their games ("Cardinals Announce..." 2018).

For Your Consideration

→ Why shouldn't athletes be allowed to take steroids if they are willing to take the health risks?

→ Assume that medical doctors can control the health risks associated with steroid use. Why shouldn't physicians be allowed to prescribe steroids to athletes?

→ Do you think all athletes—including those in high school and college—should be required to take drug tests? Why or why not?

Research Findings: Narcotics—From Opium to Heroin and Morphine

4.10 Summarize research findings on heroin and morphine.

To understand narcotics, it is necessary to start with a pretty flower—a little flower that is at the center of law making and law breaking.

Heroin

The flower that has become the root of so much controversy is the opium poppy. The reason for this controversy is that the narcotic heroin comes from this flower. Look at Figure 4.5 to see how heroin is derived from the poppy flower.

Heroin and Addiction: Conflicting Reports

Beyond a certain frequency need of heroin knows absolutely no limit or control. In the words of total need: "Wouldn't you?" Yes, you would. You would lie, cheat, inform on your friends, steal, do anything to satisfy total need. Because you would be in a state of total sickness, total possession, and not in a position to act in any other way.... A rabid dog can't choose but bite.

This is how novelist William Burroughs (1975:135) described his own addiction to heroin. His description matches the common view that heroin is so addictive and its withdrawal pains so severe that addicts will do anything to avoid withdrawal. Is it true?

When a team of sociologists headed by Bruce Johnson (Johnson et al. 1985) explored heroin addiction, they found something different. They rented a storefront in a Harlem neighborhood that had "the highest number of street-level heroin abusers in the country." For two years, a research staff of former heroin users built rapport with 201 current users. From the day-to-day reports they collected, the researchers found that many heroin users are *not* physically addicted. They use heroin once or twice a day for a period of time, and then—without suffering withdrawal symptoms—they go for several days without the drug. Other researchers have noted that some people use heroin on an occasional basis, such as at weekend parties, without becoming addicted (Spunt 2003; Gillespie 2013).

Then there are the U.S. soldiers who returned from Vietnam. About 14 percent had used heroin in Vietnam, a heroin far stronger than any available back home. After the soldiers came home, were reunited with family and friends, and went back to work, most stopped using heroin. Few had any physical problems. As the assistant secretary of defense for health and environment said, "Everything that I learned in medical school—that anyone who ever tried heroin was instantly, totally, and perpetually hooked—failed to prepare me for dealing with this situation" (Peele 1987:211).

These findings so contradict reports of William Burroughs and other addicts that it can make your head swim. Certainly, Burroughs did not make up his description of his own overwhelming addiction to heroin. Nor did the sociologists who studied addicts in Harlem make up their findings. How, then, can we reconcile such contradictory reports? The simplest explanation seems to be that heroin is addicting to some people, but not to others. Some users of heroin do become addicts and match the stereotypical profile. Others are able to use heroin on a recreational basis.

Researchers have serious disagreements about the causes of addiction. Many are convinced, and this seems to be the dominant view, that addiction is "a disease that changes the structure and function of the brain" (Heather 2017). Others take the position that addiction is much more than a "brain malfunction," that we need to consider "social, psychological, cultural, political, legal, and environmental contexts" (Heather et al. 2017). The hard research that gives us definitive answers is yet to appear—and granted the fundamental and rancorous disagreements among scientists, I doubt that we shall see accord for decades.

Baby Addicts A separate issue are the babies who are born addicted to heroin (or to alcohol, cocaine, barbiturates, or any other addicting drug). These babies lived in an environment of drug abuse, the womb of their mother. Whenever the mother took the drug, the baby was drugged. Its developing body grew dependent on the drug, and at birth, these tiny, helpless newborns go through panful withdrawal. Suffering from what is called **neonatal abstinence syndrome**, the babies scream for help. They have tremors, and they can't sleep. In distress, they frantically suck their tiny fists (Hamdan 2010; Rosen 2017).

Morphine

The poppy flower also yields morphine, an unusually strong painkiller. This drug came to the public's attention during the Civil War, when doctors used it on the battlefield to give soldiers relief from their wounds (Carroll 2016). An unfortunate aspect of morphine

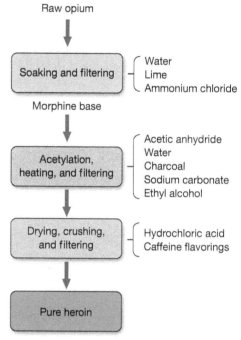

Figure 4.5 How Opium Is Converted into Heroin

Raw opium

Soaking and filtering — Water / Lime / Ammonium chloride

Morphine base

Acetylation, heating, and filtering — Acetic anhydride / Water / Charcoal / Sodium carbonate / Ethyl alcohol

Drying, crushing, and filtering — Hydrochloric acid / Caffeine flavorings

Pure heroin

Source: By the author. Based on *Newsday 1974* and Drug Enforcement Agency 2001

is that it is highly addicting, and many wounded soldiers who managed to cheat death during the Civil War came home slaves to morphine.

Morphine is still used as a painkiller on today's battlefields. And because its addictive power also remains, the federal government controls morphine, making it available only for limited medical use.

Heroin, Crime, and the Law

Heroin causes crime and destroys people's motivation to work.

Everyone knows that this statement is true. But is it? Once again, let's compare sociology and commonsense assumptions about social life.

Do you think physicians who become addicted to narcotics hold up cabbies? Do you think they mug pedestrians, burgle houses, or become prostitutes? Do you think they stop being doctors and sit in a daze on street corners and in parks?

As I'm sure you guessed, this is not what happens. Addicted doctors continue to shower, eat good food, see patients—and get high (Winick 1961; Grinspoon 2016).

Why aren't addicted doctors like street addicts? You probably can guess this one, too. The answer lies in their social position. Like streetcorner addicts, the physicians also need narcotics to avoid withdrawal pains. But unlike poor street addicts, the physician addicts have no need to prey on others. By diverting (stealing) the narcotics from legal medical sources and using samples from pharmaceutical companies, they have access to a cheap supply of drugs. The common stereotypes about narcotics causing crime and destroying the incentive to work are simply not true.

Narcotics, then, do *not* cause the things we commonly associate with them: robbery, burglary, prostitution, and unemployment. Yet these things are common to narcotic addicts—that is, to *poor* street addicts. *Life circumstances make the difference, not addiction to narcotics.*

Social Policy

4.11 Explain why it is difficult to establish social policy on drug use and abuse.

To try to determine rational social policy for drug use and abuse is to land in a minefield of emotions, contradictions, and dilemmas. Let's see why.

The Dilemma Facing Policy Makers

The major dilemma in social policy is the negative consequences that come from satisfying the public's demand to "get tough."

The "Get Tough" Approach   The middle class continuously calls for tougher laws. Throw those no-good addicts (street addicts, that is) in jail and throw away the key. Do you recall from the beginning of this chapter the severe penalties that officials once used as they tried to get rid of coffee and tobacco? Mutilations, beatings, and death. Did they work? Look around. Do you see anyone smoking cigarettes or drinking coffee?

One of the most pernicious consequences of get-tough policies is that they fuel black markets, producing fountains of profits for those who are willing to take the risk of supplying banned drugs. This harsh reality surfaced with Prohibition, when the United States made selling and drinking alcohol a criminal act. An underground network sprang up to keep that drug supply going—as it will for any drug that we make illegal.

The latent dysfunctions of criminalizing drugs are horrible. They include the bankrolling of organized crime, as the rich and poor and those in between buy the banned drugs. There is also an increase in muggings, burglaries, and thefts as poor addicts prey on others to get the money to purchase addicting drugs. And we can't forget the tens of thousands of premature deaths of those who overdose on street drugs. Are these latent dysfunctions not worse than the original problem that the laws address?

Lurking in back of a "get-tough-and-lock-'em-up" approach is the assumption that to jail a dealer is to eliminate that dealer's drug deals. Such an assumption is naïve at best. It certainly flies in the face of an unwelcome and abundant reality. The arrest of a dealer is a business opportunity for wanna-be dealers who are eager to take over vacated territory. Get rid of one dealer, and two or more jostle to take his or her place.

The profits in the black market for drugs are so huge that they can finance armies and threaten to topple governments. Look at what is happening in Mexico today, the topic of the following *Global Glimpse.*

A Global Glimpse

Drugs, Death, and Corruption in Mexico

It was a typical night at El Sol y Sombra in Uruapan, a little town in Michoacán, Mexico. Some couples were dancing to Norteño, while others were flirting. As the drinks took effect, the problems of life receded.

The reverie was broken abruptly when several men burst into the nightclub, waving machine guns and shooting into the air. The music stopped, and the revelers, their alcohol-induced escape suddenly cut short and fearing that their time had come, huddled against the walls. Instead of more shooting, the men threw a garbage bag onto the middle of the emptied dance floor.

Five human heads rolled out, the eyes staring ghastly into space, the blood still dripping from the freshly severed necks.

"Now that's something you don't see every day," said a bartender, in what surely is an understatement, when reporters talked to him later. "Very ugly."

Even in Michoacán, where drug-related violence is part of daily life, throwing severed heads onto a dance floor sends an impressive message.

Since some people—although it's hard to imagine—might not get the message, the dealers sometimes attach notes to the heads. At *El Sol y Sombra,* the note said, "The family does not kill for money. It does not kill women. It does not kill innocents. It kills only those who deserve to die. Everyone should know, this is divine justice."

"The family" (*la familia*) is the term this group has given itself.

At another location, this note accompanied severed heads: "See. Hear. Shut up. If you want to stay alive."

Not surprisingly, the police are finding it difficult to locate anyone who has seen or heard anything.

The death toll of Mexico's drug violence is staggering. The last 5 years have averaged 23,293 homicides per year (Calderon et al. 2018). This comes to more than 400 a week, 63 a day, 2 to 3 an hour, with these killings continuing year after year. Since the start of the twenty-first century, more than a quarter of a million people have been murdered in Mexico.

The gangs mark for death mayors who won't take bribes and journalists who criticize them. They also kill judges and prosecutors—or anyone else who stands in their way.

Associated Press

Tens of thousands of people have been killed in Mexico's war on drugs. From this photo taken in Saltillo, Mexico, you can see that the drug police wear masks. If not, drug lords would know who they are and order their kidnapping, torture, and execution—and perhaps that of their families as well.

If the drug dealers can, they will take over Mexico. The government of Mexico knows this, and it has declared war on the cartels. A real war? Using its navy and army, the government has sent soldiers to attack gangs, with a focus on arresting or assassinating the heads of the cartels. The cartels have not backed down. They shot down a Cougar EC 725 helicopter from the Mexican Air Force. They also have raided police stations with machine guns, grenades, and bazookas (McKinley 2006a, 2006b; Caldron et al. 2018).

Despite its press releases, the government of Mexico has failed to even slow up the drugs and killings. At the heart of its failure are vast amounts of drug money. Flowing through Mexico, this dark money corrupts both police and politicians. Some bosses of drug cartels even work at local police stations (Steinberg 2014). Corruption is so extensive that the head of Mexico's drug enforcement agency had to resign. Apparently, even he was on the gangs' payroll.

With drug money flowing amid rampant corruption, the line between government and drug cartels has grown incredibly thin. When 46 college students spoke out against the corruption of their local government, the police arrested the students. Then they handed them over to the crime bosses. Their bodies are reported to have been burned in a garbage dump—or dissolved in acid. Or were the students merely stealing a bus, and unknown to them it contained a load of cartel drugs? And was the Mexican military behind their kidnapping, torture, and death?

After the anguish of the parents of these 46 students reached a feverish pitch, there was an international outcry. A thorough investigation by neutral experts followed. The results? After confronting lies and not-to-be-believed tortured confessions and coverups by politicians and the military, what happened remains a blur (Devereaux 2017).

One of the first casualties of corruption is truth.

For Your Consideration

→ What do you think can be done to solve this problem?
→ The drug violence is fueled by a war over drug profits. What stops us from striking the problem at its root? If drugs were made legal, the profits would disappear overnight.
→ What social problems do you think that legalizing drugs that are now illicit would produce?

To combat the black market in marijuana, as highlighted in the following *Global Glimpse*, Uruguay has come up with a social policy that is getting worldwide attention.

A Global Glimpse

Uruguay's Solution to the Marijuana Problem

Let's eavesdrop on an imaginary conversation:

"The problem with laws against marijuana is their consequences. We can make marijuana illegal, but this doesn't reduce its demand. With so much money to be made, we've got rivalries and violence among the dealers," said one official in Uruguay.

"Yes, of course. We all know this," replied another official. "And we know there isn't much we can do about it."

"Yes, there is," said the first official. "We can legalize marijuana. The United States has been bullying us with its drug policies for years. They think that whatever they want is right. They've got most of the users, and the money flows down from them and creates violence here in South America."

"Right. But what do you mean by legalize? Doesn't marijuana need controls?"

"Sure it does. And it can be a source of profit, too, which can go to the government instead of the criminals. What I propose is that we license the farms where marijuana will be grown, the factories to manufacture marijuana cigarettes, and we sell the packages of cigarettes. Only those 18 and over can buy them."

"Sort of like we do with tobacco cigarettes?"

"Exactly," said the first official. "You've got the idea."

"Then we solve the crime problem and get more taxes. This could even fund our police budgets."

"Right."

"I'm on board. Let's get busy and convince the others."

"And," added the first official, "our grass is going to be the best. It will be legal, reasonably priced, and high quality. We'll drive the illegal drug dealers out of business."

This idea, quite bold and somewhat radical, was proposed in Uruguay, a little South American country of less than 4 million people. The lawmakers debated the proposal and decided to grant licenses to two companies to grow marijuana to be sold in pharmacies. Three types of marijuana are available—low, medium, and high potencies, all at $1.30 a gram. Purchasers are limited to 40 grams per month. Individuals can register with the government and grow up to six plants for personal use. And no sales to tourists (Castaldi 2015; Turner 2017).

Canada has taken the same path as our South American neighbor—with the use of marijuana for pleasure legal across the nation.

For Your Consideration

→ What do you think about the Uruguayan plan?
→ Do you think Uruguay's and Canada's approach to marijuana is the wave of the future? Why or why not?
→ Would you vote for this plan in the United States it? Why or why not?

Deciding Social Policy

Nothing is easy in determining social policy on drugs, for like abortion, the drug problem is immersed in strong opinions, emotions, and stereotypes. Complicating social policy even further are contrasting subcultural values and moralities. Consider this: The health findings on alcohol suggest that we should encourage light to moderate drinking but discourage heavy drinking. Which of our high schools and colleges—or our churches and state governments—would promote such a policy? ("Okay, class, this is why you should drink a beer or two almost every day.")

Within this morass of dilemmas and contradictions, let's try to suggest social policy that has a rational basis and might have a chance of accomplishing something.

Banning Advertising An adequate social policy can begin by banning *all* advertising for drugs known to be harmful. Nicotine is certainly a case in point. As it now stands, when young people open magazines and newspapers, smiling, happy, healthy young people beckon them to join their carefree lifestyle of pleasurable smoking. To ban all advertising for cigarettes and tobacco products would remove this source of enticement.

Drug Education To be effective, drug education should be based on scientific studies, not on anyone's ideas of which drugs are "good" or "bad." This will require that we determine *both* the beneficial and the harmful effects of drugs—and that we communicate these findings, even if they go against our personal biases. For example, if scientific evidence shows that marijuana is safer than alcohol and tobacco, which appears to be the case, then, like it or not, we need to communicate this information. We cannot shy away from communicating either the good or the bad effects of marijuana—or any drug—because we have a bias for or against a drug. With the changes occurring in the marijuana laws, we shortly should have vast scientific information on the effects of marijuana on health.

Drug Addiction Jailing addicted people is a failed social policy. Upon release, most go back to their drugs. A successful program cannot treat addicts as though they live in a social vacuum. It must take into account the context of an addict's life. Addiction is often part of subcultural orientations and deprivations—usually poverty, unemployment, dropping out of school, and a bleak future. To be successful, drug programs must reflect the life realities of drug abusers.

People who become drug dependent are strongly motivated to continue their drug use. With cigarettes available legally, smokers have no difficulty obtaining their drug. Tobacco crops are even subsidized by the Department of Agriculture. With the one-pack-a-day smoker paying an average of $2,600 a year, smokers do not mug, steal, or kill to obtain their drug. In contrast, heroin and cocaine users depend on a black market. The price of their drugs is high, and many commit crimes to support their addiction.

A successful drug addiction program, then, might include free or inexpensive drugs. For example, heroin addicts could be prescribed heroin by physicians who would treat them as patients. This would break the addicts' dependence on the black market, removing a major source of profit for organized crime. It would also eliminate the need for addicts to prey on others. If the program provided only such benefits, it would be a night-and-day improvement over our present situation. But for success, we would still need a three-pronged attack: counseling for personal problems, practical help in seeking and maintaining employment, and clinical services for those who want to end their addiction.

Methadone maintenance illustrates how significant the labels *illegal* and *legal* are in social policy. Methadone, a synthetic narcotic, was developed by the Germans during World War II as a painkiller for wounded soldiers (Fernandez 2011). *Although methadone is addicting, it is given orally in clinics to help break addiction to heroin.*

Why transfer someone's addiction from one narcotic to another? The major reason is that this frees the addicts from the black market, removing the need to commit crimes to support their drug habit. But if we are going to supply drugs to addicts, why not simply give them the drugs to which they already are addicted? The answer goes back to the labels attached to drugs, their social reputation: The narcotic heroin is evil (illegal); the narcotic methadone is good (legal).

Methadone maintenance programs were supposed to include counseling for patients and job training. To save money, these programs were cut, leaving only the "bare bones" of the original plan—giving methadone to addicts. This failing alerts us to a danger of social policy: Politicians who fund a program seldom see it in the same way as do the professionals who designed it. If politicians and bureaucrats cut costs, they can dismantle a program in all but name.

Everybody wants those addicted to drugs to be helped, but nobody wants a clinic in *their* neighborhood. After years of legal battle, this one opened in Spring Hill, Florida.

Alcoholics Anonymous Alcoholics Anonymous (AA) is a successful treatment program whose principles have been applied to other addiction treatment programs, such as Cocaine Anonymous. Started in 1935 in Akron, Ohio, by two alcoholics, AA has grown into a worldwide organization. It has more than 2 million members around the world, about half in the United States ("AA Fact File" 2018). AA is directed and staffed by people who have experienced alcohol addiction themselves—and have overcome it. They know firsthand what addicts go through. Intimately familiar with the addicts' orientations, they can talk their language on a "gut level."

The essentials of Alcoholics Anonymous are summarized in what this group calls the Twelve Steps. To overcome addiction to alcohol, you must:

1. Admit you are powerless over alcohol and your life has become unmanageable.
2. Believe that a power greater than yourself can restore you to wholeness.
3. Make a decision to turn your will and life over to God, as you understand God.
4. Make an honest moral inventory of yourself.
5. Admit to God, yourself, and another human being exactly what you have done wrong.
6. Be ready to have God help you remove your defects of character.
7. Ask God to remove your shortcomings.
8. Make a list of every person you have harmed and be willing to make amends to them.
9. Make amends whenever possible, except where it would harm them or others.
10. Continue to take personal inventory, and promptly admit your wrongs.
11. Through prayer and meditation, seek to improve your contact with God, as you understand God, praying for knowledge of God's will for yourself and the power to carry it out.
12. Have a spiritual awakening as a result of these steps; try to carry this message to other alcoholics; and practice these principles in all your dealings with others.

To put these steps into practice, members meet weekly with others who have overcome alcohol addiction or who are struggling to overcome it. From their fellow members, they draw encouragement to continue abstinence. They also carry the telephone number of a mentor, "someone who has been through it." They can call this person at any hour for personal support, learning to handle crises without turning to alcohol.

AA is not without its critics. Rival counseling programs reject what they see as AA's faith and abstinence approach (Lopez 2018). The goal of many other programs is not abstinence but to resolve emotional problems thought to be the underlying reason for the abuse.

Medical Treatment   Then there is the elusive but intriguing search for the "magic pill," the drug that will drive away people's urges to use and abuse addicting drugs. No such potion has yet been discovered, but research has turned up some drugs that hold at least limited promise. The standard drug, Antabuse, which makes people nauseous when they drink alcohol, also raises their blood pressure and blurs their vision. Less extreme is Naltrexone, which blocks the pleasant effects of alcohol. Another drug, Gabapentin, reduces the withdrawal symptoms that alcoholics experience when they try to stop drinking, and if they stop drinking, Acamprosate helps reduce their craving for alcohol (Wilkinson 2017). Researchers are also experimenting with implanting electrodes in abusers' brains to alter their neurocircuitry (Peisker et al. 2018).

Principles of Successful Social Policy

To be effective, social policy must match the culture of its target group—the group members' age, race–ethnicity, gender, and social class, as well as their values, lifestyle, and problems. This means that different groups need programs with different emphases. For example, a program that is successful with middle-class youth will fail if it is transferred without modification to inner-city youth.

To be effective, drug programs should reward conventional behavior, integrating drug abusers into a community of people where "straight" values are dominant. This will require social networks that value employment and nonexploitative relationships. Without job training and placement, poor addicts are left where they started, with little way out.

Finally, if a drug program is to be successful, it must be tied into *the realities of the users.* Nonusers' ideas about morality and the risks of using drugs, for example, are not the same as those of users. To try to impose some outside reality onto drug users is a recipe for failure.

The Future of the Problem

4.12 **Explain the likely future of the social problem of drug abuse.**

As with the anti-smoking and pro-marijuana social movements, many forces for change are at work within our society. Pressures build slowly, mostly out of sight. Then reaching a breaking point, they burst into view, bringing with them unexpected change. These two social movements have only now broken the surface. The directions seem firm, with cigarette smoking on a sharp downward path and subjective concerns about marijuana on a similar trajectory. Firm directions, however, have been known to confront oppositional forces and to change course. We shall await the final results.

The psychedelics, a unique class of drugs, open a glimpse into a potential unique future. The psychedelics are undergoing a renaissance, a reevaluation by scientists who are considering their potential for curing mental illnesses such as depression and anxiety as well as trauma and addiction (Pollan 2018). If this potential, first explored in the 1960s but then banned and cast underground, produces fruit, we will see a new wave of drug therapy.

Regardless of these specifics, the social reputations and acceptability of drugs will continue to influence people's lives profoundly. Some drugs will remain in disrepute, their users disgraced and stigmatized, while other drugs will maintain their social approval. Advertised in glossy magazines and on television, they will continue to be an accepted part of social life.

If the "good" people continue to view those who are addicted to drugs as "bad" people, they will continue to turn a blind eye to what happens to these "bad" people. The devastating consequences of anti-drug laws will be written off as things these "bad" people deserve. Lurking in the shadows of social policy, this perspective of "us" and "them" needs to be brought into the light, where it can be examined thoroughly.

Summary and Review

1. What constitutes *drug abuse* is a matter of definition. What is considered drug use at one time or in one society may be considered drug abuse at another time or in another society. And this view can switch once again, the course marijuana is following.

2. Some drugs are disreputable, and those who use them are considered to be part of a social problem. People generally consider the particular drugs that they use to not be part of a social problem.

3. A major problem in drug abuse is *addiction*—becoming dependent on a drug so that its absence creates the stresses of withdrawal. One of the most highly addicting drugs is nicotine. Heroin appears to be less addicting than previously thought.

4. Symbolic interactionists emphasize the social meanings of drugs. Prohibition, for example, has been analyzed as a symbolic crusade: As the old order lost political control, it attempted to dominate society morally by wrapping itself in abstinence (morality) and associating drunkenness (immorality) with the newcomers.

5. Functionalists stress not just that legal drugs are functional for the medical profession, their patients, and those who manufacture and sell these drugs, but also that illegal drugs are functional for their users, manufacturers (or growers), and distributors.

The dysfunctions of drugs include problems with the law and abuse that harms people physically and socially.

6. Conflict theorists stress how the criminalization of drugs is related to power. Opium, for example, was made illegal in an attempt to overcome the economic threat that Chinese immigrants posed to white workers. Similarly, marijuana legislation was directed against the Mexican working class in the United States.

7. Pharmaceutical companies and medical professionals play a central role in getting Americans to define drugs as *the way* to relieve the stresses of everyday life. Defining problems of living as medical matters, known as *the medicalization of human problems,* includes defining unruly children as having an illness for which they need medication.

8. Of all the drugs that Americans use, nicotine causes the most harm. Overall, alcohol is the next most harmful. The social setting in which people learn to drink influences their chances of becoming problem drinkers. We need more studies to determine the effects of marijuana and other drugs. Cocaine's social history illustrates how a drug's reputation depends on the people with whom it is associated.

9. Narcotics themselves do not cause crime or destroy people's desire to work. Addicted doctors maintain normal lives because they need not deal with a black market and are able to obtain pure drugs.
10. At a minimum, an adequate social policy would involve drug education that presents scientific findings honestly, whether they are favorable or unfavorable to any particular drug. It should also break the addicts' dependence on a black market and provide help for their problems. Alcoholics Anonymous appears to be a model recovery program.
11. We can anticipate that the future will bring new drugs from the pharmaceutical companies and social policies that penalize the users of drugs that are in disfavor. A "good people" versus "evil drug users" thinking is likely to continue.

Thinking Critically about Chapter 4

1. Which perspective—symbolic interactionism, functionalism, or conflict theory—do you think best explains drug policies in the United States? Why?
2. Should we make all drugs legal? If not, what criteria should we use in making a drug illegal?
3. What do you think is the best social policy regarding drug addiction? How should social policy depend on whether the drug to which someone is addicted is legal or illegal?

Key Terms

alcoholics, 91
attention-deficit hyperactivity
   disorder (ADHD), 84
binge drinking, 87
cravings, 79
drug, 78
drug abuse, 78
drug addiction, 79

fetal alcohol spectrum disorders (FASD), 93
fetal alcohol syndrome (FAS), 93
medicalization of human problems, 84
methadone maintenance, 107
moral entrepreneurs, 94
neonatal abstinence syndrome, 103
psychological dependence, 79
withdrawal, 79

Chapter 5
Violence in Society: Rape and Murder

Scott Olson/Staff/Getty Images News/ Getty Images

 ## Learning Objectives

After reading this chapter, you should be able to:

5.1 Explain the sociological perspective on violence.

5.2 Explain why violence is a social problem— its subjective and objective dimensions.

5.3 Explain the sociological perspective on violence and compare the symbolic interactionist, functionalist, and conflict perspectives on violence.

5.4 Explain how rape was transformed from a personal problem to a social problem.

5.5 Be familiar with the social patterns of rape.

5.6 Summarize the reactions to rape.

5.7 Analyze the social patterns of murder.

5.8 Discuss the findings on mass murder and serial murder.

5.9 Identify social policies that can reduce or prevent violence.

5.10 Discuss the likely future of violence.

Most faculty meetings are rather dull. The tedium is occasionally interrupted by a colleague who is upset about something and says a few choice words. Even this seldom happens, and when it does, it's usually nothing more than a little venting about something the dean or some other administrator has done. Faculty meetings like this are typical, including those at the University of Alabama at Huntsville.

> ## She took the usual pen and notebook to the faculty meeting. She also took a loaded handgun.

This one, though, was different, destined to go down in the history books.

Amy Bishop, assistant professor in the Department of Biological Sciences, took the usual pen and notebook to the faculty meeting. She also took a loaded handgun. As she sat in the meeting, she fumed that these imbeciles, so beneath her, had the temerity to reject her. None of them had invented an automatic cell incubator, as she had. They were so jealous that they had denied her tenure, and now she would have to look for a faculty position elsewhere. With four children and a husband tied to his job in Huntsville, this wouldn't be easy.

Amy's anger grew as she listened to Gopi Podila, chair of the department, drone on and on about trivial matters. And here she was, facing this momentous event in her life that *he* had caused. And these other morons, just sitting there and nodding like pigeons as he talked, *they*, too, were the cause of her problem. She couldn't stand it any longer. She had an answer for these idiots.

Amy had been fingering the pistol in her purse, quietly wondering whether she should go through with her plan, but the more she thought about what these people were doing to her, the more she knew they deserved it. She silently took the gun from her purse, and aiming it at Gopi, pulled the trigger. Then she turned the gun on the others who were staring at her in stunned disbelief. Amy continued to fire as they scrambled away, killing three and wounding three more.

Amy walked calmly out of the room, as though she had just attended a regular faculty meeting. She called her husband, told him the meeting was over, and asked if he could pick her up.

What the Huntsville administrators didn't know when they hired Amy was that in addition to getting her Ph.D. in microbiology from Harvard, she also had been a suspect there. Amy had an argument with a professor, and someone mailed him a pipe bomb. Fortunately for him, it had not gone off.

The university also didn't know that Amy had hit a woman on the head at IHOP because the woman had taken the last booster seat. Amy wanted that seat for her child.

There was also one other little incident that the university didn't know about. When Amy was 19, she shot her brother with a shotgun. He died on the kitchen floor, bleeding from massive chest injuries. The killing had been ruled an accident.

Amy's lawyer says that Amy doesn't recall the faculty meeting.

—Based on Dewan and Zezima 2010; Sweet et al. 2010; Remkus 2016.

The Problem in Sociological Perspective

5.1 Explain the sociological perspective on violence.

Whether we see violence on the street or on television, it grabs our attention, The more gruesome the violence—or the more unusual it is, as with Amy Bishop—the greater our attention. **Violence**, the use of force to injure people or to destroy their property, goes far beyond individuals or what some term "violent personalities." As you will see, violence has a basic *social* nature.

To zero in on the social aspect of violence, let's begin with this: Sociologists note that some societies encourage violence, while others discourage it. As a result, some societies have high rates of violence, and others have low rates. The sociological question is, *What is it about a society that increases or decreases the likelihood of violence?* Throughout this chapter, we shall grapple with this central question.

The Scope of the Problem

5.2 **Explain why violence is a social problem—its subjective and objective dimensions.**

Before we look at how extensive rape and murder are in the United States, we need to distinguish between violence as a personal problem and violence as a social problem.

What Makes Violence a Social Problem?

If two people get into a fight and end up in the hospital, this is their *personal* problem. The same is true if a woman, enraged at discovering her husband with a lover, shoots them to death. And the same is true if a man rapes a woman. Although these examples involve severe, bitter violence, they portray only objective conditions. To be a *social* problem, violence must also arouse widespread subjective concerns. A large number of people must be upset and want something done about it.

The Subjective Dimension of Violence *Subjective concerns* of violence are widespread. As you can see from Figure 5.1, about one-third of Americans are afraid to walk alone at night.

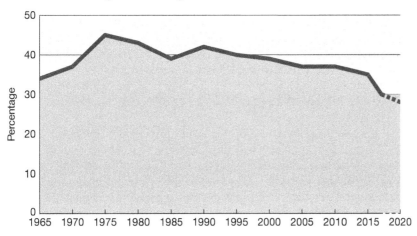

Figure 5.1 Fear of Walking Alone at Night Near Your Home

Percentage of adults who say they would be afraid to walk alone at night in their neighborhood

Source: By the author. Based on Gallup Poll. "Americans' Fear of Walking Alone Ties 52-Yar Low." November 2, 2017.

Women are more afraid than men, and there is good reason for this (Gallup Poll 2015). Seldom is it a woman who abducts a man, raping and killing him. Women feel especially vulnerable as they get on elevators, and many are fearful as they walk alone at night from their classrooms to their cars. They feel relief when they get inside their cars—after they've shut and locked their car doors.

The Objective Dimension of Violence How much violence is there in the United States? Is the country more dangerous now than in the past? These are reasonable questions. To answer them, let's look at the **rate of violence**, the number of violent crimes for each 100,000 Americans. If, over a 10-year period our population increases 10 percent and rape and murder also increase 10 percent, there would be more rape and murder, but the rate would be the same. The increase in rape and murder would simply have kept pace with the increase in population. People's chances of being raped or murdered would be the same in the two periods of time.

Now look at Figure 5.2. You can see that from 1960 to 1991, the rate of violent crime soared. It didn't just double or even triple, but it jumped *4.7 times* (from 161 to 758 violent crimes per 100,000 people). By 1991, people's chances of being a victim of violent crime were *almost five times* what they were in 1960. If the U.S. population had not increased by a single person, there would have been 4.7 times as many violent crimes in 1990 as there were in 1968.

Figure 5.2 The Rate of Violence

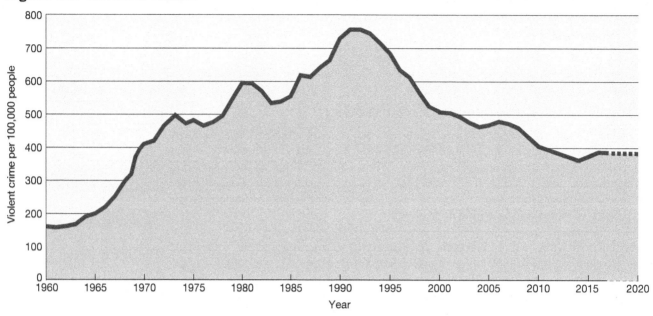

Source: By the author. Based on various editions of *Uniform Crime Reports and Crime in the United States* 2017:Table 1.

Figure 5.2 also shows the good news. In 1992, the rate of violent crime began to drop, and it dropped sharply. Today's rate of murder, rape, robbery, and aggravated assault is *less than half* (48 percent) of what it was in 1991. Despite this huge drop in violence, however, you can see that our streets are still much more dangerous than they were in 1960.

In the last couple of years, there has been a slight increase in the rate of violent crime. This could be just a blip like the one you can see in 2006, or it could be the start of a long upward trend. We'll find out shortly.

Figure 5.3 is one way of visualizing the extent of violent crime in the United States. On average, a woman is raped every 4 minutes; every 39 seconds or so, someone attacks someone else (aggravated assault); and every half hour or so, an American dies from these attacks (homicide or murder). When we refer to violent crime in the United States, we are not talking about an occasional rape, a fistfight here and there, or isolated incidents of spouses turning on one another.

Figure 5.3 The Clock of Violence

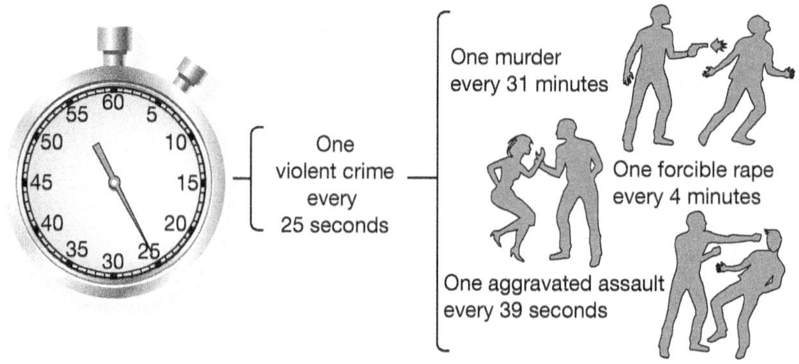

One violent crime every 25 seconds

One murder every 31 minutes

One forcible rape every 4 minutes

One aggravated assault every 39 seconds

Source: FBI 2017.

You know that when people search for an apartment or a house, they are concerned about the neighborhood's safety. But few people realize how much of a difference social location makes: If you live in Washington, D.C., your chances of being murdered are *22* times greater than if you live in New Hampshire. African American males are *8* times more likely than white males to be murdered, and men of any race-ethnicity are four times more likely than women to be murdered. In terms of age and sex, those most likely to be murdered are men in their 20s (*Statistical Abstract* 2018:Tables 334, 337, 338).

Despite the high rate of U.S. violence, it is far from the highest in the world. In Figure 5.4, you can see how the U.S. rate compares with some other countries. From this figure, you can also see how rape and murder tend to happen together. Most countries that have a high murder rate also have a high rape rate—and vice versa.

Figure 5.4 How Countries Compare in Rape and Murder

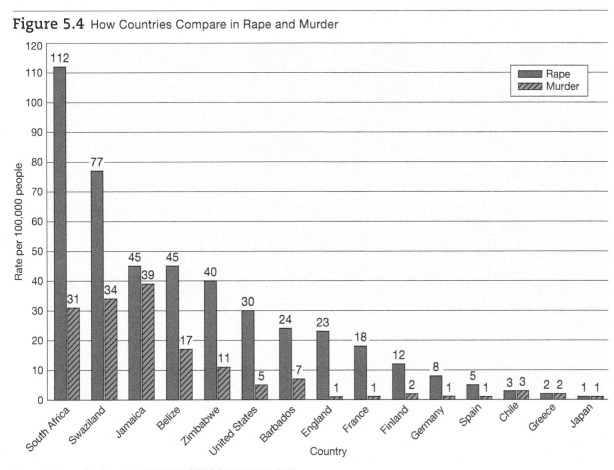

Source: By the author. Based on FBI 2017; UNODOC 2010, 2014, 2018.

But statistics can be misleading, as we discuss in the following *Thinking Critically about Social Problems.*

Thinking Critically about Social Problems

Why So Few Pakistani Women Are Raped—Or Why We Have to Be Cautious about Crime Statistics

In the United States, about 95,000 women reported that they were raped last year, but in Pakistan, only 76 women reported that they were raped.

Don't believe it. Official statistics can be totally inaccurate. Let's see why.

Let's start by noting that statistics are not things that exist in nature. They are not like apples that you pick from a tree. They are human creations, products of bureaucrats. If data are gathered freely and openly, statistics can be quite revealing of what they are intended to represent. But crime statistics can also be severely misleading.

To make themselves look better, countries have been known to fake data. The Soviets are an outstanding example. Their official statistics often did not represent reality but were intended to hide problems with their political-economic system and to make their society look better. Every government would love to produce statistics that make it look more favorable to others. The usual deception is more subtle than faked data, however. Government agencies sometimes make themselves look better by redefining key terms such as "unemployment," "production," "efficiency," and so on.

Culture can also influence the production of statistics. In Islamic countries, rapes are so underreported that I have not included their statistics in Figure 5.4. Pakistan is a remarkable example. This country reports an impossible rape rate of 0.04 per 100,000 people. This is four rapes per 10 million people. With a population of 190 million, this comes to about 76 women.

Why is this rate inaccurate, and ridiculously so? Because only a few Pakistani women report their rapes. Why? For a Westerner, it is difficult to grasp, but if a woman reports a rape, the police almost always look down on her and say, "Why do you want to report this and bring shame on yourself and your family?" (Zaman 2013)

There is more. Until recently, when a married Pakistani woman was raped and the accused man was found not guilty, the woman was automatically guilty of adultery. ("She said they had sex, and the judge found the man not guilty of rape, so this means the woman consented.") When an unmarried woman was raped, and the accused man was found not guilty, she was automatically guilty of fornication ("Cross National..." 2004). The punishment for a Pakistani woman guilty of adultery or fornication? Besides being publicly whipped, she can be stoned to death.

Mukhtaran (Bibi) Mai was gang raped on orders of village elders who were retaliating against her 12-year-old brother who was (falsely) accused of having sex with an older woman of higher caste. Mai, who protested her rape in the courts, an extraordinary act in Pakistan, has become a symbol of strong women who survive sexual violence—and thrive.

You can see what a strong deterrent there is in Pakistan for a woman to report that she was raped. Although the law has changed to provide more protection for women, little has changed in how the law is carried out (Khan and Gul 2017).

When it comes to statistics on rape, there are also other problems. There is even the question of "What is rape?" The answer differs from place to place—and the answer changes. Not only do some countries use different definitions of rape, but even in the United States the definition has changed over the years. Under the prodding of feminists, more behaviors are considered rape today than in years past.

For Your Consideration

→ What does the author mean when he says that "statistics are not like apples on trees"?
→ Why do we have to be careful of official statistics?
→ How do you think we can overcome the limitations built into official statistics?

Looking at the Problem Theoretically

5.3 Explain the sociological perspective on violence and compare the symbolic interactionist, functionalist, and conflict perspectives on violence.

Now let's look at some of the theories social scientists use to explain violence. First, let's consider two non-sociological explanations of violence, and then see how the sociological approach differs.

Comparing Non-Sociological and Sociological Approaches to Understanding Violence

Theorists from different backgrounds have distinctive ways of understanding violence. Let's contrast biological and learning theories with the sociological approach.

Biological Explanations Seeing biology as the cause of violence goes back to at least the 1800s, when Cesare Lombroso (1835–1909), an Italian physician, treated prisoners. He was struck by how different the prisoners looked from his regular patients. They had lower foreheads, larger ears, and receding chins. Lombroso (1911) concluded that violent people (and other criminals) are *atavistic;* that is, they are biological throwbacks to an earlier violent, primitive period of humanity.

Anthropologist Konrad Lorenz (1966) also claimed that evolution was the key to explaining violence, but his explanation was quite different. He said that humans are not equipped well for killing: We don't have claws, slashing teeth, or great strength. Because of this, we did not develop an inhibitory mechanism that stops violence. When dogs, wolves, and baboons fight, an inhibitory mechanism kicks in when the enemy becomes submissive, and they stop their violence. But we have a powerful intellect, which allowed us to make weapons. The combination of having weapons but not having a mechanism that blocks violence produces terrible bloodshed. In our anger or attempts to dominate, we use weapons to destroy one another. As Lionel Tiger and Robin Fox (1971:210) remarked, if baboons carried hand grenades, there would be few baboons left in Africa.

Today, another biological explanation of violence is being proposed. It goes like this: We are the product of millions of years of natural selection. During this time, people who were violent were more likely to survive and to pass on their genes. We carry those genes. Just as groups differ by skin color, hair texture, and bone and facial structure, so some groups carry genes that make them more violent than others. This explains why males are more violent than females. During the eons that humans developed, women were more limited by pregnancy, more concerned about child care, and smaller than men. They engaged in fewer violent behaviors because those behaviors could bring harm to themselves or to their children. Women, then, were less likely than men to pass on genes for violence. Geneticists are now trying to identify specific genes that code for violence (Tilhonen et al. 2015; Xu 2017; NCBI 2018).

Learning Theories   Learning theories, which go back about 75 years, are still being developed (Beane 2018). They can be traced to B. F. Skinner (1948, 1953, 1971), who did research on **operant conditioning**. By this term, Skinner meant that we tend to repeat behaviors that are rewarded ("reinforced") and drop behaviors that are not rewarded. The "reward" (or "reinforcement") can be any gain—material items such as candy or food or symbolic items such as status or even a smile. For a rapist, the reward may be power and sex. For a killer, the reward might be money, revenge, or satisfaction at eliminating an enemy.

Some violence is learned through **modeling**, copying another person's behavior. In the 1960s, psychologists Albert Bandura and Richard Walters did simple experiments that are still widely quoted (Shipancer 2017). They had some children watch an adult hit a Bobo doll (a blow-up clown) and others watch a film of an adult doing this. Other children played in the same setting but did not have the model of violence. Those who saw others hitting the Bobo doll, either in person or on film, tended to do the same thing themselves. Children who had not seen this behavior were less likely to be violent to the doll.

The Sociological Approach   Sociologists do not look for the causes of violence *within* people, as do those who propose genes as its cause. Rather, sociologists focus on matters *outside* people. Although sociologists find learning theory more compatible with their thinking because it examines factors external to people, they find it limiting because its focus is on individuals and not groups. Sociologists place the focus on the broader picture. Their basic approach is to understand how the social environment, *social life*, encourages—or discourages—violence. For example, in one society, violence may be channeled into the social roles of warrior, boxer, or football player. Other societies, in contrast, may downplay violence and develop mechanisms to ensure that it rarely occurs.

Let's apply the three sociological perspectives to violence. As we do so, let's try to understand why males are more likely than females to be violent and why violence is higher among members of the working or lower classes.

Symbolic Interactionism

Michael Franzese, a college-educated member of the Mafia, said:

> *If somebody were to dishonor my wife or my child, I would view it as something that I had to take into my own hands. I don't see why I have to go to the police. As a man, I would feel that it was an obligation that I had to take care of. And I would have to be prepared in my own mind to kill this guy. This is a basic principle (Barnes and Shebar 1987).*

Why do people kill? As we look at two theories that symbolic interactionists have developed, you will see their connection to Franzese's statement.

Edwin Sutherland: Differential Association   Sociologist Edwin Sutherland (1937) stressed that people learn criminal behavior by interacting with others. In its simplest form, Sutherland's theory goes like this: People who associate with lawbreakers are more likely to break the law than are people who associate with those who follow the law. Sutherland used the term **differential association** to describe this process.

Let's apply Sutherland's theory to violence:

1. The mechanisms for learning violence and nonviolence are the same.
2. People learn violence from others—not just techniques of violence, but also attitudes, motives, and rationalizations for violence.

3. People who are violent have learned more attitudes (or definitions) that favor violence than they have learned attitudes (or definitions) that favor nonviolence. (Sutherland called this an *excess of definitions*.)

4. The most significant learning (of violence or nonviolence) is that which occurs early in life and in interactions that are frequent, long-lasting, and emotional or meaningful.

Marvin Wolfgang: Subcultures of Violence Sociologist Marvin Wolfgang developed **subcultural theory**. In a nutshell, this theory says that people who grow up in a subculture that approves of violent behavior have a high chance of becoming violent. Wolfgang wanted to know why the homicide rate is high among lower-class African American men. Wolfgang's 1958 research on convicted murderers in Philadelphia has become a classic in sociology.

Just as the quotation from the Mafia member that opened this section stresses, Wolfgang found that the men connected honor and manliness with violence. For them, insults were a challenge to their manliness or honor, and violence was the appropriate response to the insult. Situations that others might perceive as trivial were *not* trivial to them. Anyone who backs down from a confrontation (even if it is about a "little" thing) is seen as less than a real man. Others view him as a "chicken" or a "girl"—and ridicule him. With their "rep" at stake, the young men carry weapons both for protection and as a symbol of masculinity. As a result, confrontations that in other groups would be passed over result in homicide.

The findings from this classic research from such a long time ago apply as vibrantly today as they did back then (Peterson and Ward 2015). Sociologist Victor Rios (2011, Rios 2017), who did participant observation of young male African American and Latino gang members in Oakland, California, reports that these same ideas of masculinity continue. This approach to life continues to produce high rates of violence.

Fitting the Theories Together Differential association and subcultural theory fit together well. Subcultural theory stresses that violence is woven into the life of some groups, and differential association explains how people in these groups learn that violence is an appropriate way to deal with problems.

It is not just the boys and men in these groups who associate violence with "being a man." The girls and women also feel the same way. Living in neighborhoods where violence is common, they assume that "their man" will protect them. He might manage this with threats, but if threats aren't enough, he must be ready to fight. If a fight escalates, he might have to use a knife or a gun. To do less would lower his image in the eyes of not just other men, but of the women as well.

Can you explain why this photo illustrates differential association? How about subcultural theory?

MBI/Stockbroker/Alamy Stock Photo

You can see how the idea that someone should be ready to be violent to protect his image or his friends would lead to violence. As sociologist Elijah Anderson (1990, 2006, 2012) documents, young African American men in the inner city live in a world that presents many challenges to their masculinity. As a defensive measure, so no one will "mess" with them, these men project masculinity through looking tough, as though they are ready to be violent.

Chicano gang members also connect masculinity and violence (Rios 2017). Sociologist Ruth Horowitz, who did participant observation of Chicano gangs in Chicago, found that these young men sometimes even seek violence to prove their manliness. In the following *Spotlight on Social Research,* Horowitz shares insights that she gained from her research.

Spotlight on Social Research

Studying Violence among "The Lions"

Courtesy of Ruth Horowitz

When she was a graduate student at the University of Chicago, **RUTH HOROWITZ** *(now professor of sociology at New York University) did participant observation of young people in a Chicano community in Chicago. Her purpose was not to understand violence, but to understand poverty. She wanted to see how the explanations of poverty that sociologists had developed matched what she observed in "real life."*

Two major explanations of poverty are the culture of poverty and the social structure of poverty. According to the *culture of poverty,* poor people have different values than the middle class, and this is why they act as they do. According to the *social structure of poverty,* the poor act as they do because, unlike middle-class people, they do not have the same opportunities to attend good schools or to obtain good jobs. Consequently, the poor turn to illegal opportunities, and crime becomes part of their life.

One afternoon, a month after I met the "Lions" gang and shook hands with all of them in the park, several 16-year-old young women introduced themselves. They asked me several questions about myself, and they were able to give me a definition of sociology. They told me about school and their trips around the city. Several of these women went on to college; others became pregnant and married. The life experience of siblings varied, too; some went to school and became white-collar workers, while others ran afoul of the legal system and went to prison.

When I first began my research, the "Lions" were 15 to 17 years old, had guns, and did a lot of fighting. Some had after-school jobs and dressed in tuxedos for *quinceañeras* and weddings. In the streets, these same young men had developed a reputation by being tougher than other gangs. They would even seek opportunities to challenge others. At home and during most parties, in contrast, they were polite and conformed to strict rules of etiquette.

For seven years, I did participant observation with these youths. When I returned after a three-year absence, many of the "Lions" were still hanging out together, but quite a few were working, had married, and had children. A few of the gang members attended college, and others remained in the street. One had been killed in a drug deal gone wrong. A major change was their relationship to violence. Instead of provoking incidents, now they responded only when someone challenged their reputations.

The two models of poverty did apply. Violence had been part of the culture they had learned, and a lack of opportunities did contribute to a sense of being left out. But there was more to it. Actual violence depended on how the "Lions" defined a particular situation. As sociologists phrase this: Violence was situational and constructed interactionally.

In Sum   "Manliness" (or "masculinity") is a powerful symbol, something to which boys and men aspire. To associate violence with manliness encourages violence. Working-class males tend to incorporate violence into their views of appropriate male behavior, leading to their higher rates of violence. As a result, year after year, across racial–ethnic lines and in every region of the United States, violence is more prevalent among males than females and among working-class males than males from other social classes. Until the association between masculinity and violence is broken, you can expect these patterns to continue.

Functionalism

As we consider the functionalist approach to understanding violence, keep the sociological question of violence in mind: How does the social environment encourage or discourage violence?

Emile Durkheim: Asking the Sociological Question The first person to ask *What is it about a society (or social life) that increases or decreases the likelihood of violence?* was Emile Durkheim, the first university professor to be formally identified as a sociologist. In the 1800s, Durkheim examined murder rates in Paris and suicide rates in several European countries (1897/1951, 1904/1938). He was struck by how consistent these rates were over time. Year after year, the countries that had high rates of violence continued to have high rates, and those with low rates continued to have low rates. Durkheim called this **normal violence**—the violence that a group normally (or usually) has.

Durkheim found this regularity intriguing. Since murder and suicide rates represent the number of deaths by *individuals*—with all their particular frustrations, depressions, and other emotions and situations—why don't the rates jump all over the place? To explain this, Durkheim developed the *sociological perspective:* He concluded that *society regulates individual impulses and desires,* resulting in consistent rates of violence.

To appreciate Durkheim's conclusion, consider what life used to be like in farming communities. Children followed in their parents' footsteps and either worked in the village in which they were reared or farmed nearby land. They spent their entire lives in a village where everyone knew one another. Their close bonds and their need of the community to survive helped to restrain individual impulses to lash out violently. Their close relationships (high social integration, as Durkheim called it) and their need to maintain good reputations kept overall rates of violence low.

Now let's add rapid social change to this picture. Imagine that the society is industrializing. The villagers move to the city to take jobs where they know few people. Living in the midst of strangers, they face being fired by bosses who care about profits, not workers. They face evictions by landlords who care more about collecting rent than about what happens to a family. Unlike the factors that promote cohesion in a little village, the city does the opposite. Urban life loosens social bonds. In the city, people are more anonymous, have fewer ties with one another, and the old rules no longer fit. Durkheim gave the name **anomie** (an'-uh-me) to such feelings of being unconnected and uprooted. Under these circumstances, impulses to violence are not as restrained as they are in the village. As a result, the city is a more dangerous place.

Robert Merton: Strain Theory Another functionalist, Robert Merton (1968), who applied *anomie* to crime in the United States, developed what is called **strain theory**. Success in the form of money or material goods, said Merton, is a **cultural goal**, a goal held out for all Americans. The socialization is highly effective, and almost all Americans learn to want a lot of money and material goods. Society also offers approved (or legitimate) ways to reach success, especially through education, jobs, and career training. Merton called these approved ways **cultural means**. The cultural means, however, are limited and not distributed evenly. Those who find their path to success blocked experience what Merton called *strain* (frustration and anxiety). These people still want the goal, however, and many turn to illegitimate means to reach it. This is why robbery, theft, and violence are concentrated among the poor: They have less access to the approved means to achieve success.

Reckless, Gottfredson, and Hirschi: Control Theory Strain theory does not explain why some people become violent while others do not (Broidy and Santoro 2018). We all face obstacles to success, but few of us attack others. To answer this question, sociologist Walter Reckless (1973) developed **control theory**. This theory assumes that all of us have a natural tendency toward violence, and it asks what forms of social control overcome our natural tendencies. Reckless identified *inner* controls (our inner capacity to withstand pressures to commit crime or to be violent) and *outer* controls (groups such as family, friends, and the police that divert us from violence). If our control systems are stronger than the pushes and pulls toward violence, we are not violent. If they are weaker, we are violent.

Sociologists Michael Gottfredson and Travis Hirschi (1990) refined control theory by focusing on the inner controls. They concluded that people who have low self-control get in trouble with the law because they are impulsive risk-takers. These traits also make it difficult for them to stay married, to keep a job or friends, to meet long-term commitments, and to be good parents. Low self-control comes from ineffective parenting. The parents did not adequately monitor the child's behavior, ignored or did not recognize deviant behavior when it occurred, or were unfair and inconsistent in their rewards and punishment. These patterns make a child less capable of delaying gratification, less sensitive to the needs of others, and less willing to hold back impulses. One of the consequences is a tendency to violence.

Conflict Theory

As you might expect by this point in the text, to analyze violence conflict theorists look to the capitalist/working class division in society.

Violence Is Inherent in Society   As you will recall, the focus of conflict theory is groups competing with one another for limited resources. Conflict can lie hidden beneath surface cooperation and even goodwill, but the true nature of human relationships is adversarial, which often results in violence.

Social Class and Violence: The Working Class   The social classes are among the groups competing for society's limited resources. The essential division is between those who own the means of production—the factories, the machines, and capital (investment money)—and those who work for the owners (Marx and Engels 1848/1964, Marx and Engels 1906). The workers, who must struggle to put food on the table, pay rent, and buy clothing, are at the mercy of the owners, who make their decisions on the basis of profit, not the workers' welfare. For example, in their search for cheap labor, the owners can close a factory in the United States and open another in China or India.

Finding their economic security fragile, working-class men experience high frustration. They are paid little, and unskilled jobs are drying up. These men commit more violent

How do conflict theorists relate violence and the economic insecurity of the working class?

Jetta Productions Inc/DigitalVision/Getty Images

crimes than do either working-class women or men from higher social classes. For the same reasons, working-class women commit more violent crimes than do women from higher social classes. And the most deprived—those who are confined to the inner city—have the highest rates of violence as they desperately strike out at one another.

Social Class and Violence: The Capitalist Class   "The working class is what you see when you look at individual violence," say conflict theorists. "But when you look at large-scale group violence, you see that the capitalist class is actually *more* violent than the working class. The wealthy control the police powers of the state, which they use to suppress the lower social classes. They also control the armed forces, which they send out to protect their investments. They care little how many they kill in the process. Unlike the working class, the capitalists don't kill with their own hands, but their toll on human life is much higher. It is not violence but the *form* of violence that distinguishes workers from capitalists."

In Sum   Violence is part of all human societies, and true to their calling, sociologists look for *social* causes of violence, factors outside the individual. They want to know why some societies have more violence than others, as well as why some groups in the same society are more violent than others. As usual, the theoretical orientations focus on different aspects of violence.

Symbolic interactionists stress that some groups prefer nonviolent ways of handling disagreements, while other groups consider violence an appropriate response to many situations. To resolve conflicts, the middle and upper social classes usually turn to the legal system, which transcends personal confrontation. The lower social classes, in contrast, are likely to take matters into their own hands—which breeds violence. The groups with which people associate (differential association) increase or decrease people's likelihood of becoming violent.

Functionalists emphasize that conditions that strengthen social bonds reduce violence, and conditions that produce *anomie* increase violence. Violence tends to be higher among groups whose access to culturally approved goals is blocked. Whether an individual will be violent depends on his or her inner and outer controls.

Conflict theorists stress that class exploitation underlies violence. Seldom do members of the working class direct their violence against their oppressors, for the capitalists are able to use the powers of the state to protect their privileged positions. Instead of targeting their oppressors, workers almost always misdirect their violence, aiming it at one another. The capitalists, though, are more violent than the working class, for their wars and destruction of the environment in the pursuit of profits claim far more victims.

Now that we've reviewed basic theories of violence, let's turn to research findings on rape and murder.

■ Research Findings: Rape

Our focus is **forcible rape**—an assault where one individual forces another to have any type of sex. Consent is considered absent if the victim is threatened or if the victim's judgment is impaired, such as being intoxicated. **Statutory rape**, in contrast, refers to sexual intercourse between an adult and a minor, even if the minor consents. By law, minors cannot consent.

Let's begin by looking at how rape became a social problem.

The Natural History of Rape as a Social Problem

5.4   Explain how rape was transformed from a personal problem to a social problem.

Believe it or not, but rape was labeled a social problem only during the last third of the last century. How did this new view of rape come about?

The Feminist-Conflict View:
Transforming Rape from a Personal to a Social Problem

Rape has been part of society from its beginnings to the present. The Old Testament has accounts of rape from 3,000 years ago and longer. There also are accounts of rape in Greek mythology and in the literature of other ancient peoples. But like the other social problems we discuss in this text, that rape exists does not make rape a social problem. Besides an objective condition, we must also have abundant subjective concerns.

Traditional Gender Relations To gain a fuller background, we need to understand something about the history of gender relations. A woman used to be considered the legal property of her father, property that he passed on to his daughter's husband. At that time, rape was a crime against a man's property, either the father's or the husband's. The rapist had "spoiled" (damaged) a man's property (Ullman 2007). Although this patriarchal perspective is no longer part of the Western view, remnants of it do manage to hang on. Some men and women still consider a woman who has been raped to be "spoiled goods." In their eyes, the victim of a rape is somehow less than a woman who has not been a victim of this crime.

Until recently, both women and men perceived rape as a personal problem. The woman was often blamed. Men were seen as being easily aroused sexually, and perhaps the woman, even unintentionally, had aroused the man. Perhaps she had worn revealing clothing or said the "wrong" things.

Changed Gender Relations Then how was rape transformed from a personal to a social problem? Let's go back to the 1960s, when Western women were questioning their traditional roles and redefining their place in society. At this time, their roles revolved around husband, home, and children. As women discussed their growing dissatisfactions, more and more women began to think of themselves less as individuals who were facing unique circumstances in life and more as members of a social group that shared the same problems (Friedan 1963; Millett 1970). This was a fundamental change in thinking.

Feminists first questioned, then challenged, the view that rape is an act of passion. They said that the traditional view of rape represents flawed reasoning. It assumes that men are barely able to keep their sexual passions in check. It also assumes that a woman did something that excited the man, so he lost control and took her by force. This view makes rape the woman's fault, as it was her sexual cues that stimulated the attack.

Changed Views of Rape *As feminists campaigned against rape, they emphasized that the root of rape is power, not sexual arousal.* Rape, they said, is one of the ways that men control women. The fear of rape makes women submissive, helping men maintain **patriarchy**— men's dominance of women. For example, with the threat of rape looming over them, women are not as free as men to move around society. Women constantly face situations that are similar to an unarmed man going out at night into a crime-ridden part of the city.

This new view made rape a form of violence by predators, not an act of passion by sexually stimulated men. It also removed the blame from the victim to the one(s) who committed the rape. Gradually, as this new feminist view took hold, rape was transformed from a personal problem to a social problem.

This feminist view does not suggest that men deliberately use rape to frighten women into submissive positions in society. The practice of power by men is both deeper and subtler than this. Both men and women learn to associate power and dominance with masculinity and submissiveness and weakness with femininity. As boys learn that "masculine" is tied to strength, dominance, and aggression, they assume these characteristics as part of their gender identity. They learn, too, that "real" men don't take "No" for an answer: Real men pursue a goal until they reach it. They also learn that a woman might say "No" when she doesn't really mean it. From pornography, they might even learn that women like to be forced into sexual acts.

One of the women's reactions to the threat of rape is self-defense classes. Shown here is another reaction, one that goes a step further.

You can see how sharply the feminist view of rape as dominance contrasts with the view of rape as an act of passion. Many states have incorporated this new view into their legal systems, replacing the legal charge of rape with **criminal sexual assault**. This crime is much broader, including both completed and attempted sexual assaults against both males and females.

The Social Patterns of Rape

5.5   Be familiar with the social patterns of rape.

On the surface, rape might seem random, but it is far from this. The patterns of rape that researchers have found point to its social nature, which takes us far from explaining rape as the act of "sick" individuals. Let's look at rape's basic social patterns.

Basic Social Patterns

The first social pattern that we want to look at is the number of rapes. These totals come from official statistics, and we need to question them.

Official Statistics: Why We Question National Numbers   According to the FBI, 96,000 Americans are forcibly raped each year (*Crime in the United States* 2017:Table 1). This is the official total, the number reported to the police. The actual total is 4 times higher. This means that each year, about 400,000 Americans are raped. About 15 percent of the victims are males (*Statistical Abstract of the United States* 2018:Table 341).

You might be wondering how we know that forcible rape is 4 times higher than the official total. In what is called *The National Crime Victimization Survey*, researchers interview 135,000 U.S. households each year. They ask 225,000 people about the crimes that have happened to them and whether they reported those crimes to the police. About one-fourth (23 percent) of rape victims report this crime to the police (Morgan and Kena 2017:Tables 5, 6).

Specific Patterns   You might be interested in the specific patterns that researchers have discovered about rape. Here is a brief summary:

Acquaintanceship: A woman is more likely to be raped by someone she knows than by a stranger. Seven of 10 rapes are committed by a relative of the victim or by someone she knows well or at least casually.

Place: Women who live in cities are more likely to be raped than women who live in small towns.

Age: The most common age of victims is 21 to 24.

Income: Poor women are more likely to be raped. Women with household incomes less than $15,000 are *six* times as likely to be raped as women with higher household incomes.

Weapon: About eight out of 10 rapists use no weapon. They depend on surprise, threats, and physical strength.

Season: Rapes are more likely to occur in summer than in winter.

(I abstracted these six patterns from *Sourcebook of Criminal Justice Statistics* 2012:Table 3–16; Lauritsen and White 2014; *FBI Uniform Crime Report* 2015:Table 1; *Statistical Abstract* 2018:Tables 333, 341.)

Because these patterns show up year after year, sociologists conclude that rape is not the act of a few sick men, but, rather, *rape is linked to social factors.* Some of these factors are apparent, such as those related to place and season. For others, we have some indication, such as a greater tie-in of violence with masculinity among men in poverty.

The following Social Map makes visible another pattern. As you look at this map, you might be surprised at how widely the states differ in their rates of rape. I wish I could give you the reasons for these differences, but we do not know the social factors that make some states safer or more dangerous than others. The range of danger is certainly severe. At the extreme, women in Alaska are 7 times more likely to be raped than women in New Jersey.

Figure 5.5 The "Where" of Rape: The Rape Rate by State

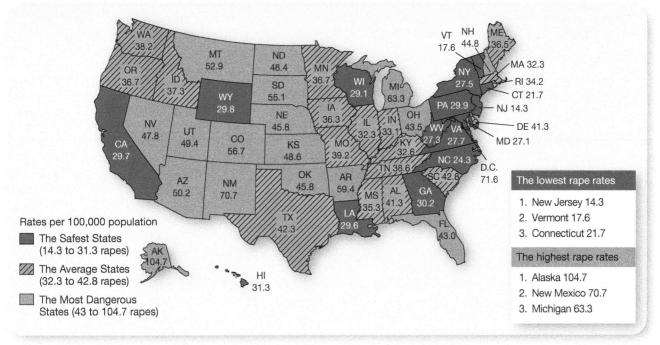

Source: By the author. Based on *Statistical Abstract of the United States* 2017:Table 334.

Groups That Are Overrepresented Rape is committed almost exclusively by young men. From Figure 5.6, you can see how arrests for rape peak at ages 15 to 24 and then drop with each age group after that. Although only 14.2 percent of males in the United States are ages 15 to 24, they account for one third of those arrested for rape (*FBI 2017*:Table 20; *Statistical Abstract* 2018:Table 6). Similar findings hold true for race–ethnicity: Only about 13 percent of the U.S. male population is African American, but African American men account for 29 percent of the men who are arrested for rape. Similarly, Latino males make up about 18 percent of the population, but 27 percent of those arrested for rape are Latinos (*FBI* 2017:Table 21a; *Statistical Abstract* 2018:Table 9).

Figure 5.6 Arrests for Rape, by Age

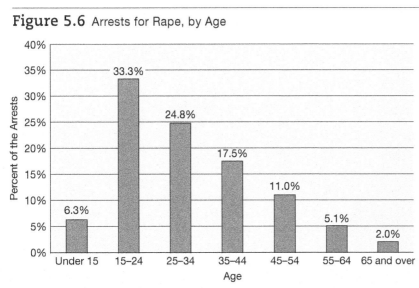

Source: By the author. Based on *Crime in the United States* 2017:Table 20.

Why are African American and Latino men overrepresented in rape statistics? For this answer, let's turn to the three sociological theories. The first two focus on social class to explain why lower-class men commit more forcible rapes (or are arrested most often). Following *symbolic interactionism*, we would stress that the lower social classes are more likely to attach violence to the meaning of masculinity. To this, we would add *conflict theory*, that the lower classes are oppressed. As we reviewed earlier, violence is one reaction to oppression. Because African American and Latino men are overrepresented in the lower social classes, they are involved in rape disproportionately. *Functionalism*, specifically *strain theory*, would stress something similar, how these men are often blocked from legitimate avenues of attaining social status. These frustrations may lead them to turn against those less powerful than themselves. For some, then, rape can be a way of gaining power (Yonack 2017).

Injury, Rape, and Resistance   Researchers are in agreement that resistance reduces rape. Women who use many forms of resistance (scratching, biting, gouging, kicking, hitting, screaming, running) are less likely to be raped (Tark and Kleck 2014; Wong and Balemba 2016). Women who resist their attackers are less likely to be raped, but are they less or more likely to be injured? Unfortunately, we don't know the answer yet (O'Neal et al. 2015). Research shows mixed results, some that resistance brings more injury to the victim, others that it does not (Tark and Kleck 2014). Researchers have found that men who use a weapon or who are violent at the beginning of a rape become even more violent when a woman resists them (Balemba et al. 2012).

Even if we knew the average results, there is no way to predict what would happen in an individual situation. Not all rapists are the same, and fighting back will discourage some rapists, even scare them away, but resistance can enrage other attackers, causing them to inflict even more injury. There also are rapists who want their victims to struggle because this excites them sexually. *Although a woman who is being attacked by a stranger doesn't know what kind of rapist she is facing, and she cannot know what the results of her resistance will be, women who resist reduce their chances of being raped.*

Women Rapists   Although we have concentrated on women as victims of rape, women also rape. Some women rape other women, and others rape men (Stemple and Meyer 2014). When a man reports that he was raped by a woman, officials have a difficult time believing that rape occurred. An underlying assumption is that men welcome all sex, so if sex occurred it could not have been rape. Legal practice is slowly catching up with the research findings that raped men no more welcomed the sex than did raped women.

Profiling the Rapist

I have developed the following 10 profiles of rapists based on men who have been arrested. Although these profiles illustrate many motivations for rape, I do not know the proportion of rapists within each type or what other types exist.

The Woman Hater   At some point in his life, the *woman hater* was hurt by a woman who was significant to him. In many cases, this woman was his mother. This hurt inflicted an emotional wound that never healed, leaving a hatred of women. By sexually assaulting women, this man gains a sense of personal power. By degrading his victim and sometimes brutally assaulting her, he retaliates for his festering wound.

The Sadist   Although the *sadist* has no particular negative feelings toward women, he beats his victims because he has learned to receive pleasure from hurting others. By raping women, he combines the pleasure he receives from inflicting pain with the pleasure he receives from sex. Because he enjoys it when his victim begs, pleads, and shows fear, the sadist is likely to increase his sexual excitement by beating or torturing his victim before sexual penetration. He sometimes prolongs his pleasure by continuing to inflict pain on her during and after the rape.

Nicolas Cocaign, a French prisoner convicted of rape, ripped a lung out of his cellmate while he was still alive. He then ate it. Cocaign says he had a bad childhood and his action was a "cry for help." What do you think?

The Generally Violence-Prone   For the *generally violence-prone* man, rape is just *one more* type of violence. He sees the world as a violent affair. If he is going to get anything—and this includes sex—he must force it from others. Unlike the previous two types of rapists, his pleasure in rape is rooted in sex, not in violence. He uses only enough violence to make the woman submit. If she resists, he feels that she deserves to be hurt because she is "holding out" on him.

The Revenger   The *revenge* rapist uses rape to get even with someone. His victim may be the person he is angry at, or she may be a substitute for his real target. In Pakistan, the brother of a girl who has been raped sometimes avenges the rape by raping the rapist's sister. In one case that came to the public's attention, both families agreed to this arrangement, and both families watched as the brother of the raped girl raped the rapist's younger sister (Adnan 2018). The Pakistani police generally don't get involved in "family matters," but in this case they did.

The Political   The *political* rapist also chooses his victim as a substitute for his enemy. Much of the raping by soldiers during war is this type. The soldiers are not motivated by hatred of women, but by hatred of the enemy. Raping "the enemy's women" shows contempt for the enemy and is a badge of their own superiority.

The Walter Mitty   Generally passive and submissive, the *Walter Mitty* rapist has an unrealistic image of masculinity. He uses rape to bridge the gap between the way he perceives how men ought to be and the way he perceives himself. He fantasizes that his victims enjoy being raped—for he is an excellent sex partner. Some carry their fantasy one step further, calling the victim later and trying to make a date with her. The Walter Mitty rapist is unlikely to beat his victim, but he will use as much force as necessary to make her submit.

The Opportunist   Unlike the first six types of rapists, the *opportunist* does not set out to rape. Rather, he takes advantage of an unexpected opportunity, often during a robbery or burglary. For example, one man drove to a local supermarket looking for a robbery victim. The first person he found was a pregnant woman. As he threatened her with a knife, the woman, scared out of her wits, blurted out that she would do anything if he didn't hurt her. At that point, he forced her to a deserted area where he raped her. He explained, "I wasn't thinking about sex. But when she said she would do anything not to get hurt, probably because she was pregnant, I thought, 'why not'" (Scully and Marolla 1985).

The Recreational Rapist   For the *recreational* rapist, rape is an activity to be enjoyed with friends, a sort of risky sport or game. As sociologists Diana Scully and Joseph Marolla (1985) discovered in their interviews of rapists in prison, one man may make a date with a victim and then drive her to a predetermined location, where he and his friends rape her. One man said that this practice had become such a part of his group's weekend routine that they had rented a house just for the purpose of recreational rape.

The Husband Rapist   There is also the *husband* rapist, a man who attacks his own wife. Contrary to common opinion, marital rape is real, not simply a husband who insists on having sex when his wife doesn't want to. After interviewing wives who had become victims of their husbands, sociologists have concluded that marital rape can involve violence and sadism every bit as horrible as any we have discussed. Some wives are forced to flee their own homes in terror (Yllo and Torres 2016).

The Date Rapist   Also called *acquaintance rapists*, the *date rapists* often feel that they deserve sex because they have invested time and money in a date or sexual seduction. For them, the rape is a way of collecting a sexual "payoff" for their investment. It is uncommon for date rapists to be reported to the police or to be convicted if they are. Police, prosecutors, judges, and juries tend to think that date rape is not "real" rape, as it does not match their stereotypes. For similar reasons, the victims also often feel that it is not the same as rape. A woman may feel guilt, thinking that she contributed to the situation by going with the man or inviting him into her home.

   As the following *Issues in Social Problems* shows, contrary to popular belief, date rape consists of much more than a man being more insistent than he should.

Issues in Social Problems

Making Campuses Safer: Date (or Acquaintance) Rape

The public has little understanding of date rape. Some seem to think that it involves a reluctant woman who needs a "push" to go along with what she really wants. Consider these two cases:

Amy had just turned 18, and it looked as if her dreams had come true. It was only the beginning of her freshman year, and yet she had met Tom, the all-state quarterback. At Wiggins Watering Hole, the college bar, he had walked over to her table and made some crack about the English comp professor. She had laughed, and the two had spent most of the evening talking.

When Tom asked to take her back to the dorm, Amy didn't hesitate. This was the man all the girls wanted to date! At the dorm, he said he would like to talk some more, so she signed him in. Once in the room, he began to kiss her. At first, the kisses felt good. But Tom was not about to stop with kissing. He forced her to the bed and, despite her protests, began to remove her clothing.

With his 240 pounds, and her 117, there wasn't much of a contest. Amy always wondered why she didn't cry out; she was asked this at the trial, at which Tom was found not guilty. This brutal end to her virginity also marked the end of her college career. Unable to shake the depression that followed, Amy left college and moved back with her parents. After a hearing, the university suspended Tom for a few games. Tom then resumed his life as before. He still goes to Wiggins Watering Hole.

* * * * * *

For Letitia, age 21, the evening started out friendly enough. After a cozy dinner at her apartment, her boyfriend suggested that she lie down while he did the dishes. She grabbed this unexpected opportunity.

As she lay on the bed, though, he walked in with a butcher knife. Her formerly tender lover bound and brutally raped her. When it was over, he fell asleep.

Convictions are difficult to get in date-rape cases. Some prosecutors discourage women from even bringing charges of date rape. A social worker at a rape treatment center summarized the problem when she said, "Most people are sympathetic when a stranger breaks into your house with a gun and rapes you, but if you say you made a date with the rapist, they always wonder how far you went before you said no."

What can be done? Campus anti-rape groups—composed of both women and men—offer one remedy. Lectures and workshops introduce incoming college women to the reality and perils of date rape and to defensive measures they can take. They also stress to men that when a woman says "no," it really is no and they must stop their advances—and that an intoxicated woman cannot give consent. Well-publicized prosecutions can help reduce the risk, and anti-rape groups can encourage women to press charges and insist that prosecutors file charges. Student groups can also pressure college administrators to react strongly to date rape. As one activist said, "If there were a pattern of assaults on quarterbacks, universities would respond very quickly."

Based on Bucher and Manasse 2011; Kingcade 2014; Tolentino 2018a.

For Your Consideration

→ Why do you think date rape is so difficult to prosecute?
→ Besides the suggestions made here, what else do you think can be done to reduce date rape?

Reactions to Rape

5.6 Summarize the reactions to rape.

Let's consider what happens to rape victims after they are attacked. We will focus first on personal reactions and then on how the criminal justice system treats rape victims.

The Trauma of Rape: A Spiral of Despair

Disbelief and shock are the first reactions reported by rape victims (Regehr et al. 2013). The event is so sudden, frightening, and alien that most victims report they could not believe it was actually happening.

The trauma of rape does not end with the physical attack. The woman typically finds her self-concept so wounded and her emotions in such tatters that her whole life is disrupted. Some rape victims deal with their trauma in an *expressive* style, venting their fear, anger, rage, and anxiety by crying and sobbing or by restlessness and tenseness. Others react in a *controlled* style, carefully masking their feelings behind a calm and composed exterior. Investigators often expect an expressive style, and talking with victims who seem calm can confuse them, even make them wonder whether a rape actually occurred (Miller and Armstrong 2018).

After a rape, life and relationships are no longer the same. Doubt, distrust, and self-blame plague rape victims. Some feel guilty for having been alone in that place at that time. Others feel it was their fault for getting in a compromising situation. If they didn't scream and fight back, this bothers them. They feel that there must have been something—*anything*—that they could have done—or not done—that might have changed the situation. As you can see, such self-doubt is bottomless.

Anxiety, depression, and thoughts of suicide plague many rape victims. So do nightmares and fears—fears of being alone, of the dark, of walking on the street, or of doing such ordinary things as shopping and driving. Anything that reminds them of the rape can send them into anxiety and depression—and they never know what will trigger the painful memories. The victim's personal relationships may deteriorate, for, feeling hurt, fearful, and less trusting, some women feel less capable of intimacy and withdraw emotionally. To complicate matters even further, some husbands and boyfriends wonder what "really" happened, with their suspicions feeding this spiral of despair.

Dealing with the Legal System

Because of pressure from rape-victim advocates and feminists, police departments have trained women officers to do the interviewing and to collect the evidence needed to pursue a criminal case. Yet the way the criminal justice system operates continues to add to the victim's suffering, sometimes even placing at least some of the blame on the victim (Chemaly 2014; McMillan 2016).

To conduct their investigation, the police must collect evidence about the attack. Because the victim's body is the crime scene, they must ask about intimate details, which can embarrass both the victim and the officers. Some officers are insensitive. Others don't believe the attack qualifies as rape if the woman doesn't have bruises and cuts. Some suspect that the victim is using the police to "get even" with a boyfriend. Because some rape charges are bogus, this is a concern (McMillan 2016).

Just when the woman needs compassion the most, when her world has been turned upside down, she can find herself disbelieved, an object of suspicion.

> Two male detectives in the state of Washington were taking a report from a woman who said she had been raped. As the woman was talking, she began to recall more details. The detectives thought that her account was inconsistent. They accused her of lying and charged her with filing a false police report. The rapist was later arrested and convicted in a string of rapes in Colorado (Miller and Armstrong 2018).

Even if a woman is fortunate enough to be questioned by sensitive, compassionate police officers who have been trained in rape investigations, this is just the beginning of her experience in the criminal justice system. The victim faces a dilemma: If she fails to press charges, the rapist goes free—and he may well rape again. But if she does press charges, she must relive her attack, perhaps repeatedly, as she goes over the details with the prosecuting attorney. Then she must describe everything in a courtroom in front of her rapist, his attorney, a judge, perhaps a jury and journalists, and even the general public. The defense attorney may attack her character, for in some states her prior sex life can be examined on the witness stand. Everything she says can and will be challenged. Any fuzziness in her account is an opportunity for the defense attorney to attack her credibility. In the courtroom, the victim can become the accused.

Some call this process a "second victimization." Others call it a "legal rape" of the victim. Some of this is inevitable. The authorities must first establish that a crime took place. Then at trial, the accused has the right to confront the accuser face to face, to question her, and to challenge her testimony. On top of this, remnants of the traditional/patriarchal view of rape remain. If the victim was raped by a stranger who grabbed her as she was walking on the street or who broke into her home, judges and jurors have no trouble seeing her as a victim. If the woman was on a date with the man she is accusing of rape, however, or if she knows him, or if he was her boyfriend, some jurors wonder whether the woman changed her mind just before consensual sex and the aroused man just continued with what they both had previously intended. In the traditional/patriarchal view, the woman does not have the right to change her mind.

When the Legal System Fails   Although the U.S. legal system is flawed, it does reduce rape (and murder). Compare this flawed legal system with the account in the following *Global Glimpse*, a depressing situation where the legal system is grossly ineffective.

A Global Glimpse

When Gangs Take Control

What would society be like if gangs ruled?

Look no further than El Salvador, a small country of 6 million in Central America. La Mara Salvatrucha, better known as MS-13, rules segments of El Salvador's towns and cities—and life is bitter for their residents.

Basically, the gang does what it wants. For them, forcing protection money from shopkeepers is just one of minor infractions. Their major infraction, also common, is raping and killing—all without penalty.

La Mara Salvatrucha started out as a group of teenaged stoners, Los Angeles immigrants from El Salvador who liked to get high. A few of them worshipped Satan and mutilated animals as sacrifice to their god. This—and such things as drinking their own blood at the initiation of new members—gave them an aura of mystery. As MS-13 grew, claiming and defending turf from rival gangs, the gang found that the more violent they were, the more respect—and fear—they received.

U.S. authorities grew eager to deport members of MS-13, and they did so whenever they could.

Deported to El Salvador, the gang members brought their violent ways with them. Banding together as fellow deportees with similar experiences in what to them was an unfamiliar country, they recruited young, poor El Salvadoran boys who were attracted to

their lifestyle—the money, sex, and power that membership offered. MS-13 then spread to other countries, especially to neighboring Honduras and Guatemala.

MS-13's violence grew even more extreme—torturing rival gang members, chopping off body parts with machetes, and decapitating them. Their motto became "mata, viola, controla," which translates as "kill, rape, control."

In areas where MS-13 is dominant, citizens live in fear. No one dares report them, even when they rape their daughters. They know the reprisal—killing the men in the family and gang raping the women.

Based on Harris et al. 2016; Miller 2017; O'Toole 2018.

For Your Consideration

→ What do you think Central American authorities can do to solve their gang problem? Keep in mind that most people in El Salvador, Guatemala, and Honduras live in poverty.

→ When the United States deports MS-13 gang members, it adds to the gang problem in the country that receives those deported. Because of this, do you think the United States has an obligation to help these countries solve their gang problems? Why or why not?

■ Research Findings: Murder

Americans are fascinated with murder. Every night, Americans watch reenactments of bashings, beatings, bombings, drownings, poisonings, shootings, slashings, stabbings, stompings, strangulations, and other mayhem on television. Beyond this entertainment are the real-life killings and the real-life killers. Like any murder mystery, let's look at the who, what, when, where, and why of murder.

The Social Patterns of Murder

5.7   Analyze the social patterns of murder.

The good news came so unexpectedly that it left the experts shaking their heads. After the murder rate peaked in 1991 at 9.8 killings per 100,000 Americans, it plunged to 4.4 in 2014, an incredible drop of 55 percent. Then came the bad news. Just as unexpectedly, this welcome decrease in murder was followed by a jump to 5.3 in 2016, an increase of 20 percent in just two years (*Crime in the United States* 2016:Table 1). Since then, this rate has fallen (Asher 2018; FBI 2018).

Why was there this little spike in murder? Just as with the huge drop, criminologists can come up with 20 possible reasons for it, but to be frank, no one really knows. However, our murders do show some major social patterns. Let's tease them out and see where they lead.

The "Who" of Murder

Although the fear of murder centers mostly on strangers, most murders are committed by someone the victim knew—and often knew well. Look at Table 5.1, which shows victims' relationships to their killers. As you can see, strangers account for only 19 percent of U.S. killings. About four of five murder victims are killed by members of their family or by their lovers, friends, neighbors, or other acquaintances.

Table 5.1 Murder Victims: What Is Their Relationship to the Killer?

Family	25%	Other People They Knew 56%		People They Did Not Know 19%	
Wife	7.3%	Acquaintances	39.7%	Strangers	19.2%
Son	3.4%	Girlfriend	6.5%		
Father	2.5%	Friend	5.7%		
Daughter	2.4%	Boyfriend	2.4%		
Mother	2.2%	Neighbor	1.5%		
Husband	1.5%				
Brother	1.3%				
Sister	0.4%				
Other Family	3.9%				

Note: These relationships refer to cases in which the relationship between the killer and victim is known. In 50 percent of killings, this relationship is unknown, either because the crime was not solved or because the police did not report the relationship.
Source: By the author. Based on *Crime in the* United States, Expanded Homicide Data, 2016:Table 10, U.S. Department of Justice.

These relationships, which the police can trace, are one of the main reasons that, as Figure 5.7 shows, murder is the most likely violent crime to be solved.

The social class, sex, age, and race–ethnicity of killers are similar to those of rapists. Those in poverty are the most likely to kill. So are younger people. Consider this astounding fact: Only 9 to 10 percent of the U.S. population consists of young men ages 17 to 29. Yet of all murders in the United States where the killer is known, *44 percent* come from this group (*Crime in the United States,* Expanded Homicide Data, 2017:Table 3; *Statistical Abstract* 2018:Table 6).

Figure 5.8 illustrates how much more likely men are to kill than women. Men kill about 89 percent of everyone who is murdered in the United States. Although women make up 51 percent of the U.S. population, they commit only about 11 percent of the murders. As you saw in Table 5.1, husbands are five times more likely to kill their wives than the reverse. You also saw that boyfriends are three times as likely to kill their girlfriends as girlfriends are to kill their boyfriends.

Similar startling differences appear in comparing the murders of African Americans and whites. Although African Americans make up only about 13 percent of the U.S. population, in 54 percent of the cases where the race–ethnicity of the killer is known, the murderer is an African American (*Crime in the United States* 2017:Table 3).

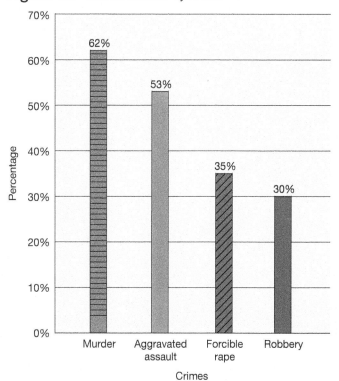

Figure 5.7 Crimes Cleared by Arrest

Source: By the author. Based on *Crime in the United States* 2016:Table 17.

Figure 5.8 Killers and Their Victims

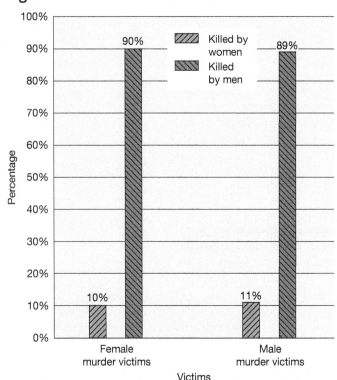

Source: By the author. Based on *Crime in the United States* 2015:Table 6, U.S. Department of Justice.

From Table 5.2, you can see that murder is overwhelmingly *intraracial*—80 percent of white victims are killed by whites, and 88 percent of blacks are killed by blacks.

The "What" of Murder

Although people use a variety of weapons to commit murder, year after year the number one weapon is the gun. The breakdown of murder by weapon is shown in Figure 5.9. Guns may be the favorite choice for two obvious reasons: They are highly effective, and they are readily available in the United States. More subtle reasons may be that men identify guns as masculine, and as you saw in Figure 5.8, men are far more likely to be the killers. Significant cultural stereotypes reinforce this image. For example, our culture romanticizes the use of guns among cowboys, hunters, and villains. To settle a quarrel, then, men are much more likely to reach for a gun than, say, a kitchen knife or a bottle of poison.

Table 5.2 Race–Ethnicity of Killers and Their Victims

		Killers	
		White	**Black**
Victims	White	80%	16%
	Black	9%	88%

Note: The source subsumes Latinos into White and Black. The percentage is less than 100 because of the killers whose race-ethnicity is not known.

Source: By the author. Based on *Crime in the United States* 2015:Table 6, U.S. Department of Justice.

Figure 5.9 Americans' Choice of Murder Weapons

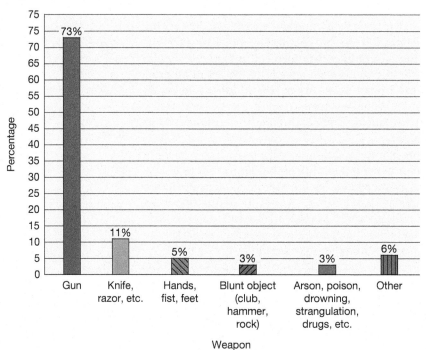

Source: By the author. Based on *Crime in the United States*, Expanded Homicide Data, 2016:Table 4.

The "When" of Murder

Like rape, more murder occurs during the summer months, during weekends, and at night, a timing that reflects social life. Because people are more likely to get out of the house and socialize during warm weather, murder is higher during the summer months and lower during the winter months. Murders are less frequent during weekdays when people are working and meeting personal and family responsibilities and higher on weekends when people are more likely to be socializing in public, drinking, and using drugs, with the peak of violence occurring on Saturday night.

The "Where" of Murder

From the following Social Map, can you see how geography plays a role in murder? Look at the general pattern of the northern states being safer than the southern states. Since we've had records, now for more than a century, the South's murder rate has been higher than that of the rest of the country. Because the South's higher murder rate persists year after year, some researchers conclude that there is a *southern subculture of violence.* In this subculture, southerners learn more violent ways to resolve disagreements. More violent themes also run through southern music, literature, and jokes. Apparently, southerners are more likely to own guns and to use them during quarrels. Sociologists find these explanations suggestive, but not satisfactory (Doerner 1978; Pridemore and Freilich 2006; Grosjean 2014). We need more research to establish adequate explanations.

Besides regional differences, this Social Map shows how the murder rate varies from state to state. Here is the extreme: People in Louisiana are 11 times more likely to be murdered than people in New Hampshire. In a class by itself is Washington, D.C, where the murder rate is one and a half times greater than that of Louisiana, 18 times that of New Hampshire.

Figure 5.10 The "Where" of Murder: The Murder Rate by State

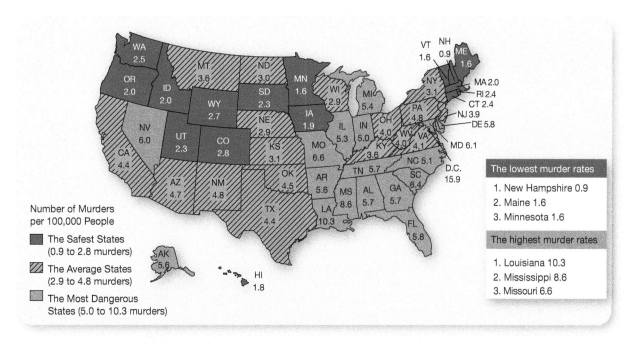

Source: By the author. Based on *Statistical Abstract of the United States* 2017:Table 334.

Many people think the chances of getting murdered are greater in the city than in the country—and they are right. Our largest cities have the highest murder rate. The rate is slightly less in smaller cities, and the suburbs and rural areas are the safest (*Crime in the United States* 2016:Table 11). From Table 5.3, you can see how uneven the murder rate is among U.S. cities.

Table 5.3 Murder: The Ten Safest and Most Dangerous U.S. Cities

The Safest			The Most Dangerous		
Rank	City	Murders per 100,000 People	Rank	City	Murders per 100,000 People
1	Chandler, AZ	0.4	1	St. Louis, MO	50
2	Henderson, NV	1.1	2	New Orleans, LA	39
3	Plano, TX	1.4	3	Baltimore, MD	34
4	San Diego, CA	2.3	4	Newark, NJ	33
5	Lincoln, NE	2.6	5	Buffalo, NY	23
6	Chula Vista, CA	2.7	6	Pittsburgh, PA	22
7	Mesa, AZ	2.8	7	Atlanta, GA	21
8	Aurora, CO	3.1	8	Memphis, TN	21
9	El Paso, TX	3.1	9	Cincinnati, OH	20
10	San Jose, CA	3.2	10	Oakland, CA	20

Source: By the author. Based on *Statistical Abstract of the United States* 2017:Table 335.

The "Why" of Murder

Now that we have looked at the "who," "what," "when," and "where" of murder, let's examine the "why." This will help make more visible how the social patterns of murder reflect our society.

Explaining the Social Patterns   Murder has several clear patterns. As we examine them, I shall intersperse occasional sociological explanations.

Acquaintanceship   As you saw, most murder victims are killed by someone they knew. With most murders being crimes of passion spurred by heated arguments, many analysts have pointed out that we are much more likely to argue with people we know than with strangers. It is with people we know that we share our money, property, and emotions—which fuel the kinds of quarrels that sometimes lead to violent death.

Social Class: Poverty   Why are poor people more likely to commit murder? To explain their higher murder rate, *functionalists* use both strain theory and control theory. Using strain theory, they emphasize that people's stress increases when they are blocked from achieving their goals, and that people with greater stress are more likely to strike out at others. Using control theory, functionalists point out that the poor have weaker controls to inhibit their desires to strike out at others. For example, the poor have "less to lose" if they go to jail—they are less likely than people from higher social classes to own their own homes, and their jobs pay relatively little. In addition, a jail sentence does not carry the same stigma as it does among the higher social classes. *Conflict theorists* add that because most murder victims are also poor, people in poverty are striking out at one another instead of at their oppressors.

To these explanations, *symbolic interactionists* add that the social classes have different ways of resolving disputes. Middle-class people are likely to call the police or talk to a lawyer. Poor people, in contrast, can't afford lawyers, and many don't trust the police. They admire someone who will personally stand up to an adversary. Direct confrontations over passionate issues lead to heated words, physical assault, and sometimes death.

Sex: Males and Dominance   Why are men so much more likely than women to kill? One reason is that dominance is considered an essential element of masculinity. Among working-class boys and men—and not limited to them—is the view that a "real man" is tough. Their standing in the group may depend on being known as "the kind of guy who can't be pushed around." Not fighting back when insulted is to be a coward, to show a lack of masculinity (Rios 2011, 2017).

Symbolic interactionists stress that while men learn to associate masculinity with acting tough and, when necessary, being violent, women tend to learn less violent ways of handling problems. As a result, *in every society around the world*, men kill at a rate several times that of women (Chernoff and Simon 2000; UNODOC 2013:Table 2.2.10). (Biological and evolutionary theorists point to this worldwide pattern of killing as evidence of genetic inheritance. We will continue with a sociological focus on environmental theories.)

Racial–Ethnic Differences Why do African Americans kill at a higher rate than other racial–ethnic groups? Let's start with symbolic interactionism. It is important to note that almost all murder by African Americans occurs among the very poor. In this subculture, masculinity is highly prized—and the form of masculinity dominant among the poor centers on the willingness to defend oneself aggressively. Functionalists would add that African Americans are socialized to strive for the cultural goal of material success, but discrimination and life situations block many of them from reaching that goal. This increases their strain, leading to a higher rate of violence, most of which is directed against people nearby.

How about the interracial pattern of murder that we reviewed, often called black-on-black murder? This is related to segregated living and housing patterns. Then what about violence that crosses racial lines? Functionalists stress our society's pattern of money and race–ethnicity. If a robbery (or mugging or burglary) results in a murder across racial lines, it is most likely to involve a poor African American robbing a white, not a poor white robbing an African American. If African Americans possessed more wealth than whites, we would expect this pattern to be reversed.

Mass Murder and Serial Murder

5.8   Discuss the findings on mass murder and serial murder.

Let's look at two patterns of murder that have gripped the public's attention: mass murder and serial murder.

Mass Murder

Mass murder, a national concern, has been defined by the U.S. Congress as the killing of three or more people in a single event (*Congressional Record* 2013). One of the most notorious mass murderers is Richard Speck, who slaughtered eight nursing students in Chicago one night in 1966. In 1981, Priscilla Ford deliberately drove her car into a crowd at a Thanksgiving Day parade in Reno, Nevada, killing six. James Huberty shot 21 people at a McDonald's in 1984. In 1991, Julio Gonzalez, unhappy that his girlfriend was breaking up with him, killed 87 people by torching the Happy Land Social Club in the Bronx. In 2007, Seung-Hui Cho shot to death 32 students and faculty members at Virginia Tech. In 2016, Omar Mateen shot to death 49 people at Pulse, a gay nightclub in Orlando, Florida. In 2018, Nikolas Cruz killed 17 students at a high school in Parkland, Florida, and that same year Stephen Paddock, shooting from the 32nd floor of a Las Vegas hotel, killed 59 people at a music festival.

The largest mass murder by a single individual in the United States occurred in 1995, when Timothy McVeigh killed 168 people by blowing up a federal building in Oklahoma City, Oklahoma. McVeigh's stunning number of victims was overshadowed on September 11, 2001, of course, when about 3,000 people lost their lives. This was a different form of mass murder, involving many people who made plans for years, with many people carrying them out. September 11 is better thought of as an act of war.

Amy Bishop appearing in court after her arrest. Dr. Bishop's murders are the topic of this chapter's opening vignette.

Serial Murder

Killing people in three or more separate events is called **serial murder**. The murders may occur over several days, weeks, or even years. The elapsed time between murders distinguishes serial killers from mass murderers. Serial killers are generally less spontaneous and do more planning than mass murderers. But not always, with Timothy McVeigh the prime example.

Some serial killers are motivated by lust and are aroused sexually by killing. The FBI refers to this type of killing as "lust murder." These serial killers like to take souvenirs ("trophies") from their victims. The victims' jewelry, underwear, even body parts remind them of the pleasure the killing gave them (Chi and Lee 2014). One of the most bizarre serial killers was Jeffrey Dahmer of Milwaukee, Wisconsin. Dahmer had sex with the dead bodies of the young men he killed, and he fried and ate parts of his victims. In 2009, Anthony Sowell was found to be living with decaying corpses in his home in Cleveland, Ohio. He was charged with killing 11 women. The serial killer in recent history who has the most victims is Harold Shipman, a quiet, unassuming physician in Manchester, England. From 1977 to 2000, he killed 275 elderly women patients, giving them lethal injections while making house calls.

Almost all serial killers are men, but there are exceptions. Here are three. In the 1980s, Genene Jones, a nurse, killed small children in her care in a hospital and a pediatrics clinic in Kerrville, Texas. In 1988, Dorothea Montalvo Puente killed seven senior citizens so she could keep cashing their Social Security checks. In 2002, Aileen Wuornos was executed for killing five men after she had sex with them.

In the following *Spotlight on Research*, I discuss my research on a teenager who became a serial killer.

Spotlight on Social Research

Doing Research on a Serial Killer

The TV reports were shocking: Decaying bodies, one after another, were being dug up from a boat storage shed in Houston, Texas. All the corpses seemed to be teenagers.

I wanted to find out more. Summer classes were ending in just a few days, and as soon as I taught my last class, I took off for a straight-through drive from Illinois.

It turned out that Dean Corll, age 33, of Houston, Texas, had raped, tortured, and killed 27 teenage boys. Two teenagers helped him, Elmer Wayne Henley, 14, and David Brooks, 15. Neither boy had a father living at home, and Corll had become a father substitute who molded the boys into killers. Henley and Brooks helped Corll pick up young hitchhikers. They even brought him their own neighbors and high school classmates to torture, rape, and kill.

The police had no idea of what was happening until Henley shot Corll to death.

Elmer Wayne Henley in Corpus Christi, Texas, who was sentenced to six life sentences for his involvement in the kidnapping, torture, rape, and murder of teenaged boys.

When I got to Houston, I went to the "morgue," the office where newspapers store their back issues. There I read the reports, from the first revelation of the killings to their current coverage. The accounts included the addresses of the local victims. On a city map, I marked their home, as well as the homes of the killers. As I drove around the neighborhoods, map in hand, at one of the addresses I saw a man painting his porch. I stopped my car, went over and introduced myself. I asked him if he were the father of a boy who had been killed. Although reluctant to talk about his son's death, he did so. His son had left the house one Saturday to go for a haircut. He never made it home. He told me bitterly that the police had refused to investigate. They insisted his son was a runaway.

Elmer Wayne Henley lived just down the street.

As I drove by Henley's home, I decided to stop and try to get an interview. As I was knocking on the door, Henley's mother and grandmother came around the side of the house, carrying bags of groceries. I told them who I was and what I wanted. Henley's mother said that her attorney had ordered her not to talk to anyone. I explained that I had driven all the way from Illinois to talk to her, and I promised that I would keep whatever she said private until after her son's trial. She agreed to be interviewed, and I went inside her home. While I was talking to her and her mother, three of Henley's friends came over. I was also able to interview them.

To prevent contamination—what one person says in an interview influencing others—I interviewed each person separately. I recorded the interviews in Henley's bedroom, with the door closed. My interviews revealed what since has become common knowledge about serial killers: They lead double lives that catch their friends and family unaware. Henley's mother swore to me that her son was a good boy, that he couldn't possibly be guilty. His high school friends stressed that Elmer couldn't be involved in homosexual rape and murder because he was interested only in girls. For proof of Elmer's innocence, his friends pointed to a pair of girls' panties that were hanging in his bedroom.

Henley and Brooks, though, had delivered hitchhikers and acquaintances to Corll, and the three of them had raped, tortured, killed, and buried the boys. Henley and Brooks were sentenced to life terms in Texas prisons, where they remain today.

For Your Consideration

→ What punishment do you think is appropriate for serial killers? Why?

Have Mass and Serial Murders Become More Common?

Many assume that mass and serial murders are more common now than they used to be, but we can't draw this conclusion. In the past, police departments had little communication with one another, and when killings occurred in different jurisdictions, the killings were seldom linked. Today's computer programs and more efficient investigative techniques make it easier for the police to recognize that a serial killer is operating in an area.

And anyone who thinks serial killing began recently misses the mark rather widely. If we look into history, we can find numerous examples. One of the most infamous is Gilles De Rais, a man of nobility, who in the 1400s in France tortured, raped, and killed several hundred children. In the 1800s, Fritz Haarmann raped and killed 27 boys and men. He also cut up their bodies and sold the meat to unsuspecting shoppers. Then, of course, there is the serial killer from the 1800s with whom everyone is familiar, Jack the Ripper.

Social Policy

5.9   Identify social policies that can reduce or prevent violence.

While I could suggest many policies for dealing with offenders and their victims, the primary concern is the prevention of violence. Let's look at the potential.

Global Concerns: Preventing Violence

Here are four social policies that can reduce or prevent violence:

Equality   First, researchers have documented that rape is higher in societies in which women are devalued (Lalumiere et al. 2005). The implications for social policy are profound. We can reduce rape by increasing the social value of women. To do this, we need programs in churches and schools and portrayals on television and movies that stress equality.

The Cost of Rape   Second, researchers have also documented that rape is lower when the perceived cost of raping is high (Lalumiere et al. 2005). Put more simply, if men think they will be punished, they are less likely to rape. This finding also has profound implications for social policy: To reduce rape, we need social policies that increase the likelihood that rapists will be punished. Of the many possibilities, here is just one. Some men are serial rapists, who commit a large number of rapes. Some rape several times a month until they are caught—which can take years. Long sentences for repeat offenders—with little chance of parole—will prevent many women from being raped. For a related social policy, read the following *Issues in Social Problems*.

Issues in Social Problems

Rape Kits: A Shameful Neglect

When a woman reports a rape, the police gather evidence from her body. Part of that evidence consists of swabs taken from wherever the rapist has penetrated her, as well as any residue that is on her body and clothing. This evidence is placed in a rape kit and sent to a state laboratory for analysis. DNA evidence from the crime scene is compared with a national DNA database. If there is a "hit," a match with DNA records, the police know they are dealing with a serial rapist.

But while rape kits go untested, rapists continue to ravage new victims.

Angela was just 15 years old. As she was walking home on a pleasant June day, a man stopped his pickup, pointed a pistol at her, and forced her into his vehicle. He drove to Denver's South Platte River where he brutally raped her. When he was finished, he ordered her out, and then shot her in the face. He threw her into the river, like a bag of garbage.

Angela crawled to shore and somehow managed to walk a half mile for help.

In the hospital, the police swabbed Angela's body to collect evidence of the rape. They placed the evidence in a rape kit. Then they placed the rape kit on a shelf in the Denver police department's evidence room.

Seventeen years later, the rape kit was tested. There was a "hit," a match with a suspect (Harrison 2015).

Why have rape kits—a staggering total, perhaps several hundred thousand—collected dust for years, some even for decades? Testing is expensive, about $1,000 a kit, and cities and states are short on money.

Facing outrage from advocacy groups, the federal government appropriated $80 million to test the backlog (Hernandez

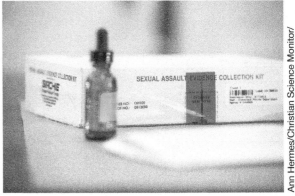

Ann Hermes/Christian Science Monitor/Getty Images

2015). In Houston, 9,500 rape kits were tested, some 35 years old. The tests brought 1,000 hits, but in Texas, rapes that occurred more than ten years ago cannot be prosecuted (Oberg and Seibert 2015). Testing in Detroit got more than 800 hits with serial rapists, men who had raped other women, even children (Saul 2017).

When women are told of a hit, some are relieved. The man who haunted their dreams is behind bars. But not all are pleased. Some get upset, saying, "Why would you do this to me? I put that away a long time ago, and I've gotten on with my life." This response upsets officials, who are trying to do their best, making them hesitant to contact women (Contrera 2018).

For Your Consideration

→ Why do you think the states and cities neglected the testing of rape kits? Could money have been the only reason?

→ Why did it take decades for the federal government to offer grants to states and cities to test rape kits?

The Climate of Violence

Third, policy makers can support research to determine how our culture creates a climate of violence. Remember the sociological question that was posed at the beginning of this chapter: What in a society increases or decreases the likelihood of violence? As indicated in the first two policies I suggested, we do have some answers to this question. But we need more research to determine what aspects of our culture produce high rates of violence and how they do so. I suggest that researchers:

1. Examine cultures with low violence to determine factors that minimize violence
2. Find ways to teach young men to channel their aggression constructively
3. Find ways to increase equality and respect among men and women
4. To the degree that rape and murder are based on economic inequality and blocked goals to opportunities, develop programs that open opportunities for the disadvantaged

Henslin, James M.

Visitors from other countries, such as this European woman visiting a "gun shop," are often shocked at how many Americans own guns and how easily guns can be purchased.

Keeping the Issue Alive The next suggestion follows the feminist/conflict view. If we are going to reduce rape further, we need to keep this issue before the public. Only by publicizing the issue did rape change from a personal to a social problem. We must keep publicizing rape as a pressing and avoidable social problem so our politicians and other officials will spend the resources needed to develop programs to reduce rape. This applies also to murder.

Gun Control To close this section, in the following *Thinking Critically about Social Problems,* let's look at gun control, a social policy that divides the nation.

Thinking Critically about Social Problems

Enough Is Enough: The Social Movement to Limit Gun Ownership

For the past 50 years or so, voices have been raised to protest the availability and use of guns in the United States. The voices, aroused after some shooting that makes headlines, always fade quietly into the background. With the shooting deaths of 17 students at Marjory Stoneman Douglas High School in Parkland, Florida, where the school's resource officer, an armed sheriff's deputy, stood outside the school and cowardly let the killings continue, the voices of protest grew louder than ever, reaching a national crescendo. For the first time, the voices were joined by masses of youth, even by survivors of the Parkland shooting. More protesters gathered in

Washington, D.C., than those who gathered for the inauguration of President Trump.

The results of this sudden massive protest are unknown as I write this. Voices once again subdued? Or voices, louder than ever and continuing to clamor for change, effective this time? Whatever the outcome, like abortion, gun control has two ardent opposing sides. Each views the other as unreasonable and unrealistic, extremes that illustrate why it is difficult to establish social policy for the prevention of violence. In the following summary of the opposing positions, I try to be fair to both sides of this issue.

Pro-Gun Control: Ban or Limit Guns

The basic position of proponents of gun control is that gun owner-ship is an outdated custom that has no relevance to modern so-ciety. They argue that limiting gun ownership through a system of strict licensing will reduce senseless killings, from school shootings to murders on the streets of Chicago and Detroit. The only common theme in this social movement is "fewer guns." At the extreme are those who take the position that guns should be banned, that guns should no longer exist except for emergency use by the police and military. There also are the moderates, those who say that we need to limit gun ownership, that we should register all guns and license all gun owners.

Anti-Gun Control: "Don't Mess with the Constitution"

Opponents of gun control argue that gun ownership is like vot-ing and free speech, a right guaranteed by the U.S. Constitution. They argue that guns are not the problem. The problem is the misuse of guns by criminals and crazies. Many take the position that Americans need more guns, not fewer. They say that if all law-abiding citizens had guns and were trained in their use, few rapists and killers would break into homes—and of those who did, not many would survive to do it again. They point out that prolifera-tion of guns does not increase murders, that Americans have more guns now than ever before, and the murder rate has dropped.

The Future of the Problem

5.10 Discuss the likely future of violence.

Let's use our theoretical perspectives to glimpse the future of the social problem of vio-lence. *Conflict theory* indicates that tensions will always exist between groups that are competing for scarce resources. Short of revolution (which has proven no panacea for any society), the wealthy will retain control, and discrimination will continue. The poor, espe-cially minorities—who suffer the double-edged sword of poverty and discrimination—will continue to show up disproportionately in crime statistics. The *functionalist* perspec-tive stresses that violence is functional enough to continue: People do get revenge and feel other satisfactions from killing their enemies. Rape does make some men feel domi-nant and powerful. The *symbolic interactionist* perspective focuses on the association of masculinity and violence. As long as these two potent symbols are intertwined, we can expect violence to continue as men try to live up to valued cultural images.

It is essential to use the *sociological* perspective to understand both the present and future of violence. Our high rate of rape and murder *cannot* be laid at the feet of an unusu-ally large number of sociopaths. There are sociopaths, to be sure, but our social patterns of rape and murder are primarily products of our history and our current social struc-ture. Without structural change that reduces social inequality, high rates of violence will remain. Understanding the *social* basis of violence can be the key to bringing change that decreases violence.

Summary and Review

1. Sociologists analyze how *violence* is rooted in society. How a society is organized—its social structure—increases or decreases its amount of violence.
2. Each society has a rate of violence that, without major social change, is fairly constant over time. Sociologists call this a society's *normal violence.*
3. Biologists, anthropologists, and psychologists have theories to account for violence. The sociological response is that whatever predispositions humans might have toward violence are encouraged or inhib-ited by the society in which they live.
4. Symbolic interactionists use two theories to explain violence. The first, *differential association*, stresses that

violence is learned in association with other people. The second, *subcultural theory*, emphasizes that some groups are more approving of violence than others. People who grow up or associate with groups that approve of violence are more likely to learn violence.
5. Functionalists stress that some people become discon-nected from cultural norms. Durkheim used the term *anomie* to describe this uprooting and estrangement. Anomic individuals are more likely to rape and to kill. Merton's *strain theory* suggests that violence is an alternative path that some people choose when they find the *cultural means* (such as jobs and career train-ing) to reach *cultural goals* (such as financial success)

blocked. *Control (or containment) theory* suggests that the inner and outer controls of rapists and murderers are weaker than their pushes and pulls to commit these acts.

6. Conflict theorists emphasize that the groups that form a society compete for scarce resources. The major division is between those who own the means of production and those who do not. Those at the mercy of the owners have few resources, and they lash out violently—misdirecting their violence onto one another.

7. Feminists challenged the traditional view of rape as a personal problem, a crime of passion. Under their prodding, rape became a social problem; that is, it came to be considered a crime of dominance and violence rooted in the structure of relationships between men and women.

8. Rape and murder are not random acts. They reflect society's larger patterns: social class, gender, age, race–ethnicity, timing, location, and acquaintanceship.

9. To prevent violence requires restructuring those aspects of society that foster violence. To determine a rational basis for social policy on these emotionally charged issues, we need research on the social causes of violence.

10. We can reduce rape through social policies that increase equality, the value of females, and the perceived costs of raping. To keep rape from fading from the public's mind as a social problem and to find workable solutions, we must keep this issue alive.

Thinking Critically about Chapter 5

1. What is the *sociological question* of violence? What materials in this chapter indicate that this is the right question to ask?

2. Which four of the profiles of rapists do you think are the most common? Explain why you think so.

3. As a social policy to reduce rape, the author suggests that we promote programs that increase the social value of females. What programs do you think would work?

Key Terms

anomie, 120
control theory, 120
criminal sexual assault, 124
cultural goal, 120
cultural means, 120
differential association, 117
forcible rape, 122
mass murder, 135
modeling, 117

normal violence, 120
operant conditioning, 117
patriarchy, 123
rate of violence, 113
serial murder, 136
statutory rape, 122
strain theory, 120
subcultural theory, 118
violence, 112

Chapter 6
Crime and Criminal Justice

Avid_creative/E+/Getty Images

Learning Objectives

After reading this chapter, you should be able to:

6.1 Explain what crime is, why crime is relative, and how something becomes a crime.

6.2 Explain why both crime and the criminal justice system are social problems and why crime is universal.

6.3 Explain how symbols (labels) affected the lives of the Saints and the Roughnecks, the role of symbols in police discretion, and why this makes us cautious about crime statistics.

6.4 Explain how core social values produce crime and how crime is related to the "opportunity structure."

6.5 Explain how power and social class are related to social inequality in the legal system.

6.6 Explain how juvenile delinquency developed, the extent of juvenile crime, the delinquent career, neutralization techniques, and how education is related to delinquency.

6.7 Be familiar with criminogenic cultures, lethal white-collar crime, embezzlement, theft, and the relationship of gender and social class to white-collar crime.

6.8 Know what professional crime is and how professional criminals maintain their secrecy and values.

6.9 Know what organized crime is and reasons for the Mafia's past success and current weakness.

6.10 Explain why plea bargaining, bias, recidivism, the death penalty, and the prison experience are part of the criminal justice system as a social problem.

6.11 Discuss retribution, deterrence, rehabilitation, and incapacitation as goals of social policy.

6.12 Explain the likely future of crime and criminal justice.

I was recently released from solitary confinement after being held therein for 37 months (months!). A silent system was imposed upon me and to even whisper to the man in the next cell resulted in being beaten by guards, sprayed with chemical mace, blackjacked, stomped and thrown into a strip-cell naked to sleep on a concrete floor without bedding, covering, wash basin or even toilet. The floor served as toilet and bed, and even there the silent system was enforced.... I have filed every writ possible against the administrative acts of brutality. The courts have all denied the petitions. Because of my refusal to let the thing die down...I am the most hated prisoner in (this) penitentiary, and called a "hard-core incorrigible."

> **I now think of killing—killing those who have beaten me and treated me as if I were a dog.**

Maybe I am an incorrigible.... I know that thieves must be punished and I don't justify stealing, even though I am a thief myself. But now I don't think I will be a thief when I am released. No, I'm not that rehabilitated. It's just that I no longer think of becoming wealthy by stealing. I now think of killing—killing those who have beaten me and treated me as if I were a dog. I hope and pray for the sake of my own soul and future life of freedom that I am able to overcome the bitterness and hatred which eats daily at my soul.

—A letter from a prisoner in a state prison, as quoted in Zimbardo 1972

The Problem in Sociological Perspective

6.1   Explain what crime is, why crime is relative, and how something becomes a crime.

Crime is a fascinating area of human behavior. You may feel almost spellbound as you learn about a crime that is particularly gruesome, or even about a crime that was committed in some unusual way. It is my hope that this chapter provides you an excellent context for understanding crime.

The first step to better understand crime is to ask this simple question: What is crime? To answer this question takes us into the essential nature of crime and then quickly into politics.

The Essential Nature of Crime: The Law

Let's start by looking at what people call "dumb laws."

> In Texas, you'll break the law if you sell your eye.
>
> In California, animals cannot have sex within 1,500 feet of a church.
>
> In Florida, it is illegal to sell alcohol before 1 p.m. on Sunday.
>
> In Arkansas, schoolteachers who cut their hair short cannot get a raise.
>
> The Florida constitution guarantees that pregnant pigs cannot be put in cages.
>
> In New York, women can go topless in public as long as they do not profit from the behavior.

More than likely, your state has "dumb laws," and I'm sure that it has laws that make something legal at one time during the day or night and illegal at another time. For example, to sell whiskey, wine, or beer one minute before "closing hour" is legal; to sell them one minute later is a crime.

It might sound strange, but these laws illustrate *the essential nature of crime.* No activity is criminal in and of itself. **Crime** *is the violation of law.* If there is no law, there is no crime. Although we may agree that stealing, kidnapping, and rape are immoral or harmful, only the law can define them as crimes.

The Relativity of Crime

The principle that law defines crime has many implications. One is that *crime is culturally relative;* that is, because laws differ from one society to another, so does crime. Travelers are sometimes shocked when they find that some behavior they take for granted at home is a crime abroad—or that what is illegal at home is taken for granted elsewhere. For example, although eating pork and drinking alcohol are illegal in some Muslim societies, a man there may take several wives as long as he can support them.

The relativity of crime is so great that even within the same society, behavior that is criminal at one time can later be encouraged as a virtue. In China, for example, selling things to make a profit used to be such a serious crime that it was punishable by death. To teach everyone a lesson, "profiteers" were hung in the public square. When Chinese officials adopted capitalism in the 1990s, however, they decided that letting people make profits would help their economy. The change has been so thorough that now "profiteers," Chinese capitalists, have become role models and can join the Communist party.

The relativity of crime is so extreme that the same act can be a crime at one point in time and later be encouraged as a contribution to humanity. One hundred years ago, birth control information and devices could not be sent in the U.S. mail because they were "obscene, lewd, and lascivious." Margaret Sanger, a pioneering feminist, was arrested for breaking this law. Today, most people consider teaching birth control to be a service to an overpopulated world that is running low on natural resources.

Making Something Criminal: A Political Process

Abortion was the social problem featured in Chapter 1. As we reviewed there, before 1973, abortion was a crime, and anyone who performed it was put in prison. After the U.S. Supreme Court made its 1973 *Roe v. Wade* decision, abortion was no longer a crime. If the antiabortion groups succeed in amending the Constitution or if the Supreme Court reverses its 1973 ruling, abortion will again become a crime. As you can see from this example, determining which behavior shall be criminal is a *political process*. The definition of some act as illegal is the outcome of a struggle among groups that have different interests and viewpoints. Perhaps the most striking current example is the legalization of marijuana in some states.

In Sum   These three principles are essential to understand crime: Law defines crime, which makes crime relative, and crime is the outcome of a political process. These principles, in turn, take us to the significance of **power**, being able to get what you want despite resistance. To understand crime, then, we need to be asking questions such as these: What groups in a society have the power to get their views written into law? How do they get authorities to pass laws? Why do some societies punish a behavior while others ignore—or even encourage—the same behavior? Perhaps these questions can be summarized into one: Whose interests do laws protect?

The Scope of the Problem

6.2   **Explain why both crime and the criminal justice system are social problems and why crime is universal.**

In considering crime as a social problem, we must also analyze the **criminal justice system**—those agencies that respond to crime: the police, courts, jails, and prisons. On the one hand, crime is a social problem when large numbers of people are upset about it, when they feel that crime threatens their safety, peace, or quality of life. On the other hand, the criminal justice system is a social problem if people are upset about it—perhaps how it fails to prevent crime, fails to rehabilitate offenders, or discriminates against some citizens.

In this chapter, we will discuss both crime and the criminal justice system as a social problem. Let's begin by looking at crime.

Why Is Crime a Social Problem?

As you will recall, to have a social problem we need both objective conditions and subjective concerns. You read in the previous chapter that the **crime rate**—the number of crimes per 100,000 people—has plunged. Today's homicide rate is less than half of what it was in 1991, yet even with this remarkably lower rate, 13,000 Americans are murdered each year. The rape rate, too, has dropped, yet as you also read in the previous chapter between 96,000 and 300,000 Americans are raped a year. Another 1,100,000 are robbed or have their cars stolen, and still another 3 million have their homes broken into (*Statistical Abstract* 2018:Tables 336, 340).

These objective conditions arouse intense subjective concerns. Over and over, people's concerns about their safety are fed by sensationalized cases in the news or by something that happened in their neighborhood. With this heightened awareness of danger, each urban resident knows which areas of the city to avoid. As you saw in Figure 5.1 of the previous chapter, both men and women have fears about their personal safety. Women, though, are more fearful, especially about abduction and rape, and they are more careful about where they go.

Why Is Crime Universal?

Some societies have much lower crime rates than ours, but no society or nation is free of crime—nor can it ever be. As Emile Durkheim, one of the earliest sociologists, pointed out in 1897, the very nature of crime makes it universal. Each society passes laws against behaviors that it considers a threat to its well-being. (Tribal groups don't have written laws. Their rules are part of an oral tradition, with penalties for those who violate them.) Passing a law never eliminates a behavior—it just marks it as illegal. As Durkheim stressed, where there are laws (or rules), there always will be criminals (or rule breakers).

As we consider the social problem of crime, let's first apply our theoretical perspectives to the criminal justice system.

■ Looking at the Problem Theoretically

As we saw in Chapter 5, each theoretical perspective provides different insights into the problem of criminal violence. Let's see how these perspectives apply to crime and the criminal justice system.

Symbolic Interactionism

6.3   **Explain how symbols (labels) affected the lives of the Saints and the Roughnecks, the role of symbols in police discretion, and why this makes us cautious about crime statistics.**

As you know, the focus of symbolic interactionism is symbols (or meanings). Sociologists want to know what meaning people place on things and how that meaning influences their interaction. Let's begin with the Saints and the Roughnecks.

The Saints and the Roughnecks: Social Class and Labeling

For two years, sociologist William Chambliss (1933–2014) observed two groups of adolescent lawbreakers at "Hanibal High School." He labeled one group the "saints" and the other the "roughnecks."

Chambliss describes the saints as "promising young men, children of good, stable, white, upper-middle-class families, active in school affairs, good pre-college students." He adds that the saints were some of the most delinquent boys in the school. They were "constantly occupied with truancy, drinking, wild driving, petty theft, and vandalism." Yet their teachers and families considered the boys "saints headed for success." Not one saint was ever arrested.

The "roughnecks," Chambliss said, were also white boys of the same age who went to the same high school. These boys, too, were delinquent, although Chambliss estimates that they committed somewhat fewer criminal acts than the saints. Their teachers considered these boys "roughnecks headed for serious trouble," and the police often dealt with them.

Why did the community perceive these boys so differently? Chambliss argues that this was due to *social class*. As symbolic interactionists emphasize, social class affects our perception and behavior. The saints came from respectable middle-class families, the roughnecks from less respectable working-class families. These backgrounds led teachers and authorities to expect good behavior from the saints and trouble from the roughnecks. Like the rest of us, the teachers and police saw what they expected to see.

The boys' social class also affected their *visibility*. The saints had cars, and they did their drinking and vandalism out of town. Because the roughnecks didn't own cars, they hung around their own street corners, where their rowdy behavior drew the attention of police. This confirmed the ideas that the community had of them.

Social class also equipped the boys with distinct *styles of interaction*. When police or teachers questioned the saints, the boys were apologetic. They showed respect for authority, so important for winning authorities' favor. Their show of respect elicited positive reactions from teachers and police, allowing the boys to escape problems with school authorities and the law. Chambliss says that the roughnecks were "almost the polar opposite." When questioned, they were hostile. Even when they tried to put on a veneer of respect, the teachers and police saw through it. The teachers came down hard on the roughnecks, and the police were quick to interrogate and arrest them rather than to warn them.

The saints and the roughnecks illustrate the differential association and subcultural theories introduced in Chapter 5. Although both the saints and the roughnecks were immersed in vandalism and theft, they were reared in different subcultures. The saints learned that college was their birthright; the roughnecks did not. The saints wanted good grades; the roughnecks didn't care. The saints learned middle-class demeanor, which showed in their choice of words, tone of voice, and body language; the roughnecks did not. The reactions by authorities to these subcultural or social class "signals" deeply affected the boys' lives.

Chambliss' research illustrates what sociologists call *labeling*, a process that can set people on different paths in life. You can see what different expectations the labels "saint" and "roughneck" carry. They influence people's perceptions and channel behavior in different directions. All but one of the saints went to college. One became a doctor, one a lawyer, one earned a Ph.D., and the others went into management. Two of the roughnecks won athletic scholarships, went to college, and became coaches. One roughneck became a bookie. Two dropped out of high school, were convicted of separate killings, and ended up in prison. No one knows the whereabouts of the other. Although outcomes like these have many "causes," the boys lived up to the labels the community gave them.

"You look like this sketch of someone who's thinking about committing a crime."

David Sipress/The New Yorker Collection/The Cartoon Bank

Bias in the criminal justice system against individuals because of their race or ethnicity can tear up people's lives. Contrary to stereotypes, sociological research indicates that bias also favors minorities. Have you had experiences with the police that indicate bias either for or against you?

Police Discretion The saints and the roughnecks had different styles of interaction, which made a difference to the teachers and the police. Running through their interaction was respect or the lack of respect. How people react to the police is significant in how the police react to them. And what a difference it made in how the police dealt with these boys.

This is a very important point. The police react more positively to those who show respect for them. To apply this—well, you know what the application is. Regardless of your feelings, when stopped by the police, show respect. You might not be as fortunate as the saints, but you set up a much better chance for a good outcome.

Violating the law is so common that as the police go about their work, they can't possibly react to all crimes. Their choosing to react to a crime or not, and how to do so, is called **police discretion**. Many things influence police discretion, from an order from their chief to a crackdown on crime in a certain neighborhood to stereotypes the police hold about who is likely to be a criminal. In many instances, showing respect for the police can be a factor that tips police discretion in a favorable direction.

Caution about Crime Statistics   These examples illustrate why sociologists approach crime statistics with caution. As noted in Chapter 2, the "facts" of a social problem are not objective: Social "facts" are produced within a specific social context for a particular purpose. According to official statistics, working-class boys are much more delinquent than middle-class boys. Yet, as we have just seen, social class influences the reactions of authorities, affecting who shows up in official statistics.

In Sum   Symbols are an essential part of living in society. As we go through everyday life, we use symbols to interpret what happens to us. Among the symbols that affect our perception and behavior are social class, reputation, and demeanor. Such symbols also affect the perception and behavior of teachers and the police, having far-reaching effects on people's lives.

Functionalism

6.4   Explain how core social values produce crime and how crime is related to the "opportunity structure."

Functionalists consider crime to be a natural part of society. They say that crime can even reflect a society's core values. Let's see how this can be.

Crime and Society's Core Values

As sociologists Richard Cloward and Lloyd Ohlin (1960, 2011) pointed out, our society has to fill many positions (dentist, lawyer, teacher, and so on) that require high ability and diligence. To fill them, we must locate and train the most talented people of each generation—whether they are born in wealth or poverty. But there is no way of looking at babies and knowing who the talented and hardworking adults will be. Our society, then, motivates *everyone* to strive for success, provoking an intense competition that allows some of the talented to emerge as victors.

"Regardless of race, sex, or social class, success can be yours" becomes the American mantra. Repeated throughout our schools and media, it motivates the young to compete intensely. By making success a universal goal, our society ensures its survival.

What does "success can be yours" have to do with crime? Almost all of us learn to want success, but the playing field isn't level. As you know so well, some people have many resources to help them become successful, while others have few. Wanting success but being cut off from the approved means to reach it leads to strain. Look at Table 6.1, which is how sociologist Robert Merton summarized this aspect of *strain theory*.

Table 6.1 Strain Theory: How People Match Their Goals to Their Means

Do They Feel the Strain That Leads to Anomie?	Mode of Adaptation	Cultural Goals	Institutionalized Means
No	Conformity	Accept	Accept
Deviant Paths:			
Yes	1. Innovation	Accept	Reject
	2. Ritualism	Reject	Accept
	3. Retreatism	Reject	Reject
	4. Rebellion	Reject/Replace	Reject/Replace

The first classification is those who don't feel the strain that leads to *anomie*. These people, the conformists, have access to approved resources, and they strive for success. The others feel strain because for them there is a gap between society's goals and the approved means to reach them. As you can see from this table, people react to strain in four primary ways:

Innovation: The innovators accept the cultural goals, but they substitute other means of reaching them. An example is someone who pursues wealth through fraud instead of hard work.

Ritualism: The ritualists have given up on achieving success, but they still work in culturally approved ways. An example is a worker who no longer hopes to get ahead but does just enough to avoid getting fired.

Retreatism: The retreatists reject both the societal goal and the means to achieve it. Some retreat into drugs, others into convents.

Rebellion: The rebels are convinced that society is corrupt and reject both societal goals and the means to achieve them. They seek to replace the current social order with a new one.

Innovation is the response that interests us. This is the tie-in of crime and core values that I mentioned. Finding the legitimate means to the cultural goal of success blocked, innovators strive for the goal, but they turn to *illegitimate* means to reach it.

Social Class and Illegitimate Opportunities

Strain theory helps us understand why the poor commit so many burglaries and robberies. Functionalists stress that society has no problem getting the poor to want material success. Television bombards them with seductive messages. The vivid images of upper-middle-class lives suggest that full-fledged Americans should be able to possess the goods and services portrayed in commercials and programs. Education is the primary approved means of reaching success, but its doors open only reluctantly to the poor.

To see what I mean by this, you must understand that the schools are middle class, and in the schools contrasting worlds meet head-on. In school, the children of the poor confront a bewildering world, one of strict rules and "proper" speech. Their grammar and profanity mark them as different from the children of the middle class. In addition, children in poverty usually attend schools that are inferior to those that educate children from higher social classes (Chaudry et al. 2017). These barriers to success create high dropout rates among working-class students, blocking them from many legitimate avenues to financial success.

Often, however, a different door opens to the children of the poor, one that Cloward and Ohlin (1960, 2011) called **illegitimate opportunity structures**. These are opportunities woven into the texture of life in urban slums: burglary, drug dealing, gambling, pimping, prostitution, robbery, and other income-producing crimes or "hustles." The "hustler," or "player," becomes a model for young people—one of the few in the neighborhood whose material success comes close to the mainstream cultural stereotype.

White-collar criminals generally receive light sentences. Bernie Madoff, shown here, who had the longest-running and largest Ponzi scheme in history, is an exception. Sentenced to 150 years in prison, Madoff exchanged his yachts, homes in Florida and France, and stays in expensive hotel suites for a prison cell.

The middle and upper classes are not free of crime, of course. Functionalists point out that *different* illegitimate opportunities attract them, ones that make *different forms* of crime functional. Instead of pimping, burglary, or mugging, members of the middle and upper classes commit white-collar crimes—tax evasion, bribery of public officials, advertising fraud, price fixing, and securities violations. Martha Stewart is a remarkable example. She made over $1 billion the day her company, Martha Stewart Omnimedia, went public on the New York Stock Exchange. Yet, to gain a few thousand dollars, not even chump change for her, Stewart committed insider trading (trading stock on the basis of secret information). She was forced to resign her position as head of the company she founded, and she served a few months in a "country club" prison.

Bernard Madoff made the list of infamous scoundrels when he was convicted for running a global Ponzi scheme. A **Ponzi scheme** consists of paying "investment profits" to clients, not from profits, but from the money that other clients invest. Madoff's $50 billion fraud is the largest in history. He defrauded wealthy, sophisticated investors as well as average

HRC/WENN/Newscom

retired people who were devastated by their losses. He did not receive the slap on the wrist usually given to white-collar offenders. He was sentenced to 150 years in prison. He has a life expectancy of only a few years, so the length of his sentence is largely symbolic. It could just as well have been 1,000 years. Madoff is serving his sentence at New York's Butner prison, which doesn't have bars—but it does have a gym, a library, pool tables, a chapel, a volleyball court, and an Indian sweat lodge (Fishman 2010).

In Sum   Functionalists view property crime as *inherent* in societies that socialize people of all social classes to desire material success when the legitimate means to achieve success are limited. Some who find their legitimate means to success blocked turn to illegitimate means. Since there is no ending point of "success," some people, like Stewart and Madoff, who have ample access to legitimate means, turn to illegitimate means so they can achieve even "more success."

The cartoonist pinpoints an essential principle that is highlighted by functionalists—that crime is functional for individuals and society.

Conflict Theory

6.5   **Explain how power and social class are related to social inequality in the legal system.**

> *Sioux Manufacturing in North Dakota made helmets for U.S. troops in Iraq and Afghanistan. They used Kevlar—a fabric that deflects some shrapnel and bullets. The company was accused of using less Kevlar than it was supposed to. This would reduce costs and increase profits—but it would endanger U.S. soldiers, perhaps causing some to die.*

> *Would anyone actually do such a thing to save a few bucks? Investigators found that the accusation was true. Employees had even doctored records to show that the company had used the correct amount of Kevlar (Lambert 2008).*

What was the punishment for a crime this serious? How long did the executives of Sioux Manufacturing who ordered this crime spend in prison? Not one spent even a single night in jail. The company paid a fine—and then the government gave it another contract to make more helmets.

Contrast this with poor people who are caught stealing a $5,000 car and sent to prison for years. How can a legal system that proudly boasts "justice for all" be so inconsistent?

Power and Social Class: Inequality in the Legal System

Conflict theorists stress that every society is marked by power and inequality. The most fundamental division of a capitalist society is that between those who own the means of production, called *the ruling class,* and those who sell their labor, called *the working class.*

The working class is made up of three major groups: (1) the upper-level managers and professionals, who hold secure positions that pay well; (2) the stable working class, white-collar and blue-collar workers whose jobs are less secure and who are paid less, although their pay is adequate for survival; and (3) the marginal working class, who have little job security and whose labor is in low demand. This group includes most of the unemployed and people who are on welfare. From the marginal working class (also called the "reserve army" of the unemployed) come most burglars, muggers, armed robbers, and car thieves.

Conflict theorists emphasize that the law is quite unlike the ideal we learn in grade school: an institution that administers impartial justice for those accused of crimes. Rather, the ruling class controls the criminal justice system, which uses it to maintain its own privileged position in society. Because of this, the police and courts do not harshly punish the owners of corporations, but instead focus their attention on the marginal working class.

Violations by company owners and other members of the ruling class cannot be ignored totally. If their crimes became too flagrant, they could provoke an outcry among the working class and, ultimately, foment revolution. To prevent this, an occasional violation by the powerful is prosecuted—and given huge publicity—as was the case with Stewart and Madoff. Public floggings like these reassure the working class that the criminal justice system applies to all. This helps to create a sense of justice and prevent an uprising.

It is rare, however, for white-collar criminals to appear in court. Most go before a state or federal agency (such as the FTC, the Federal Trade Commission), which has no power to imprison. Headed by people of privilege, the FTC levies fines and orders offenders to stop doing what they were doing. Cases of illegal sales of stocks and bonds, price fixing, restraint of trade, and so on are handled by "gentlemen overseeing gentlemen." In contrast, the property crimes of the working class—burglary, mugging, armed robbery, and petty theft—threaten not only the sanctity of private property but also, if allowed to continue, the positions of the powerful. These offenders are channeled into a court system that does have the power to imprison.

In Sum   Conflict theorists regard the criminal justice system not as a system to dispense justice, but as a device used by the powerful to keep themselves in power. This power elite uses law enforcement to control workers, mask injustice, and prevent revolt.

■ Types of Crime

We'll come back to the criminal justice system, but to better understand crime as a social problem, let's first review research on juvenile delinquency, white-collar crime, professional crime, and organized crime.

Juvenile Delinquency

6.6   **Explain how juvenile delinquency developed, the extent of juvenile crime, the delinquent career, neutralization techniques, and how education is related to delinquency.**

Did you know there used to be no juvenile delinquency? Not a bit. How could this be? Read on.

The Origin of Juvenile Delinquency: A Perceptual Shift

Our 21st-century views of child development make it difficult to realize how differently children used to be perceived and treated. Earlier generations did not make the distinctions between children and adults that we do. Historically, children who committed crimes were treated the same as adults—and just as severely. In the 1700s, girls as young as 13 were burned at the stake for their crimes, and 8- and 10-year-old boys were hanged for theirs (Blackstone 1899).

Over the years a shift occurred in how children were viewed. As part of this cultural transformation, "teenagers" became a separate class of people. Previously, the teen years were just an age, much as ages 30 to 35 are now—there was nothing distinctive about them. As views changed, laws were passed that classified "juveniles" as a separate category in the criminal justice system. This change in the law produced a new category of crime—**juvenile delinquency**—crime committed by those under age 18.

Subjective Concerns about Juvenile Crime

Some juvenile delinquents commit what are called **status crimes**, behavior that is illegal only because of the individual's age. Examples include drinking alcohol, running away from home, or violating curfew. Some of these things bother people, but subjective concerns center primarily on the other crimes that juveniles commit—their robberies, burglaries, and even some rape and murder.

The good news is shown in Figure 6.1. You can see that like their adult counterpart, crime by juveniles has been dropping. The one category that has increased is illegal drugs. Perhaps changes in state marijuana laws will reduce this total.

A major trend is the increasing numbers of women who are involved in crime. Unlike this woman, however, few of them are elderly.

Figure 6.1 Number of Juveniles[1] Arrested by Type of Offense

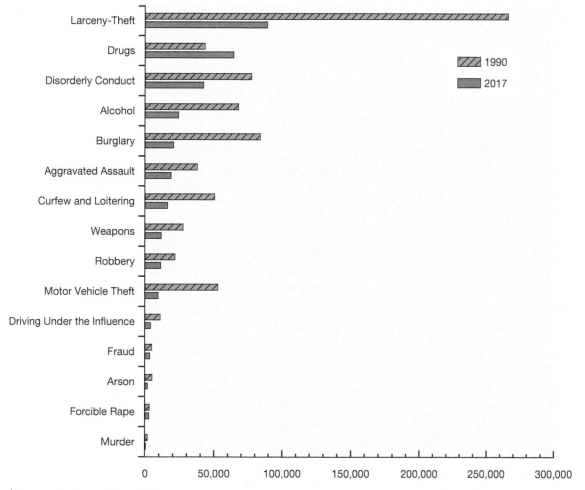

[1]Persons under the age 18 arrested in one year.
Source: By the author. Based on Crime in the United States 2010:Table 32; 2017:Table 32.

One of the fascinating aspects of people who break the law is how they set up personal defenses to protect their self-concepts. Let's look at how juvenile boys do this.

Neutralizing Deviance

Although juvenile delinquents know that their crimes are condemned by society, many don't feel guilty about what they do. How they manage this is the focus of the next *Thinking Critically about Social Problems.*

Thinking Critically about Social Problems

How to Be "Bad" But Think of Yourself as "Good"

Back in 1957, sociologists Gresham Sykes and David Matza did an analysis that has never been superseded. I think you'll agree that their analysis remains as insightful today as when they did it so long ago. These two sociologists were doing research on juvenile delinquents, and they were struck by how little guilt the boys felt about their crimes. As they listened to the boys, they uncovered what they called **techniques of neutralization**, ways that people deflect social norms. These techniques also apply us, but let's look at how the boys used them.

If this individual stabs someone, what techniques of neutralization do you think he will use?

Colin Edwards/Photofusion Picture Library/Alamy Stock Photo

1. *Denial of responsibility.* The boys think of themselves as propelled by forces beyond their control. Their unloving parents, bad companions, or bad neighborhoods cause them to break the law. By denying responsibility, they break the link between themselves and their acts. ("I'm just a billiard ball on the pool table of life.")

2. *Denial of injury.* The boys admit that their acts are illegal, but they deny that they hurt anyone. They call their vandalism "mischief," "pranks," or "just having a little fun." This breaks the link between them and the consequences of their acts.

3. *Denial of a victim.* If the boys admit that they have done harm, they claim that the injury was not wrong "under the circumstances." The person they hurt was not really a victim. All they did was just "get even" for some wrong. Vandalizing a school, for example, is revenge on unfair teachers; theft is retaliation against gouging storekeepers. Someone they beat up deserved it because he mouthed off to them. With no victims, they transform themselves from wrongdoers into avengers.

4. *Condemnation of the condemners.* Delinquents also take the offensive. They call those who condemn them hypocrites. They accuse the police of being brutal, dishonest, or picking on people. By attacking others, they deflect attention away from their own behavior.

5. *Appeal to higher loyalties.* Some delinquents see themselves as caught between a rock and a hard place. The law pulls them one way, loyalty to friends another. In this war of incompatible expectations, loyalty to friends wins out. If a rival gang hurts a friend, for example, to retaliate is "more moral" than to ignore the injury.

These techniques allow delinquents to neutralize society's norms. Even if delinquents have internalized mainstream values—and not all have—these rationalizations let them commit crimes with a minimum of guilt or shame.

For Your Consideration

I mentioned that these five techniques of neutralization also apply to us. We usually precede our neutralizations (rationalizations) with something like, "I couldn't help it because..." or "I know I shouldn't have, but I did it because..."

→ How have you or people you know used each of these five techniques of neutralization?

→ Which technique did you use most recently? Under what circumstances?

Delinquent Subcultures

Some delinquents have little or no need to neutralize their lawbreaking. They grow up in **delinquent subcultures** where criminal activities are a normal part of everyday life. In these subcultures, they learn norms that support crime, as well as techniques for committing burglaries, robberies, and other crimes (Fabio et al. 2011). In the next *Thinking Critically about Social Problems*, we focus on such a subculture.

Thinking Critically about Social Problems

Islands in the Street: Urban Gangs in the United States

For more than 10 years, sociologist Martín Sánchez-Jankowski (1991) did participant observation of 37 gangs in Boston, Los Angeles, and New York City. The gangs were made up of African Americans, Chicanos, Dominicans, Irish, Jamaicans, and Puerto Ricans. They earned money through gambling, arson, mugging, armed robbery, and selling moonshine, drugs, guns, stolen car parts, and protection. Sánchez-Jankowski ate, slept, and some-times fought with the gangs, but by mutual agreement he did not participate in drug dealing or in other illegal activities. He was seriously injured twice during the study.

Sánchez-Jankowski's research breaks stereotypes. The motive for joining a gang was not to escape a broken home (there were as many members from intact families as from broken homes); nor was it to seek a substitute family (the same number of boys said they were close to their families as those who said they were not). They said that the gangs gave them access to money, protec-tion, and anonymity in committing crimes. They also said that the gangs are a source of fun (this included access to girls and drugs).

The boys also gave a reason that might sound strange to your ears—they wanted to help the community. To understand this, you

Mark Allen Johnson/ZUMAPRESS/Newscom

Sánchez-Jankowski looked beyond the exterior to get the inside story of gang members. This photo, taken in Los Angeles, California, is of two members of the Gape Street Crips before they left to participate in a revenge shooting of the East Coast Crips. Both gangs are located in Watts.

need to know that in some neighborhoods gangs protect residents from outsiders and spearhead political change (Martinez 2003). There was one more reason: The boys saw the gang as an alternative to the dead-end—and deadening—jobs held by their parents.

Neighborhood residents are ambivalent about gangs. On the one hand, they fear the violence. On the other hand, many adults once belonged to these same gangs, the gangs often provide better protection than the police, and gang members are the children of people who live in the neighborhood.

Particular gangs will come and go, but gangs will likely always remain part of the city. As functionalists point out, gangs fulfill needs of poor youth who live on the margins of society.

For Your Consideration

→ What are the needs that youth gangs meet (the functions they fulfill)?

→ Suppose that you have been hired as an urban planner by the City of Los Angeles. How could you arrange to meet the needs that gangs are meeting in ways that minimize violence and encourage youth to follow mainstream norms?

Education and Delinquency

Here is a common view: "If we can keep them in school, we can keep them out of trouble. If they drop out, they're lost." For the most part, this idea is borne out by sociological re-search. Those who graduate from high school are less likely to commit crimes–and about 30 percent of inmates in our prisons have not finished high school (ACS 2017). It costs about $11,000 to educate one high school student for one year, but it costs about $28,000 to keep one person in prison for one year (BJS 2012; *Statistical Abstract* 2018:Table 259). There are also other huge costs—what people in prison could have been contributing to society and what victims lose, not just money and property, but also in injuries and lost sense of security.

White-Collar Crime

6.7   Be familiar with criminogenic cultures, lethal white-collar crime, embezzlement, theft, and the relationship of gender and social class to white-collar crime.

When corporate scandals hit the news, we learn that top executives have stolen outrageous amounts of money. Later, in almost all cases, we learn that they have been given a slap on the wrist. Only a handful of white-collar criminals receive stiff sentences, and as you saw with Bernie Madoff, they often serve their time in what are called "country club" prisons.

Let's explore this.

Criminogenic Subcultures

The term **white-collar crime** refers to crimes committed by people of higher social status in the course of their occupation. Examples are lawyers who rob people not by guns but by pens, executives who authorize defective products that they know will harm people, and corporations that gain sales by false advertising.

Some executives work within a **criminogenic subculture**; that is, their work environment encourages and supports the commission of crime. In a subculture where there is high pressure to increase profits and to climb the corporate ladder, cutting corners can be winked at, even encouraged. In a climate of ethical numbness, if you don't go with the flow, you'll soon be on the outside looking in.

Imagine that you are working in the sales department at Wells Fargo, one of the largest banks in the United States. Your job is to open new bank accounts and to sign up customers for the Wells Fargo credit card. You do your best, but you find that your sales are lagging behind everyone else. Your supervisor tells you that if your sales don't improve soon, you're out. Then you discover the magic that the others are using. To meet quotas, they're filling out the credit card applications with the names and addresses of people who don't know they are being signed up. They are even making up fake email addresses. Thousands of them. Tens of thousands. Everyone in your office is all smiles. The supervisor is smiling, too—she is getting her bonus for meeting quotas, and she knows that many of the new accounts are fake.

You are probably thinking that this couldn't be possible. But it did happen like this. Wells Fargo opened *1.5 million* fake bank accounts and a half million unauthorized credit cards (Corkery 2016). Anyone go to jail? No. Anyone get arrested? No. But 5,000 "sales" agents were fired, and the government fined Wells Fargo $185 million.

White-Collar Crimes That Kill

Some white-collar crime has devastating results. Listeria is a deadly disease that food factories must continually guard against. If they let their guard down, they can poison their customers. In a Sara Lee factory producing Ball Park Franks, the company cut costs and stopped testing for listeria. Fifteen people who ate Sara Lee's infected hot dogs died. How many executives do you think were sent to prison for life for these murders? None. How about for even 10 or 15 years? Not a chance. Sara Lee pled guilty to two misdemeanors and paid a fine (Mauer 2004).

Some "household name" corporations have produced criminogenic subcultures so cold-blooded that their executives have planned murder for profit. You might think I'm exaggerating—and I wish I were—but look at this list from the automobile industry:

- Ford in the 1970s. Their car, the Pinto, had a little problem: It exploded in rear-end crashes. *For $11 per car, the problem could be fixed.* Ford executives met to discuss the problem and decided not to pay the $11. They figured the lawsuits would be cheaper than fixing the problem. Several hundred people burned to death (Dowie 1977).
- GM in the 1990s. The same problem. Their car, the Oldsmobile Cutlass, exploded in accidents. An even cheaper fix was available—just $4.50 per car. GM executives met. Same decision. They, too, figured the

The top photo shows a 1973 Pinto that exploded when tested by Ford. At the bottom is the 1973 Pinto that Ford sold, knowing it was a ticking time bomb. Three teenaged girls burned to death when this car was rear-ended.

Associated Press

lawsuits would be cheaper than fixing the problem. Let them burn to death (Boot 1998).

- GM again. This time in the 2000s. The Cobalt. Test drivers of the new models reported a little problem with the ignition switch. On bumpy roads, the ignition switch could move to the off position, cutting the car's electrical power, making the driver lose control, and causing the air bags not to deploy. Engineers wrote memos, but GM executive chose to do nothing. Failed ignition switches left 124 people dead and another 17 with amputations, burns, and brain damage (Jennings and Trautman 2016).

Cold, calculating, decisions to kill customers by respected executives. How many went to jail? You know the answer. Not one.

Let's reverse the situation. What do you think would happen if drivers who were dissatisfied with their cars killed a couple hundred automobile executives? How about if they killed just one or two? In asking these questions, with their obvious answers, we uncover the stunning contrast in how white-collar crime and street crime are treated in the criminal justice system.

The exploding cars and failing ignitions confirm the perspective of conflict theorists: The powerful can and do manipulate our legal system. They can and do escape punishment for their crimes, including—and let's coin a term—*serial manslaughter.*

Embezzlement and Employee Theft

Two common types of white-collar crime are embezzlement and employee theft. Let's see what patterns they have.

Embezzlement   The essence of embezzlement is a violation of trust. Someone who has been entrusted to oversee someone else's money, to deposit it or invest it, secretly steals it instead. Why does someone embezzle? The simplest answer, of course, is that they want the money. In most cases, they find themselves in a financial jam, and they "borrow" the money, telling themselves that they will pay it back shortly. This is common among compulsive gamblers (Bindle 2016).

Sociologists call this *the fraud triangle: opportunity,* access to other people's money; *need,* which drives the individual to embezzle; and *rationalization,* the techniques of neutralization the individual uses to justify the embezzlement.

When they aren't able to return the money—to repay the "loan," as they think of it—the embezzlers develop deeper rationalizations to justify their secret theft (Cressey 1953; Binde 2016). Some tell themselves that they deserve the money because they aren't being paid what they are worth or because their employer has somehow taken advantage of them. As with juvenile delinquents, their techniques of neutralization are usually effective: Although they are stealing from their company, even from a boss they might like and have known for years, they still consider themselves to be respectable, law-abiding citizens.

Not all embezzlers neutralize their crimes. Some embezzle without trying to justify anything. They do it just because they can (Benson 1985; Green 1993). Embezzlers also have many motives besides financial problems. Some embezzle on an impulse, and seeing that it was easy, they continue. I am sure that there is even a "revenge embezzler," one who embezzles to get even with the boss, perhaps for some slight the employee feels. There is probably the "daring embezzler," too, one who embezzles for the thrill of the act. And I am sure there are "upwardly mobile" embezzlers, those who steal in order to "better" themselves and gain a more prominent place in the community. These motives, and whatever others there might be, are yet to be borne out by research.

Employee Theft   When you think of employee theft, you are likely to think of employees stealing things that their company sells or manufactures. The restaurant employee shoving steaks out the back door might come to mind. This type of employee theft is common,

From mayor of a major city to felon. Women have joined men not only in positions of power but also in positions of crime. Shown here is Megan Barry, former mayor of Nashville, TN, who pleaded guilty to felony theft.

but employee theft comes in many forms. Some steal company secrets, such as formulas, manufacturing processes, or marketing plans. A gray area emerges when an employee goes to work for a competitor and brings knowledge inside his or her head. No documents are stolen, making this crime difficult to prove.

A case that made headlines was the theft of the Bratz dolls. Actually, it was just the idea and sketch of the dolls that were stolen. Carter Bryant was a designer working for Mattel, the maker of the iconic Barbie doll. Bryant made some sketches of an idea he had for a new doll. He later went to work for MGA Entertainment, which turned his ideas into the Bratz dolls.

The Bratz were a thundering success—about $3 billion a year—threatening Barbie's dominance of the doll market. After a lot of detective work, Mattel was able to prove that Bryant had drawn his sketches while he was under contract to Mattel. The court ruled that Mattel, not MGA, had the rights to the Bratz dolls. MGA was also ordered to pay $100 million to Mattel.

As you can see, white-collar crime can be 49 shades of gray. With the Bratz dolls, a judgment call could have gone either way. Perhaps Bryant made the sketches on his own time. As sketches, they certainly weren't valuable, just a jumble of lines. The sketches became valuable only when the idea was turned into a successful product. Essentially, this is what an appeals judge decided, for in a later ruling a judge decided that MGA could keep the Bratz—and even that Mattel owed $310 million to MGA (Lepore 2018).

Social Class and Crime

The examples I have reviewed are typical. It is rare for executives to be arrested for their crimes, much less convicted or to serve even a single day in prison. While bank robbers risk their lives for $10,000 and are sentenced to years in prison, corporate executives who manipulate documents worth millions of dollars are at low risk of discovery—and practically none of punishment. In short, white-collar criminals enjoy a privileged position within the criminal justice system. Because of their social position and ability to manipulate the law, few are punished. Some even get away with murder, as we saw with the Pinto, Cutlass, and Cobalt.

Gender in White-Collar Crime

As the corporate doors have opened to women, so have the enticements to white-collar crime. Like men, many women who join the corporate world are tempted by its illegal opportunities. They, too, want the finer things in life, and they, too, often take shortcuts, especially if they think the chances of getting caught are slim. From Table 6.2, you can see how the arrests of women for white-collar crime have increased over the years. The last reporting year shows an unexpected and unexplained drop in women's arrests since 2000 in 3 of the 4 types of white-collar crime.

Table 6.2 Arrests for White-Collar Crimes, by Sex

	1981		2000		2010		2017	
	Male	Female	Male	Female	Male	Female	Male	Female
Embezzlement	70%	30%	50%	50%	50%	50%	51%	49%
Fraud	58%	42%	55%	45%	58%	42%	62%	38%
Forgery and counterfeiting	68%	32%	61%	39%	62%	38%	65%	35%
Stolen property	88%	12%	83%	17%	80%	20%	78%	22%

Source: By the author. Based on *FBI Uniform Crime Reports*, various editions, including *Crime in the United States* 2001:Table 42; 2011: Table 42; 2018:Table 42, FBI 2017:Table Arrestees Sex by Arrest Offense Category.

Professional Crime

6.8 **Know what professional crime is and how professional criminals maintain their secrecy and values.**

For some people, *crime is their work.* People who consider crime to be their occupation are called **professional criminals**. Jewel thieves and counterfeiters—so highly romanticized in movies and novels—are examples of professional criminals. So are fences—those who buy stolen goods for resale. The activities of professional criminals, although illegal, are a form of work, and they pride themselves on their skills and successes.

Professional criminals organize their lives around their "work," much as people who work at legal jobs do. Professional thieves, for example, plan where and how they will steal, and they make arrangements to get it done. They may steal almost every day of the year, but they take vacations and days off to celebrate birthdays, anniversaries, and holidays. They associate with like-minded people who share their scorn for the "straight world," as well as support their values of secrecy and loyalty. They also teach one another skills for committing crimes and ways to avoid detection. Sociologists have observed these aspects of professional thieves since the 1930s, and they have not changed (Sutherland 1937; Matlock 2018).

Unlike amateurs, professional criminals are not troubled by their criminality. For them, crime is simply a way to make a living, and they are ultra-successful at neutralizing societal norms. They see themselves as businesspeople, no different from clerks who sell shoddy merchandise or surgeons who perform unnecessary operations. As you can see from the following *Personal Account,* they view their activities as just another way of "making it" in U.S. society.

Personal Account

Operating a "Chop Shop"

I was teaching an undergraduate course in the sociology of deviance. The usual problem of "What should I write about for my term paper?" came up. When a student told me about the connections he had with a "chop shop," I encouraged him to write his term paper on this topic.

Apparently, each large metropolitan area has at least one "chop shop," a place where stolen cars are "chopped," broken into their various parts. The owner of this "chop shop" in St. Louis, Missouri, kept informed of what parts were in demand. He would then order specific cars to be stolen, paying set prices according to the makes and models he ordered. He and his workers used acetylene torches and other tools to disassemble the cars. They sold the fenders, motors, transmissions, seats, doors, and so on to dealers in used auto parts. The small amount of metal left over was hauled away by an older man who sold it for scrap.

Like small business owners across the country, the owner-manager of the "chop shop" had a great deal of responsibility. He made the business decisions, paid the rent on the shop, and met his weekly payroll. Unlike "straight" employers, however, he paid wages in cash and did not pay taxes. He also had to arrange for a surreptitious supply of oxygen for the acetylene torches. To buy oxygen from regular sources would have aroused suspicion, as he had no legitimate reason for the oxygen.

Like employees of any legitimate business, the workers at the "chop shop" formed a team, each performing specific tasks. The difference, of course, was that each knew that they were

A "chop shop" in Missouri mysteriously burns after the police raided it earlier in the day. The gasoline can in the foreground could have something to do with it.

working on stolen cars, a secret knowledge that bound them together. Because their work was risky, with the threat of arrest and prison hanging over their heads, the men developed ways to maintain their loyalty, trust, and dependence on one another. In addition to the usual joking and bragging that working class men do at work, they also built a life together outside of work. After work and on weekends, they drank at the same tavern, a bar where they could relax, since it was frequented by other professional criminals. They also visited one another's homes. By integrating their working and social lives, these men minimized the intrusion of straight values, kept close tabs on one another, and reinforced ideas that the way they made a living was right and desirable.

In their research, sociologists report that professional criminals scorn the values of the straight world, pride themselves on their specialized skills, organize their lives around their work, and depend on in-group loyalty. My student found these traits to be evident among the workers in this "chop shop."

For Your Consideration

A basic principle of sociological research is to cause no harm to your subjects. Even though this was secondary or indirect research, I was careful not to ask my student about his relationship with the owner or workers of the "chop shop." It is likely that one was his relative, or perhaps a neighbor, a friend, or the relative of a friend. He might have even worked there himself.

→ Do you think that sociologists are wrong to take this approach?
→ Could you ever be a professional criminal? Why or why not?

Organized Crime

6.9 **Know what organized crime is and reasons for the Mafia's past success and current weakness.**

The professional criminals we just discussed are local and independent. Now let's turn to **organized crime**, criminals who are part of a larger network, perhaps even national or international in scope.

The Mafia: Origins and Characteristics

The most famous organized crime group, the **Mafia**, originated in Sicily. As *The Godfather* series depicts, the Sicilian government was weak, and local strongmen united to protect their families and communities from bandits. After establishing control over an area, these men functioned as a private government. Like a government, they collected taxes (payments, tribute) in return for protecting their communities from other strongmen (Catanzaro 1992; Dimico et al. 2017). As the formal government extended its power from the capital, these men, entrenched in power, maintained their control over areas of Sicily. After the 1860s, they became known as the Mafia. Even today, organized crime remains powerful in Sicily and other parts of Italy (Rakopoulos 2018).

Unlike the myth, the Sicilians (or Italians) did not introduce organized crime to the United States. To the contrary, organized crime has gone through several ethnic successions. In New York City, the Irish used to dominate organized crime. They were succeeded by the Jews. Only after that did the Italians take over (Bell 1960). Today, several ethnic groups are involved in organized crime—not just Sicilians and Italians, but among others also African Americans, Chinese, Colombians, Cubans, Irish, Japanese, Puerto Ricans, and Russians (Barrett and Gardiner 2011; Albanese 2014).

In the Sicilian U.S. Mafia, about 5,000 members belonged to about 24 "families" of 200 to 700 members each. The families are linked to each other by understandings and "treaties." The leaders of the most powerful families formed a "commission" or "combine" to which the weaker families pay deference (Windle et al. 2018). Members call this structure the Mafia, or **Cosa Nostra** ("our thing").

Why Was the Mafia Successful?

Central to the Mafia's organization are two principles that separate group members from outsiders: *omertá*, its vow of secrecy, and family. To maintain close connections, the Mafia encourages marriage among its members and *fictive kinship* (assigning obligations to people who are not related; a godfather, for example, unites two families).

Why does the Mafia continue to exist despite decades of efforts of the U.S. government to put it out of business? In addition to family ties and *omertá*, here are four more reasons:

1. Organized crime *is* organized. The Mafia has a *bureaucracy* with individuals specializing in different criminal activities.
2. Organized crime offers illegal *services in high demand* (prostitution, gambling, and loan-sharking)—with customers who participate willingly and do not complain to the police.

3. Organized crime wields influence through *political corruption.*
4. Organized crime uses *violence and intimidation* to control victims and its own members.

The Mafia was once so influential in the United States that from time to time the U.S. ruling class called on it for help (Simon 1981). During the 1920s and the 1940s, periods of great labor unrest, corporations hired gangsters to break strikes and infiltrate unions, especially those among autoworkers and longshoremen. During World War II, U.S. Navy Intelligence asked Mafia boss Charles "Lucky" Luciano to protect the New York docks from sabotage. Luciano, who was directing Mafia operations from prison, agreed to do so. Luciano also helped get the Sicilian Mafia to support the U.S. invasion of Sicily, likely saving the lives of many U.S. soldiers. As a reward for his help, after the war Luciano was released from prison. Luciano thought he would be given citizenship, but he was deported to Italy.

After Luciano left, the Mafia continued to gain power. It eventually controlled the labor unions, construction trade, and garbage hauling in New York and other cities (Trust 1986; Albanese 2014; Windle et al. 2018). On a national level, the Mafia controlled the Teamsters, dominating the trucking of goods across the nation.

The Godfather, one of the most successful movies of all time, has become the basis for a stereotype of the Sicilian Mafia. As the text explains, there are other mafias as well and various forms of organized crime.

The Weakening of the Mafia

The U.S. government's perpetual war against the Mafia has left it in a weakened state. An example is the Mob and Las Vegas. Although the Mafia began the gambling industry in Las Vegas, with Bugsy Siegel opening The Flamingo in 1946, the Mafia's presence there is now mostly relegated to memorabilia in Las Vegas' Mob Museum.

Especially effective has been the FBI's use of undercover agents to infiltrate the organization. With powerful surveillance devices, grand jury indictments, and a witness protection program that elicits cooperation by providing new identities, even top Mafia bosses have been convicted.

One of the Mafia bosses, John Gotti, captured the public's attention. Despite his crimes, which included murder, Gotti was romanticized and became a darling of the media. After Gotti was convicted and died in prison, his son, also named John, took over the Gambino crime family. When the son was put on trial, he amazed law enforcement by convincing jurors that he had seen the light and left his criminal ways (O'Connor 2010). After four trials that ended in hung juries, the government gave up. Gotti then wrote a book about how it was to be raised in organized crime (Gotti 2015).

Although the Mafia is in decline, it is premature to write its obituary. An "old line" business that remains is loan-sharking, making private, illegal loans at outrageous rates of interest. ("Pay or we break your leg.") But for decades, this group has been adapting to changing circumstances, and it likely will continue to do so. Recently, the Mafia has come to realize that there are enormous amounts of money to be made in computer crimes, including identity theft.

The Criminal Justice System

6.10 Explain why plea bargaining, bias, recidivism, the death penalty, and the prison experience are part of the criminal justice system as a social problem.

We cannot fully understand crime as a social problem without examining the criminal justice system. To illustrate how this system works, let's follow the case of Buddy, Gary, and Clyde.

Plea Bargaining

On a Saturday night, Buddy Hudson, a 19-year-old African American, teamed up with two whites, Gary Carson, 34, and Clyde Johnson, 21, to rob a liquor store. The robbery netted them $2,590. After a week's spending spree—their dreams of drugs and women realized—they tried their luck again. This time, though, their luck ran out. When an alarm went off, they fled, but a patrol car was in the area, and they were arrested.

To ensure that the courts could not throw the case out for violating the suspects' rights, the arresting officers read the men the 1966 Miranda warning:

1. *You have the right to remain silent.*
2. *If you do not remain silent, what you say can and will be used against you.*
3. *You have the right to be represented by a lawyer during questioning and thereafter.*
4. *If you cannot afford an attorney, the state will provide one at its expense.*

The state did provide an attorney. Her advice was to say nothing. She would talk to the prosecuting attorney, who would determine what crimes the suspects would be charged with. After meeting with the state's attorney, she told the men that the evidence against them was solid. They would be charged with armed robbery, resisting arrest, and assault with a deadly weapon. They could go to prison for up to 40 years. She added that she thought she could "cut a deal" and get the charges of assault and resisting arrest dropped in return for a guilty plea to armed robbery. If so, she could get them a five-to-seven (a minimum of five years and a maximum of seven years in state prison).

The men figured that they could do better if they went to trial. Clyde's mother put up $20,000 to secure her son's release on bond. Unable to raise bond money, Buddy and Gary remained in jail during the nine months *it took for their case to come to trial. Just before the trial, to everyone's surprise, Clyde pled guilty. The judge suspended Clyde's sentence and placed him on probation for five years. Buddy and Gary were found guilty of armed robbery. The judge gave Gary a six-year sentence and Buddy a sentence of 10 to 15 years.*

When a reporter asked about the differences in sentencing, the judge replied, "I have to show consideration for the defendant who cops a plea. It saves the court the expense of a trial." He added that Clyde had a job and that to send him to prison would serve no purpose. Letting him keep his job, however, would increase Clyde's chances of staying out of trouble. When the reporter cautiously said that some people might think that Buddy's longer sentence might have something to do with Buddy being an African American, the judge said, "Race has nothing to do with this case. These are just facts: Gary Carson is older, but he has fewer 'priors' (previous arrests). He doesn't need as stiff a sentence to teach him a lesson. Buddy's 'priors' tell me he's more dangerous."

Note the principles from this case that illustrate how the criminal justice system can be "more criminal than just."

1. Some of the poor spend months (even years) behind bars awaiting trial, while those with money use the bond system to buy their release.
2. Defense attorneys encourage plea bargaining, *whether or not the individual is guilty*. In urging his client to accept a jail sentence, one public defender said, "Even if you're innocent, it's a good deal" (Penn 1985).
3. Prosecutors use threats of longer sentences to get guilty pleas. ("Plead guilty to this charge, or they'll charge you with this additional crime, which carries a longer sentence.")
4. Judges dislike "unnecessary trials" and impose harsher sentences on those who insist on them (Work 2014).
5. Age, employment, and the number of previous arrests affect sentencing. Even when offenses are the same, those who have better employment histories are given more lenient sentences.
6. The *number of arrests,* not the seriousness of the charges, influences a sentence. Judges often discount the type of charge because they know that plea bargaining changes what people are officially charged with.

Assembly-Line Justice

What is wrong with plea bargaining? We can start with something quite basic: The Sixth Amendment to the Constitution guarantees people accused of a crime the right to be judged by their peers in a "speedy and public" trial. As with Buddy, Gary, and Clyde, in *90 percent* of cases the trial has been replaced with plea bargains, arrangements worked out behind closed doors (Bagaric et al. 2018). To get people to plead guilty and avoid a trial, prosecutors charge them with more serious crimes and then offer to accept a guilty plea to lesser offenses.

What about defense attorneys, provided for free to the poor? Despite their obligation to *defend* their clients, public *defense* attorneys usually suggest to them that they plead guilty. Despite their formal job description, public defenders develop "implicit understandings" about what their job *really* is: to be team players who produce "assembly-line justice" for the poor (Blumberg 1967; Levintova et al. 2013; Bagaric et al. 2018).

Before you go to the next section, read the following *Issues in Social Problems,* which builds on what you have just read.

Issues in Social Problems

You Don't Have to Be Poor to Go to Jail—But It Helps

Richard Garrett of Harpersville, Alabama, who is unemployed, couldn't pay his fine for traffic and license violations. He spent 24 months in jail. The interest and collection fees keep growing, and Garrett now owes $10,000.

Then there is Marilyn Roberts' son in Olympia, Washington, who flicked a cigarette at a police officer. He spent 97 days in a county jail, most of them alone in a cell 23 hours a day.

It isn't a crime to be poor, but poverty doesn't help when you're in trouble with the law. If you can't pay a fine, you go to jail.

"It's the only practical alternative," said Woodrow Wilson, a judge in Bastrop, Louisiana. "Otherwise, some people would never be punished."

In courtrooms across the nation, defendants with ready cash pay and leave. Those without money are ushered from the courtroom to jail to pay their debts with days rather than dollars—or to wait until someone bails them out.

Authorities jail defendants who can't pay fines for minor crimes such as public drunkenness and speeding. Although legal aid lawyers protest that it is unjust to give better treatment to defendants who have money, indigent defendants keep winding up in jail. During the economic crisis, some courts even began adding "user fees" to those who "use" the courts—that is, to those who are arrested.

Judges and prosecutors claim not to know which defendants are poor. "If they raised the issue, they wouldn't be put in jail," said an Aurora, Colorado, city attorney, "but I don't see that it's the responsibility of the court or the prosecutor to check out their ability to pay fines."

It certainly must be difficult to tell the difference. Are the people sitting in jail for petty offenses poor? Or do they have plenty of money but prefer jail rather than going home with their families? Really hard to tell.

Some officials have tried, or at least have given the appearance of trying. In Monroe, Louisiana, officials hired a priest to evaluate defendants' finances. They let him go, though, because he sided with the poor too often.

This prisoner is meeting her public defense attorney for the first time. How do you think her poverty might influence her chances of conviction?

Thinkstock/Stockbyte/Getty Images

The sheriff in charge of the 8,000 inmates of Chicago's Cook County Jail said that 1,500 of them could be free if they had $5,000 and 200 if they had just $500. "The situation is ridiculous," he said. "One homeless man was arrested for allegedly trespassing at a gas station. His bond was $100, which he didn't have. In the seven weeks he was in my jail, at $143 a day, his stay cost the county $7,000" (Dart 2016).

As Jackie Yeldell, an attorney, said, "You can be sure there aren't any wealthy persons in jail."

Based on Schmitt 1982; Bronner 2012; Palazzolo 2015; Stuart 2016; Copp and Bales 2018.

For Your Consideration

→ Do you agree with the judge who said that the only practical alternative is to put poor people in jail, "otherwise, some people would never be punished"?

→ What alternatives can you think of?

Bias in the Criminal Justice System

Let's discuss racial–ethnic discrimination in the criminal justice system. As you will recall, Buddy, the only African American in the trio, received the most severe sentence. The judge claimed that this was because of Buddy's "priors." What is the answer?

The issue of bias is complicated. At first glance, the judicial system certainly seems to discriminate along racial–ethnic lines, especially when it comes to African Americans.

Figure 6.2 U.S. Prisoners, by Race-Ethnicity

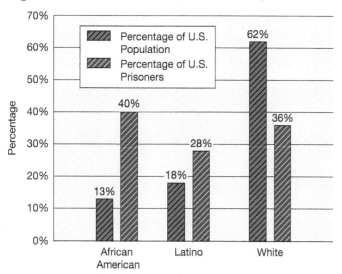

Source: By the author. Based on "Prisoners in 2016." NCJ 251149. U.S. Department of Justice, January 2018.

Figure 6.2 shows the huge disparities between a group's percentage of the population and its percentage of prisoners. You can see that the percentage of African American prisoners is triple what you would expect from their percentage in the U.S. population. For Latinos, it is 55 percent higher, and for whites, it is 42 percent less.

Now look at the racial–ethnic make-up of the prisoners on death row. From Table 6.3, you can see that the percentage of African Americans on death row is also triple what you would expect from their percentage in the U.S. population. For Latinos and whites, however, it is less than you would expect. Overall, the criminal justice system has an overwhelming impact on African Americans: On any given day, one of every 14 black males ages 25 to 34 is in prison—and this does not include the tens of thousands who are in jail (Guerino et al. 2011). Some estimate that one-fourth of all black males born today will spend time in prison (Kessler 2010).

These data do *not* let us draw conclusions about bias, however, because they do not take into account differences in crime among racial–ethnic groups. We need to compare

Table 6.3 Prisoners on Death Row, by Race–Ethnicity

Race–Ethnicity	Number on Death Row	Percentage of Death Row Inmates	Percentage of U.S. Population	More (+) or Less (–) Than What You Would Expect from the Group's Percentage of the U.S. Population[1]
White	1,181	42.3%	61.3%	−31%
African American	1,162	41.6%	13.3%	+312%
Latino	368	13.1%	17.8%	−26%
Asian American	53	1.9%	5.7%	−67%
Native American	27	1.0%	1.3%	−23%
Totals	2,792	100%	100%	

[1] This total is computed by dividing the difference between the group's percentage of the U.S. population and its percentage of death row inmates by its percentage of the U.S. population.

Sources: By the author. Based on NAACP 2017; *Statistical Abstract of the United States* 2018:Table 10.

arrest rates and crime rates. We can do this by comparing the arrest rates with what crime victims in the National Crime Victimization Survey report about the race–ethnicity of their offenders. When we do this, we find that crimes of violence are higher for African Americans than their percentage of the population and lower for Latinos and whites (Morgan 2017:Table 1). African Americans are also more likely to use a weapon than are Latinos and whites (Morgan 2017:Table 7). These findings would account for some of the difference in the groups' make-up of the prison population, but far from all of it.

How does bias work in the criminal justice system? This question takes us to a morass of conflicting research results. Here is some research that shows bias. Sociologist Gary LaFree (1980) examined the court records of a Midwestern city and found that African Americans who raped white women received more severe sentences than white men who raped white women. African Americans who commit the same crimes as whites and whose background is similar receive longer sentences (USSC 2017).

Other studies show that bias works in *both* directions: Whites sometimes get more favorable treatment, but at other times minorities do. Here is some of this research. African Americans are given longer prison terms for rape and drugs, but whites receive longer sentences for murder (Butterfield 1999). Latinos and whites receive about the same sentences for assault, robbery, burglary, theft, and forgery, but when it comes to drug offenses, Latinos are more likely to be sent to prison (Klein et al. 1990). In areas where blacks are a numerical majority, whites are more likely than blacks to be sentenced to prison (Myers and Talarico 1986:246).

Then there is this amazing finding. To test bias, juvenile offenders were randomly assigned to white and to African American judges (Depew et al. 2017). African American judges gave longer sentences to African American offenders, and white judges gave longer sentences to white offenders. This in-group bias was a surprise to everyone.

We are quite sure that bias is at work, but at this point, the evidence is mixed and inconclusive. We don't know to what extent bias exists, much less the directions it takes under different circumstances. Research that cuts through this morass is yet to appear.

The Revolving Door of America's Prisons

Recidivism refers to the commission of crimes by people who have been released from prison. If the goal of prisons is to rehabilitate their guests, they are gross failures. Look at Figure 6.3, which reports a follow-up study of 405,000 people who were released from prison. Within just six months, more than a third (37 percent) were arrested. Within three years of their release from prison, two out of three prisoners had been arrested, and over half were back in prison. Within five years, 77 percent, about 312,000 people, had been arrested (Durose et al. 2014).

Figure 6.3 Recidivism: What Happens After Prison?

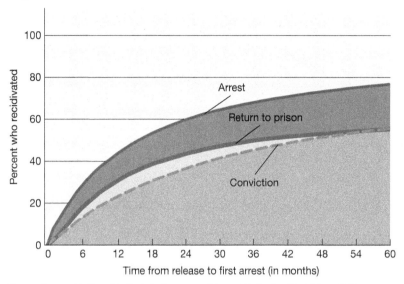

Source: Durose, Matthew R., Alexia D. Cooper, and Howard N. Snyder. "Recidivism of Prisoners Released in 30 States in 2005: Patterns from 2005 to 2010." *Special Report*, U.S. Department of Justice, April 2014.

You might be wondering about the crimes that former prisoners commit after their release from prison. These statistics, too, are enlightening—and, some would say, frightening. Table 6.4 summarizes the crimes of the 312,000 recidivists. In addition to what you

Table 6.4 Recidivism: Committing Crime After Prison

Type of Crime	Percentage of Prisoners Charged with the Crime
Violent Crimes	29%
Murder	1%
Rape/Sexual Assault	2%
Robbery	6%
Assault	23%
Other	4%
Property Crimes	38%
Burglary	10%
Larceny/Motor Vehicle Theft	21%
Fraud	12%
Other	19%
Drug Crimes	39%
Possession	27%
Trafficking	13%
Other	20%
Public Order Crimes	58%
Weapons	9%
Probation Violations	25%
Driving under the Influence	9%
Other	40%

Note: Arrests exceed 100 percent because some individuals were arrested more than once and some were charged with multiple crimes. It is the same for the subcategories, which total more than the percentage of the main categories.

Source: Durose, Matthew R., Alexia D. Cooper, and Howard N. Snyder. "Recidivism of Prisoners Released in 30 States in 2005: Patterns from 2005 to 2010." *Special Report*, U.S. Department of Justice, April 2014.

see on this table, keep in mind that few individuals are arrested the first time they commit a crime. Researchers have found that the average former prisoner commits four crimes before being arrested. In short, these individuals committed a vast number of crimes and hurt many people.

Now look at Table 6.5 to see how recidivism differs by age, sex, and race–ethnicity. Women, whites, and older former prisoners are less likely to get in trouble with the law again. Age at release is especially interesting. The older that people are when they come out of prison, the less likely they are to be rearrested and go back to prison. It might be that the older former convicts have learned to stay away from crime. Or it could be that they have learned to avoid getting caught. Or maybe they are just tired.

Table 6.5 Recidivism by Age, Sex, and Race–Ethnicity

	Length of time after release from prison		
	1 Year	**3 Years**	**5 Years**
Age			
Under 24	51%	76%	84%
25 to 39	44%	70%	78%
40 and over	37%	60%	69%
Sex			
Male	45%	69%	78%
Female	35%	59%	68%
Race–Ethnicity			
Whites	40%	64%	73%
Latinos	46%	68%	75%
African Americans	46%	72%	81%

Source: By the author. Durose, Matthew R., Alexia D. Cooper, and Howard N. Snyder. "Recidivism of Prisoners Released in 30 States in 2005: Patterns from 2005 to 2010." *Special Report*, U.S. Department of Justice, April 2014.:Tables 12, 14, 15,U.S Department of Justice.

Researchers have found that, when they are released, *those who have been in prison the most often have a higher chance of going back to prison.* Grasp the significance of this finding: If prisons were rehabilitating their inmates, the *opposite* of this would happen.

Why Do Our Prisons Fail to Rehabilitate?

There are many reasons that our prisons fail to rehabilitate, but here is one: Prisons are socializing agents for criminal behavior. People who have been declared unfit to live in normal society are housed together. Crime is one of their favorite topics of conversation. Just as most men boast of their accomplishments to one another, these men boast of theirs—the crimes they've gotten away with and the crimes they'd like to commit. Older, more experienced prisoners also teach younger ones how to commit crimes. It is an irony, of course, that the models for the younger prisoners are criminals who have failed: All these mentors have been caught and are serving time in prison.

Here is another reason for our high rate of recidivism: When prisoners are released, they go back to their old environment with no new skills to lead a straight life. Here's how sociologist Gregg Scott (2004) put it:

> *Over two million men and women are confined to jails and prisons in the U.S. Ninety percent of them eventually return home. After having served a median prison term of 15 months, approximately 1,600 inmates disgorge from state and federal prisons every single day of the week. In the greater Chicago metropolitan area alone roughly 1,500 male ex-convicts return to their neighborhoods each month. They arrive home "wearing an X" on their backs, possessing meager skills of limited portability, and enjoying scanty resources on which to draw in their efforts to "make good," or live a life on the straight and narrow path of desistance. They almost always return to the same disaffected, marginalized neighborhoods in which they resided prior to incarceration but which now offer even fewer legitimate opportunities than before. The majority will stray from the path and wander into a gnarled grove of institutional failure, criminal opportunity, and the uniquely rewarding but ultimately self-defeating whorl of drug dealing and otherwise hustling street gangs.*

The Death Penalty

If you bring up the death penalty, or **capital punishment**, in a discussion, you are sure to touch raw nerves. Like attitudes about abortion, opinions are strong. Let's get a little sociological background on the death penalty.

Race–Ethnicity   Early research into bias of the death penalty brought chilling results. As he practiced law in Virginia, Donald Partington was disturbed at what he saw in the courtrooms. Deciding to do some research, he examined all executions for rape and attempted rape in that state between 1908 and 1963 (Partington 1965). Convicted of these crimes were 2,798 men (56 percent whites and 44 percent African Americans). Forty-one of these men were executed for rape and another 13 for attempted rape. *All the executed men were African Americans. Not one white man was executed for this crime.*

When judges used to give the death penalty for rape, what really made the difference was the race of the attacker *and* the race of the victim. Sociologists even found that the best predictor of whether a man would be sentenced to death was knowing that the victim was white and the accused black (Wolfgang and Reidel 1975).

In 1972, bias in the death penalty was brought before the Supreme Court. The justices looked at data such as those in the top half of Table 6.6. You can see that at that point, 3,859 prisoners had been executed: 54 percent African American and 45 percent white. The Court ruled in *Furman v. Georgia* that capital punishment was being applied unconstitutionally—in a discriminatory fashion. In response to this decision, the states rewrote their laws, and since then 56 percent of those put to death have been white and 34 percent African American.

Throughout history, many methods of execution have been used, such as stoning, suffocating, bleeding, firing squads, gas chambers, eletrocution, and lethal injection. Shown here is the last public hanging in the United States. In this photo taken in Owensboro, Kentucky, on August 15, 1936, Rainey Bethea is ascending the steps to the gallows. The execution was a public spectacle, with thousands gathering to watch it.

Table 6.6 Prisoners Executed, by Race–Ethnicity

Year	White Number	White Percentage	African American Number	African American Percentage	Native American/Asian American Number	Native American/Asian American Percentage	Latino Number	Latino Percentage	Total
Before the death penalty was abolished									
1930–39	827	50%	816	49%	24	1%			1,667
1940–49	490	38%	781	61%	13	1%			1.284
1950–59	336	47%	376	52%	5	1%			717
1960–69	98	51%	93	49%	0	0%			191
Totals	**1,751**	**45%**	**2,066**	**54%**	**42**	**1%**			**3,859**
Since the death penalty was reinstated									
1970–79	3	100%	0	0%	0	0%	0	0%	3
1980–89	60	51%	48	41%	0	0%	9	8%	117
1990–99	271	58%	163	35%	10	0%	34	7%	478
2000–09	338	57%	200	34%	4	1%	48	8%	590
2010–17	138	51%	91	33%	10	3%	31	11%	270
Totals	**810**	**56%**	**502**	**34%**	**24**	**2%**	**122**	**8%**	**1,458**

Note: Until the 1970s, the Native American/Asian American category was "Other" and included Latinos. The source says that Latinos have been counted separately since 1977. This is most doubtful, as no Latinos are listed as executed until 1985, and until 2010 the number is disproportionate to the percentage of Latinos in the population. It is likely that until recently, most Latinos were counted as whites.

Sources: By the author. Based on *Sourcebook of Criminal Justice Statistics* 1998:Table 6.88; 2004:Table 6.86; 2012:Table 6.86; Death Penalty Information Center 2018.

Gender The death penalty seems to show a strong gender bias: Of the 5,317 prisoners who have been executed since 1930, only 45 have been women, a mere 0.9 percent. Since 1976, 1,346 men have been executed, and only 13 women (*Statistical Abstract* 2018:Table 384). At present, only 1.8 percent of prisoners on death row are women (Davis and Snell 2018). Do these totals indicate gender bias or real differences in the crimes they committed? We need more research to find out.

Geography Geography certainly makes a huge difference in a person's chances of being executed, and there is no doubt about this factor. From the Social Map, you can see that 31 states have the death penalty while 19 states do not. You can also see how much more willing some states are to execute prisoners than are others. Look at Texas. At 550, Texas holds the record for number of executions. Since executions resumed in 1977, more than one of every three (38 percent) have taken place in Texas. Texas has a large population, though—28 million people. With its much smaller population of just 4 million and its 112 executions since 1977, Oklahoma has executed a higher proportion of its criminals.

Figure 6.4 Executions in the United States, by State

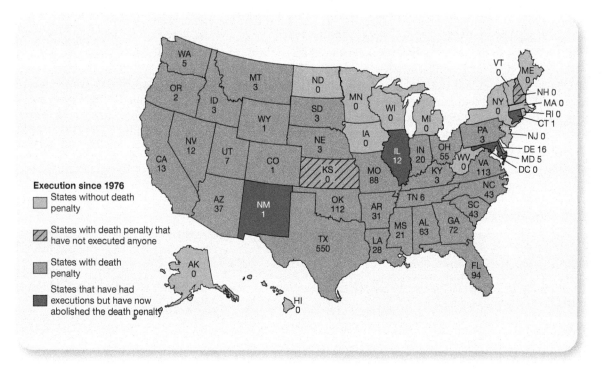

Source: By the author. Based on *Statistical Abstract of the United States* 2018:Table 385. Death Penalty Information Center 2018.

The Prison Experience: The Zimbardo Experiment

Let's close this section by looking at a fascinating experiment that can help us understand what goes on behind prison bars. Philip Zimbardo, a social psychologist, conducted an experiment that has become a classic in the social sciences. Using paid volunteers, Zimbardo (1972/2014) matched 24 college students on the basis of their education, race, and parents' social class. He randomly assigned one group as guards and the other as prisoners. Without warning, one night real police cars arrived at the homes of those who had been designated prisoners. They were "arrested," finger-printed, and taken to the basement of the psychology building at Stanford University, which had been turned into a prison. Both "guards" and "prisoners" were given appropriate uniforms.

Subject to the arbitrary control of their captors, the prisoners felt a loss of power and personal identity. The guards, in contrast, felt an increase in social power and status. They also developed strong in-group loyalty. After several days, the guards heard rumors that there was going to be a prison break. They reacted brutally, with about a third treating the prisoners as though they were subhuman. Things started to get out of hand, and after six days Zimbardo stopped the experiment.

Zimbardo's experiment illustrates fundamental sociological principles: First, our ideas about the self and other people arise from the way society is structured and the groups to which we belong. Second, from these orientations come the ways we act toward one another. How a prison is organized, then, is more important in determining how guards and prisoners act than are guards' individual personalities. As guards work in a prison, they come to see themselves as representing morality and the prisoners as enemies who need to be subdued, not people who need to be helped. The guards see their job as maintaining order and upholding authority. If this requires brutality to accomplish, so be it. Being rough is justified. As the guards perform their role within this structure, they eventually come to see prisoners as "animals" who understand nothing but violence.

Zimbardo's experiment was important. It provides insight into what is wrong with our prisons. From it, we can see why prisons, as they are set up, fail to reduce crime. This experiment, though, created a stir in the scientific community. Some fellow social scientists accused Zimbardo of being cruel and irresponsible. With the publicity surrounding this and some other experiments, the federal government developed strict guidelines for research on human subjects. Today, Zimbardo's research couldn't be done, at least in the way he did it.

Shaming: An Alternative to Prison?

If prisons are not the answer, then what is? For an interesting alternative, read the following *Thinking Critically about Social Problems*.

Thinking Critically about Social Problems

Public Shaming as Social Policy

"Shame on you!"

Do you remember those horrifying words from your childhood? If your childhood was like mine, you do. The words were accompanied by an index finger that pointed directly at me, while another index finger, rubbing on top of it, seemed to send shame in my direction.

With a harsh voice or one that showed disappointment, this gesture was effective. I always felt bad when this happened. It bothered me, too, to see the looks of disappointment or disgust on the faces of my parents or grandparents in response to my

Ullstein Bild/The Image Works

Shaming is an old method of punishment, intended to humiliate violators so they conform. This 1910 photo is from China.

childish offense, whatever it may have been.

If you have read Nathaniel Hawthorne's *The Scarlet Letter*, you know about shaming. Hester Prynne, who committed adultery, a serious offense at the time because it struck at the community's moral roots, had to wear a red "A" on her clothing. For life, wherever she went, she was marked as a shameful adulteress.

This old-fashioned device is coming back. Not the scarlet "A," but its equivalent:

An Arizona sheriff makes inmates work in chain gangs, with the men dressed in pink.

A judge ordered thieves to wear sandwich boards that said, "I stole from this store." They had to parade back and forth outside the stores they stole from.

A Texas judge ordered a piano teacher who pled guilty to molesting his young students to give away his prized $12,000 piano and to not play the piano for 20 years. If you don't think this was harsh, consider the shaming that accompanied this punishment: He had to post a sign prominently on the door of his home declaring himself a child molester.

Judges have ordered drunk drivers to put bright orange bumper stickers on their cars that say, "I am a convicted drunk driver. Report any erratic driving to the police."

The Minneapolis police department has organized "shaming details." Prostitutes and their johns must stand handcuffed in front of citizens who let loose with "verbal stones," shouting things like "You're the reason our children aren't safe in this neighborhood!"

Kansas City tried a different approach to prostitution. "John TV" shows the mug shots of men who have been arrested for trying to buy sex and of the women who have been arrested for selling it. Their names, birth dates, and hometowns are displayed prominently.

Do you want to know where convicted sex offenders live? Just go online. Type sex offender and a ZIP code into your search engine, and with a couple more clicks they'll pop up on your computer screen. You can see their photos, names, addresses, dates of birth, a description of the offense, convictions, and their current address. Some sites have clickable neighborhood maps on which the offenders' homes pop up. While this information is supposed to be intended to alert citizens to potential danger, it certainly is a powerful shaming device.

Does shaming work? No one knows whether it reduces lawbreaking. But shaming certainly can be powerful. A woman who was convicted of welfare fraud was given the choice of going to jail or wearing a sign in public that said, "I stole food from poor people." She chose jail.

Even if shaming doesn't work, it does satisfy a strong urge to punish, to get even, what sociologists call retribution. In today's eager-to-punish climate, perhaps retribution is purpose enough. And perhaps it does help to restore a moral balance.

Based on Gerlin 1994; Belluck 1998b; Billeaud 2008; Earl 2017.

For Your Consideration

→ If you were convicted of shoplifting, would you choose to go to jail for three days or to spend three Saturdays from 9 A.M. to 9 P.M. walking back and forth in front of the store you stole from while holding a large sign that says, "I am a thief. I stole from this store"? Why?

→ For what offenses do you think shaming would be effective?

→ Do you think judges should use more shaming techniques and less jail time? Why or why not?

Social Policy

6.11 Discuss retribution, deterrence, rehabilitation, and incapacitation as goals of social policy.

We can never eliminate these twin social problems of crime and criminal justice, but we can build a more just society. Here are two basic principles to help us do so. For *criminal justice, laws fairly administered:* The enforcement of laws should be evenhanded throughout society, regardless of people's race–ethnicity, gender, social class, or any other characteristic. For *crime, reducing poverty:* Because street crime bothers Americans the most, and street crime is linked to poverty, the *best policy* would be to reduce poverty. Education is an effective way to reduce poverty because, on average, the further that people go in school, the better the jobs they get and the more they earn. In addition, because those who drop out of high school are more likely to end up in prison, programs that help students graduate from high school help prevent crime, reducing its cost to victims and to society in general.

We will, of course, always have criminals, so we need effective policies for dealing with them. Let's consider the four basic approaches: retribution, deterrence, rehabilitation, and incapacitation.

Retribution: Paying for the Crime

The basic idea of retribution is to *punish* criminals to demonstrate to others that criminal behavior will not be tolerated. Offenders are thought of as needing to "pay for the crime" or "make up" for what they've done. The punishment, then, should fit the crime. The *public shaming* that you just read about is an example of retribution. In the photo in that section, you could see the humiliation the Chinese women were going through.

Besides direct punishment, another form of retribution is **restitution**, making offenders compensate their victims for the harm they have done. If people have stolen, for example, they are required to pay the money back. Restitution is practical for property crimes, when the offender can repay the victim. It is less practical for offenders who don't have jobs, although some judges require the unemployed to "work their debt off" in a variety of creative ways. Here are examples of trying to "make the punishment fit the crime":

> *A Memphis judge invited victims to visit the thief's house and "steal" something back (Stevens 1992).*

> *A Florida judge sentenced a white man who had harassed an interracial couple to work weekends at an African American church.*

> *A Texas judge ordered a deadbeat who had fathered 13 children to attend Planned Parenthood meetings (Gerlin 1994).*

> *For throwing beer bottles at a car and taunting a woman, a judge in Ohio sentenced two men to walk down the town's main street dressed in women's clothing (Leinwand 2004).*

For crimes of violence, retribution might call for unusual measures, such as castration of rapists—acts that courts would declare unconstitutional. A California judge, for example, wanted to withhold AIDS treatment from a man who had raped two teenagers after he was released from prison for a previous rape (Farah 1995). He was not allowed to do so. Those who agree with the judge's view that those who commit severe crimes deserve severe retribution say that if it is necessary, we should change the Constitution.

Deterrence: Frightening People Away from Crime

The purpose of **deterrence** is to make people afraid of being punished so they won't commit crime. This approach views offenders as rational people who weigh the possible consequences of their actions. They will avoid crime if punishment seems likely. Only a few sociologists have taken this "get tough" position. Back in the 1970s, criminologist Ernest van den Haag (1975; van den Haag and Conrad 1983) proposed that we treat juveniles who commit violent crimes the same way we treat adults ("adult crime, adult time"). He also said that we should abolish parole boards and put prisoners to work. With citizens demanding strong action, attempts at deterrence are popular.

Two Principles of Deterrence   Researchers have discovered two significant principles regarding deterrence. First, the longer the time between a crime and its punishment, the less the deterrence, or fear of the punishment. This underscores the need for speedy trials, already guaranteed by the Constitution, and for swift punishment of the guilty. Second, the more uncertain the penalty, the less deterrence works. To meet this principle, some propose **uniform sentencing**, the same sentence given to everyone convicted of the same crime. The problem, of course, is that crimes are seldom "the same." Each crime involves many circumstances that judges and juries need to consider.

Irrationality: Impulse and Taking Chances   Critics of deterrence point out that offenders are not always rational about committing crime. Many act on impulse. Others take such chances that you know they are not weighing the consequences of their actions in the same way most of us would. For example, back in the 1700s in England, pickpockets were hung in public. One might think that this punishment would stop this crime. Instead, when a pickpocket was being hung, other pickpockets worked the crowd. With the crowd's attention riveted on the gallows, the hanging provided easier victims (Hibbert 1963).

"Scared Straight": A Program That Backfired   The mass media once trumpeted a program of deterrence called "Scared Straight." Delinquents were given prison tours,

When inmates like this man told teenaged boys what they can expect if they go to prison, the results were the opposite of what was expected.

with the expectation that a close-up view of prison would "scare them straight." Leering and shouting obscenities, the inmates said they could hardly wait for the youths to be sent to prison so they could rape them. Those who operated the program reported that it kept 80 percent to 90 percent of the youths from further trouble with the law.

Follow-up studies by sociologists, however, showed that the program had actually done the opposite of what it was intended to do. Criminologist James Finckenauer (1982) matched delinquents on the basis of their sex, race–ethnicity, age, and criminal acts. He then compared those who had been exposed to "Scared Straight" (the experimental group) with delinquents who had not been exposed to it (the control group). Within six months, 41 percent of the experimental group were in trouble with the law while only 11 percent of the control group were in trouble. Further research confirms that "Scared Straight" programs increase delinquency (Petrosino 2014).

"Scared Straight" seems like it would work. How could it backfire? Finckenauer suggests that boys were impressed by the macho performance of hypermasculine, in-charge men. (Let your imagination go a little here: You've probably seen photos or TV programs that show the tattoos and muscles and threatening posture that many male convicts display.) The boys want to be powerful men, and this is how they perceived the convicts. Committing a crime after going through the program was one way they could show their peers that the talk hadn't frightened them, that they, too, were macho and couldn't be scared.

The Need for Research The failure of "Scared Straight" does not mean that programs of deterrence cannot work. It does, however, underline the need for sociological research to find out what does and does not work. We cannot *assume* that a program is successful just because it sounds good, because it appeals to our common sense, or because its operators say that it works. If we are to develop sound social policy, we need solid research to evaluate programs.

Rehabilitation: Resocializing Offenders

The goal of **rehabilitation** is to resocialize offenders, to help them stop committing crimes and become conforming citizens (Lippke 2018). Rehabilitation programs include teaching high school and college courses in prison, probation, parole, and halfway houses.

The transition from prison to freedom requires numerous adjustments in attitudes and behavior. This woman is reading a self-help book on her first day in a halfway house.

Another form of rehabilitation is **diversion**, diverting offenders *away from* the criminal justice system. Instead of having criminal trials, those accused of minor offenses are dealt with by community organizations or administrative hearings or are sent to drug counseling. Diversion has two goals: to avoid stigmatizing offenders and to keep them out of jails and prisons, the crime schools that socialize their guests into committing more crime.

The public is fed up with failed attempts at rehabilitation (Farmer 2014). Probation is scorned as an opportunity for felons to commit more crime. As you saw in Figure 6.3 and Table 6.4, this perception is accurate. However, the concept of probation is not unsound, although its implementation is. To improve its success, probation can be limited to convicts with the most promise. They need to receive follow-up counseling from trained probation officers who have small caseloads. This is expensive, however, and the public is also fed up with spending money on criminals.

If rehabilitation programs were successful, almost everyone would favor them. The cost of successful rehabilitation is much less than the price of crime—the cost to victims and the cost of maintaining people in prisons. We need solid research to evaluate programs of rehabilitation, to determine which programs work and the conditions that make them successful.

Incapacitation: Removing Offenders from Society

With the perception that "nothing works," the public clamors for **incapacitation**, getting offenders off the streets. This view is direct and to the point: Everything else has failed. We can't change people who don't want to change. Get them off the streets so they can't hurt people. Some offenders are "career criminals," committing crime after crime year after year, so let's free ourselves of these people.

The usual form of incapacitation is putting people in jail and prison, but new technology has brought new forms of incapacitation, such as electronic monitoring, the ankle monitor that allows officials to keep track of where an offender is at all times. The individual's approved schedule of "when and where" is programmed into a central computer. If the individual deviates from the schedule, a computer notifies the police to make an arrest. In the future, it is possible that a device will be inserted into an offender's brain that will send pain if the individual deviates from scheduled activities. As technology develops, there might even be implants that direct an individual's movements.

Controversy and Debate   As you probably have been thinking, the capacity to monitor—and perhaps to control—people leads to several issues. It would be unconstitutional for courts to order anyone to have implants inserted in their bodies, so it is likely that the courts will be limited to enforcing wearable monitoring devices. How about abuse by authorities? Could ordering monitoring devices on felons be a step toward monitoring all citizens? With the ongoing erosion of our civil rights in the name of protecting us from terrorism, along with the desire of authorities to expand their power, this is not an unrealistic question.

Incapacitation has aroused debate among the public and among sociologists. Most sociologists argue for better programs of rehabilitation, but the response of those proposing incapacitation is simple: Incapacitation works. As evidence, they point to our safer streets and neighborhoods, arguing that the crime rate dropped as we put more offenders in prison. Those who propose rehabilitation argue that the drop in crime also came from other factors: more police, less use of heroin and crack, less teenage pregnancy, the greying of America (fewer young offenders), and even abortion and less lead poisoning. Neither side convinces the other, and we can expect this discussion to continue for many years.

Let's turn to the most extreme form of incapacitation.

Extreme Incapacitation: Capital Punishment   Proponents of the death penalty argue that it incapacitates totally: The dead don't commit more crimes. They also argue that death is an appropriate punishment for heinous crimes. Opponents reply just as passionately that killing is never justified. They add that capital punishment does not deter others from killing. If capital punishment did deter criminals, then states with the death penalty should have a lower homicide rate than those without it. But they don't. In fact, it is just the opposite. On average, the murder rates of states with the death penalty are *higher* than those of states without the death penalty (Cochran et al. 2016). This doesn't faze those favoring the death penalty. They reply that this just goes to show that the states that have the death penalty really need it.

Opponents also argue that the death penalty is capricious—jurors deliberate in secret and indulge their prejudices as they recommend death (Becket and Evans 2014). They add that judges are irrational—giving mercy to some but not to others. Proponents reply that in their opinion judges and juries are doing a good job under difficult circumstances. Opponents stress that innocent people have been executed: They point to the men released from death row because of DNA testing. Proponents reply that they are happy we have DNA testing, that now we can be even more certain of the guilt of the killers we execute. Each side stands firm, neither convincing the other.

Electronic bracelets have become popular around the world to monitor those accused of crimes without having to keep them in jail. This photo was taken in Russia.

RIA-Novosti/The Image Works

Figure 6.5 Comparing Men's and Women's Attitudes on the Death Penalty

A nationally representative sample of Americans was asked: "Are you in favor of the death penalty for a person convicted of murder?"

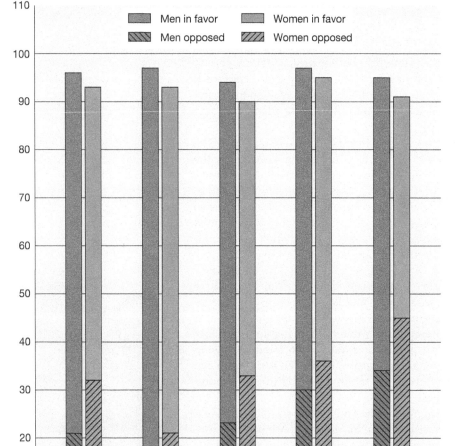

Year

¹1995 was not reported, so the average of 1994 and 1996 was used
Source: By the author. Based on *Sourcebook of Criminal Justice Statistics* 1994:Table 2.58; 2003:Table 2.50; 2005:Table 2.52; 2010:Table 2.52; 2012:Table 2.52; Gallup Poll 2013; "Less Support…" 2015; Pew Research Center 2016, 2018.

As you can see from Figure 6.5, most Americans favor the death penalty, with men consistently favoring it more than women do.

From Figures 6.6 and 6.7, you can see how the times have changed. As the states have grown more reluctant to execute prisoners, the number of executions has dropped. The courts, though, continue to sentence offenders to death.

Goals and Principles of Sound Social Policy

The United States has tried a variety of approaches to solve its crime problem. A basic problem with our attempts is that we have no agreement on what we are trying to accomplish. Is it prevention? Retribution? Deterrence? Rehabilitation? Incapacitation? Our solutions are inconsistent and in tatters.

If we are going to reform our criminal justice system, we need to have clear goals and principles. I suggest the following:

1. Laws based on the broadest possible consensus, rather than on the interests or moral concerns of small groups.
2. Swift justice based on evidence presented in adversarial proceedings. This would eliminate plea bargaining and guarantee a speedy trial for all who plead not guilty. It also would require more courts, more judges, and longer working hours for judges.
3. More rehabilitation programs, including diversion for most first offenders who did not commit violent crimes. The goal would be to integrate first-time, low-level offenders into the community.
4. Removing the constraints of uniform sentencing and allowing judges to determine sentences based on a crime's severity and harm to others.
5. Task forces to investigate organized crime and white-collar crime. These groups must have the power to subpoena. For a specified time, such as five years after they leave a task force, members should not be able to accept employment from the corporations they have investigated.
6. Prison reform, including making the position of prison warden a civil service job, training prison guards rigorously and paying them well, giving prisoners the right to continue their education, allowing prisoners to have conjugal visits, and giving *to the nonviolent* the right to visit friends and family on the outside.

Figure 6.6 Executions in the United States

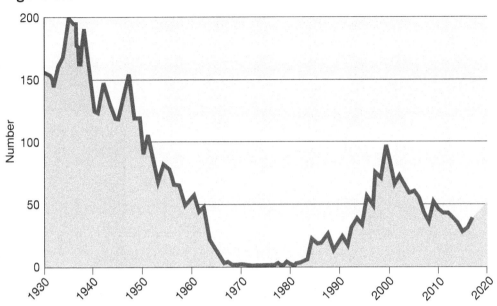

Source: By the author. Based on various editions of Sourcebook of Criminal Justice Statistics, including 1998:Table 6.88; 2012:Table 6.85; "Facts about the Death Penalty" 2018.

Figure 6.7 Persons under Sentence of Death

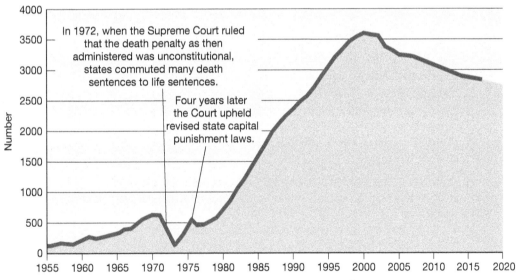

Source: By the author. Based on Greenfield 1991; Snell 2014; Death Penalty Information Center 2018.

7. Unbiased research to determine what prevents crime and changes lawbreakers. In the ideal case, we would compare experimental and control groups. We certainly have the capacity to make such determinations, but we need government officials to approve and fund the research.

In the following *Spotlight on Social Research,* sociologist William Chambliss makes suggestions for reforming the criminal justice system that you might want to consider.

Spotlight on Social Research

Doing Research on Criminals

Courtesy of William Chambliss

WILLIAM CHAMBLISS (1933–2014) *was professor of sociology at George Washington University in Washington, D.C. He became interested in criminology during his junior year in high school. That summer, he and a friend hitchhiked from Los Angeles to Walla Walla, Washington, where they worked with convicts picking peas. As Chambliss got to know the men, he was fascinated to discover what the bank robbers, drug dealers, burglars, and thieves were planning to do when they were released from prison—commit more crimes. Here is what he wrote for you.*

After my experiences that summer, I knew that I wanted to be a criminologist. When I went to UCLA, I was exposed to sociology and criminology. There, I developed a passion for both that has never waned.

After college, I was drafted into the Army and sent to Korea, where I spent 18 months as a special agent with the Counterintelligence Corps. I was exposed to an immense amount of crime. But it was the crimes of the state and of the U.S. military that most interested me. They were the most egregious, not the crimes of the petty thieves and burglars or even what today we would call "terrorists." Between the pea fields of Walla Walla and the rice paddies of South Korea, I came to ponder what a short step it is from legitimacy to crime, from interrogation to torture, and from fighting soldiers to shooting and raping civilians.

Over the years, I have done research on organized crime, economic crime, juvenile gangs, and the creation of laws in the United States. I have also studied crime in England, Sweden, Norway, Nigeria, Zambia, and Thailand. Everywhere I have gone, from the slums and drizzling rain of Seattle to the steamy heat of Nigeria, I found the same story: Some of the worst offenders are the least likely to experience the sting of the criminal justice system, while the less powerful fill the courtrooms and the prisons. This bothers me. It just isn't justice.

In one of my books, *Power, Politics and Crime* (2001), I suggest these social policies:

1. Mandatory minimum sentences should be abolished (including three-strikes laws), and, in general, the trend toward more severe punishments should be reversed.
2. Crime statistics should be gathered by agencies that are independent of law enforcement agencies.
3. Law enforcement agencies should be put under civilian control.
4. The prosecuting attorney's office should be depoliticized (removed from political influence or control).
5. Drugs should be decriminalized. The primary reason for this is that the enforcement of drug laws results in systemic bias against the poor and ethnic minorities.

My journey of discovery in criminology has exposed many shortcomings in the world we live in. It has also given me an opportunity to meet and work with wonderful people, some labeled criminals, others labeled heroes. Although I sometimes wish that "I didn't know now what I didn't know then," more often I am eternally grateful for the opportunity to explore the world of crime and crime control and to do what I can to help make it more equitable—which is its supposed purpose.

The Future of the Problem

6.12 Explain the likely future of crime and criminal justice.

Will crime increase or decrease? As you saw in Chapter 5 (Figure 5.2), the rates of violent crime have been dropping for 20 years. If the reason for this decrease is because lawmakers and judges have put huge numbers of people behind bars, then if the incarceration rate remains high, crime should continue to drop. As indicated, the experts disagree on why crime has declined. Each suggested cause lands in a pile of ideology, where people pounce on evidence that favors their views and ignore evidence that doesn't match what they think reality is. It is disturbing so see such bias among professionals who are supposed to dispassionately follow the evidence, but so it is. Perhaps there will be less ideology in the future, but this is not likely.

Changes in Crime

If more women continue to take paid jobs, then crimes by women will continue to increase. Jobs outside the home expose women to more opportunities for crime, and like men, they are attracted to illegitimate opportunities.

We won't be able to tell whether white-collar crime increases or decreases. With so much white-collar crime going undiscovered and handled informally, we simply have no baseline from which to draw accurate comparisons. If more white-collar crime is handled by the judicial system, it will *appear* to increase, but official statistics could jump, and we still would not know whether this was a real increase.

Organized crime will continue, taking different forms as social conditions change. The old standbys of gambling, loan-sharking, and prostitution will remain standard activities, but we can expect greater involvement in computer crimes such as identity theft. If anti-crime efforts directed against one part of organized crime, such as the Sicilian American Mafia, succeed, that group, much to its distaste, will turn increasingly to legitimate businesses. The Mafia will remain criminal, however, as crime is the heart of its existence.

The Criminal Justice System

The ruling class of each society controls its judicial system. With this control essential to maintain privilege and power, there is no reason to think that this will change. Firmly entrenched in power, the U.S. ruling elite will continue to make certain that the criminal justice system focuses on street crime and mostly overlooks the crimes of the powerful.

The Need for Fundamental Change

We know that locking the poor up is a poor solution to crime. If we ever get serious about preventing the poor from being recruited to street crime, we must open the doors to legitimate ways of achieving success. The poor will need access to quality education and training for good jobs. If the private sector doesn't create enough jobs for everyone who wants to work, then the government needs to create them. These jobs must pay a living wage. Because people who have high investment in the social system commit fewer street crimes, education and good-paying jobs are fundamental to preventing this type of crime.

I don't like ending this chapter on a pessimistic note, but to increase equality and opportunity entails radical change in the social system. I anticipate that the financial costs to provide quality education and job training and creation will be resisted bitterly, making it unlikely that this fundamental need will be met.

Summary and Review

1. Whether an act is a *crime* depends on the law, which, in turn, depends on *power* relationships in society.
2. Crime is universal because all societies make rules against acts they consider undesirable. Because laws differ, crime differs from one society to another and in the same society over time.
3. The social problem of crime has two parts: the crimes committed and the criminal justice system. *Crime* is a problem because people are upset about the threat to their lives, property, and well-being. *The criminal justice system* is a problem because people are upset about its failures and want something done about it.
4. Chambliss' study of the "saints" and the "rough-necks" illustrates how social class affects the perception and reactions of authorities, as well as how crime statistics are distorted.
5. Functionalists note that property crimes represent conformity to the goal of success but rejection of the approved means of achieving success. Just as some people have more access to legitimate opportunities, others have more access to *illegitimate opportunities.*
6. Conflict theorists regard the criminal justice system as a tool that the ruling class uses to mask injustice, control workers, and stabilize the social system to keep themselves in power.
7. *Juvenile delinquents* deflect society's norms by using these *neutralization techniques:* denial of responsibility, denial of injury, denial of a victim, condemning the condemners, and an appeal to higher loyalty.
8. *White-collar crime* is extensive but underreported.
9. *Professional criminals* are people who make their living from crime. They scorn the "straight" world, have high in-group loyalty, and take pride in their specialized skills.
10. *Organized crime* is best represented by the Mafia, whose use of intimidation and violence within a highly developed bureaucracy made it quite successful. With infiltration by police agents and the breakdown of *omertá,* the Mafia is a shell of its former self.
11. The criminal justice system fails to deliver justice because of plea bargaining, a team-player system that subverts public defense attorneys, biases, and prisons that foster hostility and hatred.
12. Because our criminal justice system has no unifying philosophy, our policies of social control are in disarray.
13. To get at the root of the problem of crime and criminal justice requires reform of the criminal justice system and a basic overhaul of our social institutions, especially changes that open more opportunities to the poor.

Thinking Critically about Chapter 6

1. Which of the three theoretical perspectives (symbolic interactionism, functionalism, or conflict theory) do you think does the best job of explaining the causes of crime? Why?
2. Which of the three theoretical perspectives do you think does the best job of explaining why white-collar and street criminals are treated differently? Is your answer to this question different from your answer to Question 1? Explain.
3. Do you think that violent and nonviolent criminals should be punished differently? Why or why not? Consider the case of the criminally negligent manufacturer whose product kills people but who has no contact with the victims versus the street criminal who kills someone during a robbery.
4. Which of the four basic approaches to treating criminals (retribution, deterrence, rehabilitation, and incapacitation) do you think is the most appropriate? Why?

Key Terms

capital punishment, 165
Cosa Nostra, 158
crime, 143
crime rate, 144
criminal justice system, 144
criminogenic subculture, 154
delinquent subcultures, 152
deterrence, 169
diversion, 170
illegitimate opportunity structures, 148
incapacitation, 171
juvenile delinquency, 151
Mafia, 158

organized crime, 158
police discretion, 146
Ponzi scheme, 148
power, 144
professional criminals, 157
recidivism, 163
rehabilitation, 170
restitution, 169
status crimes, 151
techniques of neutralization, 152
uniform sentencing, 169
white-collar crime, 154

Chapter 7
Economic Problems: Poverty and Wealth

Spencer Platt/Staff/Getty Images News/Getty Images

 Learning Objectives

After reading this chapter, you should be able to:

7.1 Summarize the major economic problems facing the United States, the three types of poverty, and the problems with the poverty line.

7.2 Explain how subjective concerns have changed the social problem of poverty over time, structural inequality, the basic distribution of income and wealth in the United States, and the impact of poverty.

7.3 Summarize the different pictures that emerge when you apply symbolic

interactionism, functionalism, and conflict theory to the social problem of poverty.

7.4 Summarize research findings on who the poor are, a culture of poverty, who rules the United States, and explanations of global poverty.

7.5 Explain how shifting views have influenced social policy, what progressive taxation is, and what social programs to relieve poverty are being implemented or considered.

7.6 Contrast the unlikely and likely futures of the social problem of poverty.

At age 17, Julie Treadman was facing more than her share of problems. Her boyfriend had deserted her when she told him that she was pregnant. Exhausted and depressed, Julie dropped out of high school. At five months pregnant, she wondered about her child's future.

When Julie had severe stomach pains, a neighbor called an ambulance, and she was rushed to Lutheran Hospital. When hospital administrators discovered that neither Julie nor her mother had insurance, money, or credit, they refused to admit her. Before they could transfer her to a public hospital, however, Julie gave birth to a stillborn baby.

> **Julie gave birth to a stillborn baby.**

This situation perplexed hospital administrators who didn't want to serve those who couldn't pay. They ordered the ambulance driver to take Julie—dead baby, umbilical cord, and all—to the public hospital.

—Based on an event in St. Louis, Missouri

The Problem in Sociological Perspective

7.1 **Summarize the major economic problems facing the United States, the three types of poverty, and the problems with the poverty line.**

Why was Julie Treadman treated so horribly? This question takes us to **social inequality**, a society's unequal distribution of wealth, income, power, and opportunity. All societies have social inequality, but the inequality of some societies is much greater than others. Like many societies, the United States has depths of poverty and heights of wealth. These divisions are called **social classes,** large groups of people who not only have similar income, but also similar education and job prestige. Picture the social classes like a ladder, going from the bottom rung, the least educated and very poor, to the top rung, the more educated and very wealthy. On each rung of the ladder are clustered people who have similar income and education, and whose jobs bring similar prestige.

It certainly is much more pleasant to discuss wealth, opportunity, and success than what happened to Julie Treadman, who was denied not only medical treatment but also human dignity. Because this book is about social problems, however, our focus in this chapter is on the negative aspects of social inequality. This chapter should give you greater understanding of this broader context that has such significant influence on your life, both now and in your future.

Economic Problems Facing the United States

How well will you do after college? Because your welfare is tied up with the U.S. economy, let's begin by looking at three economic problems facing the United States.

Booms and Busts The **economy** is the social institution that produces and distributes goods and services. At any given time, the U.S. economy—and increasingly, the global economy as well—is moving through a "boom–bust" cycle. During a "boom," there are plenty of jobs, making the future look bright and rosy. During a "bust," the jobs dry up, and the future seems dark and gloomy. If you are lucky enough to graduate from college during a "boom," you will have your choice of jobs. But if you graduate during a "bust," even though you have worked just as hard as the earlier students and earned the same degree, you will end up struggling to find work—if there is any work to find.

Very Slow Raises Another problem is that people's **real income** (income adjusted for inflation) is much less than the dollars in their paychecks. From Figure 7.1, you can see that workers' paychecks today are *seven* times higher than they were in 1970. This is quite impressive. But look at the constant dollars, those adjusted for inflation, and you will see that it took about *50 years* for workers to get a real raise of about $1.24 an hour.

Figure 7.1 Average Hourly Earnings, in Current and Constant Dollars

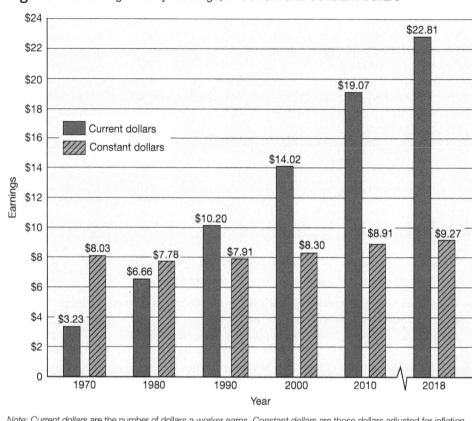

Note: Current dollars are the number of dollars a worker earns. *Constant dollars* are those dollars adjusted for inflation, with 1982–1984 as the base.

Sources: By the author. Based on *Statistical Abstract of the United States* 1992:Table 650; 1999:Table 698; 2018:Table 665; BLS 2018.

What has softened the blow for the average family is that more married women have paid jobs. In 1970, 41 percent of married women worked for wages, either full- or part-time. Today, 58 percent of married women do (*Statistical Abstract* 2018:Table 620). Families in which both husband and wife have paid jobs earn an average of 85 percent more than families in which only the husband works for a paycheck (*Statistical Abstract* 2018:Table 721).

A Debtor Nation The United States used to have a huge trade surplus, selling more goods to other nations than it bought from them. The change is so extreme that we are now the largest debtor nation in the world. We buy goods from other nations at such a frenzied pace that when you calculate what we pay for these items, minus our income from the products we sell, we end up over $700 billion short at the end of each year (*Statistical Abstract* 2018:Table 1322). We also spend vastly more on government services than we collect in taxes. Year after year, these deficits pile up, increasing our **national debt** (the total amount the U.S. government owes). To finance the national debt, which totals about $20 trillion, we pay about $475 billion a year in interest (*Statistical Abstract* 2018:Tables 497, 500). When interest rates rise, so will this national bill. Money paid for interest is money that we cannot use to build schools and colleges, hire teachers, pay for medical services or job programs for the poor, operate Head Start, or pay for any other services to help improve our quality of life.

Before closing this section, let's get an overview of one more economic problem—poverty—perhaps the most visible and bothersome of all.

What Is Poverty?

You might think that poverty would be easy to define, but its definition is neither simple nor obvious. There isn't just one kind of poverty. There are at least three types. Let's contrast the three and then consider something called the poverty line.

Andrew Toth/Stringer/ Getty Images Entertainment/Getty Images

Henslin, James M.

What a world of difference for the rich and the poor around the globe: current life circumstances, hopes for the future, and life orientations. The one is hoping for a new diamond, the other for food. The debutante on the left lives in the United States. The woman I photographed as she was searching the town garbage for salvagable discards lives in India.

Types of Poverty   The extreme form is **biological poverty**—poverty so severe that it deforms or kills people through malnutrition or starvation. Biological poverty also refers to housing and clothing so inadequate that people suffer from exposure. Our homeless endure biological poverty. So, does the young woman on the right in the photo shown here.

More common is **relative poverty**. This term refers to comparing people's standards of living and seeing that some people are worse or better off than others. A lot of relative poverty is not serious. Some people "feel poor" because they don't have a car as nice as the cars their neighbors have. You've probably experienced relative poverty yourself. Maybe you "felt poorer" when you noticed that some classmates were wearing nicer clothing or had more up-to-date, powerful laptops than you did. Or maybe some are able to go on spring break to Mexico or Bermuda, and you can't. Relative poverty also exists on a global level: What is poverty in the United States would mean very comfortable living in India, where the cost of living is low, but where most families have little clothing, little food, and live in just a room or two.

There is also **official poverty**. This is a specified income level that separates the "poor" from the "not poor." People below this **poverty line** are defined as "poor"; those above this line, even by a dollar, are "not poor." The poverty line is arbitrary. It was established in 1962 by the Social Security Administration. At that time, the poor spent about one-third of their income on food, and the poverty line was set by multiplying a low-level food budget by three. U.S. agencies adjust this rough figure annually to match the Consumer Price Index, the official gauge of inflation.

Using this rock-bottom definition, let's look at "official poverty" in the United States.

The Scope of the Problem

7.2 Explain how subjective concerns have changed the social problem of poverty over time, structural inequality, the basic distribution of income and wealth in the United States, and the impact of poverty.

I want to stress again a significant point that runs throughout this text: By themselves, objective conditions are not enough to make a social problem. Subjective concerns are also essential. When it comes to poverty, subjective concerns can be more important than objective conditions.

Subjective Concerns and Objective Conditions

How can subjective concerns be more important than objective conditions? Consider the extremes: Poverty (the objective condition) can be extensive, but if few people are bothered by it (the subjective concern), then poverty is *not* a social problem. By contrast, if poverty is rare, but people are concerned about the few cases and they want something done about it, then poverty *is* a social problem. Let's look at how these extremes have occurred in the United States.

Changing Subjective Concerns and Objective Conditions   During the early years of the United States, *most* people were poor. Yet as extensive as poverty was at this time, poverty was *not* considered a social problem. Life had always been a struggle for almost everyone in the world, so *poverty was assumed to be a natural part of life.* Then in the 19th century, industrialization progressed, producing an abundance of jobs and wealth and reducing poverty. But at this time, masses of poor people were streaming from the farms and other countries into U.S. cities. Even though the standard of living had increased, this migration made poverty more visible. Leaders began to declare that poverty was a social problem. Then, as immigrants were absorbed into the expanding workforce, poverty once again receded from sight.

When the Great Depression of the 1930s arrived, poverty again became a pressing public concern. As factories and offices around the country closed down, millions of Americans who had been in the middle class found themselves begging for food at what they called "soup kitchens." Protests erupted across the nation, and labor organizers led strikes. Concerned and fearful, politicians declared poverty to be the greatest problem facing the nation. They rushed through legislation that established emergency programs and created millions of jobs. Then came World War II. Workers were needed to run the factories that produced armaments and other war goods. Millions of others were sent overseas to fight. After the war, prosperity increased, and poverty receded from sight. Even though the objective condition—millions of people in poverty—remained, subjective concerns eased. The poor, tucked in out-of-the-way rural areas and in urban slums, once again dropped from sight.

Then in the 1960s, poverty again came to the nation's attention when John F. Kennedy made it a campaign issue in 1960, and two years later Michael Harrington published *The Other America.* The media publicized this book, policy makers read it, and sociologists assigned it to their students. This book set the stage for President Johnson to declare a "war on poverty," and Congress funded programs for the poor: child care, Head Start, legal services, medical services, job training, subsidized housing, and community health centers. To see the dramatic results, look at Figure 7.2. In about 10 years, the percentage of Americans below the official poverty line was cut almost in half. This quick, sharp reduction made it clear that poverty can be solved. We simply need effective social policies.

The Situation Today   As you can see from Figure 7.2, after the war on poverty's initial success, the war stalled. Despite the billions of dollars spent on anti-poverty programs, *during the past 50 years, we have made no progress in reducing the poverty rate.* Frustrating policy makers even further is this objective condition: With today's much larger population, many more Americans are poor now than before the war on poverty began.

And today's subjective concerns? When people manage to break through their enamored following of hot celebrities and sizzling fashions, or the latest gossip about politicians, what captures their attention is not poverty, but crime—and, for a few, global

Figure 7.2 Americans below the Poverty Line

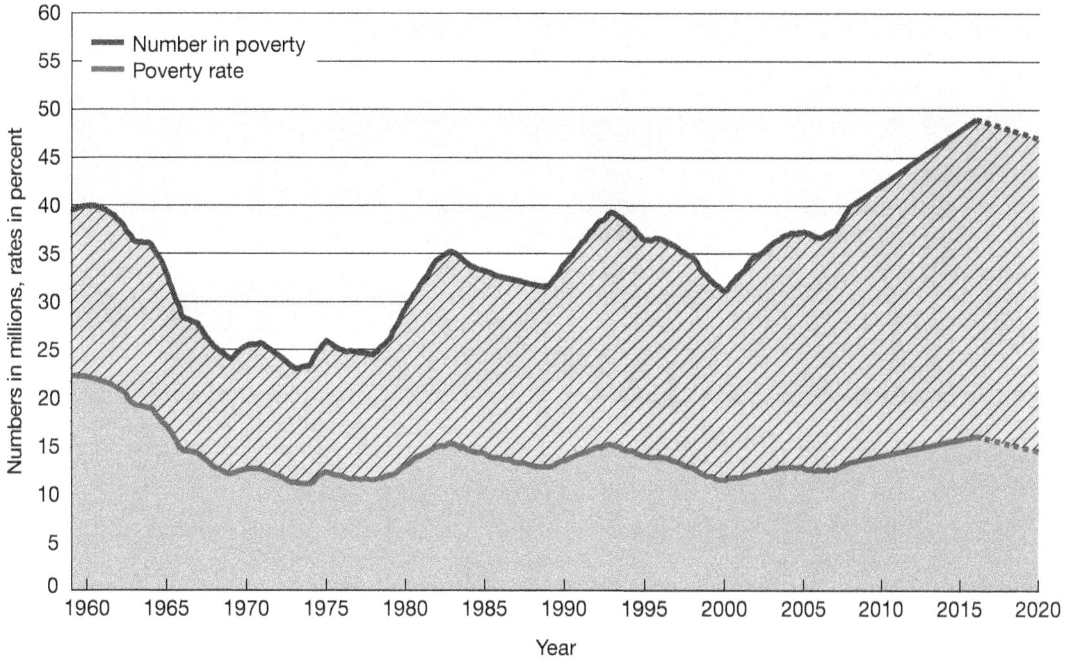

Note: Projections by the author.

Source: By the author. Based on *U.S. Census Bureau 2011*; ACS 2017b; *Statistical Abstract of the United States* 2018:Table 733.

economic threats. It is as though people are walking in a dream-like state—brought about, I would add, by the mesmerizing effects of television and the Internet, which numb consciousness about social issues. Certainly, subjective concerns about poverty are not today's issue. The homeless have not disappeared, but they seem to have become another urban fixture, although an unwelcome one. The media occasionally highlight the plight of workers in some industry, but for the most part poverty has been relegated to a back burner. Tales of woe, though, if well told and accompanied by photos of suffering children, still sell newspapers during Thanksgiving and Christmas.

The Poverty Line: Problems and Significance

Although the poverty line is the nation's official measure of poverty and is highly significant in many people's lives, it is plagued with problems. Critics say that the poverty line is stuck in a time warp that makes this measure grossly inadequate. Americans in poverty used to spend one-third of their income on food, but today it is only about one-fifth. To use this measure to determine where poverty begins, then, we should multiply a food budget by five instead of three (Chandy and Smith 2014). Another problem with the poverty line is that parents who work outside the home and have to pay for child care are treated the same as parents who don't have this expense. Still another is that the poverty line is the same for everyone across the nation, even though the cost of living is much higher in Brooklyn, New York, than in Brooklyn, Alabama.

Other critics claim that the poverty line counts too many people as poor. The problem, they say, is that the government does not count as income many benefits that people receive from antipoverty programs: Medicare, Medicaid, food stamps, HUD vouchers (government rent subsidies given to poor families), subsidized child care, and the earned income tax credit. This issue of "more or less" plagues the social problem of poverty. What should we count as income? Where should the cutoff for poverty be? Change these and we change the number of people counted as poor. In the face of these criticisms, the Census Bureau has developed alternative ways to measure poverty. These show higher poverty, but the official measure has not changed.

In the cartoon shown here you can see how Johnny Hart has picked up this arbitrary nature of the poverty line—that we can reduce or increase the number of "poor" people simply by changing the official definition of poverty.

This cartoon pinpoints the arbitrary nature of the poverty line. This makes me almost think that the creators of the Wizard of Id have been studying sociology.

WIZARD OF ID

Academics and officials can argue about the number of people in poverty (and those who do so are never in poverty themselves), but regardless of the exact numbers, poverty is a fact of life for *tens of millions* of Americans. Where you draw the poverty line is significant because it determines who is eligible for aid and who is not. The significance of poverty lies in the hardships people face. Poverty stunts people's intellectual abilities, undermines their health, and shortens their lives. Poverty also lies at the root of many other social problems. In earlier chapters, you caught a glimpse of how poverty is connected to prostitution, rape, murder, and drug abuse. In coming chapters, you will see how poverty is related to racism, physical and mental illness, and abuse in the family.

Poverty is much more than having little money. Poverty means the reduction in life chances.

Social Inequality

Let's look at how ideals confront reality and how inequality is baked into society.

Ideals versus Reality

> *"I lead a very ordinary life."*

— Ann Getty, heir to the Getty oil fortune

This is what Ann Getty told a *New York Times* reporter. *Ordinary?* Her "ordinary life" included living in a San Francisco mansion and flying to Paris to attend fashion shows and shop for clothing by top designers. On her international shopping excursions, she took her personal chef with her. She also bought $600,000 worth of clothing for her new daughter-in-law (Friedman 2010).

Let's assume that Ann Getty was serious when she made this statement, as I think she was. She was used to her way of life. This is what she experienced daily, so it was "ordinary" to her.

All of us take for granted what is usual in our environment. We also deny or explain away "inconvenient truths," things that threaten our worldview or that contradict our ideas.

As we grow up, we learn ideals about equality, opportunity, and success. Poverty is an "inconvenient truth" that contradicts these ideals. Denial is a common way of coping with this contradiction. For example, when researchers ask people what social class they belong to, most Americans—whether rich or poor—say they are middle class. With people like Ann Getty seeing themselves as living an "ordinary life," this tendency fascinates social researchers.

We know that all Americans are not equal, of course, and that the life chances of a son born to wealthy parents differ immensely from those of a daughter of a single waitress. We all know that the rich and politically connected pass advantages on to their children while the poor and powerless pass disadvantages on to theirs. Because of this, we have social programs intended to help level the playing field, such as affirmative action, college scholarships, Pell grants, and community colleges.

Structural Inequality Such programs run up against **structural inequality**, the inequality that is built into our social institutions. For example, some jobs in our economy pay higher wages and others lower wages, so automatically some people will receive more, others less. Or consider unemployment, another form of structural inequality. If a society has 100 million workers but only 90 million jobs, then 10 million workers will be unemployed, regardless of how hard they look for work. Job training programs cannot solve this structural problem. The solution requires changes in structure—that is, the creation of more jobs. No workable social system has been devised that eliminates structural inequality.

Distribution of Income and Wealth

After considering the inequality of income and wealth, we'll look at the relationship of wealth and power.

Inequality of Income Structural inequality, as you can expect, brings inequality of **income**, the money that people receive from their work and investments. You might be surprised at how vast income inequality is in the United States. From Figure 7.3, you can see that the top fifth of the U.S. population receives *51 percent* of the nation's entire income. The other "half" is divided among the remaining 80 percent of Americans. The poorest fifth of the population receives just 3 percent of the nation's income. Despite our numerous antipoverty programs, *income inequality is greater today than it was in the 1940s.*

Figure 7.3 Who Gets What? The Inverted Income Pyramid

How is the income of the United States distributed?

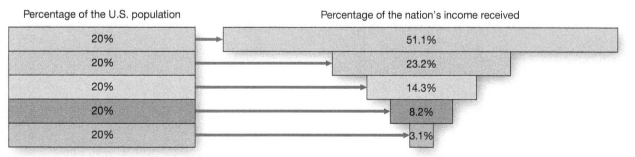

Source: By the author. Based on *Statistical Abstract of the United States* 2018:Table 720.

Figure 7.4 Income of Families by Race–Ethnicity

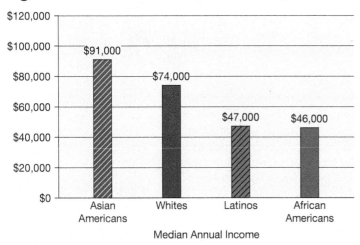

Median Annual Income

Source: By the author. Based on *Statistical Abstract of the United States* 2018:Table 723.

Figure 7.5 Who Owns the Nation's Wealth?

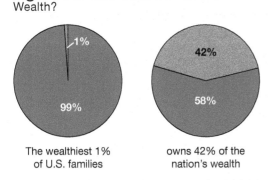

The wealthiest 1% of U.S. families

owns 42% of the nation's wealth

Source: By the author. Based on Saez, Emmanuel, and Gabriel Zucman. "Wealth Inequality in the United States Since 1913: Evidence from Capitalized Income Tax Data." Cambridge, MA: National Bureau of Economic Research, October 2014.

If we break these income totals down by race–ethnicity, as I have done in Figure 7.4, another firm pattern emerges. To the surprise of many, whites are not the top earners.

Inequality of Wealth Another way to picture financial inequality is to look at the distribution of **wealth**, the economic assets that people own, their savings, bank accounts, stocks, bonds, mutual funds, and real estate. At $62 trillion, the total of American wealth is huge (*Statistical Abstract* 2018:Table 747).

To see how the nation's wealth is distributed, look at Figure 7.5. *Forty-two percent of the nation's wealth is in the hands of just 1 percent of U.S. families.* Some suggest that this 1 percent controls corporate America. Conflict theorists come straight out and say they just buy politicians (nicely, of course) and control the entire country.

Among these one-percenters, wealth is far from divided evenly. The top tenth of the top 1 percent of U.S. families owns 22 percent of the nation's wealth. The top tenth of this small group, one hundredth of one percent of America's families, owns 11 percent of the entire country's wealth (Saez and Fry 2014). *Yes, just 16,000 families own 11 percent of the nation's wealth.*

A Note on Gates and Buffet Of the 16,000 families that own 11 percent of the nation's wealth, the two richest are those of Bill Gates and Warren Buffet. Warren Buffet is one of the world's most successful stock market investors. Bill Gates dropped out of Harvard to co-found Microsoft Corp., the world's largest software company. Gates and his employees developed MS-DOS, Windows, and Vista, popular computer operating systems. Microsoft gets a licensing fee each time a computer that uses these systems is sold.

Billions of dollars amassed by Gates and Buffet. This number trips easily off the tongue, but it is difficult to wrap your head around it. The following illustration may help you grasp the enormity of a billion dollars—*one thousand million dollars:*

> *Suppose you were born on the day Christ was born, that you are still alive today, and that you have been able to save money at the fantastic rate of one cent for every second that you lived—that is, 60 cents for every minute, $36 for every hour, or $864 for every day of your life during these past 2,000 years. At this rate, it would take you another thousand years to save $1 billion (Shaffer 1986).*

Gates and Buffet have given billions of dollars to the Gates Foundation, making these two the most generous men in human history. The money is used for global agricultural, educational, and health projects.

Wealth and Power

> *"Wealth is a good thing. Everyone ought to have some."*

> —James Smith, research scientist

If wealth is good, then what is the problem? Part of the problem is that the 1 percent of Americans who own 42 percent of the nation's wealth wield immense power over the U.S. economy. As this elite pursues even more wealth, they move production to Mexico, India, or China, where labor is cheaper. They throw hundreds of thousands of people out of work when they close factories in the United States, but this is not their concern. To them, this is merely a side effect of seizing economic opportunities. It is the wealthy who make these decisions, but it is the U.S. workers who must live with the consequences of this global game of Monopoly.

The wealthy live in a cocoon of privilege. They enjoy luxurious homes in safe neighborhoods. They are protected from unemployment, injustice in the courts, and an unresponsive political system. To perpetuate their advantages, they send their children to private schools and hire top financial advisors, attorneys, and lobbyists. At the other end of the money spectrum are those who cope with deprivation as part of everyday life. Let's turn our focus on them.

The Impact of Poverty: From Houses and Mortgages to Education and Criminal Justice

What difference does poverty make? On the most obvious level, the poor can't afford new cars, fine restaurants, and prestigious private schools. But beneath this obvious level lies a world of deprivation that enshrouds the lives of the poor. Let's look at some of these consequences of poverty.

"The poor are getting poorer, but with the rich getting richer it all averages out in the long run."

How we define reality depends to a large extent on where we are located in the social class structure. Poor Americans are not likely to have the view illustrated in this cartoon.

Housing and Mortgages

Let's start on a positive note, with a couple in poverty who, scrimping and saving for years, has managed to save enough money for a down payment on a house. They are delighted, as it has been their dream to have their own home for the children they hope to have. Unfortunately, we must follow this with bad news: In buying the house, this frugal family became the victim of predatory bankers.

As you read in Chapter 8 (Figure 8.3), bankers hit the poor—even those with good credit—with higher interest rates. Over the many years that a family makes payments on its mortgage, the higher interest can increase the amount paid by up to $100,000. Even worse, when times get tough, the higher monthly payments make it more likely that the poor will lose their homes. And if they try to negotiate lower monthly payments so they can hold onto their homes, they are unlikely to meet sympathy.

Following the economic meltdown of 2008, millions of home buyers fell behind on their mortgages. In despair, some gave the keys to their homes to the banks. Most tried to negotiate lower payments. Here is how one person described his negotiation: "I told her that I probably spend $10 a day on groceries, and she said 'Maybe you can eat less.'" (Morgenson 2008)

Would "fine, reputable" banks and loan companies really prey on the poor? This sounds so crass that it couldn't be true. The U.S. Justice Department investigated this wild charge. What did they find? Here is an example: For charging Latinos and African Americans higher interest rates, Bank of America was fined $335 million (Mayer et al. 2014).

Education The ideal behind public schools is that they will give all children an equal opportunity to succeed. The reality is that the deck is stacked against the poor. Property taxes are the main culprit. Because our schools are supported by property taxes, the property in poorer areas produces less tax revenue, and the schools that the poor attend have less money to work with. This translates into outdated textbooks, inexperienced teachers (who can be paid less), and lower test scores. Lower test scores, as you know, affect students' chances of going to college, which in turn affects their earnings. I think you see the vicious cycle here.

I'm sure it doesn't come as a surprise to you that the higher a family's income, the greater the likelihood that their children will attend and complete college. If you rank families from the poorest to the richest, at each level of family income the likelihood increases that their children will go to college. Forget test scores. Whether they score high or low on tests, children from homes with more money are more likely to go to college.

Similarly, the more money a family has, the more years of schooling their children complete (Cahalan and Perna 2015; Madland 2015).

Our educational system also matches family income. If children from poverty go to college, most attend community colleges, where many take vocational programs. In contrast, most children from middle-class homes attend state universities. And the children of the wealthy? They go to elite private colleges. Before college, many attend private high schools, where the classes are small and the teachers are paid well (Cahalan and Perna 2015; Bloch et al. 2017). At elite high schools, the college advisors have close ties with admissions officers at elite colleges. Some networks are so efficient that *half* of a private high school's graduating class is admitted to Harvard, Yale, and Princeton (Cookson and Persell 1985/2005; "Top U.S. Schools..." 2015).

Jobs and Careers   Jobs and careers follow this educational path. Beckoning children of the middle and upper classes are high-paying professions and other secure positions. To children from homes of poverty, the term "career" is a foreign word. What they have are low-paying, insecure jobs. With dead-end and often sporadic work, many don't even know from one week to the next how much they will earn—or even if there will be a paycheck at all. This makes planning uncertain and life hectic. To the stresses already knitted into their daily lives, job insecurity and unemployment create huge tensions. Not only do the poor not know if there will be enough money to buy food and pay the rent, but they also need to cope with the frustrating bureaucracies of unemployment insurance, welfare, and other social programs.

Criminal Justice   The poor are more likely to be victims of violent crimes and to commit robberies and assaults, crimes for which offenders are punished severely. As we reviewed in Chapter 6, white-collar crime is more pervasive and costly to society, but it is less visible and carries milder punishments. As also mentioned, when the poor are arrested, they lack the resources to hire good lawyers to defend themselves. Often, they cannot even post bail, and they remain in jail for months while they await trial. Most prisoners in our jails and prisons are people who were reared in poverty.

In Sum: Quality of Life   Social inequality makes a fundamental difference in people's quality of life. The low-paying jobs of the poor, when they have them, bring no security, no pensions, and no medical benefits. The poor live from paycheck to paycheck, trying to keep one step ahead of having the lights cut off or being evicted. If they get sick, their job may not be there when they return to work. Among the stark consequences: Those living in poverty don't eat as well, their children are more likely to die in infancy, they have more accidents, and they die younger. Like Julie Treadman in our opening vignette, they also have limited access to good medical care, which further jeopardizes their well-being. In short, wealth and poverty represent privilege—given or denied.

Looking at the Problem Theoretically

7.3   **Summarize the different pictures that emerge when you apply symbolic interactionism, functionalism, and conflict theory to the social problem of poverty.**

As you learned in earlier chapters, each theoretical perspective gives a different view of a social problem. Let's look at poverty through these three lenses.

Symbolic Interactionism

As you can expect, when we apply symbolic interactionism to poverty, we will be focusing on meanings. Let's begin by looking at why poverty is relative.

The Relativity of Poverty

Andy, Sharon, and their two children live in a small house in a rural area, where they farm 65 acres. To make ends meet, Andy works part-time at a local grocery store, and Sharon works *part-time as a cook at the Dew Drop Inn. Between their jobs and the farm, they make about $18,000 a year. They grow their own vegetables, raise a few chickens for eggs and meat, and fish in a nearby pond. Andy brings home a deer each hunting season. Integrated into the community and with their basic needs satisfied, they don't think of themselves as poor. Neither do their friends and neighbors.*

Leslie attends a private college. Her parents pay her tuition, fees, books, rent, utilities, medical insurance, transportation, and entertainment. They also give her about $500 a month for "extras." Unlike many of her friends, Leslie has no car, and she complains about how hard it is to get by. Her more affluent friends feel sorry for her.

Between auditions, Keith, a struggling young actor, works as a waiter. He earns about $1,400 a month, which has to cover his rent, food, and all other expenses. To make ends meet, he rooms with three other aspiring actors. "It's difficult to make it," he says, "but one day you'll see my name in lights." Keith sees himself as "struggling"—not poor. Nor do his actor friends think of him or themselves as poor.

Maria and her two children live in a housing project. Her rent is subsidized and cheap—$97 a month. Her welfare, Medicaid, and food stamps total $16,287 a year, all tax-free. Her two children attend school during the day, and she takes classes in English at a neighborhood church. Maria considers herself poor, and so do the government and her neighbors.

We have an irony here. Leslie is, by far, much better off financially than the other three, yet she *feels* poor. Why? This takes us back to *relative poverty*.

Symbolic interactionists stress that to understand poverty we must focus on what poverty *means* to people. When people evaluate where they are in life, they *compare* themselves with others. In some rural areas, simple marginal living is the norm, and people living in these circumstances don't feel poor. But in Leslie's cosmopolitan circle, people can *feel* deprived if they can't afford the latest upscale designer clothing from their favorite boutique. The meaning of poverty, then, is *relative*: What poverty is differs from group to group within the same society. Its meaning also changes from culture to culture and from one era to the next.

How people above the poverty line view poverty is also significant. If they see "the poor" as good people who are down on their luck, they are likely to offer "a helping hand" by supporting programs that provide job training and monthly support. If they view the poor as "lazy no-goods" who refuse to work—a parasitic drain on society—they are not likely to favor such social policies. As you can see, perception and meaning—main elements of symbolic interactionism—are essential for understanding poverty.

Changing Meanings of Poverty Symbolic interactionists stress that the meaning of poverty changes as social conditions change. Let's take a quick glance at how this happened in the United States.

The way people viewed poverty in the early 1700s was remarkably different than how we view it today. At that time, poverty was seen as God's will. The clergy preached that God put the poor on Earth to provide an opportunity for the rest of us to show Christian charity (Rothman and Rothman 1972). Poverty was not a social problem, but a personal problem.

At that time, few Americans lived in cities, and the poor were scattered among hundreds of villages along country roads. As cities grew, so did the concentration of the poor in those cities. By the time of the American Revolution (1775–1783), cities such as Boston, Philadelphia, and New York had set up welfare committees to distinguish between the "deserving" and the "undeserving" poor. The deserving poor were the blind, people with disabilities, and mothers of small children whose husbands had deserted them. The undeserving poor were beggars, peddlers, idlers, drifters, and prostitutes. At this point, the meaning of poverty was changing. Increasingly, poverty was viewed not just as God's will, but also as the result of flawed character.

This change meant that the development of a social problem was now in process. As the United States industrialized and its cities grew, the urban squalor bothered people of good intentions. Reformers launched campaigns to help the poor. The meaning of poverty continued to change, coming to be seen as the product of corrupt cities. People who had given in to urban temptations—alcohol, crime, and debauchery—were held in the chains of poverty (Rothman and Rothman 1972).

The idea that poverty is God's will is no longer common, but the idea that poverty ought not to exist—and the suspicion that it is the result of character flaws or the behavior of the poor—remains part of our symbolic heritage. We have vacillated between viewing the poor as worthy people who deserve our help and as undeserving people who have brought the ills of poverty down on their own heads.

Functionalism

Can poverty be functional for society? Or is poverty only dysfunctional? Let's find out what sociologists have to say about this.

How Income Inequality Helps Society   In a classic essay, sociologists Kingsley Davis and Wilbert Moore (1945) developed the functionalist perspective on social inequality. Their argument was simple: Some positions in society are more important than others for society's welfare. To attract highly talented people, these positions must offer high income and prestige. Oil, for example, is vital for the economy, but to learn the technology necessary to find oil takes years of training in geology. To motivate people to postpone gratification and continue studying for years, petroleum geologists, especially geophysicists, must be offered a substantial salary and high respect from others. In contrast, anyone can wash dishes, so these unskilled workers with little training can be given low pay. Differences in income and prestige, then, sort people by their abilities and drive to succeed. This helps society function.

How Poverty Is Functional for Society   Functionalists tend to see functions in everything. Although functionalists analyze the dysfunctions of poverty, including alienation and despair, drug abuse, street crime, suicide, and mental illness, they point out that poverty is functional for society. The following *Thinking Critically about Social Problems* summarizes the functionalist view of how poor people contribute to society's well-being.

Thinking Critically about Social Problems

Why We Need the Poor: How Poverty Helps Society

Most of us think of poverty in negative terms: Poverty is undesirable, and we should get rid of it. Functionalists, in contrast, identify the functions of poverty—that is, the positive consequences that poverty has for society. Consider these 12 functions, most pointed out by sociologist Herbert Gans (1971):

1. *The poor ensure that society's dirty work gets done at low cost.* Many factories, restaurants, farms, and hospitals could not survive in their present state without a poorly paid workforce. If there weren't poor people, who would do society's dirty jobs at low wages?

2. *The poor create jobs for others.* Think of the welfare agencies that serve the poor and—not incidentally—shield the rest of us from them. Most police officers

In tough economic times, a lot of people lose their jobs—and their homes. If this happens, how can you survive? Maybe with a smile and a sense of humor to tap the kindness of strangers. I took this photo outside Boston's Fenway Park.

would be without jobs if it weren't for the poor. And what would social workers do for a living?

3. *The poor serve as guinea pigs in medical experiments.* The rest of us benefit from these advances in medicine. How else would we test risky new medicines and surgical techniques?

4. The poor make the economy more efficient. They spend their low wages and welfare money on leftover goods such as day-old bread and the many "seconds" that our factories produce. They also buy the clothing, furniture, and cars that the rest of us discard. Where else would these items go if it weren't for the poor?

5. The poor provide an income for others, even making some wealthy. Many slum landlords, for example,

would have to get jobs if it weren't for the poor. And what would the owners of the many liquor stores in the inner city do without the poor? Or those who offer bail bonds and pay-check loans? And what about the owners of the trailer parks?

6. *The poor provide the frontline soldiers for war.* The youth from poverty can be sacrificed during battle. (German generals used to call them "cannon fodder.") Where else would we get the many people that we need to fill the "grunt" jobs in the armed services—or to test the roads for bombs in such places as Iraq and Afghanistan?

7. *The poor help stabilize our political system.* Most poor people vote for Democrats, so to the degree that this party helps the U.S. political system, the poor contribute to that effort.

8. *The poor provide entertainment.* The lives of the poor are lives of despair—which become the story lines of novels, movies, and television. News programs also attract audiences and advertising revenue by featuring the robberies, rapes, and murders committed by the poor.

9. *The poor enrich our music.* They have given us the blues, Negro spirituals, country music (from the Southern poor), rock (the Beatles came from the slums of Liverpool), and hip-hop/rap. Without the devastating experiences of the poor, the rest of us would have fewer tunes to hum.

10. *The poor help motivate us.* Our awareness of "the projects," skid row, homeless shelters, and soup lines keep us on our toes. We know that if we don't get an education and work hard—doing whatever our teachers and bosses tell us—we could end up there. The poor have replaced the "bogeyman" of years past.

11. *The poor help our self-concept.* They make the rest of us feel superior. *We* are not like *them.*

12. *The poor provide hope.* The heartwarming accounts of the poor who have "made it," overcoming huge obstacles to achievement, offer motivation for others. If those people can do it, we can, too.

By the time functionalists get through with their analysis, one wonders if society could even exist without the poor.

For Your Consideration

→ Do you think that we need some people to be poor?

→ What functions of poverty can you think of that are not included here?

→ How can the benefits that the poor provide society be replaced so we will no longer "need" people to be poor?

Conflict Theory

Why do we have social inequality? Here is the answer given by conflict theorists.

The Basic Cause of Social Inequality Central to conflict theory is the idea that a society's resources are limited and that groups compete for these resources. In each society, some group has gained control of that society's resources. This group uses those resources to make a better life for itself, to keep itself in power, and to exploit weaker groups. The result is a social class system in which the wealthy pass advantages to their children, while the poor pass disadvantages to theirs.

A General Theory of Social Class Karl Marx (1818–1883) was the first person to develop a general theory of social class. He argued that social class revolves around a single factor, the *means of production*—the tools, factories, land, and capital used to produce wealth (Marx, 1867/1967; Marx and Engels, 1848/1964). People are either capitalists (*bourgeoisie*), who own the means of production, or they are workers (*proletariat*), who serve the capitalists. The history of a society is the history of conflict between owners and workers, the wealthy and the poor. Because the owners hold the power, they manipulate society's social institutions—economic, legal, political, educational, and religious—to promote their own interests and to control workers.

Marx wrote that the owners' position of power and privilege will not continue forever. The day of reckoning will come when workers shrug off their **false class consciousness**, the delusion that they will start their own business and become wealthy. In its place will arise *class consciousness*, the realization that whether they are garbage collectors or college professors, they all are workers. With their eyes finally opened and realizing that they all are exploited, they will join together and overthrow the capitalists. Seizing the means of production, the workers will use them for the good of all. Poverty will become a distant memory.

Modifications of Conflict Theory Most sociologists acknowledge that Marx provided valuable insight into relationships between the powerful and the poor, but they find inadequate his class division of only two groups, owners and workers. In Marx's analysis, the managers of corporations are workers who serve the capitalists. This may be, but what do the top managers of corporations, whose decisions affect tens of thousands of workers, have in common with office and factory workers, whose decisions center around such things as what kind of breakfast cereal to buy? To lump corporate CEOs with factory workers is to join together people who belong on either side of a chasm. Why should people with such huge differences in power and lifestyle be included in the same group?

Feminist theorists highlight another fault with Marx's analysis. They point out that Marx analyzed the exploitation of workers in the paid sector, but he overlooked the unpaid sector, where women perform reproductive and household labor. This is another example, they stress, of men overlooking the contributions of women to the welfare of society. Feminist theorists also criticize Marx for ignoring key issues of gender, race–ethnicity, and age as areas of exploitation. They emphasize that these are just as important as the exploitation of production and workers.

In Sum   Conflict theorists stress the relationship between those who have power and those who do not. The problems of the poor are due to their deprived position in a system of stratification, to their relative powerlessness and oppression.

Summary of Theoretical Approaches

Each theoretical lens provides a unique understanding of wealth, poverty, and social inequality. Symbolic interactionists focus on the individual level, making us more sensitive to how social class works in our everyday lives. They explain, for example, why the amount of income that people have (the objective condition) is not the same as how people feel about that amount (subjective views that underlie relative poverty). Functionalists and conflict theorists look at a bigger picture. They examine social structure—in this case, the relationships between the poor and the wealthy, the powerful and the powerless. Where functionalists see inequality as originating from society's need to reward its important positions, conflict theorists stress how the means of production produce inequality.

Research Findings

7.4   Summarize research findings on who the poor are, a culture of poverty, who rules the United States, and explanations of global poverty.

As sociologists have studied poverty, they have uncovered major patterns. Let's look at them.

Who Are the Poor?

We'll begin with the most obvious pattern, low-paying jobs.

Minimum Wage Workers   People who work at minimum wage jobs are trapped in poverty. They clean motel rooms, wash dishes in restaurants, do "stoop labor" on farms, and fill the sweatshops of our cities. They have low education, bad nutrition, more sicknesses than others, and if they change jobs, it is for more minimum wage work. For most of these people, whom some refer to as an *underclass,* poverty will remain their lot in life. College students who take such jobs while they are preparing for careers that pay well are not part of this group.

State and Region   Where people live makes a huge difference in their chances of being poor. One of the most striking examples is the inner city, where poverty is concentrated. To be born or reared there obviously increases your chances of living in poverty. The rural areas of the country also have higher than average poverty, although certainly not as concentrated as it is in the inner city. As you can see from the following Social Map, poverty is also higher in some states than others. You can also see how poverty differs by regions of the country. The higher rate of poverty in the South that you see on this map has continued for about two centuries.

Figure 7.6 The Geography of U.S. Poverty

What percentage of the population is in poverty?

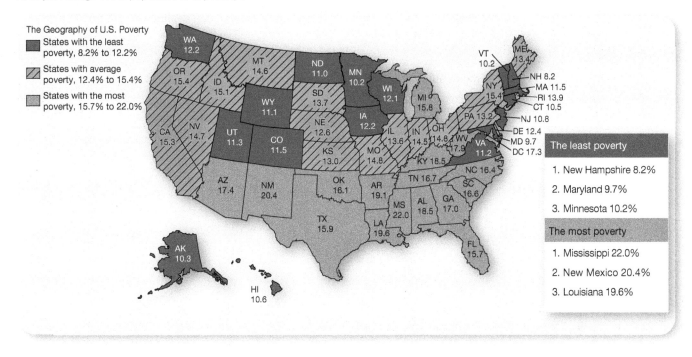

Source: By the author. Based on *Statistical Abstract of the United States* 2018:Table 729.

Race–Ethnicity   Figure 7.7 illustrates how poverty is related to race–ethnicity: African Americans, Latinos, and Native Americans are *more than twice* as likely as whites to be poor, with Native Americans having the highest rate of poverty. If their rates could be reduced to the rate of whites or of Asian Americans, many millions of people would no longer live in poverty. They would be spared its many deprivations, so hazardous to the individual and corrosive to society. We should note, however, that progress has been made. As high as these rates are, they are lower than they were several decades ago.

Figure 7.7 Minorities Are More Likely to Be Poor

What percentages of these groups are poor?

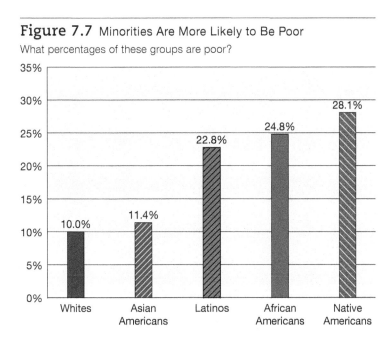

Source: By the author. Based on *Statistical Abstract of the United States* 2018:Tables 7, 35.

Age: Children and the Elderly Poverty is also related to age. The poverty rate of the elderly is lower than the national average, but the poverty rate of children is higher. As you can see from Figure 7.8, the children's rate of poverty is much higher than that of the seniors. Note how poverty among the elderly has declined while poverty among children has fluctuated.

Figure 7.8 Comparing Poverty of Children and the Elderly

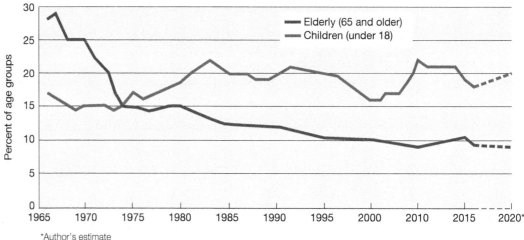

*Author's estimate

Source: By the author. Based on U.S. Census Bureau 2009; Semega et al. 2017; *Statistical Abstract of the United States* 1994:Tables 728, 731; 2018:Table 737.

Figure 7.9 Child Poverty and Race–Ethnicity

What percentage of children in these groups live in poverty?

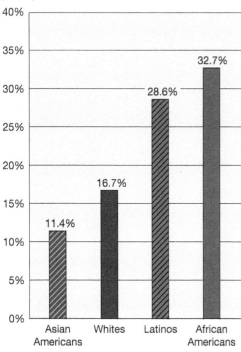

Note: Native Americans are not listed in the source. With their overall poverty rate of 28 percent, I estimate their child poverty rate to be about 35 percent.

Source: By the author. Based on *Statistical Abstract of the United States* 2018:Table 736.

To get a different view of child poverty, look at Figure 7.9, which shows poverty among children by race–ethnicity. As you can see, poverty is lowest among Asian American children and considerably higher among Latino and African American children. Such extensive poverty in childhood has severe implications for the next generation.

The Feminization of Poverty Poverty in the United States is concentrated among women and children. Sociologists call this pattern the **feminization of poverty**. Children who live with both parents are seldom poor, which is a major reason that childhood poverty is the lowest among Asian Americans. In contrast, children who live with just one parent are

Poverty in the United States is concentrated among women and children. Sociologists call this pattern the *feminization of poverty*. Poverty is especially high among teenage mothers.

often poor. The reason for this is fairly simple: Two working parents earn more. In addition, as you know, it is usually the mother who heads single-parent families. Mother-alone families average *less than half* of what families with two working parents earn (*Statistical Abstract* 2018:Table 724).

Single mothers who bear children at a young age are especially disadvantaged. With their limited skills and ongoing child-care responsibilities, how can they compete in the labor market? Women who divorce after being homemakers for years also face distinct disadvantages. Their income usually nosedives after divorce, and with their work skills rusty and no recent employer recommendations, good jobs are rare.

What about child support? As you can see from Figure 7.10, less than half of single mothers receive all the child support that the courts order the absent fathers to pay. A fourth of the fathers skip out and pay nothing. Add all these factors together, and you can see why women and children are much more likely to be poor.

Permanence of Poverty It may surprise you that most people who fall below the poverty line do not stay there. Most people are poor only for short periods—when they are injured, sick, or during layoffs or slow seasons at work. The total number of poor in the United States remains fairly constant from year to year, but there is much change *within* this total. Each year millions of people rise above the poverty line, but at the same time millions of others fall below it.

Do you want to avoid poverty? I'm sure you do. And I'm sure, too, that you would like to have a financially secure life. The following *Thinking Critically about Social Problems* can help you realize this desire.

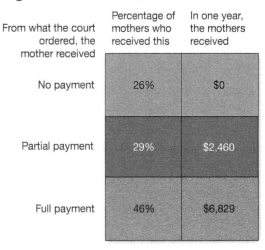

Figure 7.10 Child Support Payments

From what the court ordered, the mother received	Percentage of mothers who received this	In one year, the mothers received
No payment	26%	$0
Partial payment	29%	$2,460
Full payment	46%	$6,829

Note: These totals are based on the 46 percent of divorced mothers who had custody of their children and who were supposed to receive payments.

Source: By the author. Based on *Statistical Abstract of the United States* 2018:Table 593.

Thinking Critically about Social Problems

How to Avoid Poverty

Here are three "rules" that will help you avoid poverty:

1. Finish high school. (You've done this one.)
2. Get married before you have your first child.
3. Don't have a child until after you reach the age of 20.

   You can see why following these three "rules" helps people avoid poverty, and here are four more "rules" that can help you not only avoid poverty but also develop a more financially secure life:

4. Graduate from college. (You've started this one.)
5. Stay married.
6. Don't abuse drugs, including alcohol.
7. Avoid debt, especially on credit cards.

   Poverty among people who follow these seven rules is practically nonexistent.

For Your Consideration

→ What other "rules" would you add to this list?
→ If you or someone else has already broken one or more of these "rules," how can you overcome the consequences and avoid poverty?

Blatant Poverty in the Midst of Plenty How things have changed! Americans used to associate bread lines and soup kitchens with the Great Depression, or perhaps with Charles Dickens's description of 19th-century London. Now the homeless are part of every large city across this rich land. Most are tucked out of sight, but the presence of others on our streets and sidewalks reveals the contrast between the American Dream and its stark reality. Who are these homeless people, ravaged by hunger and dressed in mismatched layers of out-of-date clothing? How did they get that way? These questions intrigued me, so I set out on a search for answers. I spent nights with the homeless in their shelters, ate with them there, and interviewed them on the streets and in back alleys. The next *Thinking Critically about Social Problems* summarizes some of what I discovered on this sociological adventure.

Thinking Critically about Social Problems

Being Homeless in the Land of the American Dream

When I met Larry Rice, who ran a shelter for the homeless in St. Louis, Missouri, he said that as a sociologist I should learn firsthand what is happening on our city streets. I was reluctant to leave my comfortable home and office, but Larry baited a hook and lured me onto the streets. He offered to take me to Washington, D.C., where he promised that I would see people sleeping on sidewalk grates within view of the White House. Intrigued at the contrast this painted in my mind, I agreed to go with him, not knowing that it would change my life.

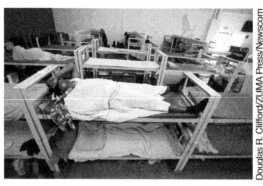

In my research, I stayed at homeless shelters like this one in Florida. They are not welcoming or appealing places. Some are so dangerous that many homeless people prefer to sleep in parks and alleys.

When we arrived in Washington, it was bitter cold. It was December, and I saw what Larry had promised: sorrowful people huddled over the exhaust grates of federal buildings. Not all of the homeless survived the first night I was there. Freddy, who walked on crutches and had become a fixture in Georgetown, froze to death as he sought refuge from the cold in a telephone booth. I vividly recall looking at the telephone booth where Freddy's frozen body was found, still upright, futilely wrapped in a tattered piece of canvas. I went to Freddy's funeral and talked with his friends. To me, Freddy became a person, an individual, not just a faceless, nameless figure shrouded by city shadows.

This experience ignited my sociological curiosity. I felt driven to learn more. I ended up visiting a dozen skid rows in the United States and Canada, sleeping in filthy shelters across North America. I interviewed the homeless in these shelters—and in alleys, on street corners, in parks, and even in dumpsters. I became so troubled by what I experienced that for three months after I returned home, I couldn't get through an entire night without waking up startled by disturbing dreams.

In this research, I discovered that there are many routes to homelessness. Here are the types of homeless people I met:

1. *"Push-outs:"* These people have been pushed out of their homes. Two common types of "push-outs" are teenagers kicked out by their parents and adults evicted by landlords.
2. *Victims of environmental disaster:* This type really surprised me, but they, too, live on our streets. The disasters I came across ranged from fires to dioxin contamination.
3. *The mentally ill:* These people have been discharged from mental hospitals. Although unable to care for themselves, they receive little or no treatment for their problems. Like the teenagers, they are easy victims of the predators who prowl our city streets.

4. *The new poor:* This group consists of unemployed workers whose work skills have become outdated because of technological change.
5. *The technologically unqualified:* Unlike the new poor, these unemployed workers never possessed technological qualifications.
6. *The elderly:* These people have neither savings nor family support; they are old, unemployable, and discarded.
7. *Runaways:* After fleeing intolerable situations, these boys and girls wander our streets.
8. *The demoralized:* After suffering some personal tragedy, these people have given up and retreated into despair. The most common catalyst to their demoralization is divorce.
9. *Alcoholics:* The old-fashioned skid-row wino is still out there.
10. *Ease addicts:* These people actually choose to be homeless. For them, homelessness is a form of "early retirement." They reject responsibilities to others, and they come and go as they please. Some, in their 20s, spend their days playing chess in the parks of San Francisco.
11. *Travel addicts:* These people also choose to be homeless. Addicted to wanderlust, they travel continuously. They call themselves "road dogs."
12. *Excitement addicts:* Among the younger of the homeless, these people enjoy the thrill of danger. They like the excitement that comes from "living on the edge." Being on the streets offers many "edge" opportunities.

As you can see, the homeless are not a single group. Rather, they arrive on our city streets by many "routes." Note how different the "routes" are for the last three types (those who choose homelessness, a minority of the homeless) than for the first nine types, who do not want to be homeless. Because there are many "causes" of homelessness, it should be obvious that there can be no single solution to this social problem. We need multifaceted programs, perhaps based on the various "routes" by which people travel to this dead-end destination.

For Your Consideration

→ Based on the types of homeless people that I found on our streets, what solutions would you suggest to homelessness? Be practical.

In Sum: Social Structure   The patterns of poverty we have reviewed do not point to laziness, stupidity, or any other personal characteristics as their cause. Instead, they point to *structural features of society*. As you have seen, poverty follows lines of geography, age, education, gender, race–ethnicity, and marital status. To understand poverty, sociologists examine features of the *social system:* discrimination, education, welfare programs, changes in the economy, and the availability of work. In later chapters, we shall discuss some of these patterns, but for now let's consider culture of poverty, an analysis that has generated considerable controversy in sociology.

Is There a Culture of Poverty?

> We boast of vast achievement and of power,
> Of human progress knowing no defeat,
> Of strange new marvels every day and hour—
> And here's the bread line in the wintry street!

—Berton Braley, "The Bread Line"

A Culture of Poverty?   Why do some people remain poor in the midst of plenty? In the middle of the last century, Oscar Lewis, an anthropologist who did participant observation with poor people, ignited a controversy that is not yet resolved. Lewis (1959, 1966) said that people who remain poor year after year develop a way of life that traps them in poverty. He called this a **culture of poverty**. These people, he said, see before them a deep canyon, one they can never bridge. They stand on one side, and on the other is mainstream society, which is almost everyone else. Feeling inferior and insecure, they become convinced that they can never get out of poverty. Turning fatalistic and passive, they develop low aspirations and think about the present, not the future. Some become self-destructive, as illustrated by their high rates of alcoholism, physical violence, and family abuse. Their lives become marked by broken marriages, desertion, single-parent households, and self-defeating despair. Their way of life, this *culture of poverty*, as Lewis called it, makes it almost impossible for them to break out of poverty.

What is controversial about a culture of poverty? Sociologists bristle at this concept because it appears to blame poor people for their poverty, emphasizing that their ideas and behavior keep them down. As I just stressed, instead of personal factors, sociologists emphasize *structural* causes of poverty. Herbert Gans, introduced in the earlier section on the functions of poverty, has written extensively on this topic. In the following *Spotlight on Social Research*, Gans explains why he loathes this concept.

Spotlight on Social Research

Demonizing the Poor

HERBERT GANS, *professor of sociology at Columbia University, is a past president of the American Sociological Association. He has written extensively on urban poverty and antipoverty policy. Here is what he wrote for you.*

Courtesy of Warna Oosterbann, photo provided by Herbert Gans

Ever since the 1950s, sociologists have led poverty researchers in studying America's victimized and demonized poor—although they have not done nearly enough research on their victimizers and demonizers.

Perhaps because I am a refugee from Nazi Germany and came to the United States dirt-poor, a significant part of my teaching and research has been about poverty and antipoverty policy. I have been concerned with the victimized and demonized, as well as the agencies and institutions that victimize and demonize the poor. In the early 1960s, I wrote *The Urban Villagers*, a book about a low-income neighborhood in Boston that was demonized as a slum, and about its residents, who were victimized when their neighborhood was torn down.

Later in the 1960s, I wrote a good deal about poverty and antipoverty policy—what is today called public sociology. Along with other sociologists, I analyzed and criticized the "culture of poverty" arguments, which suggested that the poor practice a culture that helps to keep them poor and prevents their escaping from poverty. We argued that blaming the victims for their victimization diverted attention away from what really keeps them poor: the shortage of secure and decent-paying jobs, the failures of the welfare program, and racism. Although their victimization resulted in depression and pathology, it was not a culture of poverty.

I returned to antipoverty research in the late 1980s, when a new version of, and a new term for, the culture of poverty argument appeared. This time, the poor were demonized as an "underclass," an alleged stratum that existed under respectable society. This underclass was accused of such moral shortcomings as not wanting to work, turning to welfare or street crime instead, being promiscuous, and avoiding marriage.

My interest in victimizers and demonizers made me wonder who invented and spread the new blaming term. In 1995, I wrote *The War Against the Poor*, which identified its inventors. The book also described how journalists, social scientists, and political conservatives combined to use and popularize the term.

Since the late 1990s, when welfare reform and a boom in low-wage jobs enabled more poor people to work, their demonization has declined—at least for the moment. However, if enough working poor lose their jobs to a weak economy, they surely will be demonized again—with the same old arguments, but perhaps with another new term. Then sociologists must show once more that blaming the victims only makes it harder for the poor to escape from poverty.

Revival of the Concept   Sociologists are reviving the concept of a culture of poverty, but they are treading lightly around it. Basically, they find that the concept matches a reality of life in poverty—attitudes and behaviors that hold people back versus those that help people get ahead. However, they fear that the mention of cultural factors will lead to blaming people for their poverty, and they stress the structural conditions that create attitudes and behaviors that perpetuate poverty (Bell et al. 2014; Royce 2019).

Research by sociologist Karl Alexander and his team (2014) provides a good example of the tension between structural conditions and the culture of poverty in sociology. They followed 790 children in Baltimore from age 6 to age 29. Most of the children who started life financially comfortable did well financially as adults. Most of the children who started life poor moved out of poverty, but almost half remained poor as adults. The most important structural factors that led to a secure financial future were the parents being married (or living together in a stable arrangement), stable neighborhoods, and good schools. What spelled trouble for the children's future were one-parent families, chaotic neighborhoods, and bad schools. Alexander concludes that these structural characteristics, not a culture of poverty, held the children down—or set them on paths that led to brighter futures.

Sociologist William Julius Wilson (2010) places greater stress than most sociologists on cultural factors in poverty. He points out that within the same setting are different values, belief systems, styles of presentation, and linguistic patterns. Those that people learn either help or hinder their movement out of poverty. Wilson is careful to stress that social policy needs to focus on the structural factors, such as training in marketable skills and providing jobs.

It seems fair to conclude that structural conditions are overwhelmingly the factors that keep people poor. Sociologists repeatedly find the same three structural conditions to be the most important: single-parent, female-headed families with their much lower incomes, unstable neighborhoods with crime and violence, and poor schools. In the middle of these structural conditions, however, are significant differences. Some people learn attitudes and behaviors that help them escape from poverty, while others learn attitudes and behaviors that help keep them poor, each passing distinctive ways of life on to their children. What leads to these life-significant distinctions has yet to be specified. Now that the culture of poverty is again considered, perhaps sociologists will explore and, hopefully, uncover these distinctions. If so, they may be able to pave the way for more effective social policy.

I suggest that when the dust settles on this concept, if it ever does, the term we need will be *cultures of poverty*, as it is likely that distinctive subpaths create similar results.

We have been focusing on the poor and powerless. Now let's turn to the other extreme.

Who Rules the United States?

Conflict theorists stress that to understand social life we must understand who controls society's scarce resources. Like wealth, power is a scarce resource: Some people have much of it, while others have little or none. Max Weber, an early sociologist, defined **power** as the ability to get your way despite resistance (Weber 1921/1964). The possession of power is especially significant because it determines who gets the lion's share of the other resources in society. Let's ask, then, who makes the major decisions in the United States?

The Power Elite Sociologist C. Wright Mills (1959a) argued that a **power elite** rules the United States. He said that a small group made up of the top military, political, and business leaders makes decisions that direct the country—and shake the world. Figure 7.11 illustrates Mills' view of the power elite.

Mills stressed that the power elite is not a formal group. It meets neither in secret nor in public. In fact, some members may not even think they belong to it. But, structurally, it exists. The power elite consists of top leaders whose interests have merged. White House aides join powerful law firms. A law partner joins the president's cabinet or is appointed secretary of the treasury. The head of the treasury becomes the CEO of a leading bank or corporation. An air force colonel retires and then takes over the sales division of Boeing or General Dynamics.

In its most public form, able for anyone to recognize, whether an Obama or a Trump is in the White House, you can see representatives of Goldman Sachs, the powerful financial firm. They are nominated to Cabinet positions and otherwise surround the president, protecting the interests of the nation's power elite. In effect, there is a revolving door between Wall Street and the White House.

Because the power elite share interests and experiences in business and politics, they think alike on major issues. In addition, they come from similar backgrounds, and they share similar values. Most are WASPs, White Anglo-Saxon Protestants, who attended exclusive prep schools and Ivy League colleges. Many belong to the same private clubs and vacation at the same exclusive resorts. These people, then, are united by shared backgrounds, contacts, ideologies, values, and interests (Domhoff 1974, 2017).

Mills said that the three groups that make up the power elite—the top political, military, and corporate leaders—are not equal in power. To identify who was dominant, Mills did not point to the president, however, or even to the generals and admirals, but rather to the heads of corporations. Because all three segments of the power elite view capitalism as essential to the welfare of the country, national policy centers on business interests. Making decisions that promote U.S. business works to the mutual benefit of all three groups.

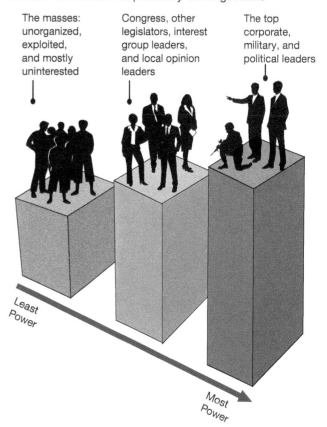

Figure 7.11 How Is Power Distributed in the United States? The Model Proposed by C. Wright Mills

The masses: unorganized, exploited, and mostly uninterested

Congress, other legislators, interest group leaders, and local opinion leaders

The top corporate, military, and political leaders

Least Power

Most Power

Source: Based on Mills, C. Wright. *The Sociological Imagination.* New York: Oxford University Press, 1959b.

Sociologist William Domhoff (2017) prefers to use the term "ruling class" instead of power elite. He studied the wealthiest 1 percent of Americans, those whom you saw in Figure 7.5, who own *42 percent* of the nation's wealth. This 1 percent controls the nation's top corporations and foundations, even the boards that oversee our major universities. They also own the nation's major newspapers, magazines, and television stations. Members of this powerful group attempt, quite successfully, to shape the consciousness of the nation. It is no accident, says Domhoff, that from this group come most of the president's cabinet and top ambassadors.

Conflict theorists stress that we should not think of the power elite or ruling class as a group that meets and makes specific decisions. Rather, with their interlocking economic and political interests, their behavior stems not from a grand conspiracy to control the country but from social ties and mutual interest in solving the problems that face big business. Able to ensure that the country adopts the social policies that it deems desirable—from interest rates to sending troops abroad—this powerful group sets the economic and political agenda under which the rest of the country lives (Burris 2005; Domhoff 2009, 2017).

Because the power elite does not meet as a group, it cannot be photographed. The Forbes are part of this group. Shown here are Malcolm Forbes and his three brothers at the Forbes Building. Their collection of nine Fabergé Imperial Easter eggs and other Fabergé objects that used to belong to the czars of Russia sold for $90 million.

David Lefranc/Gamma-Rapho/Getty Images

The Pluralist View   Not all sociologists agree that a power elite is pulling the strings behind the scenes. The **pluralists** present a contrasting view. Pluralists argue that many **interest groups**—people united by their mutual interests in some matter—are competing for social, economic, and political power. Because the country's many groups are divided by essential differences, power is dispersed, and *no single group is in control.* As unions, industries, professional associations, and the like compete with one another, consensus is reached, or at least tradeoffs are agreed on, which allows decisions to be made and society to function.

Continuing Research on the Controversy   The controversy between the pluralists and the power elitists is long-standing. The disagreements can be remarkable, especially when one researcher finds little overlap between elites and decision making, while another, looking at the same data, finds close connections between them (Dahl 1961; Domhoff 1978b). The data aren't inkblots, open to imaginative interpretations, but in some instances they seem to be treated this way.

After years of rancorous arguments by proponents of each view, researchers seemed to have come up with the answer. Political scientists Martin Gilens and Benjamin Page

(2014) reviewed 1,800 policy decisions made by the U.S. government. The evidence overwhelmingly indicated that a power elite consisting of wealthy and business groups is the major influence in U.S. policy.

With such definitive research, the controversy seemed to be settled. But far from it. The Gilens-Page research has come under a barrage of attacks. Other researchers who reviewed the data used by Gilins and Page have found that the middle class and the wealthy agreed on 90 percent of the policy decisions. In addition, when the two disagreed, they each got their way about half the time (Enns 2015; Branham t al. 2017).

At this point, then, the pluralist/elitist controversy continues.

The Culture of Wealth   Does the culture of the elite—its institutions, customs, values, worldviews, family ties, and connections—allow the rich and powerful to perpetuate their privileges? In other words, is there a **culture of wealth** that keeps people from falling down the social class ladder, just as some claim that a culture of poverty makes it difficult for poor people to climb even a single rung of that ladder? Of course there is. The elite of any city, region, or nation—indeed, of any group—tend to develop common sentiments and share similar values and goals. The sociological problem is not to determine whether this occurs but to discover how it operates.

It is precisely here that many sociologists see danger—that the concentration of wealth and power violates the democratic processes on which our country is premised. Interlocking interests by wealthy people in powerful positions can result in a few non-elected individuals wielding immense control over the country.

Those who support the power elite view say that this is not a matter of *can*, but, rather, how the country *is* run. I am certain that this debate will continue.

Inequality and Global Poverty

Just as the United States is stratified into different social classes, so the globe is stratified into rich and poor nations. The most industrialized nations, which are wealthy, have **residual poverty**, or pockets of poverty. Most of the least industrialized nations, in contrast, have **mass poverty**: In some, *most* citizens live on less than $1,000 a year. These people are malnourished, chronically ill, and die young. In the following *Global Glimpse*, we look at the abysmal conditions of some children in nations that experience mass poverty.

A Global Glimpse

Killing Kids for Fun and Profit

What is childhood like in the Least Industrialized Nations? As in the United States, the answer depends on who your parents are. If your parents are rich, childhood can be pleasant. If you are born into poverty but live where there is plenty to eat, life can be good—although you will lack books, television, and education. But you probably won't miss them. If you live in a slum, however, life can be horrible, worse than in the slums of the most industrialized nations (Davis 2018). Let's take a glimpse of the slums (*favelas*) of Brazil.

Alcoholism, drug abuse, child abuse, wife beating, a lot of crime, and not having enough food—you can take these for granted. Even in the inner cities of the most industrialized nations, you would expect these things.

Teenagers who remain in the *favela* are of no interest to the middle or mercantile classes. When they venture out of the *favela*, with no money or support, hungry and begging or shoplifting, or looking for work, they pose a threat to the social order.

You might not expect this, though: Poverty is so deep that children and adults swarm over garbage dumps to find enough decaying food to keep them alive. Sociologist Martha Huggins (Huggins et al. 2002) reported that the owners of these dumps hire armed guards to keep the poor out—so they can sell the garbage for pig food. And here's something else you might not expect: Death squads murder some of these children. Some associations of shop owners even put assassins on retainer and auction victims off to the lowest bidder! The going rate is half a month's salary—figured at the low Brazilian minimum wage. Some of the hired killers are policemen.

Life is cheap in the least industrialized nations—but death squads for children? To understand how this could possibly be, we need to note that Brazil has a fragile political structure and a long history of violence. With high poverty and a small middle class, the potential of mob violence and revolution always lurks in the background. The "dangerous classes," as they are known, cast an ominous shadow, a constant threat to the status quo. Roaming the streets are groups of homeless children, who have no jobs or prospects of getting work. To survive, these children scramble in and out of traffic to wash the windshields of cars that stop at red lights. They shine shoes, beg, steal, and sell their bodies.

For many youth in Brazil (and Central and South America), the street corner is their classroom and "the gang" their family. Crime is the name of their employer, as no one else will give them work. They live among violence, they participate in violence, and their short lives end in violence (Davis 2018).

If the children survive, will they become law-abiding, productive adults? The "respectable" classes have a ready answer: Just more criminals. Without social institutions to care for these children, one solution is to kill them. As Huggins notes, murder sends a clear message, especially if it is accompanied by torture—gouging out the eyes, ripping open the chest, cutting off the genitals, raping the girls, and burning the victim's body.

For Your Consideration

→ What can the most industrialized nations do about this situation?

→ Or is this none of our business? Is it, though unfortunate, an internal affair for the Brazilians to handle?

As with individual poverty, a similar question arises in global stratification: Why do some nations remain poor year after year? Let's try to find the answer.

Economic Colonialism   Some analysts find the answer in *economic colonialism*. To obtain raw materials, powerful nations used to invade and conquer weaker nations. After the conquest, they would post a military force in the nation and extract the resources they wanted. The times have changed, and armed conquest is politically unacceptable today. Instead of invading weaker nations, the dominant nations use **economic colonialism**: Capitalists from the most industrialized nations strike a deal with the elite that controls a nation. They gain access to raw materials at a low price—and are assured that the wages of workers will remain low. If workers protest—or, worse, riot and threaten to take control of the factories and resources—this national elite sends soldiers to quiet things down and to keep the profits rolling in. For their part, the elite receive payments for the resources (in the form of bribes and taxes). These countries are unable to keep up with their expanding populations, and with the elite siphoning off vast funds, little money goes to develop schools or industries. Year after year, these nations remain poor and under the control of a small powerful elite.

Political pressure—accompanied by the veiled and not-so-veiled threat of military intervention—is often the force that maintains economic colonialism. Consider the oil-rich nations of the Middle East. What do you think would happen if one of these nations were to become dominant in this region? Controlling the flow of oil to the West, this nation could set high oil prices—and lead the most industrialized nations by the nose. Do you think that the most industrialized nations would allow this? The answer should be obvious. When Iraq made an attempt to dominate this region, the United States and its allies invaded, supposedly on behalf of Kuwait, but those who look at history through the lens of economic colonialism see it differently. They view the Gulf Wars—both the first and second—as a response to threats to the West's economic colonialism of the Middle East.

If another country in this region tries to become dominant, we can expect another violent reprisal of some sort. To view some current events through the lens of economic colonialism will give you a different understanding of global relations.

National Power Elites   As you just saw, central to economic colonialism is a *national power elite* that uses its nation's resources as though they were its personal possession. And this is how national power elites do think of them. The elite's first goal is to keep itself in power, and it uses these resources for this purpose. The West is happy when, for example, the oil-rich nations exchange their oil wealth for jet fighters and other weapons. It is not the West's concern how a national power elite uses these weapons. Its members can exploit their citizens to their hearts' content—as long as the oil or other resources keep flowing.

The national power elites also use the nation's wealth for their own pleasure, to enjoy luxurious lifestyles, and to build prestige for themselves. These power elites live a sophisticated, upper-class lifestyle in the capital city, with vacation homes at the seashore or in neighboring countries. They send their children to elite universities, to Oxford, the Sorbonne, and Harvard. The national power elites operate businesses that are guaranteed success because they are protected from competition and given lush government contracts.

A Culture of Poverty Some suggest a third explanation for why poverty continues in the least industrialized nations—they suffer from a culture of poverty. John Kenneth Galbraith (1979), former U.S. ambassador to India, said that India has a culture of fatalism reinforced by religion. He pointed out that most of the world's poor make a living off the land. With barely enough to live on, poor farmers are reluctant to experiment with different crops or ways of farming: Trying something new might fail, which would lead to hunger or death. Their religion also teaches them to accept their lot in life as God's will and to look for rewards in the afterlife. Galbraith emphasized that poor countries are not poor because they lack resources. Their weak position in world markets, however, combined with their fatalistic culture, makes it unlikely that they will rise from poverty.

In Sum Which explanation is the right one? As you read an explanation, you probably felt inclined to agree with it, only to read another and think that it might be right. Professional analysts, too, find no agreement on these explanations, although they tend to choose one and argue it as the truth. The fairest conclusion seems to be that all three hold some degree of truth, that together they give a fuller explanation than any does separately. Also, each is lacking. None, for example, would explain the current rise of China on the world stage of power—or the coming ascent of India.

Social Policy

7.5 **Explain how shifting views have influenced social policy, what progressive taxation is, and what social programs to relieve poverty are being implemented or considered.**

In previous chapters, you have seen how social policy depends on perspectives. Let's look at how perspectives apply to social policy and poverty.

Changing Views and Changing Social Policy

How people view the causes of social problems influences the social policies they favor. As you saw, when poverty was thought to be God's will, the proper response was thought to be a personal religious duty to shelter, feed, and clothe the poor. Let's look at how these ideas have changed.

Early United States During the time of the American Revolution, poor people were viewed as wayward and lazy. Boston opened a "workhouse" where the poor had to work until they showed that they had acquired self-discipline and an appreciation of hard work. Philadelphia Quakers built almshouses that took in poor women and children. These social policies marked a departure from providing relief on an individual basis. The government was also beginning to provide institutionalized care of the poor (Nash 1979).

In the 1830s, when people believed that the squalor of cities caused poverty, a logical solution was to take the poor away from the corruptions of the city. Life in the country would restore poor people's basic sense of decency and order (Rothman 1971). This attempt failed when institutions in the country filled up and budgets were cut. The institutions then became human warehouses of the worst sort.

It is difficult to remove ourselves from the views that dominate our own historical moment, but let's try to appreciate the attitudes of the time. Consider this statement from Henry Ward Beecher, who was the most prominent clergyman of his day:

> *It is said that a dollar a day is not enough for a wife and five or six children. No, not if the man smokes and drinks beer . . . . But is not a dollar a day enough to buy bread with? Water costs nothing, and a man who cannot live on bread and water is not fit to live. A family may live on good bread and water in the morning, water and bread at midday, and good water and bread at night (quoted in Thayer 1997).*

A dollar went tremendously further in those days, to be sure, and people did pump water freely from backyard wells. But to live on only bread and water—and for that to be considered right?

The Great Depression

> *Millions of families are trying to live on incomes so meager that the pall of family disaster hangs over them day by day . . . . I see one-third of a nation ill-housed, ill-clad, and ill-nourished.*
>
> *President Franklin D. Roosevelt*
> *1937 inaugural address*

In the 1930s, the United States was thrown into the Great Depression. All over the country, businesses closed. As unemployment skyrocketed, so did poverty. Many people who previously worked hard and supported their families did not have enough food to eat. Their economic security jerked from beneath them, people who once had occupied the middle class lined up with the "old poor" in breadlines.

As masses of people became poor, once again the nation's perspective changed. No longer was poverty viewed as the result of God's will, flawed character, or the corruption of the city. Rather, poverty came to be seen as the result of institutional (economic) failure—the lack of jobs. To match this shift in view, the Roosevelt administration created job programs to build parks and public facilities across the nation. It also established basic welfare to help families survive until the husband-father could get a job.

To help those suffering during the Great Depression of the 1930s, the federal government began the Works Progress Administration (WPA). Participants followed the traditional gender roles of the time, with men doing construction and women using homemaking skills.

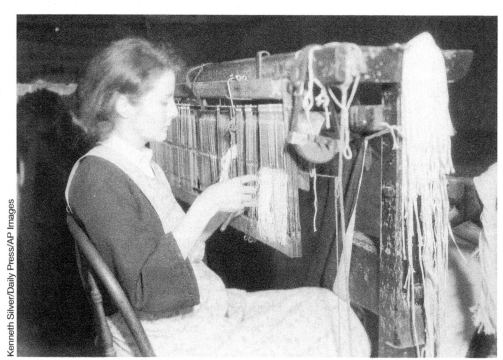

Kenneth Silver/Daily Press/AP Images

World War II   During World War II, when the economy picked up, poverty declined sharply. As jobs became available and men went back to work—and, during World War II, women also—poverty didn't disappear. It was, however, less visible. As I mentioned earlier, new programs came in when poverty was "rediscovered" in the 1960s. Some programs provided education and training so the poor could get jobs. Other programs were based on the assumption that some of the poor, such as single mothers, children, and the elderly, needed to be subsidized.

The Basic Difference—Cause as Inside or Outside of People   As you can see, views have shifted between attributing poverty to forces within the individual (laziness, stupidity, corruption) and to forces outside the individual (God, the evil city, the economy). These contrasting assumptions bring different ideas of which social policies are appropriate. To assume that the causes of poverty lie *within* people leads to such policies as teaching self-discipline and sterilization. To assume that the causes of poverty lie *outside* the individual leads to such policies as education, social reform, job training, and stimulating the economy. Our cycles of social reform still reflect this duality of internal and external forces.

Although different generations define poverty differently, in each era these two core questions remain: What is the cause of poverty and what should we do about it?

Let's look at today's social policies.

Progressive Taxation

To reduce social inequality, the United States has a policy of **progressive taxation**. This means that tax rates progress (increase) as income progresses (increases). It is important to understand that it is not just the amount of taxes that are paid, but the rate itself that increases: The higher the income, the higher the tax rate. You can see this progression on Table 7.1. As Americans earn more, they not only pay more in taxes, but they also pay a larger percentage of their income in taxes.

Table 7.1 Income Taxes Paid by Americans

Adjusted Gross Income	Number of Returns	Tax Paid as a Percentage of Adjusted Gross Income	Approximate Tax Paid by Each Individual	Total Tax Paid (in $billions)
$1,000–$4,999	10,262,000	3%	$150	$0
$5,000–$10,999	14,267,000	2%	$190	$0
$11,000–$18,999	19,022,000	3%	$540	$3
$19,000–$29,999	21,004,000	5%	$1,300	$16
$30,000–$39,999	14,600,000	7%	$2,400	$25
$40,000–$49,999	11,473,000	7%	$3,300	$32
$50,000–$74,999	19,395,000	9%	$5,300	$96
$75,000–$99,999	12,826,000	10%	$8,400	$106
$100,000–$199,999	17,501,000	13%	$17,100	$297
$200,000–$499,999	4,979,000	20%	$55,600	$276
$500,000–$999,999	835,000	26%	$174,000	$145
$1,000,000 or more	410,000	28%	$2,320,000	$380

Source: By the author. Based on *Statistical Abstract of the United States* 2018:Table 512.

Many criticisms can be leveled against our tax system. As an example, from Table 7.1, you can see that those who earn low incomes, just $11,000 to $19,000, pay $3 billion in taxes. From this table, you can also see how progressive our tax system is: The richest 410,000 Americans, those who make $1 million or more a year, pay much more taxes than the entire 123 million people in the first eight categories.

But do they pay enough? This, of course, is another issue, one based on ideas of values and fairness.

To help the poor, we have a social policy called the Per Child Tax Credit, commonly called a *negative income tax*. Parents whose income falls below a specified amount get a tax credit of $2,000 per child. If they have three children and their income is below $54,000, their tax bill will be reduced by $6,400 (Internal Revenue Service 2018).

There is no question that progressive taxation raises huge sums. The question is: What do politicians do with these immense amounts? Some of the money raised by taxing wealthier people at higher rates is redistributed to the poor through welfare, Medicaid, housing subsidies, child care, job training, and food stamps, but some of it is used to build missiles and nuclear weapons as well as bridges that go nowhere. Perhaps a reasonable social policy would be to develop a system to hold politicians accountable for how they spend our tax money. I don't want to be too critical, but if they can spend billions of dollars to bail out Wall Street bankers who made investing mistakes, as the federal government did in the Great Recession of 2008, why can't they do a better job of financing public assistance programs, such as those we will now discuss?

Public Assistance Programs

We can divide public assistance programs into the following four types.

Social Insurance   This type of program, which includes unemployment compensation and Social Security, is designed to help people help themselves. Money is deducted from workers' paychecks, and workers are able to draw on this pool when they need it. Few oppose helping workers who are laid off when an entire industry, such as steel or automobiles, is hit by recession.

Teaching Job Skills   The second type of program is intended to help the poor become self-supporting so they no longer need social welfare. Most of these programs, such as the Job Corps, center on teaching job skills. Some also teach personal grooming, punctuality, and politeness so that prospective workers can meet employer expectations.

Welfare   A third type of program is *welfare*—giving money, food, housing, and medical care to people who have a low enough income to qualify for them. The distinction between deserving and undeserving is replaced by a humanitarian notion that people in need should be helped regardless of the cause of their problems. Some of these programs, such as Temporary Assistance for Needy Families (TANF), Supplemental Nutrition Assistance Program (SNAP, commonly known as food stamps), and public housing, generate controversy because people think they encourage laziness and single women to bear children. Many also think that people who receive this help could work if they wanted to. This stereotyping of the poor has consequences for their lives, the topic of your next *Thinking Critically about Social Problems*.

Thinking Critically about Social Problems

Welfare: How to Ravage the Self-Concept

This was written by Christine Hoffman as an assignment in my introductory course in sociology. I am grateful for her permission to use it in this form.

My husband left me shortly after I was diagnosed with multiple sclerosis. At the time, I had five children. My oldest child was 14,

and my youngest was 7. My physician, believing I would be seriously disabled, helped get me on Social Security disability. The process took several months, and so it became necessary for me to go on public aid and food stamps.

By the time I needed to depend on my family in the face of a crisis, there weren't any resources left to draw on. My father had passed away, and my mother was retired, living on a modest income based on Social Security and my father's pension. Isn't it funny how there is no social stigma attached to Social Security benefits for the elderly? People look at this money as an entitlement—"We worked for it." But people who have to depend on public aid for existence are looked at like vermin and accused of being lazy.

I can tell you from my own experience that a great deal of the lethargy that comes from long periods on welfare is due primarily to the attitudes of the people you have to come into contact with in these programs. I've been through the gamut: from rude, surly caseworkers at Public Aid, to patronizing nurses at the WIC [Women, Infants, and Children] clinic ("You have *how* many children?"), to the accusing tone of the food pantry workers when you have to

Even if social workers mean well, the system, as set up and implemented, often tears at the recipient's sense of worth.

go begging for a handout before the 30-day time span has expired. After a while your dignity is gone, and you start to believe that you really are the disgusting human trash they all make you out to be.

For Your Consideration

→ If you think that the self-concept is important, why should the poor have any less right to a good self-concept than people who aren't poor?

→ Why should poor people have to endure the experiences that Christine describes?

→ Let's suppose that the president of the United States has appointed you as Head of the Department of Welfare. What would you do to improve the welfare delivery system?

Workfare A fourth type of program is *workfare.* Critics claim that welfare reduces people's incentive to work. They say, "Why will people work if they can get money, housing, and food free?" As U.S. welfare rolls swelled to 14 million people in the early 1990s, criticisms grew louder and shriller. The media ran stories about "welfare queens" who collected welfare checks and drove "welfare Cadillacs." "Welfare queen" refers to a woman who is thought to be ripping off the welfare system. She could work, but collects welfare instead, perhaps several checks under different names, often while men support her at home. This term is used to demean single mothers, especially African American women who need assistance.

As criticism mounted, the federal government passed the 1996 Personal Responsibility and Work Opportunity Reconciliation Act. This law requires states to place a lifetime cap on welfare assistance and compels welfare recipients to look for work and take available jobs. It makes 5 years the maximum length of time that someone can collect welfare. In some states, it is less. Unmarried teen parents must attend school and live at home or in some other adult-supervised setting.

It seems reasonable that the goal should not be to just cut people off welfare, but to increase their ability to compete in the job market. This takes us back to teaching job skills, so vital for avoiding welfare in the first place.

Feminized Poverty and Child Support

As we reviewed earlier, poverty is largely feminized; that is, women with children make up most of the poor. As feminist theorists point out, this imbalance exists because women do not receive equal pay. On this broader level, social policies that lead to flexible work schedules and higher pay for women will help. So will improvements in women's job training for career advancement. Social policies that promote better child care facilities and child care assistance will also help.

It also seems reasonable that absent fathers, whether or not they were married to their children's mothers, should support the children they fathered, rather than letting these children become the government's responsibility. The courts can award child care support that better reflects the father's earnings. The courts can also do a better job of making sure that fathers pay the child support that they order them to pay. Recall from Figure 7.10 that most mothers do not receive their full awards—and that one-fourth receive nothing from the fathers of their children. Some fathers, of course, are unemployed and can pay little or nothing. In those instances, it seems reasonable for the state to support those children to lift them out of poverty and to prepare them for a productive future.

Private Agencies and Faith-Based Programs

When we think of aid for the poor, we generally think of the government. The United States also has thousands of private agencies and volunteer organizations that work to help the poor. Because these groups work mainly with the desperate poor, tucked in out-of-the-way urban centers and rural areas, few Americans see them in action. The Salvation Army, for example, runs soup kitchens, food pantries, and homeless shelters, as do other religious groups. The Salvation Army's efforts on behalf of the poor include alcohol counseling and job training.

Until about 20 years ago, the federal government did not fund religious charities on the basis that doing so would violate the principle of separation of church and state. Religious charities are now allowed to compete for federal funds. Without weighing in on the issue of whether the government should fund religious charities, I will point out that without the efforts of religious groups, the social problem of poverty would be much worse. Their long history of charity hospitals and other programs for the poor is outstanding. The quality of faith-based groups, however, varies widely. When I slept and ate in the homeless shelters, I found that some have a personal, encouraging touch. Others, however, show a disgusting disrespect for the homeless people they are supposedly helping. All programs—private, government, or faith-based—must be monitored carefully.

The Purpose of Helping the Poor

What is the purpose of helping the poor? For faith-based organizations, the purpose is connected with their ideas of what God wants them to do. For private groups, the purpose is simply humanitarian: "It's good to help people." Conflict sociologists suggest that the government's motive for its welfare programs is quite different. Let's look at this view.

Regulating the Poor Conflict sociologists Frances Piven and Richard Cloward (1971, 1982, 1989, 1997) argue that because of its "booms" and "busts," capitalism needs a flexible supply of low-skilled, low-paid temporary workers. These people can be put to work when the economy expands and discarded when the economy slows. Welfare is a tool to maintain this pool of temporary workers. It keeps the temporary labor supply from starving during slowdowns so they are available during the next business expansion. To support this assertion, Piven and Cloward point to the changing rules of welfare: In times of high unemployment, when political disorder looms, welfare rules soften. This quiets the impoverished: Giving them a weekly check keeps them from starving or rioting. During "boom" times, in contrast, temporary workers are needed, and welfare rules are tightened. In short, conclude these conflict theorists, the purpose of welfare is to control the unemployed, to maintain social order, and to provide capitalists a pool of cheap labor.

Following Piven and Cloward's analysis, it is no coincidence that the Personal Responsibility and Work Opportunity Reconciliation Act was passed during a long "boom." More workers were needed, and the federal government required states to force the unemployed into the labor market by tightening their rules for welfare eligibility. Some states even fingerprinted applicants for welfare and sent investigators to their homes. During this time, the states began to emphasize job training instead of welfare. New York City even changed the name of its locations from "welfare centers" to "job centers."

This cycle of tightening and loosening eligibility for welfare continues, matching capitalism's "boom-bust" cycles.

Jobs and Child Care

A direct way to deal with poverty is to provide jobs. The federal government lifted millions out of poverty during the Great Depression by providing jobs building bridges, roads, parks, and public buildings. Programs that create jobs stimulate the economy, for the workers spend the money they earn. This, in turn, produces even more jobs. People who approve of job creation disagree violently, however, about how those jobs should be created. Some argue that it is the government's responsibility to create jobs, while others insist that this is the role of private business.

This debate may never be resolved. Rather than becoming embroiled in it, let's highlight two principles. First, regardless of the path we use to get there, what is important is that jobs be available. Second, to be effective in fighting poverty, the jobs should provide a wage that lifts people out of poverty or be a stepping-stone to jobs that do so. Dead-end jobs that keep people in poverty do not meet this goal. Additionally, jobs are often located in the suburbs, where they are inaccessible to inner-city poor. To overcome this limitation, we need to provide transportation for the poor. Finally, because much poverty clusters around women and children, we need quality child care facilities.

Education Accounts

Education is an effective way of reducing poverty. The more education people get, the less likely they are to be poor or unemployed. To spur education, we can offer *education accounts.* The government can establish a credit of, say, $100,000 for *every citizen* at age 18 who graduates from high school. Students would choose from approved colleges and technical and vocational schools. This money could be spent only for direct educational costs, such as tuition, books, and limited living expenses. To continue to qualify for the funds, students would have to make specified progress in their program.

An attractive aspect of this proposal is that ultimately it would cost little or nothing: Not only would this program reduce welfare, but it would also increase people's earning power *for their entire lives.* The additional taxes from these larger earnings would make up for the costs of the education accounts.

The Future of the Problem and Universal Basic Income

7.6   Contrast the unlikely and likely futures of the social problem of poverty.

> *In your future society, robots will do almost all the work. Automation has been proceeding for about a century, but it has picked up such speed and is becoming so extensive that new factories are conspicuous by their near absence of workers. In just a generation, the vast majority of today's work may not exist. And unlike automation of the past, our robotic future may not produce replacement jobs.*

These are serious projections by clear-headed analysts (Dillow and Rainwater 2017). Within the next 20 years, the White House Council of Economic Advisors expects that 83 percent of all jobs that pay less than $20 per hour will be replaced by robots.

Without replacement jobs, what happens to the workers? Will they be discarded like so much rubbish? Will millions upon millions of people be thrown out of their homes when they have no jobs and cannot pay rent or their mortgages?

Obviously, we cannot have a future like this. So, if we roboticize almost all jobs, how do we avoid such a bleak future?

Where are the workers? The production of cars has always taken vast numbers of employees. They held unionized jobs that paid well and provided medical and retirement benefits. Today's car factories are notable by their near absence of workers.

Sten Schunke/Westend61/Getty Images

The fascinating proposal—which also eliminates poverty—is a **universal basic income**, giving all citizens a set amount of money. Let's say this amount is $1,500 a month. No one is required to do anything in return for their monthly check. Absolutely nothing. You receive the check as long as you breathe. And you can do anything you want with it.

This is a serious proposal, and it is being tested. In a two-year experiment, a random sample of 2,000 unemployed citizens of Finland are receiving a universal basic income. The founder of eBay is financing an experiment in Kenya. In the United States, the CEO of Y Combinator is paying 50 households in Oakland, California, $1,500 a month to see what the future might look like.

Actually, experiments with a universal basic income in the United States go to back the 1970s. Random samples of poor people in Denver, Seattle, and New Jersey were given a guaranteed monthly income for either three or five years. The results were not startling. Most people continued to work as much as before, but overall they cut their work hours between 10 and 25 percent. They also spent more on durable goods (cars, refrigerators, TVs) than they did on nondurable goods (food, entertainment) (Pozdena and Johnson 1979; West and Steiger 1980).

I'm sure you would like to receive a no-strings-attached monthly $1,500. Who wouldn't? But where would the money come from? To print additional money without a matching increase in production leads to inflation, which can wipe out the value of the money, defeating the purpose of printing it.

Some say that the answer is robots, the same ones behind the problem. Robots will increase the production that is needed to back the increase in money. Nice if it works.

Will we find out? Maybe this wild experiment will be tried on the nation, but a more likely future is that the public will continue to view the poor as "deserving" and "undeserving" and that the politicians will continue their piecemeal programs. And quite discouragingly, the structural dimension of this social problem will be mostly lost from sight, with the poor continuing to be blamed for their poverty.

But cultural attitudes do sometimes undergo severe shifts. Perhaps one will occur that leads to a future of greater equality. Do you think so?

Summary and Review

1. There are several types of *poverty*. *Biological poverty* refers to starvation and malnutrition. *Relative poverty* is the feeling of being poor in comparison with others, although one may be well-off objectively. *Official poverty* refers to falling below arbitrary standards set by the government. Poverty follows lines of age, gender, geography, and race–ethnicity.

2. Symbolic interactionists examine how the meaning of *income* (for example, whether people see themselves as being rich or poor) differs from its objective measures. Functionalists emphasize that *social inequality* is a way of allocating talented people to society's more demanding tasks and less talented people to its less demanding tasks. They point out that although poverty may be dysfunctional for individuals, it is functional for society. Conflict theorists stress that those who win the struggle for society's limited resources oppress those who lose.

3. Why do some people remain in poverty year after year? Some suggest that the reason is a *culture of poverty*, self-defeating behaviors that parents pass on to their children. Most sociologists, in contrast, view the culture of poverty, to the limited extent that it exists, not as the cause of poverty, but rather as the result of poverty. Why do some countries remain in poverty year after year? Some suggest that this is because they have a national culture of poverty.

Others look to *economic colonialism* and exploitation by national elites.

Conflict theorists also stress that a *power elite* of top politicians and corporate and military leaders makes society's big decisions. *Pluralists* disagree. They view society as made up of many *interest groups* that compete with one another in a marketplace of power and ideas.

4. Policies for dealing with poverty are as diverse as the beliefs about its causes. In the 1700s, poverty was considered God's will, and it was a person's religious duty to help the poor. Personal moral failure has also been considered to be a cause of poverty. During the Great Depression, the poor were considered victims of economic conditions and were helped on a massive scale. Welfare programs cause bitter debate. Rules have been tightened to make fewer people eligible for welfare and to "encourage" the poor to take jobs. Where conservatives think that individuals should take more personal responsibility, liberals view government action as more appropriate.

5. Roboticized automation is likely to replace most jobs, and it is uncertain if replacement jobs will exist. A proposed solution is a universal basic income. In a more likely future, poverty will continue, and so will our piecemeal welfare programs and the view of the poor as "deserving" and "undeserving."

Thinking Critically about Chapter 7

1. What is your reaction to Herbert Gans' observations on how poverty helps society? Do you think Gans is serious? (See *Thinking Critically about Social Problems: Why We Need the Poor* and *Spotlight on Social Research: Demonizing the Poor*.)

2. Review the different rates of poverty by age, geography, and race–ethnicity. (See Figures 7.6, 7.7, 7.8, and 7.9.) Now explain them. To do so sociologically, you

might want to begin by asking, "Why don't all groups have the same rate of poverty?"

3. A central debate in sociology has been whether the power elite or the pluralist view is correct. Which do you think is right? Why?

4. What do you think can be done to solve the social problem of poverty?

Key Terms

Chapter 8
Racial–Ethnic Relations

Jim West/Alamy Stock Photo

Learning Objectives

After reading this chapter, you should be able to:

8.1 Distinguish between minority and dominant groups, know the origin and goals of minority groups and the policies of dominant groups, and explain why race is a social category.

8.2 Know what *racial–ethnic group* means, explain why the melting pot failed to melt, summarize basic information on institutional and unintended discrimination, and appreciate what cold numbers can represent.

8.3 Discuss the perspectives that emerge when you apply symbolic interactionism, functionalism, and conflict theory to racial–ethnic relations.

8.4 Explain why *Latino* is an umbrella term, the issue of unauthorized immigrants, the relative economic well-being of Latinos, and their political divisions and potential.

8.5 Summarize the civil rights history of African Americans, their relative economic well-being, and the controversy over race versus social class.

8.6 Discuss why *Asian American* is an umbrella term, the history of discrimination against Asian Americans, their relative economic well-being, and their political situation.

8.7 Explain why *Native American* is an umbrella term, their relations with settlers, the significance of disease, justifying labels, education and culture conflict, casinos, and self-determination.

8.8 Summarize social policy regarding cultural pluralism, preventing discrimination, and the dilemma of affirmative action.

8.9 Discuss the likely future of racial–ethnic relations.

The six or seven high school boys in Medford, New York, who hung out together liked to go "beaner hopping"—their term for hunting Latinos. They would drive around town, looking for someone they could harass and beat up. ("Beaner" refers to beans, a staple in the Hispanic diet.)

It wasn't an everyday activity—just something they did about once a week, the boys said.

On this Saturday, they began early. Seeing one man in his driveway, they stopped their SUV and shot him several times with a BB gun. That night, they came across two men walking near the train station. Surrounding the men, they called them "Mexicans" and "illegals." The boys accused them of taking money from Americans.

One of the men ran. A few boys chased after him. The other man, Marcelo Lucero, fought back. Taking off his belt, Lucero hit one of his taunters, Jeffrey Conroy, in the face. Enraged, Conroy pulled out a knife and stabbed Lucero in the chest. Lucero died a few minutes later.

> ## "They're saying that he's a supremacist. It's not true. He's a very loving person."

Was this a hate crime? It certainly seemed like it, but when details emerged, the situation grew murky. One of the defendants has a black father and a Puerto Rican mother. His lawyer claimed that because of this, he cannot be guilty of a hate crime against a Latino. Interesting position.

Then there is the swastika on Conroy's leg, usually an indicator of hate. On the other hand, Conroy's girlfriend is from Bolivia, so perhaps it wasn't a hate crime.

Conroy's Bolivian girlfriend defended Conroy. She said, "I dated him for about four years. He never said anything anti-Hispanic to me. He didn't care what you were. They're saying that he's a supremacist. It's not true. He's a very loving person."

Certainly another interesting position.

When it came to selecting a jury, the situation grew even murkier.

Hundreds of potential jurors were questioned to find a dozen people who said they could be fair. Many said they had negative feelings about the illegal immigrants in their town, and they asked to be excused from jury duty.

Then there were those who said they didn't think they could be fair because they were married to someone of Mexican descent, or they worked with Mexicans and liked them.

Hate crime? Maybe. Or maybe just guys who got a kick out of beating up people, and they found the illegal immigrants easy victims. Many are afraid of going to the police.

The jury found Conroy guilty, and the judge sentenced him to 25 years in prison.

—Based on Fernandez 2010; Ojito 2014.

The Problem in Sociological Perspective

8.1 Distinguish between minority and dominant groups, know the origin and goals of minority groups and the policies of dominant groups, and explain why race is a social category.

Prejudice, discrimination, and racial–ethnic violence are an unfortunate fact of life in the United States. Hostilities and tensions among groups surface on the street, at schools, and with occasional media-captivating events like those profiled in our opening vignette.

To better understand this social problem, let's start by looking at the bigger picture.

Minority and Dominant Groups

To see the bigger picture, you need to be able to distinguish between prejudice and discrimination and minority and dominant groups.

Prejudice and Discrimination Prejudice and discrimination are sometimes confused. **Prejudice** is an *attitude*—a prejudging of some sort. The prejudging is usually negative, but it can be positive. **Discrimination**, in contrast, is an *action*. It refers to treating someone or some group unfairly. Unfair treatment is often based on appearance—age, race–ethnicity, sex, height, weight, disability, clothing, and the like. People also discriminate against others on the basis of their income, education, language, speech patterns, sexual orientation, religion, and politics.

Prejudice and discrimination exist around the world. In Northern Ireland, Protestants and Roman Catholics discriminate against one another (Mitchell 2018). In Israel, wealthier Jews, primarily of European descent, discriminate against poorer Jews of Asian and African backgrounds (Frantzman 2015). In Europe, Muslim immigrants are singled out for harassment (Ahmed 2018). In Egypt, Muslims discriminate against Christians (Sherwood 2018). In Japan, the Japanese discriminate against just about anyone who isn't Japanese, especially the Koreans and Ainu who live there (de Graaf 2016). And to move beyond any specific group, we can note that in every society, men discriminate against women.

Minority Does Not Mean Smaller   People who are discriminated against because they belong to a particular group are called a **minority group**. As sociologist Louis Wirth (1945) defined them, these are people who are singled out for unequal treatment on the basis of their physical or cultural characteristics *and* who regard themselves as objects of collective discrimination. Discrimination denies a minority full participation in society.

Minority in this sense does not necessarily mean *numerical* minority. In colonial India, a handful of British discriminated against 350 million Indians. In South Africa, the descendants of Dutch settlers used to be in political control of the country. They discriminated against the much larger population of blacks in housing, jobs, and education. Although there are more women than men, in every society men discriminate against women. Accordingly, we refer to those who discriminate as the **dominant group**. This group, which has more power, privileges, and higher social status, can be either larger or smaller in number than the minority group.

The Origin of Minority Groups

"We didn't move across the border—the border moved across us."

—A Latino whose family has lived in New Mexico for generations

Minority groups come into existence either through political expansion or migration. As with the above quote, some groups become minorities when a government expands its political boundaries. A second way that minority groups originate is through migration— when people who have different physical characteristics or customs move to a new country.

"Minority" does not necessarily mean smaller. Less than 100,000 British troops were ruling India's 350 million people at its independence in 1947.

Hulton-Deutsch Collection/Corbis Historical/Getty Images

The migration can be involuntary, as with Africans who were forcibly brought to the United States, or voluntary, as with Turks who chose to move to Germany for work.

Minorities come into existence, then, when people who have different customs, languages, values, or physical characteristics come under control of a political system. There, some groups who share physical and cultural traits discriminate against those who have different traits. The losers in this power struggle are forced into minority-group status, while the winners enjoy the higher status and greater privileges that dominance brings.

Characteristics of Minority Groups   The classic analysis of minority groups was done by two anthropologists, Charles Wagley and Marvin Harris. They (1958) noted that minority groups share five characteristics:

1. *Ascribed status:* Membership comes through birth.
2. *Prejudice:* The dominant group holds the minority's physical or cultural traits in low esteem.
3. *Discrimination:* The dominant group treats members of the minority group unequally.
4. *Endogamy:* Minority members tend to marry within their group.
5. *Common identity:* Minority members identify with one another because of their shared physical or cultural traits—and the disadvantages these traits bring.

To sense a shared identity, especially a sense of "we" versus "them," is powerful. This identity is sometimes so strong that members of a minority group feel that they share a common destiny.

Goals of Minority Groups   The classic analysis of what minority groups want to accomplish in regard to the dominant group was done by sociologist Louis Wirth. He (1945) identified four different objectives:

1. *Assimilation:* Wanting to be treated as individuals, not as members of a separate group, members of the minority group adopt the culture of the dominant group and are absorbed into the larger society.
2. *Pluralism:* The minority wants to live peacefully with the dominant group yet maintain the differences that set it apart and are important to its identity.
3. *Secession:* Wanting cultural and political independence, the minority seeks to separate itself and form a separate nation.
4. *Militancy:* Convinced of its own superiority, the minority wants to reverse the status and dominate the society.

Policies of Dominant Groups   Dominant groups also differ in their objectives regarding minority groups. Figure 8.1 outlines six policies of dominant groups identified by

Figure 8.1 Policies of Dominant Groups toward Minority Groups

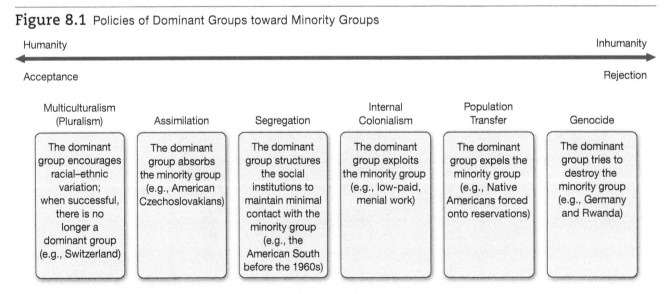

Sources: By the author. Based on Simpson and Yinger 1972; Henslin 2018.

sociologists George Simpson and J. Milton Yinger. As we review these policies, you can see how they can help or hinder minorities.

1. **Pluralism.** *Pluralism* (multiculturalism) exists when a dominant group permits or even encourages cultural differences. The "hands-off" policy toward immigrant associations and foreign-language newspapers in the United States is an example. In Switzerland, the French, Italian, German, and Romish Swiss, who live peacefully together in a political and economic unit, have retained their separate languages and other customs. None of these groups is considered a minority.

2. **Assimilation.** *Assimilation* is an attempt to eliminate the minority by absorbing it into the mainstream culture. In *forced assimilation*, the dominant group bans the minority's religion, language, and other distinctive customs. In the former Soviet Union, the Russians treated Armenians this way. *Permissible assimilation*, in contrast, lets the minority adopt the dominant customs at its own pace. In the United States, we expect that cultural minorities will gradually give up their distinctive customs, such as unique clothing and language, and adopt the customs of the dominant culture.

3. **Segregation.** *Segregation* is an attempt by the dominant group to keep a minority "in its place"—that is, subservient, exploitable, and "off by itself." In South Africa between 1948 and 1990, the small number of whites who controlled the nation established **apartheid** (ah-'pär-tāte), a system of rules that segregated blacks and whites in almost all spheres of life. In the face of international sanctions that threatened the nation's economy, the whites dismantled apartheid.

4. **Internal colonialism.** *Colonialism* refers to a more powerful nation making a colony of a weaker nation so it can exploit its resources; *internal colonialism* refers to events within the same country, where a dominant group exploits a minority group's labor.

5. **Population transfer.** In *direct population transfer*, the dominant group transfers the minority to a specified area or forces it to leave the country. In the 1400s, for example, King Ferdinand and Queen Isabella (who financed Columbus's voyage to North America) drove the Jews and Moors out of Spain. *Indirect population transfer* occurs when the dominant group makes life so miserable for a minority that its members "choose" to leave. Facing the bitter conditions of czarist Russia, for example, millions of Jews made this "choice."

6. **Genocide.** Hatred, fear, or greed can motivate the dominant group to turn to a policy of extermination, or *genocide*. The most infamous example is the Holocaust. Between 1933 and 1945, the Nazis slaughtered about 6 million Jews, hundreds of thousands of Slavs, a quarter of a million Gypsies, and unknown numbers of homosexuals, communists, people with disabilities, and the mentally ill—all people whom Hitler considered too "impure" to be part of his mythical Aryan race.

Ideas of Racial Superiority

Hitler was convinced that **race**—the inherited physical characteristics that identify a group of people—made some groups superior and others inferior. In his mind, tall, fair-skinned, mostly blond-haired people called the Aryans formed a "super race." This race, he said, was responsible for the cultural achievements of Europe. The Aryans had a destiny—to establish a higher culture, a new world order. To fulfill this destiny, the Aryans had to avoid "racial mixing," the "contamination" that comes from breeding with "inferior races." To preserve Aryan biology and culture, the "inferior races" needed to be isolated or destroyed. Some "lower races" could remain to perform tasks too lowly for Aryans to perform.

Today, most people find Hitler's ideas bizarre, but in the 1930s both the public and the scientific community took views like this seriously. Many biologists and anthropologists in Europe and the United States believed that sharp lines divided the "races" and that some "races" were inherently superior to others. It is not surprising that these scientists always concluded that Caucasians were the superior "race," for they themselves were Caucasian.

A related development of the time was *eugenics*—attempts to improve humans through selective breeding. Underlying eugenics was the assumption of racial superiority. This wasn't just Hitler's strange idea. At that time, eugenics was such a popular and dominant idea that it was approved by scientists, educators, health specialists, religious leaders, and prominent politicians of the Western nations, including the United States.

The idea of racial superiority, which justifies one group's rule over another, is certainly less popular today, but it does persist. Almost everyone assumes that "race" really exists, identifies with some "racial" group, and classifies other people into different "racial" groups. Some think that their "race" is superior to others.

Race as an Arbitrary Social Category

People have such a mixture of physical characteristics—skin color, hair texture, nose and head shapes, height, eye color, and so on—that there is no pure race. Instead, biologists have found that human characteristics flow endlessly into one another, a melding that makes any attempt to draw sharp distinctions arbitrary. Even the large groupings of humans that can be classified by blood type and gene frequencies contain tremendous variation. From the following *Thinking Critically about Social Problems,* you can see how arbitrary racial classifications are.

Thinking Critically about Social Problems

Can a Plane Ride Change Your Race?

According to common sense, the title question is nonsense—our racial classifications represent biological differences. Yet contrary to "common sense," sociologists stress that what we call races are *social* classifications, not biological categories.

Sociologists point out that *our "race" depends more on the society in which we live than on our biological characteristics*. For example, the racial categories that are common in the United States are merely one of *numerous* ways by which people around the world classify physical appearances. Although groups around the world use different categories, each group assumes that its categories are natural, merely a logical response to visible physical differences.

To better understand this essential sociological point—that race is more social than it is biological—consider this: In the United States, children who are born to the same parents are all of the same race. I am sure that you are thinking, "What could be more natural?" This is the common view of Americans. But in Brazil, children who are born to the same parents can be of different races—if their appearances differ. "What could be more natural?" assume Brazilians.

Consider how Americans usually classify a child who is born to a "black" mother and a "white" father. Why do they usually say that the child is "black"? Wouldn't it be equally logical to classify the child as "white"? Similarly, if a child's grandmother is "black" but all her other ancestors are "white," the child is often considered "black." Yet she has much more "white ancestry" than "black ancestry." Why, then, is she considered "black"? Certainly not because of biology. Rather, such thinking is a legacy of slavery. Before the Civil War, numerous children were born whose fathers were white slave masters and whose mothers were black slaves. In an attempt to preserve the "purity" of their "race," whites classified anyone with even a "drop of black blood" as "not white."

What "race" is this Brazilian mother and child? Is the mother's "race" different from her daughter's "race"? The text explains why "race" is such an unreliable concept that a person's "race" changes even with geography.

Race is so social—and fluid—that even a plane ride can change a person's race. In the city of Salvador in Brazil, people classify one another by the color of their skin and eyes, the breadth of their nose and lips, and the color and curliness of their hair. They use at least seven terms for what we call white and black. Consider again a U.S. child who has one "white" and one "black" parent. Although she is "black" in the United States, if she flies to Brazil, she will belong to one of their several "whiter" categories (Fish 1995).

On the flight just mentioned, did the girl's "race" actually change? Our common sense revolts at this, I know, but it actually did. We want to argue that because her biological characteristics remain unchanged, her race remains unchanged. This is because we think of race as biological, when *race is actually a label we use to describe perceived biological characteristics*. Simply put, the race we "are" depends on *where* we are—on who is doing the classifying.

"Racial" classifications are fluid, not fixed. Even now, you can see changes occurring in the United States. Our new terms "multiracial" and "two or more races" indicate changing ideas about race.

Who knows? Fifty years from now, we might have entirely different "racial" classifications. Many hope we would have none by then, but given our history, this is unlikely.

For Your Consideration

→ How would you explain to someone the sociological point that race is more a social classification than a biological one?

→ Can you come up with any arguments to refute the sociological view presented in this box?

→ How do you think our racial–ethnic classifications will change in the future?

Lianne Milton/Blend Images/Newscom

The Scope of the Problem

8.2   Know what *racial–ethnic group* means, explain why the melting pot failed to melt, summarize basic information on institutional and unintended discrimination, and appreciate what cold numbers can represent.

Wanting to avoid a term as imprecise as *race*, many sociologists, as I will do in this chapter, use the term *racial–ethnic group*. The term *ethnic* is derived from the Greek word *ethnos*, meaning "people" or "nation." A **racial–ethnic group** refers to people who identify with one another on the basis of their ancestry and cultural heritage. Their sense of belonging may center on unique physical characteristics, foods, dress, names, language, music, and religion. It is with this meaning that I use *race–ethnicity*. As we just reviewed, collective discrimination and intermarriage may also generate a common identity.

Let's set the stage for our discussion by identifying the largest racial–ethnic groups in the United States, which we do in Figure 8.2. As we analyze the social problem of racial–ethnic relations, we'll come back to this figure several times. In our discussion, I will stress the objective conditions and subjective concerns related to people being deprived of the rights to which citizenship entitles them—the equality guaranteed by the U.S. Constitution of "life, liberty, and the pursuit of happiness."

Figure 8.2 U.S. Racial–Ethnic Groups

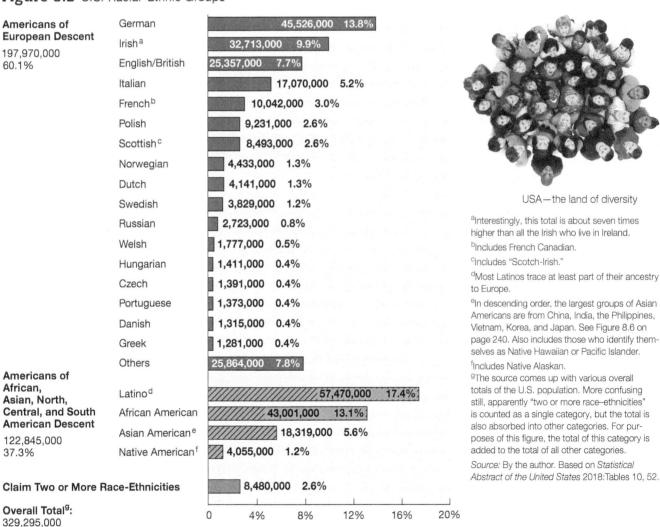

Americans of European Descent
197,970,000
60.1%

German	45,526,000	13.8%
Irish[a]	32,713,000	9.9%
English/British	25,357,000	7.7%
Italian	17,070,000	5.2%
French[b]	10,042,000	3.0%
Polish	9,231,000	2.6%
Scottish[c]	8,493,000	2.6%
Norwegian	4,433,000	1.3%
Dutch	4,141,000	1.3%
Swedish	3,829,000	1.2%
Russian	2,723,000	0.8%
Welsh	1,777,000	0.5%
Hungarian	1,411,000	0.4%
Czech	1,391,000	0.4%
Portuguese	1,373,000	0.4%
Danish	1,315,000	0.4%
Greek	1,281,000	0.4%
Others	25,864,000	7.8%

Americans of African, Asian, North, Central, and South American Descent
122,845,000
37.3%

Latino[d]	57,470,000	17.4%
African American	43,001,000	13.1%
Asian American[e]	18,319,000	5.6%
Native American[f]	4,055,000	1.2%

Claim Two or More Race-Ethnicities   8,480,000   2.6%

Overall Total[g]:
329,295,000

Percentage of Americans (0, 4%, 8%, 12%, 16%, 20%)

USA—the land of diversity

Compassionate Eye Foundation/Jasper White/DigitalVision/Getty Images

[a]Interestingly, this total is about seven times higher than all the Irish who live in Ireland.

[b]Includes French Canadian.

[c]Includes "Scotch-Irish."

[d]Most Latinos trace at least part of their ancestry to Europe.

[e]In descending order, the largest groups of Asian Americans are from China, India, the Philippines, Vietnam, Korea, and Japan. See Figure 8.6 on page 240. Also includes those who identify themselves as Native Hawaiian or Pacific Islander.

[f]Includes Native Alaskan.

[g]The source comes up with various overall totals of the U.S. population. More confusing still, apparently "two or more race–ethnicities" is counted as a single category, but the total is also absorbed into other categories. For purposes of this figure, the total of this category is added to the total of all other categories.

Source: By the author. Based on *Statistical Abstract of the United States* 2018:Tables 10, 52.

Immigrants and the Melting Pot: Invitations and Walls

"The stocks and folkways of Europe [would be], figuratively speaking, indiscriminately mixed in the political pot of the emerging nation and melted together by the fires of American influence and interaction into a distinctly new type."

—Milton Gordon, sociologist, 1964

Throughout U.S. history, immigrants have confronted **Anglo-conformity**; that is, they were expected to speak English and adopt other Anglo-Saxon ways of life. The nation's founders wanted to produce a modified version of England. Many thought that the evolving society would become a **melting pot**—that it would "melt" European immigrants into a new cultural and biological blend.

Some people were not invited to join the melting pot. Americans of Western European background set up walls to prevent nonwhites from becoming part of this new "biological mix." To protect themselves from "racial impurity," they passed laws that put blacks and whites in separate schools and made it illegal for blacks and whites to marry.

For most European immigrants, the melting pot became a reality. Most lost their specific ethnic identities and merged into mainstream culture. They might have some vague ethnic identity—"I'm three-quarters German and one-quarter mixed Italian and Greek, with some English thrown in"—but they tend to think of themselves as "just American." For some groups, however, their cultural and ethnic identities remain strong, especially recent immigrants from Mexico, Cuba, Haiti, Vietnam, Laos, India, and Islamic countries. And some who want to get "melted" have found that their appearance evokes stereotypes that make such melting elusive. This is the topic of the following *Spotlight on Social Research*.

Spotlight on Social Research

Being a "Foreign" American

NAZLI KIBRIA, *professor of sociology at Boston University, did research on second-generation Chinese and Korean Americans. She explored their experience of being identified by others as "Asian." In this essay, she reports on how "racial identities" serve as markers (or signals) in everyday social encounters. These "markers" are based on how people perceive the physical characteristics of others. This is what she wrote for you.*

Boston University © 2007, Photo provided by Nazli Kibria

I use the term "second-generation Chinese and Korean Americans" to refer to people of Chinese and Korean ancestry who were born and/or from a young age reared in the United States. Based on their encounters with people of non-Asian origin, I explored the ways in which they experience the identity marker of "Asian race" in their daily lives.

In their everyday social encounters, non-Asian Americans often assume that Chinese and Korean Americans are "foreigners." With the perception of "Asian" often comes an image of an unassimilable alien—a presence that is fundamentally and unalterably outside of, if not diametrically opposite to, what "American" is. Many of my informants said that they frequently were asked, "Where are you from?" While this question may be intended as an inquiry about one's regional origin in the United States (e.g., "Are you from Southern California?"), when asked of Asian Americans, it is often meant as a question about nationality and ethnic origins. In fact, informants told me that if they answered the question in local terms (such as, "I'm from Boston"), the person often followed up with something like, "Yes, but where are you really from?"

My informants had several ways of responding to these queries. In some situations, they interpreted the question as innocuous or even positive, as an effort on the part of the questioner to avoid making generalizations about Asian Americans and to establish the individual's specific ethnic identity. At other times, in contrast, my informants interpreted the question as an assumption that everyone of Asian origin is a foreigner and not American.

Among the strategies that my informants used to neutralize or at least to deflect the assumption of their foreignness were *dis-identifiers*. To remove an identity of "foreignness" and provide an identity of "American," they used symbols, such as language, dress, demeanor, and even the people with whom they were seen or associated. Language was one of their main dis-identifiers. During an encounter with strangers, they would deflect their presumed foreignness by speaking fluent and unaccented English. The need to use dis-identifiers produced an awareness among my informants that for Asian Americans, the achievement and acceptance of an American identity requires vigilance and work.

Ascribing "foreignness" to second-generation Chinese and Korean Americans not only casts doubt upon their identity as Americans, but also signals *authentic ethnicity*. That is, the dominant society assumes that second-generation Chinese and Korean Americans have ties to a community and culture that is either located or rooted outside the U.S. mainstream. These ties are assumed to be strong and genuine, rather than contrived or fake. My informants were especially aware of this assumption of ethnic authenticity when a non-Asian American would ask them to interpret Asian, Korean, or Chinese cultural practices or in some other way to display their ethnic cultural knowledge.

For Your Consideration

→ What does Professor Kibria mean by authentic ethnicity?
→ What is your race–ethnicity? Why do you claim this particular identity?
→ How has your race–ethnicity been an influence in your life?
→ How have others reacted to your race–ethnicity?

Stereotypes   Each group of immigrants that entered the United States confronted prejudice based on **stereotypes**—generalizations of what people are like. Some of these stereotypes were highly negative. The British immigrants provide an excellent example. Bringing prejudice with them as part of their cultural baggage, they viewed the Irish as dirty, lazy, untrustworthy drunkards.

As you know, negative racial-ethnic stereotypes have not disappeared. From the jokes you have heard, and perhaps told, you know how these stereotypes paint others in, shall we say, unflattering terms. In the next *Thinking Critically about Social Problems,* we explore an extreme: people who manipulate stereotypes to breed hatred.

Thinking Critically about Social Problems

What Should We Do about Hate Speech?

The Internet has become a marvelous source of information. This tool allows social researchers to pack an entire library, and more, in their luggage and take it with them around the world. As I write this in Latvia, I am able to keep up with political, economic, and social events by reading a couple of daily newspapers from the States. I am also able to type a few words into a search engine and bring up research articles on almost any topic. I still marvel as I use this tool, both at the information it makes available and the freedom it offers to do research around the world.

The Internet is also a remarkable source of misinformation. Anyone can put up a website or post a blog and fill it with lies or distortions of truth. They can give vent to anger, seek revenge for perceived wrongs, and spew hatred. These negative communications are upsetting. Consider these statements:

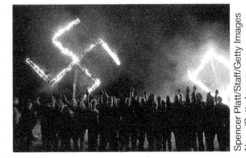

Spencer Platt/Staff/Getty Images News/Getty Images

Members of the National Socialist Movement, who met in Draketown, Georgia, are shown here at a swastika burning. Free speech, though it continues to be a contentious issue, is a basic right guaranteed by our Constitution.

Civil rights come out of the barrel of a gun, and we mean to give the niggers and Jews all the civil rights they can handle.... Our security team will see that no live targets escape from the range. Any who refuse to run or can't for any reason will be fed to the dogs. The dogs appreciate a good feed as much as we do.

—An invitation to a summer conference held by the Aryan Nations at Hayden Lake, Idaho (quoted in Murphy 1999)

Who's pimping the world? The hairy hands of the Zionist.... The so-called Jew claims that there were 6 million in Nazi Germany. I am here today to tell you that there is absolutely no...evidence to substantiate, to prove that 6 million so-called Jews lost their lives in Nazi Germany.... Don't let no hooked-nose, bagel-eating, lox-eating, perpetrating a-fraud so-called Jew who just crawled out of the ghettoes of Europe just a few days ago…

—Statements of Khalid Abdul Muhammad (quoted in Herbert 1988)

Hatred, prejudice, and stereotypes know no racial–ethnic boundaries; the first statement was made by a white, the second by an African American.

Should we ban such statements from the Internet and other forms of the mass media? Should we punish their authors as lawbreakers? Or should we allow statements like these to be circulated as part of free speech, regardless of their inflammatory rhetoric, the twisting of fact, or the hatred they spew?

Canada has banned hate speech, and several countries in Europe make it a crime to display Nazi symbols or to deny that the Holocaust took place (Elgot and Sommers 2015). Ernst Zundel, a German immigrant to Canada, ran afoul of these laws. He was arrested and deported to Germany, where he was tried on the charge of saying that the Holocaust did not happen. Zundel was found guilty and served five years in prison. When he was released from prison, supporters shouting "Bravo!" were waiting to greet him with flowers (Frey 2010; Micallef 2015).

For Your Consideration

→ Many recoil at the possibility of censoring ideas. They take the position that all censorship poses a threat to our freedoms. As much as we dislike hatred, its censorship is an attack on free speech. That people can be put in prison for expressing ideas, as with Zundel in Germany, sends a chill up the spine of the advocates of free speech. They point out that under the heavy hand of political censors any negative observations or comments about a racial-ethnic group can be construed as hatred. The next time, they say, it might be *your* ideas that are banned because some politicians decide that they don't like them. What do you think?

→ On the other side of this argument are those who say that hatred is powerful and can lead to violence. They point out that Hitler began with ideas. Passing laws against hate speech and punishing those who express those ideas, they say, is reasonable. What do you think?

Institutional Discrimination

To understand discrimination, we need to move beyond thinking in terms of **individual discrimination**, one person treating another badly on the basis of race–ethnicity. Although this certainly creates problems, it is an individual matter and does not qualify as a social problem. Sociologists encourage us to move beyond individual situations and to think in broader terms. Let's do so.

Institutional Discrimination in the Past   **Institutional discrimination** is inequality built into a social system that oppresses whole groups of people. When this occurs, not only does the dominant group take institutional discrimination for granted, but often it also assumes that this is the way life should be. When the National Association of Real Estate Boards (NAR) practiced institutional discrimination as a routine matter, this organization also defended racial discrimination as a *moral* act. Here is a statement from its 1924 code of ethics:

> *A Realtor should never be instrumental in introducing into a neighborhood…members of any race or nationality, or individuals whose presence will clearly be detrimental to property values in that neighborhood (Newman et al. 1978:149).*

Did the federal government take the NAR to court over this blatant discrimination, as it would today? On the contrary, the government *backed* the institutional discrimination. If developers of subdivisions wanted to obtain a loan from the Federal Housing Authority (FHA), *they had to exclude nonwhites* (Valocchi 1994; Oliver and Shapiro 1995). Even after World War II, the FHA denied loans to anyone who would "unsettle a neighborhood." No one was hiding this because the discrimination was considered a moral act, done to protect people's property. The FHA's manual was explicit: "If a neighborhood is to retain stability, it is necessary that properties shall continue to be occupied by the same social and racial classes" (Duster 1988:288).

As times changed, so did the NAR and the federal agencies. In 1950, under pressure, the NAR deleted the reference to race or nationality. The NAR kept resisting the change, though, and didn't take a position to support fair housing until 1972.

Institutional Discrimination Today   Many aspects of institutional discrimination, such as the discrimination practiced by the NAR, strike the contemporary ear as strange and as something from a long ago past. However, although greatly weakened, institutional discrimination continues, lurking in hidden forms. Look at Figure 8.3, which illustrates mortgage

Figure 8.3 Predatory Lending when Buying a House:
Far-Reaching Effects of Institutional Discrimination

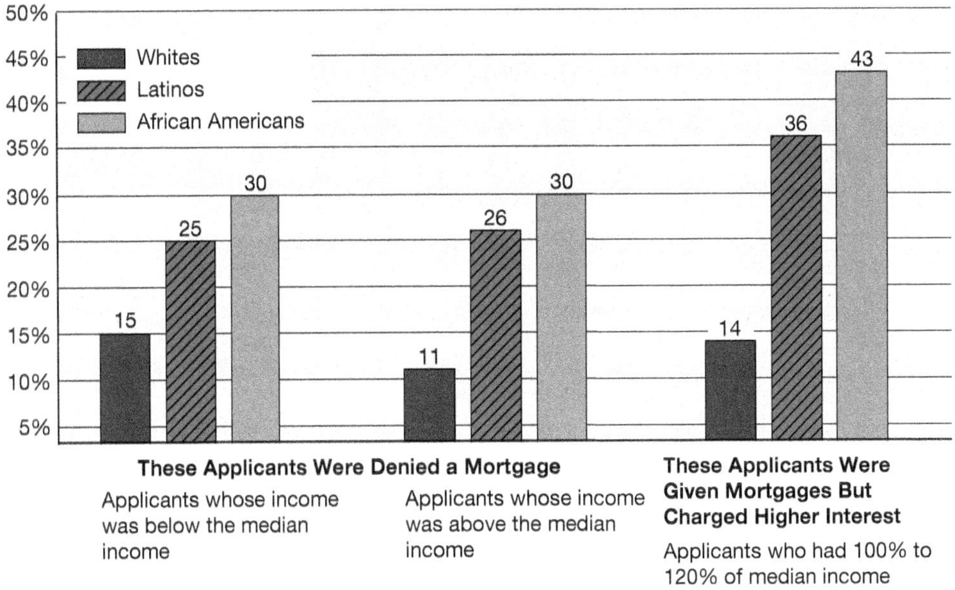

Source: By the author. Based on Kochbar and Gonzalez-Barrera, *Essentials of Sociology*, Pearson Education, 2009.

loans, another aspect of housing. You can see that *minorities are more likely to be turned down for a loan—whether their incomes are below or above the median income of their community.*

Beyond this harsh finding lies another just as devastating. In the last credit crisis that caused so many to lose their homes, African Americans and Latinos were hit harder than whites. The last set of bars on Figure 8.3 shows a major reason for this: *Banks targeted minorities to charge higher interest rates.* We are not talking about a rogue banker here or there. Like the NAR's earlier discrimination to protect neighborhoods, this discrimination, which existed across the United States, was intentional, built into the structure of banking. As we reviewed in the last chapter, the results of this *predatory banking* were devastating: If African Americans and Latinos had had the lower interest rates they qualified for, many would not have lost their homes.

Unintended Institutional Discrimination   Here is a fascinating aspect of institutional discrimination: *It can occur even when those who are doing the discriminating are unaware of it.* Let's look at IQ testing as an example.

> Imagine that you are in the fifth grade and your class is going to be given an IQ test. For "politically correct" reasons, the test has been renamed The Achievement Predictor (TAP). Your teacher tells you and your classmates to do your best because the test results are going to affect your future. This is rather vague, but it makes you feel a little nervous. You intend to do your best anyway. You don't want anyone to think you're mentally challenged.
>
> The booklets are passed out face down. You fill out the blanks on the back, carefully printing the date, your name, class, school, and teacher. At your teacher's command, for this is a timed test, you turn the booklet over, open it, and eagerly read the first question. You can hardly believe your eyes when you read:
>
> 1. *If you throw the dice and "7" is showing on the top, what is facing down?*
>
>   ____seven   ____snake eyes   ____box cars   ____little Joes   ____eleven
>
> This question confuses you. You haven't the slightest idea of what the correct answer might be. When you played Monopoly, you never looked under the dice.
>
> Since your teacher said that it is better to guess than to leave an answer blank, you put a check mark on something. Then you go to the second question, which only increases your confusion and frustration. Here is what you read:

2. *Which word is out of place here?*

____*splib* ____*blood* ____*gray* ____*spook* ____*black*

Again, you have no idea of what choice is correct, so you put a check on anything. The questions that follow are just as meaningless to you as these first two. You continue to check answers, for the most part, aimlessly. As this seemingly endless nonsense continues, somewhere in the process you give up.

No longer do you read the questions thoroughly, for it doesn't seem to affect which blank you check.

It is obvious that you performed poorly on this test. It should also be obvious why—you were being tested on things far removed from your background of experiences.

Some questions on standardized IQ tests favor children from certain backgrounds. Consider this question:

A symphony is to a composer as a book is to a(n) ____:

____*paper* ____*sculptor* ____*musician* ____*author* ____*man*

At first glance, this seems like an objective question, one that applies equally to everyone. Your experience with Little Joes and splibs, though, should have made you more aware that children from some backgrounds are more familiar with the concepts of symphonies, composers, sculptors, and musicians than are other children. Their experience tilts the test in their favor.

It is important to note that the people who write the questions for these evaluative tests are trying to be objective. They do not intend to discriminate and are unaware that they are doing so. They simply are working from within their own taken-for-granted worlds—which include symphonies and composers but not Little Joes and splibs.

The questions that "you" tried to answer were suggested by Adrian Dove (n.d.), a social worker in Watts (East Los Angeles). These questions are slanted toward a specific nonwhite, lower-class experience. With these *particular* cultural biases, can you see why children from some social backgrounds will perform better than others?

Unintended institutional discrimination also shows up in the practice of medicine (Fiscella and Sanders 2016). Researchers have found that physicians are more likely to recommend knee replacements for their white patients than for either their Latino or African American patients (Ibrahim 2010). White patients are also more likely to receive coronary bypass surgery (Smedley et al. 2003). Why should this be? Actually, no one yet knows. The nature of this discrimination is confusing, because even African American physicians are more likely to give preventive care to white patients (Stolberg 2001). Discovering how race–ethnicity becomes part of medical decision-making will be a fascinating area of future research (Hardeman et al. 2016). Perhaps you will become one of the researchers who will explore this area of social life.

In short, unintended discrimination is built into our social system. It operates throughout society—with those involved unaware of what they are doing.

Implications of Cold Numbers

Numbers can be cold, just ciphers on paper or passing digits on a screen. Look at Table 8.1 as an example. You can see that African Americans, Latinos, and Native Americans earn about 40 percent less than whites. You can see, too, that their poverty rate is about three times that of whites. But so what? You will give them a glance and probably wonder if there is something on this table that you have to memorize or recall for a coming quiz.

But underlying these abstract numbers are real people whose lives are affected adversely. As we reviewed in the previous chapter, at issue is not whether people can afford a boat, a new car, or some exotic vacation, but whether they can afford nourishing food and education. Or can they find the money to fix a broken-down car and get to work, or will they lose their job and, with it, their apartment?

Table 8.1 Indicators of Relative Economic Well-Being

	Family Income		Families in Poverty	
	Median Family Income	Compared to Whites	Percentage Below Poverty	Compared to Whites
Whites	$77,100		6.6%	
Asian Americans	$88,900	15.3% higher	8.7%	32% higher
Latinos	$46,700	39.4% lower	20.1%	205% higher
Native Americans	$46,000	40.3% lower	21.5%	226% higher
African Americans	$45,000	41.6% lower	21.6%	228% higher

Note: These totals are for families, which have less poverty than persons, the unit of the tables in Chapter 7. Because Asian American families earn more than white families, but have a higher poverty rate, it is likely that Asian American families have higher concentrations of lower-earning and higher-earning families.

Source: By the author. Based on *Statistical Abstract of the United States* 2018:Table 35.

Look at Table 8.2. These numbers might make more of an impact, as you can see that poverty even translates into life and death. Compared with white babies, African American babies are *more than twice* as likely to die before they reach their first birthday. The chances of African American women dying during childbirth are also *more than three times* as high as those of white women. Now look at life expectancy. On average, African American women die about three years younger than white women, and African American men die more than four years younger than white men. The primary reason is simple: With higher incomes, people can afford safer neighborhoods and better nutrition, housing, and medical care. The result is a longer life.

Although few, if any, tables or figures are likely to make much of an impact on you, try to appreciate that cold numbers sometimes translate into cold bodies.

Table 8.2 Health and Race–Ethnicity

	Infant Deaths[1]	Maternal Deaths	Life Expectancy	
			Male	Female
Whites	4.9	11.1	76.6	81.3
African Americans	11.4	36.5	72.2	78.5

[1]Infant deaths refer to the number of infants under 1 year old who die in a year per 1,000 live births. The source does not provide data for other racial–ethnic groups.

Source: By the author. Based on *Statistical Abstract of the United States* 2018:Tables 111, 120.

Looking at the Problem Theoretically

8.3 Discuss the perspectives that emerge when you apply symbolic interactionism, functionalism, and conflict theory to racial–ethnic relations.

Although usually much less open and direct than the events in our opening vignette, prejudice and discrimination are part of many relations between racial–ethnic groups in the United States. Let's look at how sociologists use theory to better understand prejudice and discrimination.

Symbolic Interactionism: Labels

> *"What's in a name?"* asked Juliet. *"That which we call a rose, by any other name would smell as sweet."*

What Juliet said is true of roses, but in human relations, words are not meaningless. The labels we learn both color the way we see the world and influence our behavior.

Socialization and Prejudice   No one is born prejudiced, with stereotypes, or wanting to discriminate. We are not born with even a single value or belief. But each of us is born into a particular family and racial–ethnic group. There we learn values, beliefs, and ways to perceive the world. There we also learn how to label members of other groups. We might learn prejudice and discrimination as a routine part of everyday life. Or we might learn that prejudice and discrimination are wrong.

Labels and Selective Perception   As we grow up, we learn stereotypes, ways of classifying entire groups of people—men, women, the elderly, racial–ethnic groups, people with disabilities, even people who are good at computers, math, music, or sports. Learning to classify people—to "place them in boxes"—is a normal, necessary, and inevitable part of our socialization, our learning the ways of our society. These labels or stereotypes become lenses through which we view people. They also create **selective perception**, leading us to see certain things while blinding us to others.

Many racial–ethnic labels are emotionally laden. The term "nigger," for example, is so loaded with negative emotions that most people won't say the word, using the phrase "the N word" instead. Neither is there anything neutral about "cracker," "dago," "kraut," "limey," "mick," "spic," "wetback," or the many other negative labels that people use to refer to members of racial–ethnic groups. The emotional impact of such words overpowers us, blocking perception of positive characteristics (Allport 1954). As Simpson and Yinger (1972) put it, we fit new experiences into old categories by selecting those cues that harmonize with our prejudgment or stereotype.

Labels and Morality   Dehumanizing labels are so powerful that they can help people commit acts that otherwise would challenge their moral sense. For example, by labeling Native Americans as "savages," the U.S. cavalry and settlers perceived them as something less than human. This made it easier to destroy tribe after tribe (Garbarino 1976). In South Africa, the Dutch settlers labeled the native Hottentots as jungle animals, a label that salved their consciences as they wiped out these people. In Tasmania, the labels the British settlers used were so effective that the settlers even hunted the local population for sport and dog food. In Brazil today, much as in U.S. history, miners, ranchers, and loggers are wiping out Indian tribes as they seize their lands ("Guardians of the Amazon" 2018).

Negative terms and stereotypes, then, are dangerous. They create selective perception, justify discrimination, and in extreme instances even facilitate mass murder. Groups that build an identity around hatred pose a special threat. In the following *Spotlight on Social Research*, sociologist Raphael Ezekiel discusses his research on such groups.

Spotlight on Social Research

Studying Neo-Nazis and Klans

RAPHAEL EZEKIEL, *a senior researcher with the Harvard School of Public Health, says that his interest in racism was stimulated by the contradictions he experienced as a child growing up with liberal, northern, Jewish parents in a deeply racist East Texas town. Here is what he wrote for you.*

Pearson Education, Inc.

Dear students,

Jim Henslin asked me to write about my fieldwork. I got stuck, so I decided to interview myself.

Interviewer: What did you do, Professor?

Rafe: I spent three years hanging out with a neo-Nazi group in Detroit. After that, I interviewed national leaders from neo-Nazi groups and from Klans. I also went to their national and regional meetings. My book, *The Racist Mind,* comes from that work.

Interviewer: Did they know you were a Jew?

Rafe: I made sure they knew I was a Jew and opposed to racism. Good interviewing is interplay between you and your respondent—kind of a dance. That requires trust; trust requires openness and honesty.

Interviewer: But, then, why did they talk with you?

Rafe: Because I told them the truth—that I believe every person creates a life that makes sense to him or her, and my professional work is to go onto the turf of people whose lives seem unusual to most folk and let these people tell me, in their own words, the sense their lives make to them. That made sense to them.

Interviewer: Did you find anything out?

Rafe: Yeah. The leaders and members are real different. The leaders are men—this is essentially a male movement—force, macho, blood, all that. The leaders are not motivated primarily by hate or by racism. They are motivated primarily by hunger for power: Power is the goal; racism is the tool. To move a crowd by what they say. To scare a community by saying that they're coming. To fill the media with scare stories. A whole lot of this is theater—they provide the stimulus; we provide the fantasies.

There are always suckers whom you can recruit by talking racism. If you line up 100 white Americans, ranked by how much they fear and dislike African Americans, the big leaders wouldn't be at the head of the line—they'd be about 30 places back.

Interviewer: And the ordinary members?

Rafe: That's a whole different story. This is not a movement built on hate. It's a movement built on fear. When you talk with a member, talk honestly about his life—his, again—the emotion you sense under the surface is fear. The kids in the Detroit group felt, deep down, that their own lives might be snuffed out at any moment, like a candle in the wind.

Interviewer: Do you have any hints on how to do good fieldwork?

Rafe: Yeah. First, check yourself out—why are you doing this? What does it mean to you? Second, be real—with them, with yourself. Third, field notes. When you finish your interview and start home, roll the interview around in your mind. Don't analyze, just let it play in your mind. Like remembering a dream. Don't talk to anyone—no phoning—don't listen to the radio—just keep the interview rolling around. Go straight home and start writing. Write first pure emotion—primary process stuff—associations, feelings. What's going on inside you after this interview? What does it remind you of? Then write your secondary process stuff—what went on and what you think it means. Then, in terms of your project, where does this take you? Do you need more questions? Respondents? Finally, ask yourself: "So what?" What difference does it make to the world what you think you are understanding? As you write that, you will be writing much of your book.

For Your Consideration

→ Would you have thought that it would have ever been possible for a Jew to study the Klan and other hate groups? How did Ezekiel manage to do this? He is dispassionate in this analysis, but in his book he reveals some of the fear he felt during his research.

→ Could you ever do such research?

In Sum   Symbolic interactionists examine how labels (terms, classifications, symbols, or stereotypes) affect how we look at life and how we act. They analyze how we learn labels, how we use labels to classify one another, and how our classifications create selective perception. They also analyze how labels sort people out for different kinds of life experiences and how they are used to justify discrimination and violence.

Functionalism: Costs and Benefits

Why does racial–ethnic discrimination persist in the United States—and in other parts of the world? As you may recall, functionalists argue that the benefits of a social pattern (some characteristic of society) must be greater than its costs, or else that pattern will disappear. The benefits (functions) of discrimination, then, must outweigh its costs (dysfunctions). How can this be? Let's explore this intriguing question.

Functions and Dysfunctions of Discrimination   The discrimination woven into U.S. history benefited the dominant group. By killing Native Americans or transferring them to reservations, whites gained free farmland, forests, lakes, and gold. They also benefited from owning slaves, acquiring cheap labor, and selling the slaves' labor as masons, carpenters, or factory workers. Slave labor allowed many owners to live a "genteel" life of leisure or to pursue art, education, science, and other "refinements."

Slavery and the invasion of the West also had dysfunctions at that time: deaths, broken families, rapes of female slaves, and shortened lives. They also left a legacy of dysfunction: racial–ethnic tensions, hostilities, hatreds, and fears. It would seem that such high costs would lead to the elimination of discrimination.

But because racial–ethnic discrimination remains a fact of life in the United States, functionalists search for its benefits, or functions. Just as discrimination was functional for the dominant group in the past, today's dominant group also benefits from it. Let's look at two functions of discrimination: dirty work and ethnocentrism.

Getting Dirty Work Done   **Racial–ethnic stratification**, the unequal distribution of a society's resources based on race–ethnicity, helps get society's *dirty work* done. Sociologist Herbert Gans (2007) defines **dirty work** as society's "physically dirty or dangerous, temporary, dead-end and underpaid, undignified and menial jobs." Sociologist Emile Durkheim (1893/1964) stressed that society needs a **division of labor**, people performing different or specialized tasks. Dirty work, such as collecting garbage, is one of those tasks, a necessary but rather disagreeable one.

One way to get the dirty work done is to pay high wages to compensate for the unpleasant, degrading nature of the work. Obviously, we have not chosen this road. Another is to force people to do such jobs for low wages. No one waves whips over people's heads to force them to wash dishes in a restaurant or to clean motel rooms. Stratification accomplishes this quietly and effectively. People who find the doors to higher-paying, more prestigious jobs closed to them take the dirty jobs. This makes sure the dirty work gets done and gets done cheaply.

Racial–Ethnic Succession in Dirty Work   When a racial–ethnic group climbs the social class ladder, it leaves the dirty work behind. Because the dirty work still has to be done, other groups take over those tasks. For example, many African Americans have moved

For a society to function, it must make sure that its "dirty work" is done. The text discusses the racial-ethnic succession in this process.

David Bacon/The Image Works

into the middle class, and undocumented immigrants are doing much of the work they used to do. Those who have entered the United States illegally have little control over their working conditions. They take jobs that practically no one else will do, often working long hours in crowded, dirty, and sometimes dangerous conditions. And they work cheaply, for some employers pay under the table, skipping the costs of unemployment compensation, Social Security, medical, overtime, or vacation pay.

Apart from what one could say about the injustice of this situation, it is functional. (See the *Thinking Critically* box *Why We Need the Poor* in Chapter 7. Just substitute minority group for the poor as you read it.) The dirty work gets done, and *most* Americans benefit: They eat the produce that undocumented immigrants pick and wear the clothing they make. The immigrants also benefit: They earn far more than they would in their home country. Their families, left behind in desperate conditions, also benefit as these workers in the United States send them part of their earnings. Even the government of Mexico benefits, for this vast migration siphons off millions of its more ambitious and dissatisfied citizens—those who otherwise might form a restless mass, perhaps directing their energies toward overthrowing an oppressive Mexican elite.

Ethnocentrism   Another function of racial–ethnic inequality is **ethnocentrism**, a type of prejudice that can be summarized as "My group's ways are better than your group's ways." Ethnocentrism helps the dominant group justify its higher social position and greater share of society's resources. Members of the group don't have to question why they get more than others or feel guilty about it, for aren't they superior? For proof, they simply look around and see that the other group is doing the dirty work while theirs has the more respectable, prestigious, and higher-paying jobs.

Racial–ethnic stratification also produces ethnocentrism among members of minority groups. The visible differences and the discrimination that a minority group faces because of their distinctiveness create cohesion, a sense of identity with one another. Seeing that other groups have "made it" nourishes the hope that they, too, will succeed. The ethnocentrism is quite functional: It encourages minority groups to work hard, minimizes rebellion, and makes them willing to put up with demeaning circumstances in the hope of a better future.

Destruction of Human Potential   Prejudice and discrimination also have severe dysfunctions. They interfere with people's well-being—from a diminished sense of self to inadequate nourishment and early death. Prejudice and discrimination lower children's self-esteem; they discourage high goals and decrease the capacity to succeed in school and work. Many minority children drop out of school and waste their potential in low-level jobs or street crime. Society is the ultimate loser in this destruction of human potential: It is denied the contributions that these youngsters could have made. And if a group becomes too alienated, it can riot, demanding change while venting anger and hatred in the destruction of property and lives. Under the right conditions, discrimination can also lead to revolution, whose end can be quite dysfunctional for those currently in power.

In Sum   Functionalists are often misunderstood: To identify social benefits that come from negative behaviors, such as discrimination, can be viewed as justifying that behavior. Functionalists do not defend discrimination. Rather, by uncovering the functions that underlie discrimination, they give us a better understanding of why this behavior continues. By stressing both the functions and dysfunctions of racial–ethnic stratification, they reveal some of the less visible consequences of institutional arrangements.

Conflict Theory: The Labor Market

What had seemed a personal hatred of me, an inexplicable refusal of Southern whites to confront their own emotions, and a stubborn willingness of blacks to acquiesce, became the inevitable consequence of a ruthless system which kept itself alive and well by encouraging spite, competition, and the oppression of one group by another. Profit was the word: the cold and constant motive for the behavior, the contempt and despair I had seen.

—Angela Davis, 1974

With these words, Angela Davis, an African American Marxist, recounted her understanding of U.S. racial–ethnic relations. What did she mean?

Pitting Worker Against Worker   According to conflict theory, the dominant group pits racial–ethnic groups against one another in order to exploit workers and increase profit. Here is how the process works:

The United States has a **capitalist economy**; that is, our economic system is based on investing capital with the goal of making a profit. Profit is the result of selling items for more than they cost to produce. In conflict theory, this is called extracting the **surplus value of labor**. For example, if each item that a factory produces costs the owners of the factory $1 for materials; $1 for rent, utilities, and transportation; $1 for advertising, insurance, and the cost of borrowing money; and $1 for a worker to run a machine, the total cost of the item is $4. If the owners sell the item for $5, they make a $1 profit. Conflict theorists claim that the profit represents a surplus value resulting from the labor used to produce the item. That is, the item increased in value *because* the worker added his or her labor to the item.

The Split-Labor Market   Lower wages increase profit. To keep wages low, capitalists use a **split-labor market**; that is, by splitting workers along racial–ethnic lines, they weaken their bargaining power (Reich 1972, 1981; Obinna 2018). It is difficult for workers who fear and distrust one another to unite and demand higher wages and more benefits.

To maintain a split-labor market, the unemployed are a valuable tool. If everyone who wants to work has a job, workers can threaten to quit unless they receive higher pay and better working conditions. But workers without jobs provide a pool of needy workers that owners can dip into when they need them—to expand production or to break a strike. When the economy contracts or when the strike is settled, these workers—called a **reserve labor force**—can be laid off to rejoin the unemployed, with no unsettling effects on society. Minority workers are ideal for the reserve labor force as the dominant group of white workers seldom objects to what happens to unemployed members of minority groups.

Consequences of a Split-Labor Market: "We–Them"   Splitting labor along racial–ethnic lines encourages minorities and whites to view one another as enemies, able to make

Power can come from unity. The split-labor market is used to weaken worker solidarity by exploiting racial-ethnic, gender, and age divisions.

Amble Design/Shutterstock

gains only at the expense of the other. In this "we–them" view, whites think of themselves as moral, hardworking taxpayers, and of competing minority members as lazy people who swell welfare rolls, supported by taxes that whites pay. The minority, in turn, can come to view themselves as victims, unable to get ahead because of ruthless, hate-mongering whites.

As you can see, a split-labor market produces a chasm of disunity and distrust. Instead of identifying with one another as workers, each group opposes the other as a competitor. This division and opposition prevent whites and minorities from realizing that "the other" is part of one's own class interests—that they both are workers who share the same goals. Blinded, they fail to see that each is oppressed by a common enemy, the wealthy, powerful elite, which uses racial–ethnic divisions to divide them.

Riots and other violence that result from racial–ethnic divisions threaten the power elite, who often try to defuse the situation by offering concessions. They give a little here and there, whatever seems necessary to quiet the restless, threatening, low-paid workers and the unemployed. They might increase welfare benefits, allow token representation on committees, or offer government aid to reconstruct inner cities. These acts are not coming from generous hearts intended to improve the lives of the disadvantaged. Their purpose is to defuse the situation and protect the privileged positions of the powerful.

In Sum   Conflict theorists stress that racial–ethnic antagonisms divide the working class and strengthen the position of the powerful. The split-labor market pits one racial–ethnic group against another, preventing the solidarity that would allow workers to challenge control of the United States by those who own the means of production. From the conflict perspective, racial–ethnic discrimination will end only when white and minority workers come to see that they both are oppressed and understand that they have the same oppressor. From this, conflict theorists who are Marxists, draw the conclusion that when workers unite, they can create a new social order, one in which they will receive the full value of their labor in a society characterized by racial–ethnic harmony.

Summary of the Theoretical Perspectives

None of the theoretical perspectives has an exclusive claim to truth. Rather, each focuses on selective aspects of racial–ethnic relations. Symbolic interactionists alert us to the power of labels in defining human relations, how labels are lenses through which we view ourselves and others. Labels that provide demeaning, negative views of others help people discriminate with a clear conscience. Functionalists turn our attention not only to the costs of discrimination, but also to its benefits. Conflict theorists stress how prejudice and discrimination destroy worker solidarity, enabling owners to hold down wages and increase profits. Each theoretical lens produces a unique understanding of racial–ethnic relations. Combined, these perspectives provide greater understanding of discrimination than does any one of them alone.

■ Research Findings

In this section, we have the opportunity to answer significant questions: What problems do minority groups in the United States face? How do the groups differ from one another? How are relationships between groups changing? To answer these questions, we present an overview of the four largest minority groups in the United States, from largest to smallest: Latinos, African Americans, Asian Americans, and Native Americans.

Before we do this, I want to stress that minority groups are far from distributed evenly across the nation. From the following Social Map, you can see that the extreme distributions are in Maine, where whites outnumber minorities 14 to 1, and Hawaii, where minorities outnumber whites almost 4 to 1.

Figure 8.4 The Distribution of Dominant and Minority Groups in the United States

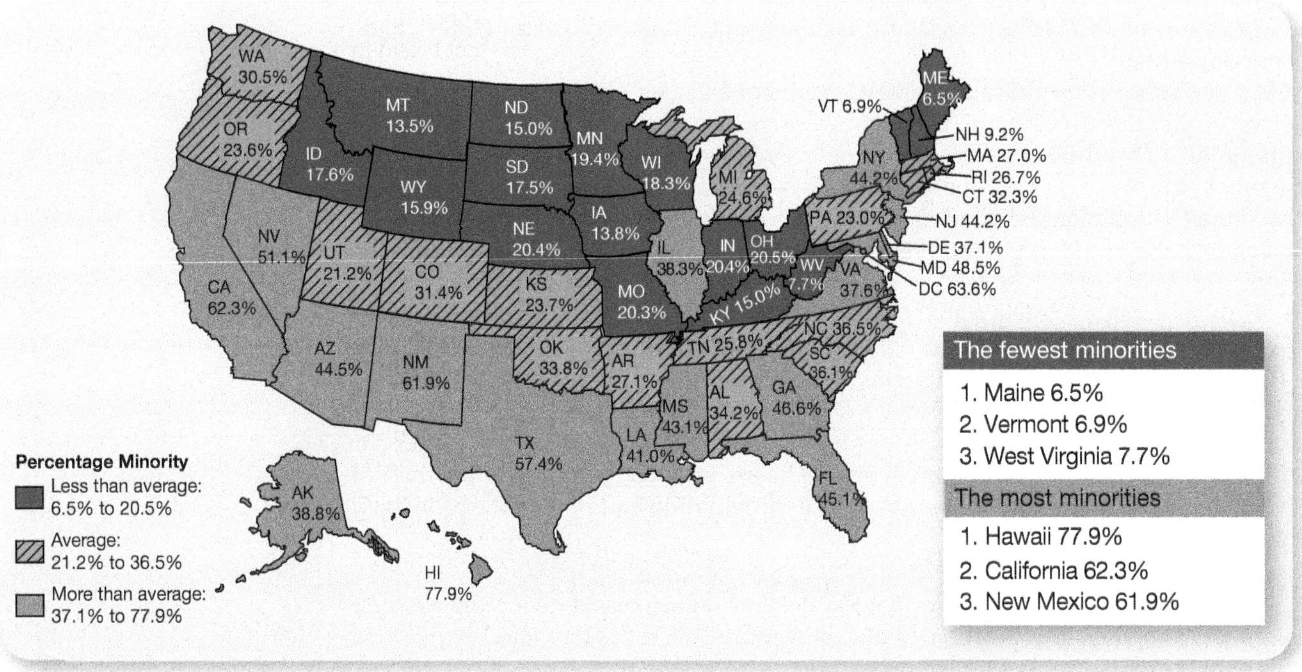

Percentage Minority

- Less than average: 6.5% to 20.5%
- Average: 21.2% to 36.5%
- More than average: 37.1% to 77.9%

The fewest minorities
1. Maine 6.5%
2. Vermont 6.9%
3. West Virginia 7.7%

The most minorities
1. Hawaii 77.9%
2. California 62.3%
3. New Mexico 61.9%

Source: By the author. Based on *Statistical Abstract of the United States* 2018:Table 19.

Latinos (Hispanics)

8.4 Explain why *Latino* is an umbrella term, the issue of unauthorized immigrants, the relative economic well-being of Latinos, and their political divisions and potential.

Let's begin with a remarkable idea: The term *Latino* does not refer to any specific group of people.

An Umbrella Term

Latino is an umbrella term that the dominant group has developed to lump people who are from different cultural backgrounds into a single category. What do these people have in common? They trace their origins to the Spanish-speaking countries of North and South America. That's it. Nothing more. Yet these peoples of diverse cultures, who are swept together into a single term, now form the largest "ethnic group" in the United States. Few people who are classified by this umbrella term, however, consider themselves to be part of a single, large, amorphous ethnic group. Instead, they think of themselves as Americans of Mexican origin (Mexicanos or Chicanos), Americans of Cuban origin (Cubanos), Americans from Puerto Rico (Puertoricanos), and so on. Nor do most identify readily with the term Hispanic, an alternative umbrella term developed by the dominant group.

It is important to be aware that the terms Latino and Hispanic lump people from many cultures into a single category. It is also important to stress that Latino and Hispanic do not refer to race, but to ethnic groups. Latinos may identify themselves as African American, white, Native American, Honduran, Uruguayan, Afro Latino, or even from some village in a remote part of a country. Because the terms Latino and Hispanic exist, however, they are taking on a life of their own. On government forms, people must select a category to which they "belong," with Latino/Hispanic being one of the choices. Eventually, the umbrella becomes the reality.

Unauthorized Immigrants

Most Latinos are U.S. citizens, but about 9 million have entered the country illegally (7 million from Mexico and 2 million from Central and South America) (Baker 2017:Appendix 2). Although fewer undocumented immigrants arrived since the Great Recession that began in 2008, the number is still so large that each year about 200,000 people are returned to Mexico or Central and South America (Homeland Security 2017:Table 41).

This massive unauthorized entry into the United States has aroused intense public concern. One reaction has been to open paths to citizenship or work permits. In 1986, the federal government passed the Immigration Reform and Control Act, which permitted undocumented immigrants to apply for U.S. citizenship. More than 3 million people applied, the vast majority from Mexico (Espenshade 1990). In 2012, President Obama signed an executive order allowing work permits to be issued to undocumented immigrants who are not over the age of 30, who arrived before the age of 16, who are in school or are high school graduates, and who have no criminal record (Preston and Cushman 2012).

Another reaction has been to prevent illegal entry and to locate and remove unauthorized residents. Agents of Homeland Security check documents at entry points to the United States, and the U.S. Coast Guard patrols the ocean borders, but the border with Mexico is the trigger point of concern. Dissatisfied with the U.S. Border Patrol's efforts to stem the flow of unauthorized immigrants, citizen groups have offered their often unwelcome help. These armed groups, such as the Texas Border Volunteers, patrol the Mexican border, but unofficially. Over the past 100 years, another preventive measure has been to build 600 miles of walls, fencing, and other barriers along this border. Proposals under President Trump to build a high wall that would seal the entire 2,000-mile border between Mexico and the United States are a divisive political issue (Mark et al. 2018).

A remarkably different response comes from groups whose goal is to save lives. As migrants try to cross Arizona's harsh Sonoran Desert, some die from the scorching heat, dehydration, and rattlesnakes. The members of such groups as Humane Borders, No More Death, and Samaritans leave water in remote locations of the desert (Mark et al. 2018).

To gain insight into why this vast subterranean migration exists, see the next *Issues in Social Problems.*

Issues in Social Problems

The Illegal Travel Guide

Manuel was a drinking buddy of Jose, a man I had met when I was living in Colima, Mexico. At 45, Manuel was friendly, outgoing, and enterprising.

Manuel, who had lived in the United States for seven years, spoke fluent English. Preferring to live in his hometown in Colima, where he could pal around with his childhood friends, Manuel always seemed to have money and free time.

When Manuel invited me to go with him on a business trip, I accepted. I never could figure out how Manuel made a living or how he could afford a car, a luxury that none of his friends had. As we traveled from one remote village to another, Manuel would sell used clothing that he had heaped in the back of his older-model Ford station wagon.

At one stop, Manuel took me into a dirt-floored, thatched-roof hut. While chickens ran in and out, Manuel whispered to a slender man of about 23. The poverty was overwhelming. Juan, as his name turned out to be, had a partial grade school education. He also had a wife, four hungry children under the age of 5, and two pigs—his main food supply. Although eager to work, Juan had no job, for there was simply no work available in this remote village.

A coyote leading 16 people across the U.S. border at Nogales, Arizona.

Manuel explained that he was not only selling clothing but was also lining up migrants to the United States. For a fee, he would take a man to the border and introduce him to a "wolf," who would help him make a night crossing into the promised land.

When I saw the hope in Juan's face, I knew nothing would stop him. He was borrowing every cent he could from every friend and relative so he could scrape the money together. Although he risked losing everything if apprehended, Juan would make the trip, for wealth beckoned on the other side. He knew people who had been there and spoke glowingly of its opportunities. Manuel, of course, stoked the fires of hope.

Amidst the children playing on the dirt floor with chickens pecking about them was a man who loved his family. In order to make the desperate bid for a better life, he would suffer an enforced absence, as well as the uncertainties of a foreign land whose customs and language he did not know.

Juan opened his billfold, took something out, and slowly handed it to me. I felt tears as I saw the tenderness with which he handled this piece of paper. It was his passport to the land of

opportunity: a Social Security card made out in his name, sent by a friend who had already made the trip and who was waiting for Juan on the other side of the border.

Only the United States could fulfill his dream.

For Your Consideration

→ Do you think this vast stream of immigrants illegally crossing the Mexican–U.S. border is destined to continue until its root causes are addressed? Why or why not?

→ What do you think is the best way to deal with this issue? Why?

Figure 8.5 Where U.S. Latinos Live

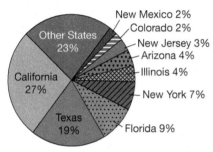

Source: By the author. Based on *Statistical Abstract of the United States* 2018:Table 19.

Residence of Latinos

The term *Latino* clusters together about 50 million people: about 35 million from Mexico, 8 million from Central and South America, 5 million from Puerto Rico, and 2 million from Cuba (*Statistical Abstract* 2018:Table 36). There has been such a vast migration from these areas that many millions more Latinos live in the United States than Canadians (36 million) live in Canada. As Figure 8.5 shows, seven of every 10 Latinos live in just six states—California, Texas, Florida, New York, Illinois, and Arizona. With its prominent Latino presence, Miami has been called "the capital of South America."

Spanish

Although not all Latinos speak Spanish, most do. About 40 million Latinos speak Spanish at home (*Statistical Abstract* 2018:Table 53). Forty percent cannot speak English or can do so only with difficulty. Being fluent only in Spanish in a society where English is spoken almost exclusively remains an obstacle.

Despite the 1848 Treaty of Hidalgo, which guarantees Mexicans the right to maintain their culture, from 1855 until 1968, California banned teaching in Spanish in school. In a 1974 decision (*Lau v. Nichols*), the U.S. Supreme Court ruled that using only English to teach Spanish-speaking students violated their civil rights. This decision paved the way for bilingual instruction for Spanish-speaking children (Vidal 1977; Lopez 1980).

The growing use of Spanish has stoked controversy. Senator S. I. Hayakawa of Hawaii initiated an "English-only" movement in 1981. The constitutional amendment he proposed never got off the ground, but the movement continues, and 32 states have passed laws that declare English their official language ("U.S. English" 2018).

Social Conditions

Latinos fare poorly on indicators of economic well-being (see Table 8.1). Their family income averages only three-fifths that of whites, and they are three times as likely as whites to be poor. In addition, their unemployment rate is twice as high as that of whites, and as Table 8.3 shows, one of three has not graduated from high school. At every level of education, from a high school diploma on, whites earn more (*Statistical Abstract* 2018:Tables 35, 254). In response to their position in U.S. society, some Latinos have begun a movement that rejects assimilation and emphasizes the maintenance of Latino culture. Others work toward faster assimilation.

Politics

Latinos hold only a fraction of elected positions. Because of their huge numbers, we might expect about 17 of the 100 U.S. senators to be Latino. How many are there? *Three.* In addition, Latinos hold only 7 percent of the seats in the U.S. House of Representatives (*Statistical Abstract* 2018:Table 450). Yet, compared with the past, even these totals represent substantial gains. On the positive side, several Latinos have been elected as state governors, including the first Latina to become a governor (Susana Martinez of New Mexico in 2010). In 2016, Catherine Cortez Masto was the first Latina to be elected to the U.S. senate. It isn't just these gains that point to a future in which Latinos soon will play a larger role in U.S. politics, perhaps one day even beyond their overall numbers. The best indicator of this coming change is that the six states in which Latinos are concentrated hold one-third of the country's 538 electoral votes: California (55), Texas (38), New York (29), Florida (29), Illinois (20), and Arizona (11).

Divisions based on country of origin hold back the potential political power of Latinos. These distinctions nourish disunity and create political discord. As I mentioned, Latinos do not think of themselves as a single people, and national origin is highly significant. People from Puerto Rico, for example, feel little sense of unity with people from Mexico. It is similarly the case with those from Venezuela, Colombia, or El Salvador. It used to be the same with Europeans who emigrated from Germany and Sweden or from England and France. With time, however, the importance of identifying with the European country of origin was lost, and they came to think of themselves as Americans. Perhaps this will happen to Latinos as well.

Catherine Cortez Masto, the former attorney general of Nevada, is the first Latina elected to the U.S. senate.

African Americans

8.5 Summarize the civil rights history of African Americans, their relative economic well-being, and the controversy over race versus social class.

It was 1955, in Montgomery, Alabama. As specified by law, whites took the front seats of the bus, and blacks went to the back. As the bus filled up, blacks had to give up their seats to whites.

When Rosa Parks, a 42-year-old African American woman and secretary of the Montgomery NAACP, was told that she would have to stand so that white folks could sit, she refused (Bray 1995). She stubbornly sat there while the bus driver fumed and whites felt insulted. Her arrest touched off mass demonstrations, led 50,000 blacks to boycott the city's buses for a year, and thrust an otherwise unknown preacher into a historic role.

Reverend Martin Luther King, Jr., who had majored in sociology at Morehouse College in Atlanta, Georgia, took control. He organized carpools and preached nonviolence. Incensed at this radical organizer and at the stirrings in the normally compliant black community, segregationists also put their beliefs into practice—by bombing the homes of blacks and dynamiting a church.

Civil Disobedience and American Apartheid

In 1943, the U.S. Supreme Court ruled that African Americans have the legal right to attend public schools with whites. Before this, they had to go to "colored" schools. In 1944, the Court ruled that African Americans could vote in southern primaries. Change was slow, and during the 1950s, the South was still practicing a form of apartheid. African Americans, then called Negroes, were not allowed to stay at hotels or to eat in restaurants that whites patronized. They had to use separate toilets, water fountains, and swimming pools. Some states had miscegenation laws prohibiting marriage between Negroes and whites, laws that were struck down in 1967 (Livingston et al. 2017).

To break institutional barriers that supported "American apartheid," Martin Luther King, Jr., led African Americans in **civil disobedience**, deliberately but peacefully disobeying laws considered unjust. Inspired by the writings of Henry David

Thoreau and the success of Mahatma Gandhi, King (1958) based his strategy on these principles:

1. Actively resist evil, but nonviolently.
2. Don't try to defeat or humiliate opponents, but try instead to win their friendship and understanding.
3. Attack the forces of evil rather than the people who are doing the evil.
4. Be willing to accept suffering without retaliating.
5. Refuse to hate the opponent.
6. Act with the conviction that the universe is on the side of justice.

King found no overnight success, but he and his followers persisted. Gradually, more barriers came down. In 1964, Congress passed the Civil Rights Act, making it illegal to discriminate in hotels, theaters, and other public places. Then, in 1965, the Voting Rights Act banned the literacy tests that whites had used to keep African Americans from voting.

Rising Expectations and Urban Revolts

Encouraged by these gains, African Americans experienced **rising expectations**; that is, they expected better conditions to follow right away. The lives of poor African Americans, however, changed little, if at all. Frustrations built, finally exploding in Watts in 1965, when residents of this central Los Angeles ghetto took to the streets in an "urban revolt." The violence, which occurred despite the protests of Dr. King, precipitated a white backlash that threatened the multiracial coalition that King had spearheaded. Congress refused to enact civil rights legislation in both 1967 and 1968. When King was assassinated on April 4, 1968, ghettos across the nation erupted in fiery violence. Under threat of the destruction of the nation's cities, Congress reluctantly passed the sweeping Civil Rights Act of 1968.

From Militancy to Moderacy

After King's death, black militants rushed in to fill the void in leadership. Like King, they emphasized black unity and black pride, but unlike King, some of them proclaimed that violence was the way to gain equality. Flashed across the nation's television screens were images of the Black Panthers, brandishing rifles and parading in military-style uniforms. The talk of revolution by black militants stirred fear and hostility among whites, and the authorities turned violently on the most outspoken leaders. In a nighttime raid in 1969,

In the 1960s, the Black Panthers sowed fear among law enforcement officers and politicians, launching a retaliation that resulted in the assassination of leaders of this group. This photo was taken on the statehouse steps of Olympia, Washington, in 1969.

State Governors' Negative Collection, 1949–1975/Black Panthers on steps of Legislative Building, Olympia/ Washington State Archives · Digital Archives

the FBI and the Chicago police assassinated Fred Hampton, the head of the Chicago Black Panthers. They shot him while he was sleeping in his bed (Haas 2009).

With photos of bloodied bodies circulating in the mass media, the black leadership fragmented. Some argued for secession from the United States, others for total integration. They disagreed over whether violent confrontation or peaceful protest was the way to go. In the end, those who made the case for integration and political action won. As more moderate approaches replaced militancy, even the Black Panthers changed their tactics. Instead of challenging white authority and confronting police, they switched to community organizing, providing breakfasts for schoolchildren, and running for political office. Lacking a charismatic leader to replace King, the momentum that had propelled the struggle for equality faded.

Continued Gains

Change has been gradual, but over time the change has been profound. Today's race relations are vastly different from those that Rosa Parks confronted when she refused to move to the back of the bus. African Americans have made remarkable gains in politics, education, and jobs. At 11 percent, the number of African Americans in the U.S. House of Representatives is *two to three times* what it was a generation ago (*Statistical Abstract* 1989:Table 423; 2018:Table 452). As college enrollments increased, the middle class expanded, and today half of African American families make more than $50,000 a year. One in five has an annual income over $100,000 (*Statistical Abstract* 2018:Table 722).

African Americans have also become prominent in politics. Jesse Jackson (another sociology major) competed for the Democratic presidential nomination in 1984 and 1988. In 1989, L. Douglas Wilder was elected governor of Virginia; in 2006, Deval Patrick became governor of Massachusetts; and in 2007, David Patterson became governor of New York. These accomplishments, of course, pale in comparison to the election of Barack Obama as president of the United States in 2008 and his reelection in 2012.

Current Losses

Despite these gains, African Americans continue to lag behind in politics, economics, and education. From their percentage of the U.S. population, we might expect about 13 African American senators. How many are there? *Two.* There have been only ten in U.S. history. As you saw in Table 8.1, the family income of African Americans is 42 percent lower than that of whites, and their poverty is much higher. From Table 8.3, you can see

In an historic first, Barack Obama was the first person who identifies as African American to be elected president of the United states. He was elected in 2008 and re-elected in 2012.

The Star-Ledger/Aristide Economopoulos/The Image Works

how African Americans compare in college education. That one of five African American families has an income over $100,000 is only part of the story. The other part is that one of every six families makes less than $15,000 a year.

Table 8.3 Race–Ethnicity and Education

Racial–Ethnic Group	Education				Doctorates		
	Less Than High School	High School	Some College	College (BA or Higher)	Number Awarded	Percentage of All U.S. Doctorates[1]	Percentage of U.S. Population
Whites	7.7%	27.9%	30.1%	34.2%	108,912	69.3%	60.1%
Latinos	34.0%	27.6%	23.6%	14.8%	11,257	7.2%	17.4%
African Americans	15.3%	31.5%	33.0%	20.2%	13,278	8.4%	13.1%
Asian Americans	13.5%	15.5%	18.7%	52.3%	19,193	12.2%	5.6%
Native Americans	20.9%	31.8%	33.2%	14.1%	884	0.6%	1.2%
Claims two or more	12.7%	22.6%	34.5%	29.9%	3,671	2.3%	2.6%
Country or Area of Origin of Latinos							
Cuban	13.8%	31.9%	21.3%	33.0%	NA[2]	NA	NA
Mexico	39.5%	29.7%	19.9%	10.9%	NA	NA	NA
Puerto Rico	19.7%	35.8%	25.1%	19.4%	NA	NA	NA
Central America	43.9%	27.2%	16.9%	12.0%	NA	NA	NA
South America	12.5%	25.8%	25.9%	35.8%	NA	NA	NA

[1]Percentage after the doctorates awarded to nonresidents (21,352) have been deducted from the total.
[2]Not available

Sources: By the author. Based on *Statistical Abstract of the United States* 2018:Tables 35, 36, 318, and Figure 8.2 of this text.

Race or Social Class? A Sociological Debate

The upward mobility of millions of African Americans into the middle class has created two worlds of African American experience—one educated and affluent, the other uneducated and poor. This division of African Americans into "haves" and "have-nots" has fueled a sociological controversy. Sociologist William Julius Wilson (2000, 2010) argues that social class has become more important than race in determining the life chances of African Americans. Before civil rights legislation, he says, the African American experience was dominated by race. Throughout the United States, African Americans were excluded from avenues of economic advancement: good schools and good jobs. When civil rights laws opened new opportunities, African Americans seized them. Just as legislation began to open doors to African Americans, however, manufacturing jobs dried up, and many blue-collar jobs were moved to the suburbs. As better-educated African Americans obtained white-collar jobs, they moved out of the inner city. Left behind were those with poor education and few skills.

Wilson stresses how significant these two worlds of African American experience are. The group that is stuck in the inner city lives in poverty, attends poor schools, and faces dead-end jobs or welfare. This group is filled with hopelessness and despair, combined with apathy or hostility. In contrast, those who have moved up the social class ladder live in comfortable homes in secure neighborhoods. Their jobs provide decent incomes, and they send their children to good schools. With middle-class experiences shaping their views on life, their aspirations and values have little in common with those of African Americans who remain poor. According to Wilson, then, social class—not race—is the more significant factor in the lives of African Americans.

Some sociologists reply that this analysis overlooks the discrimination that continues to underlie the African American experience. They note how young black males are objects of suspicion and police brutality as well as the daily indignities they experience (Brunson and Pegram 2018). Researchers have even found that an iPod sold online got 17 percent fewer offers if it was shown being held by a black hand than by a white hand (Doleac and Stein 2013). Such aspects of social life, they argue, point to racial discrimination, not to social class.

What is the answer to this debate? Wilson would reply that it is not an either-or question. My book is titled *The **Declining** Significance of Race*, he would say, not *The **Absence** of Race*. Certainly, racism is still alive, he would add, but today social class is more central to the African American experience than racial discrimination. For years, he has been stressing the need to provide jobs for the poor in the inner city—for work provides an anchor to a responsible life (Wilson 2000, 2010).

Asian Americans

8.6 **Discuss why *Asian American* is an umbrella term, the history of discrimination against Asian Americans, their relative economic well-being, and their political situation.**

It was a quiet Sunday morning, December 7, 1941, a day destined to live in infamy, as President Roosevelt was later to say.

At dawn, waves of Japanese bombers began an attack on Pearl Harbor, the major U.S. naval station in the Pacific Ocean. At Oahu, Hawaii, the Japanese pilots found the U.S. Pacific Fleet anchored in shallow waters, unprepared for battle. The Americans were sitting ducks.

In response, the United States declared war on Japan, entering World War II and leaving no American untouched. Some left home to battle overseas; others left their farms to work in factories that supported the war effort. All lived with the rationing of food, gasoline, sugar, coffee, and other essentials.

Just as waves of planes flew over Pearl Harbor, so waves of suspicion and hostility rolled over the 120,000 Japanese Americans who called the United States home (Frail 2017). Fears abounded that Japanese Americans would sabotage military installations on the West Coast. Although not a single Japanese American had committed even one act of sabotage, on February 1, 1942, President Franklin Roosevelt signed Executive Order 9066, authorizing the jailing of anyone who was *one-eighth* Japanese or more. These people were charged with no crime; they were neither indicted nor given a trial. Having one Japanese great-grandparent was sufficient reason to be locked up in a "relocation camp."

Intercontinental Railroad, Discrimination, and Segregation

This was not the first time that Asian Americans encountered discrimination. For years, Americans of European background had discriminated against Americans of Asian ancestry because of their differences in appearance and lifestyle. In the 1800s, the U.S. government promoted an intercontinental railroad to unite the east and west coasts. Short on labor, those building the railroad turned to China. Their ads and agents brought about 200,000 Chinese workers to the United States. Although 90 percent of the workers for the Central Pacific Railroad were Chinese, when the famous golden spike was driven at Promontory, Utah, in 1869 to mark the joining of the Union Pacific and the Central Pacific railroads, white workers prevented the Chinese from being in the photo of this historic event. After the railroad was finished, many Chinese settled in the West. To intimidate their new competition, white workers formed mobs and vigilante groups.

As fears of "alien genes and germs" grew, legislators passed anti-Chinese laws (Schrieke 1936). In 1850, the California Legislature passed the Foreign Miner's Act, levying a special tax on Chinese (and Latinos) of $20 a month. At this time, the average Chinese person made a dollar a day. The California Supreme Court ruled that Chinese could not testify against whites in court (Carlson and Colburn 1972). In 1882 Congress passed the Chinese Exclusion Act, suspending all Chinese immigration for 10 years. Four years later, the Statue of Liberty was dedicated. The tired, the poor, and the huddled masses it was intended to welcome obviously did not include the Chinese.

In 1942, Japanese Americans were considered a threat to the security of the United States. They were taken from their homes and locked up in detention camps patrolled by armed guards. After their release at war's end, some returned home to scenes like this.

Associated Press

In the face of such severe discrimination, Chinese immigrants formed segregated communities known as "Chinatowns." Three stages were involved in their development (Yuan 1963). In the first, *involuntary segregation*, Chinese immigrants lived in separate areas because whites refused to let them live near them. Then came *voluntary segregation:* They chose to remain in the segregated community because that was where their friends and relatives lived. There they were able to help one another, avoid language barriers, and follow their customs and traditional religions. The final stage, now in process, is *gradual assimilation:* As Chinese Americans become acculturated, they move out of Chinatown and into mainstream culture.

Spillover Bigotry

Immigrants from Japan met "spillover bigotry" that had been directed against Chinese immigrants. Even the U.S. Constitution was used against them. Although only whites could be citizens under the original Constitution, it was amended in the 1860s to include African Americans (Amott and Matthaei 1991). Because Asians had not been named in the amendments, the U.S. Supreme Court ruled that they were prohibited from becoming citizens (Schaefer 2018). This ruling provided an opportunity for California politicians. In 1913, they passed the Alien Land Act, prohibiting anyone who was ineligible for citizenship from owning land. (Most Native Americans were not granted citizenship in their own land until 1924; the Chinese gained citizenship in 1943; for those born in Japan, the exclusion remained until 1952.)

Figure 8.6 Countries of Origin of Asian Americans

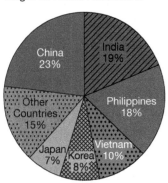

Source: By the author. Based on ACS (American Community Survey). "Total Asian Alone or in Any Combination Population." U.S. Census Bureau, October 19, 2017c.

Another Umbrella Term

As you can see from Figure 8.6, the 21 million Asian Americans living in the United States come from many different nations. As a result, Asian Americans are divided by many cultural heritages, including different languages and religions. *With no unifying culture or "race," why should people of so many backgrounds be lumped together and assigned a single label?* Think about it. What culture or race–ethnicity do people from Japan and India have in common? Or Laotians and Pakistanis? Or people from Bangladesh and those from China? Yet all these groups—and more—are lumped together and called Asian Americans. As a result, any "average" computed for Asian Americans conceals huge differences. Let's look at some of these averages.

Reasons for Financial Success

The high average income of Asian Americans noted on Table 8.1 can be traced to three major factors: family life, educational achievement, and assimilation into mainstream culture. Of all ethnic groups, including whites, Asian American children are the most likely to grow up with two parents and the least likely to be born to teenage mothers or to single mothers (*Statistical Abstract* 2018:Tables 64, 89). Common in these families is a stress on self-discipline, thrift, and hard work (Suzuki 1985; Hsin and Xie 2014). This early socialization provides strong impetus for the other two factors.

The second factor is their unprecedented rate of college graduation. As you can see from Table 8.3, 52 percent of Asian Americans complete college. To realize how stunning this is, compare this rate with that of the other groups shown on this table. This educational achievement, in turn, opens doors to economic success.

The most striking indication of the third factor, assimilation, is a high rate of intermarriage. Close to three of ten Asian Americans (29%) marry someone of a different race–ethnicity (Livingston and Brown 2017). Intermarriage is the highest among those with the most education.

Politics

With Asian Americans making up 5 to 6 percent of the U.S. population, we might expect five or six U.S. senators. How many are there? *One.* However, Asian Americans are becoming more prominent in politics. Hawaii, with about half of its citizens Asian American, has elected several Asian American governors and senators (Lee 1998; *Statistical Abstract* 2018:Table 450). The first Asian American governor outside of Hawaii was Gary Locke, elected in 1997 as governor of Washington, a state in which Asian Americans made up less than 6 percent of the population. In 2008, Bobby Jindal became the first Indian American governor when he was elected governor of Louisiana, a state in which Asian Americans made up less than 2 percent of the population. Then in 2011, Nikki Haley became the first Indian American woman to be elected a governor. In 2016, Haley resigned as governor of South Carolina to become the U.S. ambassador to the United Nations.

Native Americans

8.7 **Explain why *Native American* is an umbrella term, their relations with settlers, the significance of disease, justifying labels, education and culture conflict, casinos, and self-determination.**

> *"I don't go so far as to think that the only good Indians are dead Indians, but I believe nine out of ten are—and I shouldn't inquire too closely in the case of the tenth. The most vicious cowboy has more moral principle than the average Indian.*
>
> —Teddy Roosevelt, 1886 (President of the United States 1901–1909)

Another Umbrella Term

When Columbus arrived on the shores of the "New World," Native Americans numbered about 10 million (Schaefer 2018). They were not a single group of people living in separate tribes. They spoke over 700 languages, and their variety of cultures ranged from nomadic hunters and gatherers to farmers who lived in wooden houses. Each group had its own norms and values—and the usual ethnocentric pride in its own culture.

Four hundred years later, when Teddy Roosevelt, who spoke the words above, became president of the United States, the number of Native Americans had plunged from about 10 million to just 250,000. The reasons were the advanced weapons of the European invaders and the diseases the Europeans brought with them. Today's 4 million Native

Americans are divided among more than 500 tribes who speak 169 different languages. They do not think of themselves as a single people who fit neatly within a single label (Siebens and Julian 2011).

Relations between Native Americans and Europeans   A brief overview of early relations between Native Americans and the Europeans who arrived on their soil can help us understand the situation today.

From Peace to Conflict   At first, relations between the Europeans and Native Americans were peaceful. Some American (and Canadian) authorities even encouraged marriage between whites and Native Americans. In 1784, Patrick Henry introduced a bill in the Virginia House of Delegates offering tax relief, free education, and cash bonuses to whites and Indians who intermarried (Kaplan 1990). As more Europeans arrived, they began a relentless push westward. With Native Americans standing in the way of expansion, the Europeans adopted a policy of *genocide*. As part of this policy (which they called "pacification"), the U.S. Cavalry slaughtered tens of thousands of Native Americans. When the cavalry butchered the huge herds of buffalo on which the Great Plains Indians depended, many thousands more died from malnutrition and disease. Because Native Americans had no immunity to European diseases, more died from smallpox, measles, and the flu than from battle wounds (Kitano 1974; Dobyns 1983; Schaefer 2018).

In reading accounts from this period, I was struck by the barbarity of government agents. One of the most grisly acts was the distribution of blankets contaminated with smallpox. The blankets were given as a peace offering. Another horrific act was the Trail of Tears. In 1838, 15,000 Cherokees in the Carolinas and Georgia were rounded up and forced to march 1,000 miles to "reservations" in Oklahoma. Much of the march took place in midwinter, and these people had only light clothing. Falling from illness and exhaustion on this march, 4,000 of them, mostly elderly and children, were left to die.

The Treaties   Recognizing each tribe as a single nation, the U.S. government signed separate treaties with the tribes. These treaties granted each tribe specified lands forever. The treaties were broken when white settlers demanded more Indian land and natural resources. In 1874, for instance, when gold was discovered in South Dakota's Black Hills, whites flooded the reservation lands. The cavalry supported the settlers, resulting in the well-known defeat of "General" (actually, Lt. Colonel) Custer at Little Big Horn in 1876 (Stiles 2015). The symbolic end to Native American resistance may have been the 1890 massacre at Wounded Knee, South Dakota, where the U.S. Cavalry killed 300 (out of 350) Native American men, women, and children. After the massacre, the soldiers threw the bodies into a mass grave (Gua 2016).

Using Justifying Labels   As noted earlier, people use stereotypes and labels to justify inhumane acts. So it was with the U.S. Indian policy. The Europeans newcomers viewed Native Americans as stupid, lying, thieving, murdering, pagan "savages" (Simpson and Yinger 1972). Killing dangerous savages was viewed as a way to make the world a safer place for intelligent, civilized people. After a war, the victors, not the losers, write the history books, and the whites' choice of terms as they wrote theirs is fascinating. They called themselves "pioneers" and "settlers," not "invaders." They labeled their military successes "victories," but they gave the term "massacres" to the military victories of the Native Americans. They didn't call their seizure of Native American lands "invasion" or "theft," but, rather, "settling the land." And the Native Americans' defense of their homelands against overwhelming numbers? Not "courageous," but "treacherous" (Josephy 1970).

Education and Culture Conflict   After the federal government moved the Native Americans to reservations, the Bureau of Indian Affairs (BIA), an agency of the federal government assigned the responsibility of overseeing Native Americans, opened boarding schools in an attempt to "civilize" the Indians—that is, to replace the Native American cultures with that of the European Americans. The BIA took thousands of Native American children from their parents and forced them to attend these off-reservation boarding schools. The effects still linger, and even today many Native Americans mistrust the intentions of white authorities (McCarty 2009).

Dead center in this conflict between schools and the reservation are the children (Wong 2017). Torn between home and school, they generally choose their family and tribe. That they drop out of high school at a high rate and graduate from college at a low rate (see Table 8.3) indicates that such contrasting orientations continue.

Poverty, Alcohol, and Suicide   From Table 8.1, you can see how much lower the incomes of Native Americans are than those of whites and that their rate of poverty is about the same as those of Latinos and African Americans. Not shown on this table is the life expectancy of Native Americans: One in four Native Americans dies before the age of 25, compared with the national average of one in seven. Their suicide rate is also higher than the national average, as is their rate of alcoholism (CDC 2018d). It seems fair to conclude that it is common for Native Americans to find life in the dominant white society far from satisfying.

The Treaties   Native Americans are sometimes called the invisible minority. With one-third of Native Americans living on 557 reservations, most in just four states—Oklahoma, California, Arizona, and New Mexico—most Americans are hardly aware of their presence (Schaefer 2018). Today's conflicts center on Native Americans trying to enforce their treaties with the United States ("Seminal Supreme Court Cases…" 2016). Legal skirmishes have centered on maintaining traditional fishing and hunting rights and protesting the construction of oil pipelines (Aisch and Lai 2016). Major legal battles are being fought over the waters of the Arkansas, Colorado, San Juan, and Rio Grande rivers—which were guaranteed by treaty. Native Americans have also sued to reclaim millions of acres of land from New England to the Southwest. Originally, Congress guaranteed these lands to Native American tribes "in perpetuity"—an unlimited time, generation after generation.

The federal government's primary legal strategy has been to prevent cases being heard by making perpetual motions for postponement. In some instances, legal cases are never heard. Those who originally filed the motion die; others lose interest as proceedings drag on for years, sometimes for generations. Some tribes, however, have won legal battles. Blue Lake, in New Mexico, a heavily forested area sacred to the Taos Pueblo tribe, has been returned to the tribe. Alaskan Native Americans, primarily the Inuits and Aleuts, were awarded a cash settlement of nearly $1 billion and legal title to 40 million acres.

The vast majority of these legal claims remain undecided in court, putting "clouds" on many titles of ownership to real estate. In the state of New York, clouded titles have made it difficult for some people to sell their land even though they have owned it for 200 years (Olson 2002). Some whites have hit upon a legal strategy that goes straight to the jugular: They are trying to strip Native Americans of their legal status as separate nations. This would remove their immunity from lawsuits. So far, such attempts have failed.

The Casinos   In 1988, Congress passed a law that allows Native Americans to operate gambling establishments on reservations. Now about 250 tribes operate casinos. *They bring in $31 billion a year, more than all the casinos in Las Vegas* (RCG Economics 2018; *Statistical Abstract* 2018:Table 1277). The casinos, though, are islands of wealth in a sea of Native American poverty. Each year, the wealthiest native tribe in the country, the Mdewakanton Sioux of Minnesota, distributes $1 million to each adult member of the tribe (Rigert 2016). In contrast, most Native Americans on most reservations remain in poverty, with their tribe located too far from major population centers to make casinos profitable. The casinos have also become a source of division and bitter contention among tribes. It is not uncommon for a tribe that runs a successful casino to hire attorneys and file court cases to stop other tribes from opening their own casinos (Wiltz 2016).

Danita Delimont/Alamy Stock Photo

Wearing traditional clothing and teaching customs to children are ways by which parents and tribal leaders are trying to reclaim an authentic Native American identity, not easy to do in a society dominated by the descendants of the people who defeated their ancestors. Note the combining of cultural clothing.

And is life a bed of roses for the Mdewakanton Sioux? You would think so, with $1 million coming in each year. But to understand what happens, realize the central role that work (or going to college) plays in our lives. The $1 million erodes the incentive to work (or get an education). I mean, why bother? Idle time hangs heavily. What is it replaced with? Alcohol and other drugs. Even compulsive gambling. And the children? How are parents serving as their role models? (And they know they are going to receive $1 million a year for doing nothing when they turn 21.) A lack of purpose, addiction, isolation, the breakdown of families—not a bed of roses, but a bed of rose-covered thorns. Mdewakanton elders are working on this problem.

Self-Determination   Native Americans had no overarching term for the many tribes that inhabited North and South America. The term *Indian* was given to them by Columbus, who mistakenly thought that he had landed in India. The name stuck, and many Native Americans still use it to refer to themselves. Whites also invented the term *Native American*. Thinking of the 500 culturally distinct tribes as "one people," then, is a European American way of thought and labeling. The tribes see themselves as many nations, many peoples, and they insist on the right to self-determination—to remain unassimilated in the dominant culture and to run their own affairs as separate peoples.

That there are these many separate identities has served the dominant whites well, for they have not had to face a united Native America. Perhaps, then, the most significant change is the development of **pan-Indianism**. Emphasizing common elements that run through their many separate cultures, some Native Americans are trying to build a united identity and work toward the welfare of all Native Americans. If effective, national Native American organizations will develop. United, these groups could place greater pressure on the courts to hear Native American lawsuits. They could also develop self-help measures centering on Native American values. Pan-Indianism, however, is a controversial topic among Native Americans ("Pan-Indianism" 2015). Some stress that the many Native American tribes have their own histories, languages, and even musical styles, and they reject pan-Indianism in favor of ethnic diversity, identifying with their own tribe (Rolo n.d.).

Social Policy

8.8   Summarize social policy regarding cultural pluralism, preventing discrimination, and the dilemma of affirmative action.

A unified society certainly is desirable, especially in contrast to a broken, fragmented one, with hostile groups working at cross-currents. We have more than adequate experience, however, to know that it is futile to try to force everyone into the same mold. And which mold would it be anyway? Accordingly, it seems reasonable for social policy to center on the twin goals of encouraging cultural pluralism and preventing discrimination. What social policies might help us reach these goals?

Encouraging Cultural Pluralism and Integrating Groups into the Mainstream Culture

Let's see how we can encourage cultural pluralism and also integrate the diverse groups that make up the United States.

Appreciating Diversity   *Cultural integrity* is essential if we are to promote the first goal, that of encouraging cultural pluralism. Cultural integrity refers to accepting and appreciating diverse backgrounds. Here are steps that can bring this about:

1. Establishing national, state, and local "cultural centers" that feature a group's heritage
2. Holding "ethnic appreciation days" in public schools, featuring ethnic customs, clothing, dances, history, and food

3. Teaching history (and any courses with an historical emphasis) in ways that recognize the contributions of the many groups that make up the United States
4. Teaching foreign languages from grade school through high school—starting early enough that all students learn to converse well in one foreign language

The first two suggestions are easy to implement and go a long way toward encouraging appreciation of cultural diversity and pride in one's own heritage. Because our schools are so segregated, it would be beneficial to have cultural exchanges among public and private schools. For this proposal to be effective, the approach must be honest. Students will see through dishonest attempts to appreciate multiculturalism or to "stretch" some group's contributions to the mainstream culture. Technical advances in teaching foreign languages can make the fourth proposal a reality. As today's trade, travel, and communications expand, learning other languages could benefit the nation as a whole.

Pride in One's Heritage and Participation in the Mainstream Culture   The emphasis of cultural pluralism on pride in one's own racial–ethnic heritage does not mean a retreat into a racial–ethnic culture. Although children of minority groups should be encouraged to take pride in their rich heritage, if they are to participate in the mainstream culture, then like the children of the dominant group, they, too, need to become proficient in English and other basic skills. The school system is uniquely equipped to teach them these skills. Anyone who does not learn to speak English, or who speaks it poorly, or who fails to get a good education is at a severe disadvantage in competing for positions that pay well and offer advancement.

Using the Legal System to Prevent Discrimination

Social policy would be incomplete if we did not try to prevent discrimination, and for this the legal system is a powerful tool. It can be used to ensure that minorities are not discriminated against in jobs, housing, education, or any other area of social life. The Civil Rights Act of 1964, which forbids discrimination by race, color, creed, national origin, and sex, must be enforced. This law applies to unions, employment agencies, and, as amended in 1972, to any business with 15 or more employees. This law prohibits discrimination in voting, public accommodations, federally supported programs, and federally supported institutions such as colleges and hospitals. Preventing discrimination also requires funding the Equal Employment Opportunity Commission (EEOC)—the organization that is empowered to investigate complaints of discrimination and to recommend action to the Department of Justice.

The Dilemma of Affirmative Action

To enforce the Civil Rights Act of 1964 has presented Americans with an ongoing dilemma: How do we make up for past discrimination without creating new discrimination? Keep this dilemma in mind as you read the following cases.

The *Bakke* Case   In what has become the watershed case (*Bakke,* 1973), Allan Bakke argued that the rejection of his application to the medical school of the University of California at Davis was an act of discrimination. The school had admitted minorities who had scored lower than he had on the entrance exam and who had lower grade point averages than his. Bakke argued that had he been a member of a minority group, he would have been admitted (Epstein and Walker 2019). In other words, the university was racist—it had discriminated against him because he was white. The U.S. Supreme Court agreed, ruling that the Davis medical school had to admit Bakke because it had used illegal quotas.

Cloudy Guidance   Following the *Bakke* case, the U.S. Supreme Court issued rulings that confused everyone: Colleges cannot use quotas to determine whom they admit—but they can use race as a factor to create a diverse student body (Walsh 1996). In its 1989 *City of Richmond* decision, the Court ruled that state and local governments "must almost always avoid racial quotas" in awarding construction contracts. "Almost always" left everyone scratching their heads. No one knew where and when or in what ways preferential treatment was or was not constitutional.

Proposition 209   With the U.S. Supreme Court's cloudy guidance, this national debate continued. Few were fond of affirmative action, but no one saw alternatives to erase the consequences of past discrimination. The tide turned in 1999 when California voters passed Proposition 209, an amendment to the state constitution that banned race and gender preferences in hiring and college admissions. Despite appeals by a coalition of civil rights groups, the U.S. Supreme Court upheld the California law.

The University of Michigan Case   White applicants to the University of Michigan who had been denied admission claimed they had been discriminated against because extra points were given to applicants from underrepresented minority groups. In 2003, this case came before the Supreme Court, and the Court ruled that universities can give minorities an edge in admissions, but they cannot use a point system to do so. Race can be a "plus factor," but in the Court's words, there must be "a meaningful individualized review of applicants."

Officials found this ruling murky. To remove ambiguity, voters in California, Michigan, and Nebraska added amendments to their state constitutions that make it illegal for public institutions to consider race or sex in hiring, in awarding contracts, or in college admissions (Espenshade and Radford 2009; Perez-Pena 2012).

The New Haven Firefighters Case   To decide which firefighters should be promoted, the city of New Haven, Connecticut, gave the candidates a test. When African Americans scored poorly on the tests and all the promotions would have gone to whites and one Latino, the city decided to ignore the test results. The whites and Latino sued, and the case came before the Supreme Court, which ruled in their favor. The Court concluded that although the city's goal of diversity was fine, by ignoring the test results the city was adopting an illegal quota system (Liptak 2009).

Continuing Controversy   With laws concerning affirmative action not settled, cases continue to come before the U.S. Supreme Court. As in the *Bakke* case, Abigail Fisher, a white student who was refused admission at the University of Texas, Austin, appealed to the Supreme Court. Her claim is that she was born the wrong color: White. The Court rejected the argument, saying that universities can consider race in the goal of having a diverse student body (Barnes 2016). In a twist, Asian American students have sued, also alleging racial discrimination. Their claim is that they are rejected at top schools because there are "too many" Asian Americans already there, while whites and others with lower scores are accepted (Hartocollis 2018). This, too, will be an interesting and significant case.

Absent constitutional amendments or voter referenda that ban considerations of race-ethnicity, cities and states that want to use race–ethnicity in hiring or promotion and in college admissions have no firm guidelines to follow. As more cases come before the Supreme Court, the rulings will depend not solely on the Constitution, which is open to contradictory interpretations, but, rather, largely on the political makeup of the Court—on who retires and what justices holding what political views replace them.

The Future of the Problem

8.9   Discuss the likely future of racial–ethnic relations.

Although the future is always murky, a path strewn with unknowns, let's try to see what awaits.

Progress

Most Americans today reject the discrimination that was taken for granted in earlier times or—strange to our ears—that was even assumed to be morally correct. Over the years, progress has been slow, even inconsistent, but the result has been expanding opportunities for minority groups. Huge gaps remain, however, between our ideals of equality and the reality of racial–ethnic relations that we experience today.

In World War II, segregation extended into the armed forces, with African Americans fighting in what were called "All Negro" units. This photo was taken December 16, 1944, on the Western front, as U.S. troops were advancing on the German army.

World War II was especially significant for improving racial–ethnic relations. Prior to this war, the U.S. government supported racist policies. Segregation ("American apartheid") was assumed to be moral part of the U.S. landscape. The war brought severe dislocations that dispelled these assumptions. As war industries expanded in the North, jobs opened up and hundreds of thousands of African Americans migrated from the South to the North looking for work. Although African Americans fought in all-black units at this time, several hundred thousand African American soldiers, dislodged from the segregation back home, were thrust into cultural experiences that changed their views on racial–ethnic relations. Exposed to new ways of life in Europe, they returned home with visions of positive change. After the war, the federal government, grudgingly accepting the change from segregation to integration, broke down many of the institutional barriers that had been set up against minorities. In light of this history, we can expect the future to bring fewer barriers and greater equality.

An Ongoing Struggle

Racial–ethnic relations are haunted by barriers to equality, however, and it will require concerted effort to remove them. Affirmative action was designed to overcome these barriers, but, as you know, affirmative action has come under heavy attack. By their very nature, court rulings are victories for one side but defeats for the other. Although some legal decisions represent clear positions, giving guidance for future action, inconsistent and vague court rulings breed confusion. With a continuing need to remedy inequalities, the proper role of affirmative action in a multicultural society is likely to remain center stage for quite some time.

Jobs are likely to be the major focus in the continuing struggle for equality. Because access to jobs and careers determines much of our quality of life, we are likely to see continued efforts to reduce structural barriers and increase education. Increasingly, workers must be prepared to compete in a world that demands more technical expertise. What occurs in education, then, is of vital importance for the future of racial–ethnic relations.

Disparities in Education

For most Americans, education holds the key to the future. Those who receive the better education get the better jobs and enjoy more satisfying lifestyles. Any group that receives less schooling than the national average faces disadvantages in our technological society.

Granted this principle, then, let's see what Table 8.3 might indicate about the future. I already mentioned the outstanding rate of college graduation of Asian Americans, how it exceeds that of other groups by far. Their rate is three to four times higher than that of Latinos and Native Americans, two to three times that of African Americans, and about 60 percent higher than that of whites. They also earn doctorate degrees at more than twice their percentage of the population. You can see how this high achievement brightens the future for Asian Americans, opening doors to professions and managerial positions. This table also indicates that with their educational achievement whites will do quite well, but that the future is less bright for the other groups. They are less prepared to compete in our growing technological society.

To fall behind in education is to fall behind on almost all indicators of well-being. If you go back to Table 8.1, you can see how closely each group's relative position in income and poverty matches its attainment in education. It isn't difficult to figure out why, since you know that education opens doors of opportunity, and the lack of education closes them. To develop policies that produce greater educational achievement, I suggest the funding of a "think tank" composed of top educators from our many racial–ethnic groups. Their purpose will not be to produce more research on how education works, as we have plenty of that, but to propose testable policies that, avoiding quotas and vague "race awareness" benchmarks, will increase the educational attainment of underachieving groups–and of anyone in poverty.

An Underclass

As a nation, do we have sufficient desire to raise the educational achievement of African Americans, Latinos, and Native Americans? A disturbing possibility is that we have a permanent **underclass** (Wilson 1978, 1987, 2009). That is, society may already have thrown up its collective hands and consigned to the poverty-plagued, crime-ridden inner city an enduring underclass. This alienated group has little education and high rates of drug abuse, violent crime, and death by murder. These conditions not only make it difficult to succeed in mainstream society, but also separates people from mainstream society.

Unless we develop effective social policies to reach this underclass, the tragic cycle will continue. Many of the children born in these conditions will be fated to repeat their parents' despair. A primary structural factor that makes this sorry possibility likely is that most jobs are located in the suburbs. Those who live in the inner city lack the means of transportation to reach those jobs and the finances to move closer to them.

These disheartening conditions carry severe implications for society as a whole. When large groups of people remain isolated from mainstream society, receive a meager education, do not have access to good jobs, and are denied proper police protection, an unexpected precipitating incident can ignite the powder keg of latent and growing hostilities, resulting in an explosion of collective violence. With little being done about the problems of our inner cities, we can expect turmoil. At some point, riots are likely, and although it has become a distant memory, we may see a repeat of the 1992 Los Angeles riots.

Militancy

Militants, whether from a minority group or the dominant group, are an unpredictable factor in racial–ethnic relations. Although racial–ethnic pride is laudable—as discussed in the social policy section, such pride should be encouraged—some people mistake pride in one's own group as hostility toward other groups and the need to demean them. Groups that preach hatred will continue to appear, their leaders trying to create divisions by building on hostilities and negative stereotypes. Occasional outbursts by hate groups, though dramatic, will pose no serious threat to those working toward a future of equality.

The American Dilemma

In 1944, Gunnar Myrdal (1898–1987), a sociologist from Sweden, wrote *An American Dilemma*. Myrdal said that the United States was caught between two major forces: On one hand is prejudice and discrimination, and on the other hand is the "American creed" of equality as expressed in religion and the Declaration of Independence. Myrdal was confident that Americans would resolve racial tensions by following these higher values. Myrdal was right, and conditions are remarkably better today than they were back then. However, the dilemma that Myrdal identified remains.

With our past marked by valleys of hostilities and despair followed by peaks of goodwill and high hopes, we can expect the future to bring more of the same. Although as individuals we have little power or influence, our actions, collectively, can be powerful. Ultimately, our actions give shape to racial–ethnic relations. None of us can overcome structural barriers alone, yet, together, we can dismantle them. I do not mean to sound Pollyannaish, but I am convinced that through our collective efforts we can help to create a more equitable and positive future for us all.

Summary and Review

1. *Discrimination* occurs worldwide, as *racial–ethnic groups* living in the same society struggle for dominance. The various groups tend to perceive one another through *stereotypes*.

2. *Minority groups* share five characteristics: unequal treatment, distinctive traits, solidarity, membership by birth, and marriage within their own group. Minority groups have four objectives: *pluralism, assimilation, secession,* and *militancy*. Six policies of dominant groups are *multiculturalism (pluralism), assimilation, segregation, internal colonialism, population transfer,* and *genocide*.

3. Although the idea of *race* is significant in human behavior, biologically speaking, no human group represents a "pure race."

4. Discrimination, which affects quality of life, can be a life-and-death matter, affecting mortality rates.

5. *Individual discrimination* consists of acts by individuals. *Institutional discrimination* is discrimination that is built into the social system.

6. Symbolic interactionists focus on how symbols of race–ethnicity divide people and influence their behavior, particularly how they affect perception, sort people into different life experiences, and justify discrimination and violence. Functionalists analyze functions of discrimination, such as fostering *ethnocentrism* and ensuring that society's *dirty work* gets done. They also analyze its dysfunctions, such as destroying

human potential. Conflict theorists stress that racial–ethnic divisions among workers help capitalists control workers and increase their profits.

7. Native Americans, Latinos, and African Americans have less education, higher unemployment, lower incomes, and higher rates of poverty than whites and Asian Americans. The pressures that minority groups have placed on white-controlled social institutions have forced social change. Underlying the high social and economic gains of Asian Americans are assimilation and family values that stress hard work, thrift, and education.

8. Major cleavages along social class lines divide U.S. racial–ethnic groups. Some sociologists argue that social class has become more significant than race–ethnicity in determining an individual's life chances.

9. To be effective, social policies should encourage cultural pluralism and prevent discrimination. With the major struggle being over jobs, groups that attain the most education have the brightest future. Dilemmas concerning affirmative action continue.

10. With the continuing deprivations of the *underclass*, we can expect urban riots. In no foreseeable future will *prejudice* and *discrimination* be eliminated. A storm cloud on the horizon is the resurgence of groups that preach division and hatred.

Thinking Critically about Chapter 8

1. Minority groups share five characteristics: unequal treatment, distinctive traits, solidarity, membership by birth, and marriage within their own group. Pick any minority group in the United States and give examples of how these five characteristics apply to that group.

2. Minority groups share four objectives or goals: pluralism, assimilation, secession, and militancy. Explain how each objective applies to African Americans, to Asian Americans, to Latinos, and to Native Americans. Do these groups emphasize these objectives in the same way? If not, why do you think there are differences?

3. In their relationship to minority groups, dominant groups have six policies: multiculturalism, assimilation, segregation, internal colonialism, population transfer, and genocide. Which policies do you think that whites are following with African Americans? With Native Americans? With Latinos? With Asian Americans?

4. Which of the three sociological perspectives (symbolic interactionism, functionalism, or conflict theory) do you think best explains why prejudice and discrimination exist in the United States? Explain.

5. The author concludes this chapter on a positive note. Do you agree or disagree with his conclusion? Why?

Key Terms

Anglo-conformity, 220
apartheid, 217
capitalist economy, 230
civil disobedience, 235
dirty work, 228
discrimination, 214
division of labor, 228
dominant group, 215
ethnocentrism, 229
individual discrimination, 222
institutional discrimination, 222
melting pot, 220
minority group, 215

pan-Indianism, 244
prejudice, 214
race, 217
racial–ethnic group, 219
racial–ethnic stratification, 228
reserve labor force, 230
riots, 231
rising expectations, 236
selective perception, 226
split-labor market, 230
stereotypes, 221
surplus value of labor, 230
underclass, 248

Chapter 9
Inequalities of Gender and Sexual Orientation

Alex Menendez/Alamy Stock Photo

 ## Learning Objectives

After reading this chapter, you should be able to:

9.1 Explain why sociologists consider women to be a minority group and how gender discrimination became a social problem.

9.2 Discuss whether male dominance is universal, the sexual stratification of work, and major areas of gender discrimination.

9.3 Use the symbolic interactionist perspective to explain socialization into gender.

9.4 Discuss the two functionalist theories of the origin of gender discrimination.

9.5 Review the conflict/feminist account of women's struggle for equality in the United States.

9.6 Be able to discuss differences between the sexes, discrimination in everyday life and

in education, the portrayal of the sexes in the mass media, gender relations in politics, the gender pay gap, and sexual harassment.

9.7 Discuss changing attitudes toward sexual minorities, apply the conflict view to homosexuality, and discuss research on homosexuality.

9.8 Apply the feminist/conflict and symbolic interactionist perspectives to gendered violence.

9.9 Compare middle-of-the-road social policies with those appropriate to the radical and conservative extremists.

9.10 Discuss the likely future of gender discrimination.

"Strangling baby girls at birth might be a thing of the past."

—Promilla Kapur, sociologist in India

Strangling baby girls? Who would do such a thing?

This used to be a common practice in India. Parents would hope, pray, and offer sacrifices to their gods that their coming child would be a boy. Jobs for women, especially uneducated women, are few—and most Indian women are uneducated.

Then there are the dowries. The parents of an Indian girl have to pay dowry money when their daughter marries. This burden is costly, and most Indians are poor.

As the Indians say, "Raising a girl is like watering someone else's plant."

Today fewer baby girls are being strangled. Yet every year in India about 400,000 fewer girls are born than would happen naturally. Why? The reason is technology. The pregnant woman goes to a doctor and gets an ultrasound. Then comes the decision—if it's a girl—"Do we want to go through with the pregnancy?" If it's a boy, there is no question to ask. The parents already know the answer. When the boy becomes a man, he collects the dowry. And he helps support the parents in their old age.

Recognizing that a nation's unbalanced sex ratio is a problem and responding to an incipient women's movement, the Indian government has made sex selection abortion illegal. A doctor can lose his license.

As you know, whenever there is high demand for an illegal service, a black market pops up. For these black-market specialists, the only investment is in a small ultrasound machine (Nagar 2018).

Of course, it's a word-of-mouth kind of thing, since no one can post an ad that says, "Avoid a dowry and save a bundle of cash. Find out if you are going to have a girl."

They used to be able to do such advertising. But not under the new law. However, as with other black markets, the word gets around to those who are interested.

> ## "Raising a girl is like watering someone else's plant."

The Problem in Sociological Perspective

9.1 **Explain why sociologists consider women to be a minority group and how gender discrimination became a social problem.**

Perhaps you can see how important the sex of a child is in India, maybe even why parents who are living in poverty feel despair at the birth of a girl. They must feed and clothe her, but she can contribute practically nothing to the family income. Then she marries, and they have to pay a dowry. For this, poor families go into crippling debt to black-market money lenders. But the birth of a boy? For this, the parents rejoice. A boy will grow into a man who can help sustain them in their old age.

Women as a Minority Group

Although the Indian situation is extreme, *sex is the major sorting device in every society in the world.* In our own society, as we'll examine in this chapter, men are paid more for the same work, and, despite changes, they continue to dominate politics and public life. Even though women make up 50.8 percent of the U.S. population (*Statistical Abstract* 2018:Table 6), sociologists consider women a minority group because of their position relative to men, the dominant group.

Setting the Context: The Development of Gender Discrimination as a Social Problem

Sociologists have not always referred to women as a minority group. They attached this label only gradually, as they began to note parallels between the social positions of women and men and those of African Americans and whites. In 1944, Swedish sociologist Gunnar Myrdal mentioned these parallels in *An American Dilemma*. He noted that in the 17th century, the legal status of black slaves was derived from the legal status of women and children, whose lives were controlled by male heads of households. In 1951, an American sociologist, Helen Hacker, was the first to apply the term *minority* to women. She documented the discrimination against women at that time, how they were "barred from certain activities or, if admitted,... treated unequally."

Just as the perception of sociologists was changing, so was that of women, who began to challenge the traditional relations between the sexes. Many came to see themselves not as *individuals* who had less status than men, but as a *group* of people who were discriminated against. During the 1960s and 1970s, women publicized their grievances at being second-class citizens dominated by men. Subjective concerns grew, and large numbers of women in the United States and around the world demanded that discrimination against women be addressed. Recalling our definition of social problems, you can see that this new evaluation of the relative positions of women and men transformed what had been only an objective condition of society into a social problem. Sociologists then began to investigate **sexism**, the belief that one sex is innately superior to the other and the discrimination that results from this belief.

The Scope of the Problem

9.2 **Discuss whether male dominance is universal, the sexual stratification of work, and major areas of gender discrimination.**

The past events I just summarized help set the context for our current situation. To get a broader view of the scope of this social problem, we will consider whether male dominance is universal, look at the sexual stratification of work, and then take an eye-opening glance at sexual discrimination 65 or 70 years ago.

Is Male Dominance Universal?

When did sexism begin? Some social scientists, such as anthropologist Marvin Harris (1977:46), claim that men's domination of society "has been in continuous existence throughout virtually the entire globe from the earliest times to the present." After reviewing the evidence, historian and feminist Gerda Lerner (1986:31) agreed, saying that "there is not a single society known where women-as-a-group have decision-making power over men (as-a-group)." She also concluded that the earliest societies had the least amount of gender discrimination. In those societies, women contributed about 60 percent of the group's total food.

Don't women presidents, prime ministers, and monarchs disprove the universal domination of society by men? Sociologists point out that these are *individual* women in positions of power, not women-as-a-group in control of a society. Even those countries that are led by a woman are dominated by men, for men hold almost all key positions in politics. The global average of women in a country's house or senate is 23 percent. The extremes are Senegal with 42 percent and Papua New Guinea with 0 percent (Inter-Parliamentary Union 2018).

The Sexual Stratification of Work

Every society stratifies its members by sex; that is, they single out males and females for different activities. Around the world, for example, most work is **sex-typed**, associated with one sex or the other. At one time, sex typing was so taken for granted that many believed anatomy required men and women to be assigned particular work.

In 1937, anthropologist George Murdock blew this gender myth out of the water. He illustrated beyond doubt what we take for granted today—biology does not determine occupational destiny. Reviewing the reports that anthropologists had made on 324 societies, Murdock found that what is considered "male" or "female" work differs from one society to another. For example, in some societies the care of cattle is women's work; in others, it is men's work. He found that three types of labor were almost always defined as men's work—making weapons, pursuing sea mammals, and hunting. Four types of work were usually assigned to women—making clothing, cooking, carrying water, and grinding grain.

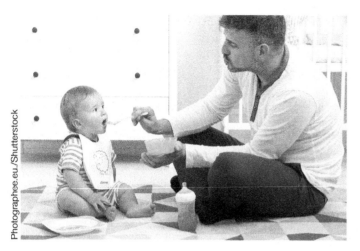

Gradually, in a process of gender modification, men are taking on more activities that previously were done almost exclusively by women.

No specific work was universally assigned to women, but one was to men—metalworking.

That one society assigns a certain kind of work to men while another assigns that same work to women—how is this relevant to a discussion of sexism? Social scientists have discovered a startling principle: *When work is assigned to men, it is considered important and given greater prestige* (Linton 1936; Rosaldo 1974; Reskin and Bielby 2005). If taking care of cattle is men's work, then cattle care is thought to be important, and it carries high prestige. If taking care of cattle is women's work, however, it is considered less important, and it carries less prestige. To cite an example closer to home, when delivering babies was "women's work," the responsibility of midwives, this job was given low prestige. But when men took over delivering babies (over the opposition of women), its prestige shot up (Ehrenreich and English 1973). *It is the sex that is associated with the work that provides its prestige—not the work itself.*

Major Areas of Discrimination

Sexism pervades every society of the world, touching almost every aspect of our social life. In her classic 1951 article, Helen Hacker listed the following types of discrimination against U.S. women at that time:

1. *Political and legal.* Women were often barred from jury duty and public office.
2. *Education.* Professional schools, such those for architecture and medicine, applied quotas for women (no more women above a certain number).
3. *Economic.* Women were usually supervised by men, where they received unequal pay, promotion, and responsibility.
4. *Social.* Women were permitted less freedom of movement; fewer deviations in dress, speech, and manners; and a narrower range of personality expression.

Hacker also described how women's three major roles—sister/daughter, wife, and mother—fit this pattern of discrimination. She said that a sister does more housework than her brother, a wife is expected to subordinate her interests to those of her husband, and a mother bears the stigma for an illegitimate child.

Sex discrimination in the United States has changed so drastically that Hacker seems to be describing another society. In a sociological sense, she is. Women are no longer barred from jury duty and public office, nor do they face quotas in professional schools. You probably noticed that on a couple of significant levels, though, Hacker's analysis remains remarkably current. Women still struggle against unequal treatment in jobs, politics, and other areas of social life.

■ Looking at the Problem Theoretically

Why are societies sexist? Let's use our theoretical lenses to see what contrasting perspectives emerge.

Symbolic Interactionism: Socialization into Gender

9.3 **Use the symbolic interactionist perspective to explain socialization into gender.**

When we consider how males and females differ, we usually think first of **sex**, the different *biological* equipment of males and females. Then we might think about **gender**, how we express our "maleness" or "femaleness." Symbolic interactionists stress that sex is biological, and gender is learned, or social. Let's look at how we learn our gender.

Socialization into Gender

Symbolic interactionists study how we are socialized into **gender roles**—the attitudes and behaviors expected of boys and men because they are male and of girls and women because they are female. The process begins *before* birth. While the woman is pregnant, traditionally-oriented couples imagine their future child's participation in gendered (sex-typed) activities. A father may see himself teaching his son how to fish or play baseball. In her mind's eye, a mother may see herself tying a little pink bow on her daughter's hair—and thinking how cute she will look.

When the child is born, the parents announce its sex to the world. Through social media, e-mails, cards, and telephone calls, they proclaim "It's a girl!" or "It's a boy!" In small towns, newspapers report this momentous event, while social media feature it as news for celebrity births. And momentous it is, for *in every society of the world this announcement launches babies into their single most significant life-shaping circumstance.* Sex is a **master trait**, cutting across all other identities in life. Whatever else we may be, we are always male or female.

Cast onto the stage of life with a gender role to play, we spend much of our childhood and young adult life learning how to manage this assignment. Throughout the world, parents are the first of many "significant others" to teach children their gender roles. In U.S. society, parents begin by dressing boy babies in blue and girl babies in pink, colors imbued with gender expectations. Parents coach their children about gender throughout childhood ("Boys don't do that!"… "Girls don't do that!"). Through their words and especially their actions, parents also teach their children about what they should be like as husband or wife.

These initial directions lay our basic foundation of gender. As we go through life, we continue to build on this foundation, refining our gender roles as we perform before different audiences. As sociologists say, we "do gender" all of our lives.

Socialization into Genders

What is femininity? What is masculinity? Each culture makes its own decisions about the behaviors and attitudes that match what they view as feminine and masculine. Definitions that once seemed to have firm edges, with everyone knowing what was expected, have weakened, and in some instances crumbled. Emerging is a mix of expectations, sometimes with masculine becoming softer and feminine becoming harder, as well as mixtures of crossovers from traditional expectations. As **transgender persons**, those whose internal gender identity does not match the gender role that society has assigned them based on their sex organs, are more accepted in society, they, too, add to changing ideas of masculinity and femininity. The future appears to be more of a more-or-less rather than an either-or.

The distinctions between sex and gender that sociologists have drawn are becoming part of public consciousness.

Interpreting Classic Research

Let's look at classic research done by psychologists Susan Goldberg and Michael Lewis (1960), who observed how mothers teach gender roles without being aware that they are doing so.

> Goldberg and Lewis recruited mothers of 6-month-olds to come into their laboratory so they could observe the development of their children. Unobtrusively, they studied how the mothers interacted with their babies. They found that the mothers kept their girls closer to them than their sons. By the time the children were 13 months old, the girls were more reluctant than the boys to leave their mothers. During play, they remained closer to their mothers and returned to them sooner and more often than the boys did.

> Goldberg and Lewis followed up their initial observations with a simple experiment. They surrounded each mother with colorful toys and placed her child on the other side of a small barrier. The girls were more likely to cry and motion for help, while the boys were more likely to try to climb over or go around the barrier.

"Sex brought us together, but gender drove us apart."

Barbara Smaller/The New Yorker Collection/The Cartoon Bank

Stills Press/Alamy Stock Photo

Gender roles are flexible, varying from culture to culture. As some entertainers such as Adam Lambert bend gender, the outer edges of gender acceptability are challenged and changed.

The researchers' conclusion? The mothers produced the different behaviors of the little girls and little boys. Without knowing it, the mothers had rewarded their daughters for passive and dependent behavior, while rewarding their sons for aggressive and independent behavior.

But are these the right conclusions? Were these differences brought about by the mother's behavior, as the researchers concluded? Or were the researchers observing genetic differences that had begun to appear by the age of 13 months? In short, had the mothers created those different behaviors, or were they merely responding to differences inherent in their children? As a sociologist, I prefer the environmental explanation, but we don't yet have enough evidence to draw a firm conclusion.

The Dominant Symbolic Interactionist Position

Most symbolic interactionists assume that gender differences like those that Goldberg and Lewis observed are learned. They emphasize how socialization produces the behaviors. It starts with stereotypes of the sexes. Since males are labeled aggressive and dominant, boys tend to fulfill those expectations by being aggressive and dominant—and they are given approval for doing so. Since females are considered more passive and submissive, girls receive approval for fulfilling those expectations. Not everyone follows gender scripts, but most do.

In Sum   Symbolic interactionists highlight how society uses the labels *male* and *female* to sort its members into separate groups, a process that starts within the family and is reinforced by other social institutions. As a result, males and females acquire different expectations of themselves and of one another, with males and females learning that certain activities—and even feelings—are appropriate for their gender. This socialization process is so effective that we all learn to evaluate ourselves on the basis of how well we "do gender."

Functionalism: Two Theories of the Origin of Gender Discrimination

9.4   Discuss the two functionalist theories of the origin of gender discrimination.

If male dominance is universal, or even nearly universal, how did this come about? Although the origins of sexism are lost in history, functionalists have developed two theories to account for it. The first is social—the necessity to survive warfare. The second is biological—based on human reproduction.

Rewards for Warriors

The first theory was proposed by anthropologist Marvin Harris (1977). His controversial explanation goes like this: In preliterate times, humans lived in small groups. Because these groups fought with one another, to survive, each group had to recruit people who would fight in hand-to-hand combat. People feared injury and death, of course, so the recruiting wasn't easy. To coax people into bravery, groups developed rewards and punishments. Because an average woman is only 85 percent the size of an average man and has only two-thirds his strength, men became the warriors. And women? They became the men's reward for risking their lives. The women were used for sexual pleasure and labor. Some groups allowed only men who had previously faced an enemy to marry. Even today, in some tribal groups such as the Barabaig of Tanzania, women are rewards for men who show bravery (Aposporos 2004).

The consequences were severe. To make the system work, men were trained from birth for combat, while women were trained from birth to be submissive to men. Men assigned the "drudge work" to women—weeding, seed grinding, fetching water and firewood, cooking, even carrying household possessions during moves. Because men preferred to avoid these onerous tasks—and could do so if they had one or more wives—offering women as a reward to men who risked their lives in combat worked.

Reproduction

The second theory for the universality of gender stratification, based on human reproduction, also goes back to early human history (Lerner 1986; Hope and Stover 1987; Friedl 1990). Since early people did not live long, for the group to survive, women had to give birth to many children. Carrying a child for 9 months, giving birth, and nursing babies limited women's activities. With a child in their wombs or at their breasts and one on their hips or on their backs, women were encumbered physically. As a result, women everywhere took on tasks associated with home and child care, while men took over hunting large animals and other tasks that required longer absence from the base camp (Huber 1990).

Again, the consequences were severe: This division of labor brought power and prestige to men. They made and controlled the weapons used for hunting and warfare. They would return triumphantly to camp with their kill, providing meat for the group. Outside the camp, the men made contact with other tribes and accumulated possessions in trade. Sometimes they would return with prisoners taken in raids. In contrast, the taken-for-granted activities of child care and cooking gave women nothing to boast about. But those who risked their lives in hunting and warfare, now that was another story. The men's weapons, their items of trade, and the knowledge they gained from their contacts with other groups became sources of power and prestige.

In Sum Whether gender stratification resulted from warfare and bravery or childbirth and child care, each theory leads to the same result—a **patriarchal society**, one in which men-as-a-group rule over women-as-a-group. To justify their dominance and privileges, men developed ideas and myths that linked manhood with superiority. To avoid "contamination" by women, now deemed inferior, men enshrouded some of their activities in secrecy and established rules and rituals that excluded women. Today's male dominance is a perpetuation of these patterns laid down in early history.

Although tribal societies developed into larger groups and hand-to-hand combat and hunting dangerous animals ceased to be routine, men, enjoying their privileges and power, held onto them. Reluctant to abandon their privileged position of dominance, men still use cultural devices to control women. For an example, see the following *Global Glimpse*.

A Global Glimpse

Female Circumcision

"Lie down there," the excisor suddenly said to me [when I was 12], pointing to a mat on the ground. No sooner had I laid down then I felt my frail, thin legs grasped by heavy hands and pulled wide apart.... Two women on each side of me pinned me to the ground...I underwent the ablation of the labia minor and then of the clitoris. The operation seemed to go on forever. I was in the throes of agony, torn apart both physically and psychologically. It was the rule that girls of my age did not weep in this situation. I broke the rule. I cried and screamed with pain ...!

Afterwards they forced me, not only to walk back to join the other girls who had already been excised, but to dance with them. I was doing my best, but then I fainted.... It was a month before I was completely healed. When I was better, everyone mocked me, as I hadn't been brave, they said (Walker and Parmar 1993:107–108).

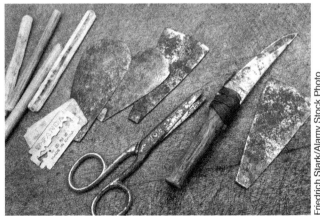

These tools were used to perform female circumcision in Kenya.

Figure 9.1 Mothers of Girls Who Are Circumcised: How They View Female Circumcision

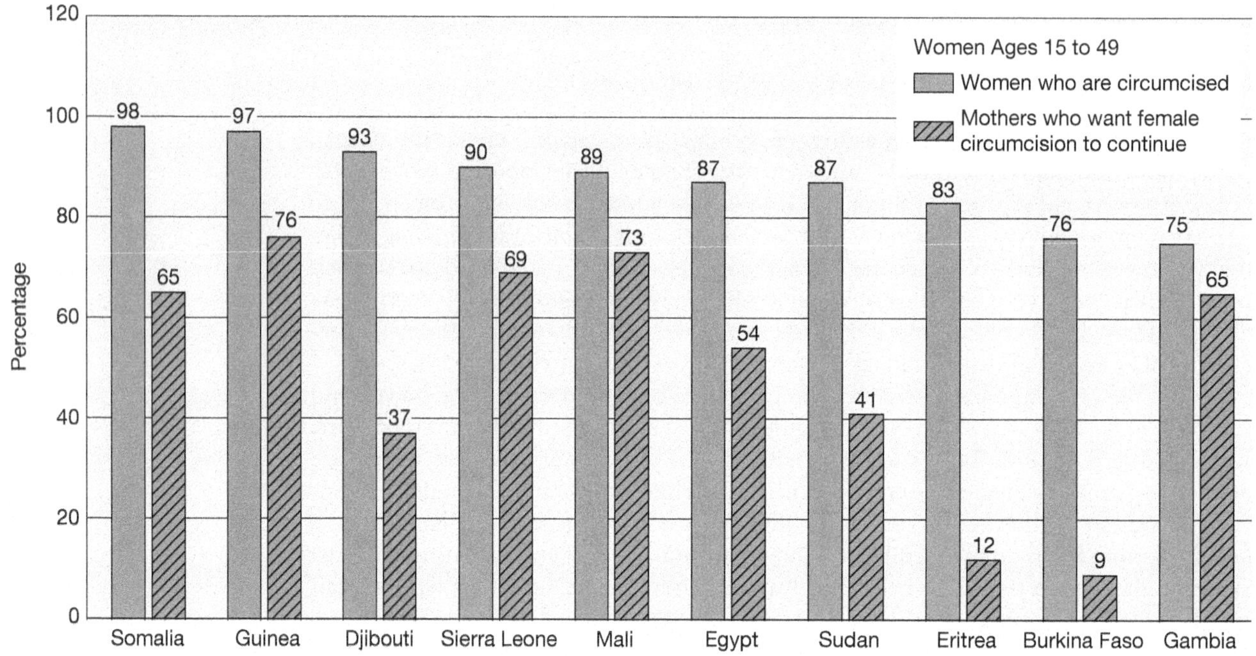

Source: Based on United Nations International Children's Emergency Fund 2016.

Worldwide, 200 million females have been circumcised, mostly in Muslim Africa and in some parts of Malaysia and Indonesia (WHO 2018). Figure 9.1 shows the ten countries where the circumcision of females is the most prevalent. The percentage of women in those countries who want female circumcision to continue might surprise you.

In some cultures, the surgery occurs 7 to 10 days after birth, but in others it is not performed until girls reach adolescence. Among most groups, the circumcision takes place between the ages of 4 and 8. Because the surgery is usually done without anesthesia, the pain is excruciating, and adult women hold the girl down. In urban areas, physicians sometimes perform the operation; in rural areas, neighborhood women usually do it.

In some cultures, only the girl's clitoris is cut off; in others, more is removed. In Sudan, the Nubia cut away most of the girl's genitalia, then sew together the remaining outer edges. They bind the girl's legs from her ankles to her waist for several weeks while scar tissue closes up the vagina. They leave a small opening the diameter of a pencil for the passage of urine and menstrual fluids. When a woman marries, the opening is cut wider to permit sexual intercourse. Before a woman gives birth, the opening is enlarged further. After birth, the vagina is again sutured; this cycle of deinfibulation and reinfibulation begins anew with each birth.

What are the reasons for circumcising girls? Some groups believe it reduces female sexual desire, making it more likely that a woman will be a virgin at marriage and, afterward, remain faithful to her husband. Others think that women can't bear children if they aren't circumcised.

As you saw in Figure 9.1, the surgery has strong support among many women. Some mothers and grandmothers even insist that the custom continue. Their concern is that their daughters marry well, and in some of these societies uncircumcised women are considered impure and are not allowed to marry.

Change is on the way: The World Health Organization, stating that female circumcision is a human rights issue, has declared an International Day of Zero Tolerance on Female Genital Mutilation/Cutting. Working with governments to pass laws and communities to change culture, success has been slow but steady. The most concrete sign of change is that globally, female circumcision has dropped by 25 percent (UNICEF 2018).

Senegal is becoming a model for how to end female circumcision. Persuaded through education programs, the elders of a village agree to stop the practice. They celebrate the change with a ceremony attended by government dignitaries. With much intermarriage among villages, a chain reaction is occurring as villages agree to stop female circumcision (Dugger 2011). On the negative side, circumcision continues in Senegal (Naib 2016).

For Your Consideration

→ Do you think the members of one culture have the right to judge the customs of another culture as inferior or wrong and to then try to get rid of those customs? If so, under what circumstances? What makes us right and them wrong?

→ Let's go further. Some oppose the circumcision of boys. One court in Germany ruled that the circumcision of boys "amounts to bodily harm even if the parents consent to the circumcision" ("German Court ..." 2012). Do you think the same principle should apply to both female and male circumcision? Why or why not?

Conflict/Feminist Theory: The Struggle for Equality

9.5 **Review the conflict/feminist account of women's struggle for equality in the United States.**

> *In the wake of the Industrial Revolution, as women acquired industrial, business, and professional skills, they increasingly sought employment in competition with men. Men were quick to perceive them as a rival group and made use of economic, legal, and ideological weapons to eliminate or reduce their competition. They excluded women from the trade unions, made contracts with employers to prevent them from hiring women, passed laws restricting the employment of married women, caricatured the working woman, and carried on ceaseless propaganda to return women to the home or keep them there (Hacker 1951).*

To gain insight into Helen Hacker's summary of the women's struggle for equality, consider the following four basic principles.

Four Principles of Power

1. Power yields privilege. In every society, the powerful enjoy the best resources available.
2. The privileged lifestyles of those in power encourage them to feel superior.
3. To support their feelings of superiority, the powerful clothe themselves with ideologies that justify their position.
4. To maintain their position in society, the powerful use the social institutions. As a group, men cling to their positions, cultivate images of female inferiority to justify their greater privilege, and use economic and legal weapons against women.

As mentioned, many feminists use conflict theory in their analyses of the relationship between women and men. Among the issues they highlight is discrimination in the workplace. The "quiet revolution"—women leaving the home for paid work—brought resistance from men, as Hacker says, but it also equipped many women for economic and emotional independence. Although multiple millions of women are in the paid labor force, today's women still face lower wages, lower prestige, and sexual harassment. We'll return to some of these issues in a moment.

The Struggle for Equality: Past and Present

What country do you think this refers to?

> *Woman are always under the legal control of a man, either her father or her husband. Women cannot vote or testify in court. Women cannot make legal contracts or hold property in their own name. Women can work for wages, but they cannot spend what they earn, as by law, their paychecks belong to the husband.*

If you guessed Saudi Arabia, you would be wrong. How about Bangladesh? No. Then maybe Somalia? No, not Somalia, either. The name might surprise you, as the country is the United States. Not now, of course, but this is a description of women's condition in the United States in the 1800s.

It is easy to lose sight of the bitter struggle by which women gained the rights we take for granted today. Women had to confront the social institutions men dominated. Men first denied women the right to speak in public. They spat upon some who did, slapped their faces, tripped them, pelted them with burning cigar stubs, and hurled obscenities at them. Despite the opposition, leaders of the women's movement persisted. They chained themselves to the iron grillwork of public buildings and went on talking while the police sawed them loose. When arrested, these women would go on hunger strikes in jail.

If you think I am exaggerating, consider what happened after feminists—then called **suffragists**—formed the National Woman's Party in 1916. To draw attention to their main goal, to attain the right to vote, in January 1917, they began to picket outside the White House. After the women had protested for six months, authorities grew tired of "the nonsense" and arrested them. The women refused to pay their fines, and judges sent hundreds of suffragists to prison, including two leaders, Lucy Burns and Alice Paul. Their treatment in jail illustrates how seriously these women had threatened male privilege:

> *The guards from the male prison fell upon us. I saw Miss Lincoln, a slight young girl, thrown to the floor. Mrs. Nolan, a delicate old lady of seventy-three, was mastered by two men... Whittaker (the Superintendent) in the center of the room directed the whole attack, inciting the guards to every brutality. Two men brought in Dorothy Day, twisting her arms above her head. Suddenly they lifted her and brought her body down twice over the back of an iron bench.... The bed broke Mrs. Nolan's fall, but Mrs. Cosu hit the wall. They had been there a few minutes when Mrs. Lewis, all doubled over like a sack of flour, was thrown in. Her head struck the iron bed and she fell to the floor senseless. As for Lucy Burns, they handcuffed her wrists and fastened the handcuffs over her head to the cell door (Cowley 1969:13).*

It is difficult to imagine any woman in the United States would be treated this way for trying to gain rights that men already possess. Despite the opposition, the early suffragists were persistent and outspoken. Using bold tactics, they forced a historical shift in the balance of power.

The suffragists spearheaded women's rights throughout the Western world. This photo was taken in London in 1905.

Manchester Daily Express/SSPL/Getty Images

Discrimination against women continues today, but it is much subtler: hidden quotas, sexist jokes, and the assumption that men are more qualified for the most responsible positions. The term **glass ceiling** describes this conceptual blockage that keeps women from achieving the higher positions in the workplace.

Although the situation is vastly different today, the struggle against discrimination is not over. Women continue to press for a greater share of society's power and privileges. They pressure lawmakers, compete for jobs, and fight obstacles that slow or prevent advancement at work.

In Sum   From the conflict-feminist perspective, the historical relationship of men and women can be written in terms of women's struggle against men's dominance. Men have controlled society's resources, and with them, women-as-a-group. Social equality comes about by forcing those in power to yield—for those in power do not willingly share their control of society's institutions.

We will examine today's ongoing struggle, but first let's pause to consider again the question of natural differences between the sexes.

Research Findings

9.6   **Be able to discuss differences between the sexes, discrimination in everyday life and in education, the portrayal of the sexes in the mass media, gender relations in politics, the gender pay gap, and sexual harassment.**

The first research findings we will look at are those that consider whether males and females have different inherent traits.

Are There Natural Differences between the Sexes?

Apart from obvious physical differences between men and women, what natural differences exist between the sexes? Is one sex innately more intelligent? More aggressive? Dominant? Protective? Nurturing? Tender? Loving? Passive? These questions are intriguing, but how do you separate culture from biology? Let's look at three research approaches.

Studies of Children   The first explanation focuses on childhood. If girls and boys show consistent differences at early ages, biology may be the cause. And researchers have found areas of consistent difference (Goldman 2017). Girls do better with words, and boys do better with numbers. Girls talk earlier than boys and form sentences at an earlier age (Espinoza 2015; Sugiura and Hata 2018). Girls also read earlier and do better in grammar and spelling (Loveless 2015). In contrast, when it comes to math, boys outperform girls. This holds true for general math, algebra, geometry, and calculus (Cunningham et al. 2015). In general, boys are better at motor and spatial tasks, while girls are superior at memory and analytical reasoning (Ingalhalikar et al. 2013).

Does biology explain these differences? Some researchers think so (Goldman 2017). For 15 years, psychologist and feminist Camilla Benbow searched for an environmental explanation. Gradually, she ruled out all possibilities and concluded—reluctantly, she stressed—that these results are due to "a basic biological difference between the sexes in brain functions" (Goleman 1987). Research on brain functioning supports this view (Ingalhalikar et al. 2013). Others say the biological view is not sufficient and we must add cultural factors. To explain young girls' higher verbal performance, these social scientists stress three social causes: (1) girls identify more with their mothers (who are more verbal), (2) both mothers and fathers hold and speak to their daughters more than to their sons, and (3) girls' games are more linguistic than boys' games (Bardwick 1971). That culture is significant, not biology alone, also becomes apparent from cross-cultural research: The gender math difference, so strongly in favor of males, is not universal. In a few societies, girls outperform boys in math (Cook 2014).

Aggression is another area in which boys and girls are different. At all ages, boys are more aggressive than girls. Boys also receive more pleasure from hurting things and from seeing "bad people" killed on television (Benenson et al. 2008). But does this mean that males are innately more "aggressive" than females? Perhaps. Aggression could be wired into boys' brains. Even if this is the case, the environment is also at work. Parents, for example, also subtly (or not so subtly) encourage their sons to be strong and tough. You've likely heard parents say to their sons, "stick up for your rights," "show you're not a sissy," or "don't let anyone push you around." At the same time, many parents express displeasure when their daughters fight, but show approval over their daughters' "cute" behavior, daintiness, and compliance. Not all parents are like this, of course, and some teach their daughters to fight back, even to be the aggressor.

The fairest conclusion seems to be that both environmental and biological influences are at work. A neuroscientist put it this way: There are slight differences between girl and boy babies' brains, but parents magnify them by reinforcing behaviors that match their gender stereotypes (Eliot 2010).

Cross-Cultural Studies   Cross-cultural research gets the sociological juices flowing, for we sociologists look for answers in social life, not in biology; and, to be frank, this research generally reinforces our mindset.

If we take a basic question like, "Are men more competitive by nature than women, and women more nurturing than men?," you will see what I mean. Seeing these two behaviors of competition and nurture attached to the sexes in similar ways over and over, it's easy to conclude that we are seeing nature in action. But here's a little cross-cultural experiment you might find interesting. For their research, a team of economists chose two contrasting societies, the Maasai in Tanzania and the Khasi in India (Gneezy et al. 2009). The Maasai are *patriarchal*. The men think of both their cattle and their wives as their property, and they care more for their cattle than they do for their wives. In contrast the Khasi are *matrilineal*. They trace their lineage through the women in the family. The women own the property and pass it on to their daughters. The Khasi women also earn more than their husbands do.

> To do their experiment, the researchers paid Maasai and Khasi men and women to throw a tennis ball into a bucket. Each had 10 tries. The men and women could choose to be paid a set amount for each successful throw. Or they could choose to be paid three times that amount for each successful throw, but only if they played against an opponent and beat that person. They could not see the opponent, who remained in another room.

> The results? The Maasai men chose to compete about twice as often as did the Maasai women. In contrast, the Khasi women were more likely than the Khasi men to choose the competitive form of payment.

Obviously, this one experiment with a few people from a few villages is not sufficient to draw firm conclusions, but it does suggest that competition is a learned form of gender behavior. In Maasai society, the men are in control. It is they who compete with one another. The Maasai men were twice as likely as the Maasai women to choose the competitive situation. But in Khasi society, the women are more competitive than the men, and the Khasi women were more likely than the Khasi men to choose the competitive situation. Again, this is only suggestive. We need a lot more research and creative experiments far beyond throwing a few tennis balls.

The Study of Vietnam Veterans   The third approach is also intriguing. The U.S. government collected data on testosterone levels among Vietnam veterans. To be certain the study was representative, the researchers chose a random sample of 4,462 men. Until this time, research on testosterone and human behavior was based on small samples. With this government study, sociologists gained access to a large random sample.

Researchers found that when the veterans with high levels of testosterone were younger, they were more likely to get in trouble with their parents, their teachers, and the law. As adults, they were more likely to use hard drugs, get into fights, end up in low-status jobs, and have more sexual partners. They were also less likely to marry. Those who did marry were more likely to have affairs, hit their wives, and, not surprising, to get divorced (Dabbs and Morris 1990; Mazur and Booth 2014).

Can we conclude that the more aggressive behavior of these men was based in biology? At first glance, it looks like this, but there is much more to it. Not all men who have high testosterone levels got into trouble with the law or mistreated their wives. The main difference—and sociologists are pleased with this—was *social class*: High-testosterone men from lower social classes are more likely to be involved in antisocial behaviors than are high-testosterone men from higher social classes (Dabbs and Morris 1990). This indicates that *social* factors (socialization, life situations, self-definitions) are a significant part of

The U.S. soldiers are carrying a wounded South Vietnamese soldier to a U.S. helicopter for evacuation to Saigon. At this time, in 1965, U.S. soldiers were still "advisers." The text describes a testosterone study of Vietnam veterans.

the explanation for these men's behavior. The task before us is to uncover the rest of the puzzle—how social factors work in combination with biological factors.

More Research on Humans Research on the effects of testosterone in humans continues. The results are intriguing. Not only do higher levels of testosterone lead to higher dominance, but the reverse is also true: Dominance behavior, such as winning a game, also produces higher levels of testosterone. This has made it difficult to determine which causes which. Controlled studies in which cause can be determined help. When researchers administer single doses of testosterone, dominance behavior increases. This is true of *both* males and females. They seek higher status and show less concern for the feelings of others (Eisenegger et al. 2011). Researchers are investigating how testosterone changes people's behaviors, which they think might be through a triggering of other hormones.

Reconciling the Findings From current evidence, we can conclude that *if* biology provides males and females different temperaments or any type of behavioral predisposition, culture can magnify or override those differences. Each culture lays out gender guidelines for its men and women, and boys and girls are socialized to do gender according to those particular guidelines. We usually are unaware of how the environment shapes children to become different types of men and women, often assuming that the differences we see are evidence of "natural" or "genetic" differences between the sexes. In the years to come, unraveling the influences of socialization and biology should prove to be an exciting—and controversial—area of sociological research.

Avoiding Ideology For science to succeed, data must be viewed with an open mind. We have difficulty opening our minds, though, as we cling to some ideas dearly. Evidence that contradicts these beliefs is threatening, as it can upset the way we see the world. To avoid this emotional challenge, we often interpret research findings through an ideological lens, accepting evidence that supports our views and rejecting that same evidence if it goes against ideas we firmly hold. Findings that support either biology or culture are like this.

Both social and biological factors underlie human behavior, with it often difficult to separate the two. Can you identify both in this photo?

This makes the question of nature or nurture both challenging and exciting. But we are far from having final answers. Some researchers are convinced that differences in aggression, nurturing, and so on are innate; others are equally convinced that they are learned. Data, not ideology, will one day answer this question once and for all. And it is likely that the answer will not be an either-or. In the meantime, almost all of us can agree on this principle: Whatever differences men and women might have in their behavior or orientations—no matter whether these differences are rooted in biology or culture or both—none provides a legitimate reason for discrimination.

Let's now turn to inequality between the sexes, with a focus on U.S. society.

Everyday Life

In everyday life, women find that many men have low regard for their interests, attitudes, and contributions. This negative, sometimes demeaning, attitude flows from a common view that masculinity represents strength, while femininity is perceived as weakness. With this orientation built into our culture, something we learn at an early age, most such perceptions are deeply rooted and lie below our awareness. Let's try to make them more visible.

We can gain clues to how femininity is devalued by looking at gender in the military. Let's go back to World War II, when a team of researchers headed by sociologist Samuel Stouffer studied combat soldiers. Out of this research came a sociological classic, *The American Soldier.* Stouffer and his colleagues (Stouffer et al. 1949:132) reported that officers motivated soldiers by using feminine terms to insult those who underperformed: "Whatsa matter, bud—got lace on your drawers?" (In the 1940s, underpants were called "drawers.") During the Vietnam War, drill sergeants mocked underperforming soldiers by saying, "Can't hack it, little girls?" (Eisenhart 1975). Today's drill sergeants do the same, shaming male recruits by comparing their performance to a woman's and calling them "girls" (Gilham 1989; Miller 2007).

You might have heard something like this in sports. If a boy misses a basket or his pass is intercepted, other boys sometimes say he is "playing like a girl." Such comments are common in football and other contact sports.

Most people dismiss such remarks as insignificant: "That's just boys talking." But this is more than "just talk." Listen more closely, and you will see that comments like these reveal a disparaging attitude toward women's abilities and accomplishments—an attitude many women face as part of their everyday lives.

Education

Let's begin by looking at how extensively deep sexism pervaded higher education in the past.

Setting the Context: Weak Women   About a century ago, leading educators claimed that women's wombs dominated their mental life. Here is a remarkable statement by Dr. Edward Clarke, a member of Harvard University's medical faculty, as he warned women that studying was dangerous for them:

> *A girl upon whom Nature, for a limited period and for a definite purpose, imposes so great a physiological task, will not have as much power left for the tasks of school, as the boy of whom Nature requires less at the corresponding epoch (quoted in Andersen 1988:35).*

To preserve their fragile health, Clarke added that young women should study only one-third as much as men. And during menstruation, they shouldn't study at all.

Views like Clarke's certainly put women at an educational disadvantage. Women who followed his warning and studied less than men would obviously do worse overall. This, in turn, would confirm the stereotype that women's brains weren't as capable as men's—and that their proper place was in the home.

As women accomplish more in areas traditionally dominated by men, it is likely that the definition of femininity will change and the devaluation of femininity decrease.

CTK/Alamy Stock Photo

Medical students at Women's Medical College in Philadelphia, Pennsylvania, about 1900. This was one of the first colleges to allow women to dissect bodies. Previously, with dissection thought inappropriate for women, they learned anatomy and physiology from skeletons.

Bettmann/Getty Images

Discrimination in Other Countries It has been a long time since American women faced overt discrimination in education, but in some countries it continues. Figure 9.2 is one of the many ways we can illustrate discrimination in education. From this figure of the five countries with the world's worst literacy rates, you can see that in all of them women are less literate than men. The limited schooling in these countries is a luxury many cannot afford, and the little that exists is parceled out first to the boys.

Figure 9.2 The Five Countries with the Least Literacy

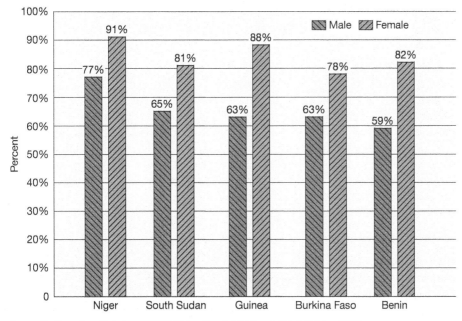

Source: By the author. Based on UNICEF. "Education: Adult Literacy Rate." October 2015.

Men Falling Behind What a vital contrast between the literacy rates shown in Figure 9.2 and the situation in the United States, where there are *3 million more women* than men in college. U.S. women even earn 57 percent of all bachelor's degrees and 60 percent of all master's degrees (*Statistical Abstract* 2018:Tables 292, 317). Could such totals indicate that we have tipped the scales the other way and even need affirmative action for men? Take a look at the following *Thinking Critically about Social Problems*.

Thinking Critically about Social Problems

Affirmative Action for Men?

Many laughed when psychologist Judith Kleinfeld (2002a) proposed that we might need affirmative action *for men.* After all, men still dominate societies around the world, as they have for millennia. To think that men would ever need affirmative action seemed humorous at best. Certainly nothing to be taken seriously.

Let's pause, step back, and try to see whether this astounding idea has any merit. Consider the statistics we just reviewed. Although our society has approximately as many men as women (women slightly outnumber men), there are 3 million more women in college. Not only do women earn most of the bachelor's and master's degrees, but they also earn more doctoral degrees than men (*Statistical Abstract* 2018:Table 317). Women have not only caught up with men in these areas, but they have also surpassed them—an accomplishment both impressive and laudable.

How does this gender gap in education apply to U.S. racial–ethnic groups? In *all* of them, more women than men are attending college and earning more bachelor's and master's degrees. This is not a temporary situation. The year-by-year national statistics show that women have been steadily increasing their college student enrollment and the degrees they earn.

Why have men fallen behind? College enrollment is open equally to both, so why don't enrollment and degrees match the relative proportions of women and men in the population (51 percent and 49 percent)? Although no one yet knows the answers—and there are a lot of suggestions being thrown about—some colleges have begun to take action. Clark University in Massachusetts was the first college to begin a support program to help men adjust to their new minority status (Gibbs 2008). Now many colleges are offering mentoring programs for men. Most

Do you think we need affirmative action for men in college?

seem geared toward African American men; however, from the data we just reviewed, men from all racial–ethnic groups could benefit from mentoring.

An Emerging Social Problem

Following the basic model of social problems I have stressed throughout this text, the changes in college enrollment and degrees reflect only objective conditions. To have a social problem, we must have widespread social concerns. If enough people become upset about the men's smaller enrollment and achievement in higher education, a new social problem will emerge. While extensive affirmative action, special scholarships, remedial help, and retention programs for men may seem unlikely, or even outrageous, this emerging social problem seems to be on its way. Similar concerns have also appeared in Great Britain (Hilman and Robinson 2016).

For Your Consideration

→ Why do you think men have fallen behind in education?

→ How can men lagging behind women in college enrollment and in earning degrees affect society? Or, is this nothing more than an interesting historical change?

→ Do you think we should start affirmative action and remedial and motivational courses for men? Why or why not?

→ To get closer to a male–female balance, some colleges have begun to reject more qualified women. What do you think about this?

Gender Tracking   There is more than meets the eye to this historical change in college attendance and degrees. Consider how some college degrees follow gender and how this *gender tracking* reinforces male–female distinctions. Here are two extremes: Men earn 94 percent of the associate degrees in the "masculine" field of construction trades, while women earn 95 percent of the associate degrees in the "feminine" field of "family and consumer sciences" (*Statistical Abstract* 2018:Table 320). Because gender socialization gives men and women different orientations to life, they enter college with gender-linked aspirations. Socialization—not some presumed innate characteristic—channels men and women into different educational paths.

A Man's World of Thought When students enter college, they study mostly male authors in their literature courses, discuss the thinking of men in their philosophy courses, and read almost exclusively about famous men in their history courses. Little is known about how this affects the orientations of female and male students, but it certainly has to be significant. Men who have taken courses in gender studies taught by women have told me how upsetting it is to be immersed in "women's world of thought." Women's immersion in what we can call the "men's world of thought" starts early and is taken for granted. Its impact, though less perceptible, is just as severe.

The Mass Media

From childhood through adulthood, the mass media help to shape our ideas about gender by portraying certain actions as "right" for boys and other actions as "right" for girls. These messages also influence our ideas about "proper" sexual relationships and body images. Let's see how some of this occurs.

Children's Books

When you were a child, picture books were probably part of your young life. Your parents might have read them to you, pausing to show you the pictures, with your little hands tracing elements of the illustrations. These books provide entertainment for children, but they do much more than this. The pictures and stories give children a view of the cultural world they are about to enter. From the characters in the stories—the illustrations and the "action"—children learn what behavior and attitudes are considered appropriate for the sexes.

So, what do children learn from their picture books? Keep in mind that imagery counts in producing attitudes and setting expectations. The top-selling children's books have more male characters than female characters, indicating that males and their activities are more important than females and their activities (Hamilton et al. 2006; McCabe et al. 2011). Males are also more often shown as providers and females as homemakers (DeWitt et al. 2013). Some parents try to counteract the stereotypes by changing "he" and "she" as they read to their children (Medley-Rath 2013).

Today's children's picture books also reflect ongoing change. One of the most significant is that they show more female characters than they used to. They also portray girls doing things that only the boys did in the older books, but boys, in contrast, are rarely portrayed in activities traditionally associated with females—caring for children, doing grocery shopping, or doing housework (Adams et al. 2011). An indication of fundamental change is that some children's books feature transgender children. Reading these books to kindergarten children has upset parents (Lambert 2017).

Video Games, Television, and, Movies

Twelve-year-old Maddie Messer loves playing video games, especially those where she has to overcome obstacles and free herself of enemies.

What Maddie doesn't like is that her character is almost always a boy.

Not only does she feel this is unfair, but also she began to wonder how common this is. This budding sociologist downloaded and analyzed the 50 most popular "Endless Running" video games for children. She found that 90 percent offered free boy characters, while only 15 percent offered free girl characters. Maddie published her research in the Washington Post (March 4, 2015).

The makers of Temple Run read Maddie's article. They said they felt embarrassed, and they added a free female character. Even Disney got in the act, dropping the $30 they had been charging for the female character in one of their games.

It is more of the same when it comes to video games, movies, and television. More main characters are male, and males have more speaking parts. Men are more likely to be

David Livingston/Getty Images Entertainment/Getty Images

Shown here is Jazz Jennings, who at the age of twelve wrote a book on her experiences as a transgender person. In her words, echoing those of so many others, she was "a girl trapped inside a boy's body." This photo was taken when Jazz was sixteen.

shown at work, and women more likely to appear as wife and mother. The most extreme imbalance is in video games, where only 8 percent of the main characters are female. The Academy Awards continue this pattern: In the films that win the Best Picture at the Oscars, men are about twice as likely as women to have speaking parts (Anderson and Daniels 2016; Lauzen 2017; Henry 2018).

But there has been fundamental change. In children's cartoons, females used to be portrayed as less intelligent, less brave, and more dependent and emotional. The female superheroes in children's cartoons today are now just as intelligent, brave, and powerful as the male superheroes. They are even portrayed as being as aggressive as the males. In HBO's *Game of Thrones*, women command fleets of ships, fight men, and even ride into battle and rescue men.

Music There are so many kinds (genres) of music that it is difficult to summarize sexism and sex roles in music, but here are a few observations. Many songs for teens and preteens have the message that boys should dominate girls. Lyrics also have lessons for girls—that they should be sexy, passive, and dependent and control boys by manipulating their sexual impulses. In music videos, sexism is especially blatant, with females often background ornaments for dominant male singers. Some rap groups glorify male sexual aggression and revel in humiliating women. Gender images, however, are far from rigid, as illustrated by Janelle Monáe. In country–western music, one theme is aggressive and dominant men and passive and dependent women. These dominant men do have a tender side, however. They cry into their beers after their cheating woman has left them. But, never mind, some honky-tonk woman is waiting to revel in her newly found, dominant man.

Advertising

You are aware that you see a lot of ads—on your phone and tablet, in magazines, on buses, on television every few minutes, and even on sports uniforms. But you might be surprised at the extent to which the media bombard you with pitches for their products. If you are average, you are exposed to several hundred thousand ads a year (Briggs 2018).

How women and men are portrayed in commercials also influences our perception of the sexes. A generation ago, commercials mainly showed women as "housekeepers, mothers, and menial workers." Men were clearly the providers. We would never describe today's situation like this, but despite many changes, women are still more likely to be shown in the kitchen and men are twice as likely to be shown with a job ("Consumers...2018).

Body Images in the Mass Media

As you know, advertisers sexualize the female body, using exposed breasts and close-ups of the female rear to sell products. To show their displeasure, some feminists spray-painted billboards, turning them into pro-woman messages (Rakow 1992). One of their more humorous examples was repainting a billboard that featured a scantily clad woman reclining on a car so it said, "When I'm not lying on cars, I'm a brain surgeon."

Body image is another key to how we do gender, and the media are effective in teaching us what we "should" look like. With most female characters below average in weight, we learn that thinness is desirable. But in addition, we are imprinted with a distorted image of women's bodies. Sociologist Lori Fowler (2008) reported that these images make such an impact on viewers that some mothers give breast implants to their daughters as high school graduation gifts—even when they are aware that the silicone can lead to health problems.

Feminists have protested exposing female bodies to sell products. It certainly is difficult to see any connection between this woman and electrolytes enhanced purified water. But sex sells, as the advertisers say. What is your position on this?

TMB/ZOJ/WENN/Newscom

With tens of thousands of commercials thrown at us, the portrayal of stereotypes powerfully influences how we see the world. Despite the attempts by feminists to reduce the exploitation of the female body in selling products, barely clothed female bodies are still used to sell new cars—whether the young, skinny women are lying on them, standing by them, or even driving them. Similar female forms are used to sell hamburgers and cruises. One major change has taken place, though—the male body is now exposed more. No longer do we see just rippling chests and biceps, but now there is also a focus on the male crotch. I suppose this is a growing equality of sorts.

Peer Groups

The mass media influence our views of the self and the world, and *our peer groups turn into their enforcing agent.* Our peers select aspects of the gender messages and ruthlessly enforce their ideas of how those images should be expressed. To read more on this topic, see the following *Spotlight on Social Research.*

Spotlight on Social Research

Sitting In on Adolescent Conversations

DONNA EDER, *professor of sociology at Indiana University, did research on gender dynamics and adolescent bullying and gossip in middle school. She explored ways that teasing, insulting, and gossiping reinforce gender roles and social status. Here she shares with you how insecure girls during middle school years try to build up their own self-esteem by making fun of social isolates.*

David Duffee

Early on in my research career, I became concerned while reading studies on adolescent girls. Many of these studies reported a drop in girls' self-esteem and self-image when they entered junior high school. I had not attended a junior high school. Instead, I went to a school for grades K-8. I was curious about what

(continued)

actually goes on in junior high or middle school, so I designed a three-year ethnographic study in a local middle school to find out. One college student later told me that middle school was such a painful time that she closed the door on that part of her life when she left and never wanted to enter another middle school again. That was when I realized that not everyone would want to undertake a study like this.

I hired both female and male assistants to observe lunchtime interaction along with me as I wanted to study both girls and boys from different social class backgrounds. We also attended after-school sports events and cheerleading practices. All of us took field notes after we left the setting and tape recorded lunchtime conversations.

Some of the things we observed were painful to watch. Through our recordings of gossip and ridicule, we learned a lot about what might make girls so insecure. For one thing, much of the gossip involved negative comments on other girls' appearance as well as their "stuck up" behavior. When we looked closely at the nature of the gossip, we found something interesting. The only time that anyone disagreed with someone's negative evaluation was if they did so early on, right after the remark was made. Once even one other person agreed with it, no one seemed willing to challenge the "group" view. So, in order to participate in the gossip, you pretty much needed to join in with the negative comments or else be sure to speak up quickly.

This is one way we saw how "meaning is constructed in the interaction"—an important concept of symbolic interactionism. When we studied teasing, we also saw the power of a response to shape the meaning of an exchange. One day during volleyball practice, a girl said that another girl was showing off her new bra through her white T-shirt. The girl responded by saying, "If I want to show off my bra I'll do it like this," lifting her shirt up. By responding playfully, she disarmed the insulter, and her teammates all joined in on the laughter.

In this large middle school, status hierarchies were based on appearance, social class, and intelligence. Since the girls had little control over most of these attributes, one way they tried to become more popular was by making friends with popular students. Of course, the popular girls (cheerleaders and those considered to be more attractive) could not befriend everyone who wanted to be their friend. This led to a cycle of popularity in which once well-liked girls became disliked and viewed as snobs for not returning others' offers of friendship.

Those at the bottom of the status rankings were isolates, eating lunch by themselves or with other low-status students. As isolates, they were frequent targets of ridicule from students trying to build themselves up by putting others down. Both boys and girls picked on the isolates, most of whom lacked the skills to turn the exchanges into playful ones.

After finishing this study, I wanted to do something constructive about the problems that we had witnessed at this middle school. I formed an after-school club which we brought to many elementary schools as part of an undergraduate service-learning experience. We called it KACTIS—Kids Against Cruel Treatment in Schools. Through KACTIS, we taught children the power of their response to ridicule, using role playing to show them how they could turn a potentially serious comment into a joking one. In one skit, the children decided that if a bully tried to keep them from using the water fountain, they would just collapse to the floor as if they were dying of thirst. When they acted this out, the bully got annoyed and walked away. After the skit, a second grader happily reported to me that they had learned how to trick the bully.

We also taught children to be more direct in their feedback to others rather than rely on gossip. In addition, we showed them how they could intervene on behalf of another child who was being bullied or ridiculed. I hope that some of these skills proved useful to these elementary students when they entered middle school. Meanwhile, my college students who provided the service-learning also learned a lot about conflict resolution, showing that we are never too old to learn new strategies to help us get through the problems we face in everyday life.

In Sum   The mass media—children's books, video games, television, movies, music, and advertising—influence our views of the self and the world. These images shape our expectations of the way we "ought" to be—how we should act and even feel. Although we aren't aware that it is occurring, we tend to view one another—even—ourselves—through the images that are presented to us as "normal" and "right." Our peer groups pressure us to conform to cultural images. Although the portrayal of boys and men as dominant continues, there has been significant change. Most remarkable is the new portrayal of girls not only as more active and dominant but also as aggressive, even fierce.

The images of the sexes that we learn as children channel our behavior along expected avenues. These images continue to influence us as we "do gender" as adults. Let's turn to how this works out in politics.

The World of Politics

Politics opens the curtain on yet another area of social life, exposing the relative positions of men and women.

The Current Situation   One of the best historical indicators is this: Since 1789, nearly 2,000 men have served in the U.S. Senate, but only 50 women have served. Similarly, only 37 women have held the office of governor, and none has ever held the office of president. Not until 1992 was the first African American woman (Carol Moseley-Braun, from Illinois) elected to the Senate. None has been elected since. As mentioned in Chapter 8, it took until 2012 for an Asian American woman (Mazie Hirono, from Hawaii) to be elected senator, and until 2016 for a Latina (Cortez Masto, from Nevada) to make it to the Senate.

U.S. politics is undergoing fundamental gender change. In 2007, Nancy Pelosi was elected speaker of the House of Representatives, the first woman to hold this position. Eighty-four of the 435 members of the House of Representatives are women, still a great underrepresentation, but the highest total ever. In the executive branch, three women have served as U.S. Secretary of State. Two women have run as vice-presidential nominees of major parties, Geraldine Ferraro as a Democrat and Sarah Palin as a Republican. In 2016, Hillary Clinton broke new ground when she became the first woman presidential nominee of the Democratic Party.

Despite these changes, men continue to dominate politics. From Figure 9.3, you can see how vastly underrepresented women are in political decision-making.

Figure 9.3 Who Controls U.S. Politics?

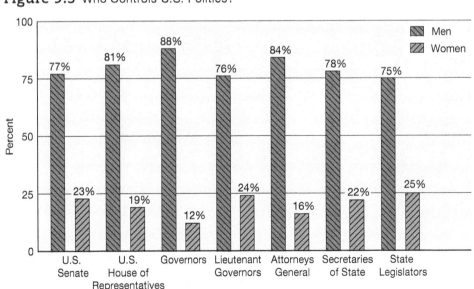

Source: By the author. Based on Center for American Women and Politics. "Women in Elective Office 2018." June 2018.

For a rough indicator of how political power is distributed between men and women on the state level, look at the Social Map. You can see that in no state legislature do women equal the number of men. You can also see the wide variation in the political power of women, from 11 percent of legislators in Wyoming to 40 percent in Arizona and Vermont.

Figure 9.4 What Percentage of Women Are in the State Legislatures?

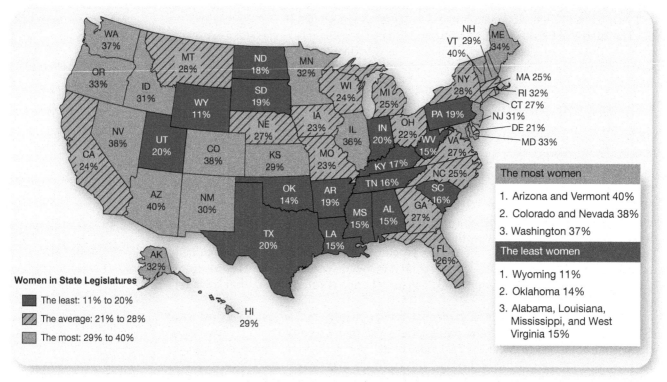

The most women

1. Arizona and Vermont 40%
2. Colorado and Nevada 38%
3. Washington 37%

The least women

1. Wyoming 11%
2. Oklahoma 14%
3. Alabama, Louisiana, Mississippi, and West Virginia 15%

Women in State Legislatures

■ The least: 11% to 20%
▨ The average: 21% to 28%
▨ The most: 29% to 40%

Source: By the author. Based on Center for American Women and Politics. "Women in Elective Office 2018." June 2018.

Why Don't Women Dominate Politics? Between *8 million and 9 million* more women than men are of voting age (*Statistical Abstract* 2018:Table 437). With their overwhelming numbers, women could take political control of the nation. Why don't they? The answer is rooted in socialization.

Women have become more prominent in politics, which has traditionally been a man's occupation/activity. Shown here is Alexandria Ocasio-Cortez, who defeated a man who had been in the House of Representatives for ten terms.

Scott Eisen/Stringer/Getty Images

The Syllogism of Masculinity   As we have seen, social institutions continue to socialize men into positions of authority and women into accepting this authority. This leads to the following reasoning:

> Dominance is masculine.
> *Politics is a form of dominance.*
> *Therefore, politics is masculine.*

The perception of politics as masculine puts severe restraints on women's recruitment, participation, and performance in politics.

The Power of Sex Roles   Other explanations for the continued dominance of politics by men center on the relative positions of men and women in other areas of society. First, women have been underrepresented in law and business, the careers from which most politicians come. Women are also less likely to have a supportive spouse who will play an unassuming background role while providing child care, encouragement, and voter appeal. Finally, until recently men have been reluctant to bring women into decision-making roles or to regard them as viable candidates.

Fundamental Changes   As you know, these restrictive patterns are loosening. As they do so, we can expect more women to seek and win political office. More women are also going into law and business, where they are doing more traveling and making statewide and national contacts. Although women still assume more responsibility for child care, these tasks are increasingly shared by both parents. And today a main focus of political parties as they select candidates is not their gender, but instead their chances of winning. This generation, then, is seeing a fundamental change in women's political participation.

The World of Work

Let's begin with a glimpse of the overall participation of women in the workforce.

The Historical Pattern   Table 9.1 traces the historical changes in women working outside the home. The first exception to the steady increase since 1890 occurred immediately

Table 9.1 Women in the Civilian Labor Force

Year	Number of Female Workers	As a Percentage of All Workers	As a Percentage of Working-Age Women
1890	4,000,000	17%	18%
1900	5,000,000	18%	20%
1920	8,000,000	20%	23%
1930	10,000,000	22%	24%
1940	14,000,000	25%	29%
1945	19,000,000	36%	38%
1950	18,000,000	30%	34%
1960	23,000,000	33%	36%
1970	32,000,000	37%	41%
1980	46,000,000	43%	52%
1990	57,000,000	45%	58%
2000	66,000,000	46%	60%
2010	72,000,000	47%	59%
2020[1]	77,000,000	47%	57%
2024[1]	77,000,000	47%	56%

[1]Estimate by the U.S. Dept. of Labor.

Note: Pre-1940 totals include women 14 and over; totals for 1940 and after are for women 16 and over.

Sources: By the author. Based on *Handbook on Women Workers 1969: Manpower Report to the President* 1971:203, 205; Mills and Palumbo 1980:6, 45; U.S. Bureau of the Census, various years; *Statistical Abstract of the United States* 2003:Table 588; 2013:Table 597; 2018:Table 610.

following World War II. By 1945, millions of men had left factory, farm, and office jobs to fight in World War II. When the men came home from the war, they reclaimed most of these jobs, and the percentage of women in the paid workforce dropped. It then started rising again, continuing for 60 years until it reached the second exception, our current era. (See the last column.) The reasons for this slight drop in the percentage of women in the paid labor force are not known (Black et al 2017).

The percentage of people ages 16 and older who are in the labor force at least part time is referred to as the **labor force participation rate**. Around 1980, for the first time in U.S. history, half of all American working-age women were employed outside the home at least part time. Today, nearly half of all U.S. workers are women. The Social Map shows how the percentage of women working for wages differs by state.

Figure 9.5 How Likely Are Women to Work for Wages?

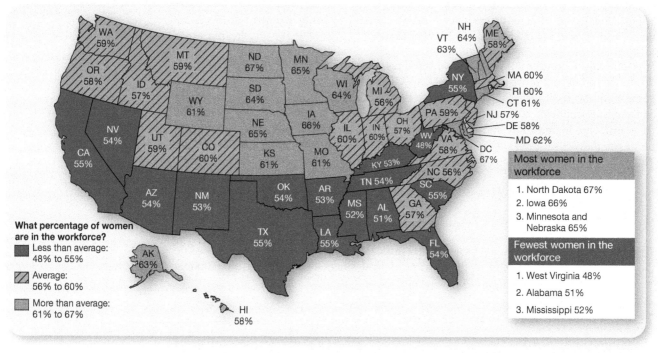

Source: By the author. Based on *Statistical Abstract of the United States* 2018:Table 617.

From these changes, you might think that work has become a level playing field for men and women. The world of work, though, is no exception to the general pattern of discrimination against women. Women come up against "old boys' networks"—social contacts that keep jobs, promotions, and opportunities circulating among men. To overcome this exclusion, some women professionals have developed "new girls' networks." They pass opportunities among one another, purposefully excluding men in order to help the careers of women.

The Gender Pay Gap

How much is that college diploma worth? It all depends on an irrelevancy: the sex equipment you were born with.

To pinpoint discrimination, we need more than anecdotes about some particular woman who is paid less than some man. We need hard numbers that apply across the nation. Figure 9.6 provides this. You can see that even though they have the same amount of education, the average man earns considerably more than the average woman. You can also see that this is true at all levels of education, whether the workers have completed only high school or are college graduates. *At all ages and at all levels of education, the average woman earns less than the average man.* This gender gap also shows up in all occupations. There isn't a single occupation in which the average woman earns more than the average man.

Figure 9.6 The Cash Penalty for Being Female (or the Cash Reward for Being Male)[1]

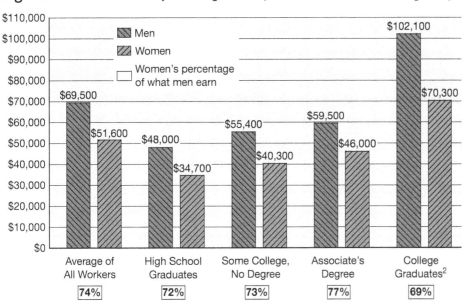

[1]These are the average (median) annual earnings of full-time workers. The percentage at the bottom of each bar indicates the women's average percentage of the men's income.

[2]Bachelor's and all higher degrees, including professional degrees.

Source: By the author. Based on *Statistical Abstract of the United States* 2018:Table 729.

This pay gap certainly will affect your future—to the advantage of the male readers of this text and to the disadvantage of the female readers. Keep in mind that Figure 9.6 does not illustrate some particular type of job. It shows the national results of *all* jobs in the United States—and only full-time, year-round workers. The women average only 74 percent of what the men make. Until 1980, women's earnings were just 60 percent of men's, which means that today's 74 percent is an improvement!

We are not talking about the difference between a hamburger and a steak. These differences translate into huge amounts of money. If you assume that a man and a woman work full-time from the age of 25 until retiring at age 65, you have 40 years of earnings. Multiply the average annual earnings shown in Figure 9.6 by 40, and you will see what an astounding total the gender gap produces in favor of men: Between the ages of 25 and 65, the average man who graduates from college will earn $716,000 more than the average woman who graduates from college.

Reasons for the Gender Pay Gap   Why do we have a pay gap between women and men? On the surface, the answer appears to be that employers simply pay women less. Probing beneath the surface, however, reveals a different answer. Using the most comprehensive data anyone has ever had access to—survey data from 8 million workers in 33 countries—researchers found three reasons for the global pay gap (Frost et al. 2016). First, women cluster in lower-paying jobs, while men cluster in higher-paying jobs. For example, 80 percent of the secretaries, nurses, and health aides in the United States are women, and globally, women make up 80 percent of the world's garment workers and 70 percent of hospitality workers. The main reason, though, is that women are overwhelmingly the ones who take care of the children. When women give birth, they—not their husbands or partners—cut back on hours at work. This slows their promotions to the higher-paid senior positions. Men don't have this slowdown, and they pass women.

As a demographic group, a global pay gap exists. Comparing the pay of women and men, women overall earn considerably less than men. The reasons for the gap, however, are a surprise. As the researchers drilled down in their data, the deeper they probed, the less pay gap they found. As they went from workers in general, then to workers within the same industry, and then to workers in the same company, the gap grew smaller and smaller. When the researchers reached workers within the same company who were at the same level of work, the gap almost disappeared, dropping to just 2 percent.

Since this research challenges the way we sociologists have viewed the pay gap, it is bound to provoke controversy. We know that basic gender discrimination is part of the world of work. Researchers who reviewed the salaries of 13,000 new MBAs found that employers offer women lower starting salaries than they offer men (Kitroeff and Rodkin 2015). The women in this research were offered an average starting salary of $98,000, while the men were offered an average of $105,000. This initial salary gap grew, and in 7 years the men were making $175,000 and the women $140,000. And here is where this research matches the global study. At this point, 7 years in, the women had had more career interruptions, primarily because of their children, and they were managing fewer people. The women also worked 24 percent fewer hours, again because of children (Kitroeff and Rodkin 2014). Underlying the gender pay gap, then, appears to be a combination of gender discrimination—though less than we had thought—and what sociologists call the *child penalty*—the missed opportunities because of giving birth and taking care of children.

In Sum   Only as we understand the reasons for a problem can we develop appropriate solutions. In this case, the reasons point directly to the need for structural changes in child care. There are two avenues to reach this solution. One is changes that would get fathers to take an equal share of child care. This would require changed cultural expectations of what fathering means. Such changes, flying in the face of history, are slow and not too encouraging. Likely to be more effective is the second avenue, structural change, such as paid parental leave from work that is equal for the father and the mother, and a system of quality child care. The emphases are on system—extensive, readily available—and quality, for without quality only desperate parents will use it.

Without a fundamental change in child care expectations and arrangements, the pay gap will not be solved.

Sexual Harassment

A severe form of discrimination is **sexual harassment**—unwanted sexual advances made by a person in power. These solicitations often are tied to promotions or demotions in the workplace. When a supervisor makes a sexual advance, the worker, who has less power, is at a considerable disadvantage in warding it off. The most vulnerable victims are those who lack job alternatives.

A Personal Problem: Just Individuals   The traditional view of sexual harassment makes it a *personal* problem, a matter of individual sexual attraction. A man gets interested in a woman and makes an advance; the woman accepts, rejects, or says "maybe." Perhaps her body language even "signals" that she *wants* to be approached sexually. There are always sexual attractions between men and women; some just happen to take place at work. From this traditional view, these are individual events and do not qualify as part of a *social* problem.

A Social Problem: Feminists and Relative Power   In 1979, Catharine MacKinnon, an attorney and professor, wrote a book on sexual harassment that changed our thinking. Rejecting the traditional view, MacKinnon argued that sexual harassment is a *structural* matter; that is, it is built into the work setting. She noted that two conditions of work encourage sexual harassment. The first is that most women occupy an inferior status in boss–worker relations. The second is an emphasis on women as sex objects. Women are sometimes hired because of their sexual attributes, a background condition that usually is hidden under the requirement that the newly hired be young, "attractive" women who will make a "good appearance" to the public. In short, sexual harassment sometimes begins with hiring procedures that judge women on their bodies, not their job qualifications.

Although MacKinnon's analysis is accepted widely now, it was controversial at the time. Until 1976, sexual harassment was literally unspeakable—because it had no name. The traditional view dominated, and women considered unwanted sexual advances as something that happened to them as individuals. They did not draw a connection between those advances and their lower position at work. As feminists raised awareness of the *group* nature of these objective conditions, women gradually concluded that the sexual advances by men in more powerful positions at work were part of a structural problem. As subjective concerns grew—more women coming to the same conclusion, being upset about it, and demanding that something be done—sexual harassment as a *social* problem was born.

The #MeToo Social Movement   When a worker is sexually harassed by a boss, she has limited options. She can object, ignore, complain, or submit, but each of these reactions carries its own risk. If she objects, she may be hounded until she quits or is fired. If she ignores it, she can get drawn into a cat-and-mouse game with few exits: If she files a complaint, she runs the risk of frustration, embarrassment, and retaliation at work. If she submits, the man may tire of her and turn to someone else, or he may fire her so he can hire a fresh victim.

With these risks, for the most part women have fended off unwanted sexual advances as best they could on an individual basis. Seldom have they rocked the boat. Then those abused learned to harness the power of the media. The case that broke the placid waters was the complaints against Harvey Weinstein, one of the most powerful men in the entertainment industry. A few, mostly anonymously, shared their stories with *New York Times* reporters. After that story broke, other women shared lurid details of Weinstein masturbating and raping. This got people's attention. Weinstein denied everything, but the shame and humiliation stuck, and he was rejected by the Hollywood community. He was forced to resign from his media empire and stripped of his membership in the Academy of Motion Picture Arts and Sciences. Criminal indictments followed. Grasping the power of public exposure in the media, women turned to the Internet. Using the hash tag, #MeToo, they began to complain publicly about bosses ogling them, pawing at them, raping them. They named and shamed.

The torrent of accusations, the "It happened-to-me-too" response by women around the country, came in a thunderous roar that awakened the public to a systemic problem. Confronted by public shaming, man after man, in industry after industry, resigned from their positions or were fired, their names scrubbed clean from boardroom lists and movie credits. The #MeToo movement revealed how far reaching sexual harassment is and how carefully it had been buried under the surface.

Not Just a Woman's Problem   I have just used "he" for the predator and "she" for the victim, but sexual harassment is not exclusively a woman's problem. As more women have moved into management, men have also found themselves victims. Men now file one of every six legal claims ("Charges Alleging..." 2016). One man claimed that his chief financial officer—a woman—made sexual advances "almost daily." Another objected that his supervisor told him she had dreamed about him naked. Men who make claims of sexual harassment often receive little sympathy. Some men don't understand why a man would take offense at sexual advances from a woman, even if she is his boss (Carton 1994; Mattioli 2010). Their response is that they would be happy for a woman, boss or not, to "hit" on them.

I anticipate that norms will change and eventually catch up with women's growing power in the workplace. At some point, perhaps soon, we will have a #MeToo movement written by men accusing women bosses. Or maybe not.

As discussed in the following *Spotlight on Social Research*, what passes for acceptable behavior in one work setting can be taken as sexual harassment in another.

Sexual Harassment at Two Magazines

KIRSTEN DELLINGER, *professor of sociology at the University of Mississippi, says her interest in gender and sexuality in organizations emerged from her own early work experiences. As she worked with autistic adults in one setting and children in another, she wondered why most workers were women and why they earned little and received little respect. From these initial observations, she turned her attention to how work is organized and the role of gender and sexuality in the work setting. Here is what she wrote for you.*

Courtesy of Kirsten Dellinger

I have been intrigued by the research that explores how organizations are "gendered" and "sexualized." One of the themes in this literature is how workplace policies create and maintain ideologies about masculinity and femininity. Another is how workers construct their gender identities through their everyday interactions. What is acceptable or not differs from one work setting to another. Take the example of sexual harassment.

Have you ever heard people say that sexual harassment is impossible to solve in the workplace because "it all depends on what an individual finds offensive"? Sally finds the joke about women's bodies funny, but Julie doesn't. Harry likes to tell stories about homosexuals, but Frank cringes when he hears them. Julie and Frank keep their mouths shut because they hold lower positions at work. Much survey research on sexual harassment emphasizes this individualistic level. Researchers ask people if, in their opinion, certain behaviors (such as patting someone's butt) are sexual harassment or not.

Instead of taking this individualistic perspective, in my research I examine how the *social context* influences how people define sexual harassment. The research I did with Christine Williams underlines the symbolic interactionist perspective that whether a behavior is sexual harassment or not depends on the definitions people apply to it. And those definitions, as we found out, depend more on the social context than on individualistic perspectives.

We studied workers at two magazines who were doing the same jobs: editors, accountants, and administrative assistants. The magazines were quite different: a heterosexual men's pornographic magazine and a feminist magazine. Workers at the men's magazine, *Gentleman's Sophisticate,* worked in a "locker room" culture. Sexual joking was common, even about the magazine itself. At the same time, these workers had strict norms against discussing highly personal aspects of their own lives. Sexual harassment was defined as a violation of personal boundaries, not by how sexual a conversation was. In contrast, workers at the feminist magazine, *Womyn,* worked in something that was closer to what you find in an all-women's dorm: They expected one another to share personal aspects about their sexual lives. They wanted to analyze them through a feminist framework. These women defined sexual harassment as an abuse of power. Editors talked about being careful with the power they had over interns, most of whom were college students. Workers at *Gentleman's Sophisticate* and at *Womyn* were using different workplace norms to define and deal with sexual harassment.

For Your Consideration

→ How would you define sexual harassment?

→ How do you think working for a year at each of these magazines might change your definition of sexual harassment?

LGBT

9.7 **Discuss changing attitudes toward sexual minorities, apply the conflict view to homosexuality, and discuss research on homosexuality.**

LGBT stands for Lesbian, Gay, Bisexual, and Transgender. That this term has moved into the mainstream media and public discourse is a sign of major social change. Let's look at this change.

Sexual Orientation as a Social Problem

As I have stressed throughout this text, for a social problem to exist, we need both objective conditions and subjective concerns. There must be a large number of people who are upset by some objective conditions. Following this definition, when people whose sexual orientation differs from most others quietly accept the objective conditions that make them second-class citizens, we have personal problems. There is no social problem even though there are many objective conditions—the vast discrimination—from being rejected for home ownership to being dishonorably discharged from the military, from being fired at work to being bullied at school. When large numbers of people are upset by these objective conditions, however—and they may even protest them—we have the subjective concerns necessary for a social problem.

This basic analysis that runs through this text applies to people whose sexual orientation differs from the majority. It is not just lesbians and gays who now openly object to their status in society, who no longer hide in the closet, quietly accepting their discrimination. Among others who are protesting and demanding change are transgender persons and **bisexuals** (those who are sexually attracted to both men and women). The concepts of objective conditions and social concerns, then, can be valuable tools for understanding the changes occurring in society.

Setting the Context: Laws and Attitudes The social institutions of U.S. society presume the norm of **heterosexuality**, a sexual orientation involving an attraction to or a preference for people of the opposite sex. Until 1960, *all states* had laws that made even private, consensual sexual acts between adults of the same sex illegal. In 2003, 12 states still had these laws on their books, but in that year the U.S. Supreme Court, in *Lawrence et al. v. Texas,* struck these laws down (Papandrea 2018).

Since 1977, the Gallup polling organization has asked Americans about their attitudes toward lesbians and gays. From Figure 9.7, you can see how extensively these attitudes have changed.

Figure 9.7 Changing Attitudes toward Lesbians and Gays

National samples of Americans were asked:

Do you think gay or lesbian relations between consenting adults should or should not be legal?

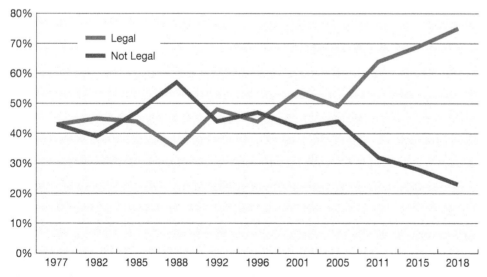

Note: The totals do not equal 100% because of those who say they don't know or refuse to answer.

Source: By the author. Based on Gallup Poll. "In Depth Topics A to Z: Gay and Lesbian Rights." 2016, Gallup Management consultant company.

Karin Hildebrand Lau/Shutterstock

Activism by LGBT people and supporters has had astounding results both legally and in social change. In what has become a global social movement, the activism continues.

Most Americans (75 percent) now think homosexual relations between consenting adults should be legal. But note that a sizable number of Americans, almost one in four, think homosexual relations—even between consenting adults—should be illegal. Because this research is from well-chosen national samples, it allows us to generalize to the U.S. population. From other surveys, we know that attitudes toward lesbians and gays follow social paths—the same that we've seen before: age, income, and education. Those most likely to give a "Yes, legal" reply to the question asked in Figure 9.7 are younger people and those who have higher incomes and higher education.

Hate Crimes The term **homophobia** was first used in an academic publication by psychologist Kenneth Smith (1971) and popularized by psychologist George Weinberg (1972). The meaning of the term has changed since then. It originally referred to fear of homosexuals, but its general meaning today is dislike or intolerance of homosexuals. The term **homophobe** is used to refer to a person who has such attitudes.

Over the years, lesbians and gays have been the victims of violence because of their sexual orientation, but until 1990 there was no way of tracking their victimization. In that year, Congress passed the Hate Crime Statistics Act, and the FBI began to collect data on **hate crimes**. These are crimes such as assault or vandalism that are motivated by dislike or hatred of the victim's race, religion, ethnicity, sexual orientation, disability, or national origin. Each year, more than 1,000 crimes are committed against people because of their sexual orientation. As you can see from Table 9.2, the vast majority of victims are gays and lesbians. You can compare these larger numbers to the 13 heterosexuals who are victimized by homosexuals. Since not all victims file reports, and not all police agencies report these data to the FBI, the actual numbers are higher.

Table 9.2 Hate Crimes Based on Sexual Orientation

Crime Against Whom	Number of Victims	Number of Offenders
Gays	787	806
Lesbians	147	127
Lesbians, Gays, Bisexuals, Transgendered Persons[1]	271	254
Bisexuals	27	25
Heterosexuals	23	13
Totals	1,255	1,225

[1]A mixed group in the statistics, apparently used when the authorities cannot determine a more specific target.
Source: By the author. Based on *FBI* 2018:Hate Crime Statistics Table 1.

The 2016 terrorist attack at Pulse, a gay nightclub in Orlando, Florida, a shooting that left 49 dead and 43 wounded, is the single largest hate crime directed at homosexuals in the United States.

Lesbians and gays face considerably less discrimination today than they did a decade or two ago. Supported by the American Civil Liberties Union, gay liberation groups campaigned to repeal oppressive laws. The Civil Service Commission used to deny federal employment to homosexuals, but no longer. Similarly, corporations such as AT&T, Ford, GM, and IBM used to discriminate against homosexuals in hiring and promotions, but because of a change in federal law (the 2003 Employment Equality Regulations), they no longer do so.

The U.S. Department of Defense is an outstanding example of the change. The military used to discharge any soldier who was discovered to be homosexual. Then it eased up, with a policy called "Don't Ask, Don't Tell," which lasted from 1993 to 2011. Lesbians and gays could serve in the military as long as they kept their sexual orientation a secret. Today, they can openly identify themselves as homosexual and continue to serve in the military.

The military ban of transgender people continued until 2016. In that year, after much pressure, the U.S. Secretary of Defense, lifted the pentagon's ban on transgender people.

No longer could they be discharged from the military for being transgender. The ban again went into effect in 2018 (Gore 2018).

In order to better understand homosexual–heterosexual relations, let's use the lens of conflict theory.

Homosexuality Viewed Theoretically: Applying Conflict Theory

Lesbians and gays have found politics a useful tool to bring about the social change we have been discussing. *Coming out of the closet*—publicly asserting a gay identity—they marched in protest and affirmation of identity and campaigned for legal reform. Beginning with local campaigns in San Francisco and New York to demand equality and basic human rights, homosexuals expanded their campaigns and made an impact on national politics. As a result, politicians now study homosexual voting patterns so they can target the "gay vote."

After struggling for decades, lesbians, gays, and transgender people made their civil rights a prominent social issue. Despite the major gains I have mentioned, their struggle is far from over. Many people, especially because of firmly held religious beliefs, continue to view **homosexuality** as immoral. It is important to note that people who view same-sex sexual relations as part of an immoral lifestyle differ considerably from individuals who dislike and even hate homosexuals. This distinction, however, is lost on many.

A major issue has been marriage. Lesbians and gays fought fierce opposition for the right to marry legally. Statewide campaigns led to divergent decisions, with some states granting same-sex couples the right to marry, and others denying them marriage. This led to the ludicrous situation of a couple being lawfully married in one state, but not so if they moved to another state, the situation once faced by African Americans and whites who married. The Supreme Court resolved such inconsistencies in its 2015 *Obergefell v. Hodges* ruling, which allows same-sex couples to wed in all 50 states.

Having tasted this victory, lesbians and gays are not about to stop their struggle until they attain not just the right to marry but equal rights in housing and employment, including the right to work in all occupations with open homosexual identities. As you can see, with opposing sides holding down firm lines, especially over such matters as openly identified lesbians and gays teaching grade school, the controversy will not end soon.

Research on Homosexuality

Let's review three major studies on homosexuality.

The Kinsey Research Alfred Kinsey and his associates shocked Americans with their pathbreaking 1948 study, *Sexual Behavior in the Human Male*. Based on case histories of about 5,300 males, Kinsey found that 37 percent of men in the United States had at least one sexual experience with a same-sex partner that resulted in orgasm. Such experiences, however, did not translate into homosexuality. As Kinsey pointed out, most of these homosexual behaviors were a form of experimentation, and almost all of these males went on to live heterosexual lives. Kinsey concluded that about 4 percent of American males are exclusively homosexual.

We can dismiss Kinsey's findings as unscientific. Kinsey used a biased sample, and we cannot generalize from his findings. Kinsey recruited men who had been in prison and reform schools. He also interviewed only lower-class white males. Obviously, these men do not represent the general population (Himmelhoch and Fava 1955). An occasional uninformed writer will still quote Kinsey, however, as though what Kinsey reported had something to do with people other than those in his sample.

The battered wall by which the Orlando, Florida, police entered Pulse nightclub to try to stop the slaughter.

For all the turmoil the issue of same-sex marriage created in society, since the Supreme Court made its landmark decision, the result has mostly been quiet acceptance.

The Laumann Research A beautifully contrastive study was carried out by a team of researchers headed by sociologist Edward Laumann (1994). This research was not without opposition, as Laumann explains in his *Spotlight on Social Research* in Chapter 3. Because Laumann interviewed a representative sample of the U.S. population, we can generalize his findings to the entire U.S. population. As you can see from Figure 9.8, during the preceding five years, 2.2 percent of women and 4.1 percent of men in the United States had sex with a same-sex partner. When the time period is extended to include all the years of their lives, these totals increase to 3.8 percent for women and 7.1 percent for men. You can see what a far cry this is from Kinsey's 37 percent for men.

As Figure 9.8 also shows, 1.4 percent of U.S. women and 2.8 percent of U.S. men identify themselves as homosexuals. These percentages are almost identical to those who reported that they had sex with a same-sex partner during the preceding year (1.3 percent of women and 2.7 percent of men). These figures may be slightly high, as the Laumann researchers included bisexuals in the homosexual data.

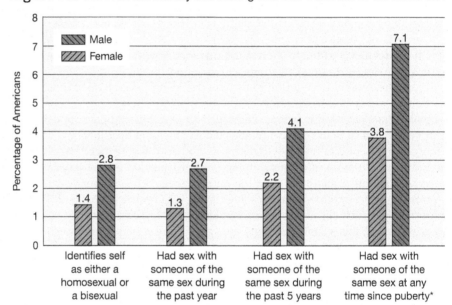

Figure 9.8 Homosexual Identity and Having Sex with Someone of the Same Sex

Note: Another form of this question yielded 4.3 percent for women and 9.1 percent for men.

Source: Based on Laumann, Edward O., John H. Gagnon, Robert T. Michael, and Stuart Michaels. *The Social Organization of Sexuality: Sexual Practices in the United States.* Chicago: University of Chicago Press, 1994.

As you might recall from Chapter 2, sociologists do quantitative and qualitative research. Laumann did quantitative research, using a sampling technique that allows us to generalize his findings to the U.S. population. Sociologists who do qualitative research, in contrast, focus on the smaller picture, helping us understand people's interactions, perspectives, and motivations. As we learn how people construct their worlds, we have a better understanding of how and why they make their decisions. Let's turn to qualitative research.

The Humphreys Research Sociologist Laud Humphreys, then a graduate student in sociology, did creative but widely criticized research. Humphreys knew that some men have impersonal sex in public restrooms, meeting places they call "tearooms." He began hanging around these restrooms in St. Louis' Forest Park. He would take the role of "watch queen," the individual who warns participants when strangers approach the restroom. Humphreys (1970/1975) recorded how the men use a system of gestures to initiate sex at the urinal and then move to a toilet stall for fellatio (oral sex). The sex was quick and anonymous, usually occurring without the exchange of a single word.

Humphreys noticed that many of the men having tearoom sex wore wedding rings, and he wanted to know why these married men engaged in homosexual acts. He decided to interview them, but he knew they would run from a researcher. The men parked nearby, and

Humphreys wrote down their license plate numbers. Using a contact in the police department, he traced their home addresses. With the cooperation of his professors, who were conducting a health survey, he had these men added to their sample. Humphreys then interviewed the men in their homes, supposedly for the purpose of the medical research but really to get background information on the tearoom participants. For this deception, Humphreys was criticized severely, and he came close to having his Ph.D. revoked.

Thirty-eight percent of the tearoom participants that Humphreys observed were married men who identified themselves as heterosexuals. In the interviews, the married men reported that their wives often refused to have sex. Humphreys concluded that tearoom sex was like stopping at a convenience store on the way home from work, except that this stop offered free oral sex. Unlike an affair with a woman, the quick, anonymous sex in a tearoom did not threaten the men's emotional attachment to their wives. In essence, the tearoom functioned as a free house of prostitution, a place where the men could obtain quick oral sex with no emotional entanglements. Similar behavior occurs elsewhere, including at truck stops, where heterosexual truckers have sex with homosexuals who search out partners (Corzine and Kirby 1977; Habib 2012; Brewer 2018).

This research underscores the distinction that sociologists make between *homosexual behavior* and *homosexuality*. Homosexual behavior characterized the married men who visited the tearooms for quick sex, while homosexuality was the orientation of the men in the tearooms who gave the oral sex.

Prison rape is vastly under reported. If you were a man in prison and some of these men raped you, and you were still living among them, what are the chances that you would report their crime against you? This photo was taken at a jail in Santa Ana, California.

Bisexuala Bisexuals are people who are sexually attracted to both men and women. This does not imply that they are attracted equally to men and women. Some are. For them, it makes no difference if a sexual partner is a male or a female. In contrast, many bisexuals have sexual and romantic relationships with both males and females, but they prefer one or the other.

Our fundamental social change in sexual mores allows bisexuals to openly discuss their preferences and experiences, as they now do on TV talk shows. This does not mean wholesale approval of bisexuality, for there is a strong moral component in many people's negative reactions. Consequently, some bisexuals band together in what is called a bi-community, where they support to one another. If U.S. society continues on its current path of liberalizing sexual behavior and attitudes, it is likely that bisexuality will become a more common life choice.

Violence against Women

9.8 **Apply the feminist/conflict and symbolic interactionist perspectives to gendered violence.**

As our final topic, let's look at gendered violence.

Gendered Violence: Rape, Murder, and Abuse in the Family

Fears of rape and murder surround girls and women in this society. They are aware that they can be attacked while on a routine errand or on the way to school. We have already discussed rape and murder in Chapter 5, and there is no need to go beyond what we reviewed in that chapter. We need to stress one of the main points of that chapter, though: Women tend to be the victims, men the rapists and killers.

In the family, too, females are also disproportionately the victims of abuse, whether incest or battering by a spouse. These are topics we will review in Chapter 11, so it is sufficient to just mention them now. Earlier in this chapter, we discussed female circumcision as a form of violence against women.

Another form of violence, one alien to Western culture, is "honor killing." In some societies, such as Pakistan, Jordan, and Kurdistan, a woman who is thought to have brought disgrace to her family is killed by a male relative—usually her brother or her husband, but sometimes her father or uncle. What threat to the family's honor can be so severe that the men kill a daughter, wife, or sister? The usual reason is sex outside of marriage. Even a woman who has been raped is in danger of becoming the victim of an honor killing (Falkenberg 2008; Yardley 2010). Killing the girl or woman removes the "stain" she has brought to the family and restores its honor in the community. Amid global protest, Pakistan has passed a law against honor killings, but the police generally ignore it, viewing honor killings as private family matters (Boone 2016).

Applying the Feminist/Conflict Perspective   To explain why girls and women are so often the victims of violence at the hands of men, some sociologists use conflict or feminist theory. They stress that violence against women is a form of power and control. Some men use violence to maintain their dominance, control, or authority over their wives and children. Violence is a way of keeping these less powerful family members "in line."

Applying Symbolic Interactionism   Sociologists also use symbolic interactionism to understand gendered violence. Strength and virility are held out as goals for boys to achieve. Both boys and girls are surrounded by men in positions of power. As they see men dominate society, they learn to associate power, dominance, strength, virility, and superiority with masculinity. Weakness then becomes equated with femininity. As boys and men come to judge themselves in these terms, violence becomes one way to assert dominance and power.

The models of violence that surround boys also encourage some to be violent. Of the many examples that we could select, let's highlight video games, whose themes are often sexist, violent, and sexually explicit. In many of these games, the goal is to hunt down and kill enemies. In some games, those to be hunted down and killed are robots and monsters, in others men, and in still others barely clad young women. Although the form may change over time, symbols of violence continue to be a constant feature of the male world.

Social Policy

9.9   Compare middle-of-the-road social policies with those appropriate to the radical and conservative extremists.

As we have seen with other social problems, social policy can be effective in reducing inequality. Let's turn to an overview of social policy as it applies to inequalities of gender and sexual orientation.

As you know, people want social policies that match their views of what is right, or of how they think things in life should be. But in our large, diverse society, people come from many backgrounds. With these vastly contrasting views, there is little agreement on social policies. Any proposal for social policy that I make, then, will land in the midst of controversy, as no matter what the proposal is, it will violate someone's ideas of what is right or wrong, desirable or undesirable. As we consider social policy for reducing sex discrimination, we will examine a wide spectrum of views. You will see what I mean as we compare social policies of the *radical extremists* and *conservative extremists*, terms I have developed to represent the views of individuals, groups, and organizations that stand on opposing sides of issues that center on gender and sexual orientation.

The Radical Extremists

Discrimination is so rooted in society, say the *radical extremists*, that the only way to get rid of it is to restructure society. As sociologists have stressed for decades, equal pay, the glass ceiling, and gender hostilities are only surface manifestations of sexism. To eradicate sexism, we need go beyond the surface and develop social policies that cut sexism's social roots.

Because the roots of sexism reach back into childhood socialization, to succeed we would need to remove distinctions between boys and girls. Girls and boys would have to be socialized in the same way. They would have to be treated equally in the family and throughout their education, from preschool to graduate school. This would include gym, sports, and sexual orientation. Husbands and wives would have to share housework equally, and both parents would have to compete equally in the world of work. Ultimately, men and women would hold all positions in our social institutions equally.

Such extreme social policies are not plausible in our society—unless we have a dictator to enforce them. These means to eliminate sexism are not likely to ever be achieved.

The Conservative Extremists

The social policies preferred by the *conservative extremists* are remarkably different. They believe gender distinctions of boys and girls and men and women are not only natural, but they also ought to be encouraged. They argue that a woman's natural and proper role is that of a homemaking wife and mother. A man's natural and proper role is that of a breadwinning husband and father. Social policy should support these basic gender distinctions. They should encourage girls to become full-time wives and mothers and boys to be the protectors and primary source of financial support of their wives and children. On a practical level, children's picture books and school texts should present women and men in these traditional roles, tax breaks should go to full-time homemakers, and job preference and higher pay should be given to men who are supporting dependents.

Again, absent a dictator, these social policies are not plausible in our diverse society. These goals, too, are not likely to ever be achieved.

Middle-of-the-Road Policies

Innumerable positions fall between these two extremes. It is likely that some of the more middle-of-the-road policies reflect your views and the causes you support: policies that would reduce or end the gender pay gap, the right for both mother and father to take extended leaves from work when a child is born or sick, protection of sexual minorities from discrimination, tough enforcement of court-ordered child support, and, at home, more child care by fathers and more equitable distribution of housework.

The Future of the Problem

9.10   Discuss the likely future of gender discrimination.

Although gender discrimination is likely to remain a fact of life, historical trends point toward growing equality between women and men of all sexual orientations. The future will bring more attempts to break stereotypes, to eliminate the gender gap in pay, and for people of any sexual or gender orientation to gain greater access to leadership and authority, whether in business and politics or any other area of social life. The change is likely to be gradual, but as time passes, it is also likely to be significant.

Sexual Minorities and the Future

At the center of controversy over social policy about sexual orientation lies a primary issue, that of sexual minorities serving as role models. Especially controversial is sexual minorities occupying positions that mold the orientations of youth, such as public school teachers and scout leaders. This issue provokes intense disagreement between those who favor the full civil rights of sexual minorities and those who have moral objections to their activities. Although tensions run high, granted current trends, it is likely that this issue will be decided in favor of greater freedom of social participation by sexual minorities.

The World of Work: "At Work" and at Home

As women continue to join the paid workforce, power relationships between women and men at work will continue to shift toward greater equality. We will see remarkable changes in this area. This includes the world of politics—and at some point a female president.

Equal pay will remain an issue. Reaching this goal certainly will not happen overnight, but it is likely that we will gradually inch toward it. We can expect women to make greater use of the Equal Pay Act of 1963 (forbidding discrimination in salaries), Title VII of the Civil Rights Act of 1964 (forbidding discrimination on the basis of sex), and the Fourteenth Amendment (forbidding a state to "deny any person within its jurisdiction the equal protection of the laws"). Such legal pressures will not eliminate the problem, but they will continue to undermine the remaining sexist structure of work.

As more women earn paychecks and as the size of those paychecks increases, relations between husbands and wives will continue to shift. Wives who work outside the home make more family decisions than wives who work only at home, and the future will bring more family power to women. The trend is toward greater participation by wives and husbands in areas that have traditionally been seen as the proper area of one sex or another. We will also see husbands take on greater responsibilities for housework and children.

This takes us to a thorny question: What is equality of housework and child care? We will never have equality in the sense of husbands and wives working an equal number of hours per week at each task. Such a rigid view of equality does not match the way people live their lives. All tasks involve personal preferences and practical matters, which individual wives and husbands will decide for themselves. Ultimately, what one couple determines to be equality, another couple may see as inequality. This issue will always remain.

Changing Gender Stereotypes and Orientations

The increasing numbers of women in the workforce are already changing gender stereotypes, a change that will continue. Children who see both mother and father bringing home paychecks take it for granted that a man is not the exclusive breadwinner and that a woman is more than a housewife or homemaker. They grow up with a mother who more fully participates in family decisions, often is the primary decision-maker, and may outearn her husband. As gendered roles that push us into activities dictated by our culture bend, stereotypes will break, and we will see fundamental change in both self-perception and in gender relationships.

More equal gender roles will free both men and women to do activities that are compatible with their personal preferences—not because an activity matches a cultural stereotype that they must live up to. As activities become more gender-neutral, men and women will develop a new consciousness of who they are and of their potential in life. This will free men to play more supportive roles and to "get more in touch with their feelings," while it will free women to take more leadership roles and to become more assertive. For the past hundred years, sociologists have stressed that gender divisions harm both men and women, that greater gender equality will bring "greater wholeness" to men and women. We might not know the shape of such equality or what the wholeness will look like, but our major trends indicate they are on the way.

Summary and Review

1. Although there are more females than males in the world, around the globe, men discriminate against women. Consequently, sociologists refer to men as a dominant group and women as a minority group.

2. Every society *sex-types* work; that is, in each society some work is considered suitable for men and other work appropriate for women. There is no inherent biological connection between work and its assignment to women or men, for "women's work" of one society may be "men's work" in another. In all societies, "men's work" is given greater prestige than "women's work."

3. Symbolic interactionists examine *gender* (masculinity and femininity), looking at how each society socializes the sexes into its ideas of what men and women ought to be like. Socialization includes learning *sexism,* the belief that one *sex* is innately superior to the other and the discriminatory practices that result from this belief.

4. Functionalists theorize that sexual discrimination is based on the need of early human groups to engage in hand-to-hand combat. Men had the greater physical strength but needed to be motivated to become warriors. Women, offered as inducements for men to fight, were assigned the drudge work of society. A second functionalist explanation is that because women were encumbered physically through childbearing and nursing, men became dominant as they took control of warfare and trade.

5. Conflict theorists emphasize that the rights U.S. women enjoy came out of a power struggle with men. The confrontations between the sexes in the late 1800s and early 1900s have been replaced by legal pressure and economic and educational competition.

6. With the difficulty of separating nature and nurture, we do not know the extent of natural differences between the sexes. Both genetics and socialization can explain females' earlier proficiency in verbal skills and males' greater aggressiveness and abilities at mathematics.

7. Women confront discrimination in most areas of life, including a belittling attitude from men. Although women outnumber men as voters, men dominate politics. Women are challenging this dominance.

8. A gender gap in pay exists at all educational levels. Over a lifetime, the cost to the average woman who graduates from college is more than $700,000. The #MeToo social movement indicates how deeply *sexual harassment* affects women, but both heterosexual and homosexual men are also victims.

9. Applying conflict theory to *sexual minorities* uncovers fundamental tensions between them and heterosexuals, indicating an uneasy adjustment to one another.

10. Social policies to deal with inequalities of gender and sexual orientation are controversial because they represent contrasting and incompatible ideas of what is right.

11. In the future, even larger numbers of more highly educated, motivated women will be employed outside the home. This will continue to change power relationships at home and at work and further break down traditional stereotypes. The direction of the future is toward greater equality between the sexes, with emergent outcomes of changed personalities and preferences, the shape of which remains to be seen.

Thinking Critically about Chapter 9

1. List three examples of sexism in the United States. In what ways do you think your list would be different if you had written it 10 years ago? In what ways do you think it would be different if you were to write it 10 years from now?

2. Which of the three theoretical perspectives (symbolic interactionism, functionalism, or conflict theory) do you think best explains gender discrimination in the United States? Why?

3. What are the main changes you see occurring in gender roles? Why do you think we are experiencing these changes?

Key Terms

bisexuals, 279
gender, 254
gender roles, 255
glass ceiling, 260
hate crimes, 280
heterosexuality, 279
homophobe, 280
homophobia, 280
homosexuality, 281
labor force participation rate, 274

LGBT, 279
master trait, 255
patriarchal society, 257
sex, 254
sex-typed, 253
sexism, 253
sexual harassment, 276
suffragists, 260
transgender persons, 255

Chapter 10
Medical Care: Physical and Mental Illness

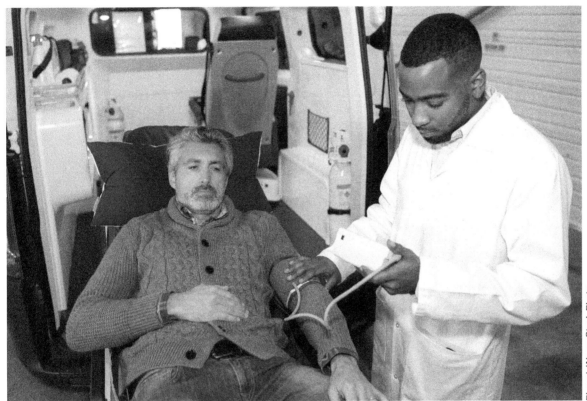

Phovoir/Alamy Stock Photo

 ## Learning Objectives

After reading this chapter, you should be able to:

10.1 Explain what is *social* about illness. Include lifestyle, iatrogenesis, changing ideas, and the environment.

10.2 Explain why the social organization of medicine is part of a social problem.

10.3 Summarize some of the aspects of physical illness that make it a social problem.

10.4 Summarize some of the aspects of mental illness that make it a social problem.

10.5 Discuss the perspectives that emerge when you apply symbolic interactionism, functionalism, and conflict theory to health, illness, and the practice of medicine.

10.6 Summarize changes in health problems and infectious diseases, the relationship of the environment and disease, and social inequalities in physical and mental illness.

10.7 Summarize social policy regarding medical care.

10.8 Discuss the likely future of medical care as a social problem.

To prepare for the birth of their first child, Kathie Persall and her husband, Hank, read books and articles about childbirth and took childbirth classes together. At 5 o'clock one morning, as Kathie woke from a fitful sleep, the protective "bag of waters" that surrounded her fetus broke.

By 10 A.M., Kathie was in the maternity ward, hooked up to an electronic fetal monitor and an intravenous feeding tube. She was informed of the hospital's rule that to prevent infection, delivery must take place within 24 hours after the waters break. At 11 A.M., the resident physician (not her own doctor) said that they would speed up Kathie's labor by using Pitocin, a powerful drug.

> **The nurse wiggled the bottle, and a large dose of Pitocin sped through Kathie's veins. Kathie writhed in pain as a massive contraction took over her body.**

Kathie's sister, Carol, knew that inducing labor could lead to cesarean section. She urged Hank to get Kathie off Pitocin, but Kathie and Hank felt that they couldn't tell the doctor what to do. By evening, the doctor decided that Kathie's cervix wasn't dilating rapidly enough, and he increased the Pitocin. A nurse, thinking that the flow of Pitocin looked blocked, wiggled the bottle. A large dose sped through Kathie's veins. Kathie writhed in pain as a massive contraction took over her body.

The fetal monitor set off an alarm, indicating that the baby's heartbeat had dropped from 160 to 40 beats per minute. The doctor rushed in, cut off the Pitocin, and gave Kathie another drug to stop the contraction. He told Kathie and Hank that a cesarean might be necessary. Hank, who had been trying to comfort Kathie, protested. The doctor told them that they needed to sign a consent form, that they could face an emergency at any time. On the form, Hank and Kathie read a long list of things that could go wrong. They didn't want to sign the form, but how could they resist? Kathie was in pain and exhausted.

At midnight, the doctor told Kathie that a cesarean was necessary because she had dilated only 5 centimeters in 13 hours of labor. At 1:10 A.M., Kathie went into surgery. When the baby was born, Kathie was vomiting severely from the anesthetic, and she could not even look at her new son. It took Kathie 7 weeks to recover physically from the cesarean surgery. She was left with a disfiguring scar, but this was nothing compared with her anger at the doctors, the hospital, and the medical procedures that had created the need for surgery, denying her and her husband the kind of delivery they had looked forward to.

Earlier, we focused on the twin problems of crime and the criminal justice system. As we consider medical care in this chapter, we again need to focus on twin problems, in this case, illness and the medical care system. Our focus will be on how social factors affect health.

The Problem in Sociological Perspective: The Social Nature of Health and Illness

10.1   **Explain what is *social* about illness. Include lifestyle, iatrogenesis, changing ideas, and the environment.**

In this chapter, we will focus on the *social* nature of health and illness and on the medical system as a social problem.

Not Just Biology

Most of us think of illness in biological terms, but there are significant social components as well. For example, what it means to be sick differs from one culture to another, and in a large, pluralistic society like ours, even from one group to another. This may seem strange—isn't a fever always a sign of illness? Not always. While some take a low-grade fever as a sign of illness, others dismiss it as "just a little temperature."

Industrialization and Lifestyle The social nature of health and illness becomes apparent when we consider industrialization and lifestyle. When the United States changed from a farming nation to one where people worked in factories and offices, heart disease became the number one killer. The primary reason? As industrialization brought higher incomes, people changed their lifestyle. They ate richer foods and weren't as physically active, which led to more heart attacks. As you know, the pursuit of pleasure is also often a cause of disease. Consider some consequences of unprotected sex—gonorrhea, herpes, syphilis, chlamydia, HIV, and genital warts. Then, too, there are the many diseases that come from smoking, drinking, and doing drugs. The social causes of illness and disease, then, take us far beyond biology.

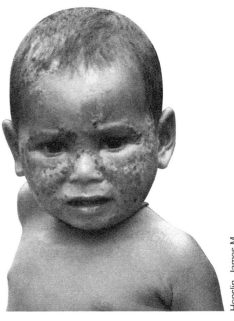

Iatrogenesis

Most doctors take great care in treating their patients. Unfortunately, not all do. At one meeting, when physicians learned that one of their colleagues had recklessly caused a patient's death, the others wanted to stand up and choke him. Instead, one of the doctors pulled a newspaper out of his pocket and slowly began to read the patient's obituary out loud. She was a dearly loved mother, daughter, and wife—and people were suffering her loss (Gupta 2012).

This statement was made by a doctor who was upset about **iatrogenesis**, medical errors that harm patients. You saw a minor example in our opening vignette. When the nurse jiggled Kathie's bottle of Pitocin, the baby's heartbeat plummeted, and Kathie and the baby needed emergency care.

You might think that iatrogenesis would be rare. It is not. It is stunningly common—and in many instances it is fatal. Each year, about 400,000 Americans die needlessly at the hands of doctors and nurses (Makary and Daniel 2016). *If the number of Americans killed by medical errors were an official classification of death, it would rank as the third leading cause of death (Statistical Abstract 2018:*Table 127).

In the following *Thinking Critically about Social Problems,* we examine medical incompetence, another aspect of iatrogenesis.

We define health and illness according to our culture. If almost everyone in a village had this skin disease, the villagers might consider it normal—and those without it the unhealthy ones. I photographed this infant in a jungle village in Orissa, India, so remote that it could be reached only by following a foot path.

Henslin, James M.

Thinking Critically about Social Problems

How Incompetent Can a Doctor Be?

When ultrasound showed that one of the twins had defects, the woman asked her doctor to abort it. He removed the healthy fetus.

Another woman went into the hospital with a problem with her lungs. Her surgeon did a hysterectomy.

Tests showed that a man had a cancerous kidney. The surgeon removed the healthy one.

A man was supposed to have a circumcision. The surgeon removed both of his testicles.

Someone hung the scan backward. The surgeon operated on the wrong side of the patient's brain.

This woman complained of severe abdominal pain after her surgery. She was told that it was normal to feel such pain. After complaining for 18 months, the doctor took this X-ray.

GRANT TURNER/Stringer/AFP/ Getty Images

And then there's the Oops! moment: In the midst of surgery, the doctor realized that he was removing the wrong leg. But it was too late. He had to complete the amputation.

No, I'm not making these up. These are actual cases (Steinhauer and Fessenden 2001; Seiden and Barach 2006; Childs 2007; Puzic 2010; Gupta 2012). There is also the woman who had the wrong foot amputated, the man who.... In fact, some physicians operate on the wrong patient altogether.

To prevent these mistakes, maybe surgeons should put a mark on the patient's body where the incision is to be made. Using indelible ink, both patient and doctor could sign their names at that spot. Before the surgeon makes an incision, he or she can check the signatures.

This suggestion may sound facetious, but you should know that it isn't. Nor is it just an idea. To prevent what surgeons call "wrong-site surgery," some hospitals have the doctor and patient mark the spot and sign it. This helps, but incredibly, surgeons sometimes can't figure out whether the mark means "Operate here" or "Operate on the other side" ("Wrong-Site . . ." 2017).

I once had such confidence in the medical profession (the tough entrance requirements for medical school, the years of study, the supervision and evaluations) that I didn't think there were incompetent doctors. Some weren't as good as others, to be sure, but they weren't incompetent. Then on a postdoctoral fellowship, I studied suicide in Missouri. As I pored over the coroner's records, I was awestruck when I saw a doctor's decision that a person who had been shot several times might have committed suicide. Later, I read about a father in Warren, Ohio, who was convinced that his 20-year-old daughter, who was found dead in a field, had not committed suicide. For 17 years, this man kept the case alive. As he doggedly pursued the issue, it eventually became apparent that the coroner had missed "obvious" clues—like "suspicious

marks" on her neck. The woman's former boyfriend was charged with strangling her.

When this case became public, the sheriff investigated the coroner. Over the years, the coroner had made these decisions:

- Suicide—the man had been run over with a bulldozer and shot
- Suicide—an inmate was found hanged on his knees with toilet paper stuffed in his mouth
- Death by carbon monoxide from a lawn mower—the lawn mower didn't work
- Death by carbon monoxide—no carbon monoxide was found in the person's blood

This coroner had served as president of the Ohio State Medical Association.

Makes you wonder, doesn't it?

For Your Consideration

→ Please suggest ways to reduce medical errors.
→ What system would you suggest to discover and remove incompetent medical students and licensed physicians?

Changing Ideas about Health and Illness

Physicians' involvement in pregnancy also highlights the *social* nature of health and illness. Physicians have defined a natural process (pregnancy and birth) as a medical problem, one that requires fetal monitors, powerful drugs, and medical supervision. As in our opening vignette, many doctors define a woman as "ill" if she does not deliver a baby within 24 hours after her water breaks. This is an arbitrary definition of "illness." It has been imposed on a natural process in which some women deliver a baby an hour after their water breaks, but others not for 48 hours or longer.

Coal mining provides another example of the social nature of "disease." Longtime miners used to complain to doctors that they were short of breath and that they were coughing up blood. The doctors said that these weren't signs of a disease. They were things that "just happened" to coal workers. To get their definition accepted, the miners had to fight the medical establishment. They did succeed, and the miners' struggle to get their disease recognized led to a new understanding of how the environment can cause illness (Hamby 2014).

The "new" disease, progressive massive fibrosis (black lung disease), turned out to be preventable. Safety measures were put into effect, and this disease among coal miners became uncommon. Now, however, with more powerful machines churning up more coal dust, this disease is again increasing (Payesco 2018).

Environment and Disease on a Global Level

Medical researchers investigate how human activities reshape the environment, and how this, in turn, has an impact on the diseases that humans experience. We explore this topic in the following *Global Glimpse*.

A Global Glimpse

Solving Medical Mysteries: Cholera, Bats, and Ticks

Back in the 1800s, fear stalked the city of London. An outbreak of deadly cholera had hit the city. There was no cure, and no one knew where this silent killer would strike next. Londoners, healthy one day, were dead a day or two later. The disease hit men and women, the elderly and the young. The public and authorities were alarmed, and London physicians were left perplexed. Nothing made sense.

John Snow, a physician, came up with a new idea. Taking a city map, he marked where each victim had lived. He saw that the marks were clustered around one of the city wells. Snow speculated that this well was contaminated, and that if it were shut down, the epidemic would end. To find out, he removed the pump handle from the well, an area where 500 people had died in just the previous 10 days (Cooper 2002; Barton 2018). The cholera was stopped in its tracks, defeated not by medicine but by medical investigation.

Researchers are studying the relationship of disease and the environment. How does clearing the forests lead to humans getting diseases from bats?

aDam Wildlife/Shutterstock

You can see how tracking the *social* causes of disease can be significant for human health and why it is an essential aspect of medicine. Medical mysteries like the cholera epidemic of London reappear. For example, asthma has doubled among preschoolers in the United States. Also, many U.S. campers come down with Lyme disease, but a few years back they didn't. Surprising changes in disease also occur in other parts of the world. Malaysia has experienced the Nipah virus and an increase in malaria.

Let's look at these health problems and see how researchers are tracing their changing patterns to changes in the environment. Let's start with the Nipah virus.

In the 1990s, Malaysians cleared a lot of forests. At the same time, there were extensive forest fires in nearby Sumatra. In these forests lived fruit bats, which carry the Nipah virus. With much of their natural habitat destroyed, the bats migrated. In their search for food, they moved closer to where humans lived, some even settling in backyard fruit trees. The Nipah virus also migrated—from the fruit bats to pigs and then to people.

Clearing the forests also brought an unexpected increase in malaria. The clearing left countless holes where the trees had been. When it rains, these holes filled with water, turning the holes into breeding grounds for malaria-carrying mosquitoes. The millions of plastic bags that people discard around the world are doing the same thing. Crumpled, they, too, collect water, becoming breeding sites for mosquitoes and contributing to an increase in malaria.

But why has asthma more than doubled among U.S. preschool children? It can't be because of clearing forests or discarding plastic bags. Researchers are narrowing the cause. The major suspect turns out to be air pollution, including diesel exhaust, that triggers asthma and magnifies its problems (Guidry 2016).

And the increase in Lyme disease? Researchers are pointing to global warming. There are more ticks because the warmer earth provides a more hospitable environment. With more ticks, more humans are bitten, leading to an increase in Lyme disease. As global warming continues, the ticks that carry Lyme disease have migrated northward. But the disease is also migrating southward, likely because suburbia is expanding into the edge of forests, producing thin forest cover, favored by deer and the white-footed mouse, hosts and transporters of the tick that passes on Lyme disease (Belluz 2018).

Medical researchers are trying to tease out more connections between human activities and disease. In Chapter 13, which focuses on the environment, I stress that "everything is connected to everything else." The relationship between human activities, the environment, and disease is an example of this principle.

For Your Consideration

→ Have you ever had an illness that was related to the environment?

→ Aren't all illnesses related to the environment in some way? So, what's new about the information in this box?

In Sum   We usually think of illness and disease as biological matters. Biology is certainly involved, but what is considered health and illness is also a *social* matter. At one point in time, a physical condition such as pregnancy can be considered as a natural event, and at another time, it can be considered a medical matter. What we think of as the causes of health problems also go beyond biology. Just as doctors once viewed "black lung problems" as "weakness" on the part of some coal miners, they now define this condition as a disease stemming from the miners' environment.

The Problem in Sociological Perspective: The Social Organization of Medicine

10.2 **Explain why the social organization of medicine is part of a social problem.**

When we look at issues of health as social problems, we look not only at illness and disease but also at the *system* of health care. To make this clearer, let's consider medical costs, cesarean births, and the quality of medical care.

An Explosion in Medical Costs

Figure 10.1 illustrates how medical costs have soared in the United States. In 1960, the nation's medical bill ran $28 billion. Today's cost has exploded to almost $4 trillion, about *150 times higher*. During this time, the cost of other goods has increased almost nine times. If medical costs had increased at the same rate as average inflation and considering that the population had also increased by about 75 percent, the nation's annual medical bill would run about *one-tenth* of what it is now.

Figure 10.1 The Nation's Medical Bill: Soaring Costs

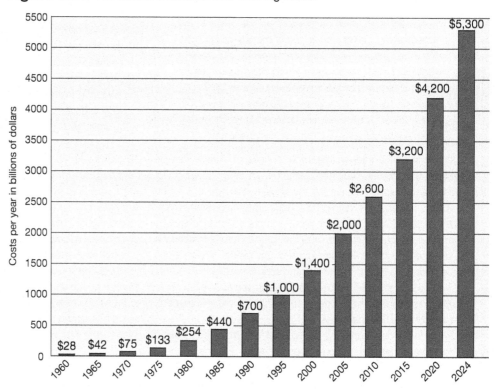

Source: By the author. Based on *Statistical Abstract of the United States* 2011:Table 130; 2016:Table 148.

Another way to illustrate the explosion in the costs of medical care is to see how little it used to cost to have a baby. Look at Figure 10.2. The 1962 bill of $113.85 included a three-day stay in the hospital for the mother, her anesthetic, lab fees, medicine, dressings, delivery room, nursery, her son's circumcision, and even his bracelet. Today, an uncomplicated vaginal delivery with a three-day stay in the hospital runs about $11,481: $6,743 for the hospital, $1,078 for the anesthesiologist, and $3,660 for the attending physician (Healthcare Blue Book 2018). A circumcision will cost an additional $286, double the entire 1962 cost.

Why did the nation's medical bill explode? There are three primary reasons: First, there are more elderly people in our population, and they need much more medical treatment than the younger. A second reason is that we have a lot of new medical technology, which is expensive. The third reason is that we approach medical care as a commodity to be sold for profit. Let's look at this third reason.

Medicine for Profit: A Two-Tier System of Medical Care

Medicine for profit is also known as a *fee-for-service medical system*. Under this system, physicians are like mechanics and plumbers: They collect a fee for each service they perform. And like mechanics and plumbers, the more services they sell, the more money they make. In a fee-for-service system, health care is a commodity to be sold—not a citizen's right.

Our fee-for-service system has led to a **two-tier system of medical care**: one for those who can afford good insurance and another for those who cannot. Because our society treats health care as a commodity to be sold to the highest bidder, our medical care ranges from the finest in the world at major universities to that provided by an underground network of unlicensed, foreign-trained physicians who can barely understand their patients.

Medicine for Profit: Cesarean Delivery

Kathie, in our opening vignette, had an expensive **cesarean section** (C-section), her baby delivered through abdominal surgery. Although a mistake by a nurse triggered events that made her surgery necessary, the extra profits that come from cesarean deliveries motivate many doctors to prefer this method of delivering babies. As shown in Figure 10.3, in 1970 about one of 19 babies was delivered by cesarean section; now the total is one of every three.

Figure 10.2 Hospital Bill for Childbirth, 1962

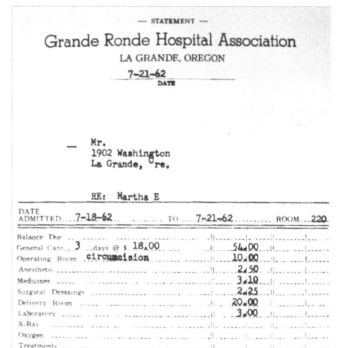

Source: From the author's files. The individual wishes to remain anonymous, so the name has been redacted.

Figure 10.3 The Increase in Cesarean Births

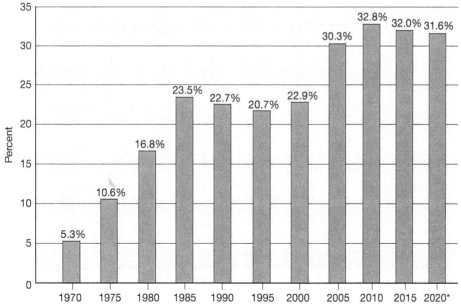

Note: *Author's estimate.

Sources: By the author. Based on *Statistical Abstract of the United States* 1990:Tables 88, 89; 2016:Table 94; *National Vital Statistics Reports* 2018.

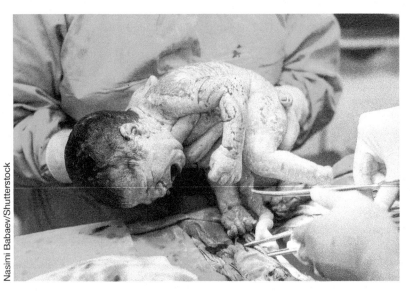

This baby has just been born by C-section. The text discusses the reasons that this medical procedure has become common.

Why the Increase in Cesarean Births? Do you think women in the United States are becoming less healthy, so that more of them need this surgery?

I'm sure you know the answer: Today's women aren't less healthy than women in the past. But did you know that today's women are actually healthier? How do we know? The best single indicator of health is longevity—how long people live. And women are living longer today. If it isn't women's health, then what is the answer? Could it be the medical system? It certainly is. We know this because some hospitals have much higher rates of cesarean delivery than other hospitals even though they are in the same city and serve patients from similar backgrounds. The doctors in some hospitals promote C-section births, while other doctors are less likely to do so (Park 2014).

In Figure 10.3, you saw how the rate of C-sections has risen—even though this type of delivery carries greater health risks for the mother: bleeding, blood clots, sterility, and ruptured uteruses (Kuklina et al. 2009; Offord 2016). Compared with women who give birth vaginally, women who have cesarean births also have to stay in the hospital longer. Their new babies are also more likely to have breathing problems, to require intensive care, and to have higher rates of asthma and diabetes (Blustein and Liu 2015; Keag et al. 2018).

And here is what many find shocking: *Most cesarean deliveries are medically unnecessary.* Then why are one-third of U.S. births by C-section? Let's look at four main reasons.

Profit: The main reason for the increase in Cesarean births seems to be more income for obstetricians—doctors who specialize in childbirth. Being able to charge much more for cesarean births motivates them to recommend the surgery. Obstetricians' income has increased so much that, with the exception of other surgeons and anesthesiologists, it is higher than that of all other medical specialties (BLS 2018).

Convenience: Another reason for this increase is that cesarean births *allow doctors to take control* of the delivery process. Instead of having to come into the delivery room at 3 A.M.—something no one likes to do—the doctor can decide when the baby will be born.

Both convenience and higher profits motivate doctors to do more C-sections. Now that births are scheduled around the physician's preference, more births occur on Tuesday than on any other day of the week (*National Vital Statistics Reports* 2018:Table 1-1).

Technology: Advanced technology is an-other reason. Almost all U.S. women who give birth do so in a hospital, and almost all of these women are attached to a fetal monitor during their labor. When the fetus is in distress, the monitor sets off an alarm, but many of these signals are false. With no standard way of interpreting the distress signals and doctors wanting to take the safest route, the use of fetal monitors increases the number of cesarean deliveries (Rosenberg and Trevathan 2018).

Preference: Finally, some women ask their doctors for a C-section because they fear the labor pains that come with vaginal childbirth or because they, too, want to control the time of delivery. It is difficult for doctors to refuse such requests—especially since a C-section means both convenience and profit (Kirkey 2016; Panda et al. 2018).

A Feminist Controversy Cesarean births have become not only a social issue but also cause for controversy among feminists. The central issue is the relative power of women. Some feminists say that cesarean delivery takes the power over childbirth away from women and puts it in the hands of doctors. Kathie, in our opening vignette, would agree. Others, in contrast, take the view that cesarean delivery can empower women. They point out that it isn't always the physician who decides that a woman will have a cesarean delivery: As just mentioned, some women tell their doctors how and when they want to deliver their children.

Amelie-Benoist/BSIP/The Image Works France

Jochen Sands/DigitalVision/Getty Images

■ The Scope of the Problem

To better understand the scope of medical problems, we will look at both physical and mental illness. Let's begin with physical illness as a social problem.

To illustrate our two-tier medical system, I chose two photos of patients waiting for the doctor. I'm sure you have no problem telling which tiers the photos represent.

Physical Illness as a Social Problem

10.3   Summarize some of the aspects of physical illness that make it a social problem.

Two ways social researchers evaluate the general health of a society are to analyze life expectancy and infant mortality.

Life Expectancy

In the United States, life expectancy has been increasing for more than a century. In 1900, the average person died before seeing the age of 50. In contrast, the average boy born today can expect to live to age 76, the average girl to age 81 (*Statistical Abstract* 2018:Table 110). These are national averages, and group averages never apply to individuals. Your particular life expectancy is not 76 or 81 or any other group average.

As with so many other conditions in society, life expectancy is related to income and education: Those who have higher incomes and education live longer. Life expectancy is also related to race–ethnicity: Whites live an average of 3.5 years longer than African Americans (*Statistical Abstract* 2018:Table 111); Asian Americans live the longest, while Native Americans have the shortest lives. If we could improve social conditions so that everyone has the same educational and environmental conditions as the wealthy, we would save five to eight lives for every one saved by advances in medicine (Woolf et al. 2010; Fauci and Eisinger 2018).

To the shock of experts, the steady upward climb of the life expectancy of Americans was interrupted with slight declines in 2015 and 2016. Several reasons have been proposed, with the main one being the many deaths from our opioid crisis (Thielking 2017).

Sociology contains a lot of practical lessons, as you've probably noticed by now. The practical lesson from this is that if your goal is to save lives, you might want to go into public health instead of medicine.

Infant Mortality

A primary reason why life expectancy has increased is the decline in the **infant mortality rate**, the number of babies who die before their first birthday, per 1,000 live births. The infant mortality rate is another way to measure a group's well-being: It reflects the quality of nutrition, the health of mothers and babies, and the quality of health care. In 1960, the U.S. rate was 26 deaths per 1,000 births. Now it is just a fourth of this, 5.8 per 1,000 births (*Statistical Abstract* 1990:Table 110; 2018:Table 1356). The following Social

Map shows how infant deaths are distributed among the states. The clustering of states that you see indicates *social* influences on health, illness, and even the death of babies. The particular social factors for this clustering, however, remain elusive.

Figure 10.4 The Geography of Death: Infant Mortality Rates

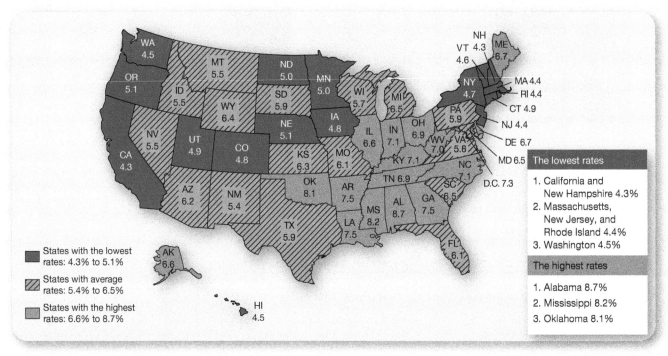

Source: By the author. Based on *Statistical Abstract of the United States* 2018:Table 121.

Although our infant mortality rate has plunged, many still find it a cause for concern. To see why, look at Figure 10.5, where you can see that the U.S. rate is higher than that of several other nations. The cold numbers on this table translate into avoidable deaths. If our rate were the same as Japan's, most of the 16,000 infants who die in the United States each year would live (*Statistical Abstract* 2018:Table 119).

Why is the U.S. infant mortality rate higher than the rates of the other nations shown in Figure 10.5? The primary reason is the huge pockets of poverty in the United States. As you saw in Chapter 7, poverty is especially high among African Americans, Latinos, and Native Americans. Their higher rates of infant mortality reflect this poverty and increase the overall U.S. rate. To put the matter in the simplest terms: To live on the edge of survival is not good for pregnant women. They get sick more often, experience more stress, have more emotional problems, don't eat as healthful foods, and receive less prenatal care.

Lifestyle

It is difficult to overstate the importance of lifestyle in determining health and illness because *lifestyle is the major cause of illness and death.* To mention the most obvious: Overeating and lack of exercise lead to heart attacks and strokes, smoking causes cancer, and the abuse of alcohol harms essential body organs. These are all part of the *social* nature of physical illness.

Sexually transmitted diseases (STDs), also called sexually transmitted infections (STIs), illustrate how lifestyle is related to health. To again state the obvious: Singles who practice abstinence run zero risk of STDs. So do couples who never had sex before they marry and then remained sexually faithful after marriage. All others are at risk—a risk that rises

Figure 10.5 Infant Mortality Rates

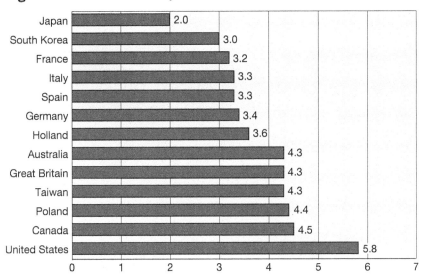

Note: These are the countries listed in the source whose rates of infant mortality are less than that of the United States. Infant mortality is defined as the babies who die before their first birthday per 1,000 live births. Belgium, Cuba, Czech Republic, Greece, Portugal, Sweden, and Switzerland, listed in earlier editions of the source as having rates of infant mortality lower than the United States, no longer appear in the current edition. It is likely that their rates are still lower.

Source: By the author. Based on *Statistical Abstract of the United States* 2018:Table 1356.

with the number of sexual partners and the amount of unprotected sex. Although people with more sexual partners and unprotected sex have a greater chance of acquiring an STD, it's possible to become infected with gonorrhea, syphilis, and even HIV with just the first sexual encounter.

Heroic and Preventive Medicine

At the core of the social problem of medical care lies this contradiction: We live in an age of *chronic* illnesses (lingering and ongoing medical problems), while our medical services are geared for *acute* illnesses (those that have a sudden onset, a sharp rise, and a short duration). Our medical approach to cancer, heart disease, and other chronic disorders is heroic, hospital-based, and expensive. Intervening after a disease is advanced requires highly trained specialists, technical equipment, and expensive drugs. Patients who have serious illnesses want the best care, and the medical world has taught us that "the best" means complex, technical, and expensive.

Unlike heroic medicine, with doctors intervening in life–death situations—popularized by movies and television—preventive medicine is not dramatic. On the contrary, preventive medicine consists of quiet, behind-the-scenes activities such as encouraging changes in people's behavior by promoting exercise and more healthful eating and reducing smoking and drug use. Yet prevention, not heroic medicine, holds the key to limiting untold suffering and saving millions of lives.

Uneven Distribution of Doctors

Another problem with the medical delivery system is an uneven distribution of doctors. Some areas have an abundance of physicians, while others have few doctors. It is difficult for small towns, which offer few cultural attractions, to attract doctors, while large cities near major hospitals have doctors in abundance. As you can see from the following Social Map, the states reflect this same unevenness. In the extreme, Massachusetts has more than twice as many doctors per 100,000 people than Oklahoma.

Figure 10.6 Where the Doctors Are

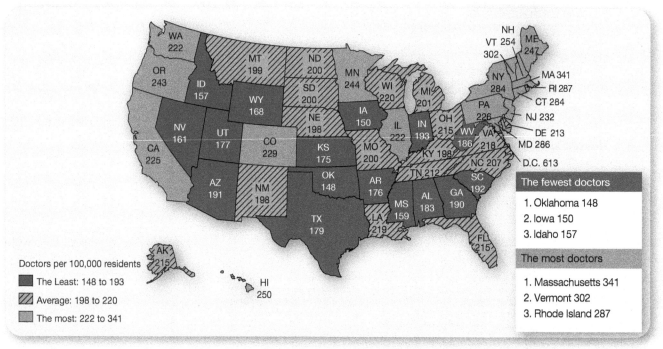

Source: By the author. Based on AAMC (Association of American Medical Colleges). "State Physician Workforce Data Report," November 2017.

Mental Illness as a Social Problem

10.4 **Summarize some of the aspects of mental illness that make it a social problem.**

We should start by asking two basic questions: Has mental illness increased? and What is mental illness?

Measuring Mental Illness

You probably are familiar with the high stress that people experience today, and you might know that our social support systems (family, friends, and community) have become weaker. Do you think, then, that mental illness has increased? This sounds good and could be true, but, frankly, it is just as possible that there is less mental illness today than in past years. Then-and-now totals are impossible to compare because we don't know how much mental illness there is today, much less how much mental illness there used to be. Any totals that any "expert" tells you are just fuzzy speculations. Experts don't even agree on how to define various forms of mental illness—and the definitions they use keep changing. We can dispense, then, with the notion that mental illness is more common today, for there is no way of knowing one way or the other.

A Two-Tier System of Mental Health Delivery

Just as problems of physical illness have two parts—the illnesses and the medical delivery system—so do problems of mental illness. Let's see how the medical delivery system is part of this problem. Here is something I observed as I was doing research on the homeless:

> I watched as an elderly nude man, looking confused, struggled to put on his clothing. With his bare hands, the man had ripped the wires out of the homeless shelter's electrical box and then, with the police in pursuit, had run from one darkened room to another.
>
> I asked the officers where they were going to take the man, and they replied, "To Malcolm Bliss" (the state hospital). When I commented, "I guess he'll be there for quite a while," an officer replied, "Probably for just a day or two. We picked him up last week when he was crawling under cars at a traffic light—and they let him out after two days."

The police explained that only people who are a danger to others or themselves are admitted as long-term psychiatric patients. Visualizing this old man crawling under cars in traffic and risking electrocution by ripping out electrical wires with his bare hands, I marveled at the definition of "danger" the psychiatrists must be using. Here in front of me, the two-tiered medical system was stripped of its coverings. A middle-class or wealthy person would have received different treatment. Of course, such a person would not have been in a shelter for the homeless in the first place.

This event exposes the lowest part of the lower level of our two-tier system of mental health care: People with more money are likely to receive individual counseling—some form of intensive, expensive "talk therapy" from a psychiatrist. People with little or no money are likely to be ignored or given some form of medication and told that "Everyone has problems, so do your best."

The homeless are the castoffs of postindustrial society. Unwanted and unneeded, they are left to wander the city streets and countryside. Only grudgingly are their needs attended to. This photo was taken in Denver, Colorado.

YAKOBCHUK VIACHESLAV/Shutterstock

The Social Nature of Mental Illness

What exactly is mental illness? This question lands us in the midst of controversy. Some psychiatrists see mental illness behind each shadow, while others deny that mental illness exists (Szasz 1961; Doward 2013). Mental illness, whatever it is, has a strong social basis. That is, people who experience more stress are more likely to also experience what are known as mental problems.

Mental problems are assumed to be the primary reason for suicide, although the matter is not this simple. In the following *Issues in Social Problems*, you can see how suicide is related to social conditions and also how suicide changed from a personal problem to a social problem and then back again to a personal problem.

Issues in Social Problems

Suicide: The Making and Unmaking of a Social Problem

Deliberately drawing a razor blade across one's wrist, putting a gun in one's mouth and pulling the trigger, or taking poison—these chill the imagination. More than 100 years ago, sociologist Emile Durkheim (1897/1951) documented how suicide is more than an individual act, how it is related to social conditions.

Regularity of Rates

When Durkheim analyzed the suicide rates of different countries, he noticed that year after year, each country's rate remained about the same. Look at Figure 10.7. Unless there is a change in

reporting from one year to the next, these rates show little change. Ten years from now, Greece and Italy will have much lower suicide rates than the United States. Suicide rates are so regular that you can expect about 40,000 to 41,000 Americans to kill themselves this year, and next year, and the year after that (*Statistical Abstract* 2018:Tables 130, 131).

Gender in Suicide

From Figure 10.7, you can see that in almost all countries men are more likely than women to kill themselves. In the United States, for every woman who kills herself, three to four men do the same. This ratio holds true year after year. Yet year after year, women *attempt* suicide more often than men. This is interpreted as meaning that women's suicide attempts are more likely to be "cries for help," but men are more likely to mean it. This is true, but there is also the matter of gender in the choice of method: Women are more likely to take pills, men to use guns. Pills allow more time for discovery before death, or even for changing one's mind. Guns, not so much.

I spent a (depressing) year studying suicide. As I reviewed my county's coroner's records, I was impressed by the role of gender in suicide. Before taking pills, women tended to "pretty" themselves with makeup and to smooth the bed cover. You could see that they had in mind an image of how they would look when they were discovered. And comfort in death: One woman turned on the gas and then rested her head on a pillow in the oven. Not all women commit suicide like this, of course. Some do blow their brains out, but this is more likely to be a man's way of death.

The Making and Unmaking of a Social Problem

In the 1960s, our suicide rates were somewhere in the middle of those of the industrialized nations. But at that time, mental health professionals began to publicize the idea that suicide was a national problem. The objective conditions hadn't changed; that is, there was no increase in suicide, but subjective concerns grew as mental health professionals and government officials used the mass media to arouse the public. The idea of swift intervention when people contemplate or attempt suicide was appealing, and across the nation the National Institute of Mental Health began to finance suicide prevention centers to conquer what had become a social problem.

Although the suicide prevention centers failed to reduce the suicide rate, subjective concerns gradually decreased. The funding dried up, and most centers closed their doors. From time to time, subjective concerns grow, such as after the suicide of a famous person or a series of suicides of teenagers. But subjective concerns have dropped to such an extent that suicide is again a personal problem, not a social problem. Note that during this social construction of a social problem the objective condition, the rate of suicide, did not change.

With an increase in U.S. rates, authorities and experts are again trying to make suicide a social problem. Their current headlines feature "alarming rates of suicide," "startling rise of suicide," and "rising tide of suicide." If these publicity efforts succeed in arousing sufficient subjective concerns, once again suicide will change from a personal problem to a social problem.

For Your Consideration

→ Can you explain why objective conditions are not sufficient to have a social problem?
→ Why did suicide change from a personal to a social problem? Why has it changed back to a personal problem?
→ Can you think of other examples of this process?

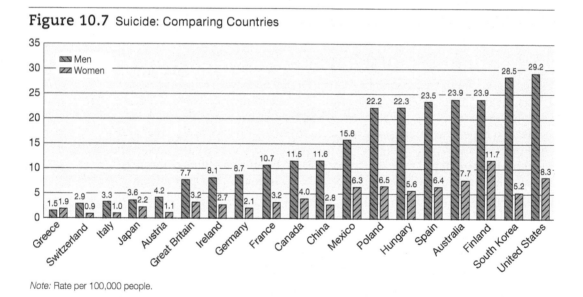

Figure 10.7 Suicide: Comparing Countries

Note: Rate per 100,000 people.

Source: World Health Organization (WHO). "Suicide Rates, Data by Country." New York: United Nations.

Looking at the Problem Theoretically

10.5   **Discuss the perspectives that emerge when you apply symbolic interactionism, functionalism, and conflict theory to health, illness, and the practice of medicine.**

Let's look at how our theoretical perspectives apply to health, illness, and the practice of medicine.

Symbolic Interactionism

As we have reviewed, symbolic interactionists focus on how people determine meaning and how those meanings influence their behavior. Let's look at how determining meaning (symbols) applies to health and illness.

The Meaning of Symptoms

> *If you feel something unusual, you will self-diagnose. That is, you will try to figure out what your out-of-the-ordinary feelings mean. Am I coming down with an illness? Should I go to bed? Call a doctor? Or just carry on with my everyday life?*

How do you determine what your feelings mean? You use definitions that your culture provides. Because social classes and subcultures equip their members with distinctive ways of viewing life, you will interpret your experience differently than will someone from a different background. Back pain is an example. People from the lower classes are likely to regard back pain as part of life. "This is what happens to people when they get older." People from the middle class, in contrast, are more likely to view back pain as a health problem that needs to be treated by a doctor. It is the same with cold or flu symptoms. For many people, these feelings indicate a need to go to a doctor and "get a shot." To those who follow alternative medicine, these same symptoms indicate the need to drink more water or to take vitamin C or other antioxidants. In short, we use cultural and subcultural symbols to determine what our symptoms mean.

The Significance of Definitions Just as social classes and subcultural groups perceive illness differently, so groups compete to get their views of health accepted. This, in turn, changes the way we view health, illness, and medicine. For example, the American Psychiatric Association (APA) used to list homosexuality as a mental illness and approved therapists who treated it. Using **conversion therapy** (sometimes called reorientation or reparative therapy), psychiatrists would attempt to change a person's sexual orientation. Homosexuals objected to being defined as mentally ill and having their sexual orientation treated as an illness. They lobbied for a change, and in 1973 the APA dropped homosexuality as a form of mental illness. Conversion therapy has fallen into such disfavor that some states have made it illegal (Leonard 2018).

Just as leaders in the fields of medicine and psychiatry can decide that some behavior is no longer an illness, so they can declare that some other behavior is an illness. What had been called drunkenness, for example, was relabeled as the disease of alcoholism. As we reviewed in Chapter 4, through a similar process, unruly and inattentive children were reclassified as children suffering from attention-deficit disorder.

The labels we apply to health and illness become lenses through which we view the world. If we define alcohol abuse as a disease, we perceive an alcohol abuser as sick; if we define the abuse as drunkenness, we might think of the person as sinful or morally weak. Such contrasting views come with matching ideas of appropriate social policy: If we consider alcohol abuse to be a disease, we might think that sympathy and medical help are appropriate responses, but if we define alcohol abuse as a moral failing, we might think that shaming or punishment is more appropriate. Because our social groups provide the symbols or definitions that we use, sociologists say our ideas of health and illness are "socially constructed."

Conflicting Referral Networks As symbolic interactionists study how meaning is determined in the practice of medicine, they analyze interactions between doctors and patients. They stress that patients and doctors use different referral networks (Friedson 1961; Lopez 2018). Patients use a **lay referral network**—family, friends, neighbors, and coworkers with whom they talk about their medical problems. This network helps the individual decide which doctor to see—or even whether to see a doctor at all. In this lay referral network, the perception of a physician's knowledge and personality is important. So is the confidence that the doctor exhibits. Doctors who show uncertainty create fear, while those who appear confident instill trust. Patients also want to be sure they get a shot or a prescription, not just advice to go on a diet or to get more rest. That advice might be the most appropriate response the physician could give, but the patient expects something "more professional," which translates into "medicine" that only a doctor can give.

The physician's frame of reference, in contrast, is a **professional referral network**—made up of other physicians and medical professionals. In this network, the meaning of "doctoring" is different, for their training in medical schools has emphasized organs, symptoms, and diseases apart from the person. Sympathy for the patient is less important than determining why some organ is malfunctioning and prescribing appropriate treatment (Conrad 1995; O'Rourke 2014).

You can see, then, how the different referral networks of patients and physicians produce contrasting definitions. Because the expectations of patients and doctors are so different, their worlds can collide. Let's look at such a collision of expectations.

Depersonalization

As Mary Duffy was lying in bed, still groggy on the morning after her breast surgery, a group of white-coated strangers filed into her hospital room. Without a word, one of them, a man, leaned over, pulled back her blanket, and stripped her nightgown from her shoulders. As the half-dozen medical students who had encircled her bed stared at Mary's naked body with detached curiosity, the doctor talked about carcinomas. Abruptly, he said to her, "Have you passed gas yet?" (Carey 2005)

It's difficult to imagine that doctors would treat a patient as an object to the extent that this surgeon did. But as you can see, some do. Sociologist call this **depersonalization**—treating a person as an inanimate object.

Depersonalization is common in some medical settings (Jauhar 2014). It is as though medical personnel think that people who check into a hospital have also checked their persona—their personal, intimate feelings and needs—into their medical folder. Sociologists who have studied depersonalization in public clinics note how the poor have to wait for hours, aren't looked directly in the eyes when spoken to, and are addressed as numbers rather than by name. If they aren't able to see a doctor that day, it's just one of those things. After all, what do poor people have to do that's important, anyway?

"Of course I'm listening to your expression of spiritual suffering. Don't you see me making eye contact, striking an open posture, leaning towards you and nodding empathetically?"

Bacall, Aaron/Cartoon Stock

Physicians are often criticized for bad communications with patients. Can we really expect them to empathize with patients when they see one sick person after another all day long?

Patients who are depersonalized feel a gap between themselves and their doctors, and they have a greater tendency to sue their doctors. The threat of malpractice suits, in turn, produces **defensive medicine**; that is, doctors order lab tests and consultations that may not be needed in order to leave a "paper trail" to show they did everything reasonable. Preparing for possible lawsuits adds billions to the nation's medical bill.

Functionalism

Functionalists assume that customs or social institutions persist because they fulfill social needs. This perspective raises interesting questions: Whose needs are met by a health care system that is hospital-based and oriented toward acute illnesses? What are the benefits of depersonalizing patients or of making childbirth a medical procedure?

Fee-for-Service Means Profits   Let's start with the obvious: It is difficult for doctors to make money from people who are healthy. Sick people mean patients for doctors, and patients mean money for them. On top of this, patients who get well quickly bring less profit. But a high-profit-producing hospital-based system oriented toward acute illness—now that's a dream come true. Everyone—doctors, nurses, hospitals, medical suppliers, and drug companies—makes money from patients who are given intensive care. Each year, about 35 million patients—one of every nine Americans—are admitted to a hospital and stay an average of 5 days (*Statistical Abstract* 2018:Table 194).

Figure 10.8 shows the average daily cost of a stay in a hospital. Like the bill for delivering a baby in Figure 10.2, this figure illustrates the skyrocketing costs of medical care better than words can say. Pay attention to the shorter bars. They represent what a day's stay in the hospital would cost if medical costs had risen at the same rate as inflation.

Figure 10.8 How Much Does It Cost to Stay in the Hospital? One Day's Cost Compared to Inflation

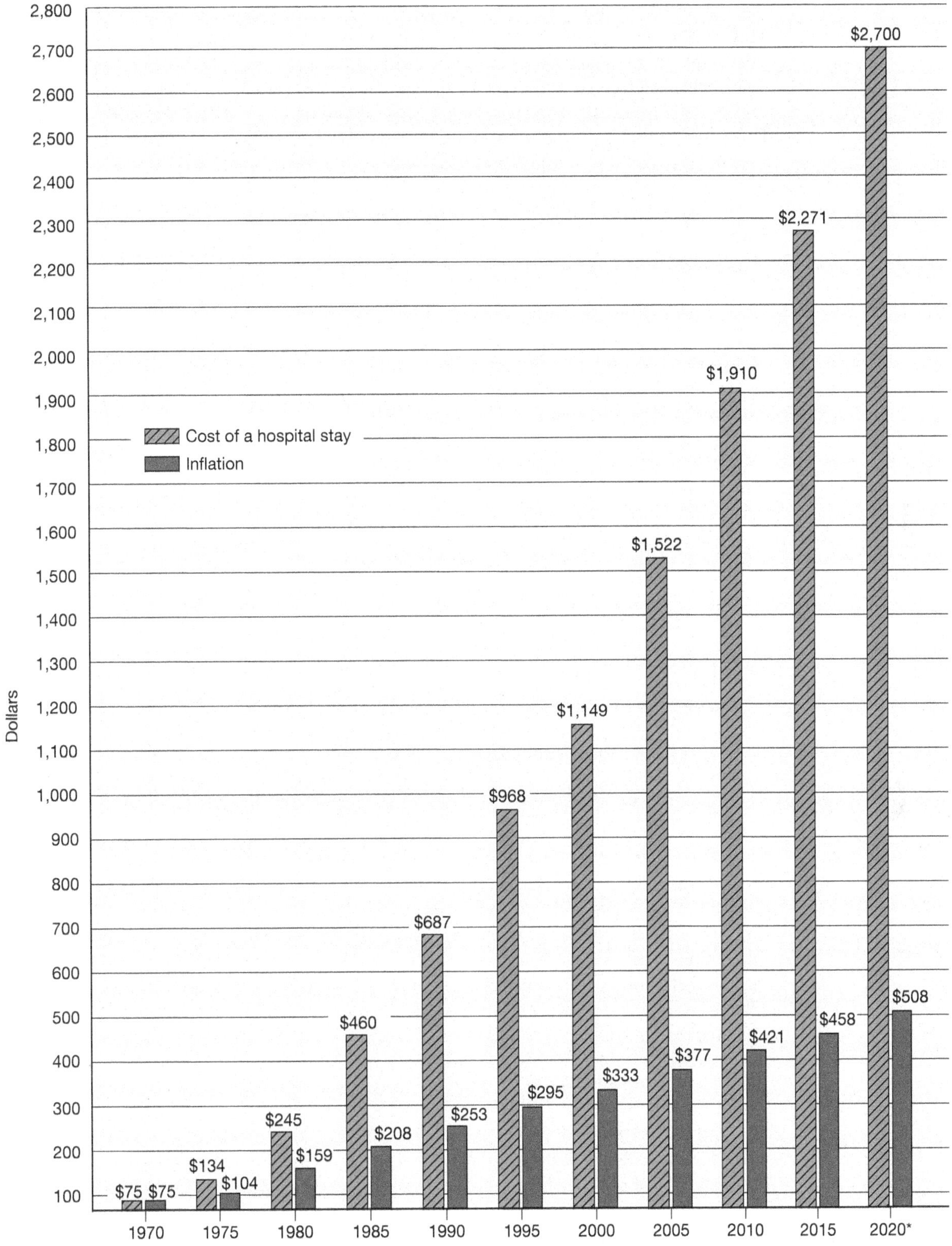

Note: *Author's estimate.

Source: By the author. Based on *Statistical Abstract of the United States* 1998:Table 137; 2018:Table 192.

Despite feeble denials from the medical profession, profits—not health care—drive the U.S. health care system. Our fee-for-service system means that the more services doctors sell and the higher price they charge, the more they earn. One result is unnecessary surgery, such as most cesarean sections. Another example is hysterectomies, which we will review in the next section on conflict theory.

Physicians, nurses, and investors in the U.S. health care industry aren't the only ones who benefit from our fee-for-service system. Patients also benefit, for this system lets them shop around. They can choose which doctor to see and what services to purchase. That this system is functional for patients is indicated by our rising life expectancy and decreasing infant mortality rates.

A Self-Correcting System   I have mentioned problems with our fee-for-service system, but functionalists reply that the system is self-correcting. For example, although the medical system is oriented to acute illnesses, after environmental health problems were recognized as serious, the government took a huge step toward preventive medicine by passing antipollution laws and establishing the Environmental Protection Agency (EPA). Medical schools also responded, adding training programs in environmental medicine. Similarly, because insurance is expensive, it has led to the development of managed care (discussed later) and outpatient surgery. In short, functionalists view fee-for-service health care as a system that responds to shifting needs of the nation.

The Global Level   Functionalists also analyze functions and dysfunctions of medicine on a global level. Exporting Western medicine to the Least Industrialized Nations provides an excellent example. The vaccines and medicines sent to these countries were functional because they reduced death rates on a global scale. But they were also dysfunctional because they set the conditions for the global population explosion that worries so many. We will discuss this topic in Chapter 12.

Conflict/Feminist Theory

As usual, conflict sociologists disagree with the functionalist view. In fact, they argue the opposite—that the U.S. medical system is *not* self-correcting. Conflict sociologists view patterns of illness and health care in the United States as the outcome of clashes between interest groups. They argue that the poor are sicker than others because they have lost the competition for high-quality education, food, housing, jobs, and medical care.

Medicaid   What about Medicaid, which benefits the poor? Conflict sociologists point out that this program developed in conflict. In the 1960s, resentment about the treatment of the poor in the medical system had grown so vocal that politicians were forced to take action. Congress saw Medicaid for the poor as the answer. However, the physicians' union, the American Medical Association (AMA), viewed Medicaid as a first step to socialized medicine. This organization feared that Medicaid was an attack on its profitable fee-for-service system, and it spent millions of dollars lobbying to prevent Congress from approving Medicaid. Caught between the public's demand for change and the intense lobbying of the AMA, Congress designed Medicaid to satisfy both—more medical coverage for the poor but retaining the doctor's profitable fee-for-service system.

Colliding Interests of Doctors and Patients   Conflict theorists also have a different view of the doctor–patient relationship. Those adhering to the Marxist perspective emphasize that doctors and patients form two classes—those who control medicine and those who receive treatment. As the dominant class, physicians try to control the doctor–patient relationship. One way they do this is to use technical medical terms, a use of language that places them above the patient. These terms emphasize their knowledge and expertise, helping to produce, maintain, and exercise authority. As conflict sociologists put it: In a capitalist system of production for profit, the relationship of physician and patient is like that of owner and worker. Conflict is built into the relationship, for the interests of the one (making a profit from the illness) oppose those of the other (getting well at the least expense).

The Internet has helped patients regain some control over their medical care. People who have rare diseases, for example, can participate in online discussion groups.

Although people don't meet personally, they share their experiences and knowledge with one another. Some doctors are surprised—and dismayed—when their patients know more than they do about a new treatment or some new research. Not only do physicians feel threatened because they no longer are the sole possessors of esoteric knowledge on rare diseases or even the treatment of common disorders, but they also fear that patients can be picking up misinformation on the Internet.

Women's Reproductive Organs   Each year, about 600,000 American women have hysterectomies, the surgical removal of the uterus, and often the ovaries. This surgery is so common that by the age of 60, more than one-third of all American women have had hysterectomies (NWHM 2018). Unfortunately, nearly one of five of these surgeries is unnecessary (Corona et al. 2015).

Why do surgeons perform unnecessary hysterectomies? In some cases, the tests that indicated the need for the hysterectomy were inadequate. The tests might indicate the presence of cancer or some other disease, but post-surgical tests indicate otherwise. In other cases, the doctors are unsure of the medical conditions, and they remove the uterus as a safe precaution. In still other cases, the dollar signs in the surgeon's eyes are the deciding factor to operate.

In Sum   From a conflict/feminist perspective, profits, not health care, are the goal of the U.S. medical system. Physicians are businesspeople, patients are customers, and health care is the commodity for sale. Conflict theorists argue that their perspective best explains why medical care for the rich is better than that for the poor: The government pays an increasing proportion of the nation's health care bill because it perpetuates and underwrites the interests of capitalist industries—including medicine. Conflict theorists argue that health care should be a right of all citizens and that people's illnesses and diseases should not be exploited for profit.

Research Findings

10.6   **Summarize changes in health problems and infectious diseases, the relationship of the environment and disease, and social inequalities in physical and mental illness.**

Sociologists do a lot of research on health problems and the medical system. In keeping with the theme of this book, our focus will be on social inequalities of health and health care. First, we will discuss physical health problems: age, race–ethnicity, and social class; our two-tier system of medicine; and how health insurance creates inequalities. We will then discuss social inequalities in mental illness.

Historical Changes in Health Problems

To examine the main causes of death in a society is to make the social nature of health, disease, and death even more apparent.

The Top 10 Killers   In Figure 10.9, you can compare today's 10 leading causes of death with those of 1900. The changes over this time make the *social* nature of death evident. As you can see, only six of today's 10 leading causes of death are the same as back then.

To see the *social* basis of even the cause of death, note that in 1900, "senility" was the ninth leading cause of death. This term seems to have been a catch-all category for "old age," which we don't consider a cause of death today. When the elderly didn't die from diarrhea, pneumonia, or something recognizable, doctors just said they died from "senility." It is likely that the category included what we call Alzheimer's disease today.

To emphasize even further the *social* nature of death, note how causes of death are related to lifestyle and environmental pollution. In 1900, lifestyle factors like smoking cigarettes and the intake of high amounts of sugar weren't common, and lung diseases and diabetes didn't make the top 10 list. With broad changes in lifestyle have come changes in leading causes of death.

Figure 10.9 The 10 Leading Causes of Death in the United States

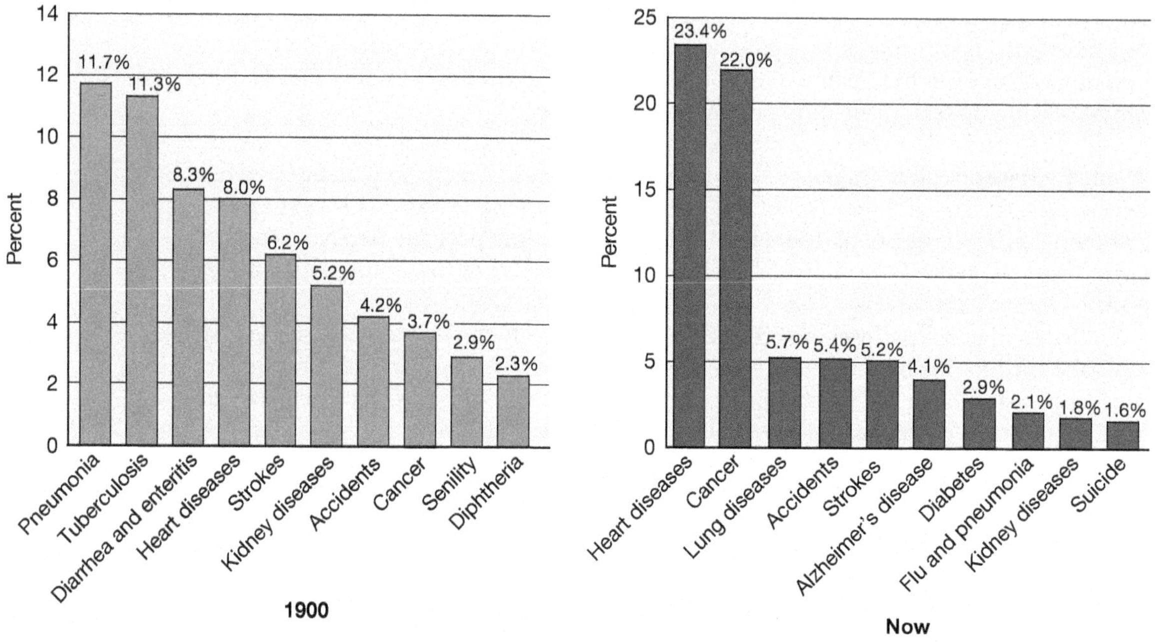

1900

Now

Sources: By the author. For 1900, CDC 2006c; For Now, *National Vital Statistics Reports* 2018:Table B.

Infectious Diseases

Infectious diseases threaten us all, but not all of us are threatened in the same way.

A Decline in Infectious Diseases   From Figure 10.9, you can see what a deadly threat infectious diseases used to be. In 1900, pneumonia was the number one killer, with tuberculosis (TB) close behind. Even diarrhea was a major killer. Every family feared polio, whooping cough, German measles, smallpox, and diphtheria. Then, during the first half of the 20th century, these diseases receded. As death rates dropped, life expectancy rose, going from 47 years to an average of 78 or 79. What happened?

The usual answer is that modern medicine wiped out these diseases. I don't want to detract from the many accomplishments of modern medicine, for most of us know someone who would not be alive if it weren't for coronary bypass surgery, cancer treatment, a pacemaker, or some organ transplant. Prescription drugs and vaccinations certainly have been significant in prolonging life by preventing and treating diseases such as syphilis, bacterial pneumonia, and hypertension.

But most infectious killers of the 19th century were declining *before* antibiotics, immunizations, or specific drugs were developed (McKeown 1980). Although medical myth has it that new drugs and vaccinations conquered TB in the 1950s, you can see from Figure 10.10 that TB had been declining since the 1800s. If modern medicine didn't conquer this infectious disease so feared by earlier generations, what did? *The answer is that cleaner public water supplies and better living conditions improved overall health.* Deaths from these infectious killers declined as people became healthier from cleaner water, better food, and better housing.

The Resurgence of Infectious Diseases

It started with a cough, an autumn hack that refused to go away.

Then came the fevers. They bathed and chilled the skinny frame of Oswaldo Juarez, a 19-year-old Peruvian visiting the United States to study English. His lungs clattered, his chest tightened, and he ached with every gasp. During a wheezing fit at 4 A.M., Juarez felt a warm knot rise from his throat. He ran to the bathroom sink and spewed a mouthful of blood.

Figure 10.10 The "Conquest" of Tuberculosis

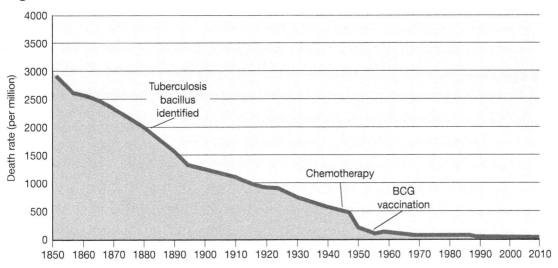

Source: McKeown 1980; *Statistical Abstract of the United States* 2018:Table 197.

"I'm dying," he told himself, "because when you cough blood, it's something really bad."

Oswaldo Juarez had been infected with extremely drug-resistant (XXDR) TB, the first case in the United States (Mason and Mendoza 2009). Since then, a handful of XXDR cases have shown up (Krapp et al. 2018).

Health officials around the world so fear a strain of TB that is resistant to all drugs, one that can spread wildly through a population, that in some countries officials arrest TB patients, keeping them locked up until their disease is cured (McNeil 2016).

Infectious diseases have surprised health experts by their capacity to fight back by developing new strains that are resistant to drugs and vaccines. This may be happening not just with TB but also with the other infectious diseases we thought our drugs had either cured or brought under control. Health experts acutely fear a global outbreak of drug-resistant typhoid (Mole 2018). The implications of the developing drug-resistant infectious diseases are severe on both a personal level, your own health, and on a global level. Let's look at some aspects of this threat to our health in the following *Technology and Social Problems*.

Technology and Social Problems

Superbugs in the Global Village

Simon Sparrow, a 17-month-old toddler, was just learning to feed himself. His family was startled out of sleep early one morning when Simon let out a primal scream. They rushed Simon to the hospital, where he was diagnosed with a virus and asthma and sent home. Fifteen hours later, he was dead (Chase 2006).

What killed Simon? It was a new strain of staph infection. This germ can penetrate bones and lungs, leaving abscesses that require surgery. Simon died so quickly that he was spared this suffering.

This new form of staph (community associated methicillin-resistant

American Red Cross in operation during the Spanish flu epidemic of 1918–1920. The flu killed 25 million people worldwide.

Staphylococcus aureus, which, fortunately has a shortened name—CA-MRSA) has alarmed health authorities. Their fear is that someone, somewhere, will come down with CA-MRSA or some other drug-resistant bacteria that is resistant to every antibiotic—and that with global travel, in just a matter of days the new strain will spread throughout the global village.

Following the discovery of penicillin in the 1940s came a

series of effective microbe killers. By the 1970s, more than 100 antibiotics sat on pharmacy shelves. The war against microbes had been won—or so the medical industry thought—and researchers stopped developing new antibiotics. So, what happened?

When hit with antibiotics, the weaker germs die off. The stronger ones, though, can mutate, survive, and multiply. This is especially likely to happen when people stop taking a drug because they feel better, instead of completing their full course of medical treatment. The more that antibiotics are used and misused, the more that drug-resistant bugs proliferate.

The misuse of antibiotics is common. One of the many reasons is that patients expect a prescription, and doctors comply. Researchers have found that *30 percent* of oral antibiotics are unnecessary (Durkin et al. 2018).

We all carry staph germs on our skin and in our nose. They don't lead to serious problems, as most of these staph germs are relatively mild. But when they are replaced by a mutant, virulent strain, even a simple cut or scrape can become a mortal wound. A patient who goes to the hospital for a sore throat or routine surgery can be carried out in a coffin.

Pharmaceutical firms are searching for the next generation of antibiotics to fight the next generation of microbes. Let's suppose that we win this race and develop new antibiotics in time to prevent a global epidemic. Will we then repeat this process—overprescribing, not completing the course of treatments—with the microbes again mutating and developing resistance to the new drugs?

Granted the past, I am certain this will happen. We have a medical establishment eager for profits and the tendency of patients to quit taking medicines when they feel better, but before their invasive microbes are destroyed totally. A sage once said that those who do not learn from history are doomed to repeat it. I would add that although we study history, and even know its lessons, in some instances we set ourselves on a course destined to repeat it. This, I fear, is one such case.

For Your Consideration

→ It is easy to stop taking medication when you feel better. It's like, "I'm cured. Why take those last six pills in that bottle?" Do you know anyone who has not completed an entire course of treatment prescribed by a physician? Have you?

→ Do you realize the global health implications of not completing a prescribed course of antibiotics?

How Disease Is Related to Behavior and Environment: HIV/AIDS and Other STDs

Most people are unaware of the dangers of drug-resistant TB and typhoid, but they do fear HIV/AIDS. Let's look at how this disease is related to behavior and the environment.

Background When HIV/AIDS first came to the public's attention, almost all victims were men who had sex with men, intravenous drug users, and hemophiliacs. Hemophiliacs and intravenous drug users were exposed to the disease through contaminated blood. Drug-addicted prostitutes also spread the disease to heterosexual men. Today, the disease affects people from all walks of life. Behavior and environment remain important in the transmission of HIV, with men who have unprotected sex with men the most likely to get this disease. Today, women account for more than one-quarter of all new HIV cases.

Orphans in Karonga, Malawi, whose parents died from AIDS are lined up at a feeding station, which they depend on for survival.

Heiner Heine/imageBROKER/Newscom

A Global Epidemic HIV/AIDS is a global epidemic. Each year, about 2 million people are infected with HIV, and about 1 million people die from AIDS. The global death toll numbers 35 million (UNAIDS FactSheet 2018). Hit the hardest is sub-Saharan Africa, where 70 percent of the world's new infections occur. HIV/AIDS is so common in this region that it has become the area's leading cause of death. The main reasons for the prevalence of this disease in sub-Saharan Africa are a lack of sex education, unprotected sex, and prostitution.

Children are also victims, and about 2 million are living with this disease. Ninety percent of these children are in sub-Saharan Africa. Some are infected through sexual violence, but most get the disease from their mother, during pregnancy, birth, or breastfeeding (Avert 2016; UNAIDS FactSheet 2018). Worldwide, more than 25 million children have been orphaned because of AIDS.

HIV/AIDS in the United States **Antiretroviral drugs** (ARVs) can slow HIV infection, preventing full-blown AIDS from appearing for up to 20 years. When ARVs were first developed, they were expensive, costing

$10,000–$15,000 per patient per year. With today's generic versions, costs have dropped to as low as $200 to treat a patient for a year (World Health Organization 2016c). Although these drugs can hold back the symptoms of AIDS, they do *not* prevent people from infecting others with HIV. In the United States, with the combination of antiretroviral drugs and education about unprotected sex, the annual new cases of HIV/AIDS has dropped from 80,000 in 1992 to 38,000 now. Annual deaths from AIDS are now just one-eighth of what they were, dropping from 50,000 in 1995 to 6,500 now (CDC 2018e; *Statistical Abstract* 1998:Table 144; 2018:Table 198).

Figure 10.11 shows how HIV/AIDS is related to race–ethnicity. The reason that racial–ethnic groups have different rates of this disease is not genetic. No group is more or less susceptible to HIV/AIDS because of biological factors. The reasons are social: different rates of multiple sex partners, unprotected sex, and drug users sharing needles.

Ominous Changes The HIV virus mutates rapidly. Some medical researchers fear that strains of HIV might develop that are resistant to the drugs being used, making them only a temporary fix to a global epidemic. If drug-resistant strains become widespread, the epidemic will surge again. Several new drugs, however, hold the promise of picking up where the current drugs leave off.

HIV is not the only sexually transmitted disease (STD), of course, and for all STDs *social* factors or behavior are important. You might be interested in following up this line of thought in the next *Thinking Critically about Social Problems*.

Figure 10.11 Adults Living with HIV/AIDS

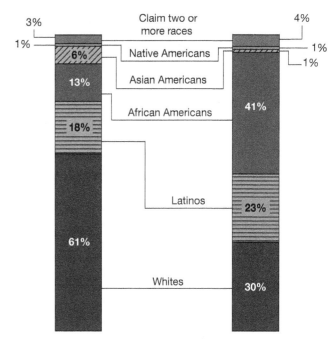

Percentage of U.S. Population | Percentage of HIV/AIDs Cases

- Claim two or more races — 3% / 4%
- Native Americans — 1% / 1%
- Asian Americans — 6% / 1%
- African Americans — 13% / 41%
- 18%
- Latinos — 23%
- Whites — 61% / 30%

Source: By the author. Based in *Statistical Abstract of the United States* 2018: Tables 10, 200.

Thinking Critically about Social Problems

"I Did Not Have Sexual Relations with That Woman": What Is Sex, and So What?

In one of President Bill Clinton's many public dramas, this one at a White House press conference televised to the nation, the then president said, "I did not have sexual relations with that woman."

Some people believed him, and some did not. Almost all were disgusted, though, with the presidency degenerating to this point. But not as disgusted as they were when the transcripts of Clinton's trials were published. And titillated, too, as they read accounts about oral-genital contact between Clinton and Monica Lewinsky, a White House intern.

Was Clinton lying at the televised press conference? At first blush, it seems so. There is no doubt that he was covering up, but was he lying? As Clinton emphasized with his famous "It depends on what 'sex' is" statement about his relationship with Lewinsky, it all depends on definitions. Just what do you mean by a particular word?

"I didn't have sex with that woman," said Bill Clinton to the nation. Considering the steamy revelations of his "whatever-it-was" relationship with Monica Lewinsky, well, you decide.

Or perhaps Clinton was simply ahead of his time. Only 20 percent of today's college students consider oral-genital contact to be sex (Hans et al. 2010).

Or Clinton could have been the leader—showing a new generation a new way to define sex.

Regardless, what is significant about this?

Unprotected sex can lead to STDs. Now everyone knows this, but those who don't think that oral-genital contact is sex might think they can't get STDs from it. I mean, how can you get a sexually transmitted disease from oral-genital contact if oral-genital contact isn't sex?

The STDs—none of them—don't care whether you call oral-genital contact sex or not. It makes no difference to them if you call it pumpkin pie. They just go ahead and do their thing—which is to spread as far and wide and fast as they can.

And they do spread—quite happily, it seems—through oral genital whatever-you-want-to-call-it.

On the list of what someone can get from unprotected (no condom) oral-genital contact is a bunch of things that no one wants: herpes, syphilis, gonorrhea, human papillomavirus, hepatitis A, and HIV. They can also get little critters called intestinal parasites.

For Your Consideration

→ Do you think that oral-genital contact is sex? Why or why not?
→ Why is the definition of what it means to have sex important?
→ Do you think the definition of sex is changing? Why or why not?

Social Inequalities in Physical Illness

As we have learned, social factors largely determine who will be healthy and who will be sick. Poor children, for example, are more likely to be undernourished or to lack a balanced diet. As a result, they are more vulnerable to disease. In general, the poorer people are, the sicker they are. Even their death rates are higher.

This takes us to the heart of the matter—social inequality—the essential factor that underlies our patterns of disease and death. Let's look at social class.

Occupational Health Hazards

On September 12, 2001, Jimmy Willis, a former subway conductor, rushed to Ground Zero to volunteer alongside thousands of workers who had been sent by the city government. For about 10 days, they helped clear out a towering six-story mass of rubble known as "the Pile." They carved a path "five feet at a time" through a morass of concrete and bodies, with little or no respiratory protection. Health problems have plagued these workers, and now 21,000 are being treated for asthma, breathing problems, blood disorders, and various forms of cancer (Chen 2007; Kim 2012; Landgren et al. 2018).

After the collapse of the World Trade Center on September 11, 2001, volunteers and city employees working at Ground Zero were exposed to severe environmental contamination. During these initial recovery efforts, most of the volunteers and employees wore inadequate protection, or none at all.

Although this was an unusual event, it illustrates this principle: Health problems that are a result of employment hit the working class harder. The executive at headquarters is less likely than the worker at the manufacturing plant to be exposed to toxic chemicals—the carbon monoxide, mercury, and uranium that destroy the kidneys, and the heavy metals that invade the nervous system. It is the same for factory noise. It is the working-class ear that is likely to be damaged, not that of the executive.

Reducing Inequalities: Health Care Reform In 2010, Congress passed the Patient Protection and Affordable Care Act. The intention of this law was to reduce the inequalities in health care by requiring all U.S. citizens and legal residents to have medical insurance. As I write this, the law is being modified. Whatever form this law may take, we can be certain that it will *not* eliminate the inequalities in health care. The inequalities are built into our social structure. People with higher incomes will always be able to afford higher-quality medical care. And, as with the example cited of Ground Zero, unless there is fundamental change—which there will not be—the poor will continue to be exposed to more harmful conditions at work. The poor will also continue to eat less healthy food, exercise less, and have a higher rate of obesity. The end result is that they will continue to suffer from more health problems and to die younger.

In every society, the poor have less access to the desirable things in their society. This includes medical care, both physical and mental. Although this woman looks abandoned, she is part of a village and receives care from relatives. I took this photo in a village outside Chennai, India.

Henslin, James M.

Social Class and Mental Illness

Do some social classes have more emotional problems than others? Sociologists have answered this intriguing question time and again. Since 1939, they have found that people's emotional well-being gets worse the lower they are on the social class ladder. Those in the lower social classes are more likely to be depressed, anxious, nervous, and phobic (fearful). Numerous studies have confirmed this finding (Faris and Dunham 1939; Srole et al. 1978; Lundberg 1991; Birzins et al. 2018).

Why do the poor have more mental disorders than people in other classes? Let's compare two competing explanations.

The Drift Hypothesis The first, the *drift hypothesis,* is based on the idea that people with emotional difficulties tend to be less successful in life. People from higher-income families who have mental problems tend to drift downward, landing in the lower classes (Crick and Cois 2018). One result is that those mental disorders thought to have a genetic base, such as schizophrenia and depression, have become concentrated among the poor. Even if these genetic predispositions once were distributed evenly among the social classes, the drift downward has redistributed them. Another result is that the poor have a larger percentage of mentally disturbed parents. Their children are more likely to learn pathological ways of coping with the world, making them less able to deal with the challenges of education and career. They, too, are more likely to end up living in poverty.

You can see how this explanation relates to the nature–nurture controversy we reviewed in the preceding chapter. There we saw how difficult it is to separate genetic influences from the effects of socialization. The many attempts to unravel this thorny problem regarding mental illness have also satisfied no one. With the decoding of the human genome system, researchers are attempting to match specific genes with mental illnesses (Wang et al. 2018).

The Environmental Hypothesis Most sociologists prefer the second explanation, the *environmental hypothesis.* To see how this works, let's rephrase the basic finding that the lower classes have more mental illnesses this way: People in the lower social classes tend to be sadder, more anxious, and more fearful, while those in the higher social classes tend to be happier, less anxious, and less fearful. Sociologists regard these differences in emotions (or "feeling states") as the product of different environments. In short, they see social class as producing "mental health" and "mental illness."

Can social class really do this? Consider how social class sorts people into different kinds of lives. Because of social class, some people enjoy job security, solid finances, and good physical health, medical care, and marriages. Not only do these people have greater security at the present, but they also have greater hopes for the future. They realistically plan and look forward to larger houses, new cars, exotic vacations, college degrees for their children, and a relaxing, enjoyable retirement. You can see how this type of life can produce better mental health.

Compare this with the stress-filled lives of people who live in poverty. Their jobs don't offer security. With low wages, they live from paycheck to paycheck. Unpaid bills pile up. They have high rates of divorce, alcoholism, violence, worse physical health, and less access to good medical care. The contrasting conditions of social class, then, either support people's mental well-being or deal severe blows to it.

Social Class Differences in Mental Health Care To better understand how mental health services are related to social inequality, let's consider types of therapy. In **individual psychotherapy**, a therapist listens and tries to guide the patient toward a resolution of emotional problems. One type of psychotherapy is **psychoanalysis**, which Sigmund Freud pioneered as a way to uncover the subconscious motives, fantasies, and fears that shape people's behavior. The patient meets an analyst several times a week and talks about whatever comes to mind, while the analyst listens for hidden patterns, particularly those that reveal unresolved conflicts from childhood. More common is **short-term directive therapy**, in which a counselor focuses on current situations to help clients understand their problems. In **group therapy**, several patients, with the guidance of a therapist, help each other cope with their problems.

Another treatment is **drug therapy**, the use of tranquilizers, antidepressants, and antipsychotic drugs to relieve people's problems and help them cope with life. As discussed in Chapters 2 and 4, some of these drugs have serious side effects. Drug therapy is often criticized as treating symptoms without offering a cure.

For some illnesses, especially depression, doctors treat some patients with **electroconvulsive therapy (ECT)** (also called electroshock therapy). They attach wires to either side of a patient's skull and send low-voltage electric shocks through the brain. Memory loss is a possible side effect.

The type of therapy that troubled people receive does not depend on what kind of problems they have, but on their ability to pay. People who have money and good insurance are more likely to be guided through their problems with **talk therapy**—psychotherapy, group therapy, and so on. "Talk" therapy is expensive, and few poor or uninsured people receive it. They are usually given drug therapy, sometimes derisively called **pharmaceutical straitjackets**—drugs that make patients drowsy, lethargic, and easier to handle.

Although the patterns of treatment differ by social class, we don't know that this represents inequality. Despite the many years these therapies have been used, we do not know which therapies work. Costly psychoanalysis could be less (or more) effective than drug therapy. It is even possible that no therapy is more effective than all of these. Since we don't know which therapies are more (or less) effective, we don't know whether the poor are receiving worse—or better—treatment for their emotional problems. We need rigorous studies to evaluate the effectiveness of therapy (Paterson et al. 2018).

In Sum   Sociologists consider social inequality to be a root cause of mental problems. Social inequality is also related to the medical treatment people receive for both physical and mental problems. Health care reform is intended to address some of these inequalities in medical care. We won't know the results of these changes in the medical delivery system for years, but we can be certain that laws will not eliminate inequality in health care.

Let's turn our focus on social policy.

Social Policy

10.7   Summarize social policy regarding medical care.

We will first review social policies that pertain to reducing the cost of medical care, then look at preventive medicine and humanizing health care.

Prepaid Medical Care

To reduce the cost of providing health care for their workers, some employers buy **prepaid** or **managed care**. The best-known type is the **health maintenance organization (HMO)**. A business pays a set fee to a medical corporation (the HMO), which covers the health needs of the company's employees. If the health care of these employees costs less than the fee, the HMO makes money; if it costs more, the HMO loses money. Because the HMO receives no more than this fee, it is motivated to reduce costs. Doctors are paid salaries, but they can receive bonuses if they reduce patient costs.

The Positive Side: Healthier Lifestyles   Because doctors make more money when patients stay well, they are motivated to treat medical problems before they become serious and more expensive. They encourage preventive care, such as immunizations, well-baby checkups, mammograms, and physicals. They urge patients to adopt a lifestyle that improves health: better diet, exercise, rest, and avoiding the abuse of drugs, including alcohol. This lifestyle reduces medical tests, surgery, and hospital admissions. HMO doctors also lower costs by keeping the length of hospital stays to the bare minimum (Purcell 2016).

The Negative Side: Profits and a Conflict of Interest

A doctor noticed a lump in one of her own breasts. When she called the radiology department of the hospital where she worked to schedule a mammogram, she was told that she would have to wait six months. The hospital's HMO allowed one mammogram every two years, and she had had a mammogram 18 months earlier. She had to appeal to the HMO's board of directors, who agreed to let her be an exception to the rule. She had breast cancer (Gibbs and Bower 2006).

This event is a succinct summary of the negative side of HMOs. By cutting down on tests and hospitalization, HMO doctors sometimes withhold *necessary* treatments, tests, and hospitalizations. A woman I know was sent home from the hospital even though she was still bleeding from her surgery. If she had remained longer, she would have used up more than her "share" of allotted costs and eaten into the HMO's profits. This would not have happened to a fee-for-service patient who could afford to pay for her health care.

Another negative is that physicians have to get permission to give certain treatments. Some administrators of HMOs, whose job is to produce profits, end up dictating to doctors what treatment they can give their patients. ("You can do that if you want to, but we won't pay for it.") Some HMOs even determine the number of patients the doctors must see each day.

Being Paid to Stay Healthy

Another attempt to reduce costs is to give workers a rebate for staying healthy—or at least for staying away from doctors. In return for accepting a high annual insurance deductible, employees who spend less than the deductible are paid the difference between it and their insurance claims. If the deductible is, say, $1,500, workers who claim only $100 for medical care collect $1,400, a nice bonus. Where this program has been tried, employee health costs go down. As one employee said, "Now I feel I have an investment in my own health."

Physician Assistants and Nurse Practitioners

Another strategy for controlling costs is to use lower-paid *physician assistants* and *nurse practitioners,* who work under the supervision of physicians. Half to three-fourths of all the problems dealt with in a typical doctor's office are aches, sniffles, and other trivial matters. Physician assistants and nurse practitioners also manage routine tasks like giving school physicals and educating patients who have chronic disorders.

An in-house rivalry has developed. Physician assistants and nurse practitioners don't like doctors breathing down their necks, and they want more independence in treating patients. Their efforts to attain greater autonomy are resisted by doctors, of course, who feel their turf is being invaded. In general, the attitude of the medical profession is, "If they want to do more, they can go to medical school."

As physician assistants and nurse practitioners have pushed the boundaries, they have gained more autonomy. They now run in-store clinics where you can get a physical, flu shot, or vaccination, and in some states they can prescribe basic medications and work free of systematic observation of physicians (Japsen 2016). Some nurses who earn a "doctor of nursing" degree call themselves "doctors," which confuses patients and infuriates physicians (Al-Agba 2017). Physicians are trying to get state legislators to limit the title of doctor only to themselves.

Training Physicians

Today, there are 82 million more Americans than 30 years ago, yet our medical schools graduate only about 2,000 physicians a year more than they did 30 years ago (Statistical Abstract 2018:Tables 2, 322).

This startling statistic should give you insight into why some areas have the doctor shortage we discussed—and how limiting the number of new physicians drives up medical costs. Although the number of graduates has had only a small increase, as you can see from Figure 10.12 a fundamental change has occurred in the gender makeup of those graduates. The gender change is likely to be irrelevant as the medical delivery system is in place, with depersonalization and the profit motive built into it. Female doctors are as likely as male doctors to be generous or greedy, to be patient- or profit oriented, and to favor heroic medicine or preventive medicine.

Figure 10.12 M.D. Degrees, by Sex

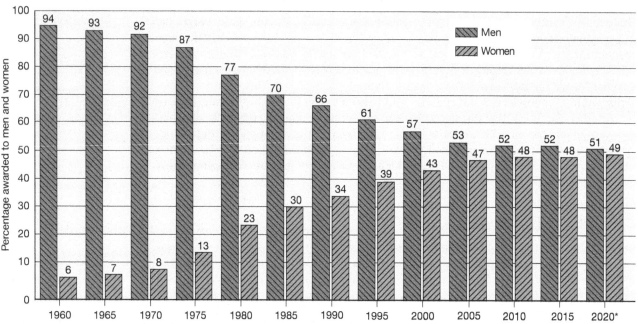

Note: Asterisk indicates author's estimate.

Source: Statistical Abstract of the United States 1994:Table 295; 2018:Table 322.

How to Solve the Doctor Shortage Here is a simple, direct, and far-reaching proposal for social policy: To reduce the costs of health care, overcome the doctor shortage, and provide more care for the poor, let's train more physicians. The government could finance new medical schools. The schools could be tuition free, and the students could be paid a monthly salary. In return, for each year the graduates were supported in medical school, they would spend one year in areas where there is a doctor shortage. These new physicians would not be given final certification until they completed their years of public service. During those years, the government would pay for their medical malpractice insurance and pay them a salary equal to what the average American earns. The United States already has the National Health Service Corps, which offers support for students in medical school, but this would be a much more extensive program. A social policy to increase competition among doctors would be met with shrill protest from the American Medical Association. The AMA stifles competition by limiting the number of medical graduates. If medical schools graduated enough new physicians to produce strong competition among doctors, the cost of medical care would drop, threatening the power of this medical monopoly.

Home Health Care

In Figure 10.8, you saw how expensive hospitalization is. To help reduce medical costs, some doctors are substituting **home health care** (also called **domiciliary care**), treatment given in a patient's home. Most elderly patients prefer home health care, not only because it is less expensive but also because they find it more humane to be treated at home than in an unfamiliar and often depersonalized nursing home or hospital.

We can extend this concept by establishing group homes and supervised apartments for the mentally disturbed and the chronically ill who have difficulty living in the community on their own. There, we can provide them home health care. Such programs would be costly, of course, and granted our ongoing, huge budget deficits, we can ill afford them. You can also anticipate the objection that we would be spending more money on the "unworthy."

Preventive Medicine

Prevention—taking steps that preserve health or avoid illness and disease—can be highly effective. The most preventable cause of premature death is smoking. Each year, a half million (480,000) Americans die from nicotine in its various forms (CDC 2017a). Many other unhealthy lifestyle choices lead to deaths at early ages, especially obesity and lack of exercise. Let's look at how we can improve health and avoid premature deaths.

Three Types of Preventive Medicine   There are three types of prevention. **Primary prevention** keeps a disease from occurring in the first place. Examples are improving nutrition and vaccinating children. **Secondary prevention** refers to detecting a disease before it comes to the attention of a physician. An example is self-examination for breast cancer. **Tertiary prevention** refers to preventing further damage from a disease that has been detected. This is often the same as regular medical care. Examples are maintaining a diabetic on insulin and inserting pacemakers in heart patients.

Food and Health   Primary prevention has a huge payoff for improving health. Proper nutrition, exercise, rest, and avoiding tobacco and the abuse of alcohol and other drugs strengthen the immune system and help people avoid many diseases. Many cancers can be prevented by a diet rich in beta-carotene, raw fruits, vegetables, and nuts. Supplements of natural vitamin C and E also reduce the risk of cancer. So do wheat bran, canola oil, soy milk, cantaloupe, avocados, olive oil, red wine, and leafy green vegetables—cabbage, broccoli, brussels sprouts, and spinach (Kohler et al. 2016; Collins 2018).

Immunizations   Immunizing children is effective primary prevention. Not only do immunizations save lives but also they save vast amounts of money that otherwise would be spent on medical treatment. Yet about 10 percent of U.S. children have not been immunized against chickenpox, diphtheria, hepatitis, measles, mumps, and polio (*Statistical Abstract* 2018:Table 232). This is the overall average. The rate of immunization is lower for children in poverty.

Preventing Drug Abuse   Although not usually thought of as preventive medicine, no program would be complete unless it also included preventing drug abuse. As we have learned in Chapter 4, to reduce drug abuse is to prevent many health problems. Drug abuse prevention programs directed against smoking and alcohol abuse could prevent the untimely deaths of hundreds of thousands of people *each year*. Drug abuse programs, then, are another way to improve the nation's health.

Eating Ourselves to Death   Something disturbing is happening in the United States, and it does not bode well for health. Let me share these two events with you:

> *While waiting for a space shot at Cape Canaveral, Florida, I struck up a conversation with a British couple in their 20s. I asked about their impression of the United States. Hesitantly, they said that they had never seen so many fat people in their lives.*

> *When a friend from Spain arrived, he asked me why there were so many fat Americans.*

Are these valid perceptions or ethnocentric observations of foreigners? Judge for yourself. In 1980, one of four Americans was overweight. This was a huge number of people. But since then, this already large percentage has jumped to seven of every ten American adults (NIH 2016; *Statistical Abstract* 1998:Table 242; 2018:Table 225). Forty percent of Americans are now obese; that is, they weigh 20 percent or more than they should. The cause is not hard to find: Americans eat too much and don't get enough exercise.

Some will say, "So what?" Isn't "fat" just an arbitrary idea of how much people should weigh? And maybe this idea came from a skinny person.

Obesity has become a major health problem in the United States. So far, attempts to solve it have failed. Over the coming years, these two high school students can expect to suffer from severe health problems because of their weight.

Andy Richter/Aurora Photos/Alamy Stock Photo

Unfortunately, we are talking about a great deal more than this. The excess fat that surrounds an obese person's vital organs is more destructive to health than alcohol abuse, with one of five deaths due to excess weight (Olson 2016). Why so many deaths? Among other reasons, people who are overweight are more likely to suffer from diabetes and to have strokes, heart attacks, and cancer (CDC 2018f). Compared with thinner people, when the obese come down with these health problems, they are more likely to die from them (Moussa 2018).

This unprecedented increase in the weight of Americans flies in the face of what we know about preventing health problems. But with cultural tastes for fattening, sweetened, processed foods, the pounds pile on. With the onslaught of advertising, many people grab a soda instead of a glass of water, and sugar-sweetened soft drinks have become one of the causes of the nation's obesity (CDC 2017b). Within this cultural setting—and because fattening, sugary foods taste good—it is difficult to halt this growing problem.

It is also significant to note that prevention is not the primary emphasis in our culture. The primary cultural orientation is to visit a doctor when health problems arise, not to avoid health problems through healthier foods and lifestyles.

The Problem with Preventive Medicine The problem with preventive medicine is that it isn't appealing—it doesn't taste good like all those sugary foods. It violates our desire to eat sweets and swill soft drinks and alcohol. And it goes against our pleasure of being lazy couch potatoes. But these things are killing us. If we want health, we have to work at it. This means eating healthfully, getting the sleep we need, and forcing ourselves to do the exercises that our bodies require to function well.

If the medical profession were to give preventive medicine the same priority it gives heroic medicine and the treatment of acute conditions, the nation's health would improve dramatically. But with its exercise and watching one's weight, preventive medicine is not appealing to a lot of people. It is also holds little appeal to medical people who have been trained for open-heart surgery, screaming ambulances, and rushing about in emergency rooms—or, if not that, at least prescribing pills. And a major problem for both the public and professionals is that, unlike antibiotics or surgery, prevention doesn't show immediate results.

To see how lifestyle can affect people's health on a national basis, read the next *Spotlight on Social Research*.

Spotlight on Social Research

Solving a Medical Mystery

WILLIAM COCKERHAM, *distinguished professor of sociology and chair emeritus at the University of Alabama at Birmingham, studies international aspects of health. He has done research on health and lifestyles in Russia, Eastern Europe, Western Europe, and the United States.*

Cockerham, William

In the mid-1990s, I attended a medical sociology conference in Vienna. Sociologists from the former socialist countries in Eastern Europe reported that their countries were in the midst of a health crisis. They said that men were dying prematurely and that the life expectancy for women had either declined or stagnated. What was striking about their presentations and in the discussions that followed was that no one could explain why this was occurring. That in peacetime an entire group of industrialized societies was experiencing a prolonged deterioration in the health of the population was unexpected.

The lack of an explanation for this crisis presented an intriguing research question. The killer turned out to be an increase in heart disease that began in the mid-1960s and lasted into the 21st century. A review of the evidence showed that infectious diseases, environmental pollution, and poor medical care were not enough to cause this surge in mortality. A clue that other social factors were important was the fact that the rise in death rates was not universal. Heart disease differed by gender, age, urban–rural locale, education, and region. Those most affected were middle-aged, urban men who did manual work.

We now knew the "what" and the "who," but not the "why." To discover the "why," I traveled to Russia and Eastern Europe. There, I collected data from clinics, hospitals, and ministries of health. I also interviewed public health experts, physicians, and sociologists. In addition, I investigated how people lived.

I uncovered three reasons for the increase in premature deaths. The first was a lack of policies addressing the increase in heart disease and adopting measures to lower smoking and drinking. The second seemed to be stress, which had increased with the collapse of communism: Workers had lost jobs and state benefits, such as housing and food subsidies. In addition, inflation had made their money worth less, driving down the value of their pensions and salaries. The third—and the primary reason—turned out to be unhealthy lifestyles. Heavy drinking and smoking and lack of exercise characterized the people who died prematurely from heart disease. To say "heavy" drinking is an understatement: Adult Russian males, who comprise 25 percent of the population, drink 90 percent of the alcohol consumed in a country that averages 14 gallons per person annually.

I did not have enough data, however, to determine conclusively that stress—which has a well-established connection to heart disease—was especially important. A grant from the European Union provided funds to survey 18,000 people in eight countries of the former Soviet Union. This survey showed that women actually are more stressed than men. While stress undoubtedly makes the women's lives less pleasant and has consequences for their health, it is not killing enough of them prematurely to come close to the mortality rates of the men. As bad as the situation may be for the women, the data showed the key to explaining the health crisis ultimately was the health lifestyles of men.

Humanizing Health Care

Jeanne Kennedy, the chief patient representative at Stanford Hospital in Palo Alto, California, broke her kneecap rushing to a meeting. A member of her staff wheeled her to the employee health department, where a nurse practitioner she had worked with for years began to arrange for her care. The nurse spoke to the woman pushing the wheelchair and ignored Mrs. Kennedy.

"It was crazy," she said, "Here I was in my own hospital, hurt but perfectly capable, and she's being very professional, but she's talking over my head as if I were a child. And we worked together. She knew me!" (Carey 2005)

Patients hate being depersonalized, but how can you overcome it? Even when medical students have a strong desire to treat patients as people, the pressures of their training, accompanied by the faculty's stress on organs, disease, and dysfunctions, change the students' attitude about patients. Listen to this medical student:

Somebody will say, "Listen to Mrs. Jones's heart. It's just a little thing flubbing on the table." And you forget about the rest of her . . . and it helps in learning in the sense that you can go in to a patient, put your stethoscope on the heart, listen to it, and walk out. . . . The advantage is that you can go in a short time and see a patient, get the important things out of the patient, and leave (Haas and Shaffir 1993:437).

Ultimately, medical training needs to stress the *inherent worth* of patients—that each individual is valuable and deserves personal attention. Achieving this is certainly an uphill battle because depersonalization has become instinctive to medical personnel. The best social policy, it seems, is the one I proposed to overcome the doctor shortage. If we train enough doctors, we will produce strong competition for patients. Of necessity, doctors will have to treat patients as people. Those who don't will have fewer patients—and less profit.

In Sum   The aim of these policies is to reduce the cost of medical care, improve health by preventing disease, and humanize the treatment of patients (see Figure 10.13).

Figure 10.13 Reducing the Cost of Medical Care

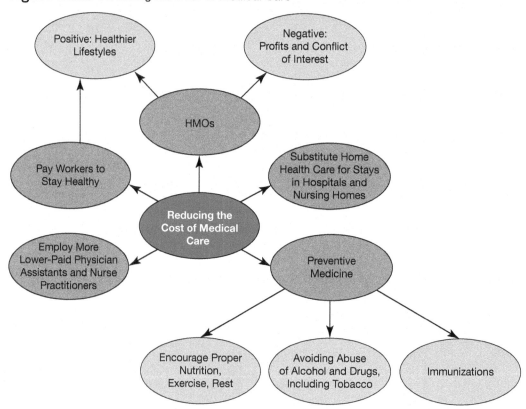

Source: By the author.

These simple, direct policies offer inexpensive alternatives to highly technological and costly medical care. But as we discuss in the next *Issues in Social Problems*, for one problem there is an even simpler solution.

Issues in Social Problems

Doctors, Please Wash Your Hands!

Do you recall the statement I made at the beginning of this chapter, that each year about 400,000 Americans die needlessly at the hands of doctors and nurses? Many of these deaths are so easily preventable that it is infuriating.

Let's look at one type, deaths from catheterization. This term simply refers to inserting a little tube in a vein to deliver drugs or other liquids. This allows a nurse to make quick, easy connections to a tube that is attached to a bag of fluids. About 40,000 patients each year were getting blood stream infections from the catheters. About 5,000 to 10,000 of the patients died from the infections.

After new procedures were followed, the infections and deaths were cut almost in half.

What new procedures could have such dramatic results? Here are the main ones:

1. The doctors wash their hands.
2. The area where the needle is inserted is sterilized.

And there is a third. Breaking with tradition, the nurse is given a checklist and is authorized to tell the doctor that he or she must wash and must follow the

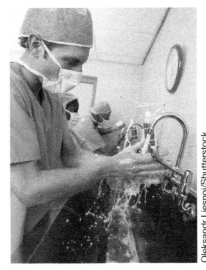

It's a chore for doctors and nurses to wash their hands before visiting each patient. When they don't, they spread disease. Fresh latex gloves for each patient visit are one solution.

checklist and to report the doctor if the doctor does not do so (Mathews 2012). Medical researchers continue to remind doctors how important these basic procedures are (Band and Gaynes 2016).

For Your Consideration

→ What is your reaction to this? To me, this is incredible, and I can hardly stop gritting my teeth at a medical profession that still kills patients out of sloth. The ignorance ended long ago when it was proven—to the amazement of physicians—that there are little things called germs and that women were dying in childbirth because the doctors were transmitting disease with their dirty hands. Reluctantly, the doctors began to wash their hands. Evidently, they have to keep learning this lesson—and evidently patients have to keep dying until they really learn it.

The Future of the Problem

10.8 Discuss the likely future of medical care as a social problem.

To try to catch a glimpse of the future, let's look at trends in medical technology and in changing the direction of medicine.

Technological Advances

Both doctors and patients derive deep satisfaction from medical technology that improves the diagnoses and treatment of medical problems. In the coming years, we can expect doctors to continue to adopt new medical technology and patients to expect their doctors and hospitals to have whatever technology is new. Within this context, the manufacturers of medical equipment will continue to develop and market cutting-edge technologies. You can expect, then, that medical costs will continue to escalate.

Ethical Dilemmas from New Technology Out of these technological advances have arisen ethical problems that plague medical professionals and laypeople alike. If people can be kept alive artificially, must doctors keep them alive? Does "brain dead" really mean "dead"? If so, should physicians be allowed to "harvest body parts" from people who (only because of machines) are still breathing? Should medical researchers be allowed to test dangerous drugs on these people because, after all, they are "really" dead?

In the following *Technology and Social Problems,* we consider how technological advances hold the potential for improving our lives as they simultaneously create ethical dilemmas.

Medical technology is advancing at a fast pace. Shown here are before-and-after photos of a human bone being grown in a laboratory.

Technology and Social Problems

"Need a New Body Part? Turn on Your Printer"

The advances in technology are mind-boggling. Some are so astounding that it is difficult to grasp that what is being developed is even possible. Let's explore one of these leap-frogging changes.

3-D printers are fascinating. Like the replicator of *Star Trek*, the technology allows us to print entire items. By laying down fine layers of whatever substance an item is made of, we can reproduce exact replicas of the item. This can be an item as simple as a cup or as complicated as a motorcycle. And you can drink from the replicated cup or ride the motorcycle, whose parts all work.

We have just begun to explore the implications of this fascinating achievement in technology. How will we apply it beyond making car parts on demand?

How about making human parts on demand? I'm talking about printing body parts such as working blood vessels, real veins and arteries that transport blood through the body. As the technology develops, we might be able to print livers and kidneys so good that we can transplant them into real people.

This isn't just some futurist's dream. 3-D bioprinters that can replicate body tissues and organs are now being developed. Their laser-guided nozzles extrude "bio-inks" of human cells onto a mold. After about 24 hours, the mold is removed, with a bioreactor keeping the tissue alive. As the tissue stitches itself together, it becomes the particular organ it was intended to be (Choudhury et al. 2018).

There are no 3-D–printed kidneys or hearts yet, but they appear to be on the way. One of the problems to be overcome is developing a capillary system to feed the developing tissue. But if you look carefully at the gleams in the bioengineers' eyes, you will see the reflection of patients' X-rays and CT scans transformed into digital diagrams for printed body parts.

What a potential future. Absolutely mind-boggling.

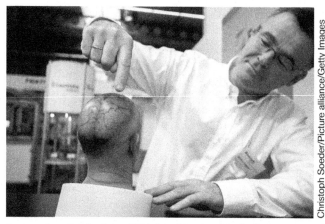

Christoph Soeder/Picture alliance/Getty Images

Are we glimpsing the future? This is a 3D-printed brain. For now, it is just a model. If a working brain is ever printed, will it come with a self? Or would a self develop? If so, would it mark the end of humans?

For Your Consideration

→ When the time comes that we can print replacement body parts—likely to occur soon—do you think we can continually replace our worn-out parts so we can live indefinitely, or at least for a couple of hundred years or so?

→ And if Mary Leticia, a star athlete, decides to enhance her running by printing out a new knee, one that improves her performance, should she be allowed to compete with people who are left with their old joints?

→ Then there is the matter of social equality. If a rich woman can pay more for a new body part, should she be given preference over a poor woman?

→ How about a prisoner convicted of rape and murder? Should he be given the same consideration as your sociology instructor?

A Final Note

You have seen how health and illness, disease and death, are much more than biological matters. Running through this chapter is an emphasis on social factors that affect who is sick and who is healthy, who gets what disease, and who dies and who lives. I have stressed the two-tier aspect of the medical delivery system, which might be tinkered with from time to time, but which I do not expect to fundamentally change. The rich will always receive better health care than the poor—and will also live healthier lifestyles.

You have seen how significant lifestyle is to health. I expect that the medical delivery system will gradually place more emphasis on "wellness," and that our future medical system will feature both heroic intervention and preventive medicine, one alongside the another.

If you take anything away from this chapter for your own life, it should be how important lifestyle is, that your lifestyle choices are so significant that they affect your health down the road. To make wise choices is up to you.

Summary and Review

1. What people consider to be health and illness varies with culture and social class. Physical and mental health problems are based on both biological and social factors.

2. Industrialization has brought better health, but with industrialization has come an increase in cancer, heart disease, drug addiction, and chronic illnesses caused by lifestyle, aging, and environmental pollution. HIV/AIDS illustrates the relationship among behavior, environment, and disease. Physical and emotional problems are more common among the poor. To explain the relationship between social class and mental illness, sociologists prefer environmental explanations rather than genetic ones.

3. The U.S. medical system is centered on specialized, hospital-based care and heroic intervention. A fee-for-service system increases medical costs. Preventive medicine redirects the emphasis to people's lifestyles and environment.

4. Social inequalities plague physical and mental health care. In our fee-for-service system, health care is not a right but a commodity sold to the highest bidder. The United States has a *two-tier system of medical care*—public clinics and poorer treatment for the poor and private clinics and better treatment for the more affluent. Despite health care reform and universal insurance, the poor and affluent will not receive the same medical treatment.

5. Two policies designed to control medical costs are to pay patients to stay healthy and to pay doctors to reduce unnecessary medical care. *HMOs* are a form of *managed care* that provides a fixed amount of money to a medical corporation to attend to the health needs of a group of people. Medical services and tests come directly off the corporate bottom line, leading to a conflict of interest in treating patients. On the positive side, it costs the HMO less if providers catch problems early and if they practice preventive medicine.

6. The medical profession is experiencing a tension among its traditional focus on heroic intervention in acute problems, the need to treat chronic problems, and the emerging focus on preventing medical problems by changing lifestyles. Within this tension, there is likely to develop increased emphasis on preventive medicine—better health habits, a cleaner environment, and education designed to teach people how to take care of themselves and to manage their illnesses.

Thinking Critically about Chapter 10

1. What do you think the government's role should be in medical care? Why?
2. Why do you think women live longer than men?
3. Which of the theoretical perspectives (symbolic interactionism, functionalism, or conflict theory) do you think best explains health care problems in the United States? Why do you think so?
4. How can you apply the content of this chapter to your own life?

Key Terms

antiretroviral drugs, 310
cesarean section, 295
conversion therapy, 303
defensive medicine, 304
depersonalization, 304
domiciliary care, 316
drug therapy, 313
electroconvulsive therapy (ECT), 314
group therapy, 313
health maintenance organization (HMO), 314
home health care, 316
iatrogenesis, 291
individual psychotherapy, 313

infant mortality rate, 297
lay referral network, 303
managed care, 314
pharmaceutical straitjackets, 314
prepaid care, 314
primary prevention, 317
professional referral network, 304
psychoanalysis, 313
secondary prevention, 317
short-term directive therapy, 313
talk therapy, 314
tertiary prevention, 317
two-tier system of medical care, 295

Chapter 11
The Changing Family

Elizabeth Crew/The Image Works

 Learning Objectives

After reading this chapter, you should be able to:

11.1 Summarize how the Industrial Revolution changed the family.

11.2 Understand how divorce, one-parent families, violence, and runaway children are part of the problem.

11.3 Discuss the perspectives that emerge when you apply symbolic interactionism, functionalism, and conflict theory to why divorce is common.

11.4 Summarize research findings on postponing marriage, couples without children, family violence, sexual abuse, the elderly, and the death of the family.

11.5 Explain the controversy over professional intrusion into the family and the dilemma of family policy.

11.6 Discuss the trends and social changes that are likely to affect family relationships.

Nancy and Antoine were pleased. Their 4-year-old daughter, Janelle, had been accepted at Rainbow Gardens Preschool in Manhattan Beach, California, a prosperous suburb of Los Angeles. The preschool came highly recommended by their close friends, whose son was attending the school. With Nancy's promotion and Antoine's new job, schedules had become more difficult, and Rainbow Gardens was able to handle their need for flexible hours.

At first, Janelle loved preschool. She would happily leave whichever parent drove her to school for the pleasures of her little friends and the gentle care of loving teachers. Then, gradually, almost imperceptibly, a change came over her. At first, Janelle became reluctant to leave her parents. Then she began to whimper in the mornings when they were getting her ready for school. And lately she had begun to have nightmares. She was waking up crying and screaming several times a week, something she had never done before. They took Janelle to a counselor. She said it was nothing to worry about, that all kids go through things like this from time to time. This was just a "developmental adjustment" and a "separation anxiety." Their daughter would be just fine in a little while.

> **Those gentle teachers, so affectionate with the children, child molesters?**

When allegations of sexual abuse of 3-, 4-, and 5-year-olds at Rainbow Gardens made headlines, parents around the nation were devastated. The unthinkable had become real. "Was it happening at our preschool, too? Could it be happening with our child?" they wondered. But for Nancy and Antoine, it was more than a nagging question. Overnight, Janelle's nightmares, her crying, and her bed-wetting took on new meaning. Those gentle teachers, so affectionate with the children, child molesters? Janelle undressed, photographed, forced to commit sexual acts with adults, and threatened with the death of her puppy if she told?

Nancy and Antoine don't know. It is either this or simply a "developmental adjustment," maybe just a normal "separation anxiety"? Now it is Nancy's and Antoine's turn for nightmares.

The Problem in Sociological Perspective

11.1   Summarize how the Industrial Revolution changed the family.

Nightmare at Rainbow Gardens could be the title of a horror movie, a real-life one for some parents. During the 1980s, rumors spread that day care centers were filled with child molesters. A kind of hysteria swept the country, with preschool teachers suspect. Some teachers were tried and convicted, sometimes on flimsy evidence (Gillies 2017). A Massachusetts man served 18 years in prison before his pleas of innocence were finally acknowledged.

Although the headlines of that time were based on hysteria, some children are abused at day school, a frightening prospect for parents. Why aren't the children at home with their families? Why are 2 million U.S. children under the age of 5 entrusted to the care of strangers in day care (*Statistical Abstract* 2018:Table 592)?

Day care is part of a sea change that has swept our society, engulfing families and forcing them to adjust. As we review problems facing families in this chapter, we'll stress this theme: the impact of social change.

Effects of the Industrial Revolution on the Family

Let's begin by looking at how the Industrial Revolution changed the family. Before industrialization, econoomic survival was perilous. It was common for families to live on the edge of disaster. There were no factories, offices, or public schools, and both parents and children worked at home together. With industrialization, production moved to factories, bringing consequences for family life that continue today.

Men Left Home   Men left home to work in factories. This created a divide between the husband-father and the other family members. During workday hours—which were long, about 12 to 14 hours a day—the husband-father was at work in the factory, while the wife and children were working at home. No longer did the family members share activities during working hours. Separated from the household, the husband-father's orientation to life changed.

Children Became an Economic Liability Industrialization transformed children from an economic asset into an economic liability. When production was farm-based, children contributed to their family's survival—they fed chickens, milked cows, and worked in the fields. After industrialization, children no longer helped produce food, but they still consumed it.

Formal Education Industrialization brought a need for more formal education and opened opportunities to acquire it. As children spent more years in school, they became dependent on their parents for a longer time. Their prolonged education and longer dependency made them even more expensive.

A Lower Birthrate The discovery of vulcanized rubber during the 1840s made large-scale production of the condom possible. With further refinements in design and manufacture in the 1920s, the condom allowed couples to limit births. The birth control pill that came in the 1970s allowed couples even more control over pregnancy. In Figure 11.1, you can see how the U.S. birthrate plunged.

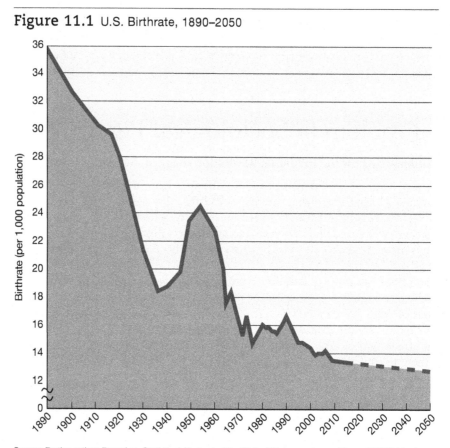

Figure 11.1 U.S. Birthrate, 1890–2050

Source: By the author. Based on *Statistical Abstract of the United States,* various editions; 2001:Table 4; 2013:Table 81; 2018:Table 3.

From Rural to Urban Industrialization also changed where people lived. In the 1800s, almost everyone lived on farms. As production moved to city factories, workers moved to where the work was. Housing in the city was more expensive, another reason for couples to have fewer children.

Loss of Functions Families used to be responsible for producing their own food and clothing, educating their children, and providing their own medical care. As industrialization spread, other institutions began to take over these functions. Factories produced food and clothing, schools educated the children, and health care systems took over the care of illness. Losing these functions weakened families.

Changes in Women's Roles Industrialization also changed women's roles. The farm wife used to be responsible for producing basic food (milk, butter, eggs, vegetables), preparing food (baking and cooking), and storing food (canning). She also made, washed, ironed, and mended the family's clothing; cleaned the house; and took care of the children, the sick, and the elderly. As her functions were reduced, the wife/mother increasingly became an "emotional provider"; that is, she spent more time giving attention to her breadwinner husband and to her diminishing number of children.

Greater Equality Industrialization also brought greater equality to husbands and wives. As men's and women's roles changed, so did ideas about how their relationship "ought to be." This change was gradual and did not happen without struggle. Men were reluctant to give up their more privileged positions. The struggle over equality (authority and decision-making) is still a primary source of tension in today's marriages.

More Divorce Before industrialization, divorce was rare. But with the changes just outlined, especially the reduced functions of the family and the lower birthrate, marriages became fragile.

Longer Lives and More Intergenerational Ties With industrialization came improvements in public health, especially a purer water supply and advances in medicine. With better health, people lived longer than ever before. One consequence is that today's children are more likely to have living grandparents, and even great-grandparents. This is new in world history. Many grandparents who live nearby provide in-home day care while the children's parents are at work. In an age of telecommunication, grandparents who live far from their grandchildren are still able to participate in their lives.

The "Quiet Revolution" One of the fundamental changes in family life was a transformation of women's roles—women leaving home to enter the paid workforce. As office work expanded, employers hired more and more women. Then during World War II (1939–1945), millions of women took over the factory jobs the men left when they went off to war. This process continued, with the 1980s marking the first time in history that half of married women worked for wages at least part-time outside the home. Today 59 percent do (*Statistical Abstract* 2018:Table 622). Because women working at paid jobs outside the home bring extensive change to family relationships, it is sometimes called the *quiet revolution.*

In Sum   For the family to provide for the well-being of its members, it must adjust to the changes that occur in society (see Figure 11.2). In some ways, the family is always in transition. Just as the family adapted to the Industrial Revolution, so today it is coping with the post-industrializing of society.

Paul Aresu/UpperCut Images/Getty Images

The family is always adjusting to changes that are taking place in society. As ideas of masculinity change, for example, behaviors that once were not acceptable for men come to be thought of as normal. After those changes become standard, a current generation may have difficulty understanding why some behaviors ever threatened men's sense of "masculinity."

John Parrot/Stocktrek Images, Inc./Alamy Stock Photo

"Man for man, America's workers and America's soldiers are the best in the world! We helped them build our nation . . . we'll help them defend it."

PRODUCE FOR VICTORY!

I chose this photo because of the message." Man for man, America's workers..." and the photo is of a woman! When millions of men were sent overseas to fight in World War II, women took their places in factories and offices. The assumption was that the women would go back to housework after the war. Many did, but an immense historical change had been set in motion.

Figure 11.2 How Industrialization Changed the Family

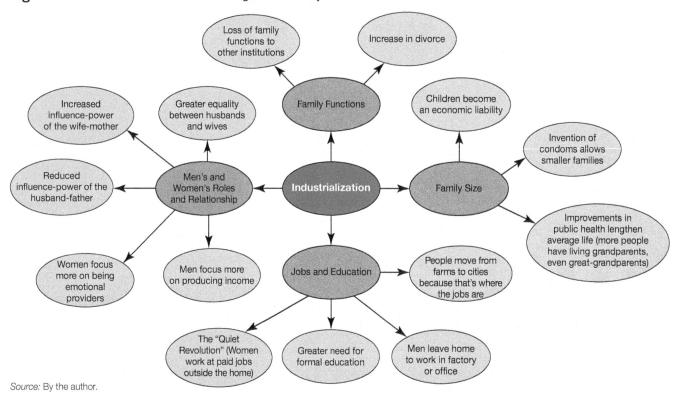

Source: By the author.

The Scope of the Problem

11.2 **Understand how divorce, one-parent families, violence, and runaway children are part of the problem.**

A lot of people are bothered by what is happening to today's families. Our current social changes are powerful, and many families are having a hard time. Some even think that the family is disintegrating. As always, we want to move beyond subjective concerns and examine objective conditions. What indications, if any, might suggest that the family is in trouble?

Divorce

When you say "family problems," divorce is one of the first things that people think of. In Figure 11.3, you can trace the changes in divorce since 1970. From something rare, divorce has become so common that it has disrupted the family life of millions of Americans.

Figure 11.3 How Many Millions of Americans Are Divorced?

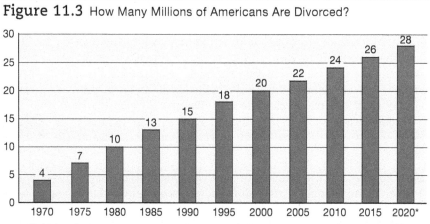

Note: *Author's estimate.

Source: By the author. Based on *Statistical Abstract of the United States* 1989:Table 50; 2013:Table 56; 2018:Table 56.

Another way to look at the trend in divorce is to compare the number of Americans who are getting married with the number who are getting divorced. As Figure 11.4 shows, for every two couples getting married, another couple is ending its marriage. Note this is not the same as saying one out of every two marriages ends in divorce. The divorces are coming from marriages of earlier years.

Figure 11.4 American Marriage, American Divorce

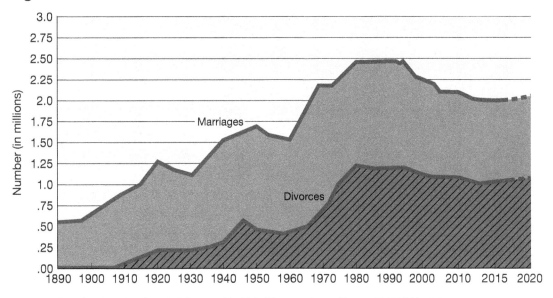

Source: By the author. Based on *Statistical Abstract of the United States*, various editions and 2018:Table 137.

Could Divorce Be a Sign of Strength?   This might surprise you, but it's possible to interpret divorce statistics as a sign that marriages are improving and families are becoming stronger. Here's the thinking: No longer willing to put up with miserable marriages, men and women end them. They then look for new partners, and most end up with more satisfying marriages. In fact, they keep divorcing and looking until they find a relationship that satisfies them enough to at least stay together.

Whether or not this interpretation is correct, if you look closely at Figure 11.4 you will see something positive about our divorce rate. After rising for about 80 years, the divorce rate peaked in 1980 and then held steady for about 15 years. After this, it started dropping and since then has been holding at the lower levels. As you can see, marriage has followed this same path. The ratio of approximately one divorce for every two marriages has also held steady.

Ripples into the Future

> At a sociology convention, I was talking to one of my former professors. After he told me how miserable he was in his marriage, I asked him why he didn't divorce. He said that he didn't want to set a bad example for his children.

What my former professor was referring to is *the divorce cycle.* When the children of divorced parents grow up and marry, they are more likely to divorce than people whose parents didn't divorce. It could be, as my former professor was indicating, that children learn from their parents that divorce is a solution to marital problems—and they run faster when problems develop in marriage. Another possibility is that as children they lived with unhappy, quarreling parents before the divorce, and they learned negative patterns of interaction with a spouse. Regardless of the root cause, and both could be part of it, on average the adult children of divorced parents are unable to cope with marriage as well as married adults whose parents did not divorce.

To see how greatly divorce rates differ from one state to another. Look at the following Social Map. In the extreme, Arkansas' divorce rate is *four* times higher than that of Iowa's.

Figure 11.5 Divorce and Geography

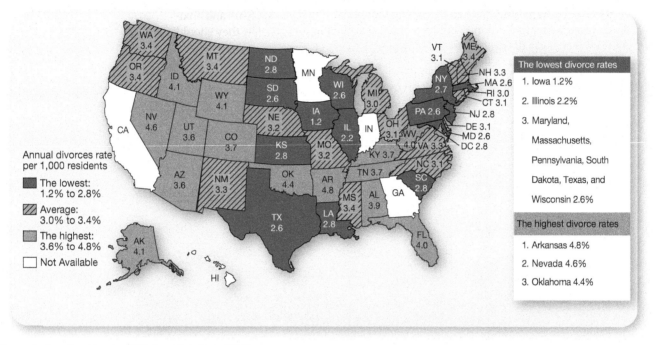

Source: By the author. Based on *"Kids Count Data Center"* 2018.

Sociologists have found that the effects of divorce don't stop with the adult children of divorced parents. Instead, they ripple across generations: Even the grandchildren of couples who divorced don't get along as well with their spouses as those whose grandparents did not divorce (Amato and Cheadle 2005; Amato 2010).

Beyond the Numbers Divorce involves things that we can't measure with numbers—the crushed hopes and dreams of adults and children; the bitterness, anger, and scarring. And on the positive side for many, relief and the hope of new beginnings. Each year, divorce disrupts the lives of about 600,000 children (*Statistical Abstract* 2018:Table 139), filling them with uncertainty, anxiety, and fear as their parents break up—and they feel deserted with an uncertain future. Divorce is so extensive that almost one of every three children lives with just one parent. This is a huge number, about 23 million children who don't live with both parents (*Statistical Abstract* 2018:Table 66). From Figure 11.6, you can see how these percentages differ with race–ethnicity.

Figure 11.6 Where Do U.S. Children Live?

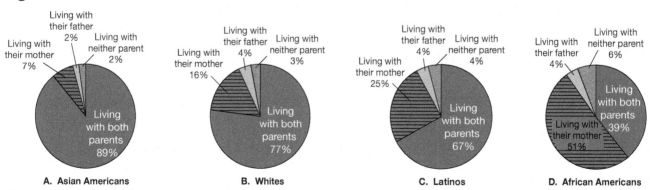

Note: The source reports these data on only these groups.

Sources: By the author. *Statistical Abstract of the United States* 2018:Table 66.

The Nagging Dilemma of Divorce   For few adults is divorce a trivial matter. The decision to divorce is usually painful, often preceded by years of dissatisfaction and unhappiness. Couples who divorce find themselves on an emotional roller-coaster, fears and anxiety looming about an uncertain future. Many try to patch things up, feeling they should "hang in there" longer, especially "for the children." Common are feelings of being torn apart as the identity markers that had become such a significant part of their lives are shredded. Many are plagued by guilt and thoughts of "what might have been." Remorse comes, too, about the years "wasted" with the wrong person. And for parents, always, nagging concerns about how their children are going to adjust.

The children of quarreling parents also find themselves embroiled in a world of turmoil, murky, with no clear answers. If their parents remain together, they live in a troubled family. If their parents divorce, they live in disturbing uncertainty. Researchers debate the effects of divorce on children: Some claim that divorce scars children for life, while others say children are better off removed from unhealthy relationships. Divorce has no single effect on children, so both claims are probably true. Divorce helps some children and hurts others. So, does the parents staying together.

One-Parent Families

A major cause of one-parent families is divorce, which we have considered. The second major cause is births to unmarried women.

Births to Unmarried Women   Figure 11.7 shows how births to single women have increased over the years. Of all babies in the United States, two of every five (40 percent) are now born to single mothers (*Statistical Abstract* 2018:Table 89). This is 50 percent higher than it was in 1990, a total that comes to 1.6 million a year.

Figure 11.7 Births to Single Women by Race–Ethnicity

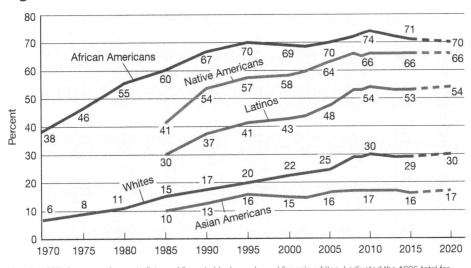

Note: In 2000, the source began to list non-Hispanic blacks and non-Hispanic whites. I adjusted the 1995 total for whites accordingly. (The source total for blacks was unchanged.) Broken lines indicate the author's estimates.

Source: By the author. Based on *Statistical Abstract of the United States* 1992:Table 87; 1998:Table 100; 2018:Table 89.

As you have seen throughout this text, social problems often follow lines of race–ethnicity. This pattern also shows up in matters of the family. From Figure 11.7, you can see how the proportion of births to single women differs among racial–ethnic groups. Births to unmarried Native American and African American women are four times higher than births to single Asian American women.

The Geography of Having Just One Parent   Divorce and births to single women can be looked at as individual matters, of course, and they are. When multiplied by millions, though, their consequences reverberate throughout society. The numbers are staggering. With our high rates of divorce and births to single women, 20 million children live without fathers at home. About *1/2 million* live without their mothers. Another 3 million have neither a mother nor a father at home (*Statistical Abstract* 2018:Table 66). As always, overall statistics conceal significant variations. The Social Map shows how the states compare in the percentage of families that are headed by single parents. You can see how single parenting is concentrated in the South.

Figure 11.8 Families Headed by Single Parents

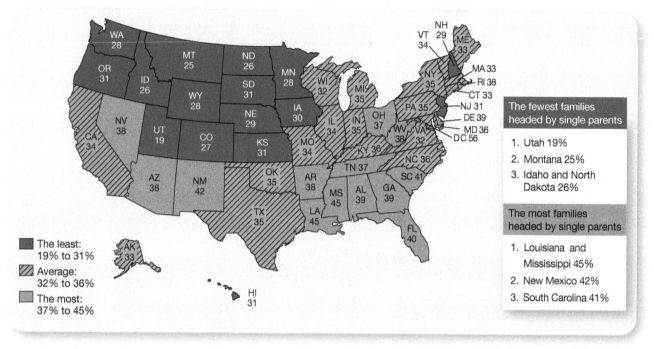

The least: 19% to 31%

Average: 32% to 36%

The most: 37% to 45%

The fewest families headed by single parents

1. Utah 19%
2. Montana 25%
3. Idaho and North Dakota 26%

The most families headed by single parents

1. Louisiana and Mississippi 45%
2. New Mexico 42%
3. South Carolina 41%

Source: By the author. Based on "Kids Count Data Center" 2018.

Impact on Children Single parents have major disadvantages in rearing children. The first is that they are likely to have less income than two-parent families. The second is that it is more difficult for a single mother or father to be an effective parent than it is for a mother and father who are working together to rear their children. The two have more time to help with homework and even to play with the children. They also are able to discuss the children's problems, decide on courses of action, and back each other up when it comes to dealing with rebellious teenagers.

One of the most remarkable consequences of one-parent families is that the children are more likely to drop out of school. This applies to every region of the country and to every racial–ethnic group. There is no group in which children reared by both parents are more likely to drop out of school. This also applies to other countries (Mikkonen et al. 2016; Nonoyama-Tarumi 2017). This statistic says nothing about the individual child, of course. Although children from mother-headed homes are more likely to drop out of school, any particular child may go far in school and become a physician or (and what can you expect of this author) a sociologist. But on average, the absence of a father leads to less education.

Absence of the Father Not having their father as a role model is significant for children. Millions of boys and girls must learn the male role from their mothers, their mother's boyfriends, and from television and the streets. They often end up with grossly inadequate role models. Some boys are fortunate in being able to learn positive masculinity from highly involved grandparents and uncles.

The impact of the father is so powerful that even fathers who do not live with the mother and children make a difference. If a nonresident father is involved in his children's everyday lives, the children are more likely to stay in school and stay out of trouble with the law. Unfortunately, involved nonresident fathers are the exception: Most fathers who don't live with their children are not involved in their children's lives (Hawkins et al. 2007; Cheadle et al. 2010).

Trying to Be Two Parents   One-parent families are not limited to those headed by mothers, of course. Children reared by their fathers also face tremendous obstacles. Some are mirror images of the mother-headed family, especially the problem of a single father teaching womanhood to his daughter, a task that in a two-parent family falls primarily on the mother. Whether man or woman, the single parent must try to be both mother and father. If not impossible, this certainly is a formidable responsibility.

Discipline   A recurring problem in all families is how to discipline children. They need guidance, role models, and corrective measures when they disobey or get in trouble. But deciding what disciplinary methods to use and how long to apply them is difficult, and it is easy to veer to excessive leniency or excessive control. The teen years are especially challenging. I survived them (barely), but it was difficult to determine when to be strict and when to be lenient—and no matter which you choose, to not know whether you are right or wrong. To find the proper balance of explanation, support, reward, and punishment is not easy for any two parents, but it is more difficult for one parent to achieve than for two, who can discuss the situation and together try to make the best choice.

The Cross-Cultural Context   Let's go beyond these findings and add cross-cultural data. Figure 11.9, which shows the rates of births to single women in 10 industrialized nations, might stretch your thinking a bit. You can see that in six of these nations the rates of births to single women are higher than ours. Yet their rates of juvenile delinquency and violent crime are lower than ours. This means that something other than single parenting is at work. That "something else" is the culture within which one-parent families live. I suggest that the significant factors are family support systems, subcultures of violence, access to guns, and perhaps views of life. We sociologists have not unraveled this thorny problem.

Figure 11.9 Births to Single Women in Ten Most Industrialized Nations

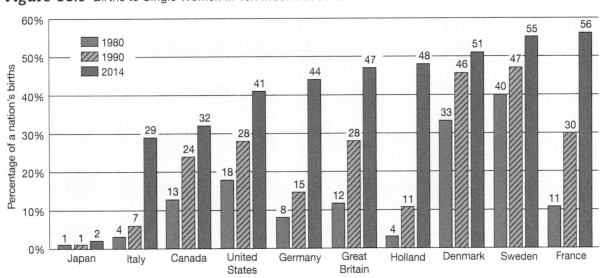

Note: The OECD source, although 2018, has statistics only to 2014.

Source: By the author. Based on *Statistical Abstract of the United States* 2013:Table 1351; 2018:Table 91; OECD Family Database 2018.

Other Problems

Two other family problems are runaway children and violence.

Runaway Children   The FBI used to report the number of runaway children each year, but it no longer does. With no central agency keeping records on runaway children, we lack good data. You might hear in the news that 1 million children run away from home each year, but this number is not real. It is made up to gain the public's attention. Whatever the total, we do know that the children are not fleeing happy homes. Some have been abused sexually at home. The parents of some of these children told them to leave ("**pushouts**"), while others knew they were leaving and did not care.

The streets are tough, and survival is precarious. Some fall into the hands of predators, making their already bruised, fragile lives even more desperate. Some **pedophiles** (adults who are sexually attracted to children) and pimps prowl about bus stations and the streets, looking for children who appear lonely, confused, and vulnerable. When children tire of sleeping in doorways, the alternative to hunger is to beg, steal, or turn to the only thing they have—their bodies. Many runaways get involved in prostitution and pornography when they have no money and no place to go.

Family Violence   Another indication of family problems is violence. Police and welfare workers know the scene all too well: the battered child, wife, husband, parent, or even grandparent. Few cases of family violence make the news, but those that do are when one (almost always the wife) calls the police, and (almost always) the husband shoots an intervening police officer. We will look at family violence in more detail later.

How times change! In the 1890s, this was standard child discipline, even the use of a special paddling board. Fathers also used their belts and switches (little branches cut from trees).

Jupiterimages/Stockbyte/Getty Images

In Sum Violence, divorce, runaway children, and so on indicate severe problems in the American family. They do not indicate, however, that the family is disintegrating. Although the contemporary family is in trouble, as a social institution it will endure. Humans have found no satisfactory substitute for the family, and millions of people report that marriage and family meet their needs for intimacy and sense of identity and belonging. The focus of this book, however, is on *social problems*, so I am not extolling the satisfactions and even joys some find in marriage and family life.

At this point, let's see what different pictures emerge when we turn our theoretical lenses on divorce, to see why it is so common.

Looking at the Problem Theoretically: Why Is Divorce Common?

11.3 **Discuss the perspectives that emerge when you apply symbolic interactionism, functionalism, and conflict theory to why divorce is common.**

For most of us, the family is our major support system. Our family nourishes and protects us when we are young. It gives us security and love and shapes our personality. Sociologists call the family that rears us our **family of orientation** because it introduces us to the world and teaches us ways to cope with life. As a result, most people around the world try to establish stability, identity, and intimacy through marriage. A married couple having its first child forms what is called a **family of procreation**.

With the high value placed on marriage and family and the many benefits they offer, why is divorce common? Let's use our theoretical perspectives to better understand how divorce is related to changes in society. As always, each perspective is a lens that yields a unique interpretation, but, as you will see, these perspectives dovetail neatly with one another.

Symbolic Interactionism: Changing Symbols

To explain why our divorce rate is so high, symbolic interactionists examine what people *expect* out of marriage.

The Love Symbol: Immersed in Unrealistic Expectations In 1933, sociologist William Ogburn noted that people were placing more emphasis on personality as they chose a husband or wife. A few years later, in 1945, sociologists Ernest Burgess and Harvey Locke observed that affection, understanding, and compatibility were becoming more central to marriage. These sociologists were observing a major shift in mate selection, a trend that has amplified until "affection, understanding, and compatibility" are now considered an essential part of a "healthy" marriage, and today's husbands and wives expect their spouse to meet most of their emotional needs. These expectations have been bound symbolically into what we call "love," idealized in phrases like "Love conquers all" and "Find your true love." Love is now so prized and expected that our "natural" response has become "Why else would you marry?"

Our cultural expectation of "finding your one true love" who will bring you "true happiness" sets us up for disappointment. We come to expect that marriage will give us some sort of perpetual emotional high. Marriage simply cannot deliver this. When disappointments arise in marriage, as they inevitably do, and usually fairly soon after the "I dos" are said, spouses tend to blame one another. Each believes that the other has somehow failed the relationship. Their engulfment in the *idea* of love—what love is supposed to do for them—blinds them to the reality of day-to-day married life. Our culture promotes an impossibility: that marriage, ideally a lifelong relationship, should be based on a temporary emotional state.

For a highly contrasting view of love and its role in mate selection, see the following *Global Glimpse*.

A Global Glimpse

Arranged Marriage in India: Probing Beneath the Surface

The idea that parents should choose their child's husband or wife shocks Western sensibilities. Arranged marriage seems to violate our basic ideas of the rights of individuals to forge their own path in life. And it does just that. In fact, this is what is wrong with the Western system, say the Indians. Young people don't have the experience to make such life-significant decisions. They need to depend on their elders, who have more experience. Their parents know them well, have their best interests at heart, and can make a much better choice of mate than they can.

Such thinking is foreign to us, of course. It is almost the polar opposite of what we expect and see as the right way to do things. The distinction gets even more complicated when we learn that Indians' ideas of love also differ from ours. We expect love to occur before marriage, and to base marriage on love. Indians expect to base marriage on wise parental decisions, and then love will develop after marriage.

We each—the Westerner and the Indian—shake our heads in wonderment at the strange customs of the other. Each wonders how life could possibly work out the way the other does things.

But each system works. So perhaps we can learn from one another. I have done work in several states of India, so let me share with you what I learned from the experience of an Indian friend. As I saw an arranged marriage unfold, I realized that there is much more to this process than met my Western eye.

My friend, Atal, began to look for a husband for his daughter, Bhanumati. From my Western perspective, this was a strange approach to marriage, but as I observed the process, my perspective changed. I saw that this was a burden for Atal. It was a part of his father role, and everyone—his wife, daughter, and son—was looking to him expectantly. They had full confidence that he would do right, a confidence that placed a heavy burden on his shoulders.

Bhanumati is a pretty young woman, age 23, intelligent, with an engaging personality. She is also educated, with a master's degree in English. Despite her education, Bhanumati would never

Even though India is embracing the capitalist system, is part of global markets, and is changing rapidly, most marriages are still arranged by the father. Shown here are newlyweds at their wedding dance.

question this process of mate selection. Nor did her brother when it came time for his marriage. This traditional way of mate selection in India makes sense to the people who live there.

I saw Atal's disappointment as he tried to fulfill his duty of arranging a good marriage for his daughter. He made several overtures to families of eligible sons, only to be rejected. My friend is a poor man, and he was unable to afford the dowry that these parents demanded. Atal's problem was unexpectedly solved when a young American visitor "fell in love" with Bhanumati. *This man, an engineer with a good job, would make a good husband. Everyone—Atal, his wife, his son, and his daughter—approved of the match. The man, of course, had to follow the Indian custom of seeing his future bride only in the presence of her parents or brother.*

Behind the scenes of arranged marriages, as you can sense, there is much more than the father's decision. The responsibility is laid on him, but to fulfill it and keep a good family life, the father must have his family's agreement. Without it, the system fails.

My friend is a good man, a gentle and considerate husband and father. Tradition laid this responsibility on him, and he fulfilled it well. You can see that other men might have used this power to benefit themselves and not their child. You can also see how this duty is an example of the *patriarchy* we reviewed in Chapter 9, of how power is vested in men.

As strange as it seems to us, the Indian view of love works. With the marriage arranged, Bhanumati is free to develop feelings of love for her husband-to-be. From marriage, the Indians say, comes love. We, of course, say that marriage comes from love. Americans and Indians confuse one another, but perhaps sharing this experience will help you to understand a different way of life.

For Your Consideration

→ Why do you think that educated Indians still go along with the custom of arranged marriages?
→ What advantages and disadvantages do you see in the Indian system of mate selection? In the U.S. system of mate selection?

Changing Ideas about Children   Ideas about children have also undergone a deep shift, so much so that some customs of earlier generations can seem strange to us. Some historians say that people in medieval society viewed children as miniature adults, and they made no sharp separation between the worlds of adults and children. Other historians disagree (Aries 1962; Corsaro 2017). Whatever the reality might be, at the age of 7, boys began to work as apprentices, learning an occupation, while girls remained at home, learning homemaking duties associated with their future wifely role.

These customs don't make sense to us. We consider age 7 to be a tender phase of early childhood, not a time for apprenticeship. In short, children have undergone a cultural transformation from learning adult occupations into impressionable, vulnerable, and innocent beings. As ideas of children have changed, so have ideas of parenting. These new expectations have placed stress on marriage.

Changing Expectations of Parenting   It might surprise you, but until about 1940 U.S. children "became adults" when they graduated from the eighth grade. For most, this was the end of their formal schooling, and they went to work. Because we now expect children to be dependent much longer, and we think of 14- and 15-year-olds as children, not as young adults, we expect parents to continue to nurture them for many more years. We have even developed new ideas of "good" parenting, notions unheard of during earlier generations, such as expecting parents to help their children achieve "self-actualization" so they can "reach their full potential." These changed expectations have placed greater responsibilities on the already burdened shoulders of the parents.

Changing Marital Roles   Just as you would expect, as parenting roles shift, so do marital roles. It used to be assumed as "natural" that the husband would be the **breadwinner**, that his earnings would be the primary source of support for the family. It was also assumed that the wife would be the **homemaker**, that she would stay home, take care of the house and children, and attend to the personal needs of her husband and children. If each did these things well, they were considered a good husband and father, wife and mother. Traditional roles—whatever their faults—provided clear-cut guidelines for newlyweds. After a couple married, each knew what to expect of the other.

Today, the roles of husband and wife are not defined clearly, and newlyweds are expected to work out their own marital realities. Although this gives them a great deal of flexibility, it also produces tension and conflict. A couple's ideas may not mesh. Who is supposed to do what housework? How should they divide child-rearing responsibilities? How much should they save? How much should they spend? On what? Wives are asking to what extent they should be career-oriented, while husbands wonder how much more they should focus on the home. When guidelines for any role, including marriage and parenting, are unclear, frustration and discontent are inevitable. How do you fulfill a marital role if you can't agree on what that role is?

In Sum   What marriage means to people has changed. The idea that love brings unlimited emotional satisfaction has become a source of shattered dreams. Our new ideas about children, parenting, and being a husband or wife also place tremendous pressure on spouses. This pressure and the tensions it brings create an "emotional overload" that becomes a push toward divorce.

Perception of Alternatives   While these historical changes in the expectations of marriage were occurring, more women began to work outside the home. This, too, changed people's ideas about marriage. As wives earned paychecks of their own, they began to perceive alternatives to living in unhappy marriages. As symbolic interactionists stress, the *perception of alternatives* is an essential first step to making divorce possible.

Childhood varies from culture to culture and changes with time. The portrait of this little girl, Mademeoiselle Busseuil, was painted by Antoine Vestier (1740–1824). Because the paintings of the 1600s and 1700s show children dressed as adults, some conclude that Europeans at this time saw children as miniature adults.

Changing Ideas about Divorce   It is difficult for us to grasp how seriously divorce was once taken. Divorce used to represent failure, irresponsibility, even immorality. Divorced people were social outcasts: Suspected of immoral behavior, they no longer were welcome as dinner guests. As divorce became more common, however, its meaning was transformed—from a symbol of failure to a "new start." Divorce no longer suggests shame and immorality, but, rather, opportunity and self-actualization. This symbolic leap added one more push toward divorce. When divorce carries a stigma, it is held in check, but to view divorce as a sign of personal change and development sets the stage for ending marriages. The thinking becomes "Maybe this is no longer right for me, if it ever was, and it is time to move on." Couples even tell others, "We just outgrew one another."

The best indicator of this fundamental change? Today's divorce parties.

Legal Changes   You might be surprised, too, at how difficult it once was to get a divorce. One spouse was required to prove severe abuse or adultery. In New York, where adultery was the only grounds for divorce, witnesses had to testify under oath at a court trial that one spouse had committed adultery. As the stigma attached to divorce shrank, laws against divorce relaxed. Today, in most states "incompatibility," which simply means that two people aren't getting along, has become adequate grounds for divorce. In many states, couples can work out their own "no-fault" divorce, and judges simply sign the paperwork. In Florida, the couple can sign papers in a lawyer's office, and they don't even have to appear in court. Such legal changes have further reduced the stigma attached to divorce, which, in turn, has contributed to the high divorce rate.

Are These Changes Good or Bad?   Symbolic interactionists take the position that nothing is good or bad in and of itself. They view "goodness" and "badness" as value judgments that people attach to behavior. Depending on its assumptions, one group is alarmed at increases in divorce and changes in marital roles, new views on parenting, and so on. Another group looks at these same changes and feels pleased that the family is evolving. Symbolic interactionists do not take a stand that either is correct or better, for symbolic interactionism has no framework for making value judgments.

Divorce is common among Americans, but far from new with them. This 1789 French painting shows a judge making decisions in a divorce—and the impatience of the new partners.

Roger Viollet Collection/Getty Images

LE DIVORCE.

In Sum   To explain why the divorce rate has increased, symbolic interactionists analyze how symbols—ideas, meanings, and expectations—associated with marriage and family life have changed. They stress that symbols both reflect and create reality. That is, symbols not only represent people's ideas but also influence people's ideas and behaviors.

Functionalism: Declining Functions

When functionalists analyze social change, they look at how change in one part of society affects its other parts. Earlier in this chapter, we examined the impact of industrialization and urbanization on marriage and family. You will recall that the birthrate fell as children became more costly. This is an example of how change in one part of the system (work) brought about change in another (family). Let's look now at how functionalists explain our high rate of divorce.

For background, we should note that functionalists have identified six key functions of the family. They point out that around the world the family provides:

1. Economic production
2. Socialization of children
3. Care of the sick and aged
4. Recreation
5. Sexual control of family members
6. Reproduction

Let's see what effects the Industrial Revolution and urbanization had on these six traditional functions of the family—and how a reduction of these functions is related to divorce.

Economic Production   Before industrialization, the members of a family worked together as an economic team. Survival was precarious. Even getting enough food and adequate clothing was a problem. To survive, the members of a family—like it or not—were forced to cooperate. *When industrialization moved production from home to factory, it disrupted this team.* No longer working as a unit, the husband-father was separated from the daily activities of the family, and the wife-mother was separated from the production of income. The older children, who went to work for wages, became less dependent on their family.

Socialization of Children   While economic production was changing, the state and federal governments were growing larger, more centralized, and more powerful. As the government spread its influence, it began to take over some of the family's functions. This weakened family relationships. For example, when lawmakers passed mandatory education laws, it became illegal for parents not to send their children to school. Parents faced fines and jail if they did not put their children in the government's care. In this one act, the government took over much of the responsibility for socializing children.

Care of the Sick and Aged   Care of the sick and aged followed a similar course. Before industrialization, medicine was a family matter. There were few trained physicians, and family members cared for their sick at home. As medical schools developed, along with hospitals and drugs, medicine came under government control. Gradually medical care shifted from the family to medical specialists. As the central government expanded and its agencies multiplied, care of the aged, too, changed from a family to a government obligation.

Recreation   As industrialization progressed, the country became more affluent, and the family's disposable income increased. Businesses sprang up to compete for that income. Before the Industrial Age, entertainment and "fun" had consisted primarily of home-based activities—card games, parlor and barn dances, sleigh rides, and so on. As family-centered activities gave way to paid events, the family lost much of its recreational function.

Seldom is the control of sexuality as direct and forceful as the chastity belt of the 1500s. A husband who was about to go on a long journey locked a chastity belt on his wife to make sure she would be loyal to him while he was away.

Control of Sexuality The family traditionally controlled the sexual behavior of its members. Only sexual relations in marriage were viewed as legitimate. Sexual relations outside marriage—even between engaged couples—were considered immoral. Although this was only an ideal, and marriage never enjoyed a monopoly on sexual relations, the **sexual revolution** opened many alternatives to marital sex. The changed standards of sexual behavior weakened the family's control over the sexuality of its members.

Reproduction Even reproduction has increasingly moved outside the traditional family unit of husband and wife. As we reviewed earlier, two of five births in the United States are to unmarried women. If the increase continues, soon half of all births will be to unmarried women. Other significant changes have altered the face of reproduction. It is especially significant that married women can get abortions without informing their husbands and that teens can obtain birth control without parental consent.

Can reproduction move even further away from the family? With the miracles of our biological/genetic laboratories, we are on the cusp of designer babies. Men or women, single or married, homosexual or heterosexual, will be able to put in orders for the kind of children they want. They will be able to specify not only the child's sex and race–ethnicity, but also its height, hair color, eye color, body type, even its intelligence, personality traits, and ability in music, art, poetry, and sports. Will we arrive at such a future? It is unlikely, as lurking behind the idea of designer children is the potential to try to produce a genetically engineered superior people. Those who recall Hitler's ideas of Übermensch shudder at such a thought.

In Sum Functionalists stress that the loss of functions has weakened the family unit. The fewer functions that family members have in common, the fewer are the "ties that bind" them together. As family bonds have weakened, the family has become fragile, with divorce the inevitable consequence of eroded functions.

Conflict and Feminist Theory: Shifting Power Relations

Conflict and feminist theorists point us in a different direction. They stress that marriage and family roles reflect the basic social inequality that runs through society. In general, men dominate and exploit women, and marriage and family life is one of the means by which they do this.

Male Domination of Marriage and Family Historically, women have served men as wife, sister, and mother. The wife was expected to prepare her husband's food, to take care of his clothing, and to satisfy his sexual and emotional needs. The woman's life was expected to revolve around her home, including the care of the children. This backstage work is called **reproductive labor**—the work that a wife performs behind the scenes that allows her breadwinner husband to flourish in his more public life.

Traditionally, fathers have controlled all the members of the family. As in India today and as discussed in the previous *Global Glimpse*, deciding who a daughter or son would marry was a father's right and responsibility. To forge alliances, kings would arrange for their daughters to marry the sons of other kings. Members of the nobility would do the same, arranging for their children to marry "suitably," which meant that the marriage would provide an advantage for the father's lineage. Over time, fathers in the West gradually lost this right. While arranged marriages are no longer part of our current marital customs, the traditional wedding ceremony reflects this lost right.

As the mother sits passively to the side, the father walks his daughter down the aisle and "gives" her to her husband. This is but a pale reflection of the power that men have wielded historically, but it is a reflection nonetheless.

Both custom and the law once allowed men to discipline not only their children, but also their wives. Not too far in our own past, a husband could spank his wife—if she "needed" it. Beating a wife was considered permissible if she became rebellious or had an affair. In some areas—such as Pakistan—husbands are still permitted to beat their wives as a form of discipline. In Chapter 9, we reviewed "honor killings," the ultimate sanction that men can give women for violating the rules by which they control them.

Marriage as an Arena for an Ongoing Historical Struggle Industrialization brought major change to husband–wife relationships. As more and more women took paid jobs, their experiences at work changed their views of the world. Increasingly, wives came to resent arrangements that women at earlier periods had taken for granted. Housework and child care (or as sociologists put it, the division of labor at home) became a pivotal source of conflict. Women started chafing—and complaining—that it was unfair for them to work at jobs outside the home and to shoulder almost all the housework and child care. The husbands resented this accusation, pointing out how many more hours they were putting in at work.

As you can see from Figure 11.10, over time the division of family labor gradually changed in the direction that the wives wanted. In 1965, husbands in two-paycheck

The 1950s marked a watershed era in U.S. middle class-families. With the husband's income adequate to support a family comfortably, the wife was expected to focus on the home. This historical period is bathed in images that characterized only a minority of families, images that form a mythical lens through which we view that "ideal" period of family life.

Figure 11.10 In Two-Paycheck Marriages, How Do Husbands and Wives Divide Up Family Responsibilities?

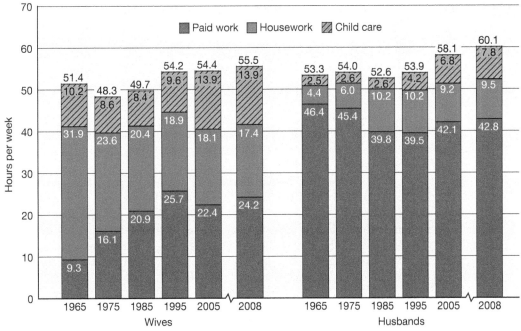

Note: Latest year available.

Source: By the author. Based on Bianchi, S.M., & Milkie, M.A. (2010). *Work and family research in the first decade of the 21st century.* John Wiley & Sons, 72, 705–725.

marriages put in 6.9 hours a week on housework and child care. By 2008, at 17.3 hours a week, their total had more than doubled. It is still considerably less than what their wives put in on these tasks, but the husbands' work hours, although reduced, remain much higher. Today's husbands and wives put in more hours per week, but with a somewhat closer balance of tasks than they used to have. Basically, though, you can see that there has been little change since 1995.

In Sum At the root of many marital problems lies the struggle of husbands and wives to achieve a satisfying balance of work, child care, and housework. Compared with the past, today's wives are considerably less dependent on their husbands for financial security. With greater independence, wives are less willing to put up with relationships that they don't find fulfilling. Conflict and feminist theorists view the high divorce rate not as a sign that the family has grown weaker, but rather as evidence that women have made headway in their millennia-old struggle with men. Today's marriage does not represent equality between men and women, but it is much closer than it used to be.

Husbands and wives view their conflict through a different lens. They don't see their marital problems as part of some flowing tide of history. Changes in historical relationships are not part of their perspective. Rather, they experience direct, personal troubles with their spouse.

Research Findings

11.4 **Summarize research findings on postponing marriage, couples without children, family violence, sexual abuse, the elderly, and the death of the family.**

Let's look at some of the major trends in marriage and family today. They are significant: marrying at a later age, cohabitation, remaining single, couples with no children, family violence, sexual abuse, and care of the elderly.

Postponing Marriage

The change in age at first marriage is startling. It is so significant that we can call it the *U-turn in age at first marriage.* During each decade from 1890 to 1950, the average age at first marriage dropped. By 1955, the typical bride had just turned 20. Having just left their teens, brides then were younger than at any other time in U.S. history. Ten years later, the average age of first-time American grooms was 22, also the youngest since the U.S. government began keeping such records. These younger ages for first marriage held steady for about 10 years or so, when they turned upward. With this U-turn, the age at first marriage for women is now 27.4 and for men 29.5 (*Statistical Abstract* 1971:Table 79; U.S. Census Bureau 2018:Table MS-2). The U-turn has been so complete that we now have the opposite situation: Today's average first-time bride and groom are older than at any other time in U.S. history.

From Figure 11.11, you can see one consequence of postponing marriage—how common it now is to be single during the late 20s. You take this for granted, of course, since this is what you see going on around you. But look how it used to be. A few decades ago, most men and women between the ages of 25 and 29 were married. Now most are single. As you can see from this figure, the percentage of single women between the ages of 25 and 29 is *five* times higher today than it was in 1970. During this same time, the number of single men of this age has more than tripled.

Figure 11.11 The Growing Number of Singles

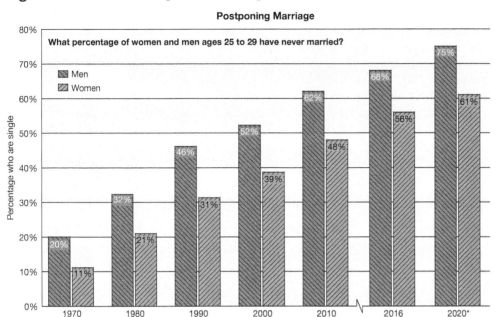

Postponing Marriage

What percentage of women and men ages 25 to 29 have never married?

- Men
- Women

Note: Author's estimate.

Source: By the author. Based on *Statistical Abstract of the United States* 2018:Table 57 and earlier years.

Why have we had this extensive change? Read on.

Cohabitation

To explain the change in age at first marriage, sociologists point to data like those shown in Figure 11.12. Look at the sharp increase in **cohabitation**, living together in a sexual relationship outside of marriage. Sociologists estimate that if cohabitation had not increased like this, so many more people would have married that we would have little change in the average age at first marriage (Manning et al. 2014).

Most couples don't cohabit because they are opposed to marriage. Rather, they figure they are not ready for marriage at this particular time in their lives. They are attracted to one another and want a relationship that is more uniting and fulfilling than just "going together" or "hooking up." But many fear that their relationship isn't strong enough to handle the commitments and responsibilities of marriage. Some hope that a strong commitment will develop, and they will marry later. Others know their relationship is temporary, and cohabiting is just a time between relationships.

There also are financial reasons. Some people do not want to commingle assets, and cohabitation makes it easier for them to keep separate bank accounts and spending patterns. With marriage usually considered a declaration of financial independence from parents, cohabitation allows many young adults, especially college students, to keep getting support from their parents. Some of the widowed cohabit so they won't lose the pension or Social Security earned by their deceased spouse. Similarly, marriage would destroy the alimony of some divorced women, but cohabitation keeps it safe.

Remaining Single

Many women who remain single into their 30s encounter stigma (DePaulo 2016). Family and friends wonder why the woman "hasn't been able to find a husband." They might question whether she is really straight, make snide remarks that she might have some huge hidden flaw, or say she is being too picky. Feelings of being an outsider are especially strong at weddings as well as at social events where most participants are couples.

Figure 11.12 Cohabitation in the United States

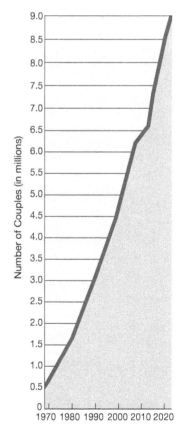

Note: The broken line is the author's estimate.

Source: By the author. Based on *Statistical Abstract of the United States* 2018:Table 57 and earlier years.

Few people view single life as a permanent alternative to marriage, but some do. Those who remain single as they age still feel a strong need for intimacy, sharing, and community (Hopper 2016; Rice et al. 2017). To attain these satisfactions, which marriage and family offer, these singles cultivate a network of people who feel the same as they do about marriage and other important aspects of life. The friendships they develop help satisfy their needs for intimacy without marriage. The same friends get together to celebrate their birthdays and holidays. They encourage and console one another. Many also try to build intimacy through sexual relationships.

Couples without Children

In the United States, about one of seven (14 percent) wives does not give birth (Livingston 2018). What term should we use to refer to married couples without children? *Childless* is the usual term, but some couples resent it. From the discussion in the following *Spotlight on Social Research*, you will see why I avoided the term *childless* in the heading above.

Spotlight on Social Research

Choosing Not to Have Children

CYNTHIA SHINABARGER REED is professor of psychology and sociology at Tarrant County College. ROBERT E. REED is adjunct instructor of sociology at Tarrant County College. This husband and wife team does research on couples without children. Here is what they wrote for you.

Cynthia Shinabarger Reed & Robert E. Reed

People who choose not to have children have received little attention from social scientists. Textbooks on sociology of the family usually include no more than a paragraph or two on this topic.

We each became interested in researching individuals who have chosen not to have children while in graduate school. We are a child-free couple, and when we learned that little research had been done on people like us, we were motivated to learn more about the child-free. One issue we encountered has to do with labeling: What should we call individuals who have chosen not to have children? Traditionally they have been referred to as "voluntarily childless" to differentiate them from people who would like to have children but have been unable to conceive ("involuntarily childless"). This term has been criticized for implying that people who choose not to have children are missing something important. Later, the term "child-free" was introduced, a term which many argued had a much more positive connotation. However, this term has also been criticized for implying that individuals who choose not to have children are free of something bad, as the terms "fat-free" and "cholesterol-free" imply. Another term that has recently been introduced is zero-child families. We perceive this term as having a negative connotation as well. This controversy led us to wonder what other people who have chosen not to have children would prefer to be called. In a recent study of men who have chosen not to have children, we found that the respondents preferred the label "child-free."

Although some couples, like us, make the decision not to have children prior to marriage, for the majority of child-free couples the decision is a gradual one that occurs after marriage. The process begins with a postponement of children for a definite period of time. The couple wants to wait until both finish school or become established in their careers. This is followed by an indefinite postponement. The couple decides "it just isn't the right time." Later, when the couple realizes that time for having children is running out, they begin to discuss the advantages and disadvantages of having children. This is followed by the acceptance of the choice to remain child-free.

People make the decision to be child-free for a variety of reasons. We have found most of these have to do with lifestyle issues. Many of the individuals we have interviewed stated they wanted more free time in order to focus on their marriage relationships and their careers. Many also mentioned the economic benefits of remaining child-free.

The United States is a pronatalist society, and people who choose not to have children are often stereotyped negatively. They are often perceived as materialistic, individualistic, career oriented, selfish, immature, child-haters, lazy, insensitive, lonely, and unhappy. Our interviews with child-free individuals have revealed that some have encountered negative reactions from family, friends, and coworkers regarding their decision. Many were asked why they made this choice, implying that there must be a reason for making such an unpopular choice. Couples who have children are not typically questioned about their decision since it is consistent with society's norms. Some of the people we interviewed stated that others reacted to their decision by looking at them as if they were crazy or by simply ignoring the decision and continuing to ask them when they were going to have children.

Our research with child-free individuals indicates that most of the stereotypes are not correct. While child-free women are typically very well educated and career-oriented, both child-free women and men usually indicate that they like children but do not want to be with children 24/7. While a few of the people we interviewed said that at some point they had reconsidered their decision, all reported being happy with their choice and satisfied with their lifestyle.

For Your Consideration

→ Are you planning on having children? Why or why not?

Choosing Not to Have Children   Some couples agree before marriage not to have children, while others plan to have children but never do (Rainey 2013). In a classic study, sociologist Jean Veevers (1973, 1980) found that women who don't make the decision before marriage go through four stages: First, they postpone getting pregnant while they work toward a goal, such as graduating from college or buying a house. Then they shift their postponement to a vague future, a "sometime," such as when they feel financially independent. This future event is vague and never seems to arrive. During the third stage, they decide that not having children isn't so bad, that they might want to remain this way. When they reach the fourth stage, they view their marriage without children as a permanent rather than a temporary state.

More recent research shows additional pathways to not having children. Some couples choose to remain without children, then decide to have children, only to find out that they cannot have them. Other couples waver throughout their marriage between wanting and not wanting children. A common reason for not having children is the couple's view that it just isn't worth it: The children will take time and money away from things they want to do, will interfere with the couple's relationship, and interfere with their lifestyle.

The situation is even more complicated than this.

> *I have friends in Spain who chose not to have children. Now in her late 40s, the wife fears that her biological clock has just about ticked its last tick, and now she wants to get pregnant. Her husband, however, has no desire to have a child, and he feels that his wife is violating their agreement. Tensions have risen in their already tense relationship. She has become resentful that he doesn't see things the way she does, and he is resentful that she has had such an abrupt change of mind. She is considering making a purchase at a sperm bank, whether he agrees or not.*

The Mythical Child   Many couples without children feel stigmatized, as friends and relatives put pressure on them to bear children. The couples sometimes talk about a "mythical child"—the one they will have "one day." Assuring one another that they will have a child in the future affirms to themselves and others that they like children. Even after the wives become too old to give birth, they still talk about the mythical child, one they might adopt "one day."

Happiness and Old Age   What about happiness? This cuts both ways. Researchers have found that on average, wives with children are slightly happier than wives without children, while husbands without children are slightly happier than those with children (Gab et al. 2013). It's difficult to decipher these differences, but there isn't much difference anyway. In general, each group is about as happy (or unhappy) as the other.

"What about when they are old?" you might ask. "Not having those intergenerational ties probably catches up with them, and at that point they pay a high cost for not having children." Researchers have investigated this, too. They have found that in old age, couples without children are just as happy as those who have children. Those without children have more social ties with nonrelatives, which provide a satisfying support system (Bures et al. 2009).

Then there is the matter of money: Those who are comfortable financially depend less on adult children for emotional support in old age, while those who are financially squeezed get more satisfaction from having adult children around (Neuberger and Preisner 2017).

Family Violence

When the frail, 70-year-old woman refused to hand over her money, the middle-aged man pushed her to the floor. She sprawled there, stunned and helpless, while he screamed insults. The woman became even more upset when the police arrived. She told them that she didn't want her attacker to be arrested.

This was not the first time—nor would it be the last—that her son would attack her.

Extent of Violence   It is a cruel irony that the family, the group we most often look to for intimacy and love, is sometimes characterized by violence. To find out how common violence is in the family, sociologists interviewed nationally representative samples. In this research, which has become a classic in sociology, the researchers analyzed slapping, pushing, kicking, biting, and the use of weapons (Straus et al. 1980; Straus and Gelles 1988). They found that the most violent family members are the children. During the year preceding the interviews, two-thirds of the children had attacked a brother or sister. Most had shoved or thrown things, but one-third had kicked or bitten a sibling. In rare instances, the attack involved a knife or gun. The researchers suggest that as high as they are, these totals are severe underestimates.

And married couples? The FBI reports violent crime as rates per 100,000 people, but sociologists have found marital violence to be so common that they report it in rates per 100 people. Each year, 16 of every 100 husbands and wives physically attack one another (Straus et al. 1980, 2017). This is one spouse out of every six. No other violent crime comes even close to this rate.

Because most couples (84 percent) were not violent during the past year and most violence is mild (such as slapping), some dismiss these figures with a "so what" attitude. To this, Straus and Gelles (1988) reply (paraphrased):

Let's suppose we are talking about a university. Would anyone say that there wasn't much of a problem because, after all, 84 percent of the faculty didn't slap a student last year? Or would anyone argue that this isn't significant because, after all, most of the 16 percent of faculty members who were violent only slapped students, rather than punching or beating them?

Experiencing Intimate Partner Violence   As you've seen in this text, sociologists do research on all kinds of topics. Sometimes they become interested in a particular social problem because of their personal experience with it. This is how it was for sociologist Kathleen Ferraro. In the next *Spotlight on Social Research*, she shares her experiences with **intimate partner violence**—physical, emotional, or sexual abuse within a relationship.

Spotlight on Social Research

Intimate Partner Violence

KATHLEEN FERRARO, *Director of Training and Curriculum of the Family Violence Institute at Northern Arizona University, wanted to be a sociologist from the time she was 12. She never imagined, though, that her research would focus on "intimate partner violence" because she never knew that this existed. Here is what she wrote for you.*

I found out about "intimate partner violence" at age 23 when I married my first husband. He went to high school with me and came from a well-respected family. He was a naturalist and a bird-watcher, did not drink or use drugs, and showed no violent tendencies. After we exchanged vows, however, he changed almost immediately, displaying the "power and control" tactics that have become so well known today. He monitored my movements, eating, clothing, friends, money, makeup, and language. If I challenged his commands, he slapped or kicked me or pushed me down.

Kathleen J. Ferraro

I left him on these occasions, staying with other graduate students at Arizona State University, but I had no way to understand what was happening. My husband always convinced me to return. He stalked and threatened to kill me, even in front of police officers, but my faculty mentor, Albert J. Mayer, and my friends hid me until my father-in-law came to take my husband back to our hometown on the other side of the country. I obtained a single-party, no-fault divorce and never saw him again.

These events took place in 1974 and 1975, before the battered women's movement transformed public understanding of "domestic violence." In a graduate class on social deviance, Erdwin Pfuhl required us to write a paper on a form of deviance with which we had personal experience. I could not think of anything. While I waited outside his office to ask for help, another woman struck up a conversation with me, and I learned that her boyfriend abused her. That was the moment that I began to think sociologically about my own experience. I discovered that there was a battered women's shelter in my city, and I began to volunteer there and to interview staff members. This was the beginning of the battered women's movement and the beginning of a lifetime of research, teaching, and activism for me. I joined with a group of people to establish another shelter, and that is where I conducted the interviews and ethnographic work for my dissertation, *Battered Women and the Shelter Movement*, and for the *Social Problems* article, "How Women Experience Battering: The Process of Victimization."

The women taught me how difficult it is to make sense of the violence and emotional abuse that come from a person they love and believe loves them. The rationalizations the women used to understand what was happening to them were similar to those used by people who commit crimes, the "techniques of neutralization" described by Gresham Sykes and David Matza. For women at the shelter, these techniques included denial of victimization, denial of the victimizer, denial of injury, denial of options, appeal to higher loyalties, and the salvation ethic. Because of fear, lack of resources, and institutional failure to respond to battering, the women found escape from violent relationships to be difficult and precarious. Leaving an abuser does not necessarily end the violence—women are often at most risk during the time they are leaving the abuser.

For Your Consideration

→ What do you think should be done to reduce spouse abuse? Be practical.

Equality of Violence between the Sexes?   This probably doesn't surprise you: Of every four of those who report to the police that they are victims of violence by an intimate partner, three are women (*Statistical Abstract* 2018:Table 344). But this might surprise you: In the classic research I just mentioned, the sociologists found that women are as likely as men to attack their intimate partner (Gelles 1980; Lussier et al. 2009; Straus 2012). In contrast, other researchers have found that men are more likely to initiate the violence (Dobash and Dobash 2014). Regardless of who is the first to be violent, when it comes to the *effects* of violence, any semblance of sexual equality vanishes. As Straus points out, even though she may cast the first coffeepot, he usually casts the last and most damaging blow. Because most men are bigger and stronger, women are at a disadvantage in this literal battle of the sexes: When intimate partners are violent, women are about four times as likely as men to be seriously hurt. Like other crimes, violence between intimate partners has dropped in recent years (*Statistical Abstract* 2018:Table 344).

Social Class and Spousal Violence   Violence between spouses occurs in all social classes, but spouses in some social classes are more likely than others to be abusers—or victims. The highest rates of violence (Gelles 1980; "Violence and…" 2018) are found among:

Low-income families

Blue-collar workers

Families in which the husband is unemployed

Families with above-average numbers of children

People with less education

Individuals who have no religious affiliation

People under 30

Why are blue-collar spouses, especially husbands, more violent than white-collar spouses? Researchers suggest that one of the reasons is that blue-collar husbands experience more stress than their white-collar counterparts. Even if blue-collar husbands do experience more stress, this does not explain why that stress gets translated into violence toward their wives. Nor does it explain why most blue-collar husbands, no matter how high their stress, do not attack their wives. We certainly need more research on family violence. Perhaps you will be the researcher who does such an enlightening study.

Figure 11.13 How Marital Violence Is Related to the Family Violence That Teenagers Experience

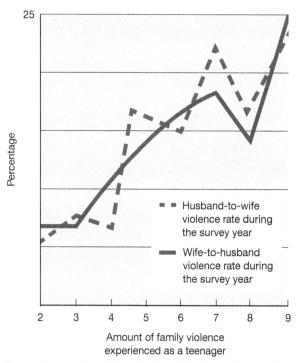

Husband-to-wife violence rate during the survey year

Wife-to-husband violence rate during the survey year

Amount of family violence experienced as a teenager

Source: Based on Straus, Murray A., Richard J. Gelles, and Suzanne K. Steinmetz. *Behind Closed Doors: Violence in the American Family.* New York: Random House, Inc., 1980.

The Social Heredity of Violence Sociologists have uncovered what they call the *social heredity of violence*—children learning from their parents that violence is a way to solve problems. After the children who grow up in violent homes marry, they apply this family lesson to their own marriage (Straus et. al 1980; Murshid et al. 2018). As Figure 11.13 shows, the more violence that children experience during their teen years, the more likely they are to be violent in their own marriage.

Here is how the researchers explain Figure 11.13:

Those with scores of zero are the people whose parents did not hit them and did not hit each other. At the other extreme are people with scores of 9. They are the people whose parents frequently hit them when they were teenagers and whose parents were frequently violent with each other.

The researchers point out that the social heredity of violence is so powerful that:

When one member of a couple had experienced the double whammy of being hit as a child and observing his or her parents hitting each other, there was a one in three chance that at least one act of violence had occurred during the year of the study! (Straus et al. 1980:113)

Why Doesn't She Just Leave? Some wives remain with husbands who abuse them. Why? This question has intrigued members of the public and sociologists alike. Researchers have studied many samples of women, and they have found remarkably consistent answers. Findings from one of these studies are featured in the next *Issues in Social Problems*.

Issues in Social Problems

"Why Doesn't She Just Leave?" The Dilemma of Abused Women

"Why would she ever put up with violence?" is a question on everyone's mind. From the outside, it looks so easy. Just pack up and leave. "I know I wouldn't put up with anything like that."

Yet this is not what typically happens (Dockterman 2014). Women tend to stay with their men after they are abused. Some stay only a short while, to be sure, but others remain in abusive situations for years. Why?

Sociologist Ann Goetting (2001) asked this question, too. To get the answer, she interviewed women who had made the break. Goetting wanted to find out what set these women apart. How were they able to leave, when so many can't seem to? She found that:

1. *These women had a positive self-concept.*
   Simply put, they believed they deserved better.

Spouse abuse, which is not limited to women victims, comes in many forms, including the one shown here.

John Rensten/Corbis/Getty Image

2. *They broke with traditional values.*

They did not believe that a wife had to stay with her husband no matter what.

3. *They found adequate finances.*

For some this was easy, but to accumulate enough money to move out, some of the women saved for years, putting away just a little each week.

4. *They had supportive family and friends.*

A support network served as a source of encouragement to help them rescue themselves.

If you take the opposite of these four characteristics, you have the answer to why some women put up with abuse: They don't think they deserve anything better; they believe it is their duty to stay no matter what; they don't think they can make it financially; and they lack a support network. These four factors are not of equal importance. For some women, the lack of finances is the most significant, while for others, it can be a low self-concept. For all women, the support network—or the lack of one—plays a significant role.

For Your Consideration

→ On the basis of these findings, what would you say to a woman whose husband or partner is abusing her?

→ Would you give a different answer to a man whose wife or partner is abusing him? Why or why not?

→ How do you think women's shelters would fit into the explanation given in this box?

→ What other parts of this puzzle can you think of—such as the role of love?

Spousal Abuse as a Defense for Homicide   Some wives, of course, leave their husbands after the first attack and never look back. Others remain in the relationship, some to murder their partners after enduring years of abuse. Being an abused wife has been used as a defense for killing husbands. Although this defense elicits sympathy from the jury and likely mitigates punishment, seldom is it successful. But sometimes it is, as in this case.

Raymond Sheehan, a 49-year-old New York retired crime scene investigator, stepped out of the shower. As he stood before the mirror shaving, Barbara Sheehan, his 47-year-old wife, pumped eleven bullets into him. She used two handguns to shoot him. When the police arrived, they found Raymond's blood-splattered body lying on the bathroom floor. The water in the sink was still running.

"He was an evil man," the wife testified at her murder trial. Clutching her heart and sobbing, she said, "He was going to kill me. I could see it in his face. I saw his eyes and I saw the gun."

"Did he have a holster in his underpants?" asked the incredulous prosecuting attorney. "You're a manipulative liar. You simply hated him, and you killed him."

The couple's 21-year-old son testified how he was going to college out of state because he feared that being around his father would drive him to suicide. He told the jury that when he was 10 years old, he saw his mother on the kitchen floor, in just a bra, hot pasta sauce thrown onto her body.

The couple's 25-year-old daughter told the jury that her father was so explosive he would punch her mother when they got stuck in traffic.

The wife recounted perverse sex acts that her husband had forced on her.

"You profited from his cold-blooded murder," the prosecutor thundered. "Your children shared with you the $660,000 they collected on his life insurance."

Barbara Sheehan broke down when she was asked to hold the gun and reenact how she had shot her husband. The judge let her use a pointed finger instead.

Victim or executioner?

The jury was deadlocked for two days. On the third day, the jurors brought in a verdict. Barbara Sheehan, they concluded, was not guilty of murder. She was guilty, though, of the illegal possession of a gun. The judge declared Barbara not guilty of murder and then sentenced her to five years in prison on the gun charge.

—Based on Bilefsky 2011a, 2011b, 2011c; Dwyer 2011; Carrega-Woodby 2014.

On an emotional, personal, and empathetic level, one can understand how years of abuse can lead to an explosive retaliation. However, no matter how understandable the desire to kill may be under conditions of abuse and brutality, this defense raises questions about justifying murder.

Bogdan Cristel/REUTERS

The Roma are an ancient people in Romania. Going back centuries, their custom of early marriage has come into conflict with modern times. This 15-year-old man, a boy by our standards, married a 12-year-old girl, a young child from our point of view. The Romanian police investigated on the basis of rape, but the court's decision was to separate the couple, require that they attend school, and make them wait until they are 18 to marry.

Sexual Abuse: Marital Rape

The prevailing idea about marital rape used to be: "It does not exist." When a couple married, it was assumed by law and common sentiment that the wife was consenting to sex for the rest of her life. Legally, then, rape in marriage was nonexistent. In some countries, it still is (Venkatesh and Randall 2018). Change came gradually in the United State and elsewhere in the West, with the push by feminists of the 1960s and 1970s leading to both fundamental legal change and different views by the public. Only about 20 years ago was marital rape recognized as a crime in all 50 states (Kreinert et al. 2018). Let's see what researchers have found concerning marital rape.

How Common Is Marital Rape? Although this area of human behavior is shrouded in secrecy, sociologists have made it a topic of their research (Michalski 2016). Classic research was done by David Finkelhor and Kersti Yllo (1985, 1989). Interviewing 330 married women in Boston, they found that at some point in the marriages, 10 percent of the husbands had used physical force to compel the wives to have sex. If this number is anywhere near accurate, it would translate into an astounding total. With 68 million married women in the United States, it would mean that close to 7 million women have been raped by their husbands (*Statistical Abstract* 2018:Table 56).

Marital rape is most likely to occur during a separation or when a marriage is breaking up. In rare instances, however, husbands rape their wives throughout marriage. In an older study, Finkelhor and Yllo interviewed one woman who had endured marital rape for 24 years. Her marriage ended only when her husband divorced her.

Types of Marital Rape   Finkelhor and Yllo found three types of marital rape:

1. *Nonbattering rape.* In about 40 percent of the cases, the husband raped his wife without intending to harm her. The attack was usually preceded by a conflict over sex, such as the husband feeling insulted when his wife refused to have sex.
2. *Battering rape.* In about 48 percent of the cases, the husband intentionally hurt his wife during the rape. He was retaliating for some supposed wrongdoing on his wife's part.
3. *Perverted rape.* In these instances, about 6 percent, the husband seemed to be sexually aroused by the violence. These husbands forced their wives to submit to unusual sexual acts.

How Does Marital Rape Affect Wives?   All we have space for is a quick summary: The short-term effects are anger, accompanied by grief, despair, shame, and feelings of "dirtiness." The most common long-term effect is the damage it does to the woman's ability to trust intimate relationships or to function sexually.

Why Do Some Women Put Up with Marital Rape?   Most women quickly leave a marriage if they are raped by their husbands. But some remain. Why? The answers are similar to the reasons some abused women stay with their husbands that we reviewed in the last *Issues in Social Problems.* Most of these women are afraid to leave. They fear that they don't have the skills to make it on their own or they lack support networks. Some are afraid that their children will suffer or that their husband will retaliate. With low self-esteem and little support, they feel they cannot survive without their husbands.

Sexual Abuse: Incest

In Australia, 61-year-old John Deaves and 39-year-old Jenny Deaves went on television. They talked about their love for one another and about their new baby.

The audience reacted with disgust. What bothered them wasn't the difference in their ages. They were upset that John is Jenny's father (Childs 2008).

Sociologists have investigated **incest**—forbidden sexual relations between relatives, such as brothers and sisters or parents and children. As they were for John and Jenny Deaves, revelations of incest are met with repugnance. As divided as Americans are on so many issues, the prohibition of incest is one on which almost all agree—and strongly. Some analysts suggest that avoidance of incest is hardwired into our brains. Around the world, incest is almost always viewed as abhorrent, sinful, or unnatural.

However, the huge variation in human behavior around the world brings exceptions to even this almost universal repugnance. These exceptions include brother–sister marriages among the Incas of Peru, the Egyptian pharaohs, and the common people of Egypt under Roman rule (Leavitt 2013). Anthropologists also have found that Thonga lion hunters of East Africa are allowed to have sex with their daughters on the night before a big hunt (La Barre 1954; Beals and Hoijer 1965).

Who Are the Offenders?   Incest can occur between any family members, but sex between children seems to be the most common form. An analysis of 13,000 cases of sibling incest showed that most incest occurs between brothers and sisters, with the sex initiated by a brother who is five years older than his sister (Krienert and Walsh 2011). In one-fourth of the cases, though, the victim is a younger brother, and in 13 percent of the cases, it is the sister who is the offender. Most offenders are between the ages of 13 and 15, and most victims are age 12 or younger. In most cases, the parents treat the incest as a family matter to be dealt with privately.

What Are the Effects on Victims?   The effects of incest can run the gamut of fear, bewilderment, resentment, withdrawal, and so on (Saunders 2017). I chose this statement from Susan Forward, a psychotherapist who was herself a victim of incest, so you can see how just one reaction, feelings of guilt, can pervade a victim's life.

I understand incest not only as a psychotherapist but as a victim. When I was fifteen my father's playful seductiveness turned into highly sexualized fondling. This is a difficult admission for me to make, but even more painful is the fact that I enjoyed my father's attentions.

I felt enormously guilty about my participation in the incest, as if I had been responsible. I know now I was not. It was my father's responsibility as an adult and as a parent to prevent sexual contact between us, but I didn't understand that at the time.

I also felt guilty about competing with my mother—who was only thirty-three and very attractive.

I was flattered by my father's attraction to me, and his caresses felt good, but after several months my guilt became too great. I somehow found the courage to tell him to stop, and he did. The psychological damage, however, had already been done.

As my guilt feelings accumulated, my self-image deteriorated. I felt like a "bad girl." I began to punish myself unconsciously, most prominently by marrying an unloving man instead of pursuing the acting career I had dreamed of since I was five. Later, when my children were in school, I finally got a job on a television series. Good jobs followed and success was within my grasp. But my guilt still fought me on a [sub]conscious level, telling me that I didn't deserve success. So I allowed myself—[sub]consciously, of course, to become overweight and matronly at twenty-eight. My acting career stagnated. My marriage was a mess. I was desperately unhappy. Yet I had absolutely no idea that there was any connection between what my father had done to me and the problems in my life (Forward and Buck 1978:1).

The Pro-Incest Lobby   A small group of people claim that incest is not a problem. The problem, they say, is the *attitude* toward incest. They argue that if people change their attitudes about adults having sex with children, then incest would not be an issue. They claim that there should be no law against incest, that prohibiting incest ruins affectionate relationships and the sexual love that can forge strong bonds between children and adults (Hari 2002; Zhou 2016).

If people with these views were to succeed in removing what has been called the "last taboo," the change could be devastating. Despite loosened sexual norms, however, the chances of incest becoming an approved behavior range from remote to impossible.

Old Age and Widowhood

Most Americans today survive to old age. As we reviewed in Chapter 2, old age brings many problems of adjustment, especially deteriorating health, the death of loved ones, and the knowledge of one's own impending death. When the elderly withdraw from productive roles, their sense of social worth can be challenged. They may even face attitudes that they have become parasites—that they are draining the health care system or robbing younger workers by bankrupting the Social Security system.

Several generations ago, Americans lived in **extended families**; that is, other relatives, perhaps grandparents or aunts and uncles, lived with the parents and their children. During this agrarian period, the aged, who owned land, could maintain positions of authority, gradually relinquishing control while easing younger family members into responsible roles. Although we cannot be sure, the transition to old age may have been smoother and perhaps less painful than it is today. Even though they may have been living in a productive extended family, however, their adjustment to deteriorating health, the death of loved ones, and the knowledge that they, too, would soon die could not have been easy.

Figure 11.14 Living Arrangements of the Elderly

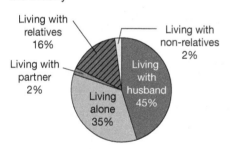

Women ages 65 and over

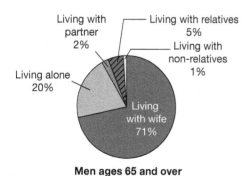

Men ages 65 and over

Source: By the author. Based on *Statistical Abstract of the United States* 2018:Table 58.

The Myth of Family Abandonment   The **nuclear family**, consisting of parents and children, has become our dominant family form. Compared with the larger extended family, the nuclear family is smaller, making it easier for its members to become isolated. The media sometimes feature some abandoned and embittered elderly person living out his or her last remorseful years stowed away in a dingy apartment crammed full of memorabilia from the past. But this grim picture doesn't hold up in the face of sociological research. Adult middle-aged children are likely to help their aged parents and receive satisfaction in doing so (Huo 2017). Figure 11.14, gives you a better perspective: 65 percent of Americans ages 65 to 74 are still living with their spouse. Only about one of five lives alone. Even among those who are age 75 and over, 46 percent live with their spouses and a little over one of three lives alone.

"Intimacy at a Distance"   Most of the elderly prefer to live near their adult children, but not with them—a situation called "intimacy at a distance." This allows the elderly to maintain their own independence, while respecting the privacy of their children and yet maintaining relationships with them. Far from abandoning their aged parents, the adult children of most elderly remain key figures in their support system (Bengtson et al. 1990; Angel 2015). With intergenerational migration, adult children often live far from their parents. Many have developed *virtual intimacy*. They use digital devices, especially those that allow the transmission of visual images to maintain a sense of closeness.

"Money can't buy happiness" is an old saying. But it is not true. Money does buy happiness. Compared with poor people, wealthier people are more satisfied with life–and more optimistic about the future. Their health is better, and they live longer. Even their marriages last longer.

The Institutionalized Elderly The 3 percent of the aged who live in nursing homes are not typical of older people. Their average age is over 80 (*Statistical Abstract* 2018:Tables 9, 68). Most are widowed or divorced, or have never married, leaving them without family to care for them. Most are in such poor health that they need help to bathe, dress, and eat (Harrington et al. 2011).

Nursing home residents who need constant care confirm stereotypes about the elderly. They certainly are not a healthy group, but remember that nursing home residents do not represent elderly people in general. On the contrary, most elderly Americans enjoy good health and the company of their family and friends.

Adjusting to Widowhood Even for people who enjoy good health and family relationships in their older years, death comes eventually. When death ends a marriage, the impact is so severe that the surviving spouse tends to die earlier than expected (Shin et al. 2018). These earlier-than-expected deaths, observed around the world, are called the *widowhood effect.* Facing life without the partner who had become such an essential part of life is traumatic. Amid disrupted family relationships and the loss of social roles, the widowed face loneliness, anxiety, depression, financial strain, and physical health problems (Shor et al. 2012; Steinberg and Roux 2018). Spouses who expect the death of their partner handle these problems better than those whose spouse dies unexpectedly (Shah et al. 2013).

The End of Marriage and the Traditional Family?

Have we come to the end of marriage and the traditional family? Let's review some of the changes in marriage and family with this question in mind.

Marriage Is Weakening Some seem to think that marriage is coming to an end. As we discussed earlier, our divorce rate is high, cohabitation has skyrocketed, and young people are postponing marriage. If cohabitation continues its rapid increase, eventually most people will live together, not marry. As you can see from Table 11.1, with women having fewer children, the size of the average family has become smaller. It's difficult to see how smaller equals stronger. On top of this, 40 percent of all U.S. children are born to unmarried women (*Statistical Abstract* 2018:Table 89). If the number of couples who cohabit continue to increase and if more and more unmarried women bear children, perhaps marriage will become a quaint custom reserved for a few traditionalists.

Table 11.1 Average Size of the U.S. Family (Persons per family)

1960	1970	1980	1990	2000	2010	2020*
3.67	3.62	3.29	3.17	3.17	3.16	3.13

* Indicates author's estimate

Source: By the author. Based on *Statistical Abstract of the United States* 1991:Table 61; 2018:Table 59.

Marriage Continues Strong But there is another side to today's marriage and family. Cohabitation has not replaced marriage. Rather, cohabitation has become a step on the way to marriage, and most people who marry today have lived with their new spouse prior to their marriage. Although people are taking longer to say "I do," they are still making these vows. Look at Figure 11.15. You can see that by the time women reach their early 30s, about two out of three are married. It takes men a little longer, but they soon hit this same total. By old age, about 96 percent of Americans have married. The older marrieds do not reflect the current wave of cohabitation, however, so the marriage rate of the elderly of the future might be lower.

Figure 11.15 The Percentage of Americans Who Have Never Married

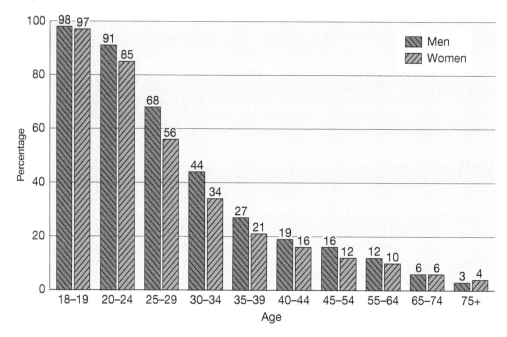

Source: By the author. Based on *Statistical Abstract of the United States* 2018:Table 57.

Is Marriage Improving? The Middletown Research Muncie, Indiana, is one of the most thoroughly researched cities in the United States, and sociological research there indicates not only that American family life is not disintegrating, it is actually improving. In the 1920s and 1930s, sociologists Robert and Helen Lynd (1929, 1937) analyzed family life in this middle-American city, which they called "Middletown." Fifty years later, other sociologists went back to Muncie to find out whether the family had declined. To see whether it had, they compared current rates of suicide, mental illness, and domestic violence with the rates from the 1920s and 1930s. To their surprise, Theodore Caplow and his fellow researchers (1982) found that these problems were less frequent in Middletown than they had been two generations earlier.

Instead of alienation, the researchers found community. Most parents and their grown children keep in close touch. The nuclear families are not isolated units, as some stereotypes paint them. Rather, the nuclear families are embedded in larger kin and friendship networks, which are vital for people's well-being. These networks help people meet their emotional needs, especially their need to feel connected to others. They also meet people's physical needs, with relatives and friends helping one another when they are sick or in financial need.

Figure 11.16 What Are Americans' Living Arrangements?

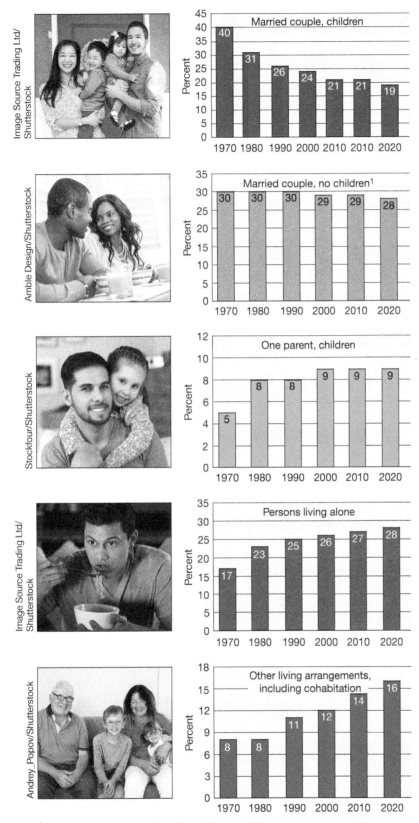

Married couple, children

1970	1980	1990	2000	2010	2010	2020
40	31	26	24	21	21	19

Married couple, no children[1]

1970	1980	1990	2000	2010	2020
30	30	30	29	29	28

One parent, children

1970	1980	1990	2000	2010	2020
5	8	8	9	9	9

Persons living alone

1970	1980	1990	2000	2010	2020
17	23	25	26	27	28

Other living arrangements, including cohabitation

1970	1980	1990	2000	2010	2020
8	8	11	12	14	16

[1]"Married couple, no children" includes childless or child-free couples, but most of these couples are "empty nesters": Their children have grown and left home.

Note: The year 2020 is the author's estimate.

Source: By the author. Based on *Statistical Abstract of the United States* 2000:Table 60; 2018:Table 59.

Perhaps these researchers' most surprising finding was that marriage had grown more vibrant. Marriage in the 1920s was shallower. At that time, husbands and wives lived more separate lives and didn't talk as much with one another. With male and female roles now more similar, husbands and wives talk things over more—and they are more satisfied with marriage. After reviewing their data, these researchers conclude: "For most of their members most of the time, Middletown's composite families provide a safe and comfortable niche in a hazardous world." *The idea that the family has declined is not correct.*

In a critique of the Middletown research, an Asian American who grew up in Muncie, points out that the research misses the experience of minorities (Gupta-Carlson 2018).

Changes and Challenges Despite such a positive assessment from the Middletown research, U.S. families face severe problems. You've read about some of them in this chapter. Look at Figure 11.16. One of the most striking aspects of this figure is the decline of married couples with children at home. In the past 40 or 50 years, this total has dropped in half. Today, only one-fifth of U.S. households consists of married couples with children. Our stereotypes of "family" will have to catch up with reality.

From Table 11.2, you can catch a glimpse of other ways that U.S. families are changing. As you can see, the four largest changes are increases in cohabitation, births to unmarried women, living alone, and children living with only one parent. At the very least, none of these indicate that marriage is strengthening.

What Do These Changes Mean? As symbolic interactionists stress, you can measure objective conditions such as the rate of divorce or the number of children who are living with one parent, but these measurements don't tell you what they mean. To understand objective conditions, you must interpret them. How shall we do this?

Let's try for a fair conclusion: American families are experiencing severe disruptions. We can see this from runaways, divorce, cohabitation, births to single women, and violence. At the same time, some areas of family life have improved over the years, especially relationships between husbands and wives. And finally, Americans retain high hope for healthy, satisfying marriage and family life. Although young people are postponing the age at which they first marry, they continue to marry at a high rate.

Table 11.2 How U.S. Families Are Changing

	2000	2016	Change Since 1980
Marriages	2,320,000	2,220,000	−4%
Divorces	940,000[1]	800,000	−15%
Married couples	56,500,000[2]	60,250,000	+7%
Unmarried couples	4,900,000[2]	6,900,000	+41%
People living alone	28,730,000	35,30,000	+23%
Married couples with children at home	25,250,000	23,780,000	−6%
Children living with both parents	49,760,000	50,660,000	+2%
Children living with one parent	19,230,000	20,280,000	+52%
Average size of household	2.62	2.53	−3%
Married women who are employed	35,000,000	36,390,000	+4%
Births to single women	1,350,000	1,600,000	+19%

[1] Beginning in 2000, several states stopped reporting divorces.
[2] Year 2000 did not include same-sex couples, but year 2016 does.
Note: Marriages, divorces, and births to single women are events that occurred in the given year. The other items are not events, but total counts.
Source: By the author. Based on *Statistical Abstract of the United States* 2018:Tables 59, 66, 70, 81, 88, 621.

Social Policy

11.5 **Explain the controversy over professional intrusion into the family and the dilemma of family policy.**

Social policy for the family is mired in controversy because every policy steps on someone's toes. In this section, we will examine this controversy.

Intrusions by Professionals and the Coming Therapeutic Society

The family is besieged by professionals—doctors, social workers, and teachers—who are trying to enlarge their own domains at the expense of the family as social historian Christopher Lasch noted back in 1977. Since then, this trend has only increased. Under the guise of helping, they have stripped the family of some of its functions, eroding its capacity to provide protective intimacy.

Consider the professionals who claim to be experts in sex. These "sexperts" flood the public with books and magazine articles about what sexual relations between husband and wife "ought" to be like. Hundreds of "Dr. Phils" and "Phil wannabes" appear as self-styled experts on radio and television and in magazines, where they proclaim their expertise. This makes husbands and wives feel less capable of working out their own sexual problems, for only "sexual experts" have the "real" answers. Or consider the professionals who stake claim to child rearing. They profess to know the best ways to rear children, sometimes even *the* correct way to do so. This makes parents worry that, as mere laypeople, they might be damaging their children through well-intended but clumsy, wrong parenting. Parents are encouraged to look to "professionals"—even though their answers conflict with one another and change over time.

We are on a road that leads to a *therapeutic society,* one in which "experts" claim that all problems—including those in the family—are their domain. The "concern" expressed by "experts" about the plight of the family, publicized on television and radio, in magazines and books, only masks what is really happening: These outside agents are trying to replace the parents' authority and put the family under their control. On top of this, there is no evidence that these so-called experts benefit the family. They market their services and products for profit, some establishing self-serving mini-empires.

As you would expect, professionals react bitterly to this attack on their skills, accomplishments, and motives. They even deny the obvious—that they have self-serving motives. On the contrary, the "professionals" say that their goal is to empower the family so it can handle the problems of life. They insist that the troubled family needs them.

The Dilemma of Family Policy: Taking Sides

With the many incompatible, contrary views in our pluralistic society, any social policy regarding family life finds itself on one side or the other of issues that divide well-meaning people who have the best interests of families at heart. Even a policy that seems totally neutral, making financial aid available to troubled families, gets embroiled in controversy. Some assume that such a policy will only help families. Others, in contrast, view providing financial aid as an attack on family self-sufficiency. They see it as discouraging families from looking out for themselves—making them further dependent on a looming welfare state.

Almost all policy falls on one side or the other of controversial, even explosive issues. In the next *Thinking Critically about Social Problems*, let's consider a more controversial matter.

Thinking Critically about Social Problems

"You Want Birth Control, Little Girl?"

Fiona is 14 years old. Her parents told her that she cannot have sex because premarital sex is a sin. Fiona is afraid that if she does not have sex with her boyfriend, he will date more cooperative girls. She also is madly in love with her boyfriend and wants to please him. She is sure he is the "right one" and that the two of them will have a marvelous life together.

Fiona went to a family planning clinic and explained her problem. The counselors encouraged her to assert herself against her domineering, old-fashioned parents. They gave her contraceptives and assured her that if she becomes pregnant, she can come to them for a free and confidential abortion.

Who is right in this example? As symbolic interactionists stress, our understanding of what "right" is depends on our values. Is a young teenager's decision to seek contraception a step forward in gaining independence? Or is giving her contraceptives an intrusion into family privacy (Joffe 1978)?

And what if we change the age in this example just a bit? How about two years up, or two years down? Assume that Fiona is 12 years old or that she is 16 years old. Your opinion about ages 12, 14, and 16, where do they come from? Or what if her boyfriend is 14? Or if he is 19? Do you see how these ages and what is appropriate for them represent your personal values? And do you see where your values come from? How, then, can one group force its values on another group?

This is the essence of the dilemma. As symbolic interactionists stress, we come from different corners of life, and in those corners we learn perspectives, views of the world. We can't help but view the world from the perspectives we learn.

For Your Consideration

→ What is your opinion about a family planning clinic giving birth control to a minor over the objection of her family? To a 12-year-old girl? To a 14-year-old? To a 16-year-old?

→ How do you think such a dilemma should be resolved?

The Future of the Problem

11.6 Discuss the trends and social changes that are likely to affect family relationships.

To close this chapter, let's take a quick look at what the future might bring American families.

Social Change

The family has already faced and successfully traversed the major upheavals of industrialization and urbanization, events so severe that they transformed almost all human relationships. Today's transforming event is the digitized world of computers and software, which is changing work, education, recreation, news, entertainment—and family relationships. Parents and children take for granted that they text one another throughout the day, giving brief updates on events and changing plans, something unknown less than a generation ago. Change is so rapid and extensive that some grown children who are visiting their parents after an absence of months or even years find that after the first hour or two they have little to talk about.

Social change, as rapid and extensive as it is, continues without let up, requiring the family to continually adapt. The specifics of future social conditions are unclear, but let's venture briefly into these uncharted waters.

Anticipating the Future

Romantic notions of love and marriage are established firmly in our culture, embedding in our cultural psyche the idea that love is the proper basis for marriage. I expect that you will agree that this will continue. Let me make a more hazardous projection, that age at first marriage will continue upward for perhaps the next 10 years, then stabilize. Cohabitation will do the same. Married women working for pay outside the home seems to have already reached a plateau. I expect marriage to become even more oriented around companionship. This orientation, coupled with wives working outside the home and with many moving into managerial positions, will be a stimulus for husbands and wives to develop more equal relationships. Women's incomes increasing relative to those of men—slowly on its way—will be another push toward greater equality. With couples marrying at older ages after attaining higher levels of education, the divorce rate will decline. Even so, marriage will remain fragile, and the United States will continue to have one of the highest divorce rates in the world. Whether you interpret such changes as good, bad, or indifferent depends, of course, on your values.

The Ideological Struggle

Finally, it seems obvious, and quite significant, that competing groups will continue to try to influence family values and family policy. With their incompatible views of what is right and of what the good life is, these groups will continue to battle one another. This struggle, which might seem theoretical or abstract, is destined to influence your family life.

Although the outcome is uncertain, the future certainly looks exciting.

Summary and Review

1. The family is always adjusting to social change. One of the most significant effects of the Industrial Revolution was the removal of economic production from the household.

2. Whether change within the family is perceived as a social problem or merely as adaptation depends on people's values. Indicators that many see as evidence of a social problem are divorce, runaway children, births to single women, one-parent families, and violence and sexual abuse in the family.

3. In analyzing why the U.S. divorce rate is high, symbolic interactionists stress the changing expectations of marriage; functionalists, the declining functions of the family; and conflict theorists, the struggle for equality in marriage.

4. The average age at first marriage declined from 1890 to about 1955, then began to increase about 1970. Today, the average age at first marriage is the highest in our history. The primary reason is *cohabitation*. As many people postpone marriage, a growing proportion of the young remain single.

5. The reasons married couples do not have children are infertility, a decision to not have children, and the postponement of children until not having them becomes inevitable. About one of seven U.S. women never gives birth.

6. Physical violence between family members is common. Regardless of who initiates the violence, wives are injured more often. People reared in violent homes are more likely to be violent to their own spouses and children. Marital rape and incest are problems of family violence and the misuse of power.

7. Most adult children and their parents keep in close touch. The elderly prefer "intimacy at a distance," living near their children, but not with them. Virtual intimacy has developed.

8. Contrary to stereotypes, the Middletown studies indicate that husbands and wives are more satisfied with married life than they were 50 years ago.

9. Social policy for marriage and family is controversial because it pits individual rights against the intervention of "experts." Some accuse "family professionals"

of trying to expand their domain at the expense of the family.

10. The future is likely to bring increases in cohabitation, later age at first marriage, increasing income to women working outside the home, and greater marital equality. Groups that are concerned about the family differ in their ideas about the way the family "should" be. It remains to be seen which groups with their clashing ideas will be most influential in determining social policy.

Thinking Critically about Chapter 11

1. What do you consider to be the three greatest benefits and the three greatest downsides of the changes in U.S. families? Do you think that these changes are bringing more negatives or positives? Explain.

2. Which perspective (symbolic interactionism, functionalism, or conflict theory) do you think best explains the changes that are taking place in U.S. families? Explain.

3. Rank the six traditional functions of the family according to how important you think they are today. Explain your rankings.

4. With the huge increase in cohabitation, the growing number of singles, the high divorce rate, and the extent of abuse in families, how can the author not conclude that marriage is doomed? Explain.

Key Terms

breadwinner, 337
cohabitation, 343
extended families, 352
family of orientation, 335
family of procreation, 335
homemaker, 337
incest, 351

intimate partner violence, 346
nuclear family, 352
pedophiles, 334
pushouts, 334
reproductive labor, 340
sexual revolution, 340

Chapter 12
Urbanization and Population

Marsha Halper/AP Images

Learning Objectives

After reading this chapter, you should be able to:

POPULATION

12.1 Discuss the evolution of cities and describe the significance of urbanization.

12.2 Explain what is *urban* about urban problems.

12.3 Discuss the perspectives that emerge when you apply symbolic interactionism, functionalism, and conflict theory to urban problems.

12.4 Summarize research findings on urban alienation and community, urban dwellers, urban violence, and transitions in power and resources.

12.5 Summarize social policy that can build community in the city.

12.6 Discuss the likely future of urban problems.

URBANIZATION

12.7 Contrast the explanations for Europe's surge in population and the views of the pessimists and the optimists.

12.8 Describe how the New Malthusians and the Anti-Malthusians view world population growth and food supply.

12.9 Discuss the perspectives that emerge when you apply symbolic interactionism, functionalism, and conflict theory to world population.

12.10 Summarize how the New Malthusians and the Anti-Malthusians interpret research findings on population change.

12.11 Compare the social policy implications of the New Malthusians and the Anti-Malthusians.

12.12 Compare the two futures as seen by the New Malthusians and the Anti-Malthusians.

Kellie Moiser was a 17-year-old high school student who worked part-time at the corner ice cream store. From childhood, she had dreamed of becoming a model. Kellie's mother encouraged her dream, hoping that it would be a way out of poverty.

But Kellie never got the chance.

Michael Hagan, 23, also lived in her area of south-central Los Angeles. He liked Olde English "800" malt liquor, especially when he smoked PCP.

He also liked guns.

And a little blood didn't bother him, either.

One Monday evening, Hagan was on a binge with other members of his gang, when they decided to go after a rival gang. They piled into an old Buick and sped toward enemy turf. There they spotted four teenagers, two boys and two girls.

And a little blood didn't bother him.

The teenagers were not gang members. They were just kids who had gone out for ice cream. When they saw the gun, they ran. Kellie didn't run fast enough. Hagan pumped 15 slugs into her, six into her back.

The police didn't have much to go on, witnesses clammed up, and detectives had other priorities.

Kellie's mother didn't have much to go on either, but she set out to find her daughter's killer. Out of a fury born of grief, she stormed the streets in search of the killers. She even barged into local drug houses. The word got around, and a sympathetic inmate in the county jail sent her a letter telling her the name of the shooter.

Kellie's mother shook her head in disbelief when she found out who had killed her daughter. She said, "I knew these gang members when they were just babies. Now look at them. They've turned into killers."

Hagan, the shooter, says, "Jail ain't bad. To me, life ain't much better on the streets than in jail. I can live here. No problem."

"The gang is your family," Hagan explains. "If you're a Crip, I fight for you, no matter what the odds. If you're the enemy, it's do or die."

Hagan adds, "If I had a son, I'd give him a choice: Either he can go to school and be a goody-goody, or he can hit the streets."

—Based on Hull 1987

In this chapter, we will look at problems related to population, where people live and world population growth.

■ Urbanization

Let's consider urban problems first.

Urbanization: The Problem in Sociological Perspective

12.1 Discuss the evolution of cities and describe the significance of urbanization.

Hagan is part of an urban nightmare—muggings on unsafe streets, drive-by shootings, senseless killings. As we look at the history of cities, we want to ask how cities can influence violent behavior.

The Evolution of Cities

Perhaps as early as 7,000 or 8,000 years ago, people built small cities with massive defensive walls, such as biblically famous Jericho (Wengrow 2010). Cities on a larger scale began to appear about 4000 B.C., around the time that writing was invented. The earliest cities emerged in several parts of the world—in Asia (Iran, Iraq, India, China), Africa (Egypt), Europe, and Central and South America.

About 5,500 years ago, Norway was home to one of the first cities in Europe. The city, which had been buried under sand, was not discovered until 2010 (Goll 2010). In the Americas, the first city was Caral, in what is now Peru (Fountain 2001). It was also discovered recently, covered by jungle growth.

Why did cities develop? The key is agriculture. Only when a society produces a surplus of food can people stop farming and gather in cities to pursue other occupations. We can even define a **city** as a large number of people who live in one place and do not produce their own food. As agricultural techniques became more efficient, they spurred urban development.

During the fourth millennium B.C., the plow was invented. As this invention spread, it brought an agricultural surplus that stimulated the development of towns and cities around the world. Although early plows were an improvement over the digging stick, they were primitive, and for the next 5,000 years there was only enough food surplus to allow a small minority of the world's population to live in urban areas.

Then came the Industrial Revolution of the 1700s and 1800s. It sparked an urban revolution around the world, one we are still experiencing today. The Industrial Revolution stimulated not only the invention of mechanical means of farming, which brought food in abundance, but also mechanical means of transportation and communication. These inventions allowed people, resources, and products to be moved efficiently—factors upon which modern cities depend.

From Rural to Urban

Cities, then, are not new to the world scene. But quite recent is **urbanization**—the movement of masses of people to cities, which then have a growing influence on society. In 1800, only 3 percent of the world's population lived in cities, but by 2008, for the first time in history, more people lived in cities than in rural areas. Urbanization is highest in the industrialized world, where 78 percent of people live in cities. This drops to 32 percent for the least industrialized nations. Globally, 54 percent of the world's people live in cities, a total expected to reach 70 percent by 2050 (Kaneda and Dupuis 2017; O'Brien 2018).

As you can see from the Social Map, urbanization in the United States also differs from state to state.

Figure 12.1 How Urban Is Your State? The Rural–Urban Makeup of the United States

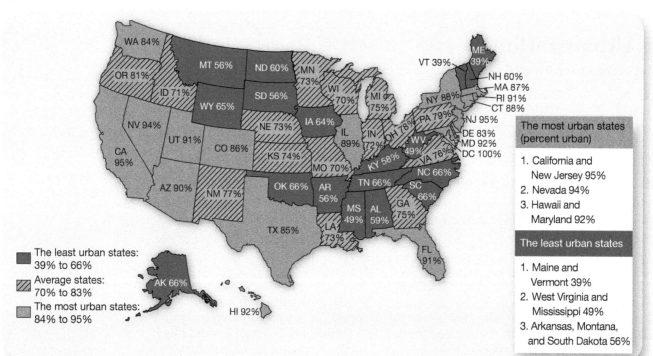

Source: By the author. Based on *Statistical Abstract of the United States* 2018:Table 26.

People expect a lot from cities—good jobs, good housing, educational opportunities, entertainment, a variety of restaurants, easy shopping, and an all-around more convenient life than they find on the farm and in villages. With their many attractions, cities are growing larger. When a city's population hits 10 million, it is called a **megacity**. In 1950, New York City and Tokyo were the only megacities in the world. Today, the world has 30 megacities, most of which are located in the least industrialized nations. Figure 12.2 shows the world's 15 largest megacities.

Figure 12.2 The World's Largest Megacities: The Top 15

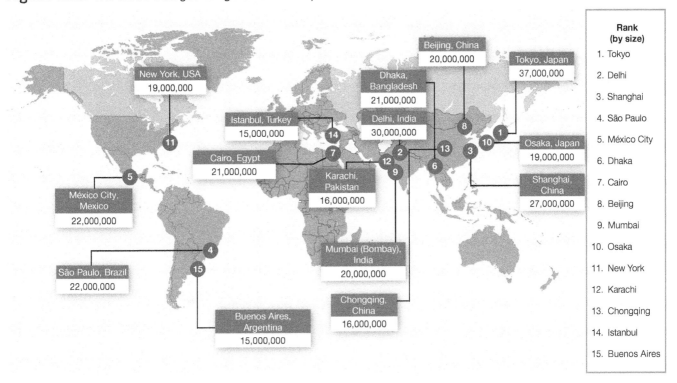

Beijing, China	20,000,000
Tokyo, Japan	37,000,000
New York, USA	19,000,000
Dhaka, Bangladesh	21,000,000
Istanbul, Turkey	15,000,000
Delhi, India	30,000,000
Osaka, Japan	19,000,000
Cairo, Egypt	21,000,000
Karachi, Pakistan	16,000,000
Shanghai, China	27,000,000
México City, Mexico	22,000,000
São Paulo, Brazil	22,000,000
Mumbai (Bombay), India	20,000,000
Chongqing, China	16,000,000
Buenos Aires, Argentina	15,000,000

Rank (by size)
1. Tokyo
2. Delhi
3. Shanghai
4. São Paulo
5. México City
6. Dhaka
7. Cairo
8. Beijing
9. Mumbai
10. Osaka
11. New York
12. Karachi
13. Chongqing
14. Istanbul
15. Buenos Aires

Note: Includes contiguous cities. Los Angeles, for example, includes Long Beach and New York includes Newark.
Source: By the author. Based on United Nations 2018:File 11a.

Why are people in the least industrialized nations flocking to the cities? Let's explore this in *A Global Glimpse.*

A Global Glimpse

Why City Slums Are Better Than Living in the Country

At the bottom of a ravine near Mexico City is a bunch of shacks. Some of the parents have 14 children. "We used to live up there," Señora Gonzalez gestured toward the mountain, "in those caves. Our only hope was one day to have a place to live. And now we do." She smiled with pride at the jerry-built shacks... each one had a collection of flowers planted in tin cans. "One day, we hope to extend the water pipes and drainage—perhaps even pave..."

And what was the name of her community? Señora Gonzalez beamed. "Esperanza!" (McDowell 1984:172)

Esperanza means "hope" in Spanish. What started as a trickle has become a torrent. In 1930, only one Latin American city had over a million people—now 55 do (Lora 2010). The world's cities are growing by more than a million people each week. The rural poor

NAIROBI, KENYA

Sean Sprague/The Image Works

are flocking to the cities at such a rate that the least industrialized nations now contain most of the world's largest cities. You might want to look at Figure 12.2 again.

The migrants settle in illegal squatter settlements outside the city. There they build shacks from scrap boards, cardboard, and bits of corrugated metal. The squatters even scavenge flattened tin cans for building material. They enjoy no city facilities, public transportation, water, sewers, or garbage pickup. After thousands of squatters have settled an area, the city reluctantly acknowledges their right to live there and adds bus service and minimal water lines. Hundreds of people use a single spigot. About 5 million of Mexico City's residents live in such squalid conditions, with tens of thousands more pouring in each year.

Why this rush to live in the city under such miserable conditions? On the one hand are the *push factors* that come from the breakdown of traditional rural life. As rural populations multiply, the parents no longer have enough land to divide among their children. With neither land nor jobs, there is hunger and despair.

On the other hand are the *pull factors* that draw people to the cities—jobs, housing, doctors, modern medicine, and even a more stimulating life. That there are schools gives the hope that their children will have a better life.

How will these nations adjust to this vast migration? Authorities in Brazil, Guatemala, and other countries have sent in the police and even the army to evict the settlers. After a violent dispersal, the settlers return—and others continue to stream in. The roads, water and sewer lines, electricity, schools, and public facilities must be built. But these poor countries don't have the resources to build them. As wrenching as the adjustment will be, these countries must—and somehow will—make the transition. They have no choice.

For Your Consideration

→ What solutions do you see to the vast migration to the cities of the least industrialized nations?

The Scope of the Problem

12.2 **Explain what is *urban* about urban problems.**

What is *urban* about urban problems? In one sense, almost all social problems are urban. Because most Americans live in cities, poverty, unemployment, spousal abuse, drug addiction, rape, murder, and so forth are concentrated in cities. None of these problems is urban by nature, because these problems can—and do—occur everywhere.

What, then, is *urban* about social problems? First, city life increases rates of social problems. For example, the rates of burglary, robbery, murder, suicide, alcoholism, and rape are higher in cities than in rural areas. As we explore city life, it will become apparent why cities increase such behaviors.

Second, the United States is facing an *urban crisis*. U.S. cities have areas that almost everyone fears and avoids. There, drug dealers openly work "their" street corners, a lucrative turf that they defend by violence. Gang members tag their turf with graffiti, and those who enter these areas do so at their peril. During economic downturns, some cities lay off teachers and shorten the school year because they cannot meet payroll. They slash budgets for the public library and garbage collection. Some even reduce police and fire protection. The term **urban crisis** refers to this cluster of interrelated urban problems. Later in the chapter, we will use sociological theory to consider solutions to the urban crisis.

Looking at the Problem Theoretically

12.3 **Discuss the perspectives that emerge when you apply symbolic interactionism, functionalism, and conflict theory to urban problems.**

As usual, our three theoretical perspectives yield contrasting insights. We will apply symbolic interactionism to the inner city, looking at the social organization of the "slum." Functionalist theory will make visible the zones of activity that develop as a city expands. Finally, using the conflict perspective, we will see how power and social class are related to urban problems.

Symbolic Interactionism

Middle-class Americans fear the inner city and avoid it—unable to understand why anyone would live "like that." Let's see why these are outsiders' views.

Gaining an Insider's View As you will recall, symbolic interactionists try to see how life looks to the people who live it. They try to discover the meanings that people attach to their experiences, how they view their situation, and how they cope with their problems. When this approach to research is applied to urban life, it sometimes is called the **Chicago School of Sociology**. This term is used because about a hundred years ago, in the 1920s and 1930s, sociologists at the University of Chicago used participant observation to produce classic studies of urban life. In 1923, Nels Anderson wrote *The Hobo,* followed in 1927 by Frederic Thrasher's *The Gang.* In 1929, in *The Gold Coast and the Slum,* Harvey Zorbaugh contrasted the rich and the poor in Chicago. Then in 1932, Paul Cressey published *Taxi-Dance Hall,* his research on women who were paid "a dime a dance" to dance with men. Making the city their sociological laboratory, these sociologists focused mostly on the lives of the poor.

Whyte's Classic Study In this tradition, sociologist William Foote Whyte lived as a participant observer in an inner city for three years. In *Street Corner Society* (1943, 1995), his classic account of his experiences, Whyte explained that what may seem disorganized to outsiders is, in fact, a tightly knit way of life. By participating in the residents' lives—hanging around the street corner with "the boys," going to dances, bowling, playing baseball—Whyte found that the young men separated themselves into two main groups: "the college boys," who were upward bound, and "the corner boys," who remained in their old neighborhood. Each group had its own statuses, norms, and ways of controlling its members.

Anderson's Studies As a graduate student at the University of Chicago, Elijah Anderson continued this type of research in another Chicago slum. Doing participant observation at Jelly's, a bar and liquor store in an African American area, Anderson (1978) uncovered intricate boundaries that unite and separate people from one another. From what might seem like a shapeless group—"just a bunch of people"—Anderson found separate clusters of people, each with its own norms, values, and ideas of life. Here are the three main groups that he found at Jelly's:

> The regulars. *These men see and present themselves as hard-working. They follow mainstream values, are proud of their involvement in families, and have aspirations of getting ahead. Their values can be summed up with the single word decency—working regularly and treating other people right.*

> The wineheads. *These men neither value work nor work regularly. Their main concern is getting enough money to buy wine. They beg from others and have low status.*

> The hoodlums. *These men pride themselves on "being tough" and having access to easy money. They are involved in petty theft, stickups, burglaries, and fencing stolen property. The other men at Jelly's do not trust them, nor do they trust one another.*

A Mosaic of Social Worlds Symbolic interactionists continue to do participant observation in the urban world (Duneier 1999; Trimbur 2016; Hansen 2018). They are fascinated with the contrasts of the city—its many groups with their distinctive ways of life. They study how people within each area of the city stake out territory, establish social boundaries, and work out a sense of identity and belonging. They remind us that when we look at a rundown area, we need to see beyond the decaying buildings. Like people everywhere, people in the inner city develop social networks and interact on the basis of background assumptions.

Symbolic interactionists also remind us that the poor do not experience urban problems in the abstract. For example, the poor do not experience the *concept* of urban decay. Rather, they deal with cutbacks in city services; buses that run late or not at all; factories that move to Mexico or China and wipe out their jobs overnight—and killers like Hagan who stalk their neighborhoods.

Functionalism

One aspect of the functionalist view of urban life is how the city develops. Let's look at the major models functionalists have produced.

A Classic Model of the City Sociologists at the University of Chicago also did urban research that reflects the functionalist perspective. Look at Figure 12.3, which is taken from one of these classic studies. You can see that Ernest Burgess identified five urban zones, each with distinct functions. He visualized the city as expanding outward from its center, the central business district (Zone I). The city's slums are in Zone II, which encircles the downtown area. To escape the slums, skilled and thrifty workers move outward, to Zone III. The better apartment buildings, residential hotels, single-family dwellings, and gated communities where the wealthy live are located in Zone IV. Still farther out, beyond the city limits, is Zone V, a commuter zone of suburbs and satellite cities.

Figure 12.3 Burgess' Concentric Zones: Illustrating the Growth of the City

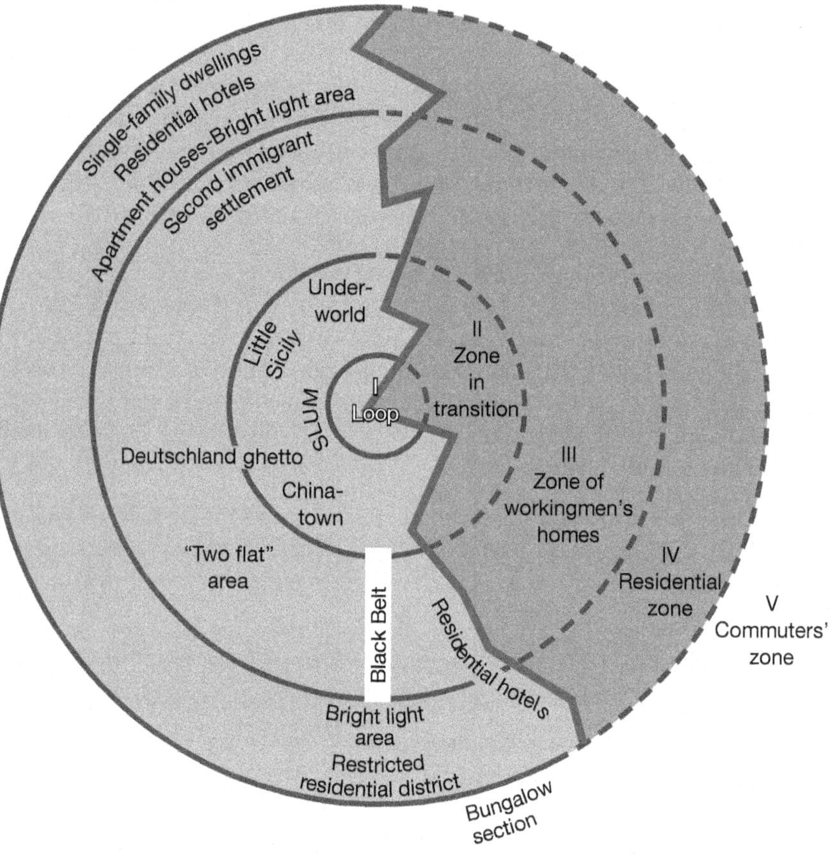

Note: This is Burgess' depiction of how concentric zones flow from the central business district as a city expands. The left side shows the city of Chicago in 1925. The jagged vertical line represents the shore of Lake Michigan.

Source: From Ernest W. Burgess, "The Growth of the City: An Introduction to a Research Project" in *The City*, Robert E. Park, Ernest W. Burgess, and Roderick D. McKenzie, eds. Chicago: University of Chicago Press, 1925. (Pages 47–62 in the 1967 edition).

Burgess said that his **concentric zone theory** explained the "tendencies of any town or city to expand radially from its central business district." He noted, however, that no "city fits perfectly this ideal scheme." Because of physical obstructions, such as lakes or mountains, some cities don't follow this model. Burgess also noted that businesses deviate from this model when they locate in outlying zones.

Mobility in the City The classic model of urban growth shown in Figure 12.3 helps us understand urban problems. Burgess stressed that city dwellers are always on the move.

In addition to commuting for work, school, shopping, and recreation, they move into better zones when they can afford to. This creates an **invasion–succession cycle** in which one group moves into an area already occupied by people who have different characteristics. The invasion creates antagonisms between the groups: One resents displacement; the other feels unwelcome. Today, however, people move not only outward, away from a city's center, but also toward it. We will come back to this recent change in urban patterns.

The Zone in Transition Burgess also noted that the most mobile areas have the most severe social problems: These areas lack a sense of community and suffer from *anomie*, or alienation. As Burgess put it, high mobility leads to juvenile delinquency, gangs, crime, poverty, the breakup of families, and—in a term seldom used today—promiscuity. Mobility and its accompanying problems are concentrated in Zone II, which Burgess called a *zone in transition*. He said that here we find the city's "poverty, degradation, and disease," the "underworlds of crime and vice." In Burgess' colorful phrase, this zone is "the purgatory of lost souls."

Social problems are clustered in the Zone in Transition, such as this area in Holyoke, Massachusetts.

This zone of "lost souls" also attracts another group, people who Burgess said are "obsessed with the vision of a new and better world." He was referring to social workers, preachers, artists, and political radicals. Since Burgess's time, something else has happened: Looking beyond the appearance of the area, some perceive "financial value." In a process called *urban renewal*, they tear down the old and build new office buildings, financial centers, stadiums, and luxury hotels. This redevelopment of the area attracts people toward the city center.

Although Burgess' concentric zone model has many critics (Alihan 1938; Waugh 2014; Chouhy 2018), our purpose here is to note how his model highlights the city's *zones of functional specialties*. All cities have areas dominated by a specific type of business or activity—clusters of warehouses, auto dealerships, boutiques, or fast-food restaurants. Cities also have zones that "specialize" in urban problems—prostitution, seedy bars, and areas of poverty, gangs, and violent crime.

Conflict Theory

Conflict theorists argue that class conflict underlies urban problems. Let's see how this happens.

Class Conflict and Urban Problems The wealthy control a city's affairs—from its newspapers and banks to its colleges and businesses. From these command posts, they make the decisions and give the orders that run the city—always based on protecting and increasing their power and privileges.

To illustrate how the business elite influence government policy to their own advantage without regard for the consequences to inner-city residents, sociologist Manuel Castells (1977, 1983, 1989) pointed to something you wouldn't expect—the development of interstate highways.

> In the late 1800s and early 1900s, business leaders built multistory buildings to house their factories. The development of assembly lines made these buildings obsolete. Instead of the efficiencies of assembly lines, they were stuck with moving raw materials and manufactured goods from one floor to another. They needed single-story factories. The interstate highways and city expressways, built at taxpayer expense, made it profitable to relocate production to the suburbs. With the suburb's lower land prices and often lower taxes as well, the factory owners were able to build single-story factories and adopt the more efficient assembly-line techniques.

Moving factories and offices to the suburbs led to the city's decline. The flight of payroll—the jobs and spending by management and workers—ravaged the city's tax base. It crippled the city's ability to maintain services and help the many poor who were left behind. As the poor became concentrated in the inner city—with its few jobs and bad schools coupled with despair and hopelessness—the city became increasingly desperate and dangerous. In effect, corporate leaders abandoned the city, which they no longer needed, leaving the poor to fend for themselves.

Today, the city remains the repository of the poor and powerless. Adjacent to the resurrected areas we just discussed live the huddled masses—the destitute of an affluent society. The poor are bypassed—another of their many forms of oppression—by leaders who pursue their own personal, political, and economic interests. Because the capacity of the underclass to riot poses a threat to the powerful and privileged, the police keep a sharp eye on the urban poor, controlling their areas with an iron fist. Legions of social workers are also dispatched into their midst, not from altruism, say conflict theorists, but to keep the poor quiet in order to preserve the status quo.

Research Findings

12.4 **Summarize research findings on urban alienation and community, urban dwellers, urban violence, and transitions in power and resources.**

As we examine research findings, let's first consider alienation and community in the city and then look in depth at the decline of the inner city, urban violence, and the changes that are affecting cities in the United States.

Alienation in the City

In a classic essay, sociologist Louis Wirth (1938) noted that urban dwellers live anonymous lives marked by segmented and superficial encounters. This type of relationship, he said, undermines kinship and neighborhood, the traditional bases of social control and feelings of solidarity. This encourages urbanites to grow aloof and indifferent to other people's problems. In short, the price of the personal freedom that the city offers is alienation. Seldom, however, does alienation get to this point:

> In crowded traffic on a bridge going into Detroit, Deletha Word bumped the car ahead of her. The damage was minor, but the driver, Martell Welch, jumped out. Cursing, he pulled Deletha from her car, pushed her onto the hood, and began beating her. Martell's friends got out to

Here is a photo I shot in Manhattan, New York. In the extremes of alienation and community in the city, where does the man on the cardboard fit? How about the couple walking by?

Henslin, James M.

watch. One of them held Deletha down while Martell took a car jack and smashed Deletha's car. Scared for her life, Deletha broke away, fleeing to the bridge's railing. Martell and his friends taunted her, shouting, "Jump, bitch, jump!" Deletha plunged to her death (Stokes and Zeman 1995). Welch was convicted of second-degree murder and sentenced to 16 to 40 years in prison.

This certainly is not an ordinary situation, although anyone who lives in a large city knows that even a minor traffic accident can explode into road rage. And you never know who that stranger in the mall—or even next door—really is. The most common reason for the city's impersonality and self-interest is not fear of danger, however, but the impossibility of dealing with crowds as individuals. To go about our tasks and get through everyday life, we need to ignore the many stimuli that barrage us in city life. If we didn't sort out what seems irrelevant, we would be living in a confused mass.

Community in the City

I don't want to give the impression that the city is inevitably alienating. Far from it. Here is another aspect of the attack on Deletha Word. After Deletha went over the railing, two men jumped in after her, risking their own lives in futile attempts to save her.

Many people find community in the city. Sociologist Herbert Gans, a symbolic interactionist who did participant observation in a rundown, poor part of Boston, was so impressed with the area's sense of community that he titled his classic book *The Urban Villagers* (1962). Here is how Gans described his introduction to the area and his changed perspective:

> *After a few weeks of living in the West End, my observations—and my perceptions of the area—changed drastically. The search for an apartment quickly indicated that the individual units were usually in much better condition than the outside or the hallways of the buildings. Subsequently, in wandering through the West End, and in using it as a resident, I developed a kind of selective perception, in which my eye focused only on those parts of the area that were actually being used by people. Vacant buildings and boarded-up stores were no longer so visible, and the totally deserted alleys or streets were outside the set of paths normally traversed, either by myself or by the West Enders. The dirt and spilled-over garbage remained, but, since they were concentrated in street gutters and empty lots, they were not really harmful to anyone and thus were not as noticeable as during my initial observations.*
>
> *Since much of the area's life took place on the street, faces became familiar very quickly. I met my neighbors on the stairs and in front of my building. And, once a shopping pattern developed, I saw the same storekeepers frequently, as well as the area "characters" who wandered through the streets every day on a fairly regular route and schedule. In short, the exotic quality of the stores and the residents also wore off as I became used to seeing them.*

To outsiders, this was a rough, crime-infested area of the city. But Gans found a *community*—people identifying with the area and with one another. The residents enjoyed networks of friends and acquaintances. Despite the area's substandard buildings, most West Enders had chosen to live here. To them, this was a low-rent district, not a slum.

Some people find community in the city through their associations: work, shopping, school, church, and, as in the photo on the left, from neighborhood activities and friendship. For others, as for the man in the photo on the right, who is considering leaping to his death, community eludes them.

Kzenon/Alamy Stock Photo

Colin Bennett/Alamy Stock Photo

Most West Enders had low-paying, insecure jobs. Other residents were elderly, living on small pensions. Unlike the middle class, these people didn't care about their "address." The area's inconveniences were something they put up with in exchange for low rent. In general, they were content with their neighborhood.

Who Lives in the City?

Whether people find alienation or community in the city depends on whom you are talking about. As with almost everything in life, social class is especially significant. Enjoying greater security and the resources to pursue rewarding activities, from fine restaurants and entertainment to participating in clubs and cultural events, the city's wealthier residents have less alienation and greater satisfaction with city life.

There also are different types of urban dwellers, each with distinctive experiences. These are depicted in Figure 12.4.

Figure 12.4 Types of Urban Residents.

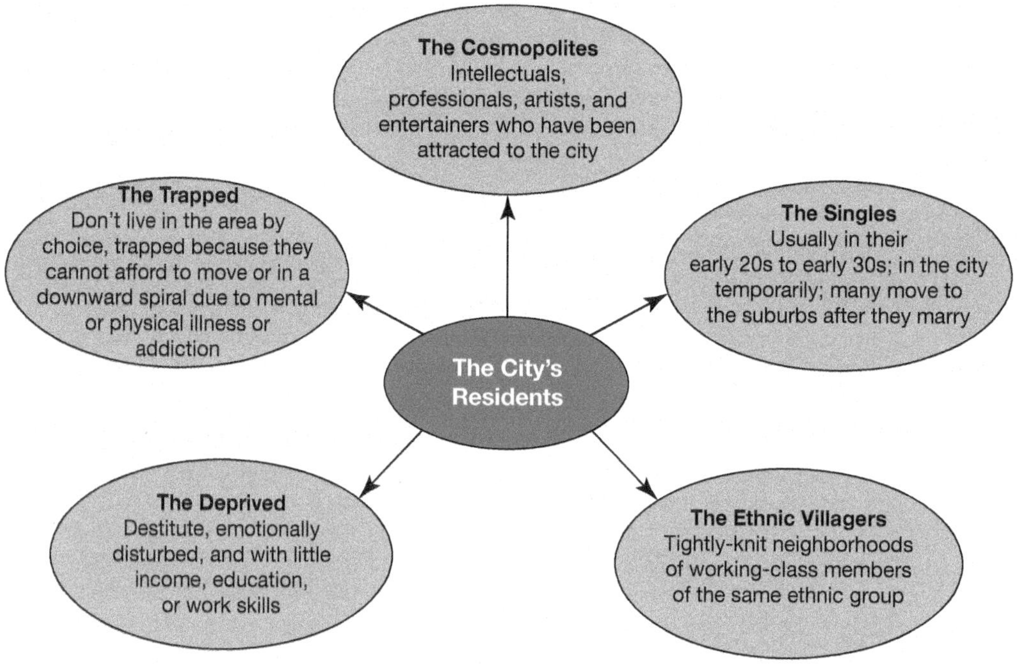

The Cosmopolites
Intellectuals, professionals, artists, and entertainers who have been attracted to the city

The Trapped
Don't live in the area by choice, trapped because they cannot afford to move or in a downward spiral due to mental or physical illness or addiction

The Singles
Usually in their early 20s to early 30s; in the city temporarily; many move to the suburbs after they marry

The City's Residents

The Deprived
Destitute, emotionally disturbed, and with little income, education, or work skills

The Ethnic Villagers
Tightly-knit neighborhoods of working-class members of the same ethnic group

Source: The author's depiction of Gans' types of urbanites.

As we review the five types that Gans (1962, 1968, 1991) identified, try to see where you fit.

The Cosmopolites. *These are the intellectuals, professionals, artists, and entertainers who have been attracted to the city. They value its conveniences and cultural benefits.*

The Singles. *Usually in their early 20s to early 30s, the singles have settled in the city temporarily. For them, urban life is a stage in their life course. Businesses and services, such as singles bars and apartment complexes, cater to their needs and desires. After they marry, many move to the suburbs.*

The Ethnic Villagers. *Feeling a sense of identity, working-class members of the same ethnic group band together. They form tightly knit neighborhoods that resemble villages and small towns. Family- and peer-oriented, they try to isolate themselves from the dangers and problems of urban life.*

The Deprived. *Destitute, emotionally disturbed, and with little income, education, or work skills, the deprived live in neighborhoods that are more like urban jungles than urban villages. Some of the deprived stalk those jungles in search of prey. Neither predator nor prey has much hope for anything better in life—for themselves or for their children.*

The Trapped. *These people don't live in the area by choice, either. Some were trapped when another group "invaded" their neighborhood and they could not afford to move. Others found themselves trapped in a downward spiral. They started life in a higher social class, but they drifted downward because of personal problems—mental or physical illness or addiction to alcohol or other drugs. There also are the elderly who are trapped by poverty and not wanted elsewhere. Like the deprived, the trapped suffer from high rates of assault, mugging, and rape.*

In Sum   Within the city's rich mosaic of social diversity, not all urban dwellers experience the city in the same way. Each group has its own lifestyle, and each has distinct experiences. Some people welcome the city's cultural diversity and mix with several groups. Others find community by retreating into the security of ethnic enclaves. Still others feel trapped and deprived. To them, the city is an urban jungle, a nightmare of threats to their health and safety.

Urban Violence: Youth Gangs

We have already discussed violence in Chapters 5 and 6. Now we look at violence in the context of urban problems, focusing first on violence by youth gangs.

The Neighborhood   As you know, the neighborhood you grow up in has a fundamental influence on your orientation to life. In some neighborhoods, violence is rare. In others, everyone knows that violence is going to happen. Even if they can't predict exactly when or where, they know there are going to be muggings and rapes, and from time to time someone is going to be knifed or shot. For these residents, armed police and wailing sirens are a taken-for-granted background expectation of "the way life is." From Ruth Horowitz's research on the Lions in Chapter 5, you saw that in some neighborhoods gang members use violence to prove themselves. By being willing to risk injury to defend themselves against insults and to protect the members of their gang, these young men receive valued recognition as worthy people. Joining one gang is also a way to protect themselves from other gangs (Brenneman 2012; Vecchio 2019). You can see that living in a neighborhood where violence is woven into the fabric of everyday life leads to a way of perceiving the world that differs radically from the way the middle class views life.

Two Classic Studies: Cohen and Miller   Sociologists have studied gangs for about a century (Thrasher 1927). Of their many studies, let's look at two classics, those by Cohen and Miller.

Sociologist Albert Cohen (1955) found two keys to understanding gangs: the desire of boys to have a valued identity and a clash between middle-class and lower-class values. The schools are located in an area of poverty, but they are run by middle-class teachers and administrators. They use middle-class standards to judge the boys' speech, behavior, and performance on tests. Confronted with these contrary values, the boys feel that they don't fit in and that their teachers look down on them. In a defensive reaction, they form a gang of like-minded boys. Their rejection of middle-class standards is so thorough that doing well in school becomes equated with girls and sissies.

Sociologist Walter Miller (1958) also studied why lower-class boys find gangs so appealing. He, too, found the key in identity. The gangs have six main values: trouble, excitement, toughness, smartness, autonomy, and fate. The better that boys demonstrate these values, the higher their status. Making trouble not only provides excitement, but it also allows the boys to show that they are tough, smart, and autonomous (independent). The boys also think of their lives as controlled by fate: If they get hurt or killed, this is because their number came up. In short, these lower-class boys reject the world of middle-class values that rejects them, crushing their spirits by marking them as failures. The gang's alternative world of values offers the boys an opportunity to achieve a sense of self-worth through the positive recognition of their peers.

National Gangs For the most part, the gangs in these classic studies were groups of adolescents who did nothing worse than get high, skip school, write graffiti, steal from parked cars, get into a fight now and then, and vandalize property. There are still some local gangs like this, but some gangs have morphed into larger organizations with national ties. The Crips, Bloods, and the many like them not only steal and deal drugs but, as with MS-13 discussed in Chapter 5 and Hagan in our opening vignette, they also kill. The findings of Cohen and Miller, however, still apply. The El Rukns/Black P. Stone Nation, the Gangster Disciples, the Vice Lords, the Latin Kings, as well as the more infamous Crips and Bloods, follow this pattern. The boys and men reject middle-class norms—which throw failure into their faces and seem irrelevant to their lives—following norms that allow them to achieve positive recognition and a sense of self-worth. The form of gangs might change over time, but the basic principles on which they operate and by which they attract lower-class boys remain the same.

Transnational Gangs The morphing has continued, with gangs expanding to other countries. There are Hells Angels in Germany and Latino gangs (their members exiled from the United States) in Honduras. The MS-13 gang in Los Angeles has branches in El Salvador, and gangs tied to Chinese Triads are found in Los Angeles; Russian gangs operate in Chicago; the Crips are in Holland; and Mexican gangs have moved into San Diego. The branches cooperate in moving drugs and women sex slaves, and even in killing. The MS-13 will smuggle a gang member from Mexico for a specific killing and then sneak him back across the border, safe from U.S. investigators (Farah 2012).

You have seen how and why gangs attract lower-class youth. It is the same with transnational gangs, which also attract the disenfranchised, the neglected, those who are left out of the legitimate political process. This takes us to a significant element that goes beyond what we have reviewed so far: Transnational gangs provide an alternative political structure. They give power to those who are bypassed by political systems. In some instances, the power of the gang is so great that the established political powers must take them into account when they develop social policy (Felker-Kantor 2018).

Gang members deported from the United States have formed violent gangs in El Salvador, Honduras, and Guatemala. Two of them, the Mara 18 and the Mara Salvatrucha, have been at war with each other. This Mara 18 inmate in a San Salvador prison is embracing his girlfriend during visitation time.

Luis Romero/AP Images

Girl Gangs Many lower-class girls also find the middle-class values of the school oppressive, and for them, too, the contrarian values of gangs beckon (Davis 2017). Some girls reject the "soft feminism" of the middle class, replacing it with toughness and aggression—characteristics that work better in their life situation. Within this framework, however, no matter their tough demeanor, the girls are expected to be submissive to the boys. Here is one indication of how dominant the boys in these groups are: When girls are initiated into the gang, the boys can require them to have sex with one or several of the male gang members. For the most part, girls play supportive roles in the boys' gangs, such as hiding weapons and drugs and providing alibis and sex. As measured by arrests, girl gangs are becoming more violent.

Urban Violence: Schools

> With events like the slaughter of kindergarten children at Sandy Hook Elementary in Newtown, Connecticut, seared in our minds—images of terrified little children cowering before a sociopath—some states require lockdown, or "Code Blue," drills: Each classroom is equipped with a phone. The classroom's doors and windows are locked. Its shades are drawn. The students are trained to remain absolutely silent. Like an armed intruder, a school official wanders the halls, listening for the slightest sound that would indicate that someone is in the classroom (Kelley 2008; Knox 2018).

> Some states have gone beyond this. Texas passed a "campus carry" law, allowing licensed gun owners, both students and professors, to bring concealed guns into the classroom. The state's attorney general warned professors who sued to block the law that they could be disciplined if they didn't allow their students to carry guns (McGaughy 2016).

What an incredible change in U.S. schools. School officials fear that "it could happen in my school." The shooting deaths of 20 kindergarten students at Sandy Hook Elementary School in Newtown, Connecticut, have confirmed their fears. Just what school is safe? And from what unknown psycho? Will teachers and school principals all over the country have to carry guns to defend students?

It isn't only students and strangers who go on killing sprees in schools. Even a college instructor can turn out to be a killer. Recall Amy Bishop who was featured in our opening vignette in Chapter 5. We can hope that this event will remain a unique case.

School violence takes many forms other than shootings, of course. Each year, about a half million students are attacked by other students. And each year, 7,000 teachers are attacked by their students (Musu-Gillette 2018:Tables 2.2, 5.1). Not everyone reports their assault, which can range from being hit to being raped. Some teachers don't report attacks because they fear reprisal from students. Guilt stops other teachers from reporting assaults; they feel that the attack would not have occurred if they had somehow done a better job in the classroom. Others find it easier to ignore an attack than to disrupt their teaching and lives by making several appearances in court.

The bottom line is that most of our interactions, whether at school or elsewhere, are based on trust. No one knows when or where someone will violate that trust, and we cannot live our lives in fear. The challenge is to identify those who are dangerous before they hurt others and to get them the help they need—without the rest of us having to give up our freedoms. This precarious balance between our needs for security and our needs for freedom of movement, association, and the expression of political opinion is a dilemma that faces not just our schools but the entire nation. We can expect many heated debates on this issue.

Population Shift: Regional Restratification

In addition to violence, U.S. cities face extensive change brought about by **regional restratification**, a shift in a region's population, wealth, and power. From Table 12.1, you can see that six of the 10 fastest-growing U.S. cities are in the West, and four are in the South. Of the 10 fastest-declining U.S. cities, five are in the Northeast, three are in the South, and two are in the Midwest. The primary reasons for the flight from the shrinking cities are loss of jobs and high crime rates. The population of the Northeast and the Midwest is not shrinking, but it is growing at a much slower pace than that of the West and South.

Table 12.1 The Shrinking and Fastest-Growing Cities

The Shrinking Cities			The Fastest-Growing Cities		
1.	−5.8%	Detroit, MI	1.	+31.5%	McKinney, TX
2.	−3.0%	Toledo, OH	2.	+25.6%	Irvine, CA
3.	−2.7%	Cleveland, OH	3.	+16.9%	Austin, TX
4.	−2.7%	Montgomery, AL	4.	+16.5%	Cape Coral, FL
5.	−2.7%	Shreveport, LA	5.	+15.9%	Orlando, FL
6.	−2.5%	St. Louis, MO	6.	+15.7%	Seattle, WA
7.	−1.0%	Buffalo, NY	7.	+15.5%	Denver, CO
8.	−0.9%	Mobile, AL	8.	+15.1%	Durham, NC
9.	−0.9%	Rochester, NY	9.	+14.7%	Fort Worth, TX
10.	−0.7%	Akron, OH	10.	+14.5%	Charlotte, NC

Note: Population change from 2010 to 2016, the latest years available.

Source: By the author. Based on *Statistical Abstract of the United States* 2018:Table 24.

It is easy to miss the deep significance of this population shift. A growing population brings with it greater wealth and political power. The tax base of the West and South is growing, and these areas are gaining representatives in Congress. The result is that these regions are gaining in wealth and power to cope with their urban problems. Other areas are losing resources, although their problems are not declining. This is a remarkable regional shift. In only one other period of U.S. history—the Civil War—has the balance of power among the states undergone such rapid and extensive change.

Let's look at the potential for improving the quality of life in U.S. cities.

Social Policy

12.5 Summarize social policy that can build community in the city.

The federal and state governments have tried many programs to solve the crises facing our cities, but some say they have accomplished nothing—except to shuffle money from one faddish urban program to another. Others even insist that government programs have made the problems worse. Shortly before she died, Jane Jacobs (2004), an influential urban expert, warned that things were getting so bad that a dark age threatened to engulf our civilization. She indicated, however, that there was still hope.

With our many resources, we can make that hope a reality. That urban problems are human problems—the products of mistakes, of bad social policy and ill-conceived decisions—means that they can be solved. We have the capacity to make our cities inviting places to live, places that add to our quality of life. The question, of course, is, do we have the will to do this?

The Goal: Establishing Community To bring about effective change, we first need to know what our goal is. As sociologists remind us, quality of social life is rooted in a sense of community (Karacor and Senik 2016; Giardello and Cuervo 2018). To reach this goal, we must preserve and develop neighborhoods that people enjoy. How can we avoid the "urban renewal" programs that Gans warned us about, those that destroy neighborhoods and social relationships? Many programs to develop community are possible, but with the space we have, we can delve into only two, empowerment zones and educating the poor.

Empowerment Zones

To have community, people need jobs. To get employers to move back into an area, many cities have developed **empowerment zones** (also known as *enterprise zones*). Empowerment zones are based on these principles:

1. Businesses that locate in a designated zone—an economically depressed area with high unemployment—receive tax breaks and wage credits for each full-time, qualified employee they hire.

2. If businesses already in an empowerment zone improve their facilities, they receive credits on their property tax.

3. Businesses that locate in an empowerment zone, or that remain there, are eligible for low-interest loans.

Empowerment zones are supposed to generate employment and stimulate economic growth, but most jobs that are transferred there are low-paying, making it difficult to reach these goals. An additional obstacle is that most businesses shy away from empowerment zones because of high crime, which can make the costs of additional security outweigh the benefits from locating there. Another problem is robbing Peter to pay Paul: Enticing businesses to move into the zone can contribute to blight in the areas they leave behind.

How have empowerment zones done? Evaluating the results is difficult. The basic problem is this: You can measure employment, earnings, and poverty in an empowerment zone, but how do you know what they would have been if the area had not been designated an empowerment zone? Overall, the results have been disappointing: Researchers have concluded that empowerment zones have had little impact (Poole 2016;Givord t al. 2018).

The potential, though, is huge. In the next *Thinking Critically about Social Problems*, we look at a success story, an outstanding exception to this evaluation of "little impact."

Thinking Critically about Social Problems

Reestablishing Community: A Twist in the Invasion–Succession Cycle

The story is well known. The inner city is filled with crack, crime, and corruption. It stinks from foul, festering filth strewn on its dangerous streets and piled up around burned-out buildings. Only people who have no choice live in these despairing areas where predators stalk their prey. Danger lurks around every corner.

What is not so well known is that affluent African Americans are reclaiming some of these areas.

The Attraction

Howard Sanders was living the American Dream. After earning a degree from Harvard Business School, he took a position with a Manhattan investment firm. He lived in an exclusive apartment on Central Park West, but he missed Harlem, where he had grown up. He moved back, along with his wife and daughter.

African American lawyers, doctors, professors, and bankers are doing the same.

What's the attraction? The first is nostalgia, a cultural yearning for Harlem past, the time of legend and folklore. It was here that black writers and artists lived in the 1920s, here that the blues and jazz attracted young and accomplished musicians.

The second reason is that Harlem offered housing values. Some homes, built in the 1800s, boasted five bedrooms and 6,000 square feet. They sold for a song, even with Honduran mahogany. Some brownstones were in good condition, although

Revitalized Harlem has brought amenities that were unheard of in this city, a former violence-ridden center of predation.

Guido Koppes/age fotostock/Super Stock

others were only shells and had to be rebuilt from the inside out.

Rebuilding Community

What happened was the rebuilding of a community. Some people who had succeeded in business and the professions wanted to be role models. They wanted children in the community to see them going to and returning from work.

When the middle class moved out of Harlem and the area was taken over by drug dealers and prostitutes, the amenities moved out, too. When the young professionals moved back in, the amenities returned. There were no coffee shops, restaurants, jazz clubs, florists, copy centers, dentist and optometrist offices, or art galleries—the types of things urbanites take for granted. Now there are.

There is also a Whole Foods market, an American Eagle, and a Burlington Coat Factory. There is even a 95-foot-square block of free Wi-Fi. Quite a change.

The police have also helped to change Harlem. No longer do they rush in, sirens wailing and guns drawn, to confront emergencies and shootouts. Instead, the police have become a normal part of this urban scene. Not only did they shut down the open-air drug markets, but they also began enforcing laws against urinating on the streets, something they used to ignore as too trivial to matter for "that area." The greater safety of the area has attracted even more of the middle class. The change is so extensive that former President Clinton chose to locate his office there, and Magic Johnson opened a Starbucks and a multiplex.

Social Class Tensions

Another side of the story has emerged—tension between the people who were already living in Harlem and the newcomers. Social class is often the source of the irritation. Each class has its own ways, and the classes often grate on each other's nerves. The old-timers like loud music, for example, while the newcomers prefer a more sedate lifestyle. Then there is the old power establishment. They feel slighted if the newcomers don't ask for approval before they open a business. For their part, the new business owners feel they don't need to get those old people's permission to open anything.

There is another issue. The large houses built in the 1800s used to sell for a song. No longer. Vacant lots now bring a million dollars. Rents have shot upward, of course. Tenants' associations protest, their moans mostly muffled and unheard.

And the poor? The same as what has happened in other gentrified areas: Most are pushed out, block by block, forced into adjoining rundown streets.

The in-fighting of this emerging drama mostly involves African Americans, but the issue is not race but social class. The "invasion–succession cycle," as sociologists call it, is continuing, but this time with a twist—a flight back in.

A New Pattern

It isn't just Harlem. In the Boyle Heights area of Los Angeles, for example, more well-to-do Chicanos are moving back. As this run-down barrio is transformed, property prices are rising, and tensions there, too, are flaring. We can expect this twist in the invasion–succession cycle to be a new pattern that will occur throughout the country.

Sources: Based on Leland 2003; Hyra 2006; Medina 2013; Kravitz 2014; Adams 2016; Mays 2017.

For Your Consideration

→ Would you be willing to move into an area of high crime in order to get a housing bargain?

→ How do you think the current residents of an area being gentrified can be protected from rising rents so they can continue to live in the area? Should they be?

Educating the Poor

You are personally familiar with the promise of education, how it can make a significant difference in people's lives. One of those differences, as you know, is to qualify people for better jobs. Schools can transform lives, but are our schools capable of handling today's urban poor?

Here is what sociologist Herbert Gans said back in the 1960s:

> The public-school system has never learned how to teach poor children, mainly because it has not needed to do so. In the past, those who could not or would not learn what the schools taught dropped out quietly and went to work. Today, such children drop out less quietly, and they cannot find work. Consequently, the schools have to learn how to hold them, not only when they drop out physically, but long before, in the early elementary grades, when they begin to drop out in spirit (Gans 1968:292).

How pitiful that a critique of our schools from the middle of the last century remains accurate today. It is even more despairing to know that our situation has grown even worse. Unlike the past, few unskilled jobs are available, and today's school dropouts live with less hope—and with a greater tendency to lash out violently.

So what can we do? Let's look at the principles that can help transform the education of the poor.

Principles for Success To start with, we need concerned teachers. The problem is not that we lack them. We have highly principled and well-intentioned teachers and administrators in abundance. These people want to make a difference in the lives of the children entrusted to their care (Ovando and Combs 2018). Educators, however, seldom measure their effectiveness, and they generally have a one-track mind when it comes to how to how to improve education: "Give us more money." Administrators become enamored with fancifully named, currently faddish, and unproved educational programs. If not this, then more money for some public monument to their own position—that is, new buildings and facilities. And as an educator, I say this with despair.

New buildings do give the impression that something is being accomplished, but new buildings don't make good schools—at least, not any more than old buildings do. The key to effective teaching is not the building, but rather what goes on within the building—nourishing the students' desire to learn. Few poor children lack the desire to learn when they begin school. As they stay in school, however, it is common for their eyes to gloss over and for them to come to view schools as irrelevant to their lives and future. The solution is not new. As sociologist Herbert Gans pointed out back in 1968, to do a better job of educating the poor, we need:

1. Motivated teachers,
2. New teaching methods,
3. Smaller classes,
4. Innovative curricula that build on the aspirations of inner-city youth,
5. A more decentralized and less bureaucratized school system,
6. Work-study programs, and
7. Scholarships to encourage adult dropouts to return to school.

I want to add that these are just some of the things we need to educate the poor and help turn our cities around. We also need cooperative learning, child care facilities, and positive reinforcement. More controversial, but quite defensible, is a renewed emphasis on basic learning in grade school (such as memorizing the multiplication tables); a de-emphasis on "feelings of self-worth" as an educational goal, replacing this with academic subjects; and a strong trades program that leads to good-paying apprenticeships. This seems to run against mainstream assumptions, but why assume that every high school student should go to college?

To see the potential that education has for making a success of our cities, read the following *Thinking Critically about Social Problems*.

Thinking Critically about Social Problems

Reestablishing Community: Educating for Success

Education is in crisis. Children are being promoted from one grade to another whether they learn or not. Some students graduate from high school not knowing how to do simple math, unable to read even help wanted ads. Many don't know how to write a résumé and have no idea how to prepare for a job interview. Budgets are cut, programs trimmed, teachers burned out, and students unmotivated.

Community involvement can produce quality education.

"Sow the wind and reap the whirlwind," said Hosea, an Old Testament prophet. And sowing a future of illiterate adults, of poverty and unemployment, welfare dependency, crime, and despair will bring a whirlwind of shattered community. Our nation will be severed in two, those who have and those who don't. We will always have inequalities, but if the divisions grow and the underprivileged feel hopeless, our inequalities can destroy society.

Can education make a difference in this sorry picture? How about for the most impoverished of society, the children of the inner city? To find out, a team from Yale worked with the staff and parents in two grade schools in New Haven, Connecticut. The schools were in low-income neighborhoods. They were 99 percent African American and plagued by the usual inner city problems.

What happened? From the lowest scores on standardized tests in the city, student achievement soared to the third and fourth highest. The students' achievement levels jumped to nine months above their grade level in one school, and 12 months ahead in the other. Attendance and behavior improved dramatically.

How was such a remarkable change accomplished? First, the team made a radical assumption, that the problem was not "poor students"—which is what most people assume—but, rather, a poor educational system. This assumption is radical because it puts the responsibility on the shoulders of the staff. It makes teachers and administrators responsible for meeting the needs that the children's background creates. Second, the staff fostered a feeling of common cause. Third, leadership was transferred from a central office to the grass roots—to those who work in the schools and rub shoulders with the students. In their new leadership position, these people were able to make decisions. And they did this as a unit, a team. Fourth, parents, staff, and students interacted frequently. This helped students identify with adults who value and encourage learning, reflecting a solid educational principle that learning is based on modeling and imitation. Fifth, a sense of community was engendered: Trust, mutual respect, and a common cause developed among not just teachers and administrators, but also parents and students.

Using this same assumption—that inadequate teaching, not inadequate students, is the reason that poor children do poorly in school—Jaime Escalante motivated his students in an East Los Angeles inner city school to perform so well on national calculus tests that officials thought the students must have cheated.

Students in poverty can do well—if schools teach well.

Based on Comer 1986; Escalante and Dirmann 1990; Jacob and Ludwig 2009; Epstein 2018.

For Your Consideration

→ How would you apply these principles to change a troubled school in your area?

→ What other principles from this text would you use?

In Sum If we have learned anything from the recent past, it is that replacing buildings does not cure urban ills. How do more attractive housing and school buildings eliminate poverty and unemployment, whose consequences reverberate throughout society? Poverty lies at the root of many of the problems we have discussed here and in earlier chapters, from violent crime to dysfunctional families. Perhaps the simplest summary is this: Greater access to jobs, education, and justice will reduce urban problems, but these problems will persist to the same degree that the inequalities that produce them persist.

The Future of the Problem

12.6 **Discuss the likely future of urban problems.**

Current trends are firmly established and are likely to persist. I foresee, then, the following.

Higher Costs and Lower Income

Our cities are caught in a bind. They face an increasing demand for services in the face of sales and property taxes that are inadequate to pay for these services. To finance many programs, our cities depend on money from the state and federal governments—which are broke and in debt. Caught in this financial squeeze, some cities lay off teachers and shorten the school year. They also cut back on street cleaning, recreation programs, and activities for children and the elderly. Cutbacks are often the hardest in a city's poor areas, because those cutbacks upset middle-class voters the least.

The Homeless

The homeless will continue to live on our city streets. Their presence will create an outcry—not over their misery but over their visibility. In response to this pressure, city officials will use the police and social workers to disperse the homeless to less visible areas. This will make the city's historical, artsy, and sports areas more appealing to tourism and business, but it will do nothing to solve the problem of homelessness or poverty.

Gentrification

Commuting long distances to work is expensive and time-consuming, and, with inflation, is likely to grow more costly. These factors will increase **gentrification**, the process in which more affluent people move into an area and rehabilitate its buildings. The attractions of the city that we discussed earlier coupled with low-priced houses in deteriorated areas will also draw more of the middle class back to the city. Although their neighborhood grows more attractive, the poor resent the invasion of people with more money. As property values increase, so do taxes and rents, pushing many of the poorer residents into other rundown, low-rent areas.

The usual pattern of gentrification is for better-off whites to move into an area of the city, displacing minority poor. As you saw in the *Thinking Critically about Social Problems* on Harlem, this isn't always the case. Even when it is, though, sociologists have found that it isn't only the whites who benefit. Gentrification also draws middle-class minorities to the neighborhood and improves their incomes (McKinnish et al. 2008). Those who are pushed out receive no such benefits.

The areas of rehabbed buildings and renewed vibrant night life are featured by city officials in slick publicity campaigns to attract businesses, new residents, and investors. Not featured, though, is the sad fact that more areas of the city are deteriorating than are gentrifying. Their declining property values remain a festering thorn in the side of city officials (Mallach 2018).

Principles for Shaping the Future

What our cities will look like in the future depends both on trends yet to appear and on the social policies we adopt now. The following three principles can provide a solid foundation for shaping that future:

1. The city is a social creation, and so are its negative features. As such, they can be overcome.
2. As a center of work and play, the city offers vast potential for satisfying people's needs, even providing a basic structure for human happiness.
3. To design a future that overcomes urban problems, social policies must satisfy basic human needs—social, psychological, physical, and spiritual. As stressed in this chapter, the shorthand word for this is *community*.

These three principles can help us forge a future that enhances the quality of life, maximizes human potential, and creates urban areas that satisfy the human need for belonging.

■ Population

Next let's look at problems and controversies related to population.

Population: The Problem in Sociological Perspective

12.7 Contrast the explanations for Europe's surge in population and the views of the pessimists and the optimists.

We have already discussed a major change in population, the historical development of cities and their current spectacular growth. Before we examine other population trends, we should define **demography**—the study of the size, composition, growth, and distribution of human populations. This definition makes demography sound like a pretty dry subject, but this area of sociology takes us to events that have a direct impact on your future, events so significant that they are reshaping global relations. But as with cities, to get to the present we first need to step through the door of history.

A Population Mystery

Here is a mystery with two solutions.

The Mystery: A Population Explosion For most of history, the world's population increased at a snail's pace. When Jesus was born 2,000 years ago, the population of the entire world was only about the same as that of the United States today. It took until 1750 for Europe to have 140 million inhabitants. Then, unexpectedly, Europe's population surged. In just 50 years, it jumped by 48 million, and in the next 50 years by 68 million, a total of 85 percent in 100 years. What caused Europe's population to explode like this?

Two Explanations: Public Health or the Potato? Demographers have come up with two radically different explanations. G. T. Griffith (1926) argued that the reason for Europe's population explosion was improved public health. He said that better medical knowledge, hospitals, housing, water, and sanitation lowered the **death rate**, the number of deaths per 1,000 people per year. As fewer children died and more people lived longer, the population jumped.

Griffith's explanation is widely accepted, and makes good sense, but some demographers suggest an entirely different reason. Thomas McKeown (1977) claimed that the population of Europe remained low until 1750 because Europeans practiced **infanticide**, killing infants shortly after birth. Then came the potato, he said, and Europe's population surged!

I know this explanation sounds a little strange, so let's probe it a little. McKeown said that food was scarce, and the Europeans practiced infanticide to keep their population in line with their available food. Without infanticide, they would have outstripped their food supply, leading to mass starvation. Then in the 1500s, the Spaniards, who conquered South America, discovered the potato, which was cultivated in the Andean highlands. They brought this unfamiliar food back with them, and gradually the Europeans adopted it. By 1800, the potato had become the main food of the poor in northern and central Europe. As this "miracle" plant expanded the food supply, the Europeans stopped practicing infanticide, and their population almost doubled in 100 years.

Did the lowly potato really have such an impact on history? Demographers still debate the cause of Europe's population explosion, but both explanations point to changes in human behavior—from adopting new medical and sanitation practices to simple changes in diet. That changing human behavior can have far-reaching effects on a population takes us into the heart of demography—and to another controversy.

Demographers in Debate

How can a debate start in the 1700s and still continue today? Let's find out.

Thomas Malthus, the Gloomy Prophet   Europe's surge in population alarmed Thomas Malthus, an English economist. Seeing this increase as a sign of coming doom, in 1798 he wrote an influential book, *An Essay on the Principle of Population*. In this book, Malthus argued that populations grow geometrically, that is, from 2 to 4 to 8 to 16 and so forth, but the food supply increases only arithmetically, that is, from 1 to 2 to 3 to 4 and so on. His book's central message was this warning: If births go unchecked, the population of the world will outstrip its food supply.

The Pessimists: The New Malthusians   Malthus set off an alarm that you can still hear today, and his conclusions are still debated. One group—let's call them the New Malthusians—argues that Malthus was right. Today's situation is as grim, if not grimmer, than Malthus imagined. The world's population has gone unchecked, and just as Malthus warned us, it has exploded.

World population is following an **exponential growth curve**, meaning that growth doubles during equal intervals of time. The implications of exponential growth are startling. To illustrate them, sociologist William Faunce (1981:84) told this parable:

> A poor man saved a rich man's life. Very grateful, the rich man offered a reward. The poor man replied that he would like his reward to be spread out over a four-week period, with each day's amount being twice what he received on the preceding day. He also said he would be happy to receive only one penny on the first day. The rich man immediately handed over the penny and congratulated himself on how cheaply he had gotten by.
>
> At the end of the first week, the rich man checked to see how much he owed and was pleased to find that the total was only $1.27. By the end of the second week, he owed only $163.83. On the twenty-first day, however, the rich man was surprised to find that the total had grown to $20,971.51. When the twenty-eighth day arrived, the rich man was shocked to discover that he owed $1,342,177.28 for that day alone and that the total reward had jumped to $2,684,354.56!

This incredible acceleration is precisely what alarms the New Malthusians. They claim that we have now entered the "fourth week" of an exponential growth curve. Look at Figure 12.5 to see why they think the day of reckoning is just around the corner. It took from the beginning of time to 1800 for the world's population to reach its first billion. It then took only 130 years (1930) to add a second billion. Like a bullet train, the process accelerated, and just 30 years later (1960), the world's population hit 3 billion. The time it took to reach the fourth billion was cut in half, to only 15 years (1975). Then just 12 years later (in 1987) the total reached 5 billion, in another 12 years it hit 6 billion (in 1999), and in yet another 12 years it hit 7 billion (in 2011).

Figure 12.5 World Population Growth Over 2,000 Years

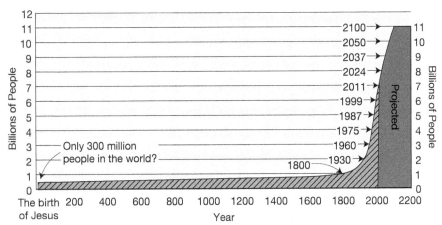

Source: Modified from Piotrow 1973, with projections based on Kaneda and Dupuis 2017.

To get another view of what alarms the New Malthusians, look at Figure 12.6. On average, every minute of every day, 169 babies are born. At sunset, the world has 243,000 more people than it did the day before. In one year, this increase totals 89 million people. In just four years, the world adds more people than the entire population of the United States. *In just the next 12 years, the world's population will increase as much as it did during the first 1,800 years after the birth of Jesus.*

Figure 12.6 How Fast is the World's Population Growing?

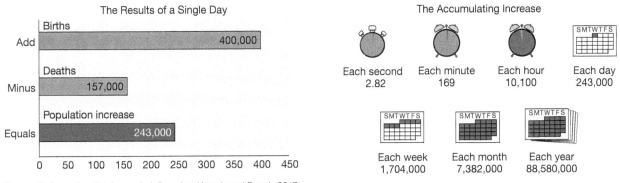

Source: By the author. Totals rounded. Based on Kaneda and Dupuis 2017.

These totals terrify the New Malthusians. In the year 2050, the population of just India and China will be as large as the world's entire population was in 1960. "We are headed for a showdown between population and food," the New Malthusians warn us. "We will run out of food if we don't curtail population growth. Soon you will see more televised images of pitiful, starving children."

The Optimists: The Anti-Malthusians All of this seems obvious, and no one wants to live shoulder-to-shoulder and fight for scraps. How, then, can anyone argue with the New Malthusians?

An optimistic group of demographers, whom we can call the Anti-Malthusians, paint a far different picture. They believe that Europe's **demographic transition** provides a more accurate glimpse of the future. Look at Figure 12.7. During most of its history, Europe was in Stage 1. Its population remained about the same from year to year, with its high death rates offsetting its high birthrates. Then came Stage 2, the population explosion that so upset Malthus. Europe's population surged because birthrates remained high while death rates dropped. Finally, Europe made the transition to Stage 3: The population stabilized as people brought their birthrates into line with their lower death rates.

Figure 12.7 The Demographic Transition

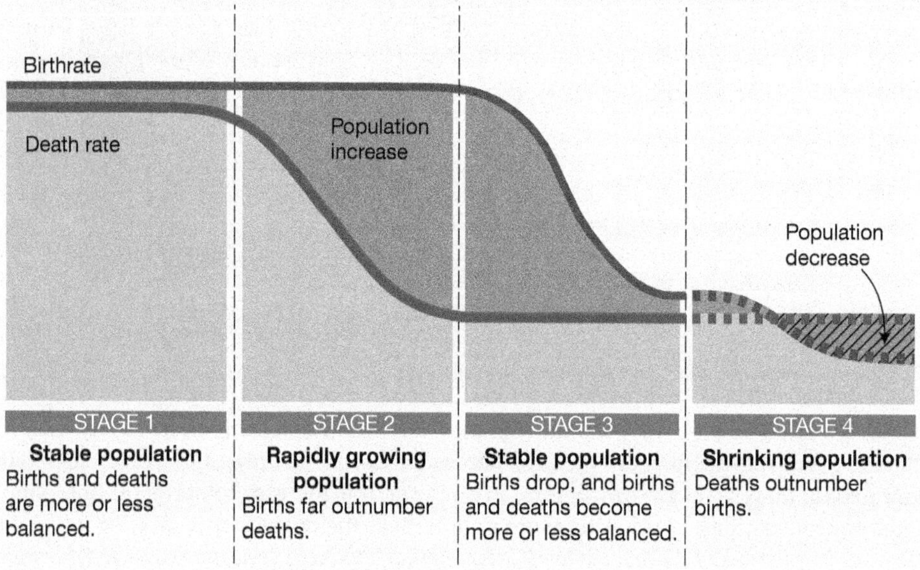

Note: The standard demographic transition is depicted by Stages 1–3. Stage 4 has been suggested by some Anti-Malthusians.

This demographic transition, say the Anti-Malthusians, will also happen in the least industrialized nations. Their current surge in population simply indicates that they have reached Stage 2 of the demographic transition. Hybrid seeds, medicine from the most industrialized nations, and purer public drinking water have cut their death rates, while their birthrates have remained high. When they move into Stage 3, as surely they will, we will wonder what all the fuss was about. In fact, their growth is already slowing.

The demographic transition was so successful that European countries, now in Stage 4, worry about not having enough babies. European leaders fear **population shrinkage**, a failure to produce enough children to replace people who die. Italy was the first country in the world to have more people over age 65 than children under age 15. Of the 38 countries of Europe, 21 are filling more coffins than cradles, shrinking a little each year. Eleven are growing, most very slowly, and six are treading water, neither growing nor shrinking (Kaneda and Dupuis 2017). You might want to jump ahead and take a peek at the global map (Figure 12.12).

Anti-Malthusians predict that this same demographic transition will occur in the poorer nations of the world. Today's rapid growth should not be a cause for concern—it merely indicates that these countries have reached the second stage of the demographic transition. Already their growth rate has slowed. Look again at Figure 12.5. It took the world's population 12 years to go from 4 billion to 5 billion, and then another 12 years to go from 5 billion to 6 billion. If population growth had kept accelerating as it had been doing, it would have taken less than 12 years each to add the world's most recent two billion new inhabitants. Instead, population growth is tapering off, the precise slowing that we would expect as these nations enter the third stage of the demographic transition.

The Scope of the Problem

12.8   Describe how the New Malthusians and the Anti-Malthusians view world population growth and food supply.

As you might suppose, with their contrary views, the New Malthusians and the Anti-Malthusians paint entirely different pictures of the scope of the population problem. Let's compare their views.

Sitting on the Shoulders of the New Malthusians

If anyone thinks we are bursting at the seams now, they need to look into the future. By the year 2050, the world will have 10 billion people—2.5 billion more people than it does now. Can the world support such a large population? To answer this question, we can ask how the world is doing right now. We find that famine and malnutrition stalk the earth. One in nine people in the world—800 million—goes to bed hungry at night ("State of Food…" 2017). In some of the world's poorest nations, such as Bangladesh, half the population never eats enough protein. In Ethiopia, which is growing so fast that by the year 2050, it might be the world's 10th-largest country, the average income is $660 for an entire year (*Statistical Abstract* 2018:Table 1364).

Sitting on the Shoulders of the Anti-Malthusians

"While the totals just cited above are correct, the conclusions are not," reply the Anti-Malthusians. The problem of malnutrition has nothing to do with the earth having too many people, nor with the earth failing to produce enough food. The amount of food available for every person on earth has been increasing, not decreasing. Every country records how much food it produces. As Figure 12.8 shows, despite the billions of people who have been added to the earth's population, *more food is available for each person now than in the past*. The nations produce so much food that obesity has become a global health problem (Kaneda and Dupuis 2017; "State of Food…" 2017).

Figure 12.8 How Much Food Does the World Produce per Person?

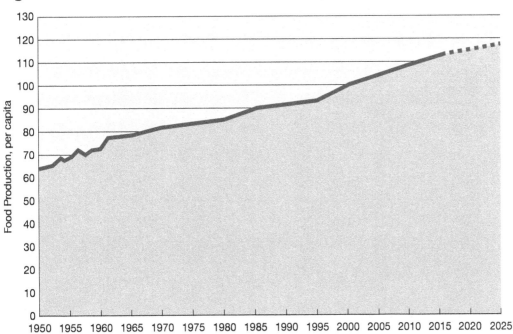

Note: Projections from 2016 are by the author.

Sources: Simon 1981:58; FAOSTAT 2015; *Statistical Abstract of the United States* 1988:Table 1411; 1998:Tables 1380–1383; 2018:Tables 1387–1391.

What about the disturbing images we see of starving children with bony arms, protruding stomachs, and flies crawling over their faces? How can anyone deny that there is a food shortage? The Anti-Malthusians reply that the starving people in those photos certainly aren't getting enough food. The reason for this, though, is not that the earth is failing to produce enough food. The problem is that the world's abundant food is not distributed adequately. If we want to, we could redistribute a small part of the world's abundant grain and prevent all the malnutrition and starvation in the entire world.

"How about the overcrowding of Africa? Everyone knows Africa has so many people that it is outstripping its food supply." What "everyone knows" can be wrong, as it is in this case. Contrary to common belief, starvation in Africa does not occur because there are too many people. Africa's population per square mile of arable land is smaller than in Western Europe (Kaneda and Dupuis 2017). The cause is quite different: drought and civil war. Civil wars in Africa disrupt food production and block humanitarian aid from reaching its suffering people ("State of Food…" 2017).

The source of starvation is not that the earth has too many people or that it does not produce enough food. This horror is caused by a combination of agricultural inefficiency, political corruption, maldistribution of the earth's abundance, and war—not too little food.

In Sum   Looking at the same evidence, the New Malthusians and Anti-Malthusians arrive at different conclusions. Much like the pessimists who look at the water in a glass and conclude that the glass is half empty, the New Malthusians conclude that population growth is out of control and we are about to run out of food. Like the optimists who consider the same glass of water half full, the Anti-Malthusians conclude that our era enjoys the greatest abundance that the world has ever known—and this abundance is growing. The scope of the population problem depends on perception—whether one sees the glass as half empty or half full.

No one can settle this argument for you. You will have to read the evidence and make up your own mind. As you do, remember the symbolic interactionist principle that facts never interpret themselves: To interpret anything, we place it within a framework that gives it meaning. As we consider issues of population and food in the coming pages, we will return to this basic principle from time to time. For now, let's apply the sociological theories.

War, not too many people, is a major cause of malnutrition and starvation in Africa. Having fled guerrilla warfare, this family in Central African Republic lives in a derelict plane.

Ton Koene/Alamy Stock Photo

Looking at the Problem Theoretically

12.9 **Discuss the perspectives that emerge when you apply symbolic interactionism, functionalism, and conflict theory to world population.**

As usual, our theoretical lenses provide contrasting perspectives. Let's compare them to see how they help us understand the social problem of population and food.

Symbolic Interactionism

Doesn't it seem obvious that if you were poor and faced hunger and disease, starvation and death, you would want to have few children? But look at Figure 12.9. You can see that the population of the least industrialized nations is growing so fast that it looks like someone marching up a steep hill. In contrast, the population of the most industrialized nations looks as if it is standing still. Why is almost all the increase in the world's population coming from the least industrialized nations?

Could it be that the adults in the least industrialized nations don't know how to prevent pregnancy? This is worth asking, but it doesn't even begin to touch the reality of the world's poor. Cheap and effective birth control techniques are available, but many of the poor won't use them. Why? Because they *want* large families.

To understand why, let's use symbolic interactionism.

Seeing the World as They See It By **taking the role of the other**—that is, seeing things from another person's perspective—we can make sense of people's experiences. Let me share with you something that happened when I was living in a remote area of Mexico:

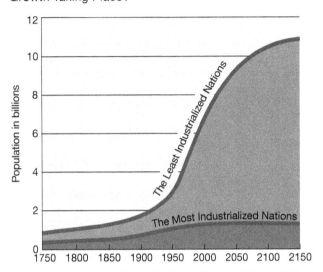

Figure 12.9 Where is the World's Population Growth Taking Place?

Sources: "The World of the Child 6 Billion" 2000; Kaneda and Dupuis 2017.

> *The image still haunts me. There stood Celia, age 30, her distended stomach visible proof that her 13th child was on its way. Her oldest was only 14 years old! A mere boy by our standards, he had already gone as far in school as he ever would. Each morning, he joined the men to work in the fields. Each evening around twilight, I saw him return home, exhausted from hard labor in the subtropical sun.*
>
> *Celia and Angel's home reflected the family's poverty. A thatched hut consisting of only a single room served as home for all 14 members of the family. At night, the parents and younger children crowded into a double bed, while the eldest boy slept in a hammock. As in many homes in the village, the other children slept on mats spread on the dirt floor—despite the crawling scorpions.*
>
> *The home was meagerly furnished. It had only a gas stove, a table, and a cabinet where Celia stored her few cooking utensils and clay dishes. There were no closets; clothes hung on pegs in the walls. There also were no chairs, not even one. I was used to the poverty in the village, but this really startled me. The family was too poor to afford even a single chair.*
>
> *Celia beamed as she told me how much she looked forward to the birth of her next child. Could she really mean it? It was hard to imagine that any woman would want to be in her situation.*

Celia meant every word. She was as full of delighted anticipation as she had been with her first child—and with all the others in between. To understand the desires of billions of poor people like Celia and Angel, we must move beyond our own culture and understand life from their perspective. For the poor in the least industrialized nations, people's identities center on their children. Motherhood is the most exalted status a woman can achieve. Through childbearing, a woman fulfills her destiny and finds personal worth. The more children she bears, the more she fulfills this purpose. Similarly, the more children that a man fathers, the more he proves his manhood. It is especially sons that he desires, for through them, his name lives on.

Most of these people live in small communities where they share values and identify with one another. In this *Gemeinschaft* community of like-minded people, pregnancy is viewed as a sign of God's favor. As people produce more children, the community grants them higher status. The barren woman, not the woman with a dozen children, is to be pitied.

For these people, children are also *economic assets*—not the costly responsibilities they are in an urbanized world. How can this possibly be? The poor in the least industrialized nations have no social security, no medical insurance, and no unemployment benefits. Most live on less than $2 a day (World Bank 2018). This motivates them to have more children because the children are their social security. When parents become too old to work, their adult children take care of them. The more children they have, the firmer their security is.

It is also useful to know that children in the least industrialized nations start to contribute financially to the family long before the parents are old. Look at Figure 12.10. This, too, should help you take the role of the other to understand why the surge in the world's population is coming from the least industrialized nations.

Figure 12.10 Why the Poor Need Children

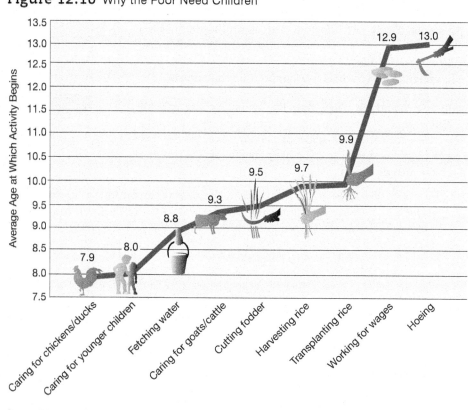

Source: U.N. Fund for Population Activities.

In Sum   People's ideas of the "right" number of children reflect their life situation. To impose our ideas onto people in other cultures is to overlook their experiences and perspectives. To understand the behavior of any group, we must see things as they see them.

Functionalism

As we apply the functionalist perspective, keep in mind that functionalists want to determine objectively the functions or dysfunctions of behaviors and events, without judging those consequences as good or bad.

Catastrophes Are Functional   As we saw with poverty, rape, murder, drug addiction, and racial–ethnic discrimination, functionalists identify functions even in deviant, illegal, or abhorrent events. With regard to the world's population growth, functionalists stress that even war, natural disasters, disease, and famine are functional. Historically, these mass killers have held the world's population in check, ensuring that humans did not outstrip their food supply.

Modern Medicine and Public Health: Latent Dysfunctions   Throughout history, the balance between population and food has been precarious. Ordinarily, high death rates have canceled out high birthrates, and populations have remained stable. Exporting modern medicine to the least industrialized nations, however, upset this balance. Along with better nutrition and sanitation, Western drugs brought under control those nations' major killers—smallpox, diphtheria, typhoid, measles, and other infectious diseases. As a result, the death rates in these nations plunged, but their birthrates went untouched. Not only did millions of people who otherwise would have died survive, but they also reproduced. This has taken the least industrialized nations into the second stage of demographic transition, which you saw on Figure 12.7.

Population Pyramids   Countries in the second stage of the demographic transition have a lot of young people, while those in the third and fourth stages have a lot of older people. Obviously, countries with more young people have higher birthrates than those with more older people. Demographers use the term *age structure* to refer to countries having larger or smaller proportions of younger and older people. To illustrate age structures, demographers produce **population pyramids**, like Figure 12.11, which contrasts Mexico, in Stage 2 of the demographic transition, with the United States, in advanced Stage 3. As you can see, different age structures produce different "shapes" of populations.

Figure 12.11   Population Pyramids of Mexico and the United States

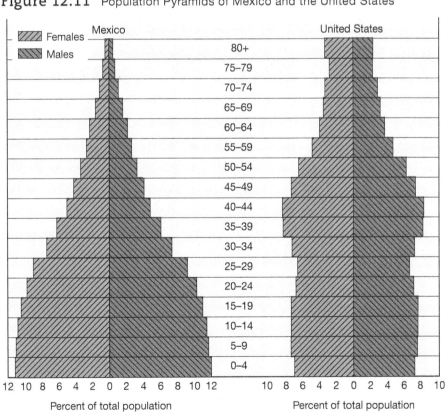

Source: By the author. Computed from the U.S. Bureau of the Census 2006b:Table 94.

To see why population pyramids are important, I would like you to imagine a miracle—that overnight, Mexico is transformed into a nation as industrialized as the United States. Imagine also that births drop and the average woman in Mexico gives birth to 2.1 children, the same as in the United States. If this happened, Mexico's population would grow at the same rate as that of the United States, right?

But this isn't what would happen. Instead, the population of Mexico would still grow faster than that of the United States. To see why, look again at the population pyramids. You can see that a higher percentage of Mexican women are in their childbearing years. Even if Mexico and the United States had the same birthrate, a larger percentage of women in Mexico would be giving birth, and Mexico's population would grow faster. As demographers like to phrase this, Mexico's age structure gives it greater population momentum.

With its higher population momentum and birthrate, Mexico's population will double in 50 years. The implications of a doubling population are mind-boggling. Just to stay even, within 50 years Mexico must double the number of available jobs and housing; its food production; its transportation and communication facilities; its water, gas, sewer, and electrical systems; and its schools, hospitals, civic buildings, theaters, stores, and parks. If Mexico fails to double them, its already meager standard of living will drop even further.

As you can see from Figure 12.12, the doubling time of the world's nations is uneven. All totals on this figure are transitory, depending on what happens with birth rates, death rates, and migration. The "Never" for Europe applies to current growth rates of its natives, but immigration and higher birthrates of immigrants can change this.

Figure 12.12 How Long Will It Take for a Population to Double?

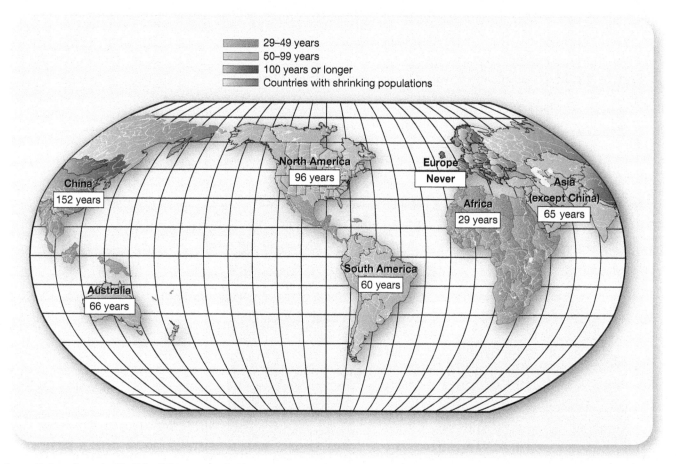

Source: By the author, using The Rule of 70 to compute doubling time from population growth rates. Based on a variety of sources, including Kaneda and Bietsch 2015; Wade 2016.

In Sum   Functionalists analyze how exporting Western medicine and public sanitation into the least industrialized nations caused a surge in their population. Their rapid population growth outstripped their food supply, resulting in malnutrition, mass starvation, and political unrest. Because these negative consequences were not anticipated or intended, sociologists call them **latent dysfunctions**.

Conflict Theory

When we look at problems of population growth and food from the conflict perspective, we get an entirely different view.

Profits, Biofuel, and Food Politics   You probably have heard a lot about the vast quantities of food that the United States ships to the poorer nations, but do you know that the least industrialized nations also send food to us? Each year, the United States imports more than $100 billion in food, much of it from India, Indonesia, Vietnam, and other least industrialized nations (*Statistical Abstract* 2018:Tables 879, 880). As social critic Michael Harrington (1977) pointed out long ago, the major profits from this food go not to the poor countries that produce it, but to corporations in the most industrialized nations that process and distribute it.

As conflict theorists stress, food is a money-making enterprise for these corporations, not a means of solving world hunger. As you know, about 10 percent of the gasoline you pump into your car is ethanol. Ethanol comes from food, primarily from corn. Each year, one-third of all corn raised in the United States, over 5 billion bushels, goes into the production of ethanol (*Statistical Abstract* 2018:Table 887). Whatever the merits were of reducing U.S. dependence on oil imports, with fracking, the United States is now a net exporter of oil, and each gallon of ethanol represents food that is needlessly no longer available to the world's population.

Even though people in some nations are starving, the U.S. government pays farmers *not* to grow crops. These government payments are huge, running about $11 billion a year (*Statistical Abstract* 2018:Table 870). Conflict theorists say that the reason for these payments is **food politics**—paying farmers to limit food production creates an artificial shortage that drives up grain prices. This caters to the farm vote by keeping grain prices high. The reason for food politics, stress conflict theorists, is profit, with no concern for what is right, just, or moral.

Population Control   To wrap up this section, let's revisit the implications of a population doubling, which can lead to a declining standard of living. Conflict theorists point out that a declining standard of living poses the threat of political instability—protests, riots, even revolution—and, in response, repression by the government. Political instability in one country can spill into others, threatening an entire region's balance of power. Fearing such disruptions, leaders of the most industrialized nations use the United Nations to direct a campaign of worldwide birth control. With one hand they give agricultural aid, IUDs, and condoms to the masses in the least industrialized nations—and with the other hand, they sell weapons to the elites in these countries. Both actions, say conflict theorists, serve the same purpose: promoting political stability in order to maintain the dominance of the most industrialized nations in global stratification.

In Sum   Conflict theorists conclude that food production and population control are political tools. The food crisis that affects the starving and undernourished is the result of food politics, not Malthusian inevitabilities.

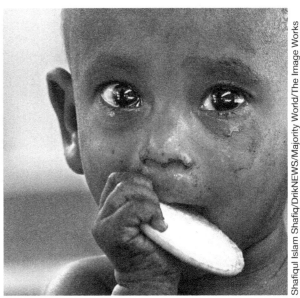

The text explains the reasons for hunger and malnourishment. This photo was taken in Bangladesh.

Shafiqul Islam Shafiq/DrikNEWS/Majority World/The Image Works

Research Findings

12.10 **Summarize how the New Malthusians and the Anti-Malthusians interpret research findings on population change.**

As we review research findings on population and food, let's continue to compare the positions of the New Malthusians and the Anti-Malthusians.

The New Malthusians

As you can expect, the New Malthusians find the research findings depressing. Let's see why.

Tsunamis and Population Growth   The worst tsunami in recorded history occurred in 2004. Its waves—30, 40, or 50 feet high, created by an earthquake on the ocean floor—rolled for hundreds and even thousands of miles before they reached land. The tsunami hit Indonesia with such force that it killed 233,000 people. At the time, Indonesia had an annual growth rate of 1.6 percent, its *rate of natural increase,* as demographers call it. With a population of 220 million, Indonesia was growing by 3,300,000 people each year, 9,041 people each day (Haub 2004). It took Indonesia *only 26 days* to replace the 233,000 people it lost to the tsunami.

The world's population growth, say the New Malthusians, is like a tsunami—a destructive wave that threatens to overwhelm us and destroy our future.

Less Food for More People   As the world's population increases, there will be less food for each person. The world's fishing grounds are threatened by pollution and overfishing. Land unsuitable for cultivation has already been pushed into production, and we are running into a global water shortage as extensive irrigation depletes the world's aquifers (Hoekstra 2018). As the wells run dry, food production will drop.

The Elusive Goal of Zero Population Growth   Let's suppose that the world somehow manages to achieve **zero population growth**—that is, adults having only enough

Is this the future of the world, as the New Malthusians fear? This photo was taken in Dalian City in northeast China's Liaoning province.

Imagine China/Newscom

children to replace themselves. On average, each woman would bear 2.1 children, the extra 0.1 child making up for those who die before reproducing. It seems obvious that the world's population problem would then disappear, right? Wrong. *The population momentum that we discussed earlier would keep the world's population growing for 50 to 70 years before it levels off.*

Consider Africa as an example. Forty-one percent of Africans are not yet age 15 (Kaneda and Dupuis 2017). This means that more Africans will enter the reproductive ages each year than will leave them. If Africa attained zero population growth now, its growth rate would fall for another 50 or 70 years, but its population would continue to increase during this time. Only then would it level off.

And, add the New Malthusians, Africa isn't even close to zero population growth. The average African woman gives birth to almost five (4.6) children, not two (Kaneda and Dupuis 2017). From the news, it often sounds as though Africa is immersed in death: HIV/AIDS, guerilla warfare, and people starving to death. Africa's population, however, is growing faster than that of any other continent in the world.

The Anti-Malthusians

And as you can expect, the Anti-Malthusians find the research encouraging.

Larger Populations Are Good The view of the Anti-Malthusians is almost the polar opposite. They even claim that more people are good for the world, that larger populations lead to higher standards of living (Simon 1977, 1982, 1991). Why? Larger populations force countries to use their land more efficiently, which increases productivity. They also create larger markets. This promotes more efficient manufacturing, lowering production costs and making more goods available. With larger populations, many social investments become profitable, especially railroads, highways, irrigation systems, and ports. These investments, which don't pay off with lower populations, spur productivity and increase a country's capacity to deliver the higher productivity to its people. Finally, a growing world population means that more geniuses will be born. They will contribute to everyone's welfare.

Food Production Is Outpacing Population Growth The Anti-Malthusians stress that the world's food production is outpacing the world's population growth. (Recall Figure 12.8.) Although the world's population has "exploded," there are now more grains and meat for each person in the entire world than there were 50 or even 100 or 200 years ago. When it comes to threats to the world's fishing stocks, human ingenuity has solved the problem. Now about half of the fish we eat come from aquaculture—and the potential of aquaculture is barely tapped (Lester et al. 2018). As a result, the world's fish harvest is growing faster than the population (*State of the World's Fisheries and Aquaculture* 2018). If the world's population increase is dramatic—and it is—then the world's food increase is even more dramatic.

Has the Population Explosion Peaked?

Do you think the population explosion has peaked? Let's see what the Anti-Malthusians and Malthusians say about this.

The Anti-Malthusians The Anti-Malthusians point out that the world's rate of population growth is slowing. Between 1965 and 1975, the world's population grew an average of 2 percent each year. During the 1980s, the growth rate dropped to 1.7 percent. Now it has dropped to 1.1 percent (UN 2017). This huge reduction in the rate at which the world's population is growing—45 percent—is evidence that the world is following the demographic transition.

I think you'll enjoy the next *Global Glimpse*, which gives insight into this process.

A Global Glimpse

"I'd Like to Have 20 Children"

In 1976, an anthropologist who was making a documentary in an African village in Kenya asked a 26-year-old mother of two how many children she wanted. The woman looked at her bulging stomach, giggled, and said, "I'd like to have 20 children."

The documentary then went into a freeze frame, with a subtitle stating that the woman had given birth to twins.

This image haunted John Tierney, a *New York Times* reporter. "What is wrong with her?" he wondered. "What would become of her family?" Ten years later, Tierney went to Kenya to follow up on the story. He found the woman, Fanisi Kalusa, living in the same hut, the twins healthy. She was now 36, with 7 children, ages 4 to 16.

When Tierney asked about her wanting 20 children, Fanisi laughed, and said, "I've rejected that idea because there is not enough food to meet the demand."

Most African men dislike birth control, but her husband had agreed to limit their family size. He had his mother put a curse on his wife to make her barren—a standard practice in the area.

Fanisi went along with the curse—but without telling her husband, she visited a clinic for a free IUD.

Initially, she wanted 20 children who would be available when she needed help on the farm and support in old age. But now, children have become expensive in Kenya. For each child, parents must pay $10 a year in tuition, a burden many poor cannot afford. In addition, many children are moving to the city, breaking close family bonds and threatening the custom of adult children providing support for their aged parents.

Fanisi told her 16-year-old daughter to have only six children. Fanisi's daughter told Tierney that she thought four would be about right.

The rapid growth of Africa's population is a global concern. Will Africa be able to feed, clothe, and educate its growing population? Will there be mass starvation? Or mass migration from Africa, upsetting populations in other regions? This photo is of children in the Samburu tribe of Kenya.

Based on Tierney 1986; Kaneda and Dupuis 2017.

For Your Consideration

→ Do you think Africa will move to the next stage in the demographic transition? Anti-Malthusians point to Fanisi Kalusa and those like her as evidence that this will happen. But the New Malthusians, well, see below.

The New Malthusians Advocates of zero population growth don't disagree that the rate of population growth has slowed, but they say that this doesn't mean what the Anti-Malthusians think it does. They stress that the world's population is still exploding. As for Africa, they point out that African women average 4.7 children each, 41 percent of Africans are under the age of 15, and by 2050 Africa' population will double from today's 1.2 billion people to 2.5 billion.

Social Policy

12.11 **Compare the social policy implications of the New Malthusians and the Anti-Malthusians.**

Because they disagree so sharply, when the New Malthusians and the Anti-Malthusians suggest social policy, they disagree on almost everything, except for the need to increase world food production. Rather than taking sides, let's consider the radically different implications of their sharply contrasting views for social policy.

Policy Implications of the Anti-Malthusians

The basic implication of the Anti-Malthusian position, though seemingly exaggerated, is this: If larger populations are good for the world, then it follows that social policy ought to encourage larger families.

Encouraging Population Growth and Technological Development   To implement the Anti-Malthusian position, we could take the following steps:

1. Reduce the age of consent to have sex to match the age at which girls are biologically able to reproduce. This would get more young women pregnant.
2. Encourage teenagers to experiment sexually.
3. Offer incentives for women to bear many children—paid maternity leave, subsidized housing and food, and free nannies, child care, and medical care—and cash bonuses for having children that would increase with each successive child.
4. Discourage the education of women, because the less education women have, the more children they bear.
5. Make abortion and birth control illegal.
6. Export Western medicine and public health techniques to the least industrialized nations. This will reduce deaths so there will be more people to reproduce.
7. Encourage science, technology, industry, and agriculture. Developments in these areas can help improve the standard of living of huge populations.

Policy Implications of the New Malthusians

The social policy implications of the New Malthusians, of course, point in a different direction. Malthus himself spelled this out. Let's see what he said.

Malthus' Machiavellian Proposal   In an essay on the principle of population (1798/1926), Thomas Malthus made these radical suggestions for limiting population:

> We should...encourage...destruction.... Instead of recommending cleanliness to the poor, we should encourage contrary habits. In our towns we should make the streets narrower, crowd more people into the houses, and court the return of the plague. In the country, we should build villages near stagnant pools, and particularly encourage settlements in all marshy and unwholesome situations.... But above all, we should reprobate [reject] specific remedies for ravaging diseases.

You can see that Malthus' suggestions to increase filth and spread disease follow logically from the New Malthusian position. Such policies, of course, have been rejected as not being humane. But let's continue on Malthus' path to see what other social policies might follow from this position.

More Generally Unacceptable Policies   If we were to implement Malthus' recommendations, some rather severe social policies would be called for. Among them would be these:

1. Encourage infanticide.
2. Refuse to send food to areas of famine and starvation.
3. Withdraw modern medicine from the least industrialized nations, including vaccines, antibiotics, and medicines for HIV/AIDS.
4. Raise the age of sexual consent and the age at which people are allowed to marry.
5. Require a license to have children.
6. Require abortions for women who become pregnant without a license.
7. Encourage homosexual unions, since they don't produce children.
8. Sterilize enough baby girls to ensure zero population growth.
9. Sterilize each woman after she gives birth to her first child.
10. Establish a national system of free abortions on demand to any woman of any age for any reason.

I know that these positions sound extreme, but some New Malthusians have gone even further. Environmentalist Pentti Linkola (2011) is the best example. He suggests that we should annihilate most of the human race. Humanity, he says, squirts all these teeming, filth-producing multitudes from out of itself, in the process suffocating its own culture to the point that people have to spasmodically search for the "meaning of life" and create an identity for themselves through petty childish arguing. Humanity is like a sinking ship with 100 passengers and a lifeboat that holds only 10. When the boat is full, those who hate life will bring aboard drowning people and sink the boat, while those who love and respect life will take the ship's axe and chop off the hands of those clinging to the boat.

Linkola also says "We need to end aid to the Third World, stop giving asylum to refugees—and a war would be good, too." To let us know that he is serious, he adds, "If there were a button I could press that meant millions of people would die, I would gladly sacrifice myself."

Achieving Zero Population Growth   Now that you have seen the extremes, let's look at less radical, more generally acceptable social policy implications of the New Malthusians. One of their common goals is to achieve zero population growth. What motivates most people to have fewer children is not some abstract notion of a world population problem but their attitudes, beliefs, and values. Let's consider what social policies might encourage such views.

1. Encourage women to go to college and to graduate school. Again, the more education women attain, the fewer children they bear.
2. Encourage women to want careers. Women with careers have fewer children.
3. Distribute free or low-cost birth control devices to everyone, including teenagers.
4. Teach zero population growth to schoolchildren, warning them about the coming tsunami of uncontrolled population growth.
5. Pay women to be sterilized. The payment can be small. One hundred dollars goes a long way in the least industrialized nations, where many annual incomes are less than $1,000. Each $100 invested now will save huge amounts in the years to come.
6. To increase food production, make international aid dependent on a country reforming its agricultural practices.

This last item, though it might seem cold and brutal, was tried successfully when India experienced mass starvation during the mid–twentieth century. Instead of just shipping supplies of food, which would have made India dependent on the West, the United States made each shipment depend on progress in meeting monthly agricultural goals.

Why is more education for girls a social policy suggestion of the New Malthusians? This photo was taken in Jordan.

Thomas Trutschel/Photothek/Getty Images

Today, not only does India feed itself, but it is a net exporter of food (Kumar et al. 2017). The food-deficient countries have the capacity to be food independent. China broke up its communal farms and, using profit-oriented incentives, now produces more food than it needs for its incredible 1.4 billion people.

The Future of the Problem

12.12   **Compare the two futures as seen by the New Malthusians and the Anti-Malthusians.**

Not surprisingly, the New Malthusians and Anti-Malthusians also disagree sharply on their perception of the future. Let's look at how they see things.

The New Malthusians: The Pessimistic View

Underlying the New Malthusians' view of the future is this hard fact: Many of the world's natural resources, such as petroleum and minerals, are finite, as are the growing capacity of our land and the carrying capacity of our oceans. Our growing populations and our prodigal use of our resources are a quick path to a gray and dismal future.

Here is what the New Malthusians foresee.

High Food Prices and Starvation   Populations will outstrip their food production. In the face of higher demand and lower supply, the price of food will increase. This will place a tremendous burden on the least industrialized nations. Already poor, and burdened by debt to the most industrialized nations, they cannot afford to import much food. With 800 million people living on less than $2 a day (World Bank 2018), the coming starvation will be severe.

More Famines and Refugees   As food shortages get worse and starvation spreads, the world will face a flood of economic refugees. Neither the least industrialized nations nor the most industrialized nations will accept these millions of poor, uneducated, culturally foreign people who seek refuge and the opportunity for a more promising, abundant life. To take them in would heighten social tensions in their lands. Millions of dislocated people will live for decades in "temporary" refugee camps.

Riots, Revolutions, and Repression   As masses of people flock to the cities of the least industrialized nations in search of work and a better life, they will be met with rising food prices and food shortages. The people's response will be food riots and revolution. The national implication: To maintain social order, governments—encouraged by their elites, who want to maintain their privileges—will become more repressive. The international implication: Because political and civil disorder can upset the global balance of power that the most industrialized nations want to maintain, the more powerful and wealthy nations will either encourage such repression or "look the other way" when it occurs.

In Sum: A Bleak Future for the World   If we paint a picture of the future of the world, we would have to use the color gray for desperate. Famine, malnutrition, and starvation, now striking at just a spot or two on the globe, are ready to stalk victims around the world. Pollution and other environmental destruction will also grow widespread as a bloated number of people try to carve out a meager living from the earth's fragile surface. As the least industrialized nations struggle for food and other resources, they will be torn apart by riots and civil wars. War will also break out as nation fights nation for control of diminishing resources.

The Anti-Malthusians: The Optimistic View

"You are using the wrong color to paint our future. You need bright colors," say the Anti-Malthusians as they scoff at the conclusions of the New Malthusians.

Let's see why the Anti-Malthusians take this position.

Two Dollars a Day First, let's get the full facts, say the Anti-Malthusians. Yes, 800 million people live in poverty. But did you know that in 1990, 2 billion people were living on less than $2 a day? While the world's population has jumped, *the number of people in poverty has been cut in half* (World Bank 2018). This marvelous achievement points to a glorious future.

Population Shrinkage If you want to peer into the future, they stress, review Figure 12.7. Many nations have entered the fourth stage of the demographic transition, and their populations have begun to shrink. The world's other nations will also enter this fourth stage. Despite their current population growth, they, too, will fill more coffins than cradles. As this process continues, the population of the world will begin to shrink. Future concerns will be the opposite of today's, shifting from what we can do about population growth to what we can do about population shrinkage. Russia and some other European countries are already trying to get women to have more children.

Technology and Abundance Our future will bring even greater abundance to the world's people. As education and knowledge increase, the world's nations will take better care of their natural systems (fishing grounds, forests, and grasslands). These are renewable resources, and, carefully managed, they will produce all that the world, even a growing one, will ever need.

In our emerging **biotech society**, bioengineers have already begun to produce pest-resistant plants that produce their own fertilizers. From gene splicing will come cereals that replace nitrogen in the soil, allowing farmers to bypass expensive petroleum-based fertilizers. We will produce low-fat cows, chickens that lay several eggs a day, and sizzling steaks made in the laboratory.

If this sounds unrealistic, note what biotech agriculture is already producing. We have not only cloned animals, but we have also produced **designer animals**, gene-spliced farm animals that produce more meat and milk. We have corn that makes its own insecticide (Kilman 2006), goats that produce spider silk, and animals that produce medicine (Kristoff 2002; Rincon 2015). Soon you will be eating meat grown in steel tanks (bioreactors) (Bunge 2016).

Which Will It Be?

Will the earth be filled with so many people that there is not enough food for them all? Or are the Anti-Malthusians right, and the world's nations will manage their resources, feed and clothe themselves, and provide an even higher standard of living for everyone? Could the future problem actually be population shrinkage rather than population explosion?

With such drastically contrasting viewpoints by experts who look at the same evidence, we cannot side with one group or the other. We can only await the future as it unfolds. Coming generations are going to wonder why we didn't see what is so obvious to them, but hindsight is so perfect—and frustrating for those of us who must peer into the future from the present. We can only anticipate what is to come based on the evidence we have at the moment. Instead of either of the extreme futures that the New Malthusians and the Anti-Malthusians foresee, another possibility is that we will end up with something in between.

Concluding Dilemma

In the following *Thinking Critically about Social Problems*, let's close this chapter on another provocative note.

Thinking Critically about Social Problems

Mass Migration: Latinos, Muslims, Conflict, and Confusion

In this chapter, you have reviewed a lot of details about population growth, the relationship of birthrates, death rates, and immigration/emigration. Many of these concepts and statistics may seem remote, even antiseptic, but their implications are relevant not only to what is happening in society but also for your life. How? Read on.

Consider the extensive Latino immigration to the United States. Many millions of people, primarily from Mexico but also from Central and South America, have moved to the United States. This vast migration has upset both white and black Americans. Whites have been upset because Latinos are bringing with them a different culture (language, family customs, ideas about life and relationships). Blacks are upset because the Latino newcomers compete for jobs. And both whites and blacks are upset because so many of the Latinos have crossed the border illegally.

Illegal immigration is both a backyard topic and a political campaign issue. What to do? Proposals from the extremes of forget it (amnesty) to legal punishment (jail and expulsion) to somewhere in between have confused almost everyone.

But this is nothing compared to what has been happening in Europe. There the migrants are from war-ravaged Syria and Afghanistan and other nearby countries. At first, Europe welcomed the refugees—mostly, kind of. Germany had the most open arms, announcing that it would take as many refugees as wanted to learn a language where the verb comes at the end of a sentence. With Germany's liberal resettlement and welfare laws and job opportunities, the refugees ignored the linguistic problems and flocked in. Soon the vast number of newcomers made Germans uncomfortable. And among the refugees were some terrorists. When they set off bombs, axed train passengers, and rammed a truck into people celebrating Christmas, it was not surprising that fears and resentment spread. When young men groped and raped women, figuring they were fair victims because they wore short skirts, the welcome mat was withdrawn. German left-wingers clucked their tongues, while German right-wingers burned down resettlement centers.

Meanwhile, in France, which already had several million Arabs who had emigrated from African countries that used to be part of the French Empire, the welcome mat wasn't quite as broad. But the European Union had rules, and France let the refugees in. As in Germany, there were two problems: The first—the migrants arrived with a different culture (language, religion, clothing, and ideas). And they did not seem inclined to accept French culture. The second problem is that among the refugees were terrorists who began to blow up French citizens, slaughtering them at concerts, in restaurants, and while they celebrated their national holiday. None of this went down well.

Desperately trying to escape war and poverty, several million people from Africa and the Middle East have fled to Europe. Shown here is a makeshift camp in Paris.

Frédéric Vielcanet/Alamy Stock Photo

Suddenly, the welcome mat was withdrawn. The British said they didn't want a part of any of this, and in a quiet British sort of way, they voted to leave the European Union. Let the others have those problems if they want them, they declared through their voting. For their part, Germany and France began to pay Turkey to block the refugees, asking Turkey to close the border and to lock refugees up in camps to keep them away. Turkey grabbed the money. Seeing the opportunity to keep those euros flowing, every now and then Turkey would hint that maybe they couldn't keep the borders closed. And those euros kept flowing.

No welcome mat. A lot of political turmoil, and upset, resentful, frightened citizens.

This is the situation as I write this text. I can't say what the situation will be in a couple of years, but I anticipate more payoffs to Turkey, new laws that allow easier expulsion of immigrants, and fierce antagonisms between the natives and the newcomers.

What lies in back of all of this turmoil? Civil war in Syria, certainly. The invasion of Iraq and Afghanistan by the United States and affiliated powers. But there is a broader background factor. The population growth rates of the countries that the migrants are coming from are high, while their economic opportunities are low. Poverty is rampant, with educational opportunities ranging from low to nonexistent. Many of these people want out. And when they escape, they want to retain their culture, which creates conflict.

There are a lot of details that you need to learn in this chapter, but keep in mind that the implications of these "boring" details are significant for your life. You, for example, might be shooting a rifle or dropping bombs because of the political unrest that comes from population growth. Or you might be marching on one side or the other in protest or support of the withdrawn welcome mats, the culture conflict, or the shooting and bombing.

For Your Consideration

→ What is the connection between Latino migrants to the United States and Syrian refugees in France?

→ What do you think the solution is to illegal immigration to the United States? Why do you think it will work?

→ What do you think the solution is to the vast immigration of Arabs to France and Germany? Why would this work?

Summary and Review

1. The world is in the middle of an urban explosion. In 1900, about 13 percent of the world's population lived in cities. Today, about 54 percent do. The U.S. total is closing in on 80 percent.

2. Symbolic interactionists emphasize that rundown areas of the city that appear disorganized and threatening to outsiders may be viable communities to those who live there. It takes an insider's frame of reference to understand these worlds.

3. According to functionalists, specialized zones develop as a city grows. Each zone meets certain needs of a city's residents, and people with distinctive characteristics live in each. Antagonisms result from the *invasion–succession cycle*, as one group displaces another. Urban problems are generally concentrated in the area adjacent to the central business district.

4. According to the conflict perspective, business leaders helped bring about the decline of the inner city by influencing politicians to build new highways. This subsidized the relocation of their businesses to the suburbs and facilitated the shipping of their products. Suburban development came at the city's expense, removing jobs, reducing its tax base, and spurring flight of the middle class.

5. Violence from youth gangs and in our schools remains a problem.

6. The *regional restratification* of the United States, a shift in population to the West and South, is leaving the cities of the North and East with fewer resources to deal with their urban problems.

7. *Demographers* study the size, composition, growth, and distribution of human populations. They disagree as to why Europe's population surged after 1750. Some cite improved public health, others a change in diet.

8. In 1798, Thomas Malthus made a prediction that is still controversial, that the world's population would outstrip its food supply. The New Malthusians fear that the population of the world is entering the latter stages of an *exponential growth curve*, with most growth in the nations least able to afford it. They

favor an immediate cutback in population. The Anti-Malthusians claim that the world is producing more than enough food; the problem is disrupted food production and distribution.

9. By applying symbolic interactionism, we can see why the birthrate is higher in the least industrialized nations. There, children, who are viewed as a blessing from God, give the parents status in the present and provide security for the future.

10. By applying functionalism, we can see that exporting medicine and public health techniques from the most industrialized nations was a *latent dysfunction* for the least industrialized nations. It upset the balance between their birthrates and death rates.

11. Conflict theorists stress that the hunger some nations experience is due to *food politics*, which intensify problems in the least industrialized nations.

12. Demographers who take a New Malthusian position stress that the world will outstrip its food supply if we fail to reduce world population growth. Even if we attain zero population growth, because of *population momentum*, it would take 50 to 70 years for the world's population to stabilize.

13. Demographers who take an Anti-Malthusian position argue that the earth can support many more people. Food production is outpacing population growth, and a growing population is a spur to greater productivity.

14. The New Malthusians recommend social policies that will curb population growth. The Anti Malthusians advocate policies that encourage (or do not discourage) population growth. Both sides agree that we should stimulate agricultural development.

15. The New Malthusians and Anti-Malthusians envision contrasting futures. The New Malthusians anticipate widespread hunger and starvation in the least industrialized nations, which will lead to political unrest and repression. The Anti-Malthusians stress that the world's nations hold the potential for meeting human needs, that one day the world will face the problem of population shrinkage.

Thinking Critically about Chapter 12

1. Which perspective do you think does the best job of explaining urban problems—the symbolic interactionist, functionalist, or conflict perspective? Why?

2. Do you think the New Malthusians or the Anti-Malthusians are right in their views of population and food? Why?

3. Which perspective (symbolic interactionism, functionalism, or conflict theory) do you think best explains the world's problems of population and food? Explain.

Key Terms

biotech society, 396
Chicago School of Sociology, 365
city, 362
concentric zone theory, 366
death rate, 380
demographic transition, 381
demography, 379
designer animals, 396
empowerment zones, 374
exponential growth curve, 380
food politics, 389
gentrification, 378

infanticide, 380
invasion–succession cycle, 367
latent dysfunctions, 389
megacity, 363
population pyramids, 387
population shrinkage, 382
regional restratification, 373
taking the role of the other, 385
urban crisis, 364
urbanization, 362
zero population growth, 390

Chapter 13
The Environmental Crisis

GM Photo Images/Alamy Stock Photo

 Learning Objectives

After reading this chapter, you should be able to:

13.1 Summarize environmental catastrophes of the past and describe the tragedy of the commons.

13.2 Explain what "everything is connected to everything else" means and how this lies at the root of environmental problems.

13.3 Discuss the perspectives that emerge when you apply symbolic interactionism, functionalism, and conflict theory to environmental problems.

13.4 Be able to summarize issues regarding pollution: air, global warming, land, water, chemical, nuclear, and food.

13.5 Compare how the pessimistic and optimistic environmentalists interpret research findings.

13.6 Know how frameworks of interpretation lead to different social policies. Summarize potential social policies to cope with environmental problems.

13.7 Discuss the likely future of environmental problems.

A great record. Seven years without a serious accident. British Petroleum (BP) officials decided that the captain and crew deserved recognition for their achievement in safety. Despite storms and other dangers in the Gulf of Mexico, the crew had drilled through 13,000 feet of rock—and this in deep water, 5,000 feet below the surface. A marvelous technological accomplishment.

The BP officials climbed out of the helicopter and scrambled aboard the *Deepwater Horizon,* a three-story-tall, intricate piece of machinery. The rig housed all the equipment needed to drill in deep water and to provide relative comfort for the 126 people who called it their temporary home.

After giving the ritual congratulations for the rig's commendable safety record, the executives would fly back to headquarters and relax in the more upscale surroundings that befit their status. The captain of the *Deepwater Horizon* would then direct the transfer of the oil rig to another site, where the crew would do more routine drilling, adding another well for a mechanized world increasingly hungry for energy.

But, first, there were a few details to take care of. One was to seal the pipe so no oil would escape. Protecting the environment and all that. A routine matter, something the experts did all the time. Then they could disconnect the rig and take off to the new assignment.

And, of course, bask in the warmth of the well-deserved commendation for safety.

Unfortunately, a little mishap stepped in to frustrate these plans.

> **An explosion blew doors off hinges, a fire melted steel equipment, and flames shot 250 feet into the night air.**

An explosion blew doors off hinges, a fire melted steel equipment, and flames shot 250 feet into the night air. Some workers were crushed by flying objects. Others panicked and jumped off the drilling platform into the frigid waters 75 feet below. In addition to the many injured, 11 men died.

For months, the world watched as 200 million gallons of oil gushed out of the broken pipe on the ocean floor, another in a long series of human-caused environmental disasters.

—Based on Blackmon et al. 2010; Boebert and Blossom 2016.

The Problem in Sociological Perspective

13.1 **Summarize environmental catastrophes of the past and describe the tragedy of the commons.**

To better understand today's environmental problems, let's start with the distant past.

Environmental Destruction in the Past: The Myth of the Noble Savage

In early history, so the story goes, humans lived in harmony with their environment. They considered themselves one with the water, earth, sky, animals, and plants. Unlike people today, who destroy their environment for shortsighted gains, people used the earth's resources wisely. Their presence did not disrupt the earth's natural systems. An old woman of the Wintu tribe explained:

> *The white people never cared for land or deer or bear. When we Indians kill meat, we eat it all up. When we dig roots, we make little holes.... We shake down acorns and pine nuts. We don't chop down trees. We only use dead wood. But the white people plow up the ground, pull up the trees, kill everything.... How can the spirit of the earth like the white man?... Everywhere the white man has touched it, it is sore (Lee 1959:163).*

The problem is that this account of the past isn't true. Although the image of earlier people living in harmony with nature is common, back in 1971 sociologist William Burch pointed out that it is a myth. He added that the social sciences should stop perpetuating romanticized views of the past and set the record straight.

Okay. Let's try. Let's peer into the past. And when we do, it isn't a pretty picture. We see humans extinguishing animals and even destroying civilizations.

The Extinction of Animals   Carnivorous kangaroos, giant lizards, and horned turtles the size of automobiles used to roam Australia. These animals became extinct when humans set fire to trees and shrubs to keep warm or to clear the land. In North America, the early inhabitants burned forests to help them hunt and to control mosquitoes. Their hunts and fires wiped out three-fourths of the animals weighing more than 100 pounds (Hotz 1999; McGlone 2012; Goudie 2019). Early humans may have extinguished more species of large animals than humans have in all the years since they invented writing.

Earlier destruction of the environment appears to have been so extensive that it even brought down entire civilizations. Environmentalists point out three examples.

The Mesopotamians   In the lush river basin of the Tigris and Euphrates, in what is now Iraq, the Mesopotamians developed a culture marked by achievements in architecture, mathematics, and science. Although scholars argue about the reason for the collapse of this civilization, one of the most persuasive explanations involves its extensive irrigation system. With irrigation providing abundant food, the Mesopotamian civilization flourished. The irrigation system did not have drainage, however, and as irrigation water evaporated, it left salty water behind (McAnany and Yoffee 2009; Held et al. 2018). Over the centuries, as this water seeped into the earth, the underground water table rose, making the land too salty for crops. Eventually, agriculture collapsed and, with it, the Mesopotamian civilization.

The Maya   In what today is Guatemala and Yucatán, another civilization met a similar fate. The Maya developed their culture over 17 centuries, reaching their peak in agriculture, architecture, and science about 900 A.D. Then, within decades, 90 percent of the Maya disappeared, their population dropping from 5 million to fewer than half a million. Scholars debate the reason, but one suggestion is environmental destruction. Samples from lake beds indicate heavy soil erosion. As the population increased, the Maya cleared the land of trees. Topsoil washed from the denuded land, and with it went the agricultural productivity on which their civilization depended (Cartwright 2014; Held et al. 2018).

As with people today, earlier humans also modified and even destroyed their environment. The rapid decline of population on Easter Island off the coast of Chile in the 1600s could have been because the inhabitants cut down all the trees on the island.

Volanthevist/Moment/Getty Images

The Anasazi   In what is now Arizona and New Mexico, the Anasazi built roads, an irrigation system, and pueblos of stone and masonry (Budiansky 1987; Kareiva and Carranza 2018). Some pueblos were four or five stories high. One had 800 rooms. As their population grew, the Anasazi cut down so many trees in the canyons that they had to travel 50 miles or more to gather wood for fuel. With the forest stripped beyond its ability to replenish itself, the civilization collapsed.

The Tragedy of the Commons

Far from being thoughtful caretakers of their environment, earlier humans were like us. They destroyed limited resources thoughtlessly. Because today's civilizations are larger, however, our capacity for destruction is greater.

Central to understanding how humans can be so thoughtless is this principle: Self-interest often works against the logic of environmental preservation (Mayumi and Giampietro 2018). Biologist Garrett Hardin (1968) explained this principle in a parable called *the tragedy of the commons.*

> *Let us picture a pasture open to everyone. The number of cattle exactly matches the amount of available grass. Each herdsman, however, will seek to maximize his own gain. He thinks to himself: "If I add a cow to my herd, I will receive all the proceeds from the sale of this additional animal. The little overgrazing that this extra animal causes will be shared by all the other herdsmen."*

> *This herdsman adds another animal to his herd. This works, so he eventually adds another . . . and another. And, for the same reason, the other herdsmen who share the commons do the same. Each is part of a system that rewards individuals for increasing the size of their herds. And therein lays the tragedy of the commons. The pasture is limited, and additional stress eventually causes it—and the civilization that depends on it—to fail. As each pursues his or her own interest, all rush to their collective ruin.*

In Sum   An irony of human life is that—just as in our opening vignette about the *Deepwater Horizon*—our efforts to survive, even to improve life, sometimes destroy the very environment on which life depends. Environmental destruction is not new; it is woven throughout human history.

The Scope of the Problem

13.2   **Explain what "everything is connected to everything else" means and how this lies at the root of environmental problems.**

You can see how humans of the past harmed their environments, sometimes to such an extent that their civilizations collapsed. Will we do the same? For the first time in world history, our earth must meet the needs of billions of people—and they are demanding an ever-increasing standard of living. Satisfying this incessant demand depends on our new technology, which, like the *Deepwater Horizon*, can fail us. Now that we have magnified our capacity for harm, the destruction of our environment is a frightening possibility.

Let's look at the scope of the problem today.

"Everything Is Connected to Everything Else"

When I first heard the words "everything is connected to everything else," they caught me by surprise. As I reflected on this statement, I began to think about the world in a different way. Let's explore some of the implications of these words.

Seeing Connections This simple statement, "Everything is connected to everything else," holds the key to understanding environmental problems. Let me begin by sharing a little story from my childhood.

> *My grandfather lived on a remote farm in northern Minnesota, way up on the Canadian border. Yet in this remote spot his actions had global consequences. He used to spray his fields with DDT, the practice at the time. The excess DDT, a virulent pesticide, ran from the fields into a creek. The creek ran into a local river. From that little river, the DDT flowed into larger rivers, and then into one that led to the Mississippi River. In this, the major watershed of the United States, the DDT my grandfather had used joined thousands of chemicals from tens of thousands of farms and businesses. Flowing into New Orleans, these chemicals helped cause the area's higher than average rates of cancer. From there, these chemicals flowed into the Atlantic, entering a food chain that ended up on people's dinner plates around the world.*

This is a homely little story, but I think it makes the point well. We tend to focus on our immediate world, the little things that affect us on an everyday level—our job or school, our families and friends, a local basketball game or a picnic in the park. It is imperative that we raise our eyes to a higher level and see interconnections. We need to become aware of how we are part of a global, interdependent system. Or, more simply put, how everything is connected to everything else.

A Lethal Legacy Threatening the Planet? Essential to our environmental problems are the population explosion we discussed in the previous chapter and the industrialization emphasized throughout this text. Each is accompanied by a relentless and global drive for higher living standards. If in this process we deplete our natural resources, as some past civilizations have, our civilization, too, will collapse. This is a fear of some *ecologists*, scientists who study **ecology**—the relationship between living things and their environment.

Of the many human actions that are upsetting our planet's precarious balance, a primary threat to humanity's welfare is **pollution**, the accumulation in the air, water, and land of substances harmful to living things. As we just saw, pollution goes far back in history, but in recent years pollution has intensified beyond anything the earth has

Poachers kill elephants so they can harvest their tusks and sell the ivory on the black market. The tusk carried by the park ranger in Tanzania was just confiscated from poachers.

ever seen. China and India have joined the world's industrial giants, which long have spewed their wastes onto our earth as though it were a sewer and not the heritage we are leaving coming generations. Are we leaving a legacy of death for the future generations that will walk the earth's fragile surface? Let's see what the problem is and whether we can avoid this lethal legacy.

Looking at the Problem Theoretically

13.3 Discuss the perspectives that emerge when you apply symbolic interactionism, functionalism, and conflict theory to environmental problems.

How did the environment become a social problem? Let's use our three theoretical lenses to trace this process.

Symbolic Interactionism

How did the environment become a social problem? The dangers seem so obvious that you might wonder why I'm even asking such a question. Just thinking of the *Deepwater Horizon* catastrophe can bring chills up the spine. Environmental decay is all around us, from the wells that used to yield pure water, now closed because of benzene poisons, to pregnant women having to limit how much fish they eat because of mercury contamination.

But it was not always this way. Just three generations ago, people rarely thought of the environment as a problem. How, then, did this social problem emerge?

Objective Conditions but Little Subjective Concern   As I have emphasized throughout this text, for a social problem to exist, it isn't enough to have harmful objective conditions. We must also have subjective concerns. In the 1800s, hundreds of coal-fired steel plants in the United States created highly visible pollution. Coal dust seeped into houses, and people coughed up black grime. But people considered this a local matter, not part of a social problem. Grit on the streets, blackened skies, and hacking coughs were thought to be just unfortunate costs of economic survival.

Even the disappearance of animal species didn't produce a social problem. The passenger pigeon, during its mass annual migration, used to darken the skies for days. Its extinction in 1914 was seen as unfortunate—an interesting bit of history, perhaps—but not tragic. The near extinction of the bison was welcomed by many European Americans as a way to defeat the Indians.

From the way we look at the world today, such events strike a strange note. They make us wonder about the way people used to think. If pollution and extinction did not bring the widespread concerns that are part of the way we look at life today, how, then, did they develop? After pollution and pesticides made headlines and became a national concern in the 1970s, sociologists decided to find out how this new concern for the environment came about Let's see what they discovered.

The Conservation Movement   Looking through the historical records, sociologists found that the environment had already become an issue in the late 1800s. At that time, Theodore Roosevelt, president of the United States from 1901 to 1909, spearheaded a conservation movement. An avid hunter, Roosevelt had become concerned that the wildlife he liked to kill was disappearing from our wilderness areas. In one of the ironies of history, Roosevelt, who liked killing animals so much that he would roam Africa in search of elephants, tigers, and lions, supported legislation to establish our system of national parks, setting aside millions of acres for public use (Buckley and Youngs 2018).

From Conservation to Environmental Concern   Obviously, conserving wilderness areas to make certain that hunters do not run out of moving targets is vastly different from concerns about the quality of our land, air, and water. How, then, did "conservation" change to "environmental concern"? Sociologists found that this transition occurred in five stages, beginning with professionals and ending with an aroused public (Schoenfeld et al.1979):

1. *Professionals* were the first to become concerned about the environment. Geographers, especially, became troubled by our rampant use of natural resources. In 1959, they began to write journal articles about environmental problems and to present papers at their conventions.
2. *Interest groups* then began to form around specific issues.
3. *Government agencies,* aroused by the activities of the interest groups, began to issue environmental reports.
4. The *news media* discovered the issue. Like everyone else, it was difficult for reporters to understand that people, resources, and technology are all part of a single, larger system. They tended to see things in terms of unrelated news stories, such as a train wreck that spilled contaminants. As reporters began to understand the basic environmental principle—that everything is connected to everything else—they grew capable of connecting events and communicating these connections to the public.
5. *The public* was aroused by the stories in the mass media. In 1962, Rachel Carson published *Silent Spring,* a book about the dangers of pesticides. This blockbuster alerted Americans to environmental hazards, but it focused on a single issue and didn't lead the public or the news media to explore the interconnections among environmental events. Then in 1969, an oil well erupted off the coast of California, and the public was outraged when the oil blackened Santa Barbara's beautiful beaches (Davies and Davies 1975). Later that same year came the single most effective environmental message of the century—the first view of Earth from the moon. This stunning glimpse of the planet from the outside helped make the public aware that we all live on a fragile, finite "spaceship"—and that for our survival we had better take good care of it.

Teddy Roosevelt, president of the United States from 1901 to 1909, kneels proudly by a jaguar he shot in Brazil in 1913. The text explains how a concern for "conserving" wilderness areas to prevent hunters from running out of moving targets evolved into today's environmental movement.

Bettmann/Getty Images

In Sum Symbolic interactionists focus on the symbols that we use to communicate our experiences in life. They look at how our symbols create and maintain our ideas of reality. A new perception emerged as professionals and reporters began to view individual events not as individual, separate occurrences, but as interconnected parts of a global problem. This transformed the way we see ourselves, our relationship with other living things, and even what we consider to be our place in the universe. The process by which this occurred—and is occurring—is depicted in Figure 13.1.

This change in how we view ourselves and our world is still in process: We still have a difficult time connecting our present actions with a distant future.

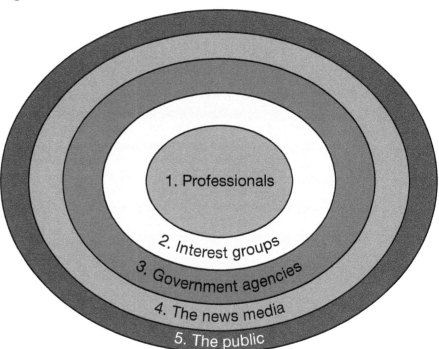

Figure 13.1 From Conservation to Environmental Concern

Source: By the author.

Functionalism

The idea that everything is connected to everything else is becoming part of our intuitive understanding of the world. We all are aware that the small groups to which we belong are parts of a larger society and that our nation is part of a global network. Slowly, we are coming to grasp that we all are part of a global social system, that what each part does—whether an individual, group, or nation—affects the other parts.

The Essence of Functionalism: Interconnections This picture of humanity forming a global network is a functional analysis. Each unit is part of a larger structure, with the activities of one part having consequences for the other parts. The more technical term for this interconnected system in the environment is **ecosystem**—all life on the planet is interconnected in finely balanced cycles that take place on the thin layer of the earth's surface.

The Ecosystem Both biologists and sociologists who work on environmental problems stress how our survival depends on the earth's *ecosystem,* on delicately balanced connections among air, water, and soil. Oxygen in the air we breathe depends on plant life. Water, to be pure, depends on plants and microorganisms in our lakes and streams. The soil depends on biological processes if it is to produce food and fuel. Anything that disrupts this finely tuned, interconnected system threatens the cycles on which our existence depends. And the major offender in disrupting the ecosystem? Humans—primarily through industrialization.

Functions and Dysfunctions of Industrialization We humans are so highly adaptable that we have expanded into every habitable region of the globe. The variety of cultures we developed has allowed us to adapt to mountains and plains, to deserts and oceans, even to steamy jungles and bitterly cold ice-bound regions. In this process, we have domesticated plants and animals and harnessed the energy of animals and rivers, the sun and the wind.

Our invention of the steam engine allowed us to harness energy on a scale unknown in history. As we saw in Chapter 11, the Industrial Revolution that followed created countless new jobs and great wealth. Because of this revolution, the average person in the industrialized world enjoys a standard of living previously attained only by the wealthy. However, in our frenetic drive to produce material wealth, we have thoughtlessly discarded our toxic industrial wastes in almost every corner of the earth. Perhaps the greatest irony in history is that we are repeating the folly of earlier peoples, with our pursuit of a better life damaging the environment that allows us life in the first place.

In Sum   Functionalists focus on how the parts of a social system are interconnected. As with earlier civilizations such as the Mesopotamians, the Maya, and the Anasazi, our economic and political systems depend on a fragile ecosystem. The failure of our ecosystem would mean the collapse of our society. Although we still have problems conceptualizing this, we have begun to think of ourselves as part of a complex, living machine called the environment.

Conflict Theory

Have you ever heard any group defend dirty water or filthy air? Of course not. Yet there are opposing sides on environmental issues. One controversy centers around those who say we need severe regulations to protect the environment and those who view such laws as unreasonable controls over private actions. Let's look at this conflict.

On One Side: Environmental Groups   On one side are environmental action groups organized to fight what they view as environmental threats. Examples are the Izaak Walton League, Greenpeace, the National Wildlife Federation, the Sierra Club, Americans for Safe Food, and Earth First! Here's how the Izaak Walton League (2018) expresses this position:

> *The greatest threat to water quality today is polluted runoff from farm fields, parking lots, industrial sites, and backyards across America. That runoff—much less visible than discharges from a factory pipe—flows unchecked and untreated into our streams and rivers. It carries animal waste, bacteria, cancer-causing chemicals, and countless other pollutants through our communities.*

Environmental action groups have become a powerful political force. With chapters across the nation, these groups hire lobbyists to promote legislation, and they pay lawyers to fight environmental cases in the courts.

On the Other Side: Polluters   The industrial polluters face a dilemma. No one would tolerate them saying that they favor pollution. Yet pollution controls are expensive and add nothing to the value of their products. Manufacturers in the most industrialized nations must compete with businesses in the least industrialized nations that enjoy a double-edged advantage: Their labor costs are low, and their governments don't require them to install costly pollution controls in the manufacturing process.

To remain competitive, U.S. manufacturers hire lobbyists to try to keep pollution laws from being passed or, if passed, to make sure their enforcement is without teeth (Attanasio 2018). You probably know that the automobile industry has opposed legal standards that require higher fuel efficiency. Some of this is just public posturing, with the real decisions made behind the scenes. Consider this historical example of how the automobile industry used its political connections so it could continue to pollute:

> *In 1951, when it was discovered that automobiles were the major cause of smog in Los Angeles, the suggestion was made to develop electric cars. The auto industry formed a committee to study this proposal. The White House stacked the committee with representatives from the auto and oil industries. Their "surprising" conclusion: a recommendation against even doing research on electric vehicles (Davies and Davies 1975).*

Industry's political clout is truly amazing. In the following *Thinking Critically about Social Problems,* you will see that the industrial giants have even been able to get laws passed that make pollution profitable.

Thinking Critically about Social Problems

How to Get Paid to Pollute: Corporate Welfare and Big Welfare Bucks

Welfare is a highly controversial topic in the United States. It arouses criticism among the wealthy and the middle class, who view welfare recipients as parasites. But have you heard about *corporate welfare?*

Corporate welfare refers to handouts given to corporations. A state will reduce a company's taxes if it will remain within the state. A state may even offer land or buildings at a bargain price to a business because it is going to hire workers.

Corporate welfare even goes to companies that are known polluters. Borden Chemicals in Louisiana has buried hazardous wastes without a permit and released clouds of chemicals so thick that the police have had to shut down the highway that runs near the plant. Borden even contaminated the groundwater beneath its plant, threatening the aquifer that provides drinking water for residents of Louisiana and Texas.

Borden's pollution cost the company dearly: $3.6 million in fines, $3 million to clean up the groundwater, and $400,000 for local emergency response units. That's a hefty $7 million. But when we take into account corporate welfare, the company didn't make out so badly. Its $15 million in reduced and canceled property taxes brought Borden a net gain of $8 million (Bartlett and Steele 1998). And that's not counting the savings the company racked up by not having to

You can see the pollution being produced by this paper factory in Port Angeles, Washington. How can we reduce the environmental costs of producing paper and the other items our society needs?

P.A. Lawrence, LLC/Alamy Stock Photo

properly dispose of its toxic wastes in the first place.

Borden shut down its chemical plant, which had made methanol—turning its focus to producing polyvinyl chloride resins ("Borden..." 2000).

Many states offer incentives to help start-up companies. Louisiana defines "start-up" somewhat strangely. Although Exxon Corporation opened for business about 125 years ago and is now Exxon Mobil, the world's largest oil and gas company, Louisiana canceled $213 million of its property taxes. Another little "start-up" was Shell Oil Company, which had $140 million slashed from its taxes (Bartlett and Steele 1998). You might be familiar with some of the other "start-ups": International Paper, Dow Chemical, Union Carbide, Boise Cascade, Georgia Pacific, and Procter & Gamble.

For Your Consideration

→ Apply the functionalist, symbolic interactionist, and conflict perspectives to corporate welfare. Which do you think provides the best explanation of corporate welfare? Why?

In Sum   As conflict theorists examine environmental problems, they focus on colliding interests. The conflict is between the environmental activists who want to eliminate what they see as dangers to the public and the groups that see profits as more important than reducing pollution. Over and over, those who campaign to develop a healthier society run head-on into groups that see the cure as worse than the problem.

Research Findings: Pollution

13.4   **Be able to summarize issues regarding pollution: air, global warming, land, water, chemical, nuclear, and food.**

How badly has our environment been hurt? Let's examine the pollution of our air, land, water, and food supply and look at energy and resources. We also want to consider whether the environmental crisis has been exaggerated.

Let's begin with air pollution.

Air Pollution

To begin, let's dip into history, not too far, about the middle of the last century, when it became apparent that the consequences of air pollution are much greater than murky air that clouds the sunshine. Here's what happened in Donora, Pennsylvania, in 1948:

> During the last five days of October, a "killer smog," a mixture of smoke and fog, settled over Donora. About 6,000 of this steel mill town's 12,000 inhabitants became sick. Twenty died.

> Donora had experienced a thermal inversion, *a layer of cold air sealing in a lower layer of warm air. Thermal inversions trap harmful smoke, exhaust, and particles.*

> The residents' reactions sound hauntingly familiar. The local doctor described the deaths as murder, but the superintendent of the steel mill said, "I can't conceive how our plant has anything to do with the condition. There has been no change in the process since 1915." The workers, who saw dense smoke and fog as part of their way of life, said, "That smoke coming out of those stacks is putting bread and butter on our tables." And the public? Most just shrugged their shoulders and went about their business (Bowen 1972; Jacobs et al. 2018).

Four years later, a killer smog hit London, leaving *4,000 dead in just five days* (Tiwary and Williams 2018).

These events, as you can well imagine, caught the public's attention. They set off a search to understand **air pollution**—poisons in the air that accumulate in the body. Besides causing eye, nose, and throat irritations, air pollution can cause bronchitis, emphysema, and lung cancer. As we have seen, it can even bring sudden death.

Causes of Air Pollution   Other than the by-products from burning coal—the cause of the Donora and London catastrophes—what causes air pollution? Let's find out.

Fossil Fuels   The main cause of air pollution is the burning of **fossil fuels**—substances derived from living things. Besides coal, examples include wood, petroleum, and natural gas. As power plants and factories burn fossil fuels to produce electricity and manufacture the goods we consume, pollutants pour into the air. The worst polluter, however, is the internal combustion engine. The exhausts of cars, trucks, and buses emit poisons—sulfur dioxide, nitrogen oxide, hydrocarbons, and carbon monoxide. Vehicles also leave behind **carcinogens** (cancer-causing substances) from the asbestos in their brake linings.

Pollution is almost always unintended. On occasion, however, pollution is the result of a deliberate, spiteful act. The most dramatic example occurred in 1991 after U.S.-led forces defeated the Iraqi army in Kuwait. During their retreat, the Iraqi military ignited more than 700 oil wells. The soot from the fires circled the globe (Simona 2018).

Waste Incineration   A second major source of air pollution is burning wastes. Burning plastics is especially damaging to our health because it creates PCBs (polychlorinated biphenyls), potent toxins. Plastics are not **biodegradable**; that is, they do not disintegrate after being exposed to normal bacteria. Even steel rusts, but plastics endure almost indefinitely. Burning is one way to get rid of them.

Fluorocarbon Gases   The Earth has its own natural sunscreen called the **ozone shield**— a layer of ozone in the upper stratosphere that screens out much of the sun's ultraviolet rays. High-intensity ultraviolet rays harm most life forms. In humans, they cause skin cancer and cataracts; in plants, they reduce growth and cause genetic mutations. When scientists realized that fluorocarbon gases—a third source of air pollution—had poked holes in the ozone shield, their use in aerosol cans, refrigerators, and air conditioners was reduced or eliminated. The ozone layer will repair itself, but it won't be fully healed until 2065 (EPA 2018a).

Changes in Air Pollution   For several decades, environmentalists protested, laws were passed, and pollution control devices were added to manufacturing processes. What a difference this has made in the air that you and I breathe. To see the huge strides we have made in cleaning up the air, look at Figure 13.2. Emissions of sulfur dioxide and volatile organic compounds have been cut sharply.

Figure 13.2 U.S. Air Quality

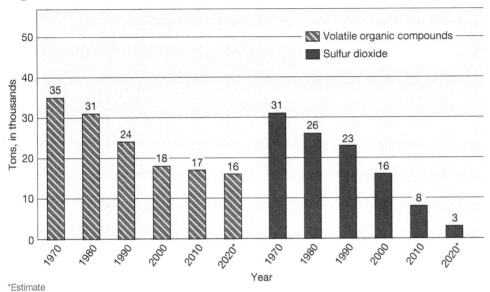

*Estimate

Source: By the author. Based on *Statistical Abstract of the United States* earlier years and 2013:Tables 379, 380; 2018:Table 409.

Not shown in this figure is the most stunning change: The amount of lead in our air is now *less than 1 percent* of what it was in 1980. The primary reason for this reduction is lead-free gasoline. (Gasoline used to contain lead as an anti-knock additive.) Despite these improvements, we still have a long way to go. About 123 million Americans live in counties that don't meet air quality standards (EPA 2017a).

Global Warming

The world is in the throes of a crisis so great that it threatens the existence of humanity. The name of the crisis is global warming.

While there is disagreement among scientists whether or not this opening statement is hyperbolic, most scientists are concerned—many alarmed—by global warming. Basic to understanding global warming is this: Carbon dioxide and water vapor form an invisible blanket around the globe that allows sunlight to enter but traps heat. Without this global blanket, temperatures would plummet, making the Earth unable to support life. But if the blanket grows too thick, it traps too much heat, creating a **greenhouse effect**, which brings devastating consequences for the earth.

Scientists gradually became concerned that the immense amounts of carbon dioxide being released because of industrialization was smudging the atmospheric window through which our earth's daily heat escapes to outer space. In 1989, they held a conference in Noordwijk, Holland, to discuss their concerns. *Since that conference, more carbons have been released into the atmosphere than in the entire history of civilization preceding it* (Rich 2018). Environmentalists refer to the earth's rising temperatures as **global warming**.

The consequences of global warming will be severe. Already, the glaciers have started to melt. Here is just one example:

The world's largest tropical glacier is in Peru. This 7.5-mile-long mountain glacier, 18,600 feet above sea level, often gets snow but never rain. The Quelcayya, as it is called, is shrinking by about 100 feet a year. As the ice receded, researchers discovered a moss-like plant that had been frozen in the glacier. Carbon dating showed the plant to be over 5,000 years old. The last time this plant wasn't covered with snow and ice, the Egyptians were busy inventing hieroglyphics (Regaldo 2004).

One likely consequences of global warming is a rise of the oceans because of the melting of glaciers, such as what remains of this one in the Antarctic.

Bernhard Staehli/Shutterstock

The Warnings   With the Earth warming and the glaciers melting, climatologists have issued grave warnings. They say that if we don't reduce the output of carbon dioxide, the world will face such severe consequences as these (National Academy of Sciences 2010; Kidwell et al. 2016; Pravalie 2018):

1. The climate boundaries will shift about 400 miles north, resulting in a longer growing season in the United States, Canada, and Russia.
2. Summers will be hotter, and there will be more forest fires, droughts, floods, and outbreaks of diseases—malaria, dengue fever, cholera.
3. Many species of plants and animals will become extinct.
4. Problems in the least industrialized nations will be worse, as they have fewer resources to meet the crisis.
5. We will have more tornados and hurricanes.
6. As the polar ice caps melt, the oceans will rise several feet, wiping out the earth's coastal cities and island nations. One of these nations, Kiribati, is making plans to move its population of 106,000 to Fiji, which is 1,500 miles away (Liljas 2014). The ministry of tourism of another, the Maldives, suggested that their national slogan should be "Come see us while we're still here" (Dickey and Rogers 2002).

The Scientific Skeptics   A small dissenting group of climatologists reply, "We need to be more cautious in drawing conclusions." This group argues that throughout history the earth has warmed and cooled, with no consistent correlation with carbon dioxide. During the earth's ice age, the atmosphere's carbon dioxide was even higher than it is today. They say that what we are now experiencing is another of the earth's natural warm/cold cycles. The causes could be changes in sun cycles or sea currents or in the cosmic rays that hit the earth (Lemonick 2010; Cook et al. 2018).

Some of the skeptics say that even if the Industrial Revolution is the cause, there is no reason for alarm. A warmer world will lower energy costs and bring fewer winter deaths and better agricultural yields (Ridley 2013).

A Healthy Debate   Do you recall the pessimists and the optimists we discussed in the previous chapter, whose views of the world's population and food are almost polar opposites? We have something similar here, but with different groups of pessimistic and optimistic scientists. Each is looking at the same evidence and drawing different conclusions. Lines between these groups have hardened, and, quite unscientifically, they have thrown verbal rocks at one another. The group that says global warming comes from human activity has accused the other of being charlatans for industry, while the group that points to natural cycles has accused the other of faking data.

Beyond the rhetoric of their hardened views, we can expect that out of open debate, climatologists will come to the right conclusions regarding the causes of global warming, its negative and positive consequences, and what actions are appropriate.

Land Pollution

It was such a beautiful day that Tamara and Bill decided to skip their social problems class and have a picnic on the beach. As they walked hand in hand, they found that they had to step around sewage that had washed ashore the night before. Their stomachs turned when they saw blood samples and contaminated needles that must have come from a hospital. All they could think of was AIDS.

They decided to leave—and didn't eat their lunch.

Garbage If you look at Figure 13.3, you will see how much garbage each American produces each day. At 4.4 pounds per person per day, we produce about 600 billion pounds of garbage each year. About a pound and a half of each person's average daily waste is recovered (paper, glass, metals, plastics, rubber, wood), but each day the average American sends between two and three pounds of solid waste to landfills (*Statistical Abstract* 2018:Table 413).

Figure 13.3 Waste Generated in the United States

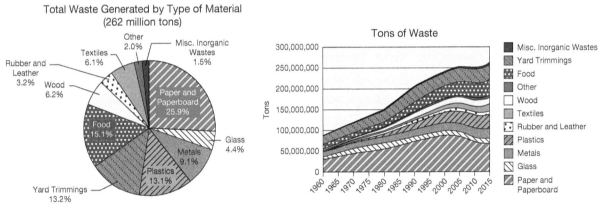

Source: *Statistical Abstract of the United States* 2018:Table 413.   Source: By the author. EPA 2018e.

Humans have always had the problem of how to dispose of their wastes. The usual solution? Dump them nearby. We can identify many Stone Age villages by the mounds of oyster and mussel shells their inhabitants left behind. Our cities used to dump their waste into a pit, light it, and forget it. But with today's awareness of how burning garbage pollutes the air and adds to global warming, cities must now use garbage incinerators—fancifully called *resource recovery plants*—that are approved by the Environmental Protection Agency (EPA). With federal regulations requiring utilities to buy power generated by these garbage-burning plants, they partially pay for themselves.

Strip Mining Another form of land pollution is **strip mining**, which occurs where coal lies so close to the surface that it can be retrieved by stripping away the soil. Strip mining, which has scarred more than 5 million acres of U.S. land, not only makes the land ugly but also poisons it. When the land is stripped bare of its forest and plant life, salt leeches from the coal. Although current federal regulations require mining companies to return land to its original condition, many believe that doing so is impossible. Today, the western areas of the United States and huge areas in Canada are vulnerable because vast amounts of shale and coal lie just beneath the surface.

Water Pollution

Of the tens of thousands of chemicals, how many do you think have been banned as harmful to people's health? You might find this hard to believe, but the answer is five. In fact, the EPA has analyzed only a handful of these tens of thousands of chemicals (McCarthy 2016).

Drinking Water

> I used to live in a town located on the banks of the Mississippi River. Although thousands of upstream industries discharge their wastes into this river, my town retrieves its drinking water from it. To "purify" this filthy river water, the water company filters out the foreign objects (condoms, worms, and the like) and then adds chemicals to the rest. Hundreds of other towns along the Mississippi do the same.

Water treated in the way I just described meets the standards set by the EPA. The drinking water of one of 14 Americans doesn't meet even these woeful health standards (Roland 2013). Of the tens of thousands of chemicals and other contaminants that exist, the EPA monitors and sets limits for only 87. Since the EPA is in charge of overseeing the nation's drinking water, this is so hard to believe that you might want to look at EPA's list yourself: https://www.epa.gov/ground-water-and-drinking-water/table-regulated-drinking-water-contaminants.

Acid Rain   Let's have a success story for a change.

In the 1980s, *acid rain*, a "chemical soup," fell from the skies, killing plants, animals, and damaging buildings. The problem arose out of a solution to a problem. When power plants burn coal and oil to produce electricity, they produce harmful smoke. To protect their communities, the utility companies built more than 175 smokestacks 500 feet tall or higher. This solved the problem for the local community, but sent high into the air, the pollutants from these megastacks remained aloft, far out of sight, for days, even weeks. As the sulfur dioxide and nitrogen oxide mixed with moisture in the air, it turned into sulfuric and nitric acid. This "airborne sewer" fell to the earth as **acid rain**.

The Clean Air Act of 1970 forced industry to reduce pollution in manufacturing and in vehicle emissions (EPA 2018b). The result was dramatic, as you saw in Figure 13.2. One consequence is that acid rain was reduced to a bad memory.

The Great Lakes   The Great Lakes of the United States form the largest surface freshwater system on Earth (EPA 2018c). This giant network of waterways—Huron, Ontario, Michigan, Erie, and Superior—contains *one of every five gallons of the entire world's surface freshwater*. The pollution comes *from* toxic chemicals used or produced by industry and runoff from farms entering the Great Lakes. Then, as the EPA (2012b) puts it:

> Small bottom-dwellers ingest the toxins as they feed in the mud. As larger animals eat these smaller animals, the toxins move up the food chain, with their concentrations getting higher, often thousands of times higher. Fish at the top of the food chain, such as lake trout and salmon, can be unsafe to eat in some areas because of the heavy concentrations of toxic substances in their tissues.

Disturbed by this pollution, environmentalists pressured Congress, which mandated that the EPA clean up the Great Lakes. Their concentration of heavy metals has been reduced somewhat, but the problem is so huge that it may take generations to solve (EPA 2012b, 2016e).

An additional problem is foreign species, some of which have hitchhiked across the world and entered the lakes from the ballast of boats (EPA 2018d). In the Great Lakes, these species no longer face the forces that keep them in check in their natural habitat. Without this, they multiply, threatening the native species. Following pressure from environmentalists, the EPA is working on this problem, too. Among their efforts is building an electric barrier to prevent invasive species from entering the Great Lakes.

Oil Spills Long gone are the days when you could insert a pipe in the ground in Texas and watch oil come gushing out. Those oil gushers have been replaced with high-tech geophysical exploration for oil in remote recesses on our planet. One of these remote spots is the deep ocean floor, bringing the consequences recounted in this chapter's opening vignette. Through miscalculations, the *Deepwater Horizon* spewed about 200 million gallons into the Gulf of Mexico.

Then there are the accidents that occur while oil is transported from where it is pumped to where it will be refined into products such as gasoline, diesel, and lubricants. The most infamous case, which got the world's attention at the time, was the rupture on the tanks of the *Exxon Valdez*, a 1,000-foot-long supertanker that ran aground in 1989. Eleven million gallons of crude oil leaked into the pristine waters of Alaska's Prince William Sound, fouling 1,300 miles of untouched coastline (Wells and McCoy 1989; Hartsig and Robbins 2018). But dwarfing both the *Exxon Valdez* and the *Deepwater Horizon* accidents are the less dramatic, not newsworthy, everyday oil spills. Here is a startling example: Each year, the aged, rusty pipelines in Russia leak two *Deepwater Horizons* of oil (Luhn 2016).

Chemical Pollution

A chemical waste dump was covered over with clay, homes were built, and hundreds of families moved in. A grade school was built there, too. Deadly poisons seeped into the yards, homes, and the school playground. The residents began to complain of urinary tract infections, swollen joints, and headaches. There were miscarriages, stillbirths, and cancers. There were also strange births. One girl was born deaf, with a cleft palate, and two rows of teeth. Another child was born with one kidney, and yet another with three ears (Brown n.d.; Shribman 1989; Newman 2016).

This was Love Canal, a little community in New York. The homes had been built next to a dump site where Hooker Chemical Company had buried 44 million pounds of waste. The home buyers didn't know about the chemical waste. They learned of it only after the health problems—and the strange births—led to an investigation.

In the 1970s, the federal government ordered all pregnant women and children under age 2 to move out of Love Canal (Brody 1976; Brown n.d.). The health problems continued, however, and in 1980 the federal government relocated 710 families and bulldozed their homes (Shribman 1989). In the 1990s, the rest of the site was renamed "Black Creek Village." Lured by low house prices and assurances that the area was safe, families bought homes and moved in. Now there are accusations—and denials—and lawsuits that the buried chemicals are again causing health problems (Newman 2016; Herbeck 2018).

Not to be too sarcastic, but there are two noteworthy improvements. One is that a fence has been built around Hooker's 20,000 tons of chemical wastes. Another is that the site is no longer called a dump. It is now a "containment area."

Residents of Love Canal sitting in front of the home they had to abandon.

Producing Chemicals The production of chemicals is essential to the world's welfare. Without them, we would not be able to feed our billions of people or enjoy the technological marvels that we take for granted, from our automobiles to televisions and computers. The production of these chemicals, though essential, poses dangers that we seldom think about. In the following *Global Glimpse,* let's turn our attention to this potential for a moment.

A Global Glimpse

The Giant Roulette Wheel of Environmental Disaster

While a scattering of people waited for early-morning trains in Bhopal, India, a maintenance worker at the nearby Union Carbide plant heard rumbling in a storage tank. Then came the sound of cracking concrete. The tank held methyl isocyanate (MIC), a chemical used in making pesticides. A white gas began seeping from the tank, then spread through the region on the northwesterly wind.

At the Vijoy Hotel near the railroad station, sociologist Swapan Saha woke up with a terrible pain in his chest. "It was like breathing fire," he said. Wrapping a damp towel around his nose and mouth, Saha went outside to investigate. Scores of victims lay dead on the platform at the train station. "I thought at first there must have been a gigantic railway accident," he recalled. Then he noticed a pall of white smoke on the ground, and an acrid smell in the air. People were retching, vomiting, and defecating uncontrollably. Dogs, cows, and water buffaloes also lay on the ground, twitching in death agonies. Saha staggered back to the hotel. Half blind by now, he sat down to write a farewell letter to his wife.

Saha survived. More than 2,500 others did not (Whitaker 1984; Mandavilli 2018).

Not all the deaths occurred immediately. The leak contaminated the area's groundwater, claiming more lives over the following years. The Indian government estimates that this accident caused 5,000 to 22,000 deaths (Hertsgaard 2004; Bhattacharya 2012). Twenty-six years later, in 2010, Indian courts convicted eight Union Carbide officials of negligent homicide. They were

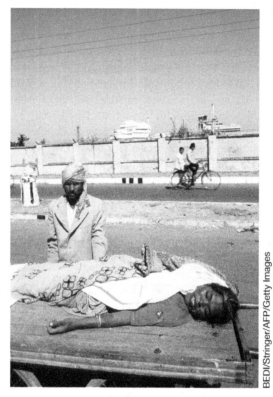

One of the many people who died from the cyanide gas released from an exploding storage tank at the Union Carbide plant in Bhopal, India.

BEDI/Stringer/AFP/Getty Images

each sentenced to two years in prison—even though one of the individuals had already died (Magnier and Rana 2010). Two years later, U.S. courts ruled that Union Carbide was not responsible for cleaning up the toxic mess. That was the responsibility of its Indian subsidiary (Bhattacharya 2012).

Effects of the accident continue today. The current generation is finding strange births, children with physical deformities, and scrambled brains that make them unable to talk or even to move (Mandavilli 2018). At least the widows are getting a pension—about $2 a month (Backhaus and Salden 2014).

Although this event took place in India, an accident like this could happen anywhere chemicals are manufactured. As an expert on workplace safety put it, "It's like a giant roulette wheel. This time the marble came to a stop in a little place in India. But the next time it could be the United States" (Whitaker 1984).

For Your Consideration

→ Do you think a similar accident could happen in the United States? Why or why not?

→ What steps do you think we should take to prevent another Bhopal disaster?

Disposing of Chemical Wastes What is the right way to get rid of chemical wastes? Companies used to simply bury their wastes, burn them, or pour them into the rivers and oceans, polluting our air and water. Today, they still do, but under the watchful eye of the EPA. Some wastes are burned in approved containers, while others are injected into the earth. Others are still buried with an "out-of-sight-out-of-mind" mentality, blindly shoved into dumps. As you saw with Love Canal, this certainly doesn't get rid of the problem. The containers buried in the dumps—fancifully renamed landfills—slowly disintegrate, allowing lethal chemical wastes to rise to the surface or to leach into rivers and groundwater.

The EPA doesn't allow all chemicals to be buried. Some must go through expensive processes to render them harmless. This has created opportunities for organized crime (Brown n.d.). Legal disposal of a tankful of chemical waste might cost $40,000, but some companies have hired criminals to dispose of it for much less. Their disposal methods weren't exactly approved by the EPA. They drove an 8,000-gallon tank truck full of liquid waste to a wooded area and dumped it in eight minutes flat. The industrial company that produced the waste (a legitimate business) feigned ignorance. On 21 acres of marshland on Staten Island, men "well known to law enforcement agents" deposited 700,000 gallons of waste oil in barrels. In North Carolina, one "midnight dumper" simply opened the spigots on a tank load of PCBs and then drove until the tank was empty.

Hazardous Waste Sites: The National Priority List With thousands of toxic dump sites, chemical wastes are a ticking time bomb. You can check to see how your state ranks on the following Social Map. This map shows the worst of the many hazardous waste sites in the United States, those so hazardous they have been placed on a national priority cleanup list. These sites pose such a risk to people's health that they need immediate attention. The sites shown on this map will be cleaned up when and *if* Congress appropriates money to do so. Since these sites remain untouched year after year, some surrounded by fences to keep people out, it is obvious that the priorities of Congress do not lie here.

Figure 13.4 Hazardous Waste Sites on the National Priority List

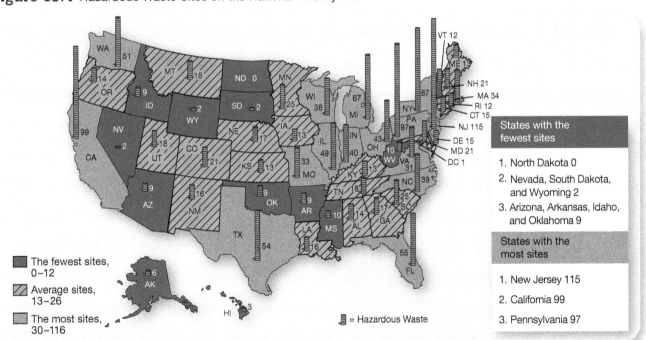

Source: By the author. Based on *Statistical Abstract of the United States* 2018:Table 420.

Nuclear Pollution

Nuclear power plants are like nuclear waste sites—who wants to live with the fear of spewing radiation? While nuclear accidents are rare, let's look at four of them.

The World's First Nuclear Waste Disaster: Kyshtym Russia's Ural River Valley is a remote place, and it was here that the Soviet government decided to develop its first atomic bomb. To obtain the necessary plutonium, the Soviets built a nuclear reactor in Kyshtym. Accounts vary as to how they disposed of the millions of gallons of nuclear waste produced by this reactor. Some say they bored holes into the ground and poured the liquid wastes into them (Solomon and Rather 1980). Others report that they piled the waste onto a dry lake bed (Clines 1998). Perhaps they did both. Either way, a chemical reaction took place. In 1957, the waste exploded, sending radioactive dust high into the air.

The radioactive fallout from the explosion devastated the area. Maps before the explosion show 30 villages and towns around Kyshtym. On maps printed after 1958, those communities are nowhere to be seen. The residents had been evacuated permanently from a 1,000-square-kilometer area.

The Puny Nuclear Reactor Accident: Three Mile Island In comparison, the worst nuclear accident in the United States is puny. In 1979 at Three Mile Island, Pennsylvania, a reactor leaked, people panicked, and 100,000 residents fled (Zaretsky 2018). The news was alarming, but the contamination was minimal, and people moved back to their homes. Despite the fright it caused, this minor loss of coolant seems to have exposed people to less radiation than you get when you have your teeth X-rayed at your local dentist (Williams 1980).

The World's Worst Nuclear Reactor Disaster: Chernobyl Then we have the other extreme. This is what happened in 1986 at Chernobyl, in the Ukraine, when it was part of the USSR:

> *Meltdown. The word froze in the mouth of the operating engineer. An explosion had blown a 1,000-ton steel cover off a nuclear reactor, obliterating the containment structure.*
>
> *It was too late to flee: No one can outrun deadly radiation. For 10 days, the world watched the drama, the fire raging and radioactive materials spewing into the air.*
>
> *Chernobyl's cloud of radioactive gases migrated slowly around the world. In two weeks, its airborne waste was detected in the United States and Tokyo (Flavin 1987). Canadians were advised not to drink rainwater, and farmers in Great Britain were ordered not to grow certain crops because of the radioactive fallout (Dufay n.d.).*

Victims of the Chernobyl nuclear disaster who are suffering from skin cancer.

More than 300,000 people were evacuated. International medical teams rushed to the scene, and despite emergency transplants of bone marrow and fetal liver cells, 31 people died during the first months. About 12,000 square miles of farm- and forestlands were so contaminated that they may be useless for two generations or longer. Some people, even though they are aware of the risk, have moved back into the contaminated areas (Dufay n.d.). "This is our home," they say. "Where else can we live?" Some farmers are again growing crops and raising livestock in areas contaminated by the Chernobyl disaster. On a personal note, when I was living in Latvia, I was warned not to eat strawberries because they had been grown in areas contaminated by the Chernobyl disaster. However, I saw others buying the strawberries.

When United Nations researchers did 20- and 30-year follow-up studies of Chernobyl, they found that the health effects were much milder than expected. Levels of leukemia—one of the main fears—turned out to be within the normal range. Cases of thyroid cancer were higher than normal. The main victims were those who had been children at the time. They had consumed milk from cows that had eaten radiation-contaminated grass. Thyroid cancer, though, is treatable and has resulted in only a few deaths ("Stakeholders and Radiological..." 2006; WHO 2016e). The researchers had a problem separating health consequences of Chernobyl from those arising from the heavy consumption of vodka. Overall, the findings are unexpectedly encouraging.

The Fukushima Nuclear Disaster   Nuclear disaster also struck Japan. In 2011, an earthquake damaged a nuclear reactor at Fukushima. While the damage was being brought under control, a tsunami hit Japan's coast, knocking out the plant's capacity to cool the reactor. This was followed by an explosion that spewed radiation. Uncooled, the nuclear fuel overheated and melted through its steel containment vessels. The nuclear fuel now lies at the bottom of the reactors, with no one knowing how to remove it. The best hope the experts have at the moment is to send in robots, draw up a plan of the unknown, and perhaps—if everything goes right—within 10 years begin to remove the molten debris (Negishi and Pfanner 2016). Meanwhile, the consequences continue: To prevent another explosion, water is being pumped onto the nuclear fuel. And the contaminated water? It ends up in the ocean ("Seven Years..." 2018).

Food Pollution

After a visit to Orlando, Florida, I drove to my home in the Florida panhandle. The night I arrived home, I came down with a fever. I decided to "tough it out" so I could continue to write, confident that the fever would subside. After three days, however, the fever persisted. In intense pain and on the verge of delirium. I gave up, drove to the nearest hospital, and went to the emergency room.

I soon found myself attached to IV bags, my body pierced with needles. Tests showed that I was infected with Escherichia coli (E. coli), which can be fatal. After a week in the hospital and being presented with a humongous medical bill, I was able to go home.

What had happened? The best guess is that some restaurant worker in Orlando who handled my food hadn't washed his or her hands after defecating. *E. coli* is a bacterium that lives in our digestive system, where it plays a beneficial role. But it becomes dangerous when our food or water is contaminated with feces. *E. coli* is only one of the many disease-causing substances in our food.

How serious is food pollution? Listen to this. Each year, *48 million* Americans get sick from food they eat. One hundred twenty-eight thousand are hospitalized, and 3,000 die (CDC 2018g).

Let's look at the three types of **food pollution**: (1) disease-causing germs like *E. coli*, (2) harmful chemicals, and (3) genetically modified food.

Diseases in Our Food   We'll begin, if you have the stomach for it, by considering how chickens are processed.

Chickens

Separate raw chicken from other foods. Do not to cut vegetables on the same surface on which you have cut chicken. Wash that surface well, preferably with bleach water. And be sure to cook chicken thoroughly. Don't forget to wash your hands.

Is this warning overblown, an example of being too cautious? Or can chicken be dangerous to your health? The findings of scientists at *Consumer Reports* (2014) are

This is how life begins on a chicken farm. When these chickens are a little older, they will live in cages so small they can hardly move. After their egg-producing days are over, once again they will be placed on a conveyor belt, this time to be sliced into parts that will reach the dinner tables of America.

Andrey Rudakov/Bloomberg/Getty Images

not encouraging. They bought chicken breasts in 26 states. Ninety-seven percent of the chicken had harmful bacteria, and two-thirds had *E. coli.* In an ironic twist, 214 of those who attended the 2014 Food Safety Summit's annual conference got sick from the chicken the catering company served (Flynn 2014).

Yes, if you handle raw chicken, do follow the warnings.

Not Just Chicken

In 2018, contaminated turkey led to salmonella outbreaks in 26 states. That same year brought salmonella infections from dried coconut, raw sprouts, chicken salad, and even Kellogg's Honey Smacks Cereal (CDC 2018h).

And health-conscious individuals received a surprise from their Romaine lettuce: 210 became sick from listeria, and five died from it (CDC 2018i).

Unfortunately, you never know what food might make you sick, or worse, kill you. Thirty-three people who sat down to enjoy their summer cantaloupe ended up in the hospital. They left in body bags (Booth 2016). Here are other foods that have claimed lives: Jalisco soft cheese (40 deaths), hot dogs from a subsidiary of Sara Lee (20 deaths), the Peanut Corp. of America (nine deaths), and Blue Bell Ice Cream (three deaths) (Burros 1999; Neuman 2010; Gasparro and Newman 2015). The killer hiding in these savory treats? Listeria.

Chemical Additives   Let's turn to the second type of food pollution: chemicals added to our food to lengthen its shelf life, enhance its appearance, or control its taste.

Food Flavorings and Colorings

How safe are the chemicals in your soft drinks, ice cream, and, yes, in your yogurt? The agency responsible for overseeing the safety of food is the Food and Drug Administration (FDA). The FDA sometimes seems less interested in protecting the health of the public than in protecting business from being inconvenienced.

What I have written above, is this an exaggeration? Judge for yourself. Red Dye No. 2 used to be the most common food coloring in the United States. After researchers found that rats and mice fed this dye developed cancer, public interest groups flooded Congress and the agency with petitions. It took five years for the reluctant FDA to ban this dye.

Many find little comfort in knowing that the food industry replaced Red Dye No. 2 with Red Dye No. 40 and other red dyes (FDA 2015). Red Dye No. 40, made from petroleum, causes cancer in animals. Although some European countries have banned Red Dye No. 40, the FDA continues to look the other way (Perry 2010; Gasparro and Newman 2014). But forget the cancer. Red Dye No. 40 makes the food looks so appealing.

If you see the words *artificial flavors* on the label of some food, you should know that this generic term hides chemicals you likely don't want to put into your mouth. Here are some: benzophenone, ethyl acrylate, eugenyl methyl ether, pulegone, pyridine, styrene, and p-menth-4(8)-en-3-one. I have chosen to list these seven because they have been identified as causing cancer ("Advocates Sue FDA…" 2018).

Where are these chemicals used? Baked goods, candy, and ice cream. They add flavor—as well as cancer, claim those suing the FDA to get them to prohibit their use in our foods.

Food Preservatives   Sulfites are used to keep food from discoloring, making them "look fresh." Sulfites are also added to baked goods, sprayed over shrimp and fish, mixed with dairy and grain products, and added to fruit juices, beer, and wine.

Some people get sick from sulfites, especially those who suffer from asthma. A few even die from allergic reactions. After years of complaints, the FDA banned sulfites from fresh fruits and vegetables and required a warning label on other products (Bahna and Burkhardt 2018). The warning label reminds me of Love Canal, putting a warning sign on a little fence around a dangerous chemical dump.

Synergism and Cumulative Effects   Food additives are *synergistic*—that is, they interact with one another. Some additives that are not hazardous by themselves can become dangerous when combined with other additives. For example, the nitrites that give hot dogs, ham, and bacon their inviting red color appear to be safe in and of themselves. In the presence of amines, however, nitrites become nitrosamines—potent carcinogens. Every organ in every species of animal ever exposed to nitrosamines developed cancer. Amines are commonly added to beer, wine, cereals, tea, fish, cigarettes, and Contac cold medicine. Hot dogs and beer, then, are an unhealthy combination. The same with a ham sandwich and a cup of tea. Figure 13.5 illustrates another surprising example of polluted food.

Figure 13.5 Bon Appétit?

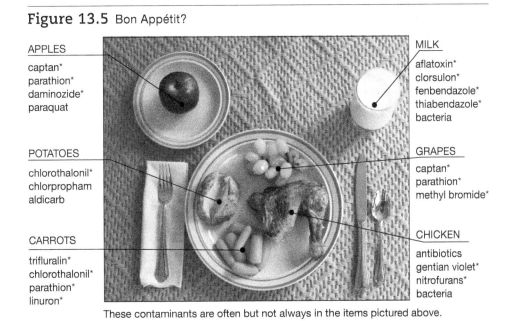

APPLES	MILK
captan*	aflatoxin*
parathion*	clorsulon*
daminozide*	fenbendazole*
paraquat	thiabendazole*
	bacteria

POTATOES	GRAPES
chlorothalonil*	captan*
chlorpropham	parathion*
aldicarb	methyl bromide*

CARROTS	CHICKEN
trifluralin*	antibiotics
chlorothalonil*	gentian violet*
parathion*	nitrofurans*
linuron*	bacteria

These contaminants are often but not always in the items pictured above.
*Known or suspected carcinogen.

Another problem is that some chemical additives that are harmless in small amounts build up in our bodies. When they reach a certain level, they begin to destroy tissues and organs. The level at which destruction begins varies both from chemical to chemical and from person to person.

Profits Ahead of Health Americans spend more money on food than on anything else. They spend $730 billion for food at home, and the same amount for food away from home (*Statistical Abstract* 2018:Table 1078). The food industry adds harmful chemicals to our food not because it is necessary but because it is profitable. The chemicals slow spoilage and increase sales by making food appeal to the public's conditioned taste and sight. Certainly the food chain is long—that is, getting food from grower to consumer is a lengthy process—and the food industry must use effective ways to preserve food. But we have many ways to do this that don't harm people's health: canning, dehydrating, freeze-drying, freezing, pickling, salting, smoking, and vacuum packing. When the food industry chooses to preserve food in ways that harm health, we can say that those who control the food industry put profits ahead of health.

Some of our food is polluted before it is processed. Animals are given antibiotics to keep them from getting sick and growth hormones to cause them to grow faster. Farmers spray pesticides on fruits and vegetables to prevent insect damage. When we eat non-organic fruits and vegetables or animals or their products, such as milk and cheese, some of these antibiotics, hormones, and pesticides end up in our bodies. Some accumulate there until they reach a tipping point or are set off by some catalyst and trigger cancer or other diseases.

Of course, we have the ever-vigilant FDA to protect us. This agency issued a dire warning that dogs could die if they chewed gum—that is, ate gum—that contains the sweetener xylitol. "Ingesting just a few pieces of gum can poison even a large dog" is the warning (Maremont 2016). And for people? No warning. It would interfere with the gum industry if they removed xylitol. So just keep chewing away. But be careful for your dog.

Genetically Modified Foods (GMOs) It doesn't take a brain surgeon to figure out that we should avoid diseased meat and that at least some chemicals added to foods are harmful. However, we land in the midst of controversy when it comes to **genetically modified foods**—foods derived from plants or animals in which genetic materials have been transferred from one species to another, or in which genes have been manipulated in a way that does not occur in nature. Some see GMOs as just another step in improving food, while others view GMOs as Frankenfoods that threaten to unleash unknown horrors onto the world.

Even placing the topic of genetically modified foods in this section of the book is controversial. It could imply that modifying foods genetically is a form of food pollution. But locating this topic here is not intended to communicate such a message, only to stress that some scientists take this position.

The issue is simply this: Modifying foods in this way scares people, who fear an increase of cancer and other diseases. U.S. companies have spearheaded the development of genetically modified foods, and they stand to reap huge profits if the new strains are accepted around the world. Even when laws were proposed to label GMO foods—not to ban them—so consumers could make a choice in the foods they buy, these U.S. agricultural giants poured millions of dollars into campaigns to fight the legislation (Doering 2014).

Are GMOs dangerous? The American Association for the Advancement of Science (AAAS) reviewed the evidence and concluded that GMOs are just as safe as conventional food (Rainie and Funk 2015). This has not hushed the controversy, however, which is a quiet affair in the United Sates but somewhat noisier in Europe, where 17 European countries have banned the cultivation of genetically modified crops (Lynas 2015). Although the AAAS has declared that GMOs are fine, one of nine U.S. scientists disagrees (Rainie and Funk 2015). Occasionally, a scientist will make a statement warning the public about the dangers of GMOs (Lathan 2015). Ultimately, scientific research will demonstrate that one or the other economic–political side is correct. It is even possible that each side is partially correct—that some genetically modified foods will prove to be harmful, and others safe. We will have to await the outcome of this controversy.

Research Findings: Conflicting Interpretations

13.5   **Compare how the pessimistic and optimistic environmentalists interpret research findings.**

Almost everything we have reviewed about the environment reflects negative findings and opinions. Before turning to a surprising contrasting view, let's continue on this negative path a while longer as we consider energy and resources.

The Pessimistic Environmentalists

One group of experts argues that we are facing energy and resource shortages so vast that they will shatter the foundations of civilization. These **pessimistic environmentalists** can't understand why most of us are so shortsighted that we become concerned only when the price of gasoline goes up. We miss the bigger picture—that for its existence, our civilization depends on substances whose supplies are limited.

Oil   The pessimistic environmentalists almost pull out their hair at the way most of us think about oil and other resources. They can't understand why we aren't alarmed about what is so obvious. No matter how ample the supply of oil might be at the present, oil reserves are not infinite. At some point, we will reach the end of being able to pump oil from the ground. As we get close to this, the price of oil will skyrocket. And when we do run out of oil, just like the Mesopotamians, Maya, and Anasazi, our civilization will collapse. Running out of oil, they stress, is not a matter of if, only of when.

Oil is not the only catastrophic depletion the world faces. Shortages of minerals and water can also bring down civilizations.

Minerals   The pessimistic environmentalists also foresee a bleak outlook for essential minerals, substances such as chromium, cobalt, copper, molybdenum, and vanadium. Without these minerals, we would have neither cars nor computers. Economies around the world are expanding ferociously. The most industrialized nations depend on an economic expansion of 2 or 3 percent a year in order to keep people employed and their standard of living increasing. At the same time, India, China, and other nations have joined the most industrialized nations in this furious competition for the earth's limited resources. The pessimists argue that we will run out of these essential minerals, that substitute materials may buy us time, but we are reaching limits that will stop the expansion of the world's economies and bring our civilizations to a screeching halt.

The Water Shortage   Then there is the issue of fresh water. We turn on the faucet, and before our eyes is an endless supply of running water. We can take showers as long as we want, or we can fill our bathtubs. We can flush the toilet as often as we want. Those who have swimming pools fill them with water. So, what is the problem?

We are slowly learning a bitter lesson. Of all the water on Earth, 97 percent is saltwater. A little more than 2 percent is frozen in glacial ice. This leaves about 1 percent for all agricultural, industrial, and personal uses. Contrary to appearance, we are entering a water crisis. Communities have begun to quarrel about who has a right to the water of the Great Lakes. California and Arizona argue about who has the right to the water of the Colorado River. States are going to court, suing each other over water rights.

To illustrate the coming crisis, consider that we are depleting the underground water of the Ogallala, the largest aquifer in the United States. As shown in Figure 13.6, the Ogallala runs from South Dakota to Texas. It is so huge that it waters the nation's breadbasket, where farmers grow one-sixth of the world's grain (Frankel 2018). In this same area, ranchers raise nearly half the nation's cattle. One scientist suggested we replant the

Figure 13.6 The Ogallala Aquifer

The Ogallala Aquifer

native prairie grasses, reintroduce the buffalo, and turn off the lights (Farney 1989). Some say that desert is the natural condition of much of this area, now in pasture and farmlands. Perhaps, then, the emptying of the Ogallala destines this area to be a tourist attraction of giant sand dunes.

Water is far more than just a U.S. problem. Around the world, nations are arguing about the right to the water in the rivers that mark their borders or that flow from one nation into another. As industry expands and populations grow, demands for water will increase. The coming confrontations over water are likely to be so severe that nations will go to war over water rights. They are already threatening to do so (Kuol 2018).

Do you think the water shortage will ever become so severe that people will resort to drinking water from the toilet? I'm sure you shook your head, but don't be so sure. Read the following *Thinking Critically about Social Problems*.

In Sum The pessimistic environmentalists stress that our resources are finite and that we are depleting them. There is only so much oil and natural gas; there are only so many mineral deposits and freshwater sources. When we run out of them, as we will, our factories will grow silent, our cars will sit in driveways, and our homes will grow cold.

Thinking Critically about Social Problems

From the Toilet to the Tap: Overcoming the Yuck Factor

Would you drink water from someone's toilet?

This is a serious question. The water shortage is becoming so severe that some people are doing exactly this.

Okay, they aren't like dogs that slurp water from the toilet. And they don't scoop it up in a glass. But they do drink it. After the toilet water (and the shower water and the dirty dishwater) goes down the drain, it ends up at a central station where the toilet paper and other "solids" are diverted and the rest is strained through holes smaller than bacteria. Then the water goes through reverse osmosis, which removes most molecules that are not water. Finally, the water is exposed to ultraviolet light. The result, say the experts, is the equivalent of distilled water.

You probably wouldn't want to scoop water out of this toilet and drink it, but what if it goes through a purification process first?

JGI/Jamie Grill/Tetra Images, LLC / Alamy Stock Photo

"Maybe so, and you can drink it if you want to, but not me" is the reaction of many.

But a lot of people are drinking this water. In Orange County, California (the home of Disneyland), 70 million gallons of such water (called "treated effluent") are returned to the aquifer each day. In Singapore, about 15 percent of the water is treated effluent.

On space missions, the astronauts drink their own recycled urine.

"From the toilet to the tap" seems to be the wave of the future.

"That's not accurate," reply the experts again. "Get it straight. It's from toilet to treatment to tap. And we call it potable reuse."

"I don't care what you call it. I wouldn't even want my cat to drink it," said one woman.

"I'll stick with bottled spring water," said one man.

"If science says it's clean, then it's fine" is another response, growing more common as people get used to the idea, the "yuck factor" receding.

Based on Barringer 2012; National Research Council 2008, 2012; "Reuse Opportunity" 2018.

For Your Consideration

→ What is your reaction to treated effluent?
→ Would you drink treated effluent? Would you drink cleaned-up toilet water? It does seem to make a difference what you call it, doesn't it?

The Optimistic Environmentalists

There is another side to this matter, one that is seldom heard. Some experts, whom I call the **optimistic environmentalists**, say that alarmist doomsayers have captured the attention of the media. With their dire predictions and woeful exaggerations, they paint a bleak picture of the future. Isolated incidents, although tragic, make sensational headlines, but they don't give us the larger picture. If we take a more realistic, dispassionate view, they say, we will see that our situation is a lot more pleasant than the pessimists make it appear. Let's look at their arguments.

Resources Are Not Getting Scarcer   Before his death in 1998, economist Julian Simon took a provocative position that seemed to fly in the face of logic and reality. He insisted that raw materials are *not* getting scarcer. He said that when something that people want grows scarce, its price increases. To see whether a raw material is becoming scarcer, he said we should just look at its price. The long-term trend is lower prices, which means *less scarcity*. Here is how Simon put it (Simon 1980:11):

> The cost trends of almost every natural resource—whether measured in labor time required to produce the resource, or even in the price relative to other consumer goods— have been downward over the course of recorded history. An hour's work in the United States has brought increasingly more of copper, wheat, and oil from 1800 to the present.... These trends imply that the raw materials have been getting increasingly available and less scarce.

To illustrate how the prices of raw materials have been falling relative to wages, Simon used copper as an example. As Figure 13.7 illustrates, over the past century, it has taken less and less time to earn enough to buy a pound of copper.

Figure 13.7 The Price of Copper Relative to Wages

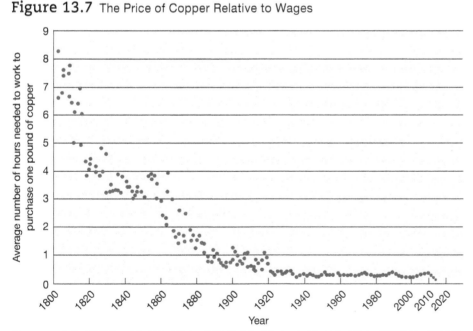

Sources: Historical Statistics of the United States 1976; Statistical Abstract of the United States 2018:Tables 665, 761.

This view so infuriated the pessimistic environmentalists that it led to one of history's famous bets. This fascinating bet is recounted in the following *Thinking Critically about Social Problems*.

Thinking Critically about Social Problems

Put Your Money Where Your Mouth Is: The Simon–Ehrlich Bet

To say that professors Julian Simon and Paul Ehrlich didn't like each other would be an understatement. *Detest* would be more appropriate. Simon was an economist who taught at the University of Maryland. Ehrlich, a demographer and biologist, taught at Stanford.

Ordinarily, their paths would not have crossed. They lived a continent apart, and they worked in different fields.

But then life changed for both of them.

Ehrlich came out swinging. In 1968, he wrote a book that scared millions of people and fueled the environmental movement. He said that the world's population was growing so fast that food would soon be scarce. Prices were going to soar, and life expectancy would drop. His book, with the pop title, *The Population Bomb,* sold 3 million copies. The book scared the American public, aroused an environmental movement, and made Ehrlich rich. From obscurity in the classroom, he was vaulted to prominence as a guest on talk shows.

Fame and fortune. A prestigious job at Stanford. Unless he started to sexually harass his students or come to class drunk, how could that be spoiled?

Then along came Simon. Simon started grumbling in public, muttering that Ehrlich's book was a piece of, well, you know what—rotten catfish. Simon even claimed that the truth was the opposite of Ehrlich's headline-grabbing screams about a dire future. Larger populations, asserted Simon, would mean more abundance, not less. Prices would drop, not increase. Life expectancy would increase, not drop.

Simon and Ehrlich began to call each other names. They wrote nasty comments about one another in academic journals. Scholars, who usually write dispassionate articles for one another, were amused at the unusual display of passion and vitriol.

Ehrlich still had the public on his side. He kept repeating his doomsday predictions. He was a founder of Earth Day, and at its first gathering in 1970 he spoke to a crowd of 200,000.

Simon was there, too, telling his side of the story. He had an audience of 16.

Simon didn't like this, but there wasn't much he could do about the public latching on to Ehrlich's ideas, not his.

Then Simon made an intriguing proposal. Without mentioning Ehrlich by name, he challenged any pessimistic environmentalist to a bet (Toth 1998). The opponent could select *any* commodity, and Simon would bet that its price would drop. "After all," he said, "contrary to common sense, resources are growing more plentiful, and they will drop in price."

"Put your money where your mouth is if you don't agree," Simon challenged, none too gently.

This was too much for Ehrlich—who knew that he was the target of the challenge. In October 1980, he accepted the bet. Then he did a little boasting of his own. He said, "I'll accept Simon's astonishing offer before other greedy people jump in" (Tierney 1990).

The bet was on. If the prices of chrome, copper, nickel, tin, and tungsten were higher in 10 years, Ehrlich would win; if they were lower, Simon would win. To be sure there could be no misunderstandings, the two wrote their bet down, signed a contract, and publicized it widely.

During the ensuing years, the two kept goading one another—and the world's population kept growing. During the next 10 years, it soared by more than 800 million people, the greatest increase in history.

Ten years later to the day, the two checked prices.

Ehrlich was chagrined. The price of all five metals had dropped. He quietly sent Simon a check. He enclosed no letter.

Simon gloated publicly. "Now you know who's right," he said. "And if you think this was just a fluke, let's do it again, Ehrlich. And this time, let's put up some real money. How about $20,000?"

Ehrlich refused, saying that the matter was of minor importance.

Simon laughed and continued to poke fun at Ehrlich. Then students started to do the same, calling Ehrlich the nuttiest professor at Stanford.

The two never reconciled.

Julian Simon died at age 65 in 1998. Paul Ehrlich stayed on at Stanford, where he continues to insist that the world is on the edge of mass starvation, to be accompanied by the collapse of civilization (Bailey 2018).

For Your Consideration

→ Do you think Simon's winning the bet with Ehrlich was a fluke?

→ With natural resources finite (a limited amount), why aren't their prices (in terms of hours worked or inflation-adjusted dollars) increasing instead of declining?

Energy And energy? Here too, Simon stressed that to get the answer we need to look at long-term prices. The historical prices of electricity and coal, for example, have moved downward, indicating a stable and even increasing supply of these forms of energy. Be sure to look at long-term trends, Simon stressed. Short-term prices, like what you pay at the gas station from week to week, give a distorted picture. Prices jump around week by week and year by year for any number of reasons, such as civil wars and hurricanes that disrupt supply.

The Technological Fix The optimistic environmentalists claim that improved technology will solve whatever threats we face. If we should ever exhaust a particular resource, our technology will produce a substitute. New technologies will replace older technologies. In fact, technology is rushing so headlong into the future that it sometimes produces new materials before the old ones are even threatened. Fiber-optic cable, for example, is rapidly replacing copper wire for the transmission of sound and images. Just a few years ago, the optimists point out, the pessimists were saying that we would run out of copper. Take another look at Figure 13.7.

It is the same for pollution. We have had predictions of disaster in the past, the optimists argue, and our technology has always seen us through. The present is no exception. To get their point across, some use a bit of humor. In 1900, the prominent urban pollution problem was manure. At that time, the main means of transportation was the horse, and ugly, festering mounds of manure would pile up on city streets. When motorized vehicles replaced horses, the manure problem disappeared. The present is no different, say the optimistic environmentalists, and we will develop technology to counter threats to our environment.

Pessimistic Environmentalists Cause Disease   The optimistic environmentalists also point out that the solutions of pessimistic environmentalists can do more harm than good. Edward Teller (1980), the man most responsible for the hydrogen bomb, said that environmental regulations cause disease. What did he mean by such a strange statement? DDT was banned, he said, when environmentalists objected that its use harmed the environment. Then mosquitoes multiplied, and in Sri Lanka alone, 2 million people came down with malaria. To combat this disease, DDT had to be brought back. Teller added, "I challenge anybody to show me a case where lack of environmental protection has made 2 million people as seriously sick as the disease caused by the environmentalists."

Things Are Getting Better   Finally, the optimistic environmentalists make this point: We can evaluate the condition of the environment in a number of ways, but the single best measure is life expectancy. When an environment deteriorates, life expectancy drops. When an environment improves, life expectancy increases. Look at Figure 13.8, which shows the consistent upward march in life expectancy. Why are Americans living longer? Because our environment has improved, not deteriorated. Don't let anyone twist reality in order to match their woeful view of life. Stop worrying about what *might* go wrong. Life is getting better, so enjoy it.

Figure 13.8 Life Expectancy in the United States, by Year of Birth

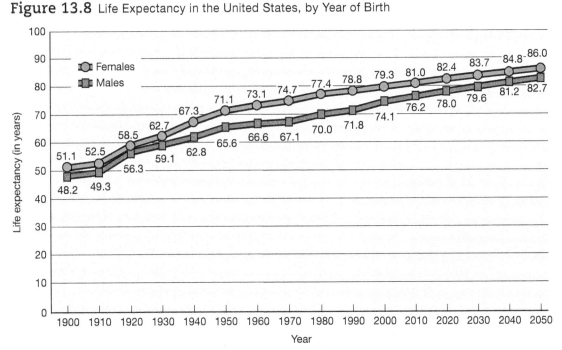

Note: Not shown is the slight drop in 2015–2017, apparently due to opioids deaths—a drop that has not yet changed the Census Bureau's projections.

Sources: By the author. Based on *Historical Statistics of the United States* 1976:Table B 116, 117; *Statistical Abstract of the United States* 2018:Table 115, with projections by U.S. Census Bureau.

In Sum   The optimistic environmentalists say that the world is improving. Our expanding industries are going to continue to bring a higher standard of living for the world's people. Life expectancy will continue to climb. If we run out of one resource, we will replace it with another. We will never run out of energy, and we will control pollution.

Reconciling the Positions

How do we reconcile such contrary positions among the "experts"?

Frameworks of Interpretation   As stressed in Chapter 2, objective conditions—or the things that we call facts—do not come with built-in meanings. We have to interpret them. All of us, as the symbolic interactionists stress, fit "facts" into some framework. The framework that we choose influences our conclusions. This basic principle applies to "experts" and "non-experts" alike.

Consider how this principle works when it comes to the environment—whether pollution, energy, or resources: If we assume that the environment is deteriorating and our resources are becoming scarce or even disappearing, we interpret data one way. In contrast, if we assume that resources are abundant and either will not shrink or will be replaced by substitutes, we make far different interpretations. The framework within which we interpret objective conditions makes the difference in how we interpret "facts."

Science at Work   Does this mean that we are left only with opinions, and opposing ones at that? Perhaps for the moment, but not indefinitely. As pointed out earlier about the controversies over global warming and genetically modified food, science is at work, and objective studies will win out. Barring political interference, as opposing sides present their evidence, air their views, and try to disprove the other, the best data will become apparent. As scientists produce more data on the environmental crisis, the exaggerations of each side will become apparent. Eventually, we will know which position has the better data on pollution, energy, and resources.

Implications of the Frameworks   Meanwhile, we must draw our own conclusions—which affect how we perceive the problem and the solutions we favor. On an individual level, our conclusions influence our choices about energy use and lifestyles. On the political level, the conclusions have far greater implications: The well-being of billions of people depends on them—including future generations. Everyone will benefit if this debate and its related research are allowed to continue unencumbered by politics, so that social policies can be based not on biases and ideology but on sound data and logic.

Resource Destruction: The Tropical Rain Forests

These two men are members of the Kenyah dayak tribe in Indonesia, one of the few hunting and gathering groups remaining on earth.

Sijori Images/Barcroft Media/Getty Images

We don't have to be alarmists to see that, at a minimum, we must reduce and properly dispose of toxic waste, provide wholesome food, and learn how to preserve and create— or at least not destroy—a healthy environment. And we don't have to be alarmists to be concerned that plant and animal species are being extinguished. Especially ominous for humanity's future is the ongoing destruction of the tropical rain forests.

The tropical rain forests have been called the "lungs of the earth." They help to regulate the earth's exchange of oxygen and carbon dioxide, and they absorb the carbon gases that many experts say underlie global warming. The rain forests also help keep the earth's climate in balance by giving off water vapor that keeps the ground from drying out. As the environmental pessimists say, the "lungs of the earth" are gasping, and if we don't take action soon, they will collapse.

Although rain forests cover only 7 percent of the earth's total land surface, they are home to *one-third to one-half* of all plant and animal species. Some of the discoveries from the rain forests have been astounding: A flower from Madagascar is used in the treatment of leukemia, and a frog in Peru produces a painkiller more powerful, but less addictive, than morphine (Wolfensohn and Fuller 1998). A chemical from a rain forest plant in Panama is thought to be effective in treating malaria (Roach 2003). A drug derived from the berry of the Blushwood tree in Australia dries up cancerous tumors (Boyle et al. 2014). We must be careful about romanticizing and mythologizing the rain forests, though, as no life-saving drugs have been found there and no diseases cured (Voeks 2018).

Even knowing that the rain forests are essential for humanity's welfare, people keep clearing them (Martins et al. 2018). In the process, they extinguish thousands of plant and animal species (Newbold et al. 2016). As biologists remind us, a species lost is a species gone forever. We are exchanging our future for some lumber, farms, and pastures.

Social Policy

13.6 **Know how frameworks of interpretation lead to different social policies. Summarize potential social policies to cope with environmental problems.**

Before we examine specific social policies, let's first consider how the contrasting frameworks of interpretation we have reviewed lead to vastly different social policies.

Oppositional Viewpoints: Pessimistic and Optimistic Assumptions

From these two strikingly different frameworks flow three approaches to social policy. As you will see, each also implies a different type of society.

The Steady-State Society As we have seen, the pessimistic environmentalists argue that it is folly to expect the world's economies and standards of living to increase endlessly. Based on their position that pollution is endangering the world and resources are diminishing, they have come up with an overarching solution called the **steady-state society**. By this term, they mean that we must stabilize industrial output at the level it is now. If we do this, we will slow the rate at which we pollute the environment and use up resources. This slowdown will give us time to solve problems of pollution and to develop alternative resources before the shortages develop that will destroy our civilization. To reach a steady-state society will require painful adjustments. It means we will have to curb our growing appetite for the material goods that support our current lifestyles.

The Scaled-Back Society A more pessimistic group of environmentalists argues that it is not enough to develop a steady-state society. The pace at which we are polluting our environment and using our resources is far beyond anything the earth can sustain. We must develop a **scaled-back society**. That is, we must reduce our industrial output and our standard of living. Only after we cut back to some optimal level—one that experts will determine—can we move to a steady-state society. This will require not "adjustments" but rather sacrifice, as we lower our material standards. Scaling back is essential for the survival of Earth. All of us, except the poorest, must learn to get by with less. Some who take this position add that once we have scaled back our expectations and have learned to live simpler, less-materialistic lifestyles, we will find life more satisfying.

The Expanding Society Optimistic environmentalists scoff at the arguments of the pessimists. Not only can we solve the current environmental crisis, they say, but we can also enjoy even higher standards of living. We can bring pollution under control through international agreements and develop alternative substances if any resources run short. As we do this, we can increase our industrial output and create a world of even greater material abundance. It is foolish to even consider a steady-state or scaled-back society. Either of these choices would deny billions of people a better life.

Specific Social Policies

Regardless of whether we agree—partially, reluctantly, or wholeheartedly—with the pessimistic or optimistic environmentalists, it seems reasonable that we need social policies regarding pollution and energy. Let's consider possible policies.

Preventing Food Pollution   Let's start with what seems a reasonable goal: All food should be safe. This applies to all "food orientations." Whether carnivore or vegan, preferring organic or dripping with animal fat, each person deserves their food of choice to be safe.

The very minimum is to never allow diseases or poisons to be transmitted in our food. Food processors have no need to add carcinogenic chemicals to our food to lengthen its shelf life. Available are alternative forms of food processing and preservation we have already reviewed. Nor do they need these chemicals to make our food look or taste better. As an example, we all like our food to come in pleasing colors, but instead of using those carcinogenic red dyes I mentioned, food processors can use tomato or elderberry to produce the color red (Gasparro and Newman 2014). At a minimum, no chemical should be added to our food until it is proven safe for human consumption.

To be effective, the legal penalties need to be directed against the managers and directors of U.S. companies that violate laws against food pollution. If the companies are outside the United States, we can ban food imports from countries that violate chemical restrictions.

Toxic Chemicals and Hazardous Waste Sites: Holding Industry Accountable
Industry must be held accountable for the toxic chemicals they produce and use. Back in 1986, Congress passed the Community Right to Know Act. This law requires that each year companies submit to a state agency and to local fire departments a list of the hazardous chemicals they use or manufacture. Some states have passed their own right-to-know laws, requiring businesses to inform their employees of the hazardous chemicals they will be exposed to at work. In general, the law is rarely and selectively enforced.

To go farther, we can follow a "cradle-to-grave" approach for all toxic chemicals. Each would be registered as it enters the marketplace and monitored throughout its lifetime. When California passed a cradle-to-grave law, environmentalists celebrated. But seven years later, the state had lost track of 3,000 truckloads of hazardous wastes (Garrison et al. 2013). Because some states are rigorous and others lax in keeping track of toxic chemicals, in 2012 Congress passed the Hazardous Waste Electronic Manifest Establishment Act. This national tracking system took the EPA seven years to implement (Vanguilder 2018). If followed through, we should never have another Love Canal.

But our current Love Canals must be eliminated, a costly venture. As you saw from Figure 13.4, more than a thousand hazardous waste sites are spread across the nation. Congress established a superfund to clean them up, and a few sites have been cleaned up. But with the cleanup costs running into the billions of dollars, the pace is slow. The choice seems to be a large bill or slow poison—whether to fund the cleanup or to build high fences around the sites and let the wastes continue to leach into our groundwater. Citizen action is needed to move past a policy of fences.

Nuclear Wastes: The Problem with No Solution   Because nuclear wastes stay lethal for thousands of years, they have perplexed the experts. Scientists are trying to figure out how to store something that is beyond human experience. We face an almost ludicrous situation: We have *160 million* pounds of radioactive waste that lasts thousands of years stored in temporary containers at 80 sites in 35 states (Pearce 2018).

Experts came up with what sounds like an ideal solution: To give these wastes a permanent home, storage chambers were carved

Chemicals that are illegal to use in the United States can be manufactured in the United States and exported to other countries, where environmental laws are weak. You can see how these young men in Albania are being exposed to the chemicals. In a boomerang effect, foods treated by these chemicals are imported to the United States and consumed, along with their chemicals.

from an ancient salt bed at Yucca Mountain near Las Vegas, Nevada (Martin 2018). Then some critics pointed out a little flaw in the plan: The containers for the waste—stainless steel lined with lead—might not last 1,000 years, much less the 15,000 years they needed. And how right they were. Just 15 years after the first radioactive wastes were placed in the containers, one began to leak.

The Greenhouse Effect and Climate Change   Because the consequences of carbon dioxide are a world problem, the world's nations must reduce the amounts they produce. In 1997, the most industrialized nations agreed in Kyoto, Japan, to do just this, and in 10 years they reduced their emissions by 20 percent (UN 2015). This encouraging progress was followed in 2016 with 175 nations signing an agreement in Paris to further limit carbon dioxide. In 2018, the United States withdrew from the Paris Agreement. Some despair that whatever we do now is too late anyway; global warming is going to hit with its full destructive force (Rich 2018).

The Rain Forests   To prevent the destruction of the world's rain forests, I propose two social policies: (1) Make it illegal to import timber that comes from rain forests. This will require an international agreement; the ban won't work if only a nation here and there passes such laws. (2) Industrialized nations can *purchase the rights to not develop the rain forests*. This policy would preserve millions of acres and tens of thousands of plant and animal species for future generations. The rights would extend indefinitely and be overseen by an international watchdog agency.

The rain forests, so significant for Spaceship Earth, depend for their existence on politics. Political leaders can protect the rain forests, as was the encouraging outcome of an accord on climate in Paris. But the election of a new leader, such as occurred in Brazil, who views the rain forests as lumber and farmland, and plans on paving a highway through them, can suddenly detour many years of effort (Maisonave 2018).

Technology and Energy   Technology is sometimes thought of as the silver bullet that will save the day. Somehow, we will develop new technology that solves our problems. And for energy, this could be the case. The most astounding new technology is *fracking (fracturing)*—using pressurized liquids to break underground shale rocks, giving us access to their pools of natural gas. The result is nothing short of amazing. So much natural gas is being tapped in the United States that its price has plummeted. Companies are building vast pipelines to transport the gas and terminals to export it to other countries.

Is there another side to this positive development? Of course. And the pessimists step right up to the plate. Breaking the shale disturbs natural rock formations and causes mini-earthquakes, and the liquids used to break up the shale will seep into the aquifers and pollute our drinking water.

Again, instead of coming down on one side or the other, we will have to let scientific studies give us the evidence we need to make a decision. But aside from new deposits of natural gas and petroleum, only two types of solutions for energy exist: alternative forms of energy and energy conservation. Let's look at these.

Alternative Forms of Energy   A variety of alternative forms of energy can reduce and even replace our dependence on fossil fuels.

Harnessing the Sun and Wind   As you know, solar power is infinite, and harnessing the sun has moved from a promise to a viable form of energy. The solar panels you see on homes are just a hint of what is to come. Germany has a social policy to become entirely independent of fossil fuels. As other countries adopt similar policies and slide off fossil fuels, solar power will be harnessed in such abundance that today's pollution might become a distant memory. Such, at least, is the potential.

Harnessing the wind is nothing new. In the 1800s, wind was a primary source of non-animal power on our farms. Each farm had a little wind mill that produced limited, basic power. Today, social policies that require utility companies to purchase the electricity generated by wind have resulted in the sprouting of wind farms in remote, windy places around the world. We shall see many more of these.

Synthetic Fuels and Others **Synthetic fuels** (called **synfuels**) can be developed from garbage and other waste. The decay of organic substances such as sewage and straw produces methane and methanol, gases that motors can burn efficiently. Synfuels offer the potential to solve two problems at once: the disposal of our organic garbage and the production of alternative fuels. We may be able to plant fields of common milkweed, turning them into "petroleum farms" as factories extract **hydrocarbons**—the backbone of motor fuels, lubricants, turpentine, and rubber—from those plants.

Hydrogen, too, holds great potential. As a basic component of air and water, hydrogen is available in limitless amounts. Carbon dioxide is also plentiful—and unloved because of its contribution to global warming. A process is being developed to turn carbon dioxide into a liquid fuel, which will also solve two problems at once, reducing global warming and providing abundant energy (Chanmannee 2016). Other alternative sources of energy include the ocean tides, **geothermal energy** (heat from beneath the earth's crust), and **nuclear fusion** (combining atoms, as opposed to nuclear fission, which splits atoms).

Energy Conservation   Here are ways we can conserve energy.

Our Homes   In reaction to the growing price of energy, and to a lesser extent to environmental concerns, we have made our homes more energy efficient. But we still have a long way to go. The future seems to point to **passive houses**, which can cut fuel bills by 90 percent (Hurley 2016). Passive houses are like a thermos bottle: Special insulation and windows retain most of the heat produced by people's bodies and appliances. A high-tech filtration system maintains the temperature and keeps fresh air flowing through the house. Germany, which is leading the energy revolution, is building entire subdivisions of passive houses.

Our Cars   We have done well in increasing the energy efficiency of our cars. The average car today gets 77 percent better mileage than cars did 45 years ago, from 13.5 miles per gallon to 23.9 miles per gallon (*Statistical Abstract* 2018:Table 1120). As electric cars replace the gas guzzlers, owners will think they are not part of the pollution problem. Following each electric car, however, is a long trail of pollution—from the manufacturing process to the pollution from the power plants that produce the electricity. Only as fossil-burning utility plants are eliminated will this trail of pollution begin to disperse.

Our Work Week   To conserve energy, businesses and factories can operate four 10-hour shifts a week instead of five 8-hour shifts. This change in working patterns would cut commuting expenses by 20 percent and allow factories to fire up their boilers less often. The potential savings are dramatic, but it does involve changing patterns of behavior that are rooted firmly in culture—hardly an easy matter.

In Sum   If the pessimistic environmentalists are correct, we soon will see the end of some of the resources on which our civilization depends. If we haven't implemented the right social policies before this happens, the coming shortages will force us to do so. If the optimists are right, we won't have to make difficult choices. Market forces will point us in the right direction. If we run short of something, the pursuit of profits will lead people to develop new technologies and alternative sources. Those convinced of this view tell us, "Just don't interfere with the market forces, and the balance will occur naturally."

To close this section, in the following *Thinking Critically about Social Problems,* we will consider moral dilemmas of social policy.

Thinking Critically about Social Problems

Social Policy and Moral Dilemmas in a Global Age

An overarching policy is to produce less of what harms the environment. We can change our production techniques and redesign our products and manufacturing. We can also do more recycling. More controversial—we can reduce what we consider to be needs. We have the capacity to take these steps, but to take them we must be convinced not only that our fragile environment is being harmed but also that it is worth the effort and costs to change our ways.

And changing our ways is never comfortable.

To return to one of the main points of this chapter: Our views—the perspectives we have–depend on the frameworks of interpretation that we choose. Because of differing perspectives, what is obvious to some is not obvious to others. And the perspectives are much more varied than simply those of pessimists and optimists. To agree on reality so we can approach the world similarly is a challenge, and it will remain so.

Social policy also touches on philosophical and moral issues. Because the environmental crisis is global, its solution requires global social policy. Some organization—whether the United Nations or the World Trade Organization or another international body—needs to take the lead in solving environmental problems by proposing international laws that benefit all nations. However, such laws will conflict with the individual sovereignty of nations, and some nations will reject the legislation as violating their national interests. This brings us face-to-face with philosophical, moral issues. Let's look at some.

As you consider the following two sets of questions, keep in mind that assumptions of a "greater good," as conflict theorists remind us, can be excuses for some nations to bully others. Dominance usually comes through an imbalance of power, which takes us to the relationship between the most industrialized and the least industrialized nations. If there is such a right, it certainly isn't likely that the weaker nations would be able to impose their ideas of pollution and resource depletion on the more powerful nations.

For Your Consideration

→ Do nations have a fundamental right to use resources in any way they wish? Do nations even have a fundamental right to pollute, if they choose to do so? If not, then do nations possess some fundamental right to impose on others their view of pollution and resources?

→ If nations have the right to impose their views on other nations, what is the basis of that right? Is it some "greater good" for the world's benefit? If so, who decides what that "greater good" is and how it should be enforced?

The Future of the Problem

13.7   Discuss the likely future of environmental problems.

If we take a very long view, many environmental problems will take care of themselves. Our groundwater, for example, will rid itself of most pollutants eventually. The problem is that the self-cleansing process takes significant time—about 1,400 years for the groundwater to cycle through the aquifers (Mitra 2015). And in 15,000 to 30,000 years, it should be safe to go near the accumulated nuclear waste.

To be practical, let's try to get a glimpse of a more immediate future, considering what is likely to take place during the coming decades. Let's first examine energy conservation and pollution. After this, we'll again look through the eyes of the pessimists and optimists.

Driverless Cars

To glimpse the potential of technology in solving our problems, consider driverless cars, the topic of the next *Technology and Social Problems.*

Technology and Social Problems

Peering into the Future: Consequences of Driverless Cars

Driverless cars are moving quickly from a wild idea to becoming part of our everyday lives. What remains is to master a few technical problems and to change laws to match the new reality.

Now imagine yourself in this future, which is almost on us.

You didn't have to buy a driverless car. You don't own any car at all. In fact, hardly anyone does. When you want to go somewhere, you just click an icon on your phone or watch. In a few minutes, a driverless car arrives to pick you up. The average car sits in the garage about 95 percent of the time, and with the cost of insurance, depreciation, interest payments, gasoline, and repairs, it is cheaper to subscribe to a car service than it is to own your own car.

When the car—perhaps a large SUV or even a small bus, depending on the area you live in—arrives, there likely will be other passengers. No problem. You don't have to talk to them. Your seat is laid out with a work space. The car has an electric motor and drives silently. You can plug in your computer and get to work. Or you can simply relax and enjoy music, movies, or talking books on your telephone or notebook. The driverless car drops you off at your destination.

There is no driver to bother you with needless chatter, and no one is waiting for a tip.

What are some consequences of this technological advance? First, with the extra time in the morning and the evening, you become more productive. This makes you more valuable to your employer, and you might earn extra raises. Second, you don't arrive at work—or at home—all frazzled because of traffic and inconsiderate drivers. This improves both your working conditions and your family life.

"You used to have to drive cars?!" your children might exclaim when you tell them about "how life used to be when you were a child." Driverless cars (and trucks and buses) are inevitable. But in a few years, will they look like this?

These are appealing consequences on a personal level, but driverless cars can also help alleviate some social problems. With most people not owning cars, traffic jams disappear. Since these are electric cars, most of the pollution created by those millions upon millions of cars with their internal combustion engines also disappears. (But once again we should note that electricity is produced in power plants, which are heavy polluters.)

Less pollution, less energy needs, and even less personal tension—sounds like a winner all around.

For Your Consideration

→ What is your view of this projected future?
→ What negative consequences could driverless cars bring?

Energy

To strive for higher standards of living is to increase our demands for energy. In Table 11.1, you saw how the size of the average household has shrunk. Yet the average size of a new home has risen by two-thirds—from 1,500 square feet to about 2,500. We also furnish our homes with more energy-eating appliances. In 1970, 34 percent of new homes had central air-conditioning; now 93 percent do (*Statistical Abstract* 1989:Tables 58, 1231; 2018:Table 996). We might complain about the price of gasoline, but we drive our cars more miles a year than we did 30 years ago (*Statistical Abstract* 2018:Table 1117).

It isn't just Americans. The demand for more energy is growing throughout the world, especially in India and China, which together hold a third of the world's population. Not only are these countries industrializing at a fast pace, which places tremendous demands on energy, but also millions of their people are joining the middle class in buying energy-eating cars and household appliances. Unless we sink into a lasting global depression, the expansion of their industrial base will continue, as will the demand for more cars and gadgets by their upwardly mobile populations. We likely will develop more technology to harness alternative forms of energy, making these sources of energy widely available at low prices. International oil companies will invest in alternative forms of energy, turning them into profitable enterprises.

Pollution

The future of pollution is positive—but haphazard.

No Master Plan   We have no overarching plans for chemical and nuclear pollution that would ensure the long-range health of our population. If bringing pollution under control required only technology, we could assume a future with cleaner air, water, and land. But politics is always involved. It is likely that we will never see a national policy that focuses on making our environment as free of pollution as possible. Outrage over some catastrophe—as with *Deepwater Horizon*—will produce specific changes from time to time, but when the crisis is over, the media's attention will turn elsewhere, with only small localized outrage remaining.

A Lack of Unity   The future of pollution depends on a fragile balance of power among groups whose interests sometimes coalesce and sometimes conflict. At this point, there is no strong environmental alliance united under a green banner. Certainly, people are concerned about the world they will leave for their children, but environmentalists, often local in orientation or fragmented by multiple visions and political strategies, lack a unifying voice. Each faction claims and jealously guards its own turf. To unite these groups and arouse general interest, it likely will take a charismatic leader or a huge calamity, each of which could be catastrophic.

The Greens   Environmentalists in Europe have formed political parties. The Green Party, as the one in Germany is called, holds seats in the national parliament and in several of Germany's states. It bargains those seats for power in coalition governments. The United States, too, has a Green Party, but it is so weak that it has a difficult time mustering enough support to even get on the ballot, much less to win elections. This could change. Some unexpected event could etch the environment onto the national consciousness, making it a top political issue. In the next *Spotlight on Social Research*, Robert Gottlieb discusses how environmentalists have begun to apply their perspective to urban life.

Spotlight on Social Research

The Marriage of Community and Environment

ROBERT GOTTLIEB, *professor of urban environmental policy at Occidental College, has found that something new is happening in the environmental movement. He calls it a marriage of community and environment. Living in Los Angeles and writing and teaching about the urban environment make this "marriage" particularly compelling for him. Here is what he wrote for you.*

When I first arrived in Los Angeles in 1969, the city, with its sprawling landscapes of subdivisions and freeways, had a reputation as the "anti-environment." I never focused on the fact that Los Angeles had a river until the 1980s, when one of my students brought to my attention the growing advocacy around the revitalization of the asphalt-and-concrete-encased Los Angeles River. Since then, I've been able to document the creation in Los Angeles of a new kind of community-based environmentalism: where urban rivers and streams and other green spaces and community places in the city are re-envisioned.

This marriage of community and environment has made an impact on environmental groups. *Open space* has long referred to places outside urban areas or at the urban edge, where there is little or no development. Earlier battles for open space sought to *preserve* environmental assets, such as habitat, wildlife, and other forms of biodiversity. Their focus was not on built environments where there is little or no existing green space, where density is high, where the land is contaminated, and where the acquisition of land for parks or recreation seems only a distant possibility.

That's changing. Environmental advocates have begun to redefine the issue of open space as the need to re-envision *community spaces* and to reclaim rather than simply preserve such places. Many environmentalists now embrace community gardens, farmers markets in low-income communities, re-landscaping projects, and recreational opportunities in densely populated areas. I had the opportunity to direct an educational program on the Los Angeles River—the very symbol of both the anti-environment and efforts to re-envision the river as a community and environmental asset.

If you define the marriage of community and environment as an effort to re-envision—or reconstruct or reclaim—these kinds of community and environmental assets, then a different kind of environmental agenda begins to emerge. This agenda would focus on a neighborhood's transportation needs, on access to and quality of food, on health concerns like asthma, and on schools as re-landscaped, livable places rather than fortress-like, asphalt jungles. In this marriage, the greening agenda becomes a justice agenda. It leads us to understand that nature belongs in the city as well as outside it.

Environmental Injustice

A special concern of sociologists is how unequal power has led to **environmental injustice**—pollution doing the most harm to minorities and the poor (Lester et al. 2018). Polluting industries locate where land is cheaper—and, as is no surprise to you, the wealthy don't build their homes on cheap land. As a result, low-income communities, often inhabited by minorities, are more likely to be exposed to pollution. In the struggle for environmental justice, sociologists have studied, formed, and joined groups that fight to stop polluting plants and block the construction of new ones. This struggle for justice is likely to continue.

The Environmental Pessimists and Optimists

Finally, let's look at the future through the eyes of the two groups who see practically nothing alike.

The Picture Painted by the Pessimists Pessimists paint a gloomy future, of course. Pollution will continue with only superficial improvements here and there, the depletion of resources will accelerate, and humanity will spiral downward. The countdown has

Is this the future of humanity? The picture painted by the environmental pessimists looks something like this photo taken in Manila, Philippines. What can we do to avoid it?

Zoriah/The Image Works

already begun, and "RDP Day" (Resource-Depletion and Pollution Day) is on its way. This is the day when we will have depleted our vital resources, and pollution will be so extensive that we won't be able to fix it. With its industrial base undermined, modern society will disintegrate, bringing tragedy to all. Desperate, people will flee. But to where? Even the countryside will be too polluted to support anything but a minimum of life.

Can such a gloomy future be averted? Yes, reply the pessimists, but only if we develop a steady-state or, better, a scaled-back society now. To level off our energy consumption or to reduce it severely, we need to cut back on our material gadgets and quit our endless striving for more material possessions. We have built our society on the assumption that resources are inexhaustible and production will always increase, so like an addict deprived of heroin, our withdrawal pains will be enormous. But once we recover from the shock of being forced into a drastically different lifestyle, we may find that a simpler way of life is rewarding: If we feel less compulsion to own things, life will slow down and we can enjoy social relationships more.

The Picture Painted by the Optimists And what does the future look like to the environmental optimists? Our present path is fine, they say. We already have more resources than we need for the foreseeable future. Scientists will continue to make technological breakthroughs, putting even more energy at our disposal. The development of technologies to harness hydrogen and carbon dioxide hold the potential for giving us energy in unlimited quantities. Perhaps from these sources alone, we might meet all the world's energy needs now and in the future.

Neither is pollution a fearsome problem. Scientists are discovering enzymes, microbes, and molecules that eat pollutants and clean up contaminated groundwater (Gupta et al. 2018). The principle underlying the solution is this: Pollution will be solved to the extent that people demand a cleaner environment and are willing to pay for prevention and cleanup. Because people are demanding it, the environment is already getting cleaner—and it will continue to improve. Consequently, the future promises a healthier environment, an even higher standard of living, and a continued increase in our life expectancy.

Who Is Right? What *is* the future of the environmental crisis? Is humanity on a course that dooms us to destruction, as the pessimists insist? Or are the optimists right, with our current course leading us to a delightful future? Or could the future turn out to be even gloomier than the environmental pessimists imagine, with nuclear war, the worst pollution of all, destroying our ecosystem—and humanity?

We who are the audience—and either the beneficiaries or the victims—of this unfolding drama will have to await its outcome.

Summary and Review

1. The destruction of the environment, which began millennia ago, may have destroyed ancient civilizations. Industrialization has intensified this process.

2. The nations of the world share a common *ecosystem*, which makes the environmental crisis a global matter: Even individual acts of *pollution* can have international consequences.

3. Symbolic interactionists have studied how the environment became a social problem, how objective conditions were translated into subjective concerns. Concerns about the environment began with professionals, were picked up by interest groups and government agencies, and then by the press, which aroused the public.

4. Functionalists stress that all life on Earth is interdependent. ("Everything is connected to everything else.") We all are part of a huge, complex, living machine called Earth. Industrialization has dysfunctional consequences for the ecosystem.

5. Conflict theorists stress the conflict between environmentalists, who battle to reduce environmental threat, and industrial leaders, who fight for the right to pollute while earning a profit.

6. Some measures of air and water pollution show improvement, but the results are mixed, and pollution continues. The *greenhouse effect* could cause a global climate change that would bring far-ranging consequences for humanity.

7. *Strip mining* and the disposal of solid wastes despoil the land. Industrial wastes haunt our drinking water and many of our lakes and rivers. *Acid rain* imperils animal and plant life.

8. Chemical pollutants pervade our environment. Leaching from landfills is extensive. Nuclear pollution is hauntingly ominous, as illustrated by the Kyshtym, Chernobyl, and Fukushima disasters. Food additives are a form of pollution. Genetic modification of foods might be another form.

9. Alarmed at the environmental crisis, pessimists advocate a *steady-state society*—one based on zero economic growth—or a *scaled-back society,* based on deliberately shrinking the economy. Optimists, convinced that we can continue industrial growth and that technology will solve environmental problems, advocate an expanding economy. Regardless of who is right, pollution is a global problem that requires international social policies.

10. The environmental pessimists and optimists paint contrasting pictures of the future. We don't yet know who is right, but with alternative forms of energy, accompanied by new technologies, our energy future looks positive. The outlook for pollution, however, is less positive. The environmental movement is fragmented, but it has the potential to become a powerful global force.

Thinking Critically about Chapter 13

1. Which of the theoretical perspectives (symbolic interactionism, functionalism, or conflict theory) do you think does the best job of explaining the environmental crisis? Why?

2. How far do you think the government should go to reduce pollution? Should the executives who run polluting corporations be jailed? Should the government shut down polluters? What else could or should the government do?

3. Some scientists argue that problems of pollution and the scarcity of resources are best solved by free enterprise. They believe the market is better equipped than governments to solve these problems. What do you think of their position?

4. Do you think the U.S. government has the power or authority to demand a steady-state society? Do you think it is advisable? Why or why not?

Key Terms

acid rain, 414
air pollution, 410
biodegradable, 410
carcinogens, 410
corporate welfare, 409
ecology, 404
ecosystem, 407
environmental injustice, 436
food pollution, 419
fossil fuels, 410
genetically modified foods, 422
geothermal energy, 432
global warming, 411

greenhouse effect, 411
hydrocarbons, 432
nuclear fusion, 432
optimistic environmentalists, 425
ozone shield, 410
passive houses, 432
pessimistic environmentalists, 423
pollution, 404
scaled-back society, 429
steady-state society, 429
strip mining, 413
synthetic fuels (synfuels), 432

Chapter 14
War, Terrorism, and the Balance of Power

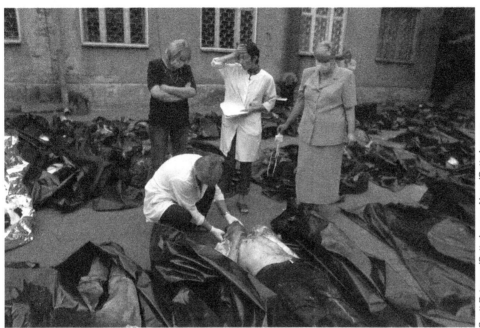

Scott Peterson/Getty Images News/Getty Images

 ## Learning Objectives

After reading this chapter, you should be able to:

14.1 Explain why war is common and know the essential conditions of war and the fuels of war.

14.2 Describe how extensive war has been and continues to be.

14.3 Discuss the perspectives that emerge when you apply symbolic interactionism, functionalism, and conflict theory to war.

14.4 Summarize what reduces war, the costs of war, dehumanization, the military–industrial complex, accidental war, and biological, chemical, and cyber warfare.

14.5 Discuss terrorism: revolutionary, repressive, state-sponsored, and criminal, as well as weapons of mass destruction.

14.6 Summarize social policies regarding terrorism, the MAD way to peace, policies that can bring peace, and how self-preservation figures in the survival of humanity.

14.7 Discuss the likely future of war and terrorism.

Some of the following events may sound strange, others humorous, perhaps even macabre. But arising from this background that follows are events that are going to have severe effects on your life.

Let's begin by noting that capitalist and socialist (or communist) economies seem to be almost mirror images of each other. Capitalists believe that socialism is immoral because it denies people the freedom of choice. People can't decide where they will live and work and go to school—others make those decisions for them. For their part, socialists believe that capitalism is immoral because it is based on making profits, which creates inequality and causes the poor to suffer. During what is called the **Cold War**, each side believed its position so strongly that they faced off, snarling, threatening, and brandishing their weapons at

Each side lived in constant fear of nuclear attack by the other.

one another. Their face-off was called a *cold* war because neither side unleashed its weapons, turning the mutual animosities hot. During this time, though, emotions did run hot, as each viewed the other as a mortal enemy that deserved to be exterminated.

I am not exaggerating. Each side barely held its war hawks in check. The leaders of each side listened to arguments about why they should strike first with nuclear weapons and obliterate the other from the face of the earth.

Each side also lived in constant fear of the other. In the 1950s, Americans were so fearful of a Soviet nuclear attack that many built bomb shelters in their homes. In the states bordering Canada, schoolchildren, even little kids in grade school, were posted on top of school buildings. They were told to look for Russian planes sneaking over the border with nuclear bombs. The children were given plane silhouettes to help them determine if a plane was American or Soviet. The silhouettes were posted next to a telephone connected to some central command. U.S. schools also held bomb drills. Children were instructed to hide under their desks in case the evil Russians dropped an atomic bomb. (Don't even try to imagine what good hiding under a desk would do. Fear gripped the country, and Americans were in a state of near panic.)

The same fear gripped the Soviet Union and its satellite nations. Students there were taught that the evil Americans might drop nuclear bombs at any time. Because the Americans might also use biological weapons (called "invasive bacteria" at the time), students were issued gas masks. Contests were held to see which students could put the gas masks on the fastest. High school students were also taught how to assemble and load Kalashnikov rifles—just as effective in coping with a nuclear attack as hiding under desks.

This is what the times were like. Both Americans and Russians thought that the Cold War might turn hot at any moment. The evil enemy (the other) stood ready to pounce and destroy.

Fear of nuclear attack was rampant in the 1950s and 1960s. Teachers taught their children to hide under desks, while others built bomb shelters in their back yards. The school photo is from 1952 in New Jersey, the bomb shelter from 1961 in California.

SAL VEDER/AP Images

Bettmann/Getty Images

Those frigid days are over. The nukes—which have been improved to kill even more—are supposedly no longer aimed at Moscow and Washington. But these former mortal enemies continue to disagree, and each nation has begun to turn up the volume of its propaganda machine.

National economic interests, which can run high and hot, often underlie war. And the confrontations have begun. In 2007, the United States announced plans to install missiles in Poland and the Czech Republic, on Russia's border, supposedly to guard against missiles launched by some "rogue nation." U.S. officials knew this announcement would provoke a strong response from Russia, but not how strong it would be. (Imagine if Russia announced plans to build a missile base in Mexico or Canada to "protect" us from some rogue nation.) Russian authorities said that if the United States put its missiles in these places, Russia would launch nuclear bombs. The United States replied defiantly that it was going ahead with its plans—but instead it quietly pulled back and did not build these missile sites.

Russia made its own announcement: It would fly bombers in the Gulf of Mexico, something that it had not done even during the coldest day of the Cold War (Cecire 2014).

Russia amassed weapons on the Ukrainian border and invaded Ukraine via non-uniformed soldiers. Succeeding in annexing the Crimean Peninsula, Russia preserved its naval base at Sevastopol (BBC 2018). Perhaps because Sevastopol had been a base for Russia's Baltic Fleet since 1783, before it was handed over to Ukraine in 1954, the United States and NATO (North Atlantic Treaty Organization) stood aside, avoiding direct confrontation.

The United States (and NATO) held some small war games in countries bordering Russia. Russia held small war games on the Ukrainian border. Russia also began to buzz U.S. ships and to fly jet fighters close to U.S. planes over the Black Sea (Sonne 2016). The escalation continues. Name calling, finger pointing, and finger giving. Small potatoes. But with the potential to get out of hand at any moment.

Welcome to the New Cold War, which at any time could be dialed down or turned off. Or, as I would like you to do as you read this chapter, ask yourself what it would take for these tensions to break out into war.

The Problem in Sociological Perspective

14.1   **Explain why war is common and know the essential conditions of war and the fuels of war.**

Let's move beyond our current situation and ask a broader question: Just why do nations quarrel and fight?

Why Is War Common?

Human groups have always fought each other (Lahr et al. 2016). Why do they do such a destructive thing?

An Instinct to Fight?   Because war has been common throughout history, some analysts suggest that humans have an instinct for aggression. At one time, said anthropologist Konrad Lorenz (1966), our instinct for aggression used to be functional. It ensured that the fittest survived. It also forced humans to colonize the entire world as they fled from one another's innate aggression. In today's society, however, as Lorenz put it, this instinct has become a "hereditary evil" left over from our primitive past.

The Sociological Answer: Societies Channel Aggression   To find the answer to why war exists, sociologists do not look *within* people. Whether humans have an instinct for aggression is not the point. People will always disagree about something, so conflicts always arise among people who live near one another. *What is significant are the norms that groups establish to deal with their inevitable conflicts.*

To illustrate this principle, let's look at two extremes. The first is a society that nourishes aggression. In the following *Global Glimpse,* you will see why the Yanomamö represent this extreme.

A Global Glimpse

Nourishing Aggression: The Yanomamö

The Yanomamö men of the Amazon rain forest often attack neighboring villages, killing the men and kidnapping the women. Villagers also fight with one another. Fights often begin over sex: infidelity, seductions, or failure to give a promised girl in marriage. Sometimes the men challenge one another to a duel. One man stands, muscles tensed, feet firmly planted, while the other hits him once as hard as he can in the chest. Then the other man gets his turn. This continues until one man can no longer return the blow. Sometimes men take turns pounding one another over the head with a long wooden club. At other times, they even use axes and machetes—and neglect to wait their turn. When relatives are drawn in, fights turn into brawls. These games can trigger feuds between Yanomamö villages. When someone is killed, relatives seek revenge. Feuds are self-feeding because each killing requires retaliation.

Why do the men fight like this? Anthropologist Napoleon Chagnon, who lived with the Yanomamö and analyzed their relationships, concluded that the basic reason is *social status*. Because violence is considered to be the mark of a true man, a reputation for violence gives a Yanomamö man high status. Almost everyone everywhere wants more status, to be looked up to by others, and the Yanomamö have developed a system that integrates violence and status.

There is also another factor, one that is less apparent: Success at violence gives men more access to women. Chagnon found that the men in this northern Venezuelan jungle who have killed at least one other person have more wives and children than those who have never killed. An especially successful warrior may have six wives. The higher status that comes with killing makes a man an attractive candidate for marriages—which are arranged by the men.

"How primitive they are!" we might say, smugly acknowledging our higher technology and education. But as Chagnon points out, the Yanomamö are not that different from us. Although we don't reward our war heroes with additional wives, we do award

The Yanomamö are a violent people. Shown here are Yanomamö men in a non-violent activity. One man is blowing ebene, a hallucinogenic drug, into another man's nose.

Robert Madden/National Geographic Image Collection/Getty Images

them medals, seats in the U.S. Senate, and sometimes even the presidency. As Chagnon points out and as presidential campaigns illustrate, the military record of candidates is important in U.S. politics.

Are we any different, then, from the Yanomamö—aside from being more indirect in the ways we reward "war behaviors"?

Based on Allman 1988; Chagnon 1988; de la Rosa 2018.

For Your Consideration

→ In what ways do we encourage (reward) and discourage human aggression?

→ In what ways do we channel human aggression into socially acceptable forms?

→ What prevents us from breaking down into little groups that are at war with one another?

The other extreme is represented by the Eskimos of East Greenland. Instead of fighting, their norms require that hostile individuals *sing* to one another! Actually, they sing about their grievances, and their song duels go like this:

> The singing style is highly conventionalized. The successful singer uses the traditional patterns of composition, which he attempts to deliver with such finesse as to delight the audience to enthusiastic applause. He who is most heartily applauded is "winner." ... One of the advantages of the song duel carried on at length is that it gives the public time to come to a consensus about who is correct or who should admit guilt in the dispute.... Gradually more people are laughing a little harder at one of the duelist's verses than at the other's, until it becomes apparent where the sympathy of the community lies, and then opinion quickly becomes unanimous and the loser retires (Fromm 1973).

Other groups channel aggression into rituals involving violence. It is common for the Tiwi of northern Australia to settle differences through spear-throwing duels.

> When a dispute is between an accuser and a defendant, which is commonly the case, the accuser ritually hurls the spears from a prescribed distance, while the defendant

dodges them. The public can applaud the speed, force, and accuracy of the accuser as he hurls his spears, or they can applaud the adroitness with which the defendant dodges them. After a time, unanimity is achieved as the approval for one or the other's skill gradually becomes overwhelming. When the defendant realizes that the community is finally considering him guilty, he is supposed to fail to dodge a spear and allow himself to be wounded in some fleshy part of his body. Conversely, the accuser simply stops throwing the spears when he becomes aware that public opinion is going against him (Fromm 1973).

In Sum   Social scientists have found that war is not universal. War is one option that some groups choose for settling disagreements, but not all societies offer this option (Fry et al. 2009; Miklikowska and Fry 2010). The Mission Indians of North America, the Arunta of Australia, the Andaman Islanders of the South Pacific, and the Eskimos of the Arctic, for example, have established ways to handle quarrels, but they do not have organized battles that pit one tribe against another. These groups don't even have a word for war (Lesser 1968). To understand war, then, sociologists look for *social* causes—conditions in society that encourage or discourage aggression and that shape aggression into organized combat between groups.

What social conditions encourage groups to choose war to handle their disagreements? Let's find out.

Why Do Some Groups Choose War?

War—an organized form of aggression that involves armed conflict between politically distinct groups—is often part of national policy. Why do some groups choose war to handle disputes when less drastic solutions are available?

Three Essential Conditions of War   Sociologist Nicholas Timasheff (1965) became intrigued by this question. After studying armed conflicts, he identified three essential conditions of war. The first is a cultural tradition for war. Because war has become part of a people's thinking, they view war as a way to resolve conflict with another nation. The second is an antagonistic situation in which groups confront incompatible objectives. Each, for example, might want the same land or resources. A cultural tradition for war and an antagonistic situation are essential, but they are not enough. They provide the fuel, but there also has to be a spark to ignite it. This third condition moves the nations from thinking about war to actually engaging in it.

Seven "Sparks" That Set Off War   To identify the sparks that ignite a war, Timasheff studied wars throughout history. He found seven sparks that ignite antagonistic situations, causing them to flame into war. They include the opportunity to:

1. Get revenge (settle "old scores" from previous conflicts)
2. Dictate one's will to a weaker nation
3. Protect or enhance prestige (to protect the nation's "honor")
4. Unite rival groups within one's country
5. Protect or exalt the nation's leaders
6. Satisfy the national aspirations of ethnic groups (to bring "our people" who are living in another country into our borders)
7. Convert others to religious and ideological beliefs

The Scope of the Problem

14.2   Describe how extensive war has been and continues to be.

You can't watch a day's news reports without hearing about a war being fought somewhere in the world. And the United States regularly sends its troops to other countries. Have countries always fought this much?

War in the History of the West

To find out how common war has been in history, sociologist Pitirim Sorokin (1937) went all the way back to 500 B.C. He identified 967 wars in Europe from then to 1925 A.D., an average of one war every two to three years. Counting the years in which a country was at war, Germany spent the least amount of time in war (28 percent) and Spain the most (67 percent). Since William the Conqueror took power in 1066, England had been at war for 56 of each 100 years. During the previous 1,000 years, Russia had only one peaceful quarter-century.

And the United States? It turns out that we are one of the most aggressive nations in the world. From 1850 to 1980, we sent troops to other parts of the world more than 150 times (Kohn 1988). That's more than once a year. We continue this tradition of warfare today. At our current rate, it won't be long before the total reaches 200. Today we are "at war" with no one; that is, Congress has not declared an official war. Despite this, we have "intervened" (as U.S. politicians like to call it) in this order: El Salvador, Honduras, Libya, Grenada, Panama, Afghanistan, Iraq, Somalia, Haiti, Bosnia, Sudan, Kosovo—back again to Afghanistan and Iraq, and then Syria. The targets of our "military interventions" differ throughout time, but not our perception of endless enemies and our readiness to attack them.

Measuring War in Terms of Deaths

War may be hell, as General William T. Sherman said, but some wars are more hellish than others. Consider the following. Since 1829, there have been approximately:

- 80 wars in which 3,000 to 30,000 people died
- 43 wars in which 30,000 to 300,000 people died
- 12 wars in which 300,000 to 3,000,000 people died
- Two wars (World Wars I and II) in which 3,000,000 to 31,000,000 people died (Richardson 1960; updated to 2018)

If your brother or sister dies in a war, of course, it matters little that there were 3,000 or 3 million other victims of that war. On a personal level, we measure things by how they affect us.

Our Growing Capacity to Kill   To understand war, we need to recognize how greatly industrialization has increased our capacity to kill. Consider bombs. When Germany and England were at each other's throats during World War I, fewer than three of every 100,000 people in these countries died from bombs. During the next 20 years, scientists "advanced" this instrument of human destruction as well as the aircraft to deliver it, and during World War II, bombs killed about 300 of every 100,000 English and Germans (Hart 1957). Scientists have continued to "advance" our killing technology, and if nations were to unleash nuclear weapons against one another today, the deaths of past wars would pale in comparison. Some of our "advanced" weapons have the capacity to destroy every living thing on Earth.

The Slaughter Continues   Many have hoped that war would become a relic of our primitive past. With higher levels of education, the thinking went, we humans would finally achieve a more advanced state. From our peaceful ways of resolving political conflict, we could look back smugly and reflect on how people used to slaughter one another.

As we all know, this description doesn't even come close to matching reality. Two generations ago, the United States fought in Vietnam for seven years—with a loss of 58,000 Americans and more than 1 million Vietnamese (Sylvester 2018). The death toll of the Soviet Union's nine-year war in Afghanistan ran about 1 million Afghans and perhaps 20,000 Soviet soldiers (Armitage 1989). Iran and Iraq fought an eight-year war at a cost of 400,000 lives. About 5,000 U.S. and other coalition soldiers died in Iraq, while estimates of Iraqi deaths run about a half million (Sheridan 2014; "Iraq Coalition..." 2018).

In Sum   War, then, as Sorokin sadly concluded in the 1930s, remains common. Sorokin added that his era was one of the bloodiest periods in the history of Western civilization—and perhaps in the history of humanity. Our era continues on this blood-soaked path. Even after generations pass, some groups claim the right to hate eternally—and to pass this bitter heritage to their children. The Israelis and Palestinians, as reported in our nightly news, each claim rightful vengeance for atrocities of the past. So do Pakistanis and Indians, Kyrgyz and Uzbeks, Georgians and Russians, and on and on. The soldiers of China, India, Israel, Russia, Iran, North and South Korea, and the United States stand armed and ready to battle. Suicide bombers continue to fuel enmities. Drones silently patrol the skies, operators far away, safely ensconced in hidden quarters, giving the command to launch missiles on the unsuspecting.

Looking at the Problem Theoretically

14.3   **Discuss the perspectives that emerge when you apply symbolic interactionism, functionalism, and conflict theory to war.**

Let's use sociological theory to better understand the social problem of war.

Symbolic Interactionism

As you know from previous chapters, symbolic interactionists emphasize how significant *perceptions* are in human behavior. You know this from your own experience, of course, because your own behavior depends on how you perceive a situation. But did you know that the fate of the world has also depended on people's perceptions? Let's see how this can be.

Perceptions and the Arms Race   As I mentioned, during the Cold War the United States and the Soviet Union viewed each other as mortal enemies. Fearing one another, each interpreted the actions of the other as evil. If one side were to underestimate the enemy, it could prove fatal. To be on the safe side, each magnified the destructive capacity of the other. Because neither had valid data, each had to *guess* what the other intended. Both used their guesses to choose what seemed to be the most practical response.

This guessing game led to an ironic self-fulfilling prophecy. When one superpower thought that the other might build a certain weapon, it rushed to build that weapon itself. Sometimes the other nation had no intention of building the weapon, but when that nation learned that the other was doing so, it felt no choice but to also build it. What were intended as countermeasures were twisted into aggressive actions. Each nation stimulated the other to build weapons it had no intention to build and could not afford.

This almost sounds like science fiction, but listen to how Robert McNamara explained it. As the U.S. Secretary of Defense, McNamara was an insider who saw this insidious process firsthand (Kurth 1974):

> In 1961 when I became Secretary of Defense, the Soviet Union possessed a very small operational arsenal of intercontinental missiles. However, they did possess the technological and industrial capacity to enlarge that arsenal very substantially over the succeeding several years. We had no evidence that the Soviets did plan, in fact, fully to use that capability. But, as I have pointed out, a strategic planner must be conservative in his calculations; that is, he must prepare for the worst plausible case and not be content to hope and prepare merely for the most probable.

> Since we could not be certain of Soviet intentions, since we could not be sure that they would not undertake a massive buildup, we had to insure against such an eventuality by undertaking ourselves a major buildup of the Minuteman and Polaris forces.... But the blunt fact remains that if we had more accurate information about planned Soviet strategic forces, we simply would not have needed to build as large a nuclear arsenal as we have today.

This buildup of **intercontinental ballistic missiles (ICBMs)** illustrates a primary principle of symbolic interactionism—that perceptions are central to human behavior. Because U.S. officials assumed that the Soviets were preparing for war, we built ICBMs so we could retaliate if we had to. This signaled to the Soviets that the United States might be preparing to attack, and they also needed to build ICBMs. The nuclear **arms race** was based on interpretations of what each nation thought the other would do.

This example illustrates how *symbols are so powerful that they can take on a life of their own.* Although McNamara's initial perception of Soviet intentions might have been wrong, our buildup of missiles became proof to the Soviets that they needed to build more missiles. When the Soviets did so, this became proof to us that our interpretation was right. To keep ahead, we then needed to build even more powerful weapons. *Perceptions, not facts, usually guide human behavior.*

Perceptions and the "First Strike"   This *principle of perceptions* is significant in all of human life. We like to think that we act on facts in our everyday lives, but we really act on our perceptions of "facts," on how we "think" things are. This basic principle of life takes on ominous significance when two nations are considering war. As long as these nations perceive war as a no-win situation, they will try to avoid it, even though they despise and fear one another.

But what if one nation thinks the other will eventually attack and that striking first will destroy the other's capacity to attack? As you might guess, that nation may strike first. This was a dilemma during the Cold War. Generals of the U.S. Air Force even argued a *first-strike policy,* that we should attack Russia if it meant that we could win the war (Kurth 1974). Apparently, Soviet generals made the same argument. You can see how tense and dangerous things were at that time. In this situation, each felt the need to signal to the other that a strike against it would be foolish. Both the Soviet Union and the United States would let information slip about new weapons and "Doomsday" systems—even if our country is destroyed by incoming nuclear weapons, our nuclear weapons will be launched automatically. It is scary to think that our lives—and those of the world—depended on each side correctly interpreting the signals of the other!

Unfortunately, the past still clings to us. Both Russia and the United States still stubbornly hold onto the right of first-strike (Sonne et al. 2016; Long 2018).

In Sum   Symbolic interactionists stress that we choose courses of action based on how we perceive events. When we apply this principle to war, we see that nations often lack facts about what an enemy is doing. In this void, they make decisions based on their perceptions of current and potential acts of the adversary. In the Cold War, this principle of perceptions led to an arms race between Russia and the United States so severe that these countries developed weapons that could destroy humanity. The need to interpret actions in order to infer intentions continues today, along with the same potential earth-shaking consequences.

Functionalism

The functionalist perspective provides another picture of war. Let's look at war's functions and dysfunctions.

The Functions of War   In 1939, the world was in turmoil. Hitler's tanks and *Luftwaffe* (air force) were rampaging through Europe. Japan had invaded China and was threatening the South Pacific. With the United States on the brink of entering the war, sociologist Robert Park (1941) decided to analyze the social functions of war. Here are the functions that he and others identified.

Extension of Territory   Park found that the world's countries had been born in war. The nations that existed in 1939—like those of today—had come into being because one group extended its political boundaries and conquered other groups. Today's United

States, for example, would not exist if it hadn't been for the Indian wars and the wars with France, Great Britain, Spain, and Mexico. A major function of war, said Park, is the *extension of territory*, an enlargement of a group's political boundaries.

Economic Gain   A second function of war is *economic gain:* access to treasure, markets, and raw materials such as oil. War also increases production, payrolls, and profits. World War II put millions of unemployed people to work and helped lift the United States out of the Great Depression. Even the threat of war can bring economic gain. As sociologist C. Wright Mills (1958) noted back in the 1950s, spending for "war readiness" benefits big business.

Social Integration   A third function of war is *social integration.* If groups within a country are in conflict, they often put aside their differences and cooperate to repel their "mutual enemy" (Timasheff 1965; Fry and Miklikowska 2012). After the war, the groups are likely to return to their unfinished conflicts. Afghanistan, for example, is fragmented into groups separated by religious, class, tribal, and clan loyalties that reach back centuries. When the Soviets invaded Afghanistan in 1979, these groups worked together to repel their common enemy. As soon as they defeated the Soviets, which took nine years, they renewed their divisions and turned on one another. That the U.S. military fought in Afghanistan and Iraq united some enemies in the Arab world. When the United States leaves this region, these enemies, as before, will again turn on one another.

The functions of the form of hostility, conquest, and killing called war are discussed in the text. This painting is of one of the numerous sea battles between the European powers in the 1500s.

Social Change   Sociologist Georg Simmel (1904) identified *social change* as a fourth function of war. The development of science and technology is one of those changes. Five centuries ago, for example, Leonardo da Vinci designed war machines for his patron. Since then, war has prompted aerodynamic designs, the harnessing of nuclear energy, and satellites. We even owe our interstate highways to war. When General Eisenhower arrived in Germany after its defeat in World War II, he was impressed by its *autobahns.* When he became president of the United States, Eisenhower decided that we needed highways like these so we could move soldiers, weapons, and supplies rapidly across the country in case the Soviets attacked. The Internet, too, came out of war; it was developed by the U.S. military as an alternative form of communication.

Other Functions   Another function of war is *ideological*—advancing a political or religious system. Between the 11th and 14th centuries, European Crusaders traveled to the Holy Land to fight Islam. Today, groups like al-Qaeda and ISIS violently advocate their ideological agenda. *Vengeance* or *punishment* is another function of war. Like people, nations can accumulate hurts and slights and, under the right circumstances, use war to "get even." Another function is *military security,* that is, a nation does not desire an asset in and of itself but attacks to prevent an enemy from using that asset against it. This is why Israel bombed Iraq's nuclear plants in 1981, bombed Syria in 2013, and targeted Palestine in 2018. Another function of war is to *increase the credibility* of a nation's threats or guarantees. By going to war, other nations will see that a nation means what it says.

Multiple Functions   No war serves a single function. A single war can involve territory, revenge, ideology, and military security. When a conflict gets drawn out, the functions can even change. The Crusades began in 1095 when Pope Urban II urged Roman Catholics to go to war and reclaim the Holy Land. Ideological purposes may have dominated at first, but the Crusades also provided treasure and territory. Nine Crusades and 200 years later, all the functions of war had been incorporated in this lengthy, sporadic war. If the "war against terrorism" goes on for decades, as seems likely, it, too, will end up serving all functions of war.

Functions for the Victors   War is usually functional for the victors. Rome, for example, conquered most of the known world, subjugating one region after another to Roman power and exploiting their resources. To the acclaim of citizens and Caesar alike, generals would return triumphantly to Rome, marching in formation down the main avenue and into the main square, laden with treasure and slaves. The treasure enriched the government and its elite. Some of the slaves brought to Rome after the fall of Greece were educated Greeks, who served as tutors for the elite's children. In the latter part of the empire, slaves provided entertainment, their deaths in the Colosseum yielding pleasure for Rome's jaded citizens.

Functions for the Losers   Although war is dysfunctional for losers, especially in terms of deaths, property destroyed, territories lost, and humiliation, losers can also benefit from war. One of the most remarkable examples occurred after World War II. After its humiliating defeat, Japan embraced Western technology. This change not only increased their standard of living and life expectancy, but also placed them in a world leadership position that they had failed to win through war. No social change is without its dysfunctions, however, and Japan's, too, has come at a price: the disruption of its traditional way of life.

Functions for Individuals   War also has functions for soldiers and leaders. Soldiers often report that battle presents the challenge to "see what I'm made of." Officers who organize battles derive satisfaction from outmaneuvering the enemy, gaining advantage through surprise attacks, and being acclaimed the victor. War also serves as an avenue of social mobility. New officer positions are created, and individuals are promoted. The prestige of winning can also bring political prominence. George Washington, Andrew Jackson, Ulysses S. Grant, and Dwight D. Eisenhower, generals of the army, were awarded the presidency of the United States. Colin Powell went from general to national security advisor. From there, he became U.S. Secretary of State, one of the most powerful positions in the world.

Dysfunctions of War   In stark contrast to the functions we reviewed are war's dysfunctions. Defeat, of course, is war's most well-known dysfunction, as are the destruction of cities, the loss of territory, and the deaths of soldiers and citizens. We can also number the fatherless and motherless children among war's dysfunctions as well as the bitterness that can span generations. Even military victory can bring dysfunctions. The victor can grow dependent on the exploitation of subjugated peoples. When that control ends, as inevitably it does, the economic pain is severe. For decades, Great Britain suffered withdrawal pains after it lost many of its colonies as a result of the fervor for independence ushered in by World War II. With the breakup of the Soviet empire, forged by war, Russia experienced this same dysfunction.

What dysfunctions of war can you identify in this photo from Iraq?

Daily Mirror Gulf coverage/Stringer/3rd Party - Misc/Getty Images

In Sum   The many functions of war include the extension of territory, economic gain, social integration of rival groups, and social change. Among the dysfunctions of war are deaths, destruction of property, and loss of territory. There can also be dysfunctions for the victors of war and functions for the losers of war.

Conflict Theory

Let's see how conflict theorists help us understand why nations go to war.

Resources, Markets, and a Military Machine   Here are three reasons stressed by conflict theorists.

Resources   Back in the 1300s, a pre-sociologist, Ibn Khaldun of Tunis, stressed that as groups struggle to survive, they compete for scarce resources. Inevitably, they come into conflict with one another, and war is one way they resolve their conflict.

Building on this explanation, conflict theorists have developed what they see as the central force in human history, the struggle for control over resources. In each society, some group gains control. This group, which conflict theorists call the **bourgeoisie**, uses society's resources to keep itself in power and to exploit the less powerful. As the bourgeoisie expands its power beyond its borders, it comes into conflict with the bourgeoisie of another country. Their quarrel over resources often leads to war. Those who hold power don't do the fighting, of course. Instead, they send young men (and sometimes young women) to battle for them. Most of these soldiers come from poor workers, the **proletariat**. The German generals used the term "cannon fodder" to refer to the young men among the poor who died in such outrageous numbers in their wars.

Expansion of Markets   The second explanation focuses on the expansion of markets. In 1902, John Hobson, an economist, noted that as capitalism grows, it develops surplus capital. Business leaders want to invest this capital, so they look for ways to expand their markets. They then persuade the government to go to war and take over other lands. The result is **imperialism**, the pursuit of profits and markets by war and threat of war.

A Military Machine   Another economist, Joseph Schumpeter, proposed a third explanation. He said (1919/1955) that the political elite build a strong military machine because it brings them power and prestige. Because the military machine was built to be used—sitting around idle is not its purpose—its very existence encourages war.

Because the military machine is so relevant for our situation today, let's look at it in more detail.

The Military Machine, the Power Elite, and the Globalization of Capitalism   Conflict theorists note that after World War I the United States dismantled its military, and U.S. war industries returned to their peacetime pursuits (Barber 1972). World War II, however, marked a turning point in U.S. history. When this war was over, the United States did not dismantle its war machine, as it had previously (Eisenhower 1961/1972). Instead, facing the Cold War, the United States, the Soviet Union, Great Britain, and France kept their military machines. Today, the U.S. military has 1,300,000 personnel on active duty (*Statistical Abstract* 2018:Table 531).

Even when its archenemy turned away from communism to transform itself into a capitalist ally, the West did not disarm and join Russia in a new world of peace. On the contrary, the West continued to arm millions of its people and to develop new weapons, some even designed to turn space into a new venue of warfare. Russia is intent on regaining its former political leverage. To propel itself as a prestigious power on the world stage, it is rebuilding its military machine. China, too, has been building its military forces. Backed by its 2 million soldiers, hypersonic missiles, and aircraft carriers, China has flexed its military muscle and thumbed its nose at the West by building artificial islands on disputed outcroppings in the East China Sea and turning them into military bases (Ait 2018).

To understand why huge military forces have become a fact of life today, conflict theorists stress that we should look at the top levels of power. There we see the *power elite*—the top leaders of the military, business, and politics. As sociologist C. Wright Mills stressed, the interests of these groups have merged, with each benefiting from a strong military. Generals always support a powerful military, of course: This is their reason for being, and greater power bolsters their position.

This isn't new, but to this picture we need to add global capitalism. Business has increasingly expanded around the globe, and business leaders want a powerful military to protect their worldwide investments. That same military can protect them at home, putting down riots by upset citizens, or even suppressing a revolution. Politicians are sensitive to what the business elite wants because they depend on them to stay in office. To finance the military machine so desired by generals and business leaders, politicians invoke the terms *national security* and *homeland security*. Who can be against the protection of the nation?

In Sum Conflict theorists stress that the interests of nations collide as they compete with one another for resources and markets. The power elite of each nation uses its military to advance its interests. The United States uses its military machine to advance capitalism around the globe. U.S. armed forces join with those of Great Britain, France, Canada, and Australia to make the world safe for capitalism. The result, says Mills (1958:2), is that "war is no longer an interruption of peace; in our time, peace itself has become an uneasy interlude between wars...."

Research Findings: War

14.4 **Summarize what reduces war, the costs of war, dehumanization, the military–industrial complex, accidental war, and biological, chemical, and cyber warfare.**

With war so prevalent—and today's weapons so powerful that they jeopardize even the existence of humanity—let's identify factors that reduce the likelihood of war. After this, we will examine the costs of war, both economic and human. Finally, we'll look at the power of the military–industrial complex in our lives, the possibility of accidental nuclear war, and biological and chemical warfare. To get an idea of the variety of research that sociologists do on war, see the next *Spotlight on Social Research*.

Spotlight on Social Research

Adventures in Military Sociology

MORTEN ENDER, professor at the U.S. Military Academy at West Point, does research on war, peace, and the military. In this essay, he discusses how he became interested in doing research on the military and his research experiences in Iraq. Here is what he wrote for you.

Although an American, I spent many years living in West Germany during the Cold War. I often reflected on the impact that World War II had on the German people as well as on the Americans living there. Both world wars had a profound impact on my own family (Ender 2018). After World War I, my maternal great-grandparents were forced to move to the hinterland of Germany and a more meager lifestyle. U.S. bombers destroyed my paternal great-grandfather's printing plant during World War II, and a generation later, my mother married an American soldier stationed in Germany. I came to the United States for the first time on a U.S. troop ship. My family's many moves during my

Dr. Morten G. Ender

formative years and the stories I heard of war sparked my interest in social change, especially radical and intense change, at the individual level.

When I began studying the military, I tried to develop knowledge in areas that had received little sociological attention, such as death and dying in a military context and military children. We learned that when a member of the military dies, the response is highly bureaucratic and task-focused, yet the notification and casualty officers keep the best interests of the survivors in mind. We also discovered that military children, who often live outside the country of their passport because of their parents' careers, have much in common with children of foreign service workers, missionaries, and those in international business.

I also had the opportunity to travel to Iraq and apply my sociological research skills to studying the Iraqi people. In a dangerous and compelling research environment, my research team helped assess the attitudes and opinions of Iraqis about their major social institutions—economics, politics, criminal justice, the family, education, the military, and medical care. We also studied Iraqi adolescents—their self-esteem and how they perceived their personal safety. Today I am studying the long-term impact of being at war in Iraq and Afghanistan on Army families.

Because I was "embedded" with U.S. soldiers in Iraq, I was able to interview them, as well as observe their day-to-day activities on and off the Forward Operating Base. Some of the topics I explored were boredom, issues with families and spouses back in the United States and Germany, and how they went about their jobs. One of the most notable findings is the decentralized nature of U.S. soldiering in Iraq. Previous wars were characterized by a hierarchical military situation; in Iraq, small groups of soldiers down to the level of 22-year-old platoon leaders make profound leadership decisions. For example, one might be responsible for training an entire police force for a neighborhood, or another might interact with the local leadership in a community, working with local mayors. This decentralized soldiering offers the opportunity to be creative and exercise autonomy. I asked soldiers an open-ended question on a survey about whether they use any creativity. A typical response was:

> Every day! This place was not what we expected and therefore we have had to adapt on many occasions. One example is up-armoring of vehicles. Soldiers are very adaptive and creative and come up with very good ideas that other units are now using. Scheduling is another example. We are short many soldiers and have had to develop shift work that fits the number of people we have.

I also studied the soldiers' morale, cohesion, preparation, leadership, and attitudes toward the mission. In many of these areas I found evidence contrary to common expectations. For example, morale was high among soldiers in Iraq—in some cases higher than when they are at home. Further, many soldiers told me they enjoyed the mission in Iraq. They liked being a part of something larger than themselves. I found the soldiers to be very focused and committed to their jobs—the small-scale, daily missions. One day, at one of the larger post-exchanges (PXs)—which was affectionately called Wal-Mart because it had everything—I struck up a conversation with a 23-year-old Army reserve specialist from Woodstock, New York. He owned a small business back home, and his brother and wife were managing it for him. He was headed home for his once-a-year two-week R&R (rest and relaxation), but with great misgivings. His job in Iraq involved responsibility for training two 44- and 47-year-old Iraqi police officers. He appeared genuinely worried that although his "guys" had received the proper socialization into the policing role, without his structure and discipline, although for only a short while, they would fall back into bad habits, possibly putting themselves and others at risk. I asked why he didn't stay, and he said his sergeant was making him take some time off.

What Reduces War?

To see what reduces war, Quincy Wright (1942), a professor of international law, studied war throughout history. His findings, combined with those of physicist-mathematician Lewis Richardson (1960), are not encouraging. Here is what they found (Nettler 1976):

1. *Type of religion* does *not* reduce warfare. A nation in which Christianity is dominant does not go to war less than a nation in which Islam is dominant.
2. *Type of government* does *not* reduce warfare. Democracies and republics are neither more nor less peaceful than dictatorships and monarchies.

3. *Prosperity* does *not* reduce warfare. Prosperous nations are neither more nor less peaceful than poor nations. Nor do periods of prosperity reduce fighting.
4. *A shared religion* does *not* reduce warfare between nations.
5. *A common language* does *not* reduce warfare.
6. *More education* does *not* reduce warfare. Education does not create an "enlightened" preference for peace; countries with high education are as likely to go to war as those with low education.
7. *Being "neighbors"* does *not* reduce warfare. Rather, the *opposite* is true: Shared boundaries stimulate fights over territory. The more boundaries that countries share, the more wars they fight with one another.

These findings are disheartening. It seems only common sense that democracy, prosperity, increased education, and a shared religion and language would reduce war. But they don't. Experts can make up fancy terms like "conflict resolution," but despite all efforts to reduce war, the world's nations are *not* becoming more peaceful. As sociologist Gwynne Nettler (1976) ruefully observed, the Nobel Peace Prize is typically awarded to a citizen of a nation that has recently been at war. Perhaps, he said, the prize is awarded on the basis of need, rather than as a recognition of achievement.

Money Spent on War

You know that war is costly. Let's get an idea of how expensive it is.

The Cold Numbers   The nations of the world spend about $1.7 trillion a year arming themselves (SIPRI 2018a). This number that trips so easily off the tongue comes to *about $225 a year for every man, woman, and child on the entire planet.*

Look at Table 14.1. You can see that the United States outspends its nearest competitor by almost three times. As a percentage of its gross national product, however, Saudi Arabia leaves the rest in its dust. (The Saudi royalty must be sitting uneasily on the throne. They certainly prefer to spend on indulgences.) You might be surprised to see that India, where most people live in poverty, appears on this list of top spenders. India is not only split by factions and needs a strong military to hold the country together, but it also faces long-feuding enemies on its borders.

Table 14.1 What Countries Spend the Most on Their Military?

Rank	Country	Amount	Percentage of GDP
1	United States	$610,000,000,000	3.1%
2	China	$228,000,000,000	1.9%
3	Saudi Arabia	$69,000,000,000	10.0%
4	Russia	$66,000,000,000	4.3%
5	India	$64,000,000,000	2.5%
6	France	$58,000,000,000	2.3%
7	Great Britain	$47,000,000,000	1.8%
8	Japan	$45,000,000,000	0.9%
9	Germany	$44,000,000,000	1.2%
10	South Korea	$39,000,000,000	2.6%

Note: These totals of a year's spending do not include the costs of military retirement.

Source: By the author. Based on SIPRI (Stockholm International Peace Research Institute). "SIPRI Fact Sheet: Trends in Military Expenditure, 2017." May 2018a.

The military spending by the United States—higher than any other country—reflects the wars in Afghanistan and Iraq as well as the cost of keeping 156,000 troops on bases around the world—the only nation to do this (*Statistical Abstract* 2018:Table 534).

What Is a Billion?   As you probably have noticed, the number *billion* flies off our politicians' tongues as easily as you and I say $10. It is difficult, if not impossible, to wrap our minds around what $1 billion is, so how can we understand the $610 billion that the United States spends each year on what it euphemistically calls national defense? Consider this:

> *Let's suppose you want to circle the earth with dollar bills. Each dollar bill is about 6 inches long. Laid end to end, it would take about 263 million bills to encircle Earth at the equator. The dollar bills of today's $610 billion "defense" budget would go around Earth 2,320 times.*

As gargantuan as it is, this total is minimal. A more realistic picture of what the United States spends on war would include the costs of running the Central Intelligence Agency, the National Aeronautics and Space Administration, the Agency for International Development, and the Department of Homeland Security. Perhaps it should also include the amounts spent on the International Monetary Fund and the World Bank. If we include these costs, we would have to keep wrapping those bills around the equator.

Another way to view the dollar costs of the military is to look at what the United States has spent to wage its wars. You can see a summary of these costs on Table 14.2. These huge amounts are rough estimates, not actual costs. They do not include the little "military interventions" in places such as Bosnia, Grenada, Haiti, Kosovo, Panama, and Somalia. The ongoing costs of involvement in Syria, not yet tallied, are also not included.

To get a better picture of what the United States spends on war, look at Figure 14.1. I expect that the U.S. spending "jumps out" at you. It does me, leaving me wondering why we have become "the police of the world" and why we must use soldiers and bombs to support our ideas and interests (and whose are they, really?).

Table 14.2 What Has the United States Spent on Its Wars?

War of 1812	$630,000,000
Mexican War	$1,155,000,000
American Revolution	$2,100,000,000
Spanish–American War	$6,300,000,000
Syria	$12,000,000.000
Civil War	$48,300,000,000
Gulf War	$152,000,000,000
Korean War	$273,000,000,000
World War I	$390,000,000,000
Vietnam War	$580,000,000,000
Afghanistan	$1,060,000,000,000
Iraq War	$1,070,000,000,000
World War II	$3,150,000,000,000
Total	$5,863,000,000,000

Note: The costs listed in *Statistical Abstract* are in 1967 dollars. To account for inflation, these amounts were increased by 355 percent, and the costs of service-connected benefits were added. Where a range was listed, the mean was used. The costs do *not* include interest payments on war loans, nor are they reduced by the financial benefits to the United States, such as the acquisition of territory, as with California and Texas in the Mexican War.

Sources: By the author. Based on *Statistical Abstract of the United States* 1993:Table 553, a table dropped after 1993. The cost for the Gulf War is from Conahan 1991, adjusted for inflation. The costs for Afghanistan and Iraq, in current dollars, are from Amadeo 2018a, 2018b.

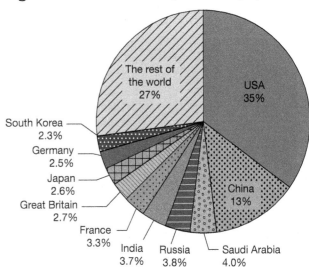

Figure 14.1 The World's Top Ten Military Spenders

USA 35%
China 13%
Saudi Arabia 4.0%
Russia 3.8%
India 3.7%
France 3.3%
Great Britain 2.7%
Japan 2.6%
Germany 2.5%
South Korea 2.3%
The rest of the world 27%

Source: By the author. Based on SIPRI 2018a.

Lost Alternatives   Many people dream of a more peaceful world in which military dollars are redirected toward education, medicine, and the enlightenment of nations. We do not live in such a world—and from all indications, we may never live in one.

Our armed forces employ 1.3 million soldiers. Add in the civilians who work for the military, those in the reserves and National Guard, and the total comes to about 3 million. For the cost of employing these men and women to fight or to be ready for war, we could pay 3 million people to work for the public good. Instead of stationing 156,000 soldiers in foreign countries, we could send tens of thousands of people to poorer countries to build schools and hospitals, and reduce suffering. You probably can think of other uses for the large amounts of money we spend on the military.

But What Choice Is There?   You might be thinking, "Yes, that's a nice thought, but it isn't practical. Without a military, an enemy would crush us." This dilemma is real. The United States does face it, just as other nations do. Although the military is costly both in money spent and benefits forgone, not spending this money would leave us vulnerable to attack. In light of the world's history, an assumption of danger is well founded, and we need a strong military. Only if all nations were to become pacifists and all dangers of attack cease would military preparedness become unnecessary. Another nice thought— and as unrealistic as mice sending cats to the moon.

However, quite different matters are the size of the armed forces, the amount of money we spend on the military, and the purposes for which the soldiers are used. And it is also worth asking why the United States is the only nation to post troops in 150 countries around the world. Just what interests are our military protecting?

Deaths from War

During the 1700s, wars were fought according to aristocratic ideals. Small professional armies waged short, limited campaigns. In battle, the soldiers, wearing brightly colored uniforms, marched in formation. Accompanying them were flying flags and teenage boys playing drums, flutes, and other musical instruments. War at this time was considered to be like a chess game, with generals from aristocratic backgrounds matching wits with one another. Military officers, viewing war as a test of bravery, looked forward to fighting on the "field of honor." Townspeople viewed military encounters as a form of entertainment. The rich would ride to the battlefield in carriages, taking with them picnic lunches and wine, all the better to enjoy the "entertainment."

This attitude toward war persisted even until the time of our Civil War, when the rich also took picnic lunches with them to watch battles (Burns 1990). But with the growing number of deaths, attitudes changed. During the four brutal years of the Civil War, 620,000 Americans died, more than in all our other wars combined, from the Revolutionary War to the present. No longer is there a "field of honor," if ever there was one. With today's mass armies and the capacity to deliver wholesale death, with industries spewing out advanced weapons, and with civilians no longer spared, an image of pageantry and games does not even come close to the reality we face today.

Most fearful of all, today's weapons are so destructive that they threaten human existence. Although more than 100 million people have died in war since 1700, by today's standards the killing was woefully inefficient (Gartner 1988). If we had another world war, the deaths could number in the hundreds of millions—if anyone were left to count them.

Dehumanization in War

Although we often calculate the cost of war in terms of money and deaths, war involves many other costs. Especially significant is war's toll on morality. War tends to break down norms that regulate human behavior. When soldiers are exposed to brutality and killing, they learn to *dehumanize* their opponents. That is, they come to see them as objects, not people. To dehumanize people removes the obligation to treat them as human beings.

Characteristics of Dehumanization   Social scientists have identified four key characteristics of **dehumanization** (Bernard et al. 1971; Kteily and Bruneau 2017; Armenta 2018):

1. *Increased emotional distance from others.* The individual stops identifying with others, seeing them as lacking basic human qualities. They become not people, but an object called "the enemy."

2. *An emphasis on following orders.* Orders and regulations become all-important. Those who do the "dirty work" don't question their orders, even if they involve atrocities. A person will say, "I don't like it, but it's necessary" or "We all have to die someday."

3. *Inability to resist pressures.* Fears of losing one's job or the respect of one's peers and supervisors or of having one's integrity and loyalty questioned become more important than morality.

4. *Diminished personal responsibility.* People come to see themselves as a small cog in a large machine. They are not responsible because they have no choice. They are simply obeying orders. The superiors know best because they have the information to judge what is right and wrong. The individual reasons, "Who am I to question this?"

When dehumanization occurs, consciences become so numbed that people can dissociate killing—even torture—from their "normal self." Torture and killing become "dirty work" that has to be done. Those who do this "dirty work" think of themselves as duty-bound to obey orders, not to question them. The "higher-ups" who make the decisions are responsible, not the simple soldier who follows orders.

Dehumanization in Prolonged Conflicts Sociologist Tamotsu Shibutani (1970) pointed out that dehumanization is especially common in prolonged conflicts. Long wars come to be viewed as a struggle between good and evil. People who don't want to torture or kill conclude that the survival of good (democracy, socialism, freedom, the nation, our way of life—whatever it may be) hangs in the balance. This requires that they suspend moral standards. War, then, exalts treachery, brutality, and killing—and we give medals to honor behavior that we would otherwise condemn.

Dehumanization by the Nazis and Japanese To participate in such acts, soldiers try to neutralize the morality they learned as children. During World War II, ordinary Germans—not Nazi ideologues—staffed concentration camps. They viewed the Jewish inmates as a blight on society. Surgeons who had been educated at top universities, whose profession called for them to be highly sensitive to people's needs, viewed the inmates as lesser humans than themselves. Methodically and dispassionately, they mutilated Jewish inmates just to study the results. Some doctors immersed Jews in vats of freezing water, considering their deaths insignificant because the results of the experiments might save the lives of German pilots shot down over the North Atlantic (Gellhorn 1959). The photos to the right are part of the research that these medical personnel produced.

The horrors of the Nazis were so extreme that no one could match them. Or so it might seem. Then we learned what the Japanese did during World War II. Here is a summary of what a Japanese soldier, a physician, confessed to a researcher:

> We strapped captured living Chinese people to tables and then, without anesthesia—because we didn't want to waste anesthesia on Chinese people—we amputated limbs, resected bowels, all sorts of things, as a matter of medical training and practice. These people died in pain.

> The researcher adds: And he did it with pride as a doctor, with a skill that would contribute to what he saw as the greater good (Lindley 2013).

In one experiment, Japanese doctors pumped U.S. prisoners full of horse blood. In another, they injected them with typhus, typhoid, smallpox, and other diseases (Daws 1994).

The extent to which dehumanization can alienate us from ordinary human feelings is incredible. To measure the effects of compression and decompression, German doctors placed this inmate of a concentration camp in a pressure chamber. As the doctors manipulated the air pressure, they observed and photographed the man's death.

Bettmann/Getty Images

Japanese soldiers beheaded some U.S. prisoners of war. Others, they buried alive (Chang 1997). In China, Unit 731 of the Japanese Army specialized in germ warfare. Using anthrax, cholera, malaria, plague, and typhoid, Unit 731 killed hundreds of thousands of Chinese (Rose 2015; Cunliffe 2018).

To those who did the experiments and killing, their victims were no longer real people. They had been transformed mentally into a "subhuman enemy."

Dehumanization by the U.S. Military   The Germans and Japanese carried dehumanization to horrifying limits, but they are not unique. U.S. soldiers in Vietnam also dehumanized their opponents. To U.S. soldiers, the Vietnamese became less than human—they were transformed into "gooks," "dinks," and "slants." Some soldiers became so effective at dehumanization that they shot mothers fleeing with their babies, the act dissociated from the self. Many found dehumanization difficult, but it was better not to question the morality of the act. It was better to think of what they did as part of the larger scheme of things, such as saving people from communism—or as rightful retaliation for fellow soldiers who had been killed: "I don't like doing this, but this is war."

Something similar is happening today. When U.S. (and coalition) forces bomb military targets, civilians are often killed. The military does not refer to them as "murdered children, mothers, and fathers." They don't even call them "dead people" or "dead civilians." Instead, the military has developed a term that removes people entirely. To refer to the unintentional deaths of civilians during combat operations, the military uses the term *collateral damage.* Talk about symbolizing people out of existence!

Children often bear the scars of war. These children are fleeing flaming napalm that was intended to root out Viet Cong. The photo was taken in 1972 in Trang Bang, Vietnam.

Nick Ut/AP images

When Dehumanization Fails   Although techniques of neutralization can protect the self, they are not foolproof. And when they fail, they can lead to crippling guilt. Tim, for example, was a Marine interrogator in Vietnam. Beating prisoners to gain information was part of his job. When beating did not work, he used electric shock by attaching "two wires of a field telephone to the earlobe, the cheek, the temple, or sometimes the balls or the crotch" (Smith 1980:27). One day while Tim was interrogating a 16-year-old girl, he began to think:

Why are we killing all these people? These aren't soldiers. I'm beating on this girl—and it all hit me. I'm beating up this girl, what for? Who am I? . . . It was as if for the first time

I was looking at myself. Here's this guy, slapping, beating on this girl—for what? . . . For the first time I was looking at this person, a detainee, as a real human being, not as a source of information.

You can see how dehumanization failed Tim. And this change in perspective—from "source of information" to "person"—had a direct effect on his job. As he said, "I wasn't a very good interrogator from that time on. I lost all motivation."

Dehumanization usually holds up well during war, when the individual is surrounded by army buddies who view the enemy in the same way. Upon returning home, however, former soldiers are resocialized into more standard norms—which tends to break down the definitions that worked for them during war. As this occurs, many former soldiers become disturbed by the harm they did during the war. Before putting a bullet in his head, here is what a soldier from California wrote in his suicide note:

I can't sleep anymore. When I was in Vietnam, we came across a North Vietnamese soldier with a man, a woman, and a 3- or 4-year-old girl. We had to shoot them all. I can't get the little girl's face out of my mind. I hope that God will forgive me. I hope the people in this country who made millions of dollars off the men, women, and children that died in that war can sleep at night (I can't, and I didn't make a cent) (Smith 1980:15).

The norms of dehumanization also failed some of the Japanese soldiers who had participated in the atrocities of World War II. After keeping quiet for 50 years, some of them publicly confessed their mass rapes and killings (Chang 1997; Demetriou 2004).

Let's turn from what has been a symbolic interactionist analysis of war to the conflict perspective and examine how organizations profit from warfare.

The Military–Industrial Complex

The military does not exist in isolation, as though it were a creature kept in a faraway cage, to be unleashed during emergencies. Rather, the military is an integrated part of U.S. society and a powerful force in the U.S. economy.

The Military as an Economic Force   Many of the billions of dollars listed on Tables 14.1 and 14.2 go to the companies that produce **armaments**—guidance systems, bombs, missiles, tanks, planes, guns, ships, submarines, and other weapons. There is no end to the need for more military weapons. Like cell phones and computers, they quickly become obsolete and need to be replaced with newer, more powerful, more sophisticated models.

The military has become a powerhouse in the U.S. economy. Contracts to manufacture airplanes and ships, bombs and missiles, guns and ammunition, boots and uniforms push billions of dollars through the nation's economy. This makes it difficult to reduce military spending. When—rarely, but occasionally—the military decides that a base is no longer needed, unions and businesses send lobbyists to Washington to fight to keep it. That the military no longer needs or wants the base pales in comparison with the state's need to retain jobs and keep the money flowing. In this case, the slogan NIMBY (Not In My Back Yard) has changed to KIMBY (Keep It In My Back Yard).

The interests of the military and defense industries have become so intertwined that the two have become known as the **military–industrial complex**. The word *incestuous* comes to mind to describe this symbiotic relationship. Here is what happens: The defense industry hires top-ranking military officers when they retire. Their job is to sell military products (planes, guns, armored vehicles, etc.). Who do they contact to make the sale? Officers in the military who are in charge of purchases, of course. Some of these officers are old friends, while others are friends of friends. Even if they don't know the individuals, their cooperation is built in as these officers are themselves eyeing high-paying jobs in the defense industry when they retire from the military.

And round and round the circle goes.

The relationship with Congress is also cozy. When the military–industrial complex asks for billions of dollars to develop new weapons and to maintain the armed forces, Congress listens. The military parades a constant stream of enemies before Congress, each of which, of course, requires more planes, missiles, bombs, bullets, and the like. Not only is it patriotic to support the military, but military spending also means that senators and representatives can channel contracts into their home districts. This makes them popular at home and increases their chance of being reelected, apparently their primary purpose in life.

How difficult it is to resist the siren call of more military spending.

The Business of Death   To analyze military spending, you might focus on sales and profits, but this would take your eyes off the fundamental characteristic of the military and the industries that support it: They represent death. Their existence depends on killing.

And the U.S. military–industrial complex is efficient at its business of death, producing ever more lethal weapons. So are the military–industrial complexes of the other top producers of military weapons: Russia, China, Great Britain, and France.

It is almost impossible to grasp the capacity these nations possess to destroy one another. Consider this:

> The explosive energy of nuclear weapons is measured in megatons. If you had 1 million tons of TNT, you would have 1 megaton. The United States has over 3,000 megatons of explosive power. Let's assume that the total of the other nuclear nations combined equals only that of the United States.

> Now think of a freight train filled with gunpowder stretching from the earth to the moon. That wouldn't even come close to the destructive power these nations have stored up. You would have to make it eight times longer, 2 million miles long (Cf. Nucleus 1981).

Poets have written elegantly about the folly of humanity, but perhaps this image of a train filled with gunpowder that is eight times longer than a trip to the moon is more vivid.

Is humanity destined by folly to obliterate itself?

A Dark Cloud   Nuclear proliferation—more and more nations possessing nuclear weapons—increases the risk of nuclear war. A related fear is that nuclear weapons will end up in the hands of a terrorist group or of nations headed by dictators. This fear was intensified when Abdul Qadeer Khan, who headed Pakistan's nuclear program, sold blueprints and parts for making nuclear bombs to Iran and North Korea (Siracusa and Warren 2018). Under a 2016 agreement with the United States, Iran suspended its nuclear program. North Korea, though, developed the bomb, and Kim Jong-un has threatened to annihilate South Korea and the United States in a nuclear storm.

A Glimmer of Hope   Amid this nuclear folly lies a glimmer of hope. Since the Cold War ended, Russia and the United States have negotiated a series of agreements to reduce their nuclear stockpiles. The latest one, called New START (New Strategic Arms Reduction Treaty), shrinks each country's nuclear arsenal from 2,200 nuclear warheads to 1,500 warheads (ACA 2018). This reduction includes SLBMs (submarine launched ballistic missiles). Surprising many, the verification process has gone well.

While the reduction of nuclear weapons makes the world safer, we need to note that New START is only a glimmer of hope. Russia and the United States are merely *reducing excess capacity*: Each nation can still destroy the other many times over—and still take the rest of the world along with it.

Perhaps one day we can have the pleasure of **nuclear disarmament**—getting rid of all nuclear weapons—but as the following global map shows, we remain far from this goal.

Figure 14.2 The Nuclear Club: Members, Former Members, and Aspiring Members

COUNTRIES THAT HAVE NUCLEAR WEAPONS
(and the year they developed them)

1. 1945, United States
Tests: Over 1,030; more than the rest of the world combined
Warheads: 1,750 on missiles, 4,700 in reserve
Has missiles on submarines
Range: Can reach any place on the globe

2. 1949, Russia
Tests: 715
Warheads: 1,600 on missiles, 5,250 in reserve
Has missiles on submarines
Range: Can reach any place on the globe

3. 1952, Great Britain
Tests: 45
Warheads: 120 on missiles, 95 in reserve
Has missiles on submarines
Range: Can reach any place on the globe

4. 1960, France
Tests: 210
Warheads: 280 on missiles, 20 in reserve
Has missiles on submarines
Range: Can reach any place on the globe

5. 1964, China
Tests: 45
Warheads: 280
Has missiles on submarines
Range: Can reach any place on the globe

6. 1967, Israel
Tests: Unknown
Warheads: 80
Range: 3,700 miles

7. 1974, India
Tests: 6
Warheads: 135
Range: 3,200 miles

8. 1987, Pakistan
Tests: 6
Warheads: 145
Range: 1,300 miles

9. 2006, North Korea
Tests: 6
Warheads: About 15
Range: 8,000 miles

COUNTRIES THAT ARE DEVELOPING NUCLEAR WEAPONS
10. Iran
Tests: None yet
Warheads: None yet
Range: 1,200 miles

Note: Many items are estimates from specialists and should be taken as approximate.

Sources: Various, including CSIS 2018; Pecanha and Collins 2018; SIPRI 2018b.

(continued)

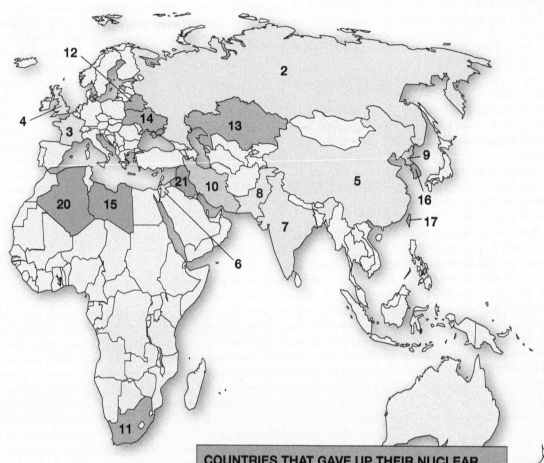

COUNTRIES THAT GAVE UP THEIR NUCLEAR WEAPONS PROGRAMS (before they developed nuclear weapons)

15. 1975 and 2003, Libya
In 1975, signed the Nuclear Non-Proliferation Treaty but violated it by continuing its nuclear program. Gave up its program in 2003

16. 1975, South Korea
Gave up its program and signed the Nuclear Non-Proliferation Treaty

17. 1978 and 1988, Taiwan
In 1978, gave up its program. Began again, and in 1988 again discontinued it

18. 1990, Argentina
Stopped its program and signed a nuclear weapons-free zone agreement in South America

19. 1990, Brazil
Stopped its program and in 1998 signed a nuclear weapons-free zone agreement in South America

20. 1991, Algeria
Dismantled its program and signed the Nuclear Non-Proliferation Treaty

21. 1991, Iraq
Program stopped with U.S.-led invasion (Gulf War)

COUNTRIES THAT HAVE GIVEN UP NUCLEAR WEAPONS

11. 1991, South Africa
Dismantled its nuclear arsenal and signed the Nuclear Non-Proliferation Treaty

12. 1991, Belarus
Returned to Russia the nuclear weapons left on its soil when the Soviet Union broke up in 1991

13. 1991, Kazakhstan
Returned to Russia the nuclear weapons left on its soil when the Soviet Union broke up in 1991

14. 1991, Ukraine
Returned to Russia the nuclear weapons left on its soil when the Soviet Union broke up in 1991

The Possibility of Accidental War

The risk of nuclear destruction comes from several directions: conflict between major powers, dictators of small nations, and terrorists from no nation. Is it also possible that nuclear missiles could be unleashed accidentally? Let's consider this chilling thought.

Forgetting Where the Nuclear Missiles Are

> In 2007, some airmen were sent to a storage room in North Dakota to pick up 12 old, unarmed nuclear missiles that were to be delivered to a "weapons graveyard." By mistake, six of the 12 that the men picked up were armed with nuclear warheads. No one noticed. The missiles were attached to a bomber and flown to an air force base in Louisiana, where they were left unguarded. Each missile's warhead was 10 times more powerful than the bomb that destroyed Hiroshima (Warrick and Pincus 2007).

Yes, it is incredible, but nuclear weapons can become just another item that needs to be inventoried and maintained, and in so doing can be misclassified.

More Human Error   The obliteration of humanity could also come from more human error. Here's another real-life event:

> On October 28, 1962, the North American Defense Command was informed that Cuba had launched a nuclear missile, and it was about to hit Tampa, Florida. The U.S. began a countdown for its retaliatory strike. Then someone noticed that there had been no explosion in Tampa (Sagan 1994).

It turned out that a radar operator had accidentally inserted into the system a test tape that simulated an attack from Cuba. If the United States had launched immediately, instead of waiting a few moments, Cuba would have been destroyed. The Soviet Union, Cuba's ally at the time, might have responded with an attack of its own.

Computer Failure   Although few people know it, we have come close to unintended launchings of nuclear missiles. Here is an actual event:

> Back in 1980, a military computer reported that Russia had fired missiles at the United States. The United States immediately went to red alert. U.S. bombers plotted courses toward pre-selected targets in the Soviet Union, and we prepared our missiles for launching. The countdown toward nuclear devastation had begun (U.S. News & World Report, June 24, 1980).

Russia had *not* launched missiles. A computer had malfunctioned. Fortunately, the error was caught in time. If it hadn't been, you wouldn't be reading this text.

Nuclear Accidents   The possibility of a nuclear accident can make your hair stand on end—since the detonation of a nuclear weapon, whether by mistake or on purpose, could lead to the end of human civilization. But here are three real-life nuclear accidents reported by a retired rear admiral:

> The George Washington, *a missile submarine, ran into a Japanese ship and sank it.*

> The Scorpion *and the* Thresher, *two nuclear attack submarines, sank in the ocean.*

> When a mechanic dropped a wrench in a missile silo in Arkansas, a missile was launched (Keyes n.d.)

Did you know that two hydrogen bombs were dropped on the United States? An accident, of course. One was kept secret from the public from 1961 until 2013, when it was revealed though a Freedom of Information Act request. A B-52 bomber was flying over North Carolina when it broke up in midair. The two Mark 39 hydrogen bombs the plane was carrying fell to the ground. The four safety switches on one bomb were triggered. The only thing that kept the bomb from exploding was the failure of a simple, low-voltage switch.

From a symbolic interactionist point of view, though, this is my favorite:

> A nuclear weapon fell from a plane into a swamp in the Carolinas. The Air Force was unable to find it! So what did they do? The solution they hit upon was Orwellian. The Defense Department bought the land, put a fence around it and called it a "nuclear safety area" (Keyes n.d.).

Fortunately for us, in none of these accidents did a nuclear weapon detonate. We have no assurance that similar accidents will not happen again or, if they occur, that the weapons will not explode. The military is well aware of the possibility of accidental nuclear war, which is one reason they want to reduce the number of nuclear missiles (Baum et al. 2018).

Nuclear Sabotage The U.S. government has repeatedly assured us—and the world—that a missile cannot be launched without official authorization. Any talk to the contrary, they say, is alarmist. Is it?

> *The year was 1962. President Kennedy had backed down in the Bay of Pigs invasion of Cuba, and the Soviet military thought that he would back down from them as well. Khrushchev, the premier of the Soviet Union, decided to ship missiles to Cuba. The CIA reported that the missiles would be capable of destroying the Pentagon, New York City, and other U.S. cities. Kennedy warned Khrushchev to order the ships back and set up a blockade to intercept them. The world waited tensely, television reporting the location of the ships as they neared the blockade.*

At the height of the Cuban crisis, though, something was taking place that the world did not know about:

> *Officers at Malmstrom Air Force Base in Montana, who doubted the resolve of President Kennedy to give the order to bomb the Soviets, did what was supposedly impossible: They manipulated their Minutemen missiles so they could launch them on their own.*

> *After the crisis, the Air Force investigated how officers at Malmstrom had given themselves the ability to launch missiles—and kept it secret (Sagan 1994).*

Nature Even natural events can set off an accidental war.

> *In 1983, the Soviets set up a new surveillance system to monitor nuclear weapons in North Dakota. The sun lined up in such a way that it fooled the system into reporting that the United States had launched five missiles at the Soviet Union.*

If the Russian military officers in charge of giving the order to launch missiles in case of an attack by the United States had been informed, you probably would not be here today. Fortunately for us and the world, the Russian officer in charge of the system had an incredibly cool head. He refused to report the launch to his superiors. He said, "When people start a war, they don't start it with only five missiles" (Lewis 2004).

The Significance of Symbolic Interaction These hair-raising events demonstrate the significance of symbolic interaction. To understand an event, we must interpret it. If the Russian in charge of the surveillance system had not interpreted the event correctly, the world might have been plunged into nuclear war. And if a missile were launched accidentally, perhaps even destroying a city, as could happen with a computer malfunction or an unauthorized launch, military and political leaders would have to answer this question: Is this an accident, an unauthorized attack by a madman, or an authorized attack?

Fortunately, the United States and Russia have agreed to notify the other if either spots a missile—and to help each other track and destroy it. Although their intention is to protect one another against missile attacks by a third nation, their cooperation also helps to prevent accidental nuclear war.

Chemical and Biological Warfare

One of the strangest quirks of human thinking is this—to kill with bullets or bombs is considered normal, but to kill with gas is deemed abnormal. During World War I, the French and Germans shocked the world by using poison gas. After that war, in 1925, the major powers met in Geneva, where they signed an agreement banning the use of poison gases in warfare. In 1997, 65 nations signed and ratified the Chemical Weapons Convention, a disarmament treaty in which they agreed not to produce, stockpile, or use chemical weapons. They also agreed to destroy their vast stockpiles of chemical weapons. Later, the rest of the world's nations signed this treaty, except for Egypt, North Korea, and South Sudan (Fraga 2018).

Chemical Agents in War   Only a few nations have ever used chemical agents as weapons. In World War I, France and Germany used mustard gas on each other. In the 1980s, Iran and Iraq also attacked each other with mustard gas. The Soviets were accused of using chemicals against their enemies in Afghanistan, but they denied the accusations (Douglass 1998). The Assad government of Syria has apparently used chemical weapons against its rebels (Rodriguez-Llanes et al. 2018). For using poison gas to quell an uprising by the Kurds, Saddam Hussein was sentenced to death. Photos of his victims helped support the U.S. decision to invade Iraq.

In the 1960s and 1970s, the United States dropped 20 million gallons of **Agent Orange**—a chemical defoliant—on Vietnam (Stellman and Stellman 2018). Agent Orange was not intended as a weapon to kill people, but as a way of destroying crops and clearing terrain. Spraying stopped when Vietnamese women gave birth to strangely malformed babies, such as the one in the adjacent photo. After the war, thousands of Vietnam veterans claimed that Agent Orange had damaged their health. In 1989, each soldier who had sued the government was awarded about $12,000. The military finally acknowledged the problem, and its budget now includes money for medical treatment of health problems caused by Agent Orange (Philpott 2018).

Biological Weapons   The end of the Cold War did not mark the end of the development of biological weapons. Russia even announced that it had genetically engineered an anthrax microbe that attacks blood cells, making vaccines useless (Broad and Miller 1998). Supposedly, Russia once armed its ICBM warheads with plague, anthrax, and smallpox (Douglass 1998). If so, we may assume that the United States did the same. The United States, Russia, France, and other countries continue their bioweapons programs, developing ever more horrible infectious substances that can destroy people's central nervous system, alter perception, or wipe out vast numbers of people. A recurring fear is that some terrorist group will get its hands on biological weapons (Charlet 2018).

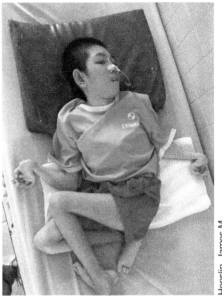

The human costs of war far outnumber the deaths of soldiers and civilians. I took this photo in Ho Chi Minh City in a hospital for victims of Agent Orange. The U.S. military did not intend or anticipate results such as this, which continue across generations.

Cyber Warfare

Like other parts of social life, warfare adapts to changing technology. The most powerful technological development within the last decades is the computer and its vast software, which are changing the face of war. In the following *Thinking Critically about Social Problems*, we will look at just one of these changes, giving us a glimpse of what is to come.

Thinking Critically about Social Problems

Cyber War and Cyber Defense

Iran's nuclear enrichment program had progressed quite well. But as 5,000 centrifuges were whirring away, Iranian scientists stared in disbelief. Although their computers reported that everything was fine, the centrifuges suddenly sped up and slowed down, ripping their delicate parts into shreds.

Iran had been hit by the Stuxnet *worm, a malware that the United States and Israel had surreptitiously entered into Iran's computer codes. Iran's goal of producing ma-*terial for a nuclear bomb had been set back by months or perhaps by years* (Sanger 2012).

Every country in conflict with another looks for an edge. The computer's marvelous strength—its capacity to store and retrieve information and to execute commands—can be turned into an Achilles heel that can bring down the powerful.

To turn strength into weakness brings both delight and fear to generals around the world. Their delight comes from the mouthwatering anticipation that they might use this capacity against their enemies. Their fear? That their enemies might use this capacity against them.

Cyber weapons offer intriguing potential for warfare (Berghel 2018). Malware can knock out power, disrupt early warning radar systems, and leave missiles that have been ordered airborne to strike enemy targets sit in their silos like frightened, wounded birds taking refuge in their nests. Computer files can display false information or computer screens can go blank. Military leaders can be left unable to communicate with their troops, open to easy attack. This fear pervades the military—on both sides, wherever those fluid sides line up today.

This is not some far-off future. As the Iranians discovered, cyber war has begun. The United States, too, is a victim, with thousands of attacks launched against its military computers. The attackers? Just round up the usual suspects: China, Russia, and North Korea. The purpose of the attacks seems to be to find the chinks in the armor, spots where malicious computer code can be installed unawares—like *Stuxnet*—to be unleashed at some designated moment. The targets extend beyond the military: a nation's electrical grid, its banking system, stock exchange, oil and gas pipelines, air traffic control system, and Internet and cell phone communications.

The nations are taking the threats of cyber warfare seriously. The United States is spending billions of dollars in preparation for cyber war. It has established the U.S. Cyber Command, giving it orders to integrate the cyber warfare capacities of the military with those of the National Security Agency.

The games have begun. The outcome, unfortunately, might not resemble a game.

For Your Consideration

→ Do you think the United States should probe the cyber weaknesses of potential enemies?

→ Do you think the United States should insert malicious codes in China's, Iran's, North Korea's, and Russia's military and central civilian computers—just in case it needs to unleash them during some future conflict?

→ If the target discovered the implanted codes, what do you think the consequences might be?

Research Findings: Terrorism

14.5   Discuss terrorism: revolutionary, repressive, state-sponsored, and criminal, as well as weapons of mass destruction.

How times change. When I wrote this section for the first edition of this text, terrorism was only a theoretical topic. There had been no terrorist attacks on U.S. soil, although a few were taking place elsewhere. The potential that I discussed back then seemed, at the time, so remote from everyday life.

Then came 9/11 and later attacks by ISIS sympathizers, which have made terrorism a part of our daily life. Although we don't live in fear, anyone who flies sees Homeland Security at work. The fear of officials that terrorists will strike again and again, hitting soft spots, has become a reality in both the United States and in Europe.

Let's take a closer look at **terrorism**, using the means of war—intimidation, coercion, and violence—to achieve objectives (Boston et al. 1977; Jensen 2018). We can divide terrorism into several types: revolutionary, repressive, state-sponsored, criminal, and using weapons of mass destruction.

Revolutionary Terrorism

The goal of **revolutionary terrorism** is to overthrow a government. Revolutionary terrorists make headlines with sudden, bloody attacks, but they don't spontaneously spring into existence as though in a social vacuum. Let's consider common background factors of revolutionary terrorists.

Background Factors   Walter Laqueur (1977), a political scientist, found these background factors to be common among revolutionary terrorists:

1. A segregated ethnic, cultural, or religious minority
2. Perceptions of being deprived or oppressed
3. Higher-than-average unemployment or inflation
4. External encouragement (often from an ethnic, cultural, or religious counterpart living elsewhere)
5. A historical "them" (a group the minority blames for its condition)
6. Frustrated elites who provide leadership and justify ideological violence

Political Theater and the Goals of Revolutionary Terrorism A group that chooses revolutionary terrorism usually has tried to change its situation by going through the official channels. Finding authorities unresponsive to their grievances, the group attempts to:

1. Publicize the group and its grievances
2. Demonstrate the government's vulnerability
3. Force political and social change

Because terrorists seek publicity for their "cause" and choose targets that will give them media attention, terrorism is sometimes called **political theater**. What often gets the publicity that terrorists seek are dead people—a lot of them, or people dying in sudden, unusual, or unexpected ways.

The drama of 9/11 served al-Qaeda well. Their two targets were carefully chosen, symbols of what al-Qaeda wants to destroy. The World Trade Center represented U.S. dominance of global capitalism, while the Pentagon symbolizes the U.S. military. The timing—a busy Tuesday workday morning—meant that a huge audience could gather immediately. The act was more effective than even the terrorists could imagine, of course, because they did not anticipate the collapse of the Twin Towers. Yet the towers did collapse and, in even more dramatic fashion, took with them over 300 firefighters. The message could not have been clearer, nor a worldwide audience summoned as quickly.

More than political theater, the attacks of 9/11 also reflect hard hatred. Americans have difficulty understanding why hatred would ever be directed against them. Conflict theorists would say the mass media have blinded Americans. As handmaidens of the state, the media deliver the soothing messages the power elite demand: America has good intentions. U.S. troops are sent abroad to protect people. The military is used to "build democracy." Many similar refrains repetitively purred into people's ears lull the public into non-thought.

At the risk, then, of provoking heretical thought and breaking ideological bubbles, take a look at the next *Global Glimpse.*

Kidnapped and forced to kill, these boy soldiers were part of the Sudan People's Liberation Army. They were told that they were fighting for their families, that "the enemy" (government soldiers) were going to kill their fathers and brothers and rape their mothers and sisters.

A Global Glimpse

Why They Hate Us: Al-Qaeda, ISIS, and Lost Power and Glory

How can we make sense of 9/11? Why would groups such as al-Qaeda love to destroy the United States? To understand this, we have to go back in history and sketch a broad background:

1. In earlier centuries, the Arabs were powerful. They had developed an advanced civilization and were world leaders in agriculture, architecture, astronomy, mathematics, medicine, and metallurgy. Their empire extended into Europe. The terraced fields the Arabs developed are still a distinctive feature of southern Spain.

2. In the late 1400s, Queen Isabella and King Ferdinand married, uniting two provinces of what is now Spain. They turned their united armies against their neighbors, including the Arabs (Moors), who ruled vast parts of this region.

3. In addition to motives of gaining territory and treasure, this was a religious war. The goal was to drive out all non–Roman Catholics from the Iberian Peninsula (Spain). The pope blessed the armies, wanting the infidels out of Europe. The Jews, who were not a political force, were given three choices: to convert to Christianity, to leave the area, or to die by the sword.

4. After a series of battles, with heavy losses on both sides, the Roman Catholic armies defeated the Islamic armies. The Arabs retreated back to Africa, although they continued to control other parts of Europe for another hundred years. Their political and economic power declined, as did their leadership in academics and the arts.

5. As the Europeans' political and military power grew, they conquered peoples around the globe. Part of this global push for dominance included the British and the French conquering Arab lands, a dominance that became especially valuable when vast pools of oil were discovered there. The British needed uninterrupted supplies of oil for their factories and homes—and for the warships with which they patrolled a globe on which "the sun never set on the British flag."

6. In the 1920s, to maintain their rule and to settle squabbles among the Arabs, who at that time were loose confederations of tribes and clans, the British divided the Arab lands

into countries. Drawing arbitrary lines on maps, they declared that those lines marked one country from another. They also set up Arab rulers in these new countries.

7. As England's power weakened, the British began to lose control over Arab lands. Wanting to protect the supply of oil coming to the West, the United States stepped in. It supported cooperative Arab leaders, keeping them submissive by giving them military aid in return for oil. At times, the Americans even set up puppets to head a country, as with the Shah of Iran, who was deposed by revolutionaries in 1979.

Having sketched this brief historical outline, let's move to the present. Using symbolic interactionism, we will try to understand why al-Qaeda and similar groups hate the West.

1. Many Arabs long for their golden past—the time when their lands were marked by grandeur and wealth, by power and prestige. Those longings stand in sharp contrast to today's shame—domination by the West and, despite vast oil wealth, most Arabs living in poverty.

2. A militant movement needs an inspirational ideology to spur people to action. When personal sacrifice is required, the cause must be greater than the individual. Islam serves this purpose. What stunning images are conjured up when al-Qaeda refers to the West as the *Great Infidel* polluting a holy land, the *Evil One* plundering resources and holding people captive through their puppet leaders, and the *Great Satan* arming Israel, the Arab's archenemy!

3. Destroying the power of the Great Infidel, then, becomes an act of service to Allah. Losing one's life in this service becomes a holy sacrifice. The loss of individual life is nothing in comparison with this noble cause.

4. The Great Infidel's vast military power—soldiers, planes, ships, missiles, and bombs—makes traditional warfare fruitless. Suicide attacks, in contrast, are effective because they can target vulnerable spots, and the enemy can't predict the target or when it will be hit. To attack the enemy on its own soil is not only daring and prestigious, but it also sows fear. This requires long-range planning, coordination, patience, and people so dedicated that they will give their lives to the holy cause.

Why are there such violent feelings against the United States, when most Americans feel they are trying to help? This photo was taken in Karachi, Pakistan.

5. The goal of suicide attacks is not for David to destroy Goliath, but rather to strike fear, create outrage, and generate publicity. If the Great Infidel can be provoked to send invading armies into sacred lands, so much the better. The more Arabs that Americans kill, the easier it is to inflame passions and recruit others to join the movement for independence.

6. The ultimate goal is pan-Arab unity, which surpasses the artificial boundaries that Western powers drew on blank maps. It will not be Iraqis, Syrians, Saudi Arabians, or any such group, but Arabs (and Persians), united by a shared vision of the glory and rightness of Islam, who will defeat the West.

7. The West will not easily give up its control over Arab oil, so the struggle will last for decades.

For Your Consideration

→ Why is this symbolic interactionist analysis so different from what you usually hear from your politicians or what you read or see in the mass media?

→ What insights do you think this analysis provides to help you to understand the terrorism directed against the United States?

→ Where do you think this analysis misses the mark? Why?

A Sense of Morality   Terrorist groups like al-Qaeda and ISIS view acts of bloodshed as righteous acts. Using the neutralization techniques discussed in Chapter 6, they justify their actions by appealing to a higher morality. It does not matter to them that almost everyone else in the world views their actions as evil—the leaders of al-Qaeda and ISIS are convinced of their moral superiority. As they see it, their "cause" justifies mass killing of civilians because these deaths can usher in their apocalyptic vision of Islamic rule.

It is this conviction of a righteous cause that makes revolutionary terrorists such formidable opponents. Some revolutionaries become so dedicated to "the cause" that they give up everything, even their lives. Listen to Karari Njama, of MauMau, a militant group whose goal was to liberate Kenya from British rule:

No one can serve two masters. In order to become a strong faithful warrior who would persevere to the last minute, one had to renounce all worldly wealth, including his family.... In fact, I had said to my wife...not to expect any sort of help from me for at least ten years' time. I had instructed her to take care of herself and our beloved daughter.

I had trained myself to think of the fight, and the African Government; and nothing of the country's progress before independence. I had learned to forget all pleasures and imagination of the past. I confined my thoughts (to) the fight only—the end of which would open my thoughts to the normal world (Schreiber 1978:32).

Repressive Terrorism

A second type of terrorism is **repressive terrorism**, that waged by a government against its own citizens. Let's look at several examples.

Argentina

Diana worked among the poor in Buenos Aires. One midnight, soldiers broke down her door, rushed in, and knocked her to the floor. They blindfolded her and beat her. They then threw her into a car and drove to a building with an underground chamber. For six straight hours, they threatened, tortured, and interrogated her about church leaders, the Vatican Council, and the Jews.

Beaten beyond all tears, she suddenly blurted, "Good God, aren't you Christians?"

Abrupt silence followed. One of the soldiers grabbed her hand and pressed her fingers to a metal cross on his chest. Afterward, they seemed to give up on her. "I'm convinced that small incident saved my life," she says. "The man apparently wanted to be recognized as a person rather than a torturer. He couldn't have that recognition without making me a person, too, rather than an object to be disposed of."

Diana was later taken back to her apartment and held there for two days by four officers who took turns raping her. The police then released her (based on Cornell 1981).

Brutality and killing are typical of repressive terrorism: In this case, the generals who headed the military dictatorship of Argentina feared that their government might collapse and fall into the hands of revolutionaries. Between 1976 and 1983, they arrested tens of thousands of people like Diana. They tortured and executed thousands, even dropping some captives alive from airplanes into the ocean.

Cambodia Pol Pot, the dictator of Cambodia who directed the Khmer Rouge, launched perhaps the most horrific repressive terrorism that any government has ever inflicted on its people. For almost four years, from April 1975 to January 1979, Cambodia was Pol Pot's private slaughterhouse. On an average day, the Khmer Rouge killed 1,500 Cambodians. In just 45 months, the government slaughtered about 2 million people (Wain 1981). Most had their heads bashed in, but many were beaten to death with rubber hoses and bamboo sticks.

The Khmer Rouge targeted *all* intellectuals because they represented an elite, and the Pol Pot government was attempting to develop a classless society. Being able to speak a foreign language was enough to merit execution. In one area of Cambodia, members of the Khmer Rouge could count only to 10. Anyone who could count higher was an "intellectual." To ferret them out, the Khmer Rouge would have someone count other people—and execute those who counted to 20, instead of counting two groups of 10. Only 50 of Cambodia's 800 doctors survived.

My visit to the Tuol Sleng prison in Phnom Penh, the capital of Cambodia, where prisoners were tortured, is still vivid in my mind.

The buildings are maintained as a museum so the people won't forget. I could see the metal cots on which the prisoners had been chained, torture devices used to break the men, women, and children before they were executed. Emblazoned on my mind is a cabinet of skulls—the larger ones of adults and the smaller ones of children—each cracked where someone struck them to death. There is also a huge vat that once had a wooden bar above it. The vat was filled with water, and the victims, hung upside down, were lowered slowly head first into the water. They could be immersed as many times as the torturers wanted, until they finally were forced to drink their death.

During its bloody rule of Cambodia from 1975 to 1979, Pol Pot's Khmer Rouge murdered about 2 million people. To save ammunition, they used hammers and axe handles to break the skulls. You can see the death blows in these skulls piled up in Siem Reap, Cambodia.

Chris Cheadle/Alamy Stock Photo

Russia Repressive terrorism is a way to silence criticism and suppress ideas. Soviet officials were sensitive to criticism of any sort, and they even persecuted poets and artists or anyone else who dared to express "incorrect" political thought. They also felt threatened by religion, with party leaders referring to the Church as "the enemy within" (Ra'anan et al. 1986). Authorities felt so threatened by alternative views that they beat to death Christians who dared to witness to Christ (Wurmbrand 1970). Andrei Sakharov (1977), a dissenter, recounted the persecution of Baptists, the True Orthodox church, Pentecostals, and Uniates:

> It is a common practice of the Russian government to take children away from parents who are evangelical; that is, they believe that Jesus of Nazareth is God incarnate or the Savior who should be placed ahead of the State. Pastors of underground churches are regularly arrested, beaten, tortured, and killed.

This changed abruptly when Russian officials switched to capitalism and allowed competing religions in the country.

State-Sponsored Terrorism

In the third type, **state-sponsored terrorism**, a government finances, trains, and arms terrorists. Colonel Muammar Gadhafi of Libya viewed terrorism as a legitimate extension of the state. He bankrolled terrorists and provided training camps for them. He also brought down a passenger plane over Lockerbie, Scotland, killing all 259 people aboard the plane (Polti 2012). After the U.S. Air Force tried to kill him by bombing his palace, Gadhafi became more clandestine in his support of terrorism. Later, after years of economic sanctions that worsened conditions in his country, Gadhafi renounced his support of terrorism and invited international inspectors to verify that he had dismantled his efforts to produce nuclear weapons.

The West continued to resent Gadhafi, however, and bankrolled rebels who overthrew his regime and killed him.

Criminal Terrorism

Some criminals use terrorism to attain their objectives. The Russian mafias are a well-known example of **criminal terrorism**. The plural is needed as there are many organized Russian crime groups. To maintain their sources of wealth, these gangsters intimidate and kill anyone who opposes them. As the executions of reporters, prosecutors, judges, and other government officials in Russia attest, death awaits those who dare to investigate or prosecute this organization.

Here is a personal observation of people who appear to be members of one of the Russian mafias.

> When I moved to Riga, the capital of Latvia, I found some of the scenes to be like the stereotypes portrayed in movies. Attended by bodyguards, men reputed to be part of the Russian mafias buzzed around the city in new shiny black cars, paying little attention to the speed limit and parking wherever they wanted. When I was looking for an apartment, one owner, burly bodyguards at his side, boasted of two special features he had installed in the apartment—the bomb-proof floor and the bulletproof door.

> The Russian mafias appear confident that they are untouchable. While eating at an outside beach restaurant run by Russians in Jurmala, Latvia, I surreptitiously watched eight muscular men, whose appearance was that of the bodyguards seen around town. They were sitting together, and as one man became animated in his conversation, my wife quietly translated for me. The others listened raptly as he told them how he had brandished a gun and boasted about the amount of money involved, proud that it all went down in only 45 minutes.

Narcoterrorism Another form of criminal terrorism, **narcoterrorism**, centers on drugs. For some narcoterrorists, drug dealing is a way to finance their goal of revolution. For most, money is the objective, with terrorism simply a way to protect and extend their drug operations. This is what is currently happening in Mexico, as recounted in Chapter 4.

In Colombia, Pablo Escobar even had justices of the supreme court assassinated, terrorizing the government until it abandoned its extradition treaty with the United States. Mehmet Ali Agca sold drugs to finance his attempted assassination of Pope John Paul II.

Weapons of Mass Destruction (WMDs)

Let's consider the possibility that terrorists will use nuclear and biological weapons.

Nuclear Terrorism   Because plutonium is often used in the manufacture of nuclear weapons, you would think it would be guarded carefully—right? Listen to this. About 5,000 pounds of plutonium are missing from U.S. nuclear facilities. A former security agent reported that protective measures at the Rocky Flats weapons factory near Denver were so lax that it was "like having a window in a bank vault" (Hosenball 1999). When asked about the missing plutonium, officials took a cavalier attitude. "What's to worry?" they said. The plutonium "probably got stuck in pipes and manufacturing tools." (2.5 tons!) The solution? Simple. The officials suspended the troublemaker who reported that the plutonium was missing.

After the collapse of the Soviet Union, some nuclear materials were said to be secured only by a chain-link fence and a night watchman (Bunn and Wier 2004). Whether it really was this bad or not, I don't know, but one worker at a nuclear plant simply hid nuclear material in his protective gloves when he walked out the gate (Zaitseva and Hand 2003). Russia and the United States ended up working together to secure and destroy the nuclear waste.

Nuclear terrorism remains a threat (Levi 2018). Terrorists don't need missiles if they can threaten with "dirty bombs" or other nuclear weapons. Because of the horrendous destruction of a nuclear attack, terrorists could hold a government captive. Tens of thousands of containers arrive each day at U.S. ports. Few are searched. What would U.S. officials do if terrorists threatened to detonate a nuclear weapon in the heart of New York City or Los Angeles?

Biological Terrorism   Perhaps an even greater threat is **biological terrorism**—the use of diseases such as anthrax, smallpox, or the plague as *bioweapons.* The knowledge of how to grow these biological agents is spreading. Especially fear-provoking is that, unlike conventional and nuclear weapons, bioweapons can be transported in tiny containers. This reality was driven home to Americans in 2001, when envelopes containing anthrax were sent through the U.S. mail. In its largest investigation ever, the FBI concluded that Bruce Ivins, a microbiologist who had worked with anthrax at the army's biodefense laboratory at Fort Detrick, Maryland, was the anthrax killer. Ivins committed suicide before he could be charged with a crime (Shane 2010a).

You can explore biological terrorism further in the following *Technology and Social Problems.*

Technology and Social Problems

Our Future: Biological Terrorism

Picture a Russian biohacker who designs a deadly form of the common flu virus and sells it on the Internet. The terrorist group that buys the design sends it to a lab tech in Pakistan, who uses tools that are widely available to make the required modifications. The product is then shipped by mail to men and women in London or Rome who infect themselves. They board airplanes headed to destinations around the world, infecting fellow passengers and people in crowded terminals. The infection spreads quickly, going global in days—long before anyone detects it (Robb 2007).

With a death toll in the millions, scenarios like this haunt U.S. officials. Few safeguards exist to protect against such an attack.

There would be no warning, no attempt to hold the United States hostage in order to extort billions of dollars. The motive would be revenge for humiliations suffered at the hands of the United States. The goal would be not profit or fear, but the annihilation of the United States itself.

How seriously officials are taking the bioterrorist threat is indicated by Congress funding Project BioShield, which is designed to provide medical countermeasures against bioweapons as well as against chemical, radiological, and nuclear weapons (DHHS 2018). Officials have stockpiled vaccines around the country and trained emergency medical teams in major cities. One of the vaccines is an antidote to anthrax.

Don Emmert/Staff/AFP/Getty Images

As in this scene in Connecticut, to prepare for what many fear will come, Homeland Security is holding mock terrorist drills in major cities across the nation.

If a biological attack occurs, U.S. officials have a plan. It is not to evacuate populations, but to try to prevent the disease from spreading by blocking roads and stopping people from fleeing cities, even if they must do so at gunpoint. Plans also include a military takeover of state and local governments to fight the chaos that would result from a biological attack (Miller and Broad 1999). For at least a while after a biological attack, the Pentagon would take direct control over the United States.

An ancient Chinese proverb states, "May you live in exciting times." This simple saying is actually a curse, the hope that an enemy's life will be chaotic. We live in exciting times. Let's hope that the curse with which we live—weapons of mass destruction, hatreds engendered by foreign domination, and retaliatory action by terrorists—does not result in our destruction.

For Your Consideration

→ What steps do you think the government should take to counter the threat of bioweapons?

→ Would you be willing to give up the freedoms you currently have to be assured you were safe from weapons of mass destruction?

Social Policy

14.6 Summarize social policies regarding terrorism, the MAD way to peace, policies that can bring peace, and how self-preservation figures in the survival of humanity.

Let's examine social policies that attempt to address two major problems we have reviewed in this chapter: political terrorism and nuclear war.

Terrorism

Social policy is often a mixture of what has developed haphazardly combined with making certain that graft continues to feed corruption or that political cronies get fed. Social policy is better if it is deigned to match principles. Let's specify the overarching principle for terrorism and then identify 10 basic policies that are derived from it.

The Overarching Principle The key principle in dealing with terrorists is "Don't give in to their demands because this encourages more terrorism." This principle poses a dilemma—not meeting demands can bring immediate costs: property damage, injuries, and deaths. Giving in to terrorists encourages terrorists—because their tactic worked.

Ten Basic Policies Anti-terrorism experts suggest the following as effective social policies (FBI 1998; "National Strategy..." 2006; Helm 2016; Nadeem 2018):

1. Promise anything during negotiations. Promises made under threat are not valid.
2. Make no distinction between terrorists and their state sponsors. Even though they hide behind the scenes, states that sponsor terrorists are not neutral and should not be treated as neutrals. This principle allows both retaliatory and preemptive acts.
3. Use economic and political sanctions to break the connection between terrorists and the states that provide them weapons, financing, safe houses, training areas, and identity documents in return for terrorism done on their behalf.
4. Treat terrorists as war criminals. Track them, arrest them, and punish them. Bomb them, if this is what it takes.
5. Discourage media coverage because publicity is a goal of terrorists. Make it illegal for the media to pay terrorists for interviews.

6. Establish international extradition and prosecution agreements. Terrorists need to know that if they are caught anywhere, they will be extradited and put on trial.

7. Offer large rewards for information leading to the capture or death of terrorists. Just as in the Old West, rewards can be paid on a "dead-or-alive" basis. With rewards of $50,000, $1 million, or $5 million, terrorists will never know whether associates can be trusted. Informants should be guaranteed safe passage and offered new identities.

8. Cut the funding of terrorist organizations so they don't have money for travel, weapons, and training.

9. Infiltrate terrorist organizations, shut down websites that are used to recruit terrorists, and develop ways to counter messages that appeal to grievances, a "cause," and adventure.

10. When someone is responsible for a terrorist attack and that person cannot be arrested, put that person on a "kill list" marked for assassination.

There are almost endless arguments to be made in support of and in opposition to these ten social policies, but the last one, which is being followed by some governments, including that of the United States, seems to be the most controversial.

A favorite way to carry out this policy, also known as *targeted killings,* is to track the person with a drone—an unmanned plane. When the individual is spotted, an operative at a remote location orders a missile to be fired. At times, the individual's family is also killed, which is marked up to the "collateral damage" we discussed earlier.

Targeted killings are also a policy of Russia's FSB and Israel's Mossad. Instead of drones and missiles, which are becoming favorite techniques of death of U.S. officials, their more usual methods are old-fashioned shootings. They sometimes are rather creative, though, and use poisoned umbrellas and nuclear isotopes. In one instance, Russian agents targeted a former colonel in the Russian intelligence who was living in England. They put Novichok, a nerve agent, on the doorknob of his apartment. Both the colonel and his daughter were poisoned as they entered the apartment, but the job was bungled, and the two survived (George and Lee 2018).

Nuclear Threats as a Path to Peace

How can the threat of nuclear attack ever be considered a path to peace? The world is filled with the unexpected. Let's look at this one.

A MAD Way to Peace   The primary policy that the United States and the former Soviet Union pursued during the Cold War was **mutual assured destruction (MAD)**. The two countries used threats and the fear of mutual destruction to prevent the other from striking first. Each was afraid to use its nuclear arsenal because even out of the ashes, missiles would be launched that would destroy the other. Because neither country would survive, there was no benefit in attacking the other.

The path to peace, then, has been a MAD one. Each superpower stockpiled weapons of mass destruction—nuclear, chemical, and biological—and signaled to the other that it was willing to unleash those weapons. The resulting balance of power—or terror— kept these two superpowers from attacking each other. Sociologist Nicholas Timasheff (1965:291) explained how it worked:

> Each party may consider that it has a fair chance to win, but each party also knows that the cost of victory would be prohibitive; physical destruction of 90–95 percent of the total population, almost complete destruction of industrial equipment, transformation of almost the total territory into an uninhabitable area because of radiation, contamination of air, water, plants and animals and other natural resources. Under these circumstances, victory can be worse than the most crucial defeat before this atomic age. Each of the parties to the possible conflict has full reason to refrain from attack.

A New Precarious Balance of Power   Canada, France, Germany, Italy, Japan, the United Kingdom, and the United States work together in an organization called G7 (sometimes G8 if Russia is on speaking terms with the other nations). G7 is working out a new balance of power—sometimes called the **New World Order**. The balance, however, is precarious. Of its many sources of disequilibrium, one is rivalries, suspicions, and unsettled grievances among nations. A second is the proliferation of nuclear weapons. Poor nations may not be able to sit at G7's bargaining table, but if they join the nuclear club, G7 will listen to them. India and Pakistan, historical enemies that still quarrel over boundaries that separate the two nations, have nuclear bombs. India has developed a missile system that can be fired from mobile launchers. Not only can India's missiles hit targets in Pakistan, but they can also reach Beijing and Shanghai. Each additional country that gains nuclear weapons increases the threat to regional balances of power.

Even local conflicts can upset this precarious balance of power, as they can heat up and bring in other nations, destabilizing an entire region. Fears of this happening led to NATO taking quick, forceful action against Serbia. Bombs speak louder than words, as Slobodan Milošević, who at the time was the president of Serbia, discovered. Serving to restrain G7, though, are the 2 million soldiers that North Korea can unleash onto South Korea and uncertainty regarding China's reaction if G7 bombs nuclear sites in North Korea.

Potential Policies for Peace

Social policies that encourage peace include disarmament, interlocking networks of mutual interests, and international law. Let's look at each.

Disarmament Although we all want a safer world, not everyone agrees with disarmament. The primary argument against disarmament is that only a strong military and the will to use it can make a nation secure. If we have adequate safeguards to protect ourselves from attack (an endless argument about what *adequate* means), eliminating biological, nuclear, and chemical weapons certainly can help make the world safer. As we discussed, progress has been made in reducing the number of nuclear weapons, but G7 fears what it calls "rogue nations." These are nations that G7 doesn't trust, currently Iran, which temporarily has suspended its nuclear program, and North Korea, which has developed nuclear weapons and the missiles to deliver them.

I need to stress that the danger of WMDs is growing, not decreasing. Bioweapons, especially, are an ominous threat to our security that continues to hang over our heads. Not only do bioweapons have the capacity to inflict mass death, but also the knowledge of how to produce them is spreading.

Interlocking Networks

The key to peace, say some, is to develop interlocking networks of mutual interests. They argue that the more a nation depends on another for its own well-being, the less likely it is to destroy that nation. If true, then we should encourage activities that make the affairs of nations more interdependent. To develop interlocking interests and stimulate peace, we can encourage trade, communication, travel, and cultural and scientific exchanges among the world's nations.

International Law International law is essential for world peace. If each nation is a law unto itself and feels free to wage war when its goals are frustrated, peace is impossible. Most nations, however, are unwilling to yield sovereignty to an international organization. We are far from having effective international law, as evidenced by NATO's bombing of Kosovo. Despite the "good" reason for the bombing—the prevention of ethnic slaughter—NATO placed itself above international law by attacking without the approval of the United Nations. Later, Russia did the same when it attacked Georgia. The United States also refuses to submit to the **International Criminal Court**, as U.S. officials fear they could be charged with war crimes (Sewall and Kaysen 2000; Beale 2018). This fear is not groundless because "one group's freedom fighter is another group's terrorist"—or more aptly phrased in this case, "one group's elected leaders are another group's child killers."

In general, the situation with international law today is disheartening, as each nation feels as though it can ignore international law when its own interests are at stake.

Survival as a Mutual Benefit

In the end, perhaps what will prevent the annihilation of humanity will be the desire for self-preservation. Leaders don't want themselves, their families, or their country destroyed. Unfortunately, as we know with suicide bombers, some individuals will sacrifice themselves in order to destroy archenemies. If terrorist groups get their hands on WMDs, they won't lack for volunteers to put them to use. And you can never be certain what any leader of a country might do in bleak and bitter moments. Albert Speer (1970), one of Hitler's close associates, noted that when Hitler realized the war was lost, he wanted to destroy his own country.

In Sum   The best social policies would be those that remove weapons of mass destruction from humanity. I foresee no social policy, though, that will eliminate these weapons. The knowledge of how to produce weapons of mass destruction has proliferated, and the best we can hope for are social policies that limit and prevent their use.

The Future of the Problem

14.7   Discuss the likely future of war and terrorism.

Here's a very quick overview of the future of arms sales, war, and terrorism.

The Global Killing Machine

A Personal Note: Each time I prepare a new edition of this book, I am appalled at the data on arms sales. To better understand the cold numbers that follow—billions here and billions there—think about what those numbers mean. In the mass media, you occasionally see men in Africa, Asia, and South America proudly posing with powerful automatic weapons. Where do these weapons come from? They don't manufacture them. Nor does any company in their country. The weapons in these photos reflect a vast global killing machine. Who are the people behind this machine, those who make fortunes selling the weapons of death? Next to trafficking in women and children for sex, this has to be the most immoral of all enterprises on Earth.

As you read this section, then, think about the blood that the following totals represent—the women who are brutally raped as they cower before men who carry the guns sold by arms merchants for their unconscionable profit, the children who are slaughtered or who live without parents, and the men and women who are killed trying to defend their families.

These aren't just numbers. You are looking at the horribly twisted face of death.

War and Terrorism Fueled by Profits   One of the easiest predictions to make in this text is that wars will continue to be fueled by the merchants of death. Look at Table 14.3. The top-selling nations produce far more weapons than their militaries can possibly use—and those behind this production are hungry for profits. As you can see, in this race to sell death, the United States far outpaces its nearest competitor. You might be surprised to see that Holland, with its carefully crafted picturesque images of tulips and windmills, is a major agent of death. The second part of Table 14.3 shows the buyers that these producers of weapons have found for their excess capacity. You can see that three of the poorest countries in the world—India, Algeria, and Pakistan—are among the top 10 buyers of the weapons of death. With those who make the profits having no concern about the destruction of human life, this merchandising in death will continue.

Why Do Poor Nations Spend So Much on Weapons?   Look again at the bottom part of Table 14.3. You can see the huge amounts that some least industrialized nations spend on the weapons of war. Algeria, Egypt, and Pakistan, who are on this list, need the money they spend on weapons to feed, house, and educate their people. The potential of aggression by neighboring countries requires a military, to be sure, but there is another reason: The power elites of these nations are insecure. They plunder their nation's resources to

Table 14.3 The Weapons of Death: 10 Years of the Global Arms Trade

The Top 10 Sellers		
Rank	**Seller**	**Value of Sales 2008–2017**
1	United States	90,000,000,000
2	Russia	66,000,000,000
3	Germany	18,000,000,000
4	France	17,000,000,000
5	China	14,000,000,000
6	Great Britain	12,000,000,000
7	Spain	8,000,000,000
8	Israel	7,000,000,000
9	Italy	7,000,000,000
10	Holland	6,000,000,000
The Top 10 Buyers		
Rank	**Buyer**	**Value of Purchases 2008–2017**
1	India	33,000,000,000
2	Saudi Arabia	19,000,000,000
3	China	13,000,000,000
4	United Arab Emirates	13,000,000,000
5	Algeria	11,000,000,000
6	Australia	11,000,000,000
7	Pakistan	11,000,000,000
8	South Korea	10,000,000,000
9	Egypt	9,000,000,000
10	United States	8,000,000,000

Note: To smooth out annual fluctuations, I have used a ten-year average of sales and purchases. The value is not in dollars, but in TIV, a unit SIPRI has developed to indicate a standard production cost. This means something to SIPRI, I suppose, but it is awkward for everyone else. To derive meaning, think of a country's amount relative to others. For example, although each of these countries spends billions of dollars on arms, you can see that India buys three times as much as Pakistan. For simplicity's sake, you can think of these totals as dollars instead of TIVs. You won't be too far off. (Turkey ranks in the top ten arms buyers, but SIPRI did not have enough information to include Turkey in this current list.)

Source: By the author. Based on SIPRI (Stockholm International Peace Research Institute). Database TIV of Arms Exports. New York: Oxford University Press, 2018c.

buy weapons to keep themselves in power. A strong military that they can control protects them from both uprisings of their own people and attacks from rival power elites within their own country. This self-feeding fear perpetuates the endless need to update their supply of powerful arms.

Want to buy machine guns? Tanks? Or how about this little baby, a "lurker bomber" that can stay aloft six hours, silently relaying information, and, on command, attack its target? All for sale to countries that can flash money or credit at arms shows, such as this one in Great Britain.

Richard Baker/Pictures Ltd./Corbis News/Getty Images

Terrorism

At this point in history, it is certain that terrorism will continue to make the news. Here are likely possibilities.

Revolutionary Terrorism Some revolutionary terrorists are motivated by bitter hatred. Others simply want political change. It seems almost inevitable that as time goes on, revolutionary terrorists, such as those who bombed the Pentagon and the World Trade Center in New York City, will acquire more sophisticated weapons. That we will one day face weapons of mass destruction—nuclear, chemical, or biological—is also likely. With advances in genetic engineering, the potential of biological weapons grows ever more ominous.

Repressive Terrorism Repressive terrorism will continue, particularly in China, Central and South America, Africa, and the Middle East. Demands for more democratic government will be met with heavy-handed repression, in some cases so extreme that the people will be cowering in fear of their own government. Political repression, in turn, may stimulate resistance—and the bloody struggles will continue.

State-Sponsored Terrorism It is likely that state-sponsored terrorism will decrease. Investigative techniques have become more powerful, enabling state-sponsored sources to be more easily tracked and destroyed. This is a powerful deterrent.

Russia After seven decades of persecution in Russia, people gained freedom of speech, press, politics, education, religion, and the arts. Increased trade and cultural exchanges with the West reduced suspicions and hostilities on both sides. Russia even joined NATO, allowing us to visualize a gentler, kinder future. Then came the backpedaling: Putin's repression, the killing of political rivals, the growing distrust between Russia and the United States, Russia's takeover of parts of Georgia and the Crimea region of the Ukraine, economic sanctions by the West, and the chills of our New Cold War.

I expect we will muddle through our current and future threats. A muddle-through future, while not exciting to contemplate, is certainly preferable to the implications of some of the problems of war and terrorism sketched in this chapter.

Red Huber/Orlando Sentinel/ Tribune News Service/Getty Images

From history, we know that world peace is an illusion, only a pause between war and violence. Yet we can hope and pray and work toward this goal. Perhaps one day ... Let's end this book on this note.

Summary and Review

1. The three essential conditions of war are a cultural tradition for war, an antagonistic situation, and a "spark" that ignites the war. Wars have occurred throughout history, but today's wars are much more destructive.

2. Symbolic interactionists analyze how symbols (perceptions) underlie war. During the Cold War, the West and the Soviets viewed each other as mortal enemies. Each felt obliged to arm itself, setting off a nuclear arms race, with nuclear weapons an indicator of one's capacity to destroy the other.

3. Functionalists identify these functions of war: the extension of political boundaries, social integration, economic gain, social change, ideology, vengeance, military security, and credibility. The dysfunctions of war are defeat, dependence, and destruction.

4. Conflict theorists identify four causes of war: competition for resources, a conflict of interests, a surplus of capital, and the dominance of a military machine.

5. Humans are no more peaceful today than in earlier times. The following do *not* diminish the chances of war: the type of government, the group's religion, prosperity, a common language or religion, shared political boundaries, or level of education.

6. Modern weapons are expensive and come at the cost of alternative expenditures. Among the non-monetary costs of war is *dehumanization*.

7. Both business and the military gain from producing, selling, and using weapons. The *military–industrial complex* is a powerful force in promoting war.

8. One of the more serious threats facing humanity is WMDs (weapons of mass destruction): biological, chemical, and nuclear. Chemical weapons seem to be under control, but unless effective international controls are put into place, biological and nuclear weapons will proliferate, one day leading to vast destruction.

9. *Political terrorism*—that is, the use of war to achieve political objectives—is of three types: *revolutionary terrorism*, waged by groups (or in rare cases, individuals) against the state; *repressive terrorism*, waged by the state against its own people; and *state-sponsored terrorism*, waged by one state against another. *Criminal terrorism* cuts across these types.

10. Disarmament, international law, and growing interlocking interests among the nations of the world point to an increase in the chances for peace. The New Cold War points in the opposite direction.

11. The future holds more terrorism and war. All-out nuclear war is unlikely because it means mutual destruction. Revolutionary terrorism will continue. This, in turn, will stimulate repressive terrorism. Al-Qaeda, ISIS, and other groups yet to appear, and their supporters, are likely to continue as agents of terrorism.

Thinking Critically about Chapter 14

1. Sociologist Nicholas Timasheff identified three essential conditions of war and seven "sparks" that can ignite these conditions into war. Analyze a war the United States has participated in. In this war, what were the essential conditions and the sparks?

2. The functions of war are the extension of political boundaries, social integration, economic gain, social change, ideology, vengeance, military security, and credibility. Apply these functions to the war on terrorism. How about the dysfunctions (defeat, dependence, and destruction)?

3. Do you think the United States has the right to intervene in another country to protect our economic or political interests? Under what conditions is intervention justified? Explain.

4. Do you think other countries have the right to intervene in the United States to protect their economic or political interests? Under what conditions is intervention justified? Explain.

Key Terms

Agent Orange, 463
armaments, 457
arms race, 446
biological terrorism, 469
bourgeoisie, 449
Cold War, 440
criminal terrorism, 468

dehumanization, 454
imperialism, 449
intercontinental ballistic missiles (ICBMs), 446
International Criminal Court, 472
military–industrial complex, 457
mutual assured destruction (MAD), 471

Glossary

A

acid rain   Rain with heavy concentrations of sulfuric and nitric acids; a result of air pollution.

addiction   Dependence on a substance to make it through the day.

Agent Orange   A chemical defoliant used in Vietnam that caused birth defects and other serious side effects.

air pollution   Air that is harmful to breathe because of burning fossil fuels and other human activities—as well as of natural events, like volcanic eruptions. Effects include eye, nose, and throat irritations as well as bronchitis, sinus infections, emphysema, and lung cancer.

alcoholic   A person with severe alcohol-related problems.

Anglo-conformity   Requiring or expecting everyone in the United States to adopt the dominant culture, the customs inherited from English settlers.

anomie   The feeling of being estranged, uprooted, unanchored, normless—not knowing what rules to apply to the situations one faces.

antiretroviral drugs (ARVs)   Medications that can slow down and even reverse the progression of HIV infection; can delay the onset of AIDS by 20 years or more.

apartheid   The enforced segregation of people on the basis of their perceived race or ethnicity.

armaments   Bombs, missiles, tanks, planes, guns, ships, submarines, and other weapons.

arms race   The attempt by nations to outmatch one another's war capabilities; usually refers to the buildup of weapons during the Cold War standoff between the Soviet Union and the West.

ascribed status   A position held as a result of one's birth.

assimilation   The absorption of a minority group or individual into the mainstream culture.

attention-deficit hyperactivity disorder (ADHD)   A condition, as defined by the medical community, that causes children not to pay attention and to disrupt classroom activities. Also known as hyperactivity, attention-deficit disorder, and hyperkinesis. The social problems associated with it include possible overmedication of children and medicalization of everyday problems.

B

binge drinking   Consuming on a single occasion five or more drinks by men or four or more drinks by women.

biodegradable   Capable of disintegrating in outdoor weather, when exposed to microorganisms.

biological poverty   Material deprivation so severe that it affects one's health (biological functioning).

biological terrorism   Use of an agent that causes disease—anthrax, smallpox, or the plague, for instance—as a weapon.

biotech society   A future society in which bioengineering (the manipulation of genetic materials) to produce food and other materials is central to that society.

bisexuals   People who are sexually attracted to both men and women.

black market   The production, exchange, and sale of goods or services not reported to government officials.

bourgeoisie   Karl Marx's term for society's power elite, which uses society's resources to keep itself in power and to exploit the less powerful; also called *capitalists*.

breadwinner   A worker whose earnings are the primary source of support for a family.

C

capital punishment   The death penalty.

capitalism   An economic system characterized by the private ownership of the means of production, market competition, and the pursuit of profit. See *socialism*.

capitalist economy   An economic system based on investing capital with the goal of making a profit.

capitalists   Owners of the means of production (land, factories, tools) who control the labor of workers.

carcinogen   A cancer-causing substance.

case study   A type of research design that focuses on a single case. The case or subject of the study can be an individual, an event, or an organization such as a church, hospital, or abortion clinic.

causation   Relationship in which one thing (variable) produces an effect on something else (another variable).

cesarean section (C-section)   A form of surgery in which a baby is delivered through an incision made in the mother's abdomen and uterus.

Chicago School of Sociology   Refers to research that stresses participant observation, symbolic interactionism, and seeing things from an insider's point of view, as practiced by the Department of Sociology at the University of Chicago in the 1920s.

city   Place of residence for a large number of people who live there permanently; city residents do not produce their own food.

civil disobedience   Deliberate but peaceful refusal to obey laws that are considered unjust.

cohabitation   Living together in a sexual relationship outside marriage.

Cold War   A period of hostilities after World War II between the former Soviet Union and nations of the West.

collateral damage   Euphemism for unintended casualties and destruction inflicted on civilians in the course of military operations.

common sense   The ideas common to a society or to some group within a society that people use to make sense out of their experiences.

community   People identifying with one another; can be on the basis of residence (a place) or an activity or interest they share.

concentric zone theory   A theory developed by Ernest Burgess suggesting that as cities expand outward from their center they develop areas, or zones, that have specialized functions. The area closest to the central business district—the zone in transition—has the most severe urban problems.

conflict theory   A sociological theory that views society as a system in competition and conflict. Each group in society attempts to further its own interests, even at the expense of others. Those who gain power exploit people and resources for their own benefit. Social problems stem from exploitation and resistance to exploitation.

control group The group in an experiment that is not exposed to an experience (or independent variable).

control theory A sociological theory that focuses on two control systems—inner controls and outer controls—which work against our tendencies to deviate.

conversion therapy A form of psychotherapy aimed at changing gay, lesbian, and bisexual people's sexual orientations to heterosexual, or at eliminating or diminishing same-sex desires and behaviors.

corporate welfare Financial benefits given to corporations, usually in the form of tax breaks; may also be reductions in rent or bargain-priced real estate.

correlation Two or more things occurring together.

Cosa Nostra The term by which East Coast mobsters refer to the Mafia. See *Mafia*.

craving An intense desire for something, often alcohol or another drug.

crime The violation of any act prohibited by law.

crime rate The number of crimes per some unit of population, most commonly the number of crimes per 100,000 people.

criminal justice system The agencies that respond to crime, including the police, courts, jails, and prisons.

criminal sexual assault Formerly called rape; includes sexual assaults, completed and attempted, aggravated and non-aggravated, against both males and females.

criminal terrorism Using terrorism to achieve criminal objectives.

criminogenic subculture Subculture that encourages and supports committing crime.

cultural feminism A branch of feminism that argues that biology leads to behavioral differences between men and women and that women and men should celebrate these differences. Cultural feminists claim that women are inherently kinder and gentler.

cultural goal A goal held out as legitimate for the members of a society.

cultural means The approved ways of reaching cultural goals.

culture of poverty Characteristics of the poor—such as dropping out of school, family violence, and alcoholism—that trap the poor in poverty.

culture of wealth Characteristics of the wealthy—such as social connections and educational achievement—that help keep them from falling down the social-class ladder.

D

death rate The number of deaths per 1,000 people per year.

defective discipline Excessive leniency or excessive control in rearing children; often a problem in single-parent households.

defensive medicine Medical procedures performed by physicians to protect themselves in case they are sued for malpractice.

dehumanization Process of viewing and treating people as objects not deserving the treatment ordinarily accorded humans.

deinstitutionalization The release of institutionalized people, especially psychiatric patients, from an institution for placement and care in the community.

delinquent subculture A group whose members are oriented toward illegal acts.

demographic transition A four-stage process of population growth. The first is high birthrates and high death rates. The second is high birthrates and low death rates. The third is low birthrates and low death rates. The fourth is birthrates so low that a population shrinks.

demography The study of the size, composition, growth, and distribution of human populations.

dependency ratio In terms of Social Security, the number of workers compared with the number of recipients.

depersonalization People being treated as inanimate objects, a characteristic found in many medical settings.

designer animals Gene-spliced farm animals.

deterrence Preventing an act by producing fear, often refers to crime or war.

differential association A symbolic interactionist theory that stresses that people learn values and behaviors by associating with people who have those values or practice those behaviors. The theory assumes people learn crime and violence in the same way people learn to follow laws or to be cooperative.

dirty work The tasks in society considered undesirable and low-level.

discrimination Singling people out for unfair treatment.

diversion A response to crime that diverts offenders away from the criminal justice system to keep them out of the courts and jails.

division of labor People performing different sets of specialized tasks.

documents Written records used as a source of information.

domiciliary care (home health care) Health care provided in the patient's home by health care professionals.

dominant group The group that has more power, privilege, and prestige and that discriminates against minority groups.

drug A substance that people take to produce a change in their thinking, consciousness, emotions, bodily functions, or behavior.

drug abuse Use of drugs in such a way that they harm one's health, impair one's physical or mental functioning, or interfere with one's social life.

drug addiction Dependence on the consumption of a drug to make it through the day. Also known as drug dependence.

drug therapy The use of drugs such as tranquilizers and anti-depressants to treat emotional problems.

dual labor market A pool of workers consisting of those who are regularly employed and better-paid and those who are temporary and low-paid.

dysfunction A part of a social system not performing its intended function adequately.

E

ecofeminism A branch of feminism that stresses that patriarchy is bad not only for women but also for the environment and that women must be leaders in preserving the environment.

ecology The study of the relationship between living things and their environment.

economic colonialism One nation dominating another nation economically to exploit that nation's people and resources.

economy A system of producing and distributing goods and services.

ecosystem The interconnection of life on the planet's outer surface; a fragile web made up of organisms and their environment.

electroconvulsive therapy (ECT) A treatment for emotional problems in which a low-voltage electric current (a shock) is sent through the brain. Also known as electroshock therapy.

endogamy The practice of marrying within one's group; can refer to a village, culture, or racial-ethnic group.

empowerment zone An area of a city where investment is encouraged by reducing taxes and government regulations.

environmental injustice The poor and minorities being harmed by polluting industries (and other forms of pollution, such as dumping) because the factories and activities are located in their neighborhoods.

ethnocentrism   The view that my group's ways are right and their group's ways are wrong.

euthanasia   Killing someone out of a sense of mercy or compassion; also called mercy killing.

experiment   A research design that divides a group into an *experimental group* (those who are exposed to some experience) and a *control group* (those who are not exposed to the experience). Measurements are taken before and after to determine the effects of the experience.

experimental group   The group in an experiment that is exposed to an experience (or independent variable).

exponential growth curve   The acceleration that appears in the later stages when growth doubles during approximately equal intervals.

extended family   A family in which relatives, such as the "older generation" or unmarried aunts and uncles, live with the parents and their children.

F

false class consciousness   Acceptance by workers of the view of the dominant class, failing to recognize they are being exploited.

family of orientation   The family into which people are born and from which they receive their basic orientations to life.

family of procreation   The family formed by marriage and that generally results in procreation, or the birth of children.

female infanticide   Killing baby girls.

feminist theory   A sociological perspective that focuses on the power relationships between men and women; comes in several varieties, usually with the aim to transform society and study it.

feminization of poverty   Poverty concentrated among women.

fetal alcohol spectrum disorder (FASD)   A cluster of congenital problems caused by the alcohol consumption of the newborn's mother; also known as fetal alcohol syndrome.

fetal narcotic syndrome   A cluster of congenital problems caused by the narcotic use of the newborn's mother.

field study (or field work or participant observation)   A method of gathering information through direct observation of some setting.

food chain   The arrangement of organisms according to food sources; each organism on the chain is a food source for the organism above it.

food politics   Controlling food production to control food prices: Paying farmers to leave their land fallow creates an artificial shortage that drives up grain prices.

food pollution   (also called *food contamination*) The transmission of disease during food processing or the addition of chemicals to food to help process it, lengthen its shelf life, or enhance its appearance or taste.

forcible rape   Forced sexual relations. See *statutory rape*.

fossil fuels   Substances (such as wood, coal, petroleum, and natural gas) used as fuels that are derived from living things.

frustration–aggression theory of violence   A psychological theory that stresses that the likelihood of aggression increases when a goal is blocked.

functions   The contribution of a part to its system, or people's actions that contribute to the equilibrium of a social system.

functionalism   (also called *functional analysis, functional theory*, and the *functional perspective*) A sociological theory that focuses on how a system consists of interconnected parts, each part contributing in some way to the equilibrium or stability of the system. The contribution of each part is called its *function*. Functionalists view social problems as *dysfunctions*, the failure of some part of the system to function correctly.

G

gender   How we express our "maleness" or "femaleness." Refers to socialization or culture. Commonly called femininity or masculinity. See also *sex*.

gender roles   The behaviors and attitudes expected of people because they are males or females.

generalize   To apply the findings learned in one setting, group, or sample to other settings or groups.

generalized other   The community or groups ("the people in general") that people take into account as they consider or evaluate a course of action.

genetically modified foods (GMF)   Foods coming from a plant or animal whose genes have been modified in a way that does not occur in nature.

genocide   The systematic killing of a people, usually racial–ethnic minorities.

genomics   The study of genes and how they relate to health and illness.

gentrification   More affluent people moving into an area and displacing poorer people and renovating their homes.

geothermal energy   Heat from beneath the earth's surface.

glass ceiling   An invisible social barrier that keeps women from rising to levels of authority within an organization.

global economy   The economic interdependence of the nations of the world.

global warming   An increase in the earth's temperature.

green party   A political party whose central issue is environmental concerns.

greenhouse effect   The concentration of gases in the atmosphere that forms a blanket around the earth, allowing sunlight to enter freely but slowing the release of heat.

group therapy   A treatment for emotional problems in which members of the group talk about their problems and help one another cope with them.

H

hate crimes   Crimes, such as assault or vandalism, motivated by dislike or hatred of the victim's race-ethnicity, religion, sexual orientation, disability, or national origin.

health maintenance organization (HMO)   An organization that has contracted to take care of the medical needs of a group for a set price; by minimizing unnecessary medical services, the HMO can make a profit.

heterosexuality   The sexual preference for people of the opposite sex.

home health care   Organized health services for people who are living at home with chronic or disabling diseases.

homemaker   The partner in a marriage, traditionally the woman, who stays home, takes care of the house and children, and attends to the personal needs of the other partner; now extended to cohabiting relationships.

homophobe   Technically, someone who fears homosexuals, but more commonly, someone who dislikes homosexuals.

homophobia   Fear, dislike, or intolerance of homosexuals.

homosexual behavior   Sexual relations between people of the same sex, regardless of their sexual preference.

homosexuality   The sexual preference for people of one's own sex.

hydrocarbons   Materials whose essential elements are hydrogen and carbon, the backbone of motor fuels and lubricants.

I

iatrogenesis Medical care that inadvertently causes an illnesses or other health problem; illnesses acquired in a hospital are iatrogenic.

illegitimate opportunity structure The opportunity built into someone's social world to learn and participate in illegal activities.

imperialism The expansion of a country and the dominance of subjugated peoples.

incapacitation A response to crime that focuses on removing offenders from circulation.

incest Sexual relations between relatives, such as brothers and sisters or parents and their children.

income The flow of money people receive from their work and investments.

incompatibility In terms of marriage and family, differences between a husband and wife that make it difficult for them to get along well.

individual discrimination Discrimination by one person against another. See also *insitutional discrimination.*

individual psychotherapy Treatment for emotional problems in which a therapist listens and tries to guide the client toward a resolution of his or her problems.

infant mortality rate The number of babies who die before one year of age, per 1,000 live births.

infanticide Killing infants shortly after birth, sometimes as a form of population control, and often directed against girls.

institutional discrimination Discrimination built into the social system that oppresses whole groups.

intercontinental ballistic missiles (ICBMs) Long-range nuclear weapons.

institutional discrimination Discrimination built into the social system that oppresses whole groups.

interest groups Groups organized around some specific interest (from the dairy industry to animal rights).

internal colonialism Exploitation by a dominant group of a minority group, where both live in the same country.

International Criminal Court (ICC) Court established in 2002 to investigate and prosecute genocide, crimes against humanity, and war crimes.

interview A method of gathering information in which the researcher asks questions. In a *structured* interview, the researcher asks preset questions; in an *unstructured* interview, people talk about their experiences, with the researcher making certain that specific areas are covered.

intimate partner violence Abuse within an intimate relationship; can be physical, sexual, or psychological.

invasion–succession cycle One group moving into an area inhabited by a group that has different characteristics. Moving in represents the invasion; dominating the area, the succession.

J

juvenile delinquency The legal term for the law-breaking behavior of children and adolescents.

L

labeling Stereotyping, or putting a tag on people, and treating them accordingly.

labor force participation rate The proportion of the population 16 years and older that is in the labor force.

latent dysfunctions The unintended consequences of people's actions that disrupt the equilibrium or stability of a social system or the adjustment of its parts.

latent functions The unintended consequences of people's actions that contribute to the equilibrium or stability of a social system or the functioning of its parts.

lay referral network Friends, relatives, and acquaintances from whom sick people get their ideas about health and illness and suggestions about who to see to treat their illnesses. See also *professional referral network.*

LGBT Lesbian, Gay, Bisexual, and Transgender.

liberal feminism A branch of feminism which stresses that oppression exists because of the way men and women are socialized.

looking-glass self Refers to our self-images being dependent on what we think others think of us. We see ourselves, in other words, as a reflection in the eyes of others.

M

Mafia An organized crime group. The Sicilian-American version is bureaucratized with specialized personnel and departmentalization.

managed care (prepaid care) Programs initiated by health insurance companies to keep health care costs down, often through financial incentives; medical decisions are often made not by patient and physician but by an insurance company employee. An HMO is one example.

manifest functions The consequences of people's actions that are *intended* to contribute to the adaptation, adjustment, or equilibrium of a social system or its parts.

masochists People who receive sexual gratification from experiencing pain. See *sadists.*

mass murder The killing of four or more people at one time in one location.

mass poverty Poverty so widespread in some location that most people are poor.

master trait A trait, such as age, disability, or sex, considered so important that it overrides an individual's other characteristics.

medicalization of human problems Making the problems of daily life a matter of sickness to be handled by the medical profession.

megacity An urban area of more than 10 million people.

megaton The explosive power of 1 million tons of TNT.

melting pot The expectation that the European immigrants to the United States would "melt" or blend together—that is, interact, intermarry, and form a new cultural and biological blend.

methadone maintenance A program for heroin addicts in which the narcotic methadone is substituted for the narcotic heroin.

military–industrial complex The merged interests of the military, business, and politicians to produce armaments.

minority group A group of people who, on the basis of physical or cultural characteristics, are singled out for unequal treatment and who regard themselves as objects of discrimination.

modeling Copying another's behavior.

moral entrepreneur A crusading reformer who wages battle to enforce his or her ideas of morality.

mutual assured destruction (MAD) The precarious balance of power between two nations that exists because neither country would survive a war, removing the benefit of attacking the other.

N

narcoterrorism Terrorism that revolves around drugs. Some narco-terrorists use drug dealing to finance their political goals.

national debt The total amount a nation owes—its total annual deficits minus its total annual surpluses.

national security   The condition of or concerns about a nation, in terms of threats from the outside and the inside.

neonatal abstinence syndrome   Withdrawal problems of babies born addicted to the drugs their mothers abused; includes fetal alcohol syndrome.

New World Order   Refers to the new balance of power attempted by the G7 nations.

normal violence   The amount of violence a group usually has.

nuclear disarmament   The process by which nations remove nuclear weapons from their arsenals.

nuclear family   A family that consists of a husband, wife, and their children.

nuclear fusion   Process of combining atoms—as opposed to nuclear fission, the splitting of atoms.

nuclear proliferation   The spread of nuclear weapons to more and more nations.

nuclear terrorism   Use of nuclear weapons, or the threat to use them, as a way to gain objectives.

O

objective condition   A condition of society that can be measured. One of the two essential characteristics of a social problem. See *subjective concern.*

observation   A means of gathering information whereby the researcher directly observes what is occurring in a setting. In the *overt* form, people know they are being studied; in the *covert* form, they do not.

official poverty   The level of income a government recognizes as constituting poverty.

operant conditioning   Principle holding that if some behavior is rewarded ("reinforced"), it will occur again.

optimistic environmentalists   Environmentalists who believe conditions are much better than the picture painted by pessimistic environmentalists.

organized crime   Organizations whose goal is to profit from criminal activities.

ozone shield   A layer of the earth's upper stratosphere that screens out much of the sun's ultraviolet rays.

P

pan-Indianism   A movement that goes beyond tribal identification to work for the welfare of all Native Americans.

participant observation (or field study)   A method of gathering information through direct observation of some setting.

passive houses   Houses that need little heating because they are built with insulation and windows that retain most of the heat produced by people's bodies and appliances.

patriarchal society   A social system in which the father is the head of the family and men have authority over women and children.

patriarchy   Rule by men-as-a-group over women-as-a-group.

pedophiles   Adults who are sexually attracted to children.

personal trouble   An individual's own experience of a social problem.

pessimistic environmentalists   Environmentalists who believe conditions are much worse than the picture painted by optimistic environmentalists.

pharmaceutical straitjacket   Refers to drugs given to patients in medical settings that make them drowsy, lethargic, and easier to handle.

plea bargaining   Pleading guilty to a lesser crime in exchange for a reduced sentence.

pluralists   Analysts who view power in society as balanced among many competing groups.

police discretion   The decisions police make about whether to overlook or enforce a law.

political process   A power struggle between groups based on their competing interests or ideologies.

political theater   A name sometimes given to terrorism because terrorists seek to use dramatic means to publicize their "cause."

pollution   The presence of substances that interferes with socially desired uses of air, water, land, or food.

Ponzi scheme   The payment of "investment profits" to clients, not from profits but from the money other clients invest.

population   In research, refers to the group one wishes to study.

population pyramid   A graphic representation of a population, showing the number in its age levels by sex.

population shrinkage   The shrinking of a country's population because its birthrate and immigration are too low to replace the people who die or emigrate.

population transfer   A minority relocating within a society or leaving the society altogether. In *direct transfer,* the minority is moved forcibly; in *indirect transfer,* the dominant group makes life so miserable for the members of a minority group that they "choose" to leave.

pornography   Writings, pictures, or objects intended to arouse sexual interest; considered offensive or filthy.

poverty line   The official measure of poverty; based on three times a low-cost food budget.

power   The capacity to get your way even in the face of opposition.

power elite   A small group of wealthy, powerful people who are said to make the major economic and political decisions of a group or country.

prejudice   An attitude whereby one prejudges others, usually negatively.

primary prevention   Measures that keep a disease from occurring, such as vaccinations. See also *secondary prevention, tertiary prevention.*

professional criminals   People who earn their living from crime.

professional referral network   The health care professionals that physicians and nurses use to evaluate their medical activities. See also *lay referral network.*

progressive taxation   Refers to tax rates progressing (increasing) as income progresses (increases).

proletariat   Karl Marx's term for the workers, whose labor is exploited by the capitalists.

prostitution   The renting of one's body for sexual purposes.

psychoanalysis   Developed by Sigmund Freud, a treatment for emotional problems whose goal is to uncover subconscious motives, fantasies, and fears by having patients speak about whatever comes to mind.

psychological dependence   The craving for a drug even though there no longer is a physical dependence on that drug.

pushouts   Children who have been kicked out of the family home by parents who no longer want them.

Q

questionnaires   A list of written questions used to gather information in research.

R

race   A group of people whose inherited physical characteristics distinguish it from others; a problematic term because it usually is used in a way that has no scientific basis; race is a social construct.

racial–ethnic group A group of people who identify with one another on the basis of their ancestry and cultural heritage. Also called an *ethnic group.*

racial–ethnic stratification Society or another group divided along racial–ethnic lines; the unequal distribution of resources on the basis of race–ethnicity.

radical feminism A branch of feminism whose position is that men and women need to be freed of rigid gender roles, which is to be accomplished by eliminating patriarchy.

random sample A sample that gives everyone in the group being studied an equal chance of being included in the research.

rate of violence The number of violent acts per some unit of population, usually per 100,000 people.

real income Income adjusted for inflation.

recidivism The commission of crimes by people who have been released from prison.

reference group A group whose standards we refer to when we evaluate ourselves.

regional restratification A shift in the population and relative wealth and power of the regions that make up a country. The current shift in the United States is toward the sunbelt.

rehabilitation A response to crime designed to resocialize or reform offenders so they can become law-abiding citizens.

relative poverty Deprivation as measured by the standards of one's society and culture. On a personal level, people think of themselves as poor or not poor on the basis of their reference groups.

repressive terrorism Terrorism directed by a government against its own citizens.

reproductive labor Labor performed by wives behind the scenes that allows the breadwinner husband to flourish in public.

research designs The methods that sociologists use to study social life. For social problems, these are case studies, experiments, field studies, and surveys.

research methods Ways of doing research.

reserve labor force The unemployed, who can be put to work during periods of labor strife or economic expansion and laid off when these conditions change. Also called *reserve labor army.*

residual poverty Pockets of poverty in an otherwise affluent society.

resource recovery plants Garbage-burning plants that generate power; utilities are required by the federal government to buy the power, which means that the plants partially pay for themselves.

restitution A form of retribution by which offenders compensate their victims.

retribution A response to crime based on restoring the moral balance upset by a criminal act. Making thieves repay what they stole is an example.

revolutionary terrorism Terrorism used in an attempt to bring about change in the political structure.

riot Violent crowd behavior aimed against people and property.

rising expectations The belief that better conditions will come soon. Rising expectations develop when institutional barriers begin to fall; if conditions do not change immediately, frustration builds, sometimes resulting in group violence.

role ambivalence Feeling both positive and negative about one's role.

S

sadists People who receive sexual gratification by inflicting pain on others. See *masochists.*

sample A relatively small number of people who are intended to represent the larger group from which they are selected.

scaled-back society Reduction of industrial output and standard of living.

secession A minority withdrawing from a society to establish its own nation.

secondary prevention Early detection and precautions that keep a disease from getting worse.

segregation Confining a group or an activity to specified geographical areas.

selective perception Seeing certain things while being blind to others.

serial murder Killing several victims in three or more separate events.

sex Sex is used in two senses. One is in reference to *gender.* In this sense, *sex* refers to a social status one inherits by birth, basically boy-girl. (The categories are expanding.) The second meaning of *sex* refers to an activity—behavior related to sexual arousal, sexual relations, or having sex.

sex tourism Travel to another country for sexual pleasure.

sex-typing Associating something with one sex or the other. "Men's work" and "women's work" are examples of sex-typing of occupations.

sexism The belief that one sex is innately superior to the other and the discrimination that supports such a belief.

sexual harassment Unwelcome sexual advances, requests for sexual favors, and other verbal or physical conduct of a sexual nature; usually connected to school or one's job.

sexual revolution Drastic relaxation in standards of sexual behavior, starting in the 1960s.

short-term directive therapy A treatment for emotional problems in which a therapist actively tries to solve the client's problems.

social class Broad grouping of people in a society based on their income, education, and occupational prestige.

social construction of reality The ways people make sense of life by giving meaning to their experiences.

social inequality The unequal distribution of wealth, income, power, and other opportunities.

social location An individual's position within society or its groups.

social problem Some aspect of society (the *objective condition*) that large numbers of people are concerned about (the *subjective concerns*) and would like changed.

socialism An economic system characterized by the public ownership of the means of production, central planning, and the distribution of goods without a profit motive. See *capitalism.*

socialist feminism A branch of feminism that believes there is a direct link between capitalism and the oppression of women.

sociological imagination (or sociological perspective) A framework of thought that looks at the broad social context that shapes people's experiences. This perspective helps people transcend personal experiences and emotions to see the larger picture that affects their situation.

sociological perspective Another term for *sociological imagination.*

sociology The systematic and objective study of the groups that make up society.

split-labor market Workers split along lines of age, race–ethnicity, or gender; those in charge try to take advantage of this split to keep wages low by sowing distrust.

state-sponsored terrorism A country supporting terrorism against another nation.

status crime   Behavior that is illegal only because of the individual's age, such as drinking alcohol, running away from home, or violating curfew.

statutory rape   Consensual sexual relations in which one person is under the legal age of consent. See *forcible rape*.

steady-state society   A society in which the economy does not grow or shrink.

stereotype   A generalization of what people are like.

strain theory   A functionalist theory that stresses how people adapt when their access to the cultural means to reach cultural goals is blocked.

strip mining   Mining coal that lies so close to the surface that it can be retrieved by stripping away the soil.

structural inequality   Inequality built into social institutions.

structure   The interrelations between the parts or subunits of society or some other social system.

structured interview   Interviews that use closed-ended questions.

subcultural theory   A symbolic interactionist theory that stresses how a group's orientations—its norms, attitudes, values, beliefs, and behaviors—influence people.

subjective concern   The concern or distress people feel about some aspect of society. One of the two essential characteristics of a social problem. See *objective condition*.

suffragists   Advocates in the 19th and early 20th centuries for more rights for women, especially the right to vote.

supergangs   Large, violent, criminal gangs; many have affiliates in other cities and even in other countries.

surplus value of labor   If an item sells for more than what it cost to produce, the profit (or surplus value) is said to result from the value of the labor that went into producing the item.

survey   Research using questionnaires or interviews that focuses on a sample of people from a target population. The sample is intended to represent the larger group from which it is selected.

symbolic interactionism   A sociological theory that focuses on the meanings that objects and events have for people and how people use symbols to communicate with one another. Social problems are the objective conditions that people have decided to call social problems.

symbols   Items of social life to which we give meaning and that we then use to communicate with one another. Symbols include signs, gestures, words, and even our posture and appearance.

synergism (literally, "working together")   Applied to groups, organizations, or even individuals, synergism refers to their interactions producing effects that are greater than those that would exist if the two (or more) had not interacted.

synfuels (synthetic fuels)   Alternative fuels developed from garbage, sawdust, and other waste.

T

taking the role of the other   Putting oneself in someone else's shoes to try to see things as that person sees them.

talk therapy   Treatments of emotional problems based on "talking" (psychotherapy, group therapy, etc.).

techniques of neutralization   Ways people justify their norm-breaking activities, making their behaviors more acceptable to themselves and others.

temple prostitution   Prostitution in a temple, as a type of worship.

terrorism   Using the means of war to create fear to achieve objectives.

tertiary prevention   Medical care of an existing disease aimed at preventing further damage.

theory   An explanation of how two or more concepts, such as age and suicide, are related to one another.

thermal inversion   A layer of cold air sealing in a lower layer of warm air.

total war   No-holds-barred warfare.

transgender persons   People whose personal gender identity does not match the gender role society has assigned them based on their sex organs.

two-tier system of medical care   A medical delivery system in which the poor receive one type of medical care and the affluent another.

U

underclass   Alienated people who live primarily in the inner cities; they have little education and high rates of unemployment, female-headed families, welfare dependency, violent crimes, drug abuse, and births to single women.

uniform sentencing   Imposing the same sentence on everyone convicted of the same crime.

universal basic income   All citizens of a country receiving a set amount of annual income from the government

unstructured interview   Interviews that use open-ended questions.

urban crisis   The interrelated problems of cities, including their governance, financing, poverty, violence, crime, and deterioration of services.

urbanization   The process by which cities grow and develop increasing influence over a region.

V

value   A belief about whether something is good or bad, desirable or undesirable.

victimless crime   An illegal act to which the participants consent.

violence   The use of physical force to injure people or to destroy their property.

W

war   Armed conflict between countries.

wealth   Savings, property, investments, income, and other economic assets.

white-collar crime   Crimes committed by executives and others in the corporate world as part of their job; for instance, knowingly producing dangerous vehicles, altering drug test data, and creating false advertising.

withdrawal   The distress people feel when they don't take a drug to which they are addicted.

Z

zero population growth   A population that is neither growing nor shrinking because women bear only enough children to replace those who die.

References

All new references are printed in blue.

"49 Bodies Found on Mexico Roadway." Associated Press, May 14, 2012.

"AA Fact File." General Service Office of Alcoholics Anonymous, 2016.

AAMC (Association of American Medical Colleges). "State Physician Workforce Data Report," November 2017.

Abbey-Lambertz, Kate. "This Group Is Raising Money to Test Decades-Old Rape Kits and Find Justice for Thousands." *Huffington Post*, January 8, 2015.

ACA (Arms Control Association). "New START at a Glance." March 2018.

Achenbaum, W. Andrew. *Old Age in the New Land: The American Experience Since 1970*. Baltimore: Johns Hopkins University Press, 1978.

Ackerman, John P., Tracy Riggins, and Maureen M. Black. "A Review of the Effects of Prenatal Cocaine Exposure Among School-Aged Children." *Pediatrics*, 125 (3), February 2010:554.

ACS (American Community Survey). "Characteristics of the Group Quarters Population in the United States, 2016." U.S. Census Bureau, October 19, 2017a.

ACS (American Community Survey). "Poverty Status in the Past 12 Months by Sex by Age." U.S. Census Bureau, October 19, 2017b.

ACS (American Community Survey). "Total Asian Alone or in Any Combination Population." U.S. Census Bureau, October 19, 2017c.

Adams, David. "Top Senator Denies Sex Tourism Claim as FBI Raids Donor's Offices." Reuters, January 30, 2013.

Adams, Michael Henry. "The End of Black Harlem." *New York Times*, May 27, 2016.

Adler, Amy. "Symptomatic Cases: Hysteria in the Supreme Court's Nude Dancing Decisions." American Imago, 64 (3), Fall 2007:297–316.

Adnan, Abidi. "Parents in Pakistan Consent to Daughter's Rape as Revenge." *The Times*, March 27, 2018.

"Advocates Sue FDA to Force Decision on Cancer-Causing Chemicals in Popular Foods." *EarthJustice*, May 2, 2018. https://earthjustice. org/news/press/2018/advocates-sue-fda-to-force-decision-on-cancer-causing-chemicals-in-popular-foods

Ahmari, Sohrab. "Helping the Escaped Slaves of ISIS." *Wall Street Journal*, November 24, 2015.

Ahmed, Akbar. *Islam, Immigration, and Identity*. Washington, DC: Brookings Institution Press, 2018.

Ahmed, Faraz, M. Zubair Shafiq, and Alex X. Liu. "The Internet Is for Porn: Measurement and Analysis of Online Adult Traffic." *IEEE Xplore*, August 11, 2016.

Aisch, Gregor, and K. K. Rebecca Lai. "The Conflicts along 1,172 Miles of the Dakota Access Pipeline." *New York Times*, December 5, 2016.

Ait, Abraham. "Will China Have Seven Aircraft Carriers by 2025?" *The Japan Times*, July 10, 2018.

Al-Agba, Niran. "MD vs. DNP: Why 20,000 Hours of Training and Experience Matter." The Health Care Blog, May 29, 2017. http://thehealthcareblog.com/blog/2017/05/29/ md-vs-dnp-why-20000-hours-of-training-and-experience-matters/

Alexander, Karl, Doris Entwisle, and Linda Olson. *The Long Shadow: Family Background, Disadvantaged Urban Youth, and the Transition to Adulthood*. New York: Russel Sage, 2014.

Alihan, Milla A. *Social Ecology*. New York: Columbia University Press, 1938.

Allen, Charlotte Low. "Anti-Abortion Movement's Anti-Establishment Face." *Wall Street Journal*, December 8, 1988:A14.

Allen, Frank Edward. "Environment." *Wall Street Journal*, May 28, 1991.

Allport, Gordon. *The Nature of Prejudice*. Reading, MA: Addison-Wesley, 1954.

Amadeo, Kimberly. "Afghanistan War Cost, Timeline and Economic Impact." *The Balance*, July 11, 2018.

Amadeo, Kimberly. "Cost of Iraq War, Its Timeline and the Economic Impact." *The Balance*, June 21, 2018.

Amato, Paul R. "Research on Divorce: Continuing Trends and New Developments." *Journal of Marriage and Family*, 72 (3), June 2010:650–666.

Amato, Paul R., and Jacob Cheadle. "The Long Reach of Divorce: Divorce and Well-Being across Three Generations." *Journal of Marriage and Family*, 67, February 2005:191–206.

Amott, Teresa, and Julie Matthaei. *Race, Gender, and Work: A Multicultural Economic History of Women in the United States*. Boston: South End, 1991.

Andersen, Margaret L. *Thinking About Women: Sociological Perspectives on Sex and Gender*. New York: Macmillan, 1988.

Anderson, D. Mark, and Daniel I. Rees. "Medical Marijuana Laws, Traffic Fatalities, and Alcohol Consumption." Bonn, Germany: IZA Discussion Paper No. 6112, November 2011.

Anderson, Elijah. *The Cosmopolitan Canopy: Race and Civility in Everyday Life*. W.W. Norton, 2012.

Anderson, Elijah. *A Place on the Corner*. Chicago: University of Chicago Press, 1978.

Anderson, Elijah. *Streetwise: Race, Class, and Change in an Urban Community*. Chicago: University of Chicago Press, 1990.

Anderson, Elijah. "Streetwise." In *Society: Readings to Accompany Sociology: A Down-to-Earth Approach, Core Concepts*, James M. Henslin, ed. Boston: Allyn & Bacon, 2006:54–63.

Anderson, Hanna, and Matt Daniels. "Film Dialogue from 2,000 Screenplays, Broken Down by Gender and Age," *The Pudding*, April 2016.

Armenta, Mika. "How Our Perceptions of Victims' Humanity Increases Some Violence, But Not All." *Chicago Policy Review*, January 19, 2018.

Angell, Marcia. "A Better Way Out." *New York Review of Books*, January 8, 2015.

Anslinger, Harry J., and Courtney Ryley Cooper. "Marijuana: Assassin of Youth." *American Magazine*, July 1937.

Apel, Robert, and Raymond Paternoster. "Understanding 'Criminogenic' Corporate Culture: What White-Collar Crime Researchers Can Learn from Studies of the Adolescent Employment-Crime Relationship." In *The Criminology of White-Collar Crime*, S. S. Simpson and D. Weisburd, eds. New York: Springer, 2009:15–33.

Aposporos, Demetra. "Hunting for Glory with the Barabaig of Tanzania." *National Geographic*, July 2004.

Aries, Philippe. *Centuries of Childhood: A Social History of Family Life*. Robert Baldick, trans. New York: Vintage, 1962.

Arlacchi, P. *Mafia, Peasants and Great Estates: Society in Traditional Calabria*. Cambridge: Cambridge University Press, 1980.

Armitage, Richard L. "Red Army Retreat Doesn't Signal End of U.S. Obligation." *Wall Street Journal*, February 7, 1989:A20.

Asher, Jeff. "U.S. Murder Rate for 2018 Is on Track for a Big Drop." New York Times, December 6, 2018.

Ashley, Richard. *Cocaine: Its History, Uses, and Effects*. New York: St. Martin's, 1975.

Atchley, Robert C. "Dimensions of Widowhood in Later Life." *The Gerontologist*, 15, April 1975:176–178.

Athens, Lonnie H. *Violent Criminal Acts and Actors: A Symbolic Interactionist Study*. Boston: Routledge, 1980.

Attanasio, John. *Politics and Capital: Auctioning the American Dream*. New York: Oxford University Press, 2018.

AVERT. "Children and HIV/AIDS." 2016. Online. http://www.avert. org/professionals/hiv-social-issues/key-affected-populations/ children.

Aydelotte, Jayson D., Lawrence H. Brown, and Kevin M. Luftman. "Crash Fatality Rates after Recreational Marijuana Legalization in Washington and Colorado." *American Journal of Public Health*, August 2017.

Backhaus, Anne, and Simone Salden. "Generations of Victims: Bhopal's Unending Catastrophe." *Der Spiegel International*, December 9, 2014.

Bagaric, Mirko, Julie N. Clarke, and William Rininger. "Plea Bargaining: From Patent Unfairness to Transparent Justice." *Missouri Law Review*, 2018.

Bahna, Sami L., and Joshua G. Burkhardt. "The Dilemma of Allergy to Food Additives." *Allergy & Asthma Proceedings*, 39 (1), Jan/Feb 2018:3–8.

Bailey, Jeff. "Economics of Trash Shift as Cities Learn Dumps Aren't So Full." *Wall Street Journal*, June 2, 1992:A1, A7.

Bailey, Ronald. "Civilization Is Doomed, Says Stanford Biologist Paul Ehrlich (Again)." *Reason*, March 22, 2018.

Bajaj, Vikas. "As Grain Piles Up, India's Poor Still Go Hungry." *New York Times*, June 7, 2012.

Baker, Bryan. "Estimates of the Unauthorized Immigrant Population Residing in the United States: January 2014." Homeland Security: Office of Immigration Statistics, Population Estimates, July 2017.

Balemba, Samantha, Eric Beauregard, and Tom Mieczkowsi. "To Resist or Not to Resist? The Effect of Context and Crime Characteristics on Sex Offenders' Reaction to Victim Resistance." *Crime and Delinquency*, 20 (10), May 2012:1–24.

Balko, Radley. "As It Turns Out Meth Laws Have Unintended Consequences." *Washington Post*, October 24, 2014.

Band, Jeffrey D., and Robert Gaynes. "Prevention of Intravascular Catheter-Related Infections." *UpToDate*, March 16, 2016.

Banda, P. Solomon. "Man, 18, Had Sex with Girl Later Found Dead." Associated Press, May 21, 2010.

Bandura, Albert, and Richard H. Walters. *Social Learning and Personality Development*. New York: Holt, 1963.

Barber, James Allen, Jr. "The Military-Industrial Complex." In *The Military and American Society: Essays and Readings*, Stephen E. Ambrose and James A. Barber, Jr., eds. New York: Free Press, 1972.

Bardwick, Judith M. *Psychology of Women: A Study of Bio-Cultural Conflicts*. New York: Harper & Row, 1971.

Barnes, Edward, and William Shebar. "Quitting the Mafia." *Life*, December 1987:108–112.

Barnes, Robert. "Supreme Court Upholds University of Texas Affirmative-Action Admissions." *Washington Post*, June 23, 2016.

Baron, Larry. "Immoral, Inviolate or Inconclusive?" *Society*, July/August 1987:6–12.

Barrett, Devlin, and Sean Gardiner. "Structure Keeps Mafia Atop Crime Heap." *Wall Street Journal*, January 29, 2011.

Barringer, Felicity. "As 'Yuck Factor' Subsides, Treated Wastewater Flows from Taps." *New York Times*, February 9, 2012.

Barron, J. "Medical Examiner Rules Ledger's Death Accidental." *New York Times*, February 7, 2008.

"Barry Bonds Prosecutor: No Jail Time 'Almost Laughable.'" *L.A. Now*, December 16, 2011.

Bart, Pauline B., and Patricia H. O'Brien. "How the Women Stopped Their Rapes." *Signs*, 10, 1984.

Bart, Pauline B., and Patricia H. O'Brien. *Stopping Rape: Successful Survival Strategies*. New York: Pergamon, 1985.

Bartlett, Donald L., and James B. Steele. "Wheel of Misfortune." *Time*, December 16, 2002:44–58.

Barton, Marc. "John Snow and the 1854 Cholera Outbreak." *Past Medical History*, January 23, 2018.

Baum, Seth, Robert de Neufville, and Anthony Barrett. "A Model for the Probability of Nuclear War." Global Catastrophic Risk Institute Working Paper 18-1, March 8, 2018.

Baumann, Mary. U.S. Senate Historical Office. Personal communication, September 14, 2006.

BBC (British Broadcasting Company). "Crimea Profile." January 17, 2018.

Beale, Sara Sun. "United States Country Report for Prosecuting Corporations for Violations of International Criminal Law." *Duke Law School Public Law & Legal Theory Series No. 2018–20*, March 28, 2018.

Beals, Ralph L., and Harry Hoijer. *An Introduction to Anthropology*, 3rd ed. New York: Macmillan, 1965.

Beane, M. (2018). "Shadow Learning: Building Robotic Surgical Skill When Approved Means Fail." *Administrative Science Quarterly*, 2018:1–37.

Beck, Allen J., and Ramona Rantala. "Sexual Victimization Reported by Adult Correctional Authorities, 2009–11." Special Report. Bureau of Justice Statistics January 2014.

Becker, Howard S. "Editor's Introduction." In *Social Problems: A Modern Approach*. Howard S. Becker, ed. New York: Wiley, 1966:1–31.

Becker, Howard S. "History, Culture, and Subjective Experience: An Exploration of the Social Bases of Drug Induced Experiences." *Journal of Health and Social Behavior*, 7, June 1967:163–176.

Beckett, Katherine, and Heather Evans. "The Role of Race in Washington State Capital Sentencing, 1981–2012." Unpublished paper, University of Washington: Law, Societies & Justice Program, January 27, 2014.

Sexual Exploitation of Children in Tourism. Madrid: World Tourism Organization, 2001.

Beech, Hannah. "Unhappy Returns." *Time*, July 26–August 2, 2004.

Bell, Daniel. *The End of Ideology*. New York: Free Press, 1960.

Bell, Monica, Nathan Fosse, Michele Lamont, and Eva Rosen. "Beyond the Culture of Poverty: Meaning-making among Low-Income Population around Family, Neighborhood, and Work." In *The Blackwell Encyclopedia of Race, Ethnicity and Nationalism*, John Stone, Rutledge Dennis, Polly Rizova, and Anthony Smith, eds. New York: John Wiley, 2014.

Belluck, Pam. "Forget Prisons: Americans Cry Out for the Pillory." *New York Times*, October 4, 1998b.

Belluz, Julia. "Lyme, the Tick-Born Disease That's Spreading Fast." *Vox*, May 29, 2018.

Bender, Jeremy, and Armin Rosen. "Mexico's Drug War Is Entering a Dark Phase." *Business Insider*, October 24, 2014.

Benenson, Joyce F., Hassina P. Carder, and Sarah J. Geib-Cole. "The Development of Boys' Preferential Pleasure in Physical Aggression." *Aggressive Behavior*, 34, 2008:154–166.

Bengtson, Vern L., Carolyn Rosenthal, and Linda Burton. "Families and Aging: Diversity and Heterogeneity." In *Handbook of Aging and the Social Sciences*, 3rd ed., Robert H. Binstock and Linda K. George, eds. San Diego: Academic Press, 1990:263–287.

Benson, Michael L. "Denying the Guilty Mind: Accounting for Involvement in White-Collar Crime." *Criminology*, 23, November 1985:585–607.

Berger, Peter. L. *Invitation to Sociology*. New York: Doubleday, 1963.

Berghel, Hal. "Bruce Schneier on Future Digital Threats." *Computer*, February 2018:64–67.

Berik, Gunseli, and Ebru Kongar. "Time Use of Mothers and Fathers in Hard Times and Better Times: The U.S. Business Cycle of 2003–2010." Levy Economics Institute: Working Paper No. 696, November 2011.

Berke, Jeremy, and Skye Gould. "This Map Shows Every State Where Pot Is Legal." Business Insider, January 4, 2019.

Berkey, C. S., W. C. Willet, A. L. Frazier, et al. "Prospective Study of Adolescent Alcohol Consumption and Risk of Benign Breast Disease in Young Women. *Pediatrics*, May 2010:2009–2347.

Bernstein, Elizabeth. "The Meaning of the Purchase: Desire, Demand, and the Commerce of Sex." *Ethnography*, 2 (3), 2001:389–420.

Bertrand, Marianne, Claudia Goldin, and Lawrence F. Katz. "Dynamics of the Gender Gap for Young Professionals in the Corporate and Financial Sectors." National Bureau of Economic Research Working Paper Number 14681, September 2009.

Bhattacharya, Prasenjit. "Union Carbide Not Liable in Bhopal Gas Cleanup, says US Court." *Hydrocarbon Processing Magazine*, July 2, 2012.

Bilefsky, Dan. "In Mother's Trial, Man Tells of His Father's Rage." *New York Times*, September 21, 2011a.

Bilefsky, Dan. "An Abused Wife or an Executioner?" *New York Times*, September 25, 2011b.

Bilefsky, Dan. "Wife Who Fired 11 Shots Is Acquitted of Murder." *New York Times*, October 26, 2011c.

Billeaud, Jacques. "Arizona Sheriff Defends Illegal-Immigrant Sweeps." *Seattle Times*, April 26, 2008.

Binde, Per. "Gambling-Related Embezzlement in the Workplace: A Qualitative Study." *International Gambling Studies, 16* (3), July 2016:391–407.

"Births: Final Data for 2013." *National Vital Statistics Report, 64*, 1, January 15, 2015:Table 1–3.

Birzins, Sandy, Robbi Babins-Wagner, and Kathleen Hyland. "Relationship of Employment Status and Socio-Economic Factors with Distress Levels and Counseling Outcomes During a Recession." *Counseling & Psychotherapy Research, 18* (2), June 2018:122–132.

BJS (Bureau of Justice Statistics). "State Corrections Expenditures, FY 1982–2010." NCJ 239672. December 10, 2012.

Black, Sandra E., Diane Whitmore Schanzenbach, and Audrey Breitwieser. "The Recent Decline in Women's Labor Force Participation." Washington, DC: Brookings, October 2017.

Blackmon, Douglas A., Vanessa O'Connell, Alexandra Berzon, and Ana Campoy. "There Was Nobody in Charge." *Wall Street Journal*, May 27, 2010.

Blackstone, Sir William. *Commentaries on the Laws of England*, 4th ed., Thomas M. Cooley, ed. Chicago: Callaghan and Co., 1899.

Bleizeffer, Dustin. "Wyoming, China Dream of a Coal-Chemical Bridge to Future Energy." August 19, 2014. Wyofile online.

Bloch, Roland, Alexander Mitterle, Catherine Paradeise, and Tobias Peter, eds. *Universities and the Production of Elites*. New York: Springer, 2017.

BLS (Bureau of Labor Statistics). "Physicians and Surgeons: Pay." *Occupational Outlook Handbook*, 2018

Blum, Richard H., Eva Blum, and E. Garfield. *Drug Education: Results and Recommendations*. Lexington, MA: Heath, 1976.

Blumberg, Abraham S. "The Practice of Law as Confidence Game: Organizational Cooptation of a Profession." *Law and Social Review, 1*, 1967:15–39.

Blumenthal, Ralph. "Polluted Midwest Rain Is Killing New York Lakes." *Alton Telegraph*, June 8, 1981.

Blustein, Jan, and Jianmeng Liu. "Time to Consider the Risks of Caesarean Delivery for Long-Term Child Health." *British Medical Journal, 350*, June 10, 2015.

Boden, Paul. "Restricting Pornography—The Slippery Slope to Censorship." *Urban Times*, May 31, 2012.

Boebert, Earl, and James M. Blossom. *Deepwater Horizon: A Systems Analysis of the Macondo Disaster*. Cambridge, MA: Harvard University Press, 2016.

Bone, James. "Prostitute Behind Spitzer Sex Scandal Revealed." *The Times*, March 13, 2008.

Boot, Max. "Your Money or Your Life? That Depends." *Wall Street Journal*, March 4, 1998:A18.

Booth, Michael. "Final Listeria Cantaloupe Death Toll at 33, CDC Says." *Denver Post*, June 23, 2016.

"Borden Chemical and Plastics to Shut La. Plant." *Columbus Business First*, November 9, 2000.

Borenstein, Seth. "Richard Muller, Global Warming Skeptic, Now Agrees Climate Change Is Real." *New York Times*, October 30, 2011.

Boston University. New England Centenarian Study. "Why Study Centenarians? An Overview." Boston University School of Medicine, 2018.

Boston, Guy D., Kevin O'Brien, and Joanne Palumbo, *Terrorism: A Selected Bibliography*, 2nd ed. Washington, DC: National Institute of Law Enforcement and Criminal Justice, March 1977.

Bowen, Crosswell. "Donora, Pennsylvania." In *Society and Environment: The Coming Collision*, Rex R. Campbell and Jerry L. Wade, eds. Boston: Allyn and Bacon, 1972:163–168.

Boyle, Glen M., Marjorie M. A. d'Souza, Carly J. Pierce, et al. "Intra-Lesional Injection of the Novel PKC Activator EBC-46 Rapidly Ablates Tumors in Mouse Models." *PLOS ONE, 9* (10), October 1, 2014.

Branham, J. Alexander, Stuart N. Soroka, and Christopher Wlezien. "When Do the Rich Win?" *Political Science Quarterly*, April 12, 2017.

Brannigan, Augustine. "Is Obscenity Criminogenic?" *Society*, July/August 1987:12–19.

Braun, Liz. "Sex Robots: The Future of Sex?" *Toronto Sun*, March 10, 2018.

Bray, Rosemary L. "Rosa Parks: A Legendary Moment, a Lifetime of Activism. *Ms., 6* (3), November–December 1995:45–47.

"Brazil Drops 'Happy Prostitute' Aids Campaign." BBC, June 4, 2013.

Brecher, Edward M., and the editors of Consumer Reports. *Licit and Illicit Drugs*. Boston: Little, Brown, 1972.

Brenneman, Robert. *Homies and Hermanos: God and Gangs in Central America*. New York: Oxford University Press, 2012.

Brenner, Grant Hilary. "4 Ways Porn Use Causes Problems." *Psychology Today*, March 5, 2018.

Breslow, Jason M. "The Staggering Death Toll of Mexico's Drug War." *Frontline*, July 27, 2015.

Brewer, Devon D., John J. Potterat, Sharon B. Garrett, et al. "Prostitution and the Sex Discrepancy in Reported Number of Sex Partners." *Proceedings of the National Academy of Sciences, 97* (22), October 24, 2000:12385–12388.

Brewer, Mick. "Good Ol' Country Boys Playin' on the Farm: Online Articulations of Rural Masculinity by Men Who Have Sex with Men." *Sexuality and Culture, 22* (2), June 2018:355–379.

Broad, William J., and Judith Miller. "Rocky Start for U.S. Plan to Stockpile Vaccines to Fight Germ Warfare." *New York Times*, August 7, 1998.

Brody, Jane E. "1,100 Tested in Michigan for Effects of Toxin That Poisoned Food in '73." *New York Times*, November 5, 1976.

Broidy, Lisa, and Wayne A. Santoro. "General Strain Theory and Racial Insurgency: Assessing the Role of Legitimate Coping." *Justice Quarterly, 35* (1), 2018.

Bronner, Ethan. "Poor Land in Jail as Companies Add Huge Fees for Probation." *New York Times*, July 2, 2012.

Bronstein, Carolyn. *Battling Pornography: The American Feminist Anti-Pornography Movement, 1976–1986*. New York: Cambridge University Press, 2011.

Brooke, James. "Deep Desert Grave Awaits First Load of Nuclear Waste." *New York Times*, March 26, 1999.

Brooks, Jack. *FDA Continues to Permit the Illegal Marketing of Carcinogenic Additives*. Twenty-fifth Report of the Committee on Government Operations. Washington, DC: U.S. Government Printing Office, 1987.

Brown, Janet Welsh. Environmental Defense Fund Letter. New York, n.d.

Brown, Letisha Engracia Cardoso. "Post-Colonial Feminism, Black Feminism and Sport." In *The Palgrave Handbook of Feminism and Sport*, Louise Mansfield, Jayne Caudwell, et al., eds 2018:479–495.

Brownmiller, Susan. *Against Our Will: Men, Women, and Rape*. New York: Simon & Schuster, 1975.

Brunson, Rod K., and Kashea Pegram. "Kids Do Not So Much Make Trouble, They Are Trouble." *Future of Children, 28* (1), Spring 2018:83–102.

Bucher, Jacob, and Michelle Manasse. "When Screams Are Not Released. A Study of Communication and Consent in Acquaintance Rape Situations." *Women and Criminal Justice, 21* (3), 2011:123–140.

Buckley, Geoffrey L., and Yolonda Youngs, eds. *The American Environment Revisited*. Lanham, MD: Rowman & Littlefield, 2018.

Budiansky, Stephen A. "The Trees Fell—And So Did the People." *U.S. News & World Report*, February 9, 1987:75.

Buff, Stephen A. "Lois Lee Takes Back Children from the Night." *ASA Footnotes, 15* (5), May 1987:1, 2.

Bunge, Jacob. "Sizzling Steaks Made in the Lab." *Wall Street Journal*, February 1, 2016.

Bunn, Matthew, and Anthony Wier. "Preventing a Nuclear 9/11." *Washington Post*, September 12, 2004.

Burby, Liza N. "Just Because I'm the Girl Doesn't Mean Caring for My Parents Should Fall on Me." *Working Mother*, February 6, 2016.

Burch, William R., Jr. *Daydreams and Nightmares: A Sociological Essay on the American Environment*. New York: Harper & Row, 1971.

Bureau of Labor Statistics. "Physicians and Surgeons." *Occupational Outlook Handbook*, U.S. Department of Labor, 2016.

Bures, Regina M., Tanya Koropeckyj-Cox, and Michael Loree. "Childlessness, Parenthood, and Depressive Symptoms Among Middle-Aged and Older Adults." *Journal of Family Issues*, 30 (5), May 2009:670–687.

Burgess, Ernest W. "The Growth of the City: An Introduction to a Research Project." In *The City*, Robert E. Park, Ernest W. Burgess, and Roderick D. McKenzie, eds. Chicago: University of Chicago Press, 1925 (pages 47–62 in the 1967 edition).

Burgess, Ernest W., and Harvey J. Locke. *The Family: From Institution to Companionship*. New York: American Book, 1945.

Burns, Kenneth Lauren. "The Civil War: A Film by Ken Burns." Public Broadcasting Service, 1990.

Burns, Steve. "GBI Charges 3 in Georgia, 76 Overall, in Child Exploitation Crackdown." *Atlanta Journal-Constitution*, March 16, 2018.

Burris, Val. "Interlocking Directorates and Political Cohesion among Corporate Elites." *American Journal of Sociology*, 111 (1), July 2005:249–283.

Burros, Marian. "Experts Worry About the Return of a Deadly Germ in Cold Cuts." *New York Times*, March 14, 1999.

Burroughs, William. "Excerpts from 'Deposition: Testimony Concerning a Sickness.'" In *Drugs in American Life*, Morrow Wilson and Suzanne Wilson, eds. New York: Wilson, 1975:133–158.

Butterfield, Fox. "Prison Population Increases as Release of Inmates Slows." *New York Times*, January 11, 1999.

Cahalan, Margaret, and Laura Perna. *Indicators of Higher Education Equity in the United States: 45 Year Trend Report*. Washington, DC: The Pell Institute, 2015.

Cahoun, L., L. Cox, and R. Chitale. "Celebrity Addictions: Painkillers and Hollywood." ABC News Medical Unit, February 22, 2008.

Calderon, Laura, Octavio Rodriguez Ferreira, and David A. Shirk. *Drug Violence in Mexico: Data and Analysis through 2017*. University of San Diego, April 2018.

Campo-Flores, Arian. "A Crackdown on Call Girls." *Newsweek*, September 2, 2002.

Caplow, Theodore, et al. *Middletown Families: Fifty Years of Change and Continuity*. Minneapolis: University of Minnesota Press, 1982.

"Cardinals Announce 2018 Promotional Giveaway Schedule." *Cardinal News*, May 5, 2018.

Carey, Benedict. "In the Hospital, a Degrading Shift from Person to Patient." *New York Times*, August 16, 2005.

Carlson, Lewis H., and George A. Colburn. *In Their Place: White America Defines Her Minorities, 1850–1950*. New York: Wiley, 1972.

Carlson, Kenneth, and Jan Chaiken. "White Collar Crime." Special Report of the Bureau of Justice Statistics. Washington, DC: U.S. Department of Justice, September 1987.

Carnevale, Mary Lu. "New Jolt for Nynex: Bawdy 'Conventions' of Buyers, Suppliers." *Wall Street Journal*, July 12, 1990:A1, A6.

Carpenter, Rhiannon, Adelle Fishlock, Ann Mulroy, et al. "After 'Unit 1421': An Exploratory Study Into Female Students' Attitudes and Behaviors Towards Binge Drinking at Leeds University." *Journal of Public Health*, 30 (1), 2008:8–13.

Carrega-Woodby, Christina. "Prison Support Group Starts Petition to Free Barbara Sheehan." *New York Post*, January 7, 2014.

Carroll, C. R. *Drugs in Modern Society*. 5th ed. New York: McGraw-Hill, 2000.

Carroll, Dillon J. "Civil War Veterans and Opiate Addiction in the Gilded Age." *The Journal of the Civil War Era*. November 22, 2016.

Carton, Barbara. "At Jenny Craig, Men Are Ones Who Claim Sex Discrimination." *Wall Street Journal*, November 29, 1994:A1, A7.

Cartwright, Mark. "The Classic Maya Collapse." *Ancient History Encyclopedia*, October 18, 2014.

"Casinos Not Paying Off for Indians." ABC News, August 31, 2016.

Castaldi, Malena. "Three Types of Marijuana to Hit Uruguayan Pharmacies in 2016." *Reuters* December 5, 2015.

Castaneda, Carlos. *A Separate Reality: Further Conversations with Don Juan*. New York: Simon & Schuster, 1971.

Castaneda, Carlos. *Tales of Power*. New York: Simon & Schuster, 1974.

Castaneda, Carlos. *The Teachings of Don Juan: A Yaqui Way of Knowledge*. New York: Ballantine, 1968.

Castells, Manuel. *The City and the Grass Roots*. Berkeley: University of California Press, 1983.

Castells, Manuel. *The Informational City*. Oxford, England: Blackwell, 1989.

Castells, Manuel. *The Urban Question: A Marxist Approach*. Alan Sheridan, trans. Cambridge, MA: MIT Press, 1977.

Catalano, Shannon M. "Intimate Partner Violence: Attributes of Victimization, 1993–2011." Bureau of Justice Statistics, November 21, 2013.

Catanzaro, Raimondo. *Men of Respect: A Social History of the Mafia*. New York: Free Press, 1992.

CDC (Centers for Disease Control). "Abortion Surveillance—United States, 2015." November 23, 2018j.

CDC (Centers for Disease Control and Prevention). "Alcohol and Pregnancy." Hyattsville, MD: Department of Health and Human Services, 2013c.

CDC (Centers for Disease Control and Prevention). "Alcohol and Public Health: Frequently Asked Questions." Hyattsville, MD: Department of Health and Human Services, 2013b.

CDC (Centers for Disease Control and Prevention). "Facts at a Glance: Suicide." 2015.

CDC (Centers for Disease Control and Prevention). "Fact Sheet: Alcohol Use and Your Health." January 3, 2018b.

CDC (Centers for Disease Control and Prevention). "Fact Sheet: Economic Facts about U.S. Tobacco." 2016a.

CDC (Centers for Disease Control and Prevention). "Fact Sheet: Smoking &. Tobacco Use." February 20, 2018a.

CDC (Centers for Disease Control and Prevention). "Fact Sheet: Tobacco Related Mortality." 2016b.

CDC (Centers for Disease Control and Prevention). "Fact Sheet: Tobacco Related Mortality." 2017a.

CDC (Centers for Disease Control and Prevention). "Fact Sheets: Alcohol Use and Your Health." 2016a.

CDC (Centers for Disease Control and Prevention). "Foodborne Illnesses and Germs." February 16, 2018g.

CDC (Centers for Disease Control and Prevention). "HIV in the United States: At a Glance." 2016c.

CDC (Centers for Disease Control and Prevention). "HIV in the United States: At a glance." July 2018e.

CDC (Centers for Disease Control and Prevention). "Investigation Notice." July 19, 2018h.

CDC (Centers for Disease Control and Prevention). "Multistate Outbreak of *E. coli* 0157:H7 Infections Linked to Romaine Lettuce." July 19, 2018i.

CDC (Centers for Disease Control and Prevention). "National Suicide Statistics at a Glance." September 30, 2009a.

CDC (Centers for Disease Control and Prevention). "Nutrition: Get the Facts: Sugar-Sweetened Beverages and Consumption." April 17, 2017b.

CDC (Centers for Disease Control and Prevention). "Overweight and Obesity." June 12, 2018f.

CDC (Centers for Disease Control and Prevention). "Reproductive Health: Abortion, Data and Statistics." February 16, 2018c.

CDC (Centers for Disease Control and Prevention). "Reproductive Health: Data and Statistics." 2016d.

CDC (Centers for Disease Control and Prevention). "Sexually Transmitted Diseases Surveillance," various years.

CDC (Centers for Disease Control and Prevention). "Suicides among American Indian/Alaska Natives." *Morbidity and Mortality Weekly Report*, March 2, 2018d.

Cecire, Michael. "Russia Tensions Move Closer to Home." *U.S. News and World Report*, November 28, 2014.

Center for American Women and Politics. "Women in Elective Office, 2016." July 2016.

Center for American Women and Politics. "Women in Elective Office 2018." June 2018.

Chagnon, Napoleon A. "Life Histories, Blood Revenge, and Warfare in a Tribal Population." *Science,* February 26, 1988:985–992.

Chambliss, William J. *Power, Politics, and Crime.* Boulder, CO: Westview Press, 2001.

Chambliss, William J. "The Saints and the Roughnecks." In *Down to Earth Sociology: Introductory Readings,* 15th ed., James M. Henslin, ed. New York: Free Press, 2017. (Originally published in Society, *11* (1), 1973:24–31)

Chandy, Laurence, and Corey Smith. "How Poor Are America's Poorest? U.S. $2 a Day Poverty in a Global Context." Washington DC: The Brookings Institution, 2014.

Chang, Iris. *The Rape of Nanking: The Forgotten Holocaust of World War II.* New York: Basic Books, 1997.

Chankova, Slavea. "Why Do Women Still Earn a Lot Less Than Men?" *The Economist,* October 20, 2017.

Chanmanee, Wilaiwan, Mohammad Fakrul Islam, Brian H. Dennis, and Frederick M. MacDonnell. "Solar Photothermochemical Alkane Reverse Combustion." *Proceedings of the National Academy of Sciences of the United States of America, 113* (10), 2016:2579–2584.

"Charges Alleging Sexual Harassment, FY 2010–FY2015." Washington, DC: U.S. Equal Opportunity Commission, 2016.

Charlet, Kate. "The New Killer Pathogens: Countering the Coming Bioweapons Threat." *Foreign Affairs, 178,* 2018.

Chase, Marilyn. "Defying Treatment, a New, Virulent Bug Sparks Health Fears." *Wall Street Journal,* January 20, 2006.

Chaudry, Ajay, Taryn Morrissey, Christina Weiland, and Hirokazu Yoshikawa. *Cradle to Kindergarten: A New Plan to Combat Inequality.* New York: Russell Sage, 2017.

Cheadle, Jacob, Paul R. Amato, and Valerie King. "Patterns of Nonresident Father Involvement." *Demography, 47,* 2010:205–226.

Chemaly, Soraya. "How Did the FBI Miss over 1 Million Rapes?" *The Nation,* June 27, 2014.

Chen, M. "Ground Zero: The Most Dangerous Workplace." *The New Standard,* 2007.

Chernoff, Nina W., and Rita J. Simon. "Women and Crime the World Over." *Gender Issues, 18* (3), Summer 2000:5–20.

Childs, Dan. "Medical Errors, Past and Present." ABC News, November 27, 2007.

Childs, Dan. "When Daddy Loves Daughter: Exploring the Incest Taboo." ABC News, April 9, 2008.

Chin, Gabriel J., and John Ormonde. "The War against Chinese Restaurants." *Duke Law Journal, 2018.*

Chiplock, Megan. "Marijuana Chemical May Slow Multiple Sclerosis." Temple University News Service, May 12, 2009.

Cho, Eunyoung, et al. "Dairy Foods, Calcium, and Colorectal Cancer: A Pooled Analysis of 10 Cohort Studies." *Journal of the National Cancer Institute, 96* (13), July 7, 2004:1015–1022.

Choi, Kwan, and Ju-Lak Lee. "Assessment of the Extent and Prevalence of Serial Murder through Criminological Theories." *Sociology and Anthropology, 2* (3), 2014:116–124.

Choudhury, Deepak, Shivesh Anand, and May Win Naing. "The Arrival of Commercial Bioprinters—Towards 3D Bioprinting Revolution!" *International Journal of Bioprinting, 4* (2), June 17, 2018.

Chouhy, Cecilia. "Segmented Assimilation, and Crime." In *Handbook on Immigration and Crime,* Holly Ventura Miller and Anthony Peguero, eds. New York: Routledge, 2018.

CIA (Central Intelligence Agency). *CIA World Factbook,* published annually.

Claudel, Matthew, and Carlo Ratti. "Full Speed Ahead: How the Driverless Car Could Transform Cities." MIT: Senseable City Lab, August 2015.

Clayton, R. R., A Catterello, and B. M. Johnstone. "The Effectiveness of Drug Abuse Resistance Education (Project DARE): 5-Year Follow-Up Results." *Preventive Medicine, 25,* 1996:307–318.

Cleaver, Eldridge. *Soul on Ice.* New York: McGraw-Hill, 1968.

Clinard, Marshall B. *Corporate Corruption: The Abuse of Power.* New York: Praeger, 1990.

Clinard, Marshall B., Peter C. Yeager, Jeanne Brisette, David Petrashek, and Elizabeth Harries. *Illegal Corporate Behavior.* Washington, DC: U.S. Department of Justice, 1979.

Clines, Francis X. "Soviets Now Admit '57 Nuclear Blast." *New York Times,* June 18, 1998.

Cloward, Richard A., and Lloyd E. Ohlin. *Delinquency and Opportunity: A Theory of Delinquent Gangs.* New York: Free Press, 1960. Reprinted by Routledge in 2011.

CMMS (Centers for Medicare and Medicaid Services). "NHE Fact Sheet." May 2018.

Cobb, Michael. *Single: Arguments for the Uncoupled.* New York: New York University Press, 2012.

Cochran, Clarke E., Lawrence C. Mayer, T. R. Carr, et al. *Public Policy: An Introduction,* 11th ed. New York: Cengage, 2016.

Code, Lorraine, ed. *Encyclopedia of Feminist Theories.* London: Routledge, 2000.

College Board. "SAT: Total Group Profile." September 30, 2016.

Collins, Karen. "Inflammation and Cancer Risk: Can Anti-Inflammatory Diets Help?" *Today's Dietitian, 20* (1), January 2018.

Collins, Laura. "Only a Paedophile Is Lower Than a Rat." *Daily Mail,* March 24, 2015.

Collins, Ronald K. L. "Comedy and Liberty: The Life and Legacy of Lenny Bruce." Social Research, *79* (1), Spring 2012:61–86.

Congressional Record. Public Law 112–265, January 14, 2013.

"Consumers: Gender Roles Have Changed. Advertising Hasn't." *Marketing Charts,* March 6, 2018.

Consumer Reports. "Dangerous Contaminated Chicken." *Consumer Reports,* January 2014.

Contrera, Jessica. "A Wrenching Dilemma." February 20, 2018.

Cook, Dianne. "The Gender Gap in Math Is Not Universal." *Chance,* November 2014.

Cook, John, Sander van der Linden, etc. *The Consensus Handbook: Why the Scientific Consensus on Climate Change Is Important.* http://www.climatechangecommunication.org/all/consensus-handbook/

Cookson, Peter W., Jr., and Caroline Hodges Persell. "Preparing for Power: Cultural Capital and Elite Boarding Schools." In *Life in Society: Readings to Accompany Sociology: A Down-to-Earth Approach,* 7th ed., James M. Henslin, ed. Boston: Allyn & Bacon 2005:175–185. (Originally published in *Preparing for Power,* by Peter W. Cookson and Caroline H. Persell, 1985.)

Cooper, P. F. "Historical Aspects of Wastewater Treatment." In *Decentralized Sanitation and Reuse: Concepts, Systems and Implementation,* P. Lens., G. Zeeman, and G. Lettinga, eds. London: IWA, 2002:11–38.

Copp, Jennifer E., and William D. Bales. "Jails and Local Justice System Reform: Overview and Recommendations." *Future of Children, 28* (1), Spring 2018:103–124.

Corcoran, Mary, Greg J. Duncan, Gerald Gurin, and Patricia Gurin. "Myth and Reality: The Causes and Persistence of Poverty." *Journal of Policy Analysis and Management, 4* (4), 1985:516–536.

Corkery, Michael. "Wells Fargo Fined $185 Million for Fraudulently Opening Accounts." *New York Times,* September 8, 2016.

Corless, Inge B., Teri Lindgren, William Holzemer, et al. "Marijuana Effectiveness as an HIV Self-Care Strategy." *Clinical Nursing Research, 18* (2), May 2009:172–193.

Cornell, George W. "Modern Persecutions Mirror Those of Jesus." Associated Press, April 13, 1981.

Corona, Lauren E., Carolyn W. Swenson, Kyle H. Sheetz, et al. "Use of Other Treatments before Hysterectomy for Benign Conditions in a Statewide Hospital Collaborative." *American Journal of Obstetrics and Gynecology, 212* (3), 2015.

Corsaro, William J. *The Sociology of Childhood,* 5th ed. Thousand Oaks, CA: Sage, 2017.

Corzine, Jay, and Richard Kirby. "Cruising the Truckers: Sexual Encounters in a Highway Rest Area." *Urban Life, 6,* July 1977:171–192.

Coscarelli, Joe, and Sheila M. Eldred. "Prince's Death Results in No Criminal Charges." *New York Times,* April 19, 2018.

Coser, Lewis A. *Masters of Sociological Thought: Ideas in Historical and Social Context.* New York: Harcourt, 1977.

Cowley, Joyce. *Pioneers of Women's Liberation*. New York: Merit, 1969.

Cressey, Donald R. *Other People's Money*. New York: Free Press, 1953.

Crider, Raquel. "Phencyclidine: Changing Abuse Patterns." In *Phencyclidine: An Update*, Doris H. Clouet, ed. Rockville, MD: National Institute on Drug Abuse, 1986:163–173.

Crime in the United States. Washington, DC: FBI (Federal Bureau of Investigation), *published annually*.

"Cross National Comparison of Rape Rates: Problems and Issues." Working Paper #18. Statistical Commission and UN Economic Commission for Europe, October 28, 2004.

Croteau, David. *Politics and the Class Divide: Working People and the Middle-Class Left*. Philadelphia: Temple University Press, 1995.

CSIS (Center for Strategic and International Studies). "Missiles of the World." CSIS Missile Defense Project. August 2018.

Cunliffe, William H. "Select Documents on Japanese War Crimes and Japanese Biological Warfare, 1934–2006." Interagency Working Group, 2018.

Cunningham, Brittany C., Kathleen Mulvaney Hoyer, and Dinah Sparks. "Gender Differences in Science, Technology, Engineering, and Mathematics (STEM) Interest, Credits Earned, and NAEP Performance in the 12th Grade." Washington, DC: National Center for Education Statistics, February 2015.

Cunningham, James K., Teshia A. Solomon, and Myra L. Muramoto. "Alcohol Use among Native Americans Compared to Whites: Examining the Veracity of the 'Native American Elevated Alcohol Consumption' Belief." *Drug and Alcohol Dependence, 160*, March 1, 2016:65–75.

Currie, Elliott. *Confronting Crime: An American Challenge*. New York: Pantheon, 1985.

Dabbs, James M., Jr., and Robin Morris. "Testosterone, Social Class, and Antisocial Behavior in a Sample of 4,462 Men." *Psychological Science, 1* (3), May 1990: 209–211.

Dahl, Robert A. *Who Governs?* New Haven, CT: Yale University Press, 1961.

Daling, Janet R., David R. Doody, Xiaofei Sun, et al. "Association of Marijuana Use and the Incidence of Testicular Germ Cell Tumors," *Cancer*, March 15, 2009:1215–1223.

Danielson, Melissa L., Rebecca H. Bitsko, Reem M. Ghandour, et al. "Prevalence of Parent-Reported ADHD Diagnosis Treatment among U.S. Children and Adolescents, 2016." *Journal of Clinical Child and Adolescent Psychology, 47* (2), January 24, 2018:199–212.

Dart, Tom. "To End Mass Incarceration, Think Local." *Wall Street Journal*, May 31, 2016.

Dash, Leon. "When Children Want Children." *Society, 27* (5), July–August 1990:17–19.

Davies, J. Clarence III, and Barbara S. Davies. *The Politics of Pollution*, 2nd ed. Indianapolis, IN: Bobbs-Merrill, 1975.

Davis, Angela. *Angela Davis: An Autobiography*. New York: Random House, 1974.

Davis, Cala P. *Girls and Juvenile Justice: Power Status and the Social Construction of Delinquency*. New York: Palgrave Macmillan, 2017.

Davis, Diane E. "The Routinization of Violence in Latin America: Ethnographic Revelations." *Latin American Research Review, 53* (1), 2018:211–216.

Davis, Elizabeth, Elizabeth, and Tracy L. Snell. "Capital Punishment, 2016—Statistical Brief," NCJ 251430, April 30, 2018.

Davis, Jordan P., Douglas C. Smith, Jason W. Morphew, et al. "Cannabis Withdrawal, Posttreatment Abstinence, and Days to First Cannabis Use among Emerging Adults in Substance Use Treatment: A Prospective Study." *Journal of Drug Issues, 46* (1), 2016:64–83.

Davis, Kingsley. "Sexual Behavior." In *Contemporary Social Problems*, 2nd ed., Robert Merton and Robert Nisbet, eds. New York: Harcourt, 1966.

Davis, Kingsley. "The Sociology of Prostitution." *American Sociological Review, 2* (5), October 1937:744–755.

Davis, Kingsley, and Wilbert E. Moore. "Some Principles of Stratification." *American Sociological Review, 10*, 1945:242–249.

Davis, Nanette J. "Prostitution: Identity, Career, and Legal-Economic Enterprise." In *The Sociology of Sex: An Introductory Reader*, James M. Henslin and Edward Sagarin, eds. New York: Schocken, 1978:297–322.

Daws, Gavin. *Prisoners of the Japanese: POWs of World War II in the Pacific*. New York: Morrow, 1994.

de Graaf, Tjeed. "The Ainu in Japan." Barcelona, Spain: Catedra UNESCO, January 19, 2016.

de la Rosa, Alexandre Coello. "The 'Fierce People' in the Context of US Foreign Politics: A Historical Anthropology to Napoleon Chagnon's Interpretation of the Yanomami." *Social Anthropology*, August 1, 2018.

de Oliveira, Jose Oswaldo. "Opiophobia and Opiophilia: The War Continues." Revista da Sociacao Medica Brasileira, *64* (5), May 2018.

de Silva, Rex. "Developing the Third World." *World Press Review*, May 1980:48.

Death Penalty Information Center. Washington, DC: 2016.

Delgado, Ysol. "Despite U.S. Ban, Bolivia Will Export Coca-Based Products to Ecuador." *PanAm Post*, November 22, 2016.

Demetriou, Danielle. "China Starts Posting Japan's War Criminal 'Confessions' Online." *The Telegraph*, July 4, 2014.

Denes, Magda. *In Necessity and Sorrow: Life and Death in an Abortion Hospital*. New York: Basic Books, 1976.

DePaulo, Bella. "Living Single: The Truth about Singles in Our Society." *Psychology Today*, 2016.

Depew, Briggs, Ozkan Eren, and Naci Mocan. "Judges, Juveniles, and In-Group Bias." *The Journal of Law and Economics, 60* (2), May 2017.

Devereaux, Ryan. "Three Years after 43 Students Disappeared in Mexico, A New Visualization Reveals the Cracks in the Government's Story." *The Intercept*, September 7, 2017.

Devine, Michael A. "A Fresh Look at Cogeneration." *Energy User News, 29*, 1, September 2004:13–15.

Devlin, Amanda, and Emma Lake. "Robot Romps." *The Sun*. March 7, 2018.

Dewan, Shaila, and Katie Zezima. "Twists Multiply in Alabama Shooting Case." *New York Times*, February 14, 2010.

Dewan, Shaila, Stephanie Saul, and Katie Zezima. "For Professor, Fury Just Beneath the Surface." *New York Times*, February 20, 2010.

DeWitt, Amy L., Cynthia M. Cready, and Rudy Ray Seward. "Parental Role Portrayals in Twentieth Century Picture Books: More Egalitarian or Ongoing Stereotyping?" *Sex Roles, 69* (2–3), July 2013:89–106.

DHHS (Department of Health and Human Services). "Public Health and Emergency Services Emergency Fund," 2018.

Diamond, Milton. "Pornography, Public Acceptance and Sex Related Crime: A Review." *International Journal of Law and Psychiatry, 32*, 2009:304–314.

Dickey, Christopher, and Adam Rogers. "Smoke and Mirrors." *Newsweek*, February 25, 2002.

Dickson, Donald T. "Bureaucracy and Morality: An Organizational Perspective on a Moral Crusade." *Social Problems, 16*, Fall 1968: 143–156.

Dillow, Clay, and Brooks Rainwater. "Why Free Money for Everyone Is Silicone Valley's Next Big Idea." *Fortune*, Jun 29, 2017.

Dimico, Arcangelo, Alessia Isopi, and Ola Olsson. "Origins of the Sicilian Mafia: The Market for Lemons." *The Journal of Economic History, 77* (4), December 2017.

Dobash, Russell P., and R. Emerson Dobash. "Women's Violence to Men in Intimate Relationships: Working on a Puzzle." *The British Journal of Criminology, 44* (3), May 1, 2004:324–349.

Dobyns, Henry F. *Their Numbers Became Thinned: Native American Population Dynamics in Eastern North America*. Knoxville: University of Tennessee Press, 1983.

Dockterman, Eliana. "Why Women Stay: The Paradox of Abusive Relationships." *Time*, September 9, 2014.

Doering, Christopher. "GMO Food Labeling Law Pressure Mounts." *Des Moines Register*, July 16, 2014.

Doerner, William G. "The Index of Southernness Revisited: The Influence of Wherefrom upon Whodunnit." *Criminology, 16*, May 1978:47–56.

Doleac, Jennifer L., and Luke C. D. Stein. "The Visible Hand: Race and Online Marketing Outcomes." *The Economic Journal, 123* (572), November 2013:F469–F492.

Domhoff, G. William, et al. Studying the *Power Elite: Fifty Years of Who Rules America?* New York: Routledge, 2017.

Domhoff, G. William. *The Bohemian Grove and Other Retreats: A Study in Ruling-Class Cohesiveness*. New York: Harper & Row, 1974.

Domhoff, G. William. *Who Really Rules?* New Brunswick, NJ: Transaction, 1978b.

Domhoff, G. William. *Who Rules America: Power and Politics*, 6th ed. New York: McGraw-Hill, 2009.

Domhoff, G. William. *Who Rules America? The Triumph of the Corporate Rich*, 7th ed. New York: McGraw-Hill, 2014.

Donadio, Rachel. "Italy's Attacks on Migrants Fuel Debate on Racism." *New York Times*, October 12, 2008.

Douglass, Joseph D. "A Biological Weapons Threat Worse Than Saddam." *Wall Street Journal*, March 10, 1998:A22.

Douvan, Elizabeth. "Is the American Family Obsolete?" University of California, University Extension, Courses by Newspaper, San Diego, 1980.

Dove, Adrian. "Soul Folk 'Chitling' Test or the Dove Counterbalance Intelligence Test." Mimeo, n.d.

Doward, Jamie. "Medicine's Big New Battleground: Does Mental Illness Really Exist?" *The Guardian*, May 11, 2013.

Dowie, Mark. "The Corporate Crime of the Century." *Mother Jones, 4*, November 1979:23–25, 37.

Dowie, Mark. "Pinto Madness." *Mother Jones, 2*, September– October 1977:18–32.

Drope, Jeffrey, and Neil W. Schluger, eds. *The Tobacco Atlas*, 6th ed. Atlanta, GA: American Cancer Society, 2018.

Drug Enforcement Administration. *Opium Poppy Cultivation and Heroin Processing in Southeast Asia*. Washington, DC: U.S. Department of Justice, 2001.

Drury, Glenys. *Contested Landscapes: An Exploration into Street-Based Sex Work and Its Implications for Urban Design in Christchurch, New Zealand*. Dissertation, Lincoln University 2018.

Dubar, Helen. "American Discovers Child Pornography." In *Human Sexuality 80/81*, James R. Barbour, ed. Guilford, CT: Dushkin, 1980.

Dufay, Joanne. "Ten Years After Chernobyl: A Witness to the Devastation." Greenpeace online, n.d.

Dugger, Celia W. "Senegal Curbs a Bloody Rite for Girls and Women." *New York Times*, October 15, 2011.

Dumas, Daisy. "'I Know They Aren't Going to Call. I Don't Want Them to Call": How Women Who Want No-strings-attached Sex Are Fuelling Boom in Gigolo Services." *Mail Online*, February 17, 2012.

Duneier, Mitchel. *Sidewalk*. New York: Farrar, Straus and Giroux, 1999.

Durken, Michal J., S. Reza Jafarzadeh, et al. "Outpatient Antibiotic Prescription Trends in the United States: A National Cohort Study." *Infection Control and Hospital Epidemiology, 39*, May 2018:584–589.

Durkheim, Emile. *The Division of Labor in Society*, George Simpson, trans. New York: Free Press, 1964. (Originally published 1893)

Durkheim, Emile. *The Rules of Sociological Method*, Sir George E. G. Catlin, ed. New York: Macmillan, 1938. (Originally published 1904; 8th ed. 1950)

Durkheim, Emile. *Suicide*, John A. Spaulding and George Simpson, trans. New York: Free Press, 1951. (Originally published 1897)

Durose, Matthew R., Alexia D. Cooper, and Howard N. Snyder. "Recidivism of Prisoners Released in 30 States in 2005: Patterns from 2005 to 2010." Special Report, U.S. Department of Justice, April 2014.

Duster, Troy. "From Structural Analysis to Public Policy." *Contemporary Sociology, 17* (3), May 1988:287–290.

Duster, Troy. *The Legalization of Morality: Law, Drugs, and Moral Judgment*. New York: Free Press, 1970.

Dwyer, Jim. "A Court Battle Over a Husband's Rage and a Wife Who'd Had Enough." *New York Times*, April 6, 2011.

Earl, Jennifer. "'It's the Shame Effect': Judge Orders Public Humiliation for Domestic Abuser." CBS News, March 31, 2017.

Eberstadt, Nicholas. "The Global War against Baby Girls." *The New Atlantis*, Fall 2011.

Eberstadt, Nick. *The Poverty of Communism*. New Brunswick, NJ: Transaction, 1988.

Edelman, Benjamin. "Red Light States: Who Buys Online Adult Entertainment?" *Journal of Economic Perspectives, 23* (1), Winter 2009:209–220.

Eder, Donna. *School Talk: Gender and Adolescent Culture*. New Brunswick, NJ: Rutgers University Press, 1995.

Edwards, Brian. "Coca-Cola's Secret Formula: Can You Make It at Home?" *The Mirror*, February 18, 2015.

EF Kessler, Glenn. "Fact Checker: The Stale Statistic That One in Three Black Males 'Born Today' Will End Up in Jail." *Washington Post*, June 16, 2015.

Ehrenreich, Barbara, and Deirdre English. *Witches, Midwives, and Nurses: A History of Women Healers*. Old Westbury, NY: Feminist Press, 1973.

Ehrlich, Paul R., and Anne H. Ehrlich. *Extinction: The Causes and Consequences of the Disappearance of Species*. New York: Random House, 1981.

Eisenegger, Christoph, Johannes Haushofer, and Ernst Fehr. "The Role of Testosterone in Social Interaction." *Trends in Cognitive Sciences, 15* (6), June 2011:263–271.

Eisenhart, R. Wayne. "You Can't Hack It, Little Girl: A Discussion of the Covert Psychological Agenda of Modern Combat Training." *Journal of Social Issues, 31*, Fall 1975:13–23.

Eisenhower, Dwight D. "From 'Farewell Address to the Nation,' January 17, 1961." In *The Military and American Society: Essays and Readings*, Stephen E. Ambrose and James A. Barber, Jr., eds. New York: Free Press, 1972:61–63.

Elgot, Jessica, and Jack Sommers. "Holocaust Denial Worries Historians and Religious Leaders as Survivors Dwindle." *Huffington Post*, January 30, 2015.

Eliot, Lise. *Pink Brain, Blue Brain: How Small Differences Grow Into Troublesome Gaps—And What We Can Do About It*. Oneworld Publications, 2010.

Ellemers, Naomi, and Jolanda Jetten. "The Many Ways to Be Marginal in a Group." *Personality and Social Psychology Review, 17* (1), 2013:3–21.

Ellis, Havelock. "Mescal: A New Artificial Paradise." *Annual Report of the Smithsonian Institution, 52*, 1897:547–548.

Ellis, Markman. *Eighteenth-Century Coffee-House Culture: Restoration Satire*. New York: Routledge, 2006.

Ellison, Graham, and Ronald Weitzer. "Young Men Doing Business: Male Bar Prostitution in Berlin and Prague." *Sexualities*, June 26, 2017.

Ellison, Graham. "Drifters, Party Boys and Incumbents: The Life Patterns of Male Street-Based Sex Workers." *Sociology*, January 13, 2017.

Ellis, Havelock. "Mescal: A Study of a Divine Plant." *Popular Science Monthly, 61*, 1902:52–71.

Emschwiller, John R. "Nuclear Waste Site Repairs Progressing." *Wall Street Journal*, February 29, 2016.

Ender, Morten. "Mom Wore Combat Boots: An Autoethnography of a Military Sociologist." In Sarah Hampson, Udi Lebel, and Nancy Tabor (eds.) *Mothers, Military, and Society*. Bradford, Ontario, Canada: Demeter Press, 2018:158–187.

Eng, James. "Texas Begins Enforcing Strict Anti-Abortion Sonogram Law." *MSNBC News*, February 8, 2012.

Engelmayer, Paul A. "Violence by Students, from Rape to Racism, Raises College Worries." *Wall Street Journal*, November 21, 1983:1, 18.

Enns, Peter K. "Relative Policy Support and Coincidental Representation." *Perspectives on Politics, 13* (4), December 2015:1053–1064.

EPA (Environmental Protection Agency). "Acid Rain and Related Programs: 2008 Highlights." U.S. Environmental Protection Agency, Office of Air Quality Planning and Standards, 2009.

EPA (Environmental Protection Agency). "Advancing Sustainable Materials Management: 2015 Fact Sheet," July 2018e.

EPA (Environmental Protection Agency). "Air Quality—A National Summary," 2016a. Online.

EPA (Environmental Protection Agency). "Great Lakes Restoration Initiative 2015 Request for Applications," 2016e. Online.

EPA (Environmental Protection Agency). "Great Lakes," 2016d. Online.

EPA (Environmental Protection Agency). "Ozone Layer Protection," 2016b. Online.

EPA (Environmental Protection Agency). "Progress Cleaning the Air and Improving People's Health," 2016c. Online.

EPA (Environmental Protection Agency). "Superfund Enforcement: 35 Years of Protecting Communities and the Environment," 2015. Online.

EPA (Environmental Protection Agency). "Air Quality—National Summary." 2017a. Online.

EPA (Environmental Protection Agency). "Great Lakes Facts and Figures." 2018c. Online.

EPA (Environmental Protection Agency). "International Activities Related to Pesticides," 2016g. Online.

EPA (Environmental Protection Agency). "Invasive Species in the Great Lakes," 2016f. Online.

EPA (Environmental Protection Agency). "Invasive Species in the Great Lakes." 2018d. Online.

EPA (Environmental Protection Agency). "Ozone Layer Protection." 2018a. Online.

EPA (Environmental Protection Agency). "Progress Cleaning the Air and Improving People's Health." 2018b. Online.

Epstein, Cynthia Fuchs. "The Nature-Nurture Controversy: Biology Versus Culture: Culture Is the Answer." In James M. Henslin, *Essentials of Sociology: A Down-to-Earth Approach*, 9th ed. Boston: Allyn and Bacon, 2011.

Epstein, Cynthia Fuchs. Letter to the author, January 26, 1989.

Epstein, Joyce Levy. New York: *School, Family, and Community Partnerships: Preparing Educators and Improving Schools*. Routledge, 2018.

Epstein, Lee, and Thomas G. Walker. Constitutional Law for a Changing America: Rights, Liberties, and Justice, 10th ed. New York: Sage, 2019.

Escalante, Jaime, and Jack Dirmann. "The Jaime Escalante Math Program." *Journal of Negro Education*, 59 (3), Summer 1990:407–423.

Espenshade, Thomas J. "A Short History of U.S. Policy toward Illegal Immigration." *Population Today*, February 1990:6–9.

Espenshade, Thomas J., and Alexandria Walton Radford. *No Longer Separate, Not Yet Equal: Race and Class in Elite College Admission and Campus Life*. Princeton, NJ: Princeton University Press, 2009.

Espinoza, Javier. "Twice as Many Boys Start School 'Unable to Speak Properly,' Report Finds." *The Telegraph*, March 26, 2015.

Fabio, Anthony, Tu Li-Chuan, Rolf Loeber, and Jacqueline Cohen. "Neighborhood Socioeconomic Disadvantage and the Shape of the Age-Crime Curve." *American Journal of Public Health*, 101, S1, 2011:S325–S331.

"Facts about the Death Penalty." Washington, DC: Death Penalty Information Center, March 11, 2016.

"Facts about Sexual Harassment." U.S. Equal Opportunity Employment Commission." Online, 2016.

FAOSTAT. "Food Production: Food per Capita Net Production by Region." Food and Agricultural Statistics Division of the United Nations, 2015.

Farah, Douglas. "Central American Gangs Changing Nature and New Partners." *Journal of International Affairs*, 66 (1), Fall/Winter 2012:53–67.

Farah, Judy. "Crime and Creative Punishment." *Wall Street Journal*, March 15, 1995:A15.

Faris, R. E. L., and W. W. Dunham. *Mental Disorders in Urban Areas*. Chicago: University of Chicago Press, 1939.

Farley, Melissa. "Risks of Prostitution: When the Person Is the Product." *Journal of the Association for Consumer Research, 3* (1), January 2018.

Farley, Melissa, Nicole Matthews, Sarah Deer, et al. *Garden of Truth: The Prostitution and Trafficking of Native Women in Minnesota*.

Saint Paul, MN: William Mitchell College of Law, October 27, 2011.

Farmer, J. Forbes. "Inmate Rehabilitation Revisited: Using Goffman and Perrow to Explain Constraints on Transformational Technologies in Prison." *Journal of Social Science Studies*, 1 (2), 2014:198–223.

Farrell, Graham. "Five Tests for the Theory of the Crime Drop." *Crime Science*, 2, 5:2013.

Fauci, Anthony S., and Robert W. Eisinger. "PREPFAR—15 Years and Counting the Lives Saved." *New England Journal of Medicine*, January 25, 2018.

Faunce, William A. *Problems of an Industrial Society*, 2nd ed. New York: McGraw-Hill, 1981.

Faupel, Charles E., and Carl B. Klockars. "Drugs-Crime Connections: Elaborations from the Life Histories of Hard-Core Addicts." *Social Problems, 34* (1), February 1987:54–68.

FBI Uniform Crime Reports. Washington, DC: U.S. Government Printing Office, annual.

FBI. *Uniform Crime Reports: Crime in the United States*. Washington, DC: U.S. Government Printing Office, annual.

FBI. *2016 National Incident-Based Reporting System*. Washington, DC: U.S. Government Printing Office, 2017.

FDA (Federal Food and Drug Administration). "Color Additive Status List." December 2015.

Feldblum, Chai R., and Victoria A. Lipnic. Select Taskforce on the Study of Harassment in the Workplace. Washington, DC: U.S. Equal Opportunity Commission, June 2016.

Feldman, Noah. "The Legal Mess Where Religion Meets Health Care." *Chicago Tribune*, June 23, 2016.

Felker-Kantor, Max. "Politicizing Youth: Police, Politics, and Gangs in the Late-Twentieth Century." *Journal of Urban History*, 2018.

Fernandez, Humberto, and Therissa A. Libby. *Heroin: Its History, Pharmacology, and Treatment*, 2nd ed. Center City, MN: Hazelden Publishing, 2011.

Fernandez, Manny. "In Jury Selection for Hate Crime, a Struggle to Find Tolerance." *New York Times*, March 8, 2010a.

Fernandez, Manny. "Layers of Contradiction in L.I. Hate-Crime Trial." *New York Times*, March 26, 2010b.

Fernandez, Manny. "L.I. Man Gets 25-Year Term in Killing of Immigrant." *New York Times*, May 26, 2010c.

Ferris-Rotman, Amie. "Putin's Next Target Is Russia's Abortion Culture." *Foreign Policy*, October 3, 2017.

"Fetal Alcohol Spectrum Disorder Among Native Americans." U.S. Department of Health and Human Services: Substance Abuse and Mental Health Services Administration, 2007.

Finckenauer, James O. *Scared Straight and the Panacea Phenomenon*. Englewood Cliffs, NJ: Prentice Hall, 1982.

Finkelhor, David, and Kersti Yllo. *License to Rape: Sexual Abuse of Wives*. New York: Holt, 1985.

Finkelhor, David, and Kersti Yllo. "Marital Rape: The Myth versus the Reality." In *Marriage and Family in a Changing Society*, James M. Henslin, ed. New York: Free Press, 1989:382–391.

Fiscella, K., and M. R. Sanders. "Racial and Ethnic Disparities in the Quality of Health Care." *Annual Review of Public Health, 37,* January 18, 2016.

Fischer, David Hackett. *Growing Old in America: The Bland-Lee Lectures Delivered at Clark University*. New York: Oxford University Press, 1977.

Fish, Jefferson M. "Mixed Blood." *Psychology Today, 28*, 6, November–December 1995:55–58, 60, 61, 76, 80.

Fisher, Gordon M. "Setting American Standards of Poverty: A Look Back." *Focus, 19* (2), Spring 1988:47–52.

Fisher, Sue. *In the Patient's Best Interest: Women and the Politics of Medical Decisions*. New Brunswick, NJ: Rutgers University Press, 1986.

Fishman, Steve. "Bernie Madoff, Free at Last." *New York Magazine*, June 6, 2010.

Fisse, B., and J. Braithwaite. "The Impact of Publicity on Corporate Offenders: Ford Motor Company and the Pinto Papers." In *Corporate and Governmental Deviance: Problems of Organizational Behavior in Contemporary Society*, M.D. Ermann and R.J. Lundman, eds., 3rd ed. New York: Oxford University Press: 1987:244–262.

Flavin, Christopher. "Reassessing Nuclear Power." In *State of the World*, Lester R. Brown, ed. New York: Norton, 1987:57–80.

Flynn, Dan. "Report: Chicken on Menu at 2014 Food Safety Summit Was Contaminated." *Food Safety News*. September 25, 2014.

Foley, Douglas E. "The Great American Football Ritual." In *Society: Readings to Accompany Core Concepts*, James M. Henslin, ed. Boston: Allyn & Bacon, 2006:64–76. (Originally published 1990)

Foley, Meraiah. "Australia to Test Web Filter to Block Banned Content." *New York Times*, December 14, 2008.

Forero, Juan. "Bolivia's Knot: No to Cocaine, but Yes to Coca." *New York Times*, February 12, 2006.

Forliti, Amy. "New Legal Issue: Payment for Child Porn Victims." Associated Press, February 8, 2010.

"Former FBI Agent Arrested on Child Porn Charges." *The Indy Channel*, May 14, 2012.

Forsyth, Craig J., Gary Asmus, York A. Forsyth, Billy R. Stokes, and Mike Mayne. "Child Delinquents: Examining the Market for Criminal Futures." *Delinquent Behavior, 32* (5), 2011:441–450.

Forward, Susan, and Craig Buck. *Betrayal of Innocence: Incest and Its Devastation*. New York: Penguin, 1978.

Fountain, Henry. "Archaeological Site in Peru Is Called Oldest City in America." *New York Times*, April 27, 2001.

Fowler, L. *Breast Implants for Graduation? Parent and Adolescent Narratives*. Dissertation, University of North Texas, 2008.

Fox, John W. "Social Class, Mental Illness, and Social Mobility: The Social Selection-Drift Hypothesis for Serious Mental Illness." *Journal of Health and Social Behavior, 31* (4), December 1990:344–353.

Frail, T. A. "The Injustice of Japanese-American Internment Camps Resonates Strongly to this Day." *Smithsonian Magazine*, January 2017.

Frankel, Jeremy. "Crisis on the High Plains: The Loss of America's Largest Aquifer—the Ogallala." *University of Denver Water Law Review*, May 17, 2018.

Frantzman, Seth. "Israel Must Banish Ashkenazi-Mizrahi Stereotypes." *New York Times*, April 5, 2015.

Freed, Anne O. "How Japanese Families Cope with Fragile Elderly." In *Perspectives in Social Gerontology*, Robert B. Enright, Jr., ed. Boston: Allyn & Bacon, 1994:76–86.

Frey, George. "Ernst Zundel Released from German Prison." Associated Press, March 1, 2010.

Friedan, Betty. *The Feminine Mystique*. New York: Norton, 1963.

Friedl, Ernestine. "Society and Sex Roles." In *Conformity and Conflict: Readings in Cultural Anthropology*. James P. Spradley and David W. McCurdy, eds. Glenview, IL: Scott, Foresman, 1990: 229–238.

Friedman, Emily. "Oil Heir Peter Getty Embroiled in Nasty Divorce." ABC News, May 20, 2010.

Freidson, Eliot. *Patient's Views of Medical Practice*. New York: Russell Sage, 1961.

Fromm, Erich. *The Anatomy of Human Destructiveness*. New York: Holt, 1973.

Frost, Benjamin, Peggy Hazard, and Desi Kimmins. "The Real Gap: Fixing the Gender Pay Divide." Korn Ferry Hay Group, 2016.

Fry, Douglas P., Bruce D. Bonta, and Karoline Baszarkiewicz. "Learning from Extant Cultures of Peace." In Joseph de Rivera, ed. *Handbook on Building Cultures of Peace*. PLACE: Springer Sciences, 2009:11–26.

Fry, Douglas P., and Marta Miklikowska. "Culture of Peace." In *Psychological Components of Sustainable Peace*, Peter T. Coleman and Morton Deutsch, eds. New York: Springer, 2012:227–244.

Fukue, Natsuko. "Aging Japan Faces Dementia Time Bomb." *Japan Times*, June 6, 2017.

Gaard, Greta. "Ecofeminism." *Companion to Environmental Studies*, 2018:286–290.

Gabb, Jacqui, Martina Klett-Davies, Janet Fink, and Manuela Thomae. "Enduring Love? Couple Relationships in the 21st Century." Open University, 2013.

Galbraith, John Kenneth. *The Nature of Mass Poverty*. Cambridge, MA: Harvard University Press, 1979.

Galliher, John R., and Allyn Walker. "The Puzzle of the Social Origins of the Marihuana Tax Act of 1937." *Social Problems, 24*, February 1977:367–376.

Gallup Poll. "Abortion." May 8–11, 2014.

Gallup Poll. "Americans' Fear of Walking Alone Ties 52-Yar Low." November 2, 2017.

Gallup Poll. "In U.S., Women, Poor, Urbanites Most Fearful of Walking Alone." November 10, 2015.

Gallup Poll. "U.S. Death Penalty Support Stable at 63%." January 9, 2013.

Gallup Poll. "In Depth Topics A to Z: Gay and Lesbian Rights." 2016.

Ganahl, Dennis J., Thomas J. Prinsen, and Sara Baker Netzley. "A Content Analysis of Prime Time Commercials: A Contextual Framework of Gender Representation." *Sex Roles, 49* (9/10), November 2003: 545–551.

Ganesan, Kavitha, and Mark V. Pellegrini. "Anabolic Steroids." *StatPearls*, National Center for Biotechnology Information, February 24, 2018.

Gans, Herbert J. *People and Plans: Essays on Urban Problems and Solutions*. New York: Basic Books, 1968.

Gans, Herbert J. *The Urban Villagers*. New York: Free Press, 1962.

Gans, Herbert J. "The Uses of Poverty: The Poor Pay All." In *Down to Earth Sociology: Introductory Readings*, 15th ed., James M. Henslin, ed. New York: Free Press, 2014. (Originally published in *Social Policy*, July/August 1971:20–24)

Gans, Herbert J. "The Way We'll Live Soon." *Washington Post*, September 1, 1991:BW3.

Garbarino, Merwin S. *American Indian Heritage*. Boston: Little, Brown, 1976.

Garner, Rob. "Antarctic Sea Ice Reaches New Record Maximum." NASA, March 26, 2016.

Garrison, Jessica, Ben Poston, and Kim Christensen. "State Fails to Keep Track of Hazardous Waste." *Los Angeles Times*, November 16, 2013.

Gartner, Michael. "A Dream of Peace, the Reality of Never-Ending Wars." *Wall Street Journal*, December 22, 1988:A13.

Gasparro, Annie, and Jesse Newman. "Blue Bell Ice Cream Recall Is a Rare Step." *Wall Street Journal*, April 22, 2015.

Gatewood, Anne G., Kelly A. Liebman, Gwenael Vourc'h, et al. "Climate and Tick Seasonality Are Predictors of Borrelia burgdorferi Genotype Distribution." *Applied and Environmental Microbiology, 75* (8), April 2009:2476–2483.

Gay, Jill. "The 'Patriotic' Prostitute." *The Progressive*, February 1985:34–36.

Gelles, Richard I. "The Myth of Battered Husbands and New Facts About Family Violence." In *Social Problems*, Robert L. David, ed. Guilford, CT: Dushkin, 1980:80–81.

Gellhorn, Martha. *The Face of War*. New York: Simon & Schuster, 1959.

Gemme, Robert. "Prostitution: A Legal, Criminological, and Sexological Perspective." *Canadian Journal of Human Sexuality, 2* (4), Winter 1993: 227–237.

General Social Survey: National Opinion Research Center. GSS 1972–2010 cumulative data file, February 2012. Documentation and Analysis archive at the University of California.

George, Susannah, and Matthew Lee. "New Russia Sanctions over Poisoning of Former Spy, Daughter." *CTV News*, August 9, 2018.

Gerlin, Andrea. "Quirky Sentences Make Bad Guys Squirm." *Wall Street Journal*, August 4, 1994:B1, B2.

"German Court Rules Religious Circumcision an Assault on Boys." Associated Press, June 26, 2012.

Giardello, Mauro, and Hernan Cuervo. "The Formation of a Sense of Belonging: An Analysis of Young People's Lives in Australian and Italian Rural Communities." In *Interrogating Belonging for Young People in Schools*, Christine Halse, ed. New York: Palgrave Macmillan, 2018:203–224.

Gibbs, Nancy. "Affirmative Action for Boys." *Time*, April 3, 2008.

Gibbs, Nancy, and Amanda Bower. "Q: What Scares Doctors? A: Being the Patient." *Time*, May 1, 2006.

Gilens, Martin, and Benjamin Page. "Testing Theories of American Politics: Elites, Interest Groups, and Average Citizens." *Perspectives on Politics*, Fall 2014.

Gilham, Steven A. "The Marines Build Men: Resocialization in Recruit Training." In *The Sociological Outlook: A Text with Readings*, 2nd ed., Reid Luhman, ed. San Diego, CA: Collegiate Press, 1989: 232–244.

Gillespie, Nick. "What's So Bad About Casual Drug Use?" *Time*, November 21, 2013.

Gillies, Esther H. "The Witch-Hunt: Narrative Reflections on Knowledge About Child Sexual Abuse and the Impact of McMartin in the State of California." *Journal of Interpersonal Violence*, 32 (6), 2017.

Givord, Pauline, Simon Quantin, and Corentin Trevien. "A Long-Term Evaluation of the First Generation of French Urban Enterprise Zones." *Journal of Urban Economics, 105*, May 2018:149–161.

Glaser, Daniel. *Crime in Our Changing Society*. New York: Holt, 1978.

Gneezy, Uri, Kenneth L. Leonard, and John A. List. "Gender Differences in Competition: Evidence from a Matrilineal and a Patriarchal Society." *Econometrica, 77* (5), September 2009:1637–1664.

Goble, Paul. "Nearly a Third of All Pregnancies in Russia Still Ended by Abortions." *Interpreter Magazine*, August 25, 2014.

Goetting, Ann. *Getting Out: Life Stories of Women Who Left Abusive Men*. New York: Columbia University Press, 2001.

Goldberg, S., and Michael Lewis. "Play Behavior in the Year-Old Infant: Early Sex Differences." *Child Development, 40*, March 1969:21–31.

Goldberg, Steven. "The Nature–Nurture Controversy: Biology Versus Culture: Biology Is the Answer." In James M. Henslin, *Essentials of Sociology: A Down-to-Earth Approach*, 9th ed. Boston: Allyn and Bacon, 2011.

Goldman, Bruce. "Two Minds: The Cognitive Differences between Men and Women." *Stanford Medicine*, Spring 2017.

Goleman, Daniel. "Girls and Math: Is Biology Really Destiny?" *New York Times*, August 2, 1987:42–44, 46.

Goll, Sven. "Archaeologists Find Mini-Pompeii." *Views and News from Norway*, October 1, 2010.

Gomez, J. Alfredo. "Hazardous Waste Cleanup: Numbers of Contaminated Federal Sites, Estimated Costs, and EPA's Oversight Role." Testimony before the Subcommittee on Environment and the Economy, Committee on Energy and Commerce, House of Representatives, September 11, 2015.

Goode, Erich. *Drugs in American Society*, 3rd ed. New York: Knopf, 1989.

Gordon, Milton. *Assimilation in American Life*. New York: Oxford University Press, 1964.

Gore, Leanda. "Pride Flags Replace Military Flags at Indiana VA Hospital for a Day." *Stars and Stripes*, June 14, 2018.

Gorman, Dennis M., and J. Charles Huber, Jr. "The Social Construction of 'Evidence-Based' Drug Prevention Programs: A Reanalysis of Data From the Drug Abuse Resistance (DARE) Program." *Evaluation Review, 33* (4), 2009:396–414.

Gottfredson, Michael, and Travis Hirschi. *A General Theory of Crime*. Stanford, CA: Stanford University Press, 1990.

Goude, Andrew S. *Human Impact on the Natural Environment: Past, Present and Future*, 8th ed. New York: WileyBlackwell 2019.

"GPS Creates Global Jail." Online, April 8, 1998.

Graff, Amy. "Jazz Jennings New Children's Book Tells Transgender Story." ISFGate, September 22, 2014.

Grant, Igor, J. Hampton Atkinson, Andrew Mattison, and Thomas J. Coates. "Report to the Legislature and Governor of the State of California Presenting Findings Pursuant to SB847 Which Created the CMCR and Provided State Funding." Center for Medicinal Cannabis Research, University of California San Diego Health Sciences, February 11, 2010.

Green, Gary S. "White-Collar Crime and the Study of Embezzlement." *Annals of the American Academy of Political and Social Sciences, 525*, January 1993:95–106.

Greenberger, Robert S. "U.S., Russia Agree to Faster Timetable for Destruction of Nuclear Arsenals." *Wall Street Journal*, September 29, 1994:A22.

Griffith, G. T. *Population Problems of the Age of Malthus*. Cambridge: Cambridge University Press, 1926.

Grillo, Ioan. "The Other Border Problem: American Guns Going to Mexico." *New York Times*, April 12, 2018.

Grinspoon, Peter. "Medical Marijuana." *Harvard Health Blog*, January 15, 2018.

Grinspoon, Peter. "Up to 15% of Doctors Are Drug Addicts. I Was One of Them." *LA Times*, June 5, 2016.

Grosjean, Pauline. "A History of Violence: The Culture of Honor and Homicide in the US South." *Journal of the European Economic Association, 12* (5), October 2014:1285–1316.

Gua, David W. *Surviving Wounded Knee: The Lakotas and the Politics of Memory*. New York: Oxford University Press, 2016.

"'Guardians of the Amazon' Seize Illegal Loggers to Protect Uncontacted Tribes," May 22, 2018. https://www.survivalinternational.org/news/11961

Guerino, Paul, Paige M. Harrison, and William J. Sabol. "Prisoners in 2010." Bureau of Justice Statistics, December 2011.

Guidry, Virginia. "May Is Asthma Awareness Month and NIEHS Highlights Research." National Institute of Environmental Health Sciences, May 2016.

Guo, Jeff. "If You're Poor, Your Mortgage Rate Can Depend on the Color of Your Skin." *Washington Post*, December 23, 2014.

Gupta, Charu, Dhan Prakash, and Sneh Gupta. "Microbes: 'A Tribute' to Clean Environment." *Paradigms in Pollution Prevention*. New York: Springer, 2018:17–34.

Gupta, Jyotsna Agnihotri. "Reprogenetic Technologies: From Desired Babies to Designer Babis." Paper presented at the International Academic Forum at Heidelberg University, September 2017.

Gupta, Sanjay. "Dr. Sanjay Gupta on Combating Medical Errors." CBS News, March 11, 2012.

Gupta-Carlson, Himanee. *Muncie, India(na): Middletown and Asian American*. Urbana: University of Illinois Press, 2018.

Gusfield, Joseph R. *Symbolic Crusade: Status Politics and the American Temperance Movement*. Urbana: University of Illinois Press, 1963.

Guttmacher Institute. "Abortion Policy in the Absence of *Roe*." available online.

Haas, Jack, and William Shaffir. "The Cloak of Competence." In *Down-to-Earth Sociology: Introductory Readings*, 7th ed., James M. Henslin, ed. New York: Free Press, 1993.

Haas, Jeffrey. *The Assassination of Fred Hampton by the FBI and the Chicago Police: Forty Years Later*. Chicago: Lawrence Hill Books, 2009.

Hacker, Helen Mayer. "Women as a Minority Group." Social Forces, 30, October 1951:60–69.

Hagedorn, John M. "The Global Impact of Gangs." *Journal of Contemporary Criminal Justice, 21* (2), May 2005:153–169.

Hall, Susan. *Gentleman of Leisure: A Year in the Life of a Pimp*. New York: New American Library, 1972.

Hamby, Chris. "A Century of Denial on Black Lung." The Center for Public Integrity, May 19, 2014.

Hamdan, Ashraf H. "Neonatal Abstinence Syndrome." *Emedicine Pediatrics*, March 3, 2010:1–25.

Hamilton, Mykol C., David Anderson, Michelle Broaddus, and Kate Young. "Gender Stereotyping and Under-representation of Female Characters in 200 Popular Children's Picture Books: A Twenty-first Century Update." *Sex Roles, 55*, 2006:757–765.

Handbook on Women Workers 1969. Washington, DC: U.S. Dept. of Labor, Women's Bureau, 1969.

Hans, Jason D., Martie Gillen, and Katrina Akande. "Sex Redefined: The Reclassification of Oral-Genital Contact." *Perspectives on Sexual and Reproductive Health*, June 2010.

Hansen, Arve. "Doing Urban Development Fieldwork: Motorbike Ethnography in Hanoi." *Sage Research Methods Cases,* 2018.

Hanson, David J. *Preventing Alcohol Abuse: Alcohol, Culture, and Control.* Westport, CT: Praeger, 1995.

Hardeman, Rachel R., Eduardo M. Medina, and Katy B. Kozhimannil. *New England Journal of Medicine, 375,* December 1, 2016:2113–2115.

Hardin, Garrett. "The Tragedy of the Commons." *Science, 162,* December 1968:1243–1248.

Harding, David, Michele Lamont, and Mario Luis Small, eds. *Reconsidering Culture and Poverty,* The Annals of the American Academy of Political and Social Science, *629,* June 2010.

Hari, Johann. "Forbidden Love." *The Guardian,* January 9, 2002.

Harrington, Charlene, Helen Carrillo, et al. *Nursing Home Facilities, Staffing, Residents and Facility Deficiencies, 2005 Through 2010.* San Francisco: University of California, October 2011.

Harrington, Michael. *The Vast Majority: A Journey to the World's Poor.* New York: Simon & Schuster, 1977.

Harris, Dan, Adam Desiderio, Jenna Millman, and Lauren Effron. "In El Salvador, the Murder Capital of the World, Gang Violence Becomes a Way of Life." *ABC News,* May 17, 2016.

Harris, Diana K., and Michael L. Benson. *Maltreatment of Patients in Nursing Homes: There Is No Safe Place.* New York: Haworth Pastoral Press, 2006.

Harris, Marvin. "Why Men Dominate Women." *New York Times Magazine,* November 13, 1977:46, 115, 117, 123.

Harrison, Wayne. *"Man Convicted in Brutal '97 Sexual Attack, Attempted Murder of Teenager in Denver." The Denver Channel,* April 8, 2015.

Hart, C. W. M., and Arnold R. Pilling. *The Tiwi of North Australia, Fieldwork Edition.* New York: Holt, Rinehart and Winston, 1979.

Hart, Carl L., and Charles J. Ksir. *Drugs, Society, and Human Behavior,* 17th ed. New York: McGraw-Hill, 2018.

Hart, Carl L., and Charles Ksir. *Drugs, Society, and Human Behavior,* 14th ed. New York: McGraw-Hill, 2011.

Hart, Hornell. "Acceleration in Social Change." In *Technology and Social Change,* Francis R. Allen, Hornell Hart, Delbert C. Miller, William F. Ogburn, and Meyer F. Nimkoff, eds. New York: Appleton, 1957.

Hartocollis, Anemoa. "Asian-Americans Suing Harvard Say Admissions Files Show Discrimination." *New York Times,* April 4, 2018.

Hartsig, Andrew, and Chris Robbins. "Exxon Valdez: 29 Years Later." *Ocean Conservancy,* March 22, 2018.

Haseeb, Sohaib, Bryce Alexander, and Adrian Baranchuk. "Wine and Cardiovascular Health." *Circulation 136* (15), October 9, 2017:1434–1448.

Haub, Carl, and Toshiko Kaneda. "World Population Data Sheet." Washington, DC: Population Reference Bureau, 2012.

Hauser, Philip, and Leo Schnore, eds. *The Study of Urbanization.* New York: Wiley, 1965.

Haveman, Robert H., and John Karl Scholz. "The Clinton Welfare Reform Plan: Will It End Poverty as We Know It?" *Focus, 16* (2), Winter 1994–95:1–11.

Hawkins, D. N., Amato, P. R., King, V. "Nonresident Father Involvement and Adolescent Well-Being: Father Effects or Child Effects?" *American Sociological Review, 72* (6), 2007: 990–1010.

Hayes, Arthur S. "How the Courts Define Harassment." *Wall Street Journal,* October 11, 1991:B1, B3.

Healthcare Blue Book, online, July 18, 2016.

HealthGrades. "Eighth Annual Patient Safety in American Hospitals Study." March 2011.

Heather, Nick, David Best, Anna Kawalek, et al. "Challenging the Brain Disease Model of Addiction: European Launch of the Addiction Theory Network." *Addiction Research and Theory,* November 2017.

Heins, Marjorie. "The War on Nudity, Continued." *Playboy,* November 1991:53.

Held, Colbert. *Middle East Patterns: Places, People, and Politics,* 6th ed. New York: Routledge, 2018.

Helm, Toby. "UK Must Be Involved in EU Anti-Terrorism Measures, Says Keith Vaz." *The Guardian,* July 23, 2016.

Helmer, J. *Drugs and Minority Oppression.* New York: Seabury, 1975.

Hendren, John. "3 Nursing Home Patients Killed by 'Chemical Restraints.'" ABC World News online. January 5, 2010.

Henn, Steve, and Jess Jiang. "A 12-Year-Old Girl Takes on the Video Game Industry." National Public Radio, April 8, 2015.

Henriques, Fernando. *Prostitution and Society.* New York: Grove, 1966.

Henry, Cole. "Feminist Frequency Breaks Down Gender Representations in Videogames at 3 2018." *Paste,* June 14, 2018.

Henslin, James M. *Essentials of Sociology: A Down-to-Earth Approach,* 12th ed. Boston: Allyn and Bacon, 2017.

Henslin, James M. *Sociology: A Down-to-Earth Approach,* 10th ed. Boston: Allyn and Bacon, 2010.

Henslin, James M. *Sociology: A Down-to-Earth Approach,* 14th ed. Hoboken, NJ: Pearson Publishing, 2018.

Hentges, Beth, and Kim Case. "Gender Representations on Disney Channel, Cartoon Network, and Nickelodean Broadcasts in the United States." *Journal of Children and Media, 7* (3), 2013.

Herbeck, Dan. "Exclusive: Are Love Canal Chemicals Still Making People Sick?" June 1, 2018.

Herbert, Bob. "Don't Flunk the Future." *New York Times,* August 13, 1998.

Herbert, Bob. "The Hate Virus." *New York Times,* August 10, 1988.

Hernandez, Vittorio. "Thousands May End in Jail as Law Enforcers Process Rape Kit Results." *International Business Times,* June 1, 2015.

Hertsgaard, Mark. "Bhopal's Legacy." *The Nation,* May 24, 2004.

Hibbert, Christopher. *The Roots of Evil: A Social History of Crime and Punishment.* New York: Minerva, 1963.

Hilman, Nick, and Nicholas Robinson. *Boys to Men: The Underachievement of Young Men in Higher Education—and How to Start Tackling It.* HEPI Report 84. Oxford, UK: Higher Education Policy Institute, 2016.

Hiltz, Starr Roxanne. "Widowhood." In *Marriage and Family in a Changing Society,* James M. Henslin, ed. New York: Free Press, 1989:521–531.

Himmelhoch, Jerome, and Sylvia Fleis Fava (eds.). *Sexual Behavior in American Society: An Appraisal of the First Two Kinsey Reports.* New York: Norton, 1955.

Himes, Christine L. "Elderly Americans." *Population Bulletin, 56* (1), December 2001:1–40.

Hinckley, David. "'White Collar Criminals' Review: CNBC Documentary Finds Prison Can Be Different for the Ultra-Wealthy." *New York Daily News,* April 29, 2015.

Hinshaw, Stephen P., and Richard M. Scheffler. *The ADHD Explosion: Myths, Medication, Money, and Today's Push for Performance.* New York: Oxford University Press, 2014.

Hirschi, Travis. *Causes of Delinquency.* Berkeley: University of California Press, 1969.

Hodgson, James F. *Games Pimps Play: Pimps, Players and Wives-in-Law.* Toronto: Canadian Scholars' Press, 1997.

Hoekstra, Arjen Y. "Global Food and Trade Dimensions of Groundwater Governance." In *Advances in Groundwater Governance.* Karen G. Villholth, Elena López-Gunn, Kirstin Conti, and Alberto Garrido, eds. New York: CRC Press, 2018:353–366.

Hoffman, Albert. "Psychotomimetic Agents." In *Drugs Affecting the Central Nervous System* (vol. 2). New York: Marcel Dekker, 1968.

Holbrook, Troy Lisa, Michael R. Galarneau, Judy L. Dye, Kimberly Quinn, and Amber L. Dougherty. "Morphine Use after Combat Injury in Iraq and Post-Traumatic Stress Disorder." *New England Journal of Medicine, 362* (2), January 14, 2010.

Holm, Erik, and Ulrike Dauer. "Insurer Hired Prostitutes." *Wall Street Journal,* May 19, 2011.

Homblin, Dora Jane. *The First Cities.* Boston: Little, Brown, Time-Life Books, 1973.

Homeland Security. *2016 Yearbook of Immigration Statistics,* November 30, 2017.

Hope, Christine A., and Ronald G. Stover. "Gender Status, Monotheism, and Social Complexity." *Social Forces, 65,* 1987:1132–1138.

Hopper, Briallen." Relying on Friendship in a World Made for Couples." *The Cut*, February 26, 2016.

Horning, Amber, and Anthony Marcus, eds. *Third Party Sex Work and Pimps in the Age of Anti-Trafficking*. Cham, Switzerland: Springer, 2017.

Horowitz, Ruth. *Honor and the American Dream: Culture and Identity in a Chicano Community*. New Brunswick, NJ: Rutgers University Press, 1983.

"Horror as Nine Bodies Found Hanged from Bridge and 14 Heads Decapitated and Dumped Along U.S. Border in Mexico." *Associated Press*, May 4, 2012.

Hosenball, Mark. "A Plutonium Mystery." *Newsweek*, May 3, 1999:62–64.

Hotz, Robert Lee. "Early Humans' Fire Use Linked to Extinctions." *Los Angeles Times*, January 8, 1999.

Hsin, Amy, and Yu Xie. "Explaining Asian Americans' Academic Advantage over Whites." *Proceedings of the National Advancement of Science*, 111 (23), 2014:8416–8421.

Huber, Joan. "Micro-Macro Links in Gender Stratification." *American Sociological Review, 55*, February 1990:1–10.

Huff, Aimee Dinnin. "Buying the Girlfriend Experience: A Exploration of the Consumption Experiences of Male Customers of Escorts." *Research in Consumer Behavior, 13*, 2011:111–126.

Huggins, Martha K., Mika Haritos-Fatouros, and Philip G. Zimbardo. *Violence Workers: Police Torturers and Murderers Reconstruct Brazilian Atrocities*. Berkeley: University of California Press, 2002.

Hull, Jon D. "Life and Death with the Gangs." *Time*, August 24, 1987.

Human Rights Watch. *"They Want Docile": How Nursing Homes in the United States Overmedicate People with Dementia*. February 2018.

Humphreys, Laud. *Tearoom Trade*. Chicago: Aldine, 1970. (Expanded version, Chicago: Aldine-Atherton, 1975.)

Huo, Meng, Jamie L. Graham, Kyungmin, et al. "Aging Parents' Disabilities and Daily Support Exchanges with Middle-Aged Children." *The Gerontologist*, September 23, 2017.

Hurdle, John. "Philadelphia Struggles to Quell an Epidemic of Gun Violence." *New York Times*, April 16, 2007.

Hurley, Amanda Kolson. "The Height of Efficiency." *The Atlantic*, January–February 2016.

Huxley, Aldous. *The Doors of Perception*. New York: Harper & Row, 1954.

Hyra, Derek S. "Racial Uplift? Intra-Racial Class Conflict and the Economic Revitalization of Harlem and Bronzeville." *City and Community, 5* (1), March 2006:71–92.

Ibrahim, Said A. "Racial Variations in the Utilization of Knee and Hip Joint Replacement: An Introduction and Review of the Most Recent Literature." *Current Orthopedic Practice, 21* (2), March–April 2010:126–131.

"Illegal Abortions Racket in Hospital Unearthed." *The Hindu*, February 3, 2018.

Inciardi, James A. *The War on Drugs: Heroin, Cocaine, Crime, and Public Policy*. Mountain View, CA: Mayfield, 1986.

Ingalhalikar, Madhura, Alex Smith, Drew Parker, et al. "Sex Differences in the Structural Connectome of the Human Brain." *Proceedings of the National Academy of Sciences, 111*, January 14, 2014:823–828.

Ingersoll, Bruce. "Faster Slaughter Lines Are Contaminating Much U.S. Poultry." *Wall Street Journal*, November 16, 1990:A1, A6.

Ingraham, Christopher. "Study: Teens Who Smoke Weed Daily Are 60% Less Likely to Complete High School Than Those Who Never Use." *Washington Post*, September 9, 2014.

Internal Revenue Service. "10 Facts about the Child Tax Credit." 2013.

Internal Revenue Service. "2018 EITC Income Limits, Maximum Credit Amounts and Tax Law Updates." April 23, 2018.

Internal Revenue Service. "What You Need to Know About the Child and Dependent Care Tax." March 9, 2016.

Inter-Parliamentary Union. "Women in National Parliaments." April 1, 2016.

Inter-Parliamentary Union. "Women in Parliament in 2017." March 2, 2018.

"Iraq Coalition Military Fatalities by Year." Icasualties.org, August 13, 2018.

"Iraq Coalition Military Fatalities by Year." icasualties.org, 2016.

Isbell, Harris. "Historical Development of Attitudes Toward Opiate Addiction in the United States." In *Man and Civilization: Conflict, and Creativity*, Seymour M. Farber and Roger H. L. Wilson, eds. New York: McGraw-Hill, 1969:154–170.

Iwersen, Sonke. "Ergo on Trial over Sex Parties." *Handelsblatt*, 2016.

Izaak Walton League of America, 2018. https://www.iwla.org/conservation/water/clean-water-challenge

Jacob, Brian A., and Jens Ludwig. "Improving Educational Outcomes for Poor Children." *Focus, 26* (2), Fall 2009:56–61.

Jacobs, Elizabeth T., Jeffrey L. Burgess, and Mark B. Abbott. "The Donora Smog Revisited: 70 Years After the Event That Inspired the Clean Air Act." *American Journal of Public Health*, April 2018.

Jacobs, Jane. *Dark Age Ahead*. New York: Random House, 2004.

Jaffe, Ina, and Robert Benincasa. "Old and Overmedicated: The Real Drug Problem in Nursing Homes." NPR, December 8, 2014.

Jaffe, Jerome H. "Drug Addiction and Drug Abuse." In *The Pharmacological Basis of Therapeutics*, Louis S. Goodman and Alfred Gilmann, eds. New York: Macmillan, 1965:285–311.

James, Susan Donaldson. "Love Canal's Lethal Legacy Persists." ABC News, August 11, 2008.

"Japan Population Drops for Third Year Straight; 25% Are Elderly." *Japan Times News*, April 15, 2014.

Japsen, Bruce. "Physician Assistants Moving into Specialties amid Doctor Shortage." *Forbes*, July 14, 2016.

Jatlaoui, Tara C., Jill Shah, Michelle G. Mandel, et al. "Abortion Surveillance—United States, 2014." *Morbidity and Mortality Weekly Report, 66* (24), November 24, 2017:1–48.

Jauhar, Sandeep. "Our Ailing Medical System." *Wall Street Journal*, August 30–31, 2014.

Jekielek, Susan M. "Parental Conflict, Marital Disruption and Children's Emotional Well-Being." *Social Forces, 76* (3), March 1998:905–935.

Jennings, Marianne M., and Lawrence J. Trautman. "Ethical Culture and Legal Liability: The GM Switch Crisis and Lessons in Governance." *22 Boston University Journal of Science and Technology Law*, 2016.

Jensen, Richard Bach. "The Rise and Fall of the 'Social Crime' in Legal Theory and International Law: The Failure to Create a New Normative Order to Regularize Terrorism, 1880–1930s." Max Planck Institute for European Legal History Research Paper Series No. 2018-02, January 2018.

Jha, Prabhat, Maya A. Kesler, Rajesh Kumar, et al. "Trends in Selective Abortions of Girls in India: Analysis of Nationally Representative Birth Histories from 1990 to 2005 and Census Data from 1991 to 2011." *The Lancet, 377*, June 4, 2011:1921–1928.

Joffe, Carole E. *Friendly Intruders: Child Care Professionals and Family Life*. Berkeley: University of California Press, 1977.

Johannes, Laura. "On the Heels of AARP." *Wall Street Journal*, March 31, 2014.

Johnson, Bruce D., Paul J. Goldstein, Edward Preble, et al. *Taking Care of Business: The Economics of Crime by Heroin Abusers*. Lexington, MA: Lexington Books, 1985.

Johnston, Lloyd D., Patrick M. O'Malley, Richard A. Miech, Jerald G. Bachman, and John E. Schulenberg. *Monitoring the Future: National Survey Results on Drug Use, 1975–2015. Overview, Key Findings on Adolescent Drug Use*. Ann Arbor: Institute for Social Research, the University of Michigan, 2016.

Johnston, Lloyd D., Richard A. Miech, Patrick M. O'Malley, Jerald G. Bachman, John E. Schulenberg, and Megan E. Patrick. *Monitoring the Future: National Survey Results on Drug Use, 1975–2017. Overview, Key Findings on Adolescent Drug Use*. Ann Arbor: Institute for Social Research, the University of Michigan, 2018.

Jones, Rachel K., and Jenna Jerman. "Abortion Incidence and Service Availability in the United States, 2014." *Perspectives on Sexual and Reproductive Health, 49* (1), 2017.

Josephy, Alvin M., Jr. "Indians in History." *Atlantic Monthly*, June 1970:67–72.

Kacen, Jacqueline J. "Advertising Effectiveness." New York: Wiley International Encyclopedia of Marketing, 2011.

Kalayjian, Tro. "Investment Opportunities in Women's Health." Seeking Alpha (online), June 4, 2010.

Kaneda, Toshiko, and Genevieve Dupuis. "World Population Data Sheet." Population Reference Bureau, August 2017.

Kaplan, Sidney. "Historical Efforts to Encourage White-Indian Intermarriage in the United States and Canada." *International Social Science Review*, 65 (3), Summer 1990: 126–132.

Karacor, Elif, and Berfin Senik. "Understanding Sense of Community through Neighborhood Satisfaction and Socio-Demographic Variables." International Journal of Humanities and Cultural Studies, 3, 2, 2016.

Kareiva, Peter, and Valerie Carranza. "Existential Risk Due to Ecosystem Collapse: Nature Strikes Back." *Futures*, January 2018.

Karmen, Andrew. "The Narcotics Problem: Views from the Left." In *Is America Possible? Social Problems from Conservative, Liberal, and Socialist Perspectives*, 2nd ed., Henry Etzkowitz, ed. St. Paul, MN: West, 1980:171–180.

Karnitschnig, Matthew. "Germany's Expensive Energy Gamble." *Wall Street Journal*, August 27, 2014.

Katz, Josh. "First Count of Fentanyl Deaths in 2016." *New York Times*, September 2, 2017.

Keag, Oonagh E., Jane E. Norman, and Sarah J. Stock. "Long-Term Risks and Benefits Associated with Cesarean Delivery for Mother, Baby, and Subsequent Pregnancies: Systematic Review and Meta-Analysis." *PloS Medicine*, 15 (1), January 23, 2018.

Keller, Christoph. "The Hip and Hop of Civilisation." Quadrant, 62 (1/2), Jan/Feb 2018:102–103.

Kelley, Tina. "In an Era of School Shootings, a New Drill." *New York Times*, March 25, 2008.

Kelly, Erin, Shane Darke, and Joanne Ross. "A Review of Drug Use and Driving Epidemiology, Impairment, Risk Factors ad Risk Perceptions." *Drug and Alcohol Review*, 23, 2004:319–344.

Kelly, Guy. "The Scary Effects of Pornography: How the 21st Century's Acute Addiction is Rewiring Our Brains." *The Telegraph*, September 11, 2017.

Kendall, Brent, Stephanie Armour, and Louise Radnofsky. "Supreme Court Invalidates State Law on Abortion Clinic Buffer Zones." *Wall Street Journal*, June 26, 2014.

Kepner, Tyler. "McGwire Admits That He Used Steroids." *New York Times*, January 12, 2010.

Keyes, Ken, Jr. *The Hundredth Monkey*. St. Mary, KY: Vision Books, n.d.

Khan, Shehar Bano, and Shirin Gul. "The Criminalisation of Rape in Pakistan." Chr. Michelsen Institute working paper number 8, September 2017.

"Kids Count Data Book: State Trends in Child Well-Being." Baltimore, MD: Annie E. Casey Foundation, 2015.

"Kids Count Data Center: Children in Single-Parent Families by State." Baltimore, MD: Annie E. Casey Foundation, 2018.

Kidwell, D M., J. C. Dietrich, et al. "An Earth's Future: Impacts of the Coastal Dynamics of Sea Level Rise on Low Gradient Coastal Landscapes." *Earth's Future*, December 12, 2016.

Kilman, Scott. "Seed Firms Bolster Crops Using Traits of Distant Relatives." *Wall Street Journal*, October 31, 2006.

Kim, Do-Hyung, Joseph O. Sexton, and John R. Townsend. "Accelerated Deforestation in the Humid Tropics from the 1990s to the 2000s." *Geophysical Research Letters*, May 7, 2015.

Kim, Hyun, Robin Herbert, Philip Landrigan, et al. "Increased Rates of Asthma among World Trade Center Disaster Responders." *American Journal of Industrial Medicine*, 55, 2012:44–53.

Kincel, Brian. "The Centenarian Population: 2007–2011." Washington, DC: U.S. Census Bureau, The Community Survey Briefs, April 2014.

King, Martin Luther, Jr. *Stride Toward Freedom: The Montgomery Story*. New York: Harper, 1958.

Kingston, S., N. Hammond, and S. Redman. *Women Who Buy Sex*. London: Routledge, 2018.

Kinsey, Alfred C., Wardell B. Pomeroy, Clyde E. Mantin, and Paul H. Gebhard. *Sexual Behavior in the Human Female*. New York: Saunders, 1953.

Kirkey, Sharon. "More Women Requesting Caesarean Birth." *Ottawa Citizen*, April 6, 2016.

Kirkpatrick, Melanie. "On the Abortion Barricades." *Wall Street Journal*, April 23, 1992:A14.

Kissinger, Henry. "Henry Kissinger on the Assembly of a New World Order." *Wall Street Journal*, August 29, 2014.

Kitano, Harry H. L. *Race Relations*. Englewood Cliffs, NJ: Prentice Hall, 1974.

Kitroeff, Natalie, and Jonathan Rodkin. "Women's Career Choices Don't Explain the Gender Pay Gap." *Bloomberg*, November 14, 2014.

Kivijarv, Leo. "Time Spent with Advertising Daily." *Research Intelligencer*, April 2, 2018.

Klein, Stephen, Joan Petersilia, and Susan Turner. "Race and Imprisonment Decisions in California." *Science*, 247 (4944), February 16, 1990:812–816.

Kleinfeld, Judith S. "Gender and Myth: Data about Student Performance." In *Through the Eyes of Social Science*, 6th ed., Frank Zulke and Jacqueline P. Kirley, eds. Prospect Heights, IL: Waveland Press, 2002a:380–393.

Kleinman, Paul H., Eric D. Wish, Shreey Deren, Gregory Rainone, and Ellen Morehouse. "Daily Marijuana Use and Problem Behaviors Among Adolescents." *International Journal of the Addictions*, 22 (12), 1987.

Knights, Roger. "Electronic Tagging in Practice." *Teleconnect*, January 22, 1999.

Knox, Michael. *Crime Scene Behaviors of Rampage School Shooters*. Doctoral dissertation. Department of Justice and Human Services, Nova Southeastern University, 2018.

Kochhar, Rakesh, and Richard Fry. "Wealth Inequality Has Widened Along Racial, Ethnic Lines Since End of Great Recession." Washington, DC: Pew Research Center, December 12, 2014.

Kohler, Lindsay N., David O. Garcia, Robin B. Harris, et al. "Adherence to Diet and Physical Activity: Cancer Prevention Guidelines and Cancer Outcomes: A Systematic Review." *Cancer Epidemiology, Biomarkers & Prevention*, June 23, 2016.

Kohn, Alfie. "Make Love, Not War." *Psychology Today*, June 1988:35–38.

Kornhauser, William. "'Power Elite' or 'Veto Groups'?" In *Culture and Social Character*, Seymour Martin Lipset and Leo Lowenthal, eds. Glencoe, IL: Free Press, 1961:252–267.

Korosec, Kirsten. "Ten Times More Deaths Linked to Faulty Switch Than GM First Reported." *Fortune*, August 24, 2015.

Kragen, Pam. "World's First Talking Sex Robot Is Ready for Her Close-Up." *San Diego Union-Tribune*, September 13, 2017.

Krapp, Fiorella, Egan A. Ozer, et al. "Case Report of an Extensively Drug-Resistant Klebsiella Pneumoniae Infection with Genomic Characterization of the Strain and Review of Similar Cases in the United States." Open Forum Infectious Diseases, 5 (5), May 2018.

Kravets, David. "U.S. Manga Obscenity Conviction Roils Comics World." *Wired*, May 28, 2009.

Kravitz, Derek. "Harlem's Mount Morris Park Sees More Change." *Wall Street Journal*, January 30, 2014.

Kriel, Lomi. "Anti-Illegal Immigration Groups Surge on Border." *Houston Chronicle*, January 5, 2015.

Krienert, J. L., and J. A. Walsh. "An Examination of Intimate Partner Violence: Comparing Marital and Nonmarital Incidents."

Krienert, Jessie L., and Jeffrey A. Walsh. "Characteristics and Perceptions of Child Sexual Abuse." *Journal of Child Sexual Abuse*, 20, 2011:353–372.

Kristof, Nicholas. "Drug Dealers in Lab Coats." *New York Times*, October 18, 2017.

Kristoff, Nicholas D. "Interview with a Humanoid." *New York Times*, July 23, 2002.

Kteily, Nour S., and Emile Bruneau. "Darker Demons of Our Nature: The Need to (Re)Focus Attention on Blatant Forms of Dehumanization." *Current Directions in Psychological Science*, 26(6), 2017.

Kuklina, Elena V., Susan F. Meikle, Dinise J. Jamieson, et al. "Severe Obstetric Morbidity in the United States." *Obstetrics and Gynecology*, 113 (2), February 2009:293–299.

Kumar, Jitendra, Meghan Pradhan, and Niti Singh. "Sustainable Organic Farming in Sikkim: An Inclusive Perspective." In *Advances in Smart Grid and Renewable Energy*, New York: Springer, 2018.

Kuol, Tito. "Looking Downstream: The Future of Nile Water Politics." *Harvard Political Review*, April 3, 2018.

Kurth, James R. "American Military Policy and Advanced Weapons." In *Social Problems and Public Policy: Inequality and Justice*, Lee Rainwater, ed. Chicago, IL: Aldine, 1974:336–352.

Kushi, Lawrence H., Colleen Doyle, Marji McCullough, et al. "Reducing the Risk of Cancer with Healthy Foods and Physical Activity." *CA: A Cancer Journal for Clinicians, 62* (1), January–February 2012:30–67.

Kutchinsky, Berl. "The Effects of Easy Availability of Pornography on the Incidence of Sex Crimes in Copenhagen: The Danish Experience." *Journal of Social Issues, 29*, 1973:163–181.

La Barre, Weston. *The Human Animal*. Chicago: University of Chicago Press, 1954.

LaBastille, Anne. "The Deadly Toll of Acid Rain: All of Nature Is Suffering." *Science Digest, 86*, October 1979:61–66.

Lacayo, Richard. "Crusading Against the Pro-Choice Movement." *Time*, October 21, 1991.

LaFree, Gary D. "The Effect of Sexual Stratification by Race on Official Reactions to Rape." *American Sociological Review, 45*, October 1980:842–854.

Lahr, M. Mirazon, F. Rivera, R. K. Power, et al. "Inter-Group Violence among Holocene Hunter-Gatherers of West Turkana, Kenya." *Nature, 529*, January 21, 2016:394–398.

Lally, Robin. "Experimental Antibiotic Treats Deadly MRSA Infection." *Science News*, June 13, 2016.

Lalumiere, Martin L., Grant T. Harris, Vernon L. Quinsey, and Marnie E. Rice. "The Causes of Rape: Understanding Individual Differences in Male Propensity for Sexual Aggression." Washington, DC: *American Psychological Association*, 2005.

Lambert, Bruce. "Manufacturer in $2 Million Accord With U.S. on Deficient Kevlar in Military Helmets." *Wall Street Journal*, February 6, 2008.

Lamberti, Rob. "Ontario Child-Porn Raids Net 55 Arrests." *Toronto Sun*, February 2, 2012.

Landgren, Ola, Rachel Zeig-Owen, Orsolya Giricz, et al. "Multiple Myeloma and Its Precursor Disease among Firefighters Exposed to the World Trade Center Disaster." *Journal of the American Medical Association Oncology, 4* (6), June 2018:821–827.

Lange, Shannon, Jurgen Rehm, and Svetlana Popova. "Implications of Higher Than Expected Prevalence of Fetal Alcohol Spectrum Disorders." *Journal of the American Medical Association, 319* (5), 2018.

Laqueur, Walter. *Terrorism*. Boston: Little, Brown, 1977.

Larned, Deborah. "The Epidemic in Unnecessary Hysterectomies." In *Seizing Our Bodies: The Politics of Women's Health*, Claudia Dreyfus, ed. New York: Random House, 1977.

Larson, Mary Strom. "Interactions, Activities and Gender in Children's Television Commercials: A Content Analysis." *Journal of Broadcasting and Electronic Media, 45*, Winter 2001:41–51.

"Las tabacaleras cortejan a las mujeres jovenes." Associated Press, AOL Noticias, May 27, 2010.

Lasch, Christopher. *Haven in a Heartless World: The Family Besieged*. New York: Basic Books, 1977.

Laslett, Barbara. "Family, Social Change Can Often Spell Trouble." University of California, University Extension, Course by Newspaper, San Diego, 1980.

Lathan, Jonathan R. "Growing Doubt: A Scientist's Experience of GMOs." *The Event Chronicle*, October 13, 2015.

Laumann, Edward O., John H. Gagnon, Robert T. Michael, and Stuart Michaels. *The Social Organization of Sexuality: Sexual Practices in the United States*. Chicago: University of Chicago Press, 1994.

Lauritsen, Janet, and Nicole White. "Seasonal Patterns in Criminal Victimization Trends." Bureau of Justice Statistics, June 2014.

Lauzen, Martha M. "Boxed in 2016–2017: Women on Screen and Behind the Scenes in Television." San Diego State University: Center for the Study of Women in Television & Film, September 2017.

Leavitt, Gregory C. "Tyler versus Westermarck: Explaining the Incest Taboo." *Sociology Mind, 13* (1), 2013:45–51.

Lee, Dorothy. *Freedom and Culture*. Englewood Cliffs, NJ: Prentice Hall, 1959.

Lee, Lois. "Communication to the author." March 20, 2019.

Lee, Soo Yeun, Seung Min Oh, and Kyu Hyuck Chung. "Estrogenic Effects of Marijuana Smoke Condensate and Cannabinoid Compounds." *Toxicology and Applied Pharmacology* 2006:214,270–278.

Lee-Gonyea, Jenifer A., Tammy Castle, and Nathan E. Gomyea. "Laid to Order: Male Escorts Advertising on the Internet." *Deviant Behavior, 30*, 2009:321–348.

Leinwand, Donna. "Judges Write Creative Sentences." *USA Today*, February 24, 2004.

Leland, John. "A New Harlem Gentry in Search of Its Latte." *New York Times*, August 7, 2003.

Lemonick, Michael D. "Climate Heretic: Judith Curry Turns on Her Colleagues." *Scientific American*, October 25, 2010.

Lender, Mark Edward, and James Kirby Martin. *Drinking in America: A History*. New York: Free Press, 1982.

Leonard, Arthur S. "Legislative & Administrative Notes." *LGBT Law Notes*, February 2018.

Lepore, Jill. "When Barbie Went to War with Bratz." *The New Yorker*, January 22, 2018.

Lerner, Gerda. *The Creation of Patriarchy*. New York: Oxford University Press, 1986.

Lesser, Alexander. "War and the State." In *War: The Anthropology of Armed Conflict and Aggression*, Morton Fried, Marvin Harris, and Robert Murphy, eds. Garden City, NY: Natural History, 1968.

Lester, James, David W. Allen, and Kelly M. Hill. *Environmental Injustice in the United States: Myths and Realities*. New York: Routledge, 2018.

Lester, Sarah E., Rebecca A. Gentry, Carrie V. Kappel, et al. "Opinion: Offshore Aquaculture in the United States: Untapped Potential in Need of Smart Policy." *Proceedings of the National Academy of Sciences of the United States of America, 115* (28), July 10, 2018.

Levi, Ori Nissim. "Failure of the Superpowers to Handle Large Nuclear Events." *Modeling the New Europe*, 2018:122–141.

Levine, Art. "Drug Education Gets an F." *U.S. News & World Report*, October 13, 1986:63–64.

Lewis, Dinah, Heidi E. Hutton, Tracy A. Agee, et al. "Alcohol Use and Unintended Sexual Consequences among Women Attending an Urban Sexually Transmitted Infections Clinic." *Women's Health Issues*, 2015.

Lewis, Jeffrey. "What If Space Were Weaponized? Possible Consequences for Crisis Scenarios." Washington, DC: Center for Defense Information, July 2004.

Lewis, Karen J. "Abortion: Judicial Control." Washington, DC: Congressional Research Service, American Law Division. Mimeo. September 13, 1988.

Lewis, Oscar. "The Culture of Poverty." *Scientific American, 115*, October 1966:19–25.

Lewis, Oscar. *Five Families*. New York: Basic Books, 1959.

Li, N., R. Hauser, T. Holford, et al. "Muscle-Building Supplement Use and Increased Risk of Testicular Germ Cell Cancer in Men from Connecticut and Massachusetts." *British Journal of Cancer*, 2015.

Lievanos, Raoul S. "Race, Deprivation, and Immigrant Isolation: The Spatial Demography of Air-Toxic Clusters in the Continental United States." *Social Science Research, 54*, 2015.

Light, Donald W. "The Overlooked Epidemic in Harmful Side Effects from Prescription Drugs." *The SSSP Newsletter, 42* (3), Fall 2011.

Liljas, Per. "The People of Kiribati Have Been Offered a Home in Fiji if Rising Seas Swamp Their Islands." *Time*, February 12, 2014.

Lindley, Robin. "James Dawes: Why Do People Commit Atrocities?" Interview on George Mason University History News Network, August 19, 2013.

Lindner, Katharina. "Images of Women in General Interest and Fashion Magazine Advertisements from 1955 to 2002." *Sex Roles, 51* (7/8), October 2004:409–421.

Linkola, Pentti. *Can Life Prevail?*, 2nd ed. Stockholm, Sweden: Arktos Media, 2011.

Linton, Ralph. *The Study of Man*. New York: Appleton, 1936.

Lippke, Richard L. "Legal Punishment and the Public Identification of Offenders." *Res Publica*, 24 (2), May 2018:199–216.

Liptak, Adam. "Blocking Parts of Arizona Law, Justices Allow Its Centerpiece." *New York Times*, June 25, 2012.

Liptak, Adam. "Supreme Court Finds Bias Against White Firefighters." *New York Times*, June 30, 2009.

Little, Jane Braxton. "The Ogallala Aquifer: Saving a Vital U.S. Water Source." *National Geographic*, March 2009.

Little, Peter D., and Michael M. Horowitz (eds.). Lands at Risk in the Third World: Local-Level Perspectives. Boulder, CO: Westview, 1987.

Livingston, Gretchen, and Anna Brown. "Intermarriage in the U.S. 50 Years after Loving v. Virginia." Washington, DC: Pew Research Center, May 18, 2017.

Livingston, Gretchen, Peter Wallenstein, et al. "Virginia Is for Lovers." *Contexts*, Winter 2018.

Livingston, Gretchen. "They're Waiting Longer, but U.S. Women Today More Likely to Have Children Than a Decade Ago." Washington, DC: Pew Research Center, January 18, 2018.

Livingston, K. "Ritalin: Miracle Drug or Cop-Out?" *The Public Interest*. April 15, 1997.

Lochner, Lance. "Education, Work, and Crime: A Human Capital Approach." *International Economic Review 45*, 3, August 2004:811–843.

Lombroso, Cesare. *Crime: Its Causes and Remedies*, H. P. Horton, trans. Boston: Little, Brown, 1911.

Long, Austin. "Russian Nuclear Forces and Prospects for Arms Control." Testimony before the Committee on Foreign Affairs Subcommittee on Terrorism, Nonproliferation, and Trade, United States House of Representatives, June 21, 2018.

Lopez, Adalberto, ed. *The Puerto Ricans: Their History, Culture, and Society*. Cambridge, MA: Schenkman, 1980.

Lopez, Ana Maria. "Telemedicine and Clinical Trials." Oncology Clinical Trials: Successful Design, Conduct, and Analysis. In William Kevin Kelly and Susan Halabi, eds. New York: Demos Medical, 2nd ed. 2018.

Lopez, German. "Alcoholics Anonymous Works for Some People. A New Study Suggests the Alternatives Do Too." Vox, March 5, 2018.

Loprest, Pamela, and Austin Nichols. "Characteristics of Low-Income Single Mothers Disconnected from Work and Public Assistance." *Low-Income Working Families Fact Sheet*. Washington, DC: The Urban Institute, 2011.

Lora, Eduardo. "Latin American Cities: Their Origin, Achievements, and Problems." In *The Quality of Life in Latin American Cities: Markets and Perception*, Eduardo Lora, Andrew Powell, Bernard van Praag, and Pablo Sanguinetti, eds. New York: the Inter-American Development Bank, 2010.

Lorber, Judith. "Beyond Equality of the Sexes: The Question of Children." In *Marriage and Family in a Changing Society*, James M. Henslin, ed. New York: Free Press, 1980:522–533.

Lorenz, Konrad. *On Aggression*. New York: Harcourt, 1966.

Loveless, Tom. "Girls, Boys, and Reading." *Brookings*, March 24, 2015.

Lucas, Ann M. "The Work of Sex Work: Elite Prostitutes' Vocational Orientations and Experiences." *Deviant Behavior, 26*, 2005:513–546.

Luckenbill, David F. "Deviant Career Mobility: The Case of Male Prostitutes." *Social Problems 33* (4), April 1986: 283–296.

Luhn, Alec. "The Town that Reveals How Russia Spills Two Deepwater Horizons of Oil Each Year." *The Guardian*, August 5, 2016.

Luker, Kristen. *Taking Chances: Abortion and the Decision Not to Contracept*. Berkeley: University of California Press, 1975.

Lund, Crick, and Annbale Cois. "Simultaneous Social Causation and Social Drift: Longitudinal Analysis of Depression and Poverty in South Africa." *Journal of Affective Disorders, 229*, March 15, 2018:396–402.

Lundberg, Ollie. "Causal Explanations for Class Inequality in Health: An Empirical Analysis." *Social Science and Medicine, 32* (4), 1991:385–393.

Lunenburg, Fred C. "School Violence in America's Schools." *Focus on Colleges, Universities, and Schools, 4* (1), 2010:1–6.

Lussier, Patrick, David P. Farrington, and Terrie E. Moffitt. "Is the Antisocial Child Father of the Abusive Man? A 40-Year Prospective Longitudinal Study on the Developmental Antecedents of Intimate Partner Violence." *Criminology, 47* (3), 2009:741–779.

Luthern, Ashley "'Notorious 'Pimpin' Paul' Sentenced to 18 Years in Federal Sex Trafficking Case in Milwaukee." *Milwaukee Journal Sentinel*, January 10, 2018.

Lutz, Harold J. *Aboriginal Man and White Man as Historical Causes of Fires in the Boreal Forest, with Particular Reference to Alaska*. New Haven, CT: Yale University School of Forestry. No. 65, 1959 [as referenced in Burch 1971].

Luy, Mary Lynn M. "Rape: Not a Sex Act—A Violent Crime, An Interview with Dr. Dorothy J. Hicks." *Modern Medicine*. February 15, 1977:36–41.

Lynas, Mark. "With G.M.O. Policies, Europe Turns against Science." *New York Times*, October 24, 2015.

Lynch, Mitchell C. "Old Ice Indicates Acid Was Present in Rain Long Ago." *Wall Street Journal*, September 18, 1980:13.

Lynd, Robert S., and Helen M. Lynd. *Middletown*. New York: Harcourt, 1929.

Lynd, Robert S., and Helen M. Lynd. *Middletown in Transition*. New York: Harcourt, 1937.

Macartney, Suzanne. "Child Poverty in the United States 2009 and 2010: Selected Race Groups and Hispanic Origin." U.S. Census Bureau, Community Survey Briefs, November 2011.

MacDougal, Gary. "A New Republican War on Poverty." *Wall Street Journal*, September 16, 2014.

Mackellar, Landis, and David Horlacher. "Population Ageing in Japan: A Brief Survey." *The European Journal of Social Sciences, 13* (4), December 2000.

MacKinnon, Catharine A. *Sexual Harassment of Working Women: A Case of Sex Discrimination*. New Haven, CT: Yale University Press, 1979.

Madland, David. *Hollowed Out: Why the Economy Doesn't Work without a Strong Middle Class*. Oakland: University of California Press, 2015.

Maisonave, Fabiano. "Amazon at Risk from Bolsinaro's Grim Attack on the Environment." *The Guardian*, October 9, 2018.

Makary, Martin, and Michael Daniel. "Medical Error—The Third Leading Cause of Death in the U.S." *British Medical Journal, 353*, May 3, 2016.

Malamuth, Neil M., Gert Martin Hald, and Mary Koss. "Pornography, Individual Differences in Risk and Men's Acceptance of Violence Against Women in a Representative Sample." *Sex Roles, 66*, 2012:427–439.

Malamuth, Neil M., Tamara Addison, and Mary Koss. "Pornography and Sexual Aggression: Are There Reliable Effects and Can We Understand Them? *Annual Review of Sex Research, 11*, 2000:26–91.

Mallach, Alan. *The Divided City: Poverty and Prosperity in Urban America*. Washington, DC: Island Press, 2018.

Malthus, Thomas Robert. *First Essay on Population*. London: Macmillan, 1926. (Originally published 1798)

Mandavilli, Apoorva. "The World's Worst Industrial Disaster Is Still Unfolding." July 10, 2018.

Manderscheid, Ronald W., Carol D. Ryff, Elsie J. Freeman, Lela R. McKnight, Satvinder Dhingra, and Tara W. Strine. "Evolving Definitions of Mental Illness and Wellness." *Preventing Chronic Disease: Public Health Research, Practice, and Policy, 7* (1), January 2010.

Manning, Jennifer E., and Colleen J. Shogan. "Women in the United States Congress: 1917–2012. Washington, DC: Congressional Research Service, January 27, 2012.

Manning, Wendy D., Susan L. Brown, and Krista K. Payne. "Two Decades of Stability and Change in Age at First Union Formation." *Journal of Marriage and Family*, 76 (2), April 1, 2014:247–260.

Manpower Report to the President. Washington, DC: U.S. Department of Labor, Manpower Administration, April 1971.

Marcus, Anthony, Amber Horning, Ric Curtis, et al. "Conflict and Agency among Sex Workers and Pimps: A Closer Look at Domestic Minor Sex Trafficking." *The American Academy of Political and Social Science*, 653 (1), May 1 2014:225–246.

Marengo, Stacy M., Jeffrey Kilbert, et al. "The Relationship of Early Maladaptive Schemas and Anticipated Risky Behavior in College Students." *Journal of Adult Development*, 2018:1–11.

Marger, Martin N. *Elites and Masses: An Introduction to Political Sociology*, 2nd ed. Belmont, CA: Wadsworth, 1987.

Marino, David. "Border Watch Group 'Techno Patriots' Still Growing." KVDA News 4, Tucson, Arizona, February 14, 2008.

Mark, Michelle, Skye Gould, and Andy Kiersz. "A Journey along the Entire 1,953-Mile U.S.-Mexico Border Shows the Monumental Task of Securing It." *Business Insider*, May 29, 2018.

Markman, Joe. "Rescued Child Prostitutes Not Receiving Help" *Los Angeles Times*, December 8, 2009.

Markowitz, Eric. "Electronic Monitoring Has Become the New Debtors Prison." *Prison Legal News*, December 23, 2016.

Maron, Dina Fine. "Has Maternal Mortality Really Doubled in the U.S.?" *Scientific American*, June 8, 2015.

Marshall, George. "Olimpias Adopts Cogeneration with AB." *Energy Live News*, June 6, 2016. Online.

Martin, Gary. "Senate Panel Again Drops Yucca Mountain Licensing Funding from Budget." *Las Vegas Review Journal*, May 24, 2018.

Martin, Joyce A., Brady E. Hamilton, Michelle J. K. Osterman, Sally C. Curtin, and T. J. Matthews, "Final Data for 2012." *National Vital Statistics Reports*. 62 (9), December 30, 2013.

Martin, Paul Schultz. "Prehistoric Overkill." In *Pleistocene Extinctions: The Search for a Cause*, Paul Schultz Martin and H. E. Wright, Jr., eds. New Haven, CT: Yale University Press, 1967.

Martinez, Juan Francisco Esteva. "Urban Street Activists: Gang and Community Efforts to Bring Peace and Justice to Los Angeles Neighborhoods." In *Gangs and Society: Alternative Perspectives*, Louis Kontos, David Brotherton, and Luis Barrios, eds. New York: Columbia University Press, 2003:95–115.

Martins, Joseph M, Fei Guo, and David A, Swanson. *Population and the Environment*. New York: Springer, 2018.

Marx, Karl. *Das Kapital*. New York: International, 1967. (Originally published 1867–1895)

Marx, Karl, and Friedrich Engels. *Capital: A Critique of Political Economy*, E. Aveling, trans. Chicago: Charles Kerr, 1906.

Marx, Karl, and Friedrich Engels. *The Communist Manifesto*, S. Moore, trans. New York: Washington Square, 1964. (Originally published 1848)

Mascio, B. *The Daughters and Sons of Elder Care*, 2007. Online. http://www.seniorsapprove.com/daughter.html.

Masisak, Corey. "Barry Bonds Earns Another Step of MLB Forgiveness." *New York Post*, February 6, 2018.

Mason, Margie, and Martha Mendoza. "First Case of Highly Drug-Resistant TB Found in U.S." *Associated Press*, December 27, 2009.

Masuchika, Glenn. "Japanese Cartoons, Virtual Child Pornography, Academic Libraries, and the Law." Reference and User Services Association, 54 (4), 2015.

Mathews, Anna Wilde. "Program Cuts Rate of Deadly Catheter Infections." *Wall Street Journal*, September 10, 2012.

Mathews, Anna Wilde. "Remember Managed Care? It's Quietly Coming Back." *Wall Street Journal*, August 2, 2012.

Matlock, Daniel. "Dr. Smiles and the 'Counterfeit' Gentlemen: Self-Making and Misapplication in Mid-Nineteenth-Century Britain." *Victorian Literature and Culture*, 46 (1), March 26, 2018.

Mattioli, Dana. "More Men Make Harassment Claims." *Wall Street Journal*, March 23, 2010.

Mauer, Marc. "Race, Class, and the Development of Criminal Justice Policy." *Review of Policy Research*, 21 (1), 2004:79–92.

Mayer, Don, Anita Cava, and Catharyn Baird. "Crime and Punishment (or the Lack Thereof) for Financial Fraud in the Subprime Mortgage Meltdown: Reasons and Remedies for Ethical Lapses." *American Business Law Journal*, 51 (3), Fall 2014:515–597.

Maynard, Douglas W. *Inside Plea Bargaining: The Language of Negotiation*. New York: Plenum, 1984.

Mayne, Susan Taylor, Dwight T. Janerich, Peter Greenwald, et al. "Dietary Beta Carotene and Lung Cancer Risk in U.S. Nonsmokers." *Journal of the National Cancer Institute*, 86 (1), January 5, 1995:33–38.

Mays, Jeffery C. "As Gas Stations Vanish, Harlem Sees Gentrification Creeping in." *New York Times*, May 28, 2017.

Mayumi, Kozo, and Mario Giampietro. "Money as the Potential Cause of the Tragedy of the Commons." *Journal for Economic Forecasting*, December 2018:151–156.

Mazur, Allan, and Alan Booth. "Testosterone Is Related to Deviance in Male Army Veterans, But Relationships Are Not Moderated by Cortisol." *Biological Psychology*, 96, 2014:72–76.

McAnany, Patricia A., and Norman Yoffee, eds. *Questioning Collapse: Human Resilience, Ecological Vulnerability, and the Aftermath of Empire*. Cambridge: Cambridge University Press, 2009.

McCabe, Janice, Emily Fairchild, Liz Grauerholz, Bernice A. Pescosolido, and Daniel Tope. "Gender in Twentieth-Century Children's Books: Patterns of Disparity in Titles and Central Characters." *Gender and Society*, 25 (2), April 2011:197–226.

McCallum, Cecilia, Greice Menezes, and Ana Paula dos Reis. "The Dilemma of a Practice: Experiences of Abortion in a Public Maternity Hospital in the City of Salvador, Bahia." *Historia, Ciencias, Saude– Manguinhos*, 23 (1), January–March 2016.

McCarthy, Gina. "TSCA Reform: A Bipartisan Milestone to Protect Our Health from Dangerous Chemicals." EPA Connect: The Official Blog of the EPA Leadership, June 22, 2016.

McCarty, Teresa L. "The Impact of High-Stakes Accountability Policies on Native American Learners: Evidence from Research." *Teaching Education*, 20 (1), 2009:7–29.

McDonald, Henry. "Sinn Fein Minister Found Guilty of Discrimination." *Guardian*, June 20, 2012.

McDowell, Bart. "Mexico City: An Alarming Giant." *National Geographic*, 166, 1984:139–174.

McGaughy, Lauren. "Professors Who Ban Guns in Their Classrooms Will Be Punished, UT Lawyer Says." *Dallas Morning News*, August 10, 2016.

McGinty, Jo Craven. "New York Killers, and Those Killed, by Numbers." *New York Times*, April 28, 2006.

McGlone, Matt. "The Hunters Did It." *Science*, 335, 6075, March 23, 2012: 1452–1453.

McKeown, Thomas. *The Modern Rise of Population*. New York: Academic Press, 1977.

McKeown, Thomas. *The Role of Medicine: Dream, Mirage, or Nemesis?* Princeton, NJ: Princeton University Press, 1980.

McKinley, James C., Jr., "With Beheadings and Attacks, Drug Gangs Terrorize Mexico." *New York Times*, October 26, 2006b.

McKinley, James C., Jr., and Marc Lacey. "Mexico's Drug War Brings New Brutality." *New York Times*, October 25, 2006.

McKinney, Sydney. "Runaway Youth: A Research Brief." *Research Briefs*, May 28, 2014.

McKinnish, Terra, Randall Walsh, and Kirk White. "Who Gentrifies Low-Income Neighborhoods?" *National Bureau of Economic Research*, Working Paper 14036, May 2008.

McLanahan, S. "Child Support Enforcement and Child Well-Being: Greater Security or Greater Conflict?" *Child Support and Child Well-Being*. Washington: Urban Institute Press, 1996:239–256.

McMillan, Lesley. "Police Officers' Perceptions of False Allegations of Rape." *Journal of Gender Studies*, 27 (1), 2016.

McNeely, R. L., and Carl E. Pope. "Socioeconomic and Racial Issues in the Measurement of Criminal Involvement." In *Race, Crime, and Criminal Justice*, R. L. McNeely and Carl E. Pope, eds. Beverly Hills, CA: Sage, 1981:31–47.

McNeil, Donald G. "Vietnam's Battle with Tuberculosis." *New York Times*, March 28, 2016.

McOrmond-Plummer, Patricia Easteal, and Jennifer Y. Levy-Peck, eds. *Intimate Partner Violence*. London: Jessica Kingsley Pub., 2014:259–269.

Medina, Jennifer. "Los Angeles Neighborhood Tries to Change, but Avoid the Pitfalls." *New York Times*, September 20, 2013.

Medley-Rath, Stephanie. "Stereotypes in Kids Books: Girl Animals Have Eyelashes." *Sociology in Focus*, February 4, 2013.

Meese Commission. *Final Report of the Attorney General's Commission on Pornography*. Washington, DC: U.S. Department of Justice, 1986.

Melloan, George. "Europe Struggles with the Burdens of Old Age." *Wall Street Journal*, December 12, 1994:A15.

Melody, G. F. "Chronic Pelvic Congestion in Prostitutes." *Medical Aspects of Human Sexuality*, 3, November 1969:103–104.

Merton, Robert K. *Social Theory and Social Structure*, enlarged ed. New York: Free Press, 1968.

Messer, Madeline. "I'm a 12-Year-Old Girl. Why Don't the Characters in My Apps Look Like Me?" *Washington Post*, March 4, 2015.

"Mexican Drug Gang Beheads Another Blogger and Dumps Body and Severed Head in Street with Bloody Warning Note." *Daily Mail*, November 10, 2011.

Meyer, Bruce D., and Nikolas Mittag. "Using Linked Survey and Administrative Data to Better Measure Income Implications for Poverty, Program Effectiveness and Holes in the Safety Net." National Bureau of Economic Research Working Paper 21676, October 2015.

Meyer, H. *Old English Coffee Houses*. Emmaus, PA: Rodale, 1954.

"MGA Entertainment Entitled To $310 Million From Mattel Over Doll Concept." *Beverly Hills Courier*, December 6, 2016.

Micallef, Shawn. "Neo-Nazi Bunker for Sale Represents Dark Era in Toronto History." *The Star*, March 5, 2015.

Michaels, Patrick J., and Paul C. Knappenberger. "Climate Models and Climate Reality: A Closer Look at a Lukewarming World." Cato Institute: Cato working paper number 35, December 15, 2015.

Michalski, Joseph H. "Ritualistic Rape in Sociological Perspective." *Cross-Cultural Research*, 50 (1), February 2016:3–33.

Michelman, Kate. As quoted in "NARAL," pamphlet published by the National Abortion Rights Action League, 1988:1.

Midling, Anne Sliper. "Fewer Heart Problems in People Who Drink Moderately but Often." *Science Nordic*, February 20, 2016.

Mikkonen, H. Maiju, Minna K. Salonen, Antti Hakkinen, et al. "The Lifelong Socioeconomic Disadvantage of Single-Mother Background—the Helsinki Birth Cohort Study 1934–1944." *BMC Public Health*, December 2016.

Miklikowska, Marta, and Douglas P. Fry. "Values for Peace: Ethnographic Lessons from the Semai of Malaysia and the Mardu of Australia." *Beliefs and Values*, 2 (2), 2010:124–137.

Mikulskaya, Elena, and Frances Martin. "Visual Attention to Motion Stimuli and its Neural Correlates in Cannabis Users." *European Journal of Neuroscience*, 47 (3), February 2018:269–276.

Milbank, Dana. "In His Solitude, A Finnish Thinker Posits Cataclysms." *Wall Street Journal*, May 20, 1994:A1, A8.

Miller, Judith, and William J. Broad. "Clinton Describes Terrorism Threat for 21st Century." *New York Times*, January 22, 1999.

Miller, Laura L. "Women in the Military." In *Down to Earth Sociology: Introductory Readings*, 14th ed., James M. Henslin, ed. New York: Free Press, 2007.

Miller, Michael E. "You Feel that the Devil Is Helping You: Ms-13's Satanic History." *The Washington Post*, December 20, 2017.

Miller, Michael W. "Quality Stuff: Firm Is Peddling Cocaine, and Deals Are Legit." *Wall Street Journal*, October 27, 1994:A1, A8.

Miller, T. Christian, and Ken Armstrong. *A False Report: A True Story of Rape in America*. New York: Random House, 2018.

Miller, Walter B. "Lower-Class Culture as a Generating Milieu of Gang Delinquency." *Journal of Social Issues*, 14, 1958:5–19.

Millett, Kate. *Sexual Politics*. Garden City, NY: Doubleday, 1970.

Millett, Kate. *The Prostitution Papers: A Candid Dialogue*. New York: Avon, 1973.

Mills, C. Wright. *The Causes of World War Three*. New York: Simon & Schuster, 1958.

Mills, C. Wright. *The Sociological Imagination*. New York: Oxford University Press, 1959b.

Mills, Karen M., and Thomas J. Palumbo. *A Statistical Portrait of Women in the United States: 1978*. Washington, DC: U.S. Government Printing Office, 1980.

Milrod, Christine, and Martin Monto. "Older Male Clients of Female Sex Workers in the United States." *Archives of Sexual Behavior*, April 5, 2016.

Mims, Christopher. "Advances in Driverless Cars Will Fuel Suburban Sprawl." *Wall Street Journal*, June 20, 2016.

Mitchell, David. "Northern Ireland's Twenty Years of Troubled Peace." *Current History*, March 2018:89–95.

Mitra, Sucharita. "Groundwater Sustainability." *International Journal of Ecosystem*, 5, 2015:43–46.

Moffitt, Robert A. "The Idea of a Negative Income Tax: Past, Present, and Future." *Focus*, 23 (2), Summer 2004.

Mole, Beth. "First XDR Typhoid Is on the Verge of Being Untreatable, Spreading Globally." *ArsTechnica*, April 17, 2018.

Moore, Brent A., Erik M. Augustson, Richard P. Moser, and Alan J. Budney. "Respiratory Effects of Marijuana and Tobacco Use in a U.S. Sample." *Journal of General Internal Medicine*, 20, 2004:33–37.

Moore, Solomon. "Justice Dept. Seeks Equity in Sentences for Cocaine." *New York Times*, April 29, 2009.

"More Bang for Your Buck." *The Economist*, August 7, 2014.

Moreno, Eduardo Lopez, Oyebanji Oyeyinka, and Gora Mboup. *State of the World's Cities 2010/2011: Bridging the Urban Divide*. London: UN Habitat, 2012.

Morgan, Rachel E. "Race and Hispanic Origin of Victims and Offenders, 2012–15." U.S. Department of Justice, October 2017.

Morgan, Rachel E., and Grace Kena. "Criminal Victimization, 2016." *Bureau of Justice Statistics Bulletin*, December 2017.

Morgenson, G. "Silence of the Lenders: Is Anyone Listening?" *New York Times*, July 13, 2008.

Mori, Kathryn, and Carolyn Scearce. "Robot Nation: Robots and the Declining Japanese Population." *ProQuest*, September 2010.

Motel, Seth. "6 Facts about Marijuana." Pew Research Center, November 5, 2014.

Moussa, O.M., S. Erridge, S. Chidambaram, et al. "Mortality of the Severely Obese: A Population Study." *Annals of Surgery*, March 8, 2018.

Mullen, Jeff M., and Adam T. Crawford. "Amphetamine Related Psychiatric Disorders." *StatPearls*, National Center for Biotechnology Information, January 23, 2018.

Mulvihill, Donald J., Melvin M. Tumin, and Lynn A. Curtis. *Crimes of Violence: A Staff Report to the National Commission on the Causes and Prevention of Violence*. Washington, DC: U.S. Government Printing Office, 1969.

Muniz-Fraticelli, Victor M. *The Structure of Pluralism*. New York: Oxford University Press, 2014.

Murphy, Kim. "Last Stand of an Aging Aryan." *Los Angeles Times*, January 10, 1999.

Murshid, Nadine Shaanta, Navine Murshid, et al. "Intergenerational Transmission of Marital Violence: Results from a Nationally Representative Sample of Men." *Journal of Interpersonal Violence*, 33 (2), 2018.

Musu-Gillette, L., A. Zhang, K. Wang, et al. "Indicators of School Crime and Safety: 2017." Washington, DC: National Center for Education Statistics, March 2018.

Myers, Martha A., and Susette M. Talarico. "The Social Contexts of Racial Discrimination in Sentencing." *Social Problems*, 33, 3, February 1986:236–251.

Myrdal, Gunnar. *An American Dilemma*. New York: Harper, 1944.

NAACP (National Association for the Advancement of Colored People). "Death Row U.S.A.," Summer 2015.

NAACP (National Association for the Advancement of Colored People). "Death Row USA." Fall 2017.

Nadeem, Meera. "Terrorism in the Age of New Media and Information Technology, Where Conventional Threats to Global Security Meet the Contemporary." *Policy Brief,* Jinnah Institute, June 20, 2018.

Nagar, Kitchu. "Government Must Check Unauthorised Ultrasound Centres." *The Tribune,* January 1, 2018.

Naj, Amal Kumar. "Kuwait Oil-Well Fires Did Little Damage to the Global Environment, Study Says." *Wall Street Journal,* May 15, 1992:B5.

Naib, Fatma. "Senegal's Anti-FGM Campaigner: 'My Child Won't Be Cut.'" *Women's Rights,* March 10, 2016.

Nash, Gary B. *The Urban Crucible.* Cambridge, MA: Harvard University Press, 1979.

National Academy of Sciences. "America's Climate Choices." 2010.

"National Assessment of Adult Literacy and Literacy among Prison Inmates." *Alaska Justice Forum,* 24 (2), Summer 2007.

National Research Council. Committee on Sustainable Underground Storage of Recoverable Water. Washington, DC: The National Academies Press, 2008.

National Research Council. Water Reuse: Potential for Expanding the Nation's Water Supply Through Reuse of Municipal Wastewater. Washington, DC: The National Academies Press, 2012.

National Science Foundation. *Science and Engineering Indicators,* 2016.

"National Strategy for Combatting Terrorism." Washington, DC: The White House, September 2006.

National Vital Statistics Reports. "Births: Final Data for 2016," January 31, 2018.

National Vital Statistics Reports. "Deaths: Final Data for 2015." November 27, 2017.

"Native American Casinos: Revenue Overview and Trend Analysis." *Cairo News Daily,* May 29, 2015.

NCBI (National Center for Biotechnology Information). MAOA Monoamine oxidase A. Gene ID: 4128, March 2018. www.ncbi. nlm.nih.gov/gene/4128?report=full_report

NCEA (National Center on Elder Abuse). "Research/Statistics Data." May 2018. https://ncea.acl.gov/whatwedo/research/statistics.html

NCHS (National Center for Health Statistics). "Provisional Drug Overdose Death Counts." April 11, 2018.

Negishi, Mayumi, and Eric Pfanner. "Japan Grapples with Fukushima Cleanup." *Wall Street Journal,* May 10, 2016.

Nelson, Dean. "Infanticide May Be Behind Boys Outnumbering Girls in Indian Village." *Telegraph Media Group,* February 3, 2014.

Nettler, Gwynn. "Embezzlement Without Problems." *British Journal of Criminology,* 14, January 1974:70–77.

Nettler, Gwynn. *Social Concerns.* New York: McGraw-Hill, 1976.

Neuman, William. "Egg Farms Violated Safety Rules." *New York Times,* August 30, 2010.

Newbold, Tim, Lawrence N. Hudson, Andrew P. Arnell, et al. "Has Land Use Pushed Terrestrial Biodiversity Beyond the Planetary Boundary? A Global Assessment." *Science,* 353 (6296), July 15, 2016:288–291.

Newman, Dorothy K., Nancy J. Amidei, Barbara L. Cater, Dawn Day, William J. Kruvant, and Jack S. Russell. *Protest, Politics, and Prosperity: Black Americans and White Institutions, 1940–1975.* New York: Pantheon, 1978.

Newman, Richard S. *Love Canal: A Toxic History from Colonial Times to the Present.* New York: Oxford University Press, 2016.

Newsday. *The Heroin Trail.* New York. Holt, Rinehart, & Winston, 1974.

Newton, David E. *Marijuana: A Reference Handbook,* 2nd ed. Santa Barbara, CA: ABC-CLIO, 2017.

NIH (National Institute of Diabetes and Digestive and Kidney Diseases). "Overweight and Obesity Statistics," 2016.

NIH (National Institute on Drug Abuse). "National Survey of Drug Use and Health."

Nonoyama-Tarumi, Yuko. "Educational Achievement of Children from Single-Mother and Single-Father Families: The Case of Japan." *Journal of Marriage and Family,* June 1, 2017.

Nordrum, Amy. "The New D.A.R.E. Program—This One Works." *Scientific American,* September 10, 2014.

"NRS Statistics on Runaways." Chicago, IL: National Runaway Safeline, 2015.

"Nuclear Waste Eaters: Scientists Discover Hazardous Waste-Eating Bacteria." *ScienceDaily,* September 9, 2014.

Nucleus: A Report to Union of Concerned Scientists Sponsors, 3, Spring–Summer 1981.

NWHM (National Women's Health Network). "Hysterectomy."

O'Brien, Geoff. "Cities—Good for the Environment?" *International Journal of Environmental Studies,* 75 (1), 2018.

O'Connor, Anahad. "Government Ends Case Against Gotti." *New York Times,* January 14, 2010.

O'Hanlon, Michael E., and Ian Livingston. "Iraq Index: Tracking Variables of Reconstruction & Security in Post-Saddam Iraq." Brookings, May 25, 2010.

O'Hare, William P. "America's Minorities: The Demographics of Diversity." *Population Bulletin,* 47 (4), December 1992:1–47.

O'Keefe, James H., Salman K. Bhatti, Ata Bajwa, et al. "Alcohol and Cardiovascular Health: The Dose Makes the Poison…or the Remedy." *Mayo Clinic Proceedings,* 84 (3), March 2014.

O'Neal, Eryn Nicole, and Kimberly A. Kaiser. "Resistance Strategies and Sexual Assault Outcomes: Do Measurement Decisions Influence Empirical Findings?" *Criminology, Criminal Justice, Law & Society* 16(2), 2015:56–73.

O'Rourke, Meghan. "Doctors Tell All—and It's Bad." *The Atlantic,* November 2014.

O'Toole, Molly. "El Salvador's Gangs Are Targeting Young Girls." *The Atlantic,* March 4, 2018.

Oberg, Ted, and Trent Seibert. "Delayed DNA Testing Allowed Alleged Rapists to Commit New Crimes." *KTRK Houston,* January 29, 2015.

Obinna, Denise N. "Ethnicity, Reception and the Growth of American Immigration." *Ethnic and Racial Studies,* 41 (2), 2018.

OECD (Organisation for Economic Co-Operation and Development). "Family Database," July 2018.

"Of Birds and Bacteria." *Consumer Reports,* January 2003.

Offord, Catherine. "Restoring C-Section Babies' Microbiota." *The Scientist,* February 1, 2016.

Ojito, Mirta. *Hunting Season: Immigration and Murder in an All-American Town.* Boston: Beacon Press, 2014.

Oliver, Melvin L., and Thomas M. Shapiro. *Black Wealth/White Wealth: A New Perspective on Racial Inequality.* New York: Routledge, 1995.

Olson, Samantha. "1 in 5 Premature Deaths in America Are Due to Obesity; Men at Greater Risk Than Women." *Medical Daily,* July 15, 2016.

Olson, Walter K. "Give It Back to the Indians?" *City Journal,* Autumn 2002.

Oppel, Richard A. "Steady Decline in Major Crimes Baffles Experts." *New York Times,* May 23 2011.

Ortiz-Ospina, Esteban, and Max Roser. "World Population Growth," Our World in Data.org, 2016.

Ovando, Carlos J., and Mary Carol Combs. *Bilingual and ESL Classrooms: Teaching in Multicultural Contexts,* 6th ed. Lanham, MD: Rowman & Littlefield, 2018.

Palamar, Joseph A., Shelby Davies, Danielle C. Ompad, et al. "Powder Cocaine and Crack Use in the United States: An Examination of Risk for Arrest and Socioeconomic Disparities of Use." *Drug and Alcohol Dependency,* April 1, 2015.

Palazzolo, Joe. "Stuck in Jail Awaiting Care." *Wall Street Journal,* April 20, 2015.

Panda, Sunita, Cecily Begley, and Deirdre Daly. "Clinicians' Views of Factors Influencing Decision-Making for Caesarean Section." *Plos/One,* July 27, 2018.

"Pan-Indianism." *Native American Calling,* September 24, 2015.

Papandrea, Mary-Rose. "Sex and Religion: Unholy Bedfellows." *Michigan Law Review,* 116 (6), 2018.

Park, Alice. "The Hospitals Most Likely to Give You a C-Section, Ranked." *Time,* May 18, 2014.

Park, Robert E. "The Social Function of War." *American Journal of Sociology,* 46, January 1941:551–570.

Parker, Laura. "What Happens to the Midwest When the Water's Gone?" *National Geographic,* August 2016.

Partington, Donald H. "The Incidence of the Death Penalty for Rape in Virginia." *Washington and Lee Law Review, 22,* 1965:43–75.

Paterson, Charlotte, Thanos Karatzias, Adele Dicksonm, et al. "Psychological Therapy for Inpatients Receiving Acute Mental Health Care: A Systematic Review and Meta-Analysis of Controlled Trials." *British Journal of Clinical Psychology, 57* (4), November 2018:453–472.

Paul, Pamela. *Pornified: How Pornography Is Transforming Our Lives, Our Relationships, and Our Families.* New York: Henry Holt, 2005.

Pawar, Yogesh. "The Many Positions on Kamasutra." *DNAIndia,* October 26, 2014.

Payesco, Jenna." Resurgence of Black Lung Disease in Coal Miners." *MD,* May 22, 2018.

Pearce, Fred. "Awash in Radioactive Waste." *New York Times,* May 24, 2018.

Pearson, Erica. "Nobody Got Out of There Unscathed." *New York Daily News,* September 10, 2015.

Pecanha, Sergio, and Keith Collins. "Only 5 Nations Can Hit Any Place on Earth with a Missile, for Now." *New York Times,* February 7, 2018.

Pedersen, Katie, Melissa Mancini, and Valerie Ouellet. "Staff-to-Resident Abuse in Long-Term Homes Up 148% from 2011." *CBC News,* January 18, 2018.

Peele, Stanton. "The Addiction Experience." In Social Problems: A Critical Thinking Approach, Paul J. Baker and Louis E. Anderson, eds. Belmont, CA: Wadsworth, 1987:210–218.

Peisker, Canan B., Thomas Schuller, Jan Peters, and Jens Kuhn. "Nucleus Accumbens Deep Brain Stimulation with Substance Use Disorders and delay Discounting." *Brain Sciences, 8* (8), January 2018.

Penn, Stanley. "How Public Defenders Deal with the Pressure of the Crowded Courts." *Wall Street Journal,* July 5, 1985:1, 22.

Penn, Stanley. "Organized Crime Finds Rich Pickings in Rise of Union Health Plans." *Wall Street Journal,* October 5, 1982:1, 26.

Perez-Pena, Richard. "To Enroll More Minority Students, Colleges Work Around the Courts." *New York Times,* April 1, 2012.

Perl, Raphael F. "Taliban and the Drug Trade." CRS Report for Congress, October 5, 2001.

Perry, Susan. "Food-∂ye Warning Labels Are Now Required in Europe; Will the FDA Do the Same?" MinnPost.com, July 29, 2010.

Pesticides: Demand and Sales Forecasts, Market Share, Market Size, Market Leaders. Cleveland, OH: Freedonia Group, 2016.

Petersen, Nick, and Geoff Ward. "The Transmission of Historical Racial Violence: Lynching Civil Rights-Era Terror, and Contemporary Interracial Homicide." *Race and Justice,* 2015:1–30.

Petersilia, Joan. *Racial Disparities in the Criminal Justice System.* Santa Monica, CA: Rand, June 1983.

Peterson, Iver. "1993 Deal for Indian Casino Is Called a Model to Avoid." *New York Times,* June 30, 2003.

Petrosino, A., C. Turpin-Petrosino, M. E. Hollis-Peel, et al. "Scared Straight and Other Juvenile Awareness Programs for Preventing Juvenile Delinquency." *The Crime Prevention Research Review, No. 12.* Washington, DC: Office of Community Orienting Police Services, 2014.

Petsonk, Edward L., Cecile Rose, and Robert Cohen. "Coal Dust Lung Disease: New Lessons an Old Exposure." *American Journal of Respiratory and Critical Care Medicine, 187* (11), June 1, 2013:1178–1185.

Pew Research Center. "Public Support for the Death Penalty Ticks Up." June 11, 2018.

Pew Research Center. "Support for Death Penalty Lowest in More Than Four Decades." September 29, 2016.

Pham, Sherisse. "China Has Found a New Way to Block Banned Words." *CNNtech,* March 1, 2018.

Philpott, Tom. "Shulkin Says He Would, If He Could, Add Agent Orange Vets, Ills." March 22, 2018. https://www.military.com/militaryadvantage/2018/03/22/shulkin-says-he-would-if-he-could-add-agent-orange-vets-ills.html

Pierson, Ransdell. "Lilly Profit Beats Forecast; Focus on New Drug Data." Reuters, April 25, 2012.

Pilkington, Ed. "U.S. Nearly Detonated Atomic Bomb over North Carolina—Secret Document." *The Guardian,* September 20, 2013.

Pillemer, Karl, and David W. Moore. "Abuse of Patients in Nursing Homes: Findings from a Survey of Staff." *The Gerontologist, 29* (3), 1989:314–320.

Piven, Frances Fox, and Richard A. Cloward. *The Breaking of the American Social Compact.* New York: New Press, 1997.

Piven, Frances Fox, and Richard A. Cloward. *The New Class War: Reagan's Attack on the Welfare State and Its Consequences.* New York: Pantheon, 1982.

Piven, Frances Fox, and Richard A. Cloward. *Regulating the Poor.* New York: Vintage, 1971.

Piven, Frances Fox, and Richard A. Cloward. *Why Americans Don't Vote.* New York: Random House, 1989.

Pollan, Michael. *How to Change Your Mind: What the New Science of Psychedelics Teaches Us about Consciousness, Dying, Addiction, Depression, and Transcendence.* New York: Penguin Random House, 2018.

Polosa, R., C. Russell, J. Nitzkin, and K. E. Farsalinos. "A Critique of the U.S. Surgeon General's Conclusions Regarding E-Cigarette Use among Youth and Young Adults in the United States of America." *Harmful Reduction Journal, 14* (1), September 6, 2017.

Polti, Daniel. "Death of a Terrorist." *New York Times,* May 22, 2012.

Poole, Heather. "Enterprise Zone Program Overview." Connecticut General Assembly, Research Report 2016–R–0033. May 26, 2016.

Pope, Carl E. "The Family, Delinquency, and Crime." In *Mental Illness, Delinquency, Addictions, and Neglect,* Elam W. Nunnally, Catherine S. Chilmam, and Fred M. Cox, eds. Newbury Park, CA: Sage, 1988:108–127.

"Possession of Rape Video Warrants Restitution; Victim Awarded Over $1 Million Thus Far; Supreme Court Grants Cert." *Prison Legal News,* February 14, 2014.

Potter, Claire. "Not Safe for Work: Why Feminist Pornography Matters." *Dissent,* Spring 2016.

Potterat, John J., Donald E. Woodhouse, John B. Muth, and Stephen Q. Muth. "Estimating the Prevalence and Career Longevity of Prostitute Women." *Journal of Sex Research, 27* (2), May 1990:233–243.

Powell, Michael, and Janet Roberts. "Minorities Hit Hardest by Foreclosures in New York." *New York Times,* May 15, 2009.

Powers, Ashley. "Male Prostitution Is Nevada's Newest Legal Profession." *Los Angeles Times,* January 6, 2010.

Pozdena, Randall J., and Terry R. Johnson. *Income Maintenance and Asset Demand.* Menlo Park, CA: SRI International, March, 1979.

Pravalie, Remus. "Major Perturbations in the Earth's Forest Ecosystems: Possible Implications for Global Warming." *Earth-Science Reviews, 185,* October 2018:544–571.

"Prenatal Substance Exposure: Factsheet." Berkeley, CA: National Abandoned Infants Assistance Resource Center, April 2008.

(The) President's Commission on Combating Drug Addiction and the Opioid Crisis." Washington, DC: November 1, 2017.

Preston, Julia, and John H. Cushman, Jr. "Obama to Permit Young Migrants to Remain in U.S." *New York Times,* June 16, 2012.

Preston, Julia. "Homeland Security Cancels 'Virtual Fence' after Billion Is Spent." *New York Times,* January 14, 2011.

Pridemore, William Alex, and Joshua D. Freilich. "A Test of Recent Subcultural Explanations of White Violence in the United States." *Journal of Criminal Justice, 34,* 2006:1–16.

"Prisoners in 2014." Bureau of Justice Statistics, September 2015.

"Prisoners in 2016." NCJ 251149. U.S. Department of Justice, January 2018.

"'Professor for a Day'" Provides 26 CSUDH Alumni Opportunity to Teach." CSUDH Campus News Center, April 13, 2016.

"Project Bioshield Annual Report: January 2014—December 2014." U.S. Department of Health and Human Services. Online.

Pruitt, A.D., and Peter Grant. "Tribal Casino Rules Revisited." *Wall Street Journal,* September 21, 2009.

Prus, Robert, and Styllianoss Irini. *Hookers, Rounders, and Desk Clerks: The Social Organization of the Hotel Community.* Salem, WI: Sheffield, 1988.

"Public Opinion on Abortion." Pew Research Center, July 7, 2017.

Pulliam, Susan, and Chad Bray. "Rajaratnam Slapped with 11-Year Prison Term for Orchestrating Insider Scheme." *Wall Street Journal*, October 14, 2011.

Purcell, Jim. "Confessions of a Health Plan CEO." *The Health Care Blog*, April 23, 2016.

Puzic, Sonja. "Windsor Dr. Barbara Heartwell's Surgical Privileges at Hotel-Dieu Grace Hospital Reinstated." *Windsor-Star*, March 12, 2010.

Ra'anan, Uri, Robert L. Pfaltzgraff, Jr., Richard H. Shultz, Ernst Halperin, and Igor Lukes, eds. *Hydra of Carnage: The International Linkages of Terrorism and Other Low-Intensity Operations, The Witnesses Speak.* Lexington, KY: Lexington Books, 1986.

Rabinowitz, Dorothy. *No Crueler Tyrannies: Accusation, False Witness, and Other Terrors of Our Times.* New York: Simon & Schuster, 2004.

Radnofsky, Louise. "New Approach Unleashed in Abortion Fight." *Wall Street Journal*, July 29, 2015.

Rainey, Sarah. "Helen Mirren Confronts the Final Female Taboo." *The Telegraph*, February 4, 2013.

Rainie, Lee, and Cary Funk. "An Elaboration of AAAS Scientists' Views." Pew Research Center, July 3, 2015.

Rakopoulos, Theodoros. "The Social Life of Mafia Confession: Between Talk and Silence in Sicily," *Current Anthropology, 59* (2), April 2018:167–191.

Rakow, Lana F. "'Don't Hate Me Because I'm Beautiful': Feminist Resistance to Advertising's Irresistible Meanings." *Southern Communication Journal, 57* (2), Winter 1992:132–142.

Ray, Oakley, and Charles J. Ksir. *Drugs, Society, and Human Behavior*, 10th ed. New York: McGraw-Hill, 2004.

RCG Economics. "Nevada by the Numbers," March 28, 2018.

Reasons, Charles E., ed. *The Criminologist: Crime and the Criminal.* Pacific Palisades, CA: Goodyear, 1974.

Reckless, Walter C. *The Crime Problem*, 5th ed. New York: Appleton, 1973.

Regaldo, Antonio. "When a Plant Emerges From Melting Glacier, Is It Global Warming?" *Wall Street Journal*, October 22, 2004:B1.

Regehr, Cheryl, Ramona Alaggia, Jane Dennis, et al. "Intervention to Reduce Distress in Adult Victims of Sexual Violence and Rape: A Systematic Review." *Campbell Systematic Reviews, 3*, March 1, 2013.

Reiss, Albert J. "The Sociological Integration of Queers and Peers." *Social Problems, 9*, Fall 1961:102–120.

Remkus, Ashley. "Supreme Court Won't Hear Appeal in 2010 University of Alabama in Huntsville Murders." *Real Time News in Huntsville*, October 14, 2016.

Reskin, Barbara, and Denise D. Bielby. "A Sociological Perspective on Gender and Career Outcomes." *Journal of Economic Perspectives, 19* (1), Winter 2005:71–86.

"Reuse Opportunity, The." Wastewater Report of the International Water Association, 2018.

Reynolds, Carl, and Jeff Hall. "Courts Are Not Revenue Centers." Conference of State Court Administrators, 2011–2012 Policy Paper, 2012.

Reynolds, Janice. "Rape as Social Control." In *Social Problems in American Society*, 2nd ed., James M. Henslin and Larry T. Reynolds, eds. Boston: Holbrook, 1976:79–86.

Rice, Doyle. "175 Nations Sign Historic Paris Climate Deal on Earth Day." *USA Today*, April 22, 2016.

Rice, F. Philip, Nick Stinnett, et al. *Intimate Relationships, Marriages, and Families*, 9th ed. New York: Oxford University Press, 2017.

Rich, Nathaniel. "Losing Earth: The Decade We Almost Stopped Climate Change." *New York Times Magazine*, August 1, 2018.

Richardson, Lewis F. *Statistics of Deadly Quarrels.* Chicago: Quadrangle, 1960.

Richey, Warren. "Supreme Court Refuses to Resolve Confusion over Child Pornography Law." *Christian Science Monitor*, November 28, 2011.

Ridley, Louise. "Rio Child Sex Trafficking 'Epidemic' Could Rocket During The 2016 Olympics—Here's Why." Huffington Post, August 17, 2016.

Ridley, Matt. "Whatever Happened to Global Warming?" *Wall Street Journal*, September 5, 2014.

Ridley, Matt. "Why Climate Change Is Good for the World." *The Spectator*, October 19, 2013.

Riesel, Victor. "Racketeers Infest New Jersey Construction Trade." Syndicated column, January 25, 1982.

Riesman, David, Nathan Glazer, and Reuel Denney. *The Lonely Crowd: A Study of the Changing American Character.* New Haven, CT: Yale University Press, 1951.

Rigert, Joe. *The Dependency Curse.* Createspace Independent Publishing Platform, 2016.

Riley, K. Jack. "Crack, Powder Cocaine, and Heroin. Drug Purchase and Use Patterns in Six U.S. Cities." National Institute of Justice, online, December 12, 1998.

Riley, Kate, Frank A. Blethen, Donna Gordon Blankenship, et al. "U.S. House Must Support Child-Pornography Victim Restitution." *Seattle Times*, March 15, 2018.

Rincon, Paul. "Is the World Ready for GM Animals?" *BBC News*, February 25, 2015.

Rios, Victor M. *Punished: Policing the Lives of Black and Latino Boys.* New York: New York University Press, 2011.

Roach, John. "Rain Forest Plan Blends Drug Research, Conservation." *National Geographic News*, October 7, 2003.

Robertson, Campbell. "In a Mississippi Jail, Convictions and Counsel Appear Absent." *Wall Street Journal*, September 24, 2014.

Rockwell, Don. "Social Problems: Alcohol and Marijuana." *Journal of Psychedelic Drugs, 5*, Fall 1972:49–55.

Rodriguez-Llanes, Jose M., Debarati Guha-Sapir, et al. "Epidemiological Findings of Major Chemical Attack in the Syrian War Are Consistent with Civilian Targeting: A Short Report." *Conflict and Health, 12* (16), April 16, 2018.

Roe, Kathleen M. "Private Troubles and Public Issues: Providing Abortion Amid Competing Definitions." *Social Science and Medicine, 29* (10), 1989:1191–1198.

Roland, Kevin. "Communities That Rely on a Contaminated Groundwater Source for Drinking Water," State Water Resources Control Board, January 2013.

Rolo, Mark Anthony. "Marked Media." *The Circle*. Online, n.d.

Rosaldo, Michelle Zimbalist. "Women, Culture, and Society: A Theoretical Overview." In *Women, Culture, and Society*, Michelle Zimbalist Rosaldo and Louise Lamphere, eds. Stanford, CA: Stanford University Press, 1974.

Rose, Alexander. "Hitting the Home Islands." *Wall Street Journal*, April 18–19, 2015.

Rose-Jacobs, Ruth, Deborah Waber, Marjorie Beeghly, et al. "Intrauterine Cocaine Exposure and Executive Functioning in Middle Childhood." *Neurotoxicology and Teratology, 31*, 2009:159–168.

Rosen, Meghan. "For Babies Exposed to Opioids in the Womb, Parents May Be the Best Medicine." *ScienceNews*, May 31, 2017.

Rosenberg, Karen R., and Wendy R. Trevathan. "Evolutionary Perspectives on Cesarean Section." *Evolution, Medicine, & Public Health, 1* (1), January, 2018:67–81.

Rosenberg, Matthew. "Transgender People Will Be Allowed to Serve Openly in the Military." *New York Times*, June 30, 2016.

Rosenthal, Norman E. "Helping 'Children of the Night'— Transcending a Different Type of PTSD." Fox News, January 27, 2012.

Rosett, Claudia. "Big Oil-Pipeline Spill in Russia May Be a Sign of Things to Come." *Wall Street Journal*, October 27, 1994:A14.

Ross, Lori E., Laurel O'Gorman, Melissa A. MacLeod, et al. "Bisexuality, Poverty and Mental Health: A Mixed Methods Analysis." *Social Science and Medicine, 156*, May 2016:64–72.

Rothman, David J. *The Discovery of the Asylum.* Boston: Little, Brown, 1971.

Rothman, David J., and Sheila M. Rothman. *On Their Own.* Reading, MA: Addison-Wesley, 1972.

Rovner, Julie. "'Partial-Birth Abortion': Separating Fact from Spin." National Public Radio Online, February 21, 2006.

Royce, Edward. *Poverty and Power: The Problem of Structural Inequality.* Lanham, MD: Rowman and Littlefield, 2019.

Rubin, Trudy. "Nuclear 'Supermarket' Another Concern for U.S." *Philadelphia Inquirer*, February 8, 2004.

Ruggles, Patricia. *Drawing the Line: Alternative Poverty Measures and Their Implication for Public Policy*. Washington, DC: Urban Institute, 1990.

Ruggles, Patricia. *Short and Long Term Poverty in the United States: Measuring the American "Underclass."* Washington, DC: Urban Institute, June 1989.

Ruiz, Rebecca R., and Danielle Ivory. "Documents Show General Motors Kept Silent on Fatal Crashes." *New York Times*, July 15, 2014.

Rumbaut, Ruben G., and John R. Weeks. "Unraveling a Public Health Enigma: Why Do Immigrants Experience Superior Perinatal Health Outcomes?" Paper presented at the annual meeting of the American Public Health Association, 1994.

Russell, James W. *Social Insecurity: 401(k)s and the Retirement Crisis*. Boston: Beacon Press, 2014.

Ruvolo, Julie. "How Much of the Internet Is Actually for Porn?" *Forbes*, September 7, 2011.

Saad, Lydia. "Americans Choose 'Pro-Choice' for First Time in Seven Years." Gallup Poll: Social Issues, May 29, 2015.

Saez, Emmanuel, and Gabriel Zucman. "Wealth Inequality in the United States Since 1913: Evidence from Capitalized Income Tax Data." Cambridge, MA: National Bureau of Economic Research, October 2014.

Sagan, Scott D. "The Perils of Proliferation: Organization Theory, Deterrence Theory, and the Spread of Nuclear Weapons." *International Security*, 18 (4), Spring 1994: 66–107.

Sakharov, Andrei. "Text of Sakharov Letter to Carter on Human Rights." *New York Times*, January 29, 1977.

Salam, Maya. "The Opioid Epidemic: A Crisis Years in the Making." *New York Times*, October 26, 2017.

Sales, Nancy Jo. "Daddies, "Dates," and the Girlfriend Experience: Welcome to the New Prostitution Economy." *Vanity Fair*, August 2016.

Sanchez, Magaly. "Insecurity and Violence as a New Power Relation in Latin America." *The Annals of the American Academy of Political and Social Science, 606*, July 2006.

Sanchez-Jankowski, Martin. *Islands in the Street: Gangs and American Urban Society*. Berkeley, CA: University of California Press, 1991.

Sanderson, Stephen K. *Religious Evolution and the Axial Age: From Shamans to Priests to Prophets*. London: Bloomsbury 2018.

Sanger, David E., John Markoff, and Thorn Shanker. "U.S. Plans Attack and Defense in Cyberspace Warfare." *New York Times*, April 27, 2009.

Santaella-Tenorio, Julian, Christine M. Mauro, Melanie M. Wall, et al. "US Traffic Fatalities, 1985–2014, and Their Relationship to Medical Marijuana Laws." *American Journal of Public Health*, February 2017.

Saul, Josh. "Untested Rap Kits Hid 817 Serial Predators in Detroit, Tens of Thousands More Concealed in Backlog Across U.S." *Newsweek*, December 19, 2017.

Saunders, Gillian. "Why I Chose Not To: A Creative Companion to the Thesis, 'It Would Kill Your Mother.'" Auckland, New Zealand: Auckland University of Technology, 2017.

Savage, Charlie, and Timothy Williams. "U.S. Seizes Backpage.com, a Site of Enabling Prostitution." *New York Times*, April 7, 2018.

"Saving Futures, Saving Dollars: The Impact of Education on Crime Reduction and Earnings." Washington, DC: Alliance for Excellent Education, 2013.

Sawhill, Isabel V. "Poverty in the U.S.: Why Is It So Persistent?" *Journal of Economic Literature, 26* (3), September 1988: 1073–1119.

Schaefer, Richard T. *Racial and Ethnic Groups*, 15th ed. Boston: Pearson, 2018.

Schaefer, Richard T. *Racial and Ethnic Groups*. Boston: Pearson Education, 2015.

Schifter, Jacobo. "Monger Culture: Sex Tourism and HIV in Costa Rica." *Wall Street International*, June 20, 2017.

Schipper, Gerard M., van Aken, A. G. Marcel, et al. "Acquiring the Competence to Drink Responsibly." In *Learning about Drinking*, Eleni Houghton and Anne M. Roche, eds. New York: Routledge, 2013.

Schmidt, Gunter, and Volkmar Sigusch. "Sex Differences in Response to Psychosexual Stimulation by Films and Slides." *Journal of Sex Research, 6*, November, 268–283.

Schmidt, Michael S., and Thom Shanker. "To Smuggle More Drugs, Traffickers Go Under the Sea." *New York Times*, September 9, 2012.

Schmitt, Richard B. "Some Towns Jail Indigents Illegally and Get Free Labor." *Wall Street Journal*, February 2, 1982:1, 16.

Schoenfeld, A. Clay, Robert F. Meier, and Robert J. Griffin. "Constructing a Social Problem: The Press and the Environment." *Social Problems, 27*, October 1979:38–61.

Schoorl, Jantiene, Sophie van Rijn, Minet de Wied, et al. "Boys with Oppositional Defiant Disorder/Conduct Disorder Show Impaired Adaptation during Stress: An Executive Functioning Study." *Child Psychiatry and Human Development, 49* (2), April 2018:298–307.

Schreiber, Jan. *The Ultimate Weapon: Terrorists and the World Order*. New York: Morrow, 1978.

Schrieke, Bertram J. *Alien Americans*. New York: Viking, 1936.

Schulenberg, John E., Lloyd D. Johnston, Patrick M. O'Malley, Jerald G. Bachman, Richard A. Miech, and Megan E. Patrick. *Monitoring the Future, National Survey Results on Drug Use, 1975–2016. Volume II: College Students and Adults Ages 19–55*. Ann Arbor: Institute for Social Research, University of Michigan, 2017.

Schultz, Colin. "Even 2-Year-Olds Are Being Prescribed Ritalin." *Smithsonian*, May 23, 2014.

Schumpeter, Joseph A. *The Sociology of Imperialism*. New York: Meridian, 1955. (Originally published 1919)

Schwartz, John. "Child Pornography, and an Issue of Restitution." *New York Times*, February 2, 2010.

Schwarz, Alan. "Risky Rise of the Good-Grade Pill." *New York Times*, June 9, 2012.

Scott, G. "'It's a Sucker's Outfit': How Urban Gangs Enable and Impede the Reintegration of Ex-Convicts." *Ethnography, 51* (1), 2004:107–140.

Scully, D., and Marolla, J. "Riding the Bull at Gilley's": Convicted Rapists Describe the Rewards of Rape. In *Down-to-Earth Sociology: Introductory Readings*, 15th ed., James M. Henslin, ed. New York: Free Press, 2014. (Originally published in *Social Problems, 32* (3), 1985:251–263)

Scully, Diana, and J. Marolla. "Riding the Bull at Gilley's: Convicted Rapists Describe the Rewards of Rape." *Social Problems, 32* (3), 1985:251–263.

Scully, Diana. "Negotiating to Do Surgery." In *Dominant Issues in Medical Sociology*, 3rd ed. Howard D. Schwartz, ed. New York: McGraw-Hill, 1994:146–152.

Scully, Diana. *Understanding Sexual Violence: A Study of Convicted Rapists*. Boston: Unwin Hyman, 1990.

Scurich, Nicholas, and Paul Appelbaum. *Journal of Law and the Biosciences, 3* (1), 2016:140–157.

Seiden, Samuel C., and Paul Barach. "Wrong-Side/Wrong-Site, Wrong Procedure, and Wrong-Patient Adverse Events." *Archives of Surgery, 141*, 2006:931–939.

Seligman, L. "Anti-Rape Group Reaches Out to Fraternities." *The Daily Pennsylvanian*, 2008. Online.

Semega, Jessica L., Kayla L. Fontenot, and Melissa A. Kollar. "Income and Poverty in the United States: 2016." U.S. Census Bureau, September 12, 2017.

"Seminal Supreme Court Cases Regarding Federal Indian Law." Online, 2016.

"Seven Years On, Radioactive Water at Fukushima Plant Still Flowing into Ocean, Study Finds." *The Japan Times*, March 29, 2018.

Sewall, Sarah B., and Carl Kaysen, eds. *The United States and the International Criminal Court: National Security and International Law*. Lanham, MD: Rowman and Littlefield, 2000.

Sewell, R. Andrew, James Poling, and Mehmet Sofuoghu. "The Effect of Cannabis Compared with Alcohol on Driving." *American Journal on Addictions, 18*, 2009:185–193.

Shaffer, Harry G. "$1,000,000,000,000." *Republic*, May 1986:24.

Shah, Sunil M., Lain M. Carey, Tess Harris, et al. "The Effect of Unexpected Bereavement on Mortality in Older Couples." *American Journal of Public Health, 103* (6), June 2013.

Shane, Scott. "F.B.I., Laying Out Evidence, Closes Anthrax Case." *New York Times*, February 19, 2010a.

Shapiro, Jacob L. "Mexico's Drug War Is No Closer to an End." February 12, 2018.

Shaw, Sue. "Wretched of the Earth." *New Statesman, 20*, March 1987:19–20.

Sheridan, Kerry. "Iraq Death Toll Reaches 500,000 Since Start Of U.S.-Led Invasion, New Study Says." *Huffington Post*, January 23, 2014.

Sherwood, Harriet. "Christians in Egypt Face Unprecedented Persecution, Report Says." *The Guardian*, January 10, 2018.

Shibutani, Tamotsu. "On the Personification of Adversaries." In *Human Nature and Collective Behavior*, Tamotsu Shibutani, ed. Englewood Cliffs, NJ: Prentice Hall, 1970:223–233.

Shin, Su Hyun, Giyeon Kim, and Soohyun Park. "Widowhood Status as a Risk Factor for Cognitive Decline among Older Adults." *The American Journal of Geriatric Psychiatry, 26* (7), July 2018:778–787.

Shipancer, Noam. "Money Laundering for the Soul." *Psychology Today*, April 5, 2017.

Shively, JoEllen. "Cowboys and Indians." In *Down-to-Earth Sociology: Introductory Readings*, 10th ed., James M. Henslin, ed. New York: Free Press, 1999:104–116.

Shor, Eran, David J. Roelfs, Misty Currell, et al. "Widowhood and Mortality: A Meta-Analysis and Meta-Regression." *Demography, 49*, 2012:575–606.

Short, Kathleen. "The Research Supplemental Poverty Measure 201." *Current Population Reports, P60–244.*" Washington, DC: U.S. Census Bureau, November 2012.

Shribman, David. "Even After 10 Years, Victims of Love Canal Can't Quite Escape It." *Wall Street Journal*, March 9, 1989:A1, A8.

Siebens, Julie, and Tiffany Julian. "Native North American Languages Spoken at Home in the United States and Puerto Rico: 2006–2010." Washington, DC: U.S. Census Bureau, December 2011.

Siegel, Larry J. *Criminology: Theories, Patterns, and Typologies*, 13th ed. Boston: Cengage, 2018.

Silins, Edmund, L. John Horwood, George C. Patton, et al. "Young Adult Sequelae of Adolescent Cannabis Use: An Integrative Analysis." *The Lancet, 1* (4), September 2014:286–293.

Silverman, Deidre. "Sexual Harassment: The Working Women's Dilemma." *Building Feminist Theory: Essays from Quest*. New York: Longman, 1981:84–93.

Simmel, Georg. "The Sociology of Conflict." *American Journal of Sociology, 9*, January 1904:490–525; March 1904:672–689; and May 1904:798–811.

Simon, Julian L. "Global Confusion, 1980: A Hard Look at the Global 2000 Report." *Public Interest, 62*, Winter 1980:3–20.

Simona, Andrei, Emil Carstea, Luminita Marmureanu, et al. "The Analysis of a Complex Fire Event Using Multispaceborne Observations." *EPJ Web of Conferences, 176*, 2018.

Simon, Julian L. *The Ultimate Resource*. Princeton, NJ: Princeton University Press, 1981.

Simpson, George Eaton, and J. Milton Yinger. *Racial and Cultural Minorities: An Analysis of Prejudice and Discrimination*, 4th ed. New York: Harper & Row, 1972.

SIPRI (Stockholm International Peace Research Institute). "Database: TIV of Arms Exports," 2016c.

SIPRI (Stockholm International Peace Research Institute). "Global Nuclear Weapons: Downsizing but Modernizing," June 13, 2016b.

SIPRI (Stockholm International Peace Research Institute). "SIPRI Fact Sheet: Trends in Military Expenditure, 2017." May 2018a.

SIPRI (Stockholm International Peace Research Institute). *Database TIV of Arms Exports*. New York: Oxford University Press, 2018c.

SIPRI (Stockholm International Peace Research Institute). Military Expenditure Database, 2016a.

SIPRI (Stockholm International Peace Research Institute). *SIPRI Yearbook* 2018. New York: Oxford University Press, 2018b.

Siracusa, Joseph M., and Aiden Warren. "The Nuclear Non-Proliferation Regime: An Historical Perspective." *Diplomacy & Statecraft, 29* (1), January 2018:3–28.

Skinner, B. F. *Beyond Freedom and Dignity*. New York: Knopf, 1971.

Skinner, B. F. *Science and Human Behavior*. New York: Macmillan, 1953.

Skinner, B. F. *Walden Two*. New York: Macmillan, 1948.

Skypala, Isabela J., M. Williams, L. Reeves, and C. Venter. "Sensitivity to Food Additives, Vaso-Active Amines and Salicylates: A Review of the Evidence." *Clinical and Translational Allergy, 5*, October 13, 2015.

Smedley, Brian D., Adrienne Y. Stith, and Alan R. Nelson, eds. *Unequal Treatment: Confronting Racial and Ethnic Disparities in Health Care*. Washington, DC: The National Academies Press, 2003.

Smith, Clark. "Oral History as 'Therapy': Combatants' Accounts of Vietnam War." In *Strangers at Home: Vietnam Veterans Since the War*, Charles R. Figley and Seymore Leventman, eds. New York: Praeger, 1980:9–34.

Smith, Douglas A., and Christy A. Visher. "Street-Level Justice: Situational Determinants of Police Arrest Decisions." *Social Problems, 29*, December 1981:167–177.

Smith, Kenneth. "Homophobia: A Tentative Personality Profile." *Psychological Reports, 29* (3), 1971:1091–1094.

Smith, Kristen F., and Vern L. Bengtson. "Positive Consequences of Institutionalization: Solidarity Between Elderly Parents and Their Middle-Aged Children." *The Gerontologist, 19*, October 1979:438–447.

Smith, Stacy L, and Crystal Allene Cook. "Gender Stereotypes: An Analysis of Popular Films and TV." Conference, The Geena Davis Institute on Gender in Media, 2008:12–23.

Snell, Tracy L. "Capital Punishment, 2013: Statistical Tables." U.S. Department of Justice, November 2014.

Snyder, Howard. *Court Careers of Juvenile Offenders*. Washington, DC: Office of Juvenile Justice and Delinquency Prevention, 1988.

Soens, Darren. "Child Porn Sweep Nets Multiple Arrests." WPRI News, April 12, 2012.

Solomon, Deborah. "Shift in Federal Bench Spurs Governors, Legislators to Battle Roe." *Wall Street Journal*, March 9, 2006.

Solomon, Jeanne, and Dan Rather. "The Kyshtym Disaster." *60 Minutes*, November 9, 1980 (Jean Solomon, producer, and Dan Rather, interviewer).

Sonne, Paul. "Russian Jet Flies 'within 10 Feet' of Navy Plane." *Wall Street Journal*, September 8, 2016.

Sonne, Paul, Gordon Lubold, and Carol E. Lee. "No First Use' Nuclear Policy Proposal Stifled by Opponents." *Wall Street Journal*, August 13–14, 2016.

Sorokin, Pitrim A. *Social and Cultural Dynamics*, 4 vols. New York: American Book, 1937, 1941.

Sourcebook of Criminal Justice Statistics. Washington, DC: U.S. Government Printing Office, published annually.

Speer, Albert. *Inside the Third Reich*, Richard and Clara Winston, trans. New York: Avon, 1970.

Spunt, Barry. "The Current New York City Heroin Scene." *Substance Use and Misuse, 38* (10), 2003:1539–1549.

Srole, Leo, et al. *Mental Health in the Metropolis: The Midtown Manhattan Study*. New York: New York University Press, 1978.

Sroufe, L. Alan. "Ritalin Gone Wrong." *New York Times*, January 28, 2012.

SSA (Social Security Administration). "Historical Background and Development of Social Security." May 2018. https://www.ssa.gov/history/briefhistory3.html

Stack, Liam. "A Brief History of Deadly Attacks on Abortion Providers." *New York Times*, November 29, 2015.

Stafford, Linda, Sonya R. Kennedy, JoAnne E. Lehman, and Gail Arnold. "Wealth in America." ISR Newsletter, Winter 1986–87.

"Stakeholders and Radiological Protection: Lessons from Chernobyl 20 Years After." Committee on Radiation Protection and Public Health. Nuclear Energy Agency, 2006.

Staples, Brent. "The Federal Marijuana Ban Is Rooted in Myth and Xenophobia." *New York Times*, July 29, 2014.

State of Food and Agriculture: Social Protection and Agriculture, Breaking the Cycle of Rural Poverty. Food and Agriculture Organization of the United Nations, 2015.

State of Food Insecurity in the World. Food and Agriculture Organization of the United Nations, 2015.

State of Food Insecurity in the World. Food and Agriculture Organization of the United Nations, 2017.

State of the World Fisheries and Aquaculture. Food and Agriculture Organization of the United Nations, 2018.

State of World's Fisheries and Aquaculture. Food and Agriculture Organization of the United Nations, 2015.

Statistical Abstract of the United States. Washington, DC: U.S. Government Printing Office. Published annually for 131 years until 2012 when the U.S. government was too broke to continue its publication. The 2013 and following editions are published by Bernan Press in Lanham, Maryland.

Statistical Handbook of Japan. Tokyo: Statistics Bureau: Ministry of Internal Affairs and Communications, 2017.

Statistical Handbook of Japan. Tokyo: The Statistics Bureau, Ministry of Internal Affairs and Communications of Japan, 2009.

Stein, Peter J. "The Diverse World of Single Adults." In *Marriage and Family in a Changing Society*, 4th ed., James M. Henslin, ed. New York: Free Press, 1992:93–103.

Steinberg, Jennifer Weathersbee, and Gayle M. Roux. "Midwestern Farm Widows: Adaptation Following Spousal Loss." *Nursing Science Quarterly, 31* (3), June 2018.

Steinberg, Nik. "Vanished: The Disappeared of Mexico's Drug War." *Foreign Policy*, January 8, 2014.

Steinhauer, Jennifer, and Ford Fessenden. "Medical Retreads: Doctors Punished by State But Prized at the Hospitals." *New York Times*, March 27, 2001.

Steinhoff, Patricia G., and Milton Diamond. *Abortion Politics: The Hawaii Experience.* Honolulu: University Press of Hawaii, 1977.

Steinmetz, Suzanne K., and Murray A. Straus (eds.). *Violence in the Family.* New York: Dodd Mead, 1974.

Stellman, Jeanne Mager, and Steven D. Stellman. "Agent Orange During the Vietnam War: The Lingering Issue of Its Civilian and Military Health Impact." *American Journal of Public Health*, June 2018.

Stemple, Lara, and Lian H. Meyer. "The Sexual Victimization of Men in America: New Data Challenge Old Assumptions." *American Journal of Public Health, 104* (6), June 2014.

Stevens, Amy. "Sensible Victims Will Be Hoping Their Burglar Drives Up in a Rolls." *Wall Street Journal*, April 8, 1992:B1.

Stevens, William K. "Great Plains or Great Desert?" *New York Times*, May 28, 1996.

Stevens, William K. "Science Academy Disputes Attack on Global Warming." *New York Times*, April 22, 1998.

Stiles, T. J. "Custer's Trials: A Life on the Frontier of a New America." New York: Alfred A. Knopf, 2015.

Stockard, Jean, and Miriam M. Johnson. *Sex Roles: Sex Inequality and Sex Role Development.* Englewood Cliffs, NJ: Prentice Hall, 1980.

Stokes, M., and D. Zeman. "Detroit: Is Apathy to Blame for a Brutal Death?" *Newsweek*, September 4, 1995.

Stolberg, Sheryl Gay. "Blacks Found on Short End of Heart Attack Procedure." *New York Times*, May 10, 2001.

Stolzenberg, Lisa, Stewart J. D'Alessio, and David Eitle. "Race and Cumulative Discrimination in the Prosecution of Criminal Defendants." *Race and Justice, 3* (4), 2013:275–299.

Stouffer, Samuel A., Arthur A. Lumsdaine, Marion Harper Lumsdaine, et al. *The American Soldier: Combat and Its Aftermath*, vol. 2. New York: Wiley, 1949.

Straus, Murray A. "Blaming the Messenger for the Bad News about Partner Violence by Women: The Methodological, Theoretical, and Value Basis of the Purported Invalidity of the Conflict Tactic Scales." *Behavioral Sciences and the Law*, 2012.

Straus, Murray A. "Explaining Family Violence." *Marriage and Family in a Changing Society*, 4th ed., James M. Henslin, ed. New York: Free Press, 1992:344–356.

Straus, Murray A., and Richard J. Gelles. "Violence in American Families: How Much Is There and Why Does It Occur?" In *Troubled Relationships*, Elam W. Nunnally, Catherine S. Chilman, and Fred M. Cox, eds. Newbury Park, CA: Sage, 1988:141–162.

Straus, Murray A., Richard J. Gelles, and Suzanne K. Steinmetz. *Behind Closed Doors: Violence in the American Family.* New York: Anchor/Doubleday, 1980.

Straus, Murray A., Richard J. Gelles, and Suzanne K. Steinmetz. *Behind Closed Doors: Violence in the American Family.* New York: Routledge, 2017 ebook.

Strobel, Lee. *Reckless Homicide: Ford's Pinto Trial.* South Bend, IN: And Books, 1980.

Stroud, Matt. "Facebook Becomes the New Front in Mexico's Drug War: The Social Narconetwork." *The Verge*, April 1, 2014.

Stuart, Forrest. *Down, Out, and Under Arrest: Policing and Everyday Life in Skid Row.* Chicago: University of Chicago, 2016.

Sugiura, L., M. Hata, H. Matsuba-Kurita, et al. "Explicit Performance in Girls and Implicit Processing in Boys: A simultaneous fNIRS-ERP Study on Second Language Syntactic Learning in Young Adolescents." *Frontiers in Human Neuroscience, 12* (62), March 8, 2018.

Surgeon General. *E-Cigarette Use among Youth and Yung Adults: Report of the Surgeon General.* Rockville, MD: Public Health Service, 2016.

Surrey, Virginia. "Faff and Fallout." *The Economist*, August 29, 2016.

Sutherland, Edwin H. "The White Collar Criminal." *American Sociological Review, 5*, 1940:1–12.

Sutherland, Edwin H. *The Professional Thief.* Chicago: University of Chicago Press, 1937.

Suzuki, Bob H. "Asian-American Families." In *Marriage and Family in a Changing Society*, 2nd ed., James M. Henslin, ed. New York: Free Press, 1985:104–119.

Swartz, James A. *Substance Abuse in America: A Documentary and Reference Guide.* Santa Barbara, CA: Greenwood, 2017.

Sweet, Laurel J., Jessica Van Sack, Jessica Fargen, and Ira Kantor. "'Oddball' Portrait of Amy Bishop Emerges." *Boston Herald*, February 15, 2010.

Sykes, Gresham M., and David Matza. "Techniques of Neutralization: A Theory of Delinquency." *American Sociological Review, 22*, December 1957:664–670.

Sylvester, Christine. "Curating and Re-curating the American War in Vietnam." *Security Dialogue, 49* (3), June 1, 2018:151–164.

Szasz, Thomas. *The Myth of Mental Illness.* Harper & Row, 1961.

Talbot, Margaret. "Why It's Become So Hard to Get an Abortion." *The New Yorker*, April 3, 2017.

Tanas, Alexander. "Moldova Detains Seven Suspected of Uranium Smuggling." Reuters, December 9, 2014.

Taormino, Tristan, Celine Parrenas Shimizu, Constance Penley, and Mireille Miller-Young, eds. *The Feminist Porn Book.* New York: The Feminist Press, 2013.

Tark, Jongyeon, and Gary Kleck. "Resisting Rape: The Effects of Victim Self-Protection on Rape Completion and Injury." *Violence Against Women, 20* (3), 2014:270–292.

Tavernise, Sabrina, and Donald G. McNeil, Jr. "Iraqi Dead May Total 600,000, Study Says." *New York Times*, October 10, 2006.

"The Tax Burden on Tobacco: Historical Compilation, 51, 1970–2016." Orzechowski and Walker, 2017.

The Tax Burden on Tobacco: Historical Compilation, 47. The Tobacco Institute, 2012.

Teisch, J., and Alex deSherbinin. "Population Doubling Time: Looking Backward." *Population Today, 23* (2), March 1995.

Teller, Edward. "The Energy Crisis: No Contingency Plan." San Diego, CA: World Research, 1980.

Tenns, Carey. "The Lasting Trauma of Rape." *Salon*, February 17, 2013.

Tewksbury, Richard Alan, and David Lapsey. "Male Escorts' Construction of the Boyfriend Experience: How Escorts Please Their Clients." *International Journal of Sexual Health, 29* (4), 2017.

Thayer, Frederick C. "The Holy War on Surplus Americans: Soviet Dogma, Old-Time Religion and Classical Economics." *Social Policy*, 28 (1), Fall 1997:8–18.

Thielking, Megan. "Life Expectancy in the U.S. Has Fallen for the Second Year in a Row." *Scientific American*, December 21, 2017.

Thier, Dave. "Time, Water Running Out for America's Biggest Aquifer." AOL News, April 21, 2010.

Thio, Alex. *Deviant Behavior*. Boston: Houghton Mifflin, 1978.

Thrasher, Frederic M. *The Gang*. Chicago: University of Chicago Press, 1927.

"Three Types of Marijuana to Hit Uruguayan Pharmacies in 2016." Reuters, December 5, 2015.

Tiger, Lionel, and Robin Fox. *The Imperial Animal*. New York: Holt, 1971.

Tiilhonen, J., M. R. Rautiainen, H. M. Ollila, et al. "Genetic Background of Extreme Violent Behavior." *Molecular Psychiatry*, 20, June 2015: 786–792.

Timasheff, Nicholas S. *War and Revolution*. Joseph F. Scheuer, ed. New York: Sheed & Ward, 1965.

Tinker, John N. "Ethnic Bias in California Courts: A Case Study of Chicano and Anglo Felony Defendants." Paper presented at the annual meeting of the Society for the Study of Social Problems, 1981.

Tiwary, Abishek, and Ian Williams. *Air Pollution: Measurement, Modelling and Mitigation*, 4th ed. Boca Raton, FL: CRC Press, 2018.

Tofte, Sarah. "Testing Justice: The Rape Kit Backlog in Los Angeles City and County." *Human Rights Watch*, March 2009.

Tolentino, Jia. "Is There a Smarter Way to Think about Sexual Assault on Campus?" *The New Yorker*, February 12 & 19, 2018a.

Tolentino, Jia. "The Promise of Vaping and the Rise of Juul." *The New Yorker*, May 14, 2018b.

Torgoff, Martin. *Bop Apocalypse: Jazz, Race, the Beats, and Drugs*. Boston: Da Capo Press, 2016.

"Top U.S. Private Schools with the Most Graduates Getting into Ivy League Universities." *The Street*, October 15, 2015.

Torry, Harriet. "German Plan Saves Energy." *Wall Street Journal*, February 27, 2013.

Townsend, Charles. *Terrorism: A Very Short Introduction*, 3rd ed. New York: Oxford University Press, 2018.

Trimbur, Lucia. *Come Out Swinging: The Changing World of Boxing in Gleason's Gym*. Princeton, NJ: Princeton University Press, 2016.

Truman, Jennifer L., and Michael Planty. "Criminal Victimization, 2011." Washington, DC: U.S. Department of Justice, Bureau of Justice Statistics, October 2012:1–19.

Trust, Cathy. "Presidential Panel Says 4 Major Unions Have Connections to Organized Crime." *Wall Street Journal*, January 15, 1986:48.

Tsang, Corey, and Anthony J. Masys. "Fentanyl Crisis: A National Security Matter." *Security by Design*, Anthony J. Masys, ed. New York: Springer, 2018:253–272.

Tsatsou, Panayiota. "Gender and Sexuality in the Internet Era." In *The Handbook of Gender, Sex, and Media*, Karen Ross, ed. New York: John Wiley, 2012:516–534.

Tsuda, S., M. Murakami, N. Matsusaka, K. Kano, K. Taniguchi, Y. F. Sasaki. "DNA Damage Induced by Red Food Dyes Orally Administered to Pregnant and Male Mice." *Toxicological Sciences*, 61 (1), May 2001:92–99.

Turner, Jonathan H. *The Structure of Sociological Theory*. Homewood, IL: Dorsey, 1978.

Turner, Taos. "Uruguay Becomes First Nation to Oversee Pot Sales, from Seed to Smoke." *Wall Street Journal*, July 19, 2017.

Tyler, Tom R. "Legitimacy in Corrections: Policy Implications." *American Society of Criminology*, 9 (1), 2010:127–134.

Ullman, Sarah E. "A 10-Year Update of 'Review and Critique of Empirical Studies of Rape Avoidance.'" *Criminal Justice and Behavior*, 34, 2007:411–429.

UN (United Nations). *World Population Prospects: The 2017 Revision, Key Findings and Advance Tables*. Working Paper No. ESA/P/WP/248.

UN (United Nations). *World Urbanization Prospects*, The 2018 Revision, June 2018.

UNICEF (United Nations Children's Fund). "Eastern and Central Africa," February 8, 2018.

UNICEF. "Education: Adult Literacy Rate." October 2015.

United Nations. *World Urbanization Prospects: The 2014 Revision*, June 2014.

United Nations. "Kyoto Protocol: 10th Anniversary." February 2015.

UNODOC (United Nations Office on Drugs and Crime). *Crime & Criminal Justice Statistics*. United Nations Publication, 2018.

UNODOC (United Nations Office on Drugs and Crime). *Global Study on Homicide 2013: Trends, Contexts, Data*. United Nations Publication, March 2014.

UNODOC (United Nations Office on Drugs and Crime). *International Statistics on Crime and Justice*. United Nations Publication, 2010.

U.S. Bureau of Labor Statistics. "Occupational Employment Statistics, May 2009 National Industry-Specific Occupational Employment and Wage Estimates." May 2010.

U.S. Census Bureau. "America's Families and Living Arrangements 2011." 2012.

U.S. Census Bureau. *Annual Social and Economic Supplement to Current Population Survey*. Washington, DC: U.S. Government Printing Office, 2010.

U.S. Census Bureau. *Current Population Survey, Annual Social and Economic Supplements, 1947 to 2015*. Washington, DC: U.S. Government Printing Office, 2016.

U.S. Census Bureau. *Current Population Survey, Annual Social and Economic Supplements*. Washington, DC: U.S. Government Printing Office, 2018.

U.S. Department of the Treasury. "Fact Sheet: History of the U.S. Tax System." March 2010.

Useem, Michael. "The Social Organization of the American Business Elite." *American Sociological Review*, 44, August 1979:553–572.

"U.S. English Efforts Lead West Virginia to Become 32nd State to Recognize English as Official Language." U.S. English: Making English the Official Language (online), March 5, 2016.

"U.S. English," 2018. https://www.usenglish.org/

USSC (Unites States Sentencing Commission). "Demographic Differences in Sentencing: An Update to the 2012 Booker Report." November 2017.

Valocchi, Steve. "The Racial Basis of Capitalism and the State, and the Impact of the New Deal on African Americans." *Social Problems*, 41 (3), August 1994:347–362.

van den Haag, Ernest, and John P. Conrad. *The Death Penalty: A Debate*. New York: Plenum, 1983.

van den Haag, Ernest. *Punishing Criminals: Concerning a Very Old and Painful Question*. New York: Basic Books, 1975.

Vanguilder, Cliff. *Hazardous Waste Management: An Introduction*, 2nd ed. New York: Mercury Learning, 2018.

Vecchio, J. Michael. "The Role of Violence within and across Self-Identified Gang Youth." Doctoral dissertation. Criminology and Criminal Justice, University of Missouri-St. Louis, 2019.

Veevers, Jean E. *Childless by Choice*. Toronto: Butterworths, 1980.

Veevers, Jean E. "Voluntarily Childless Wives." *Sociology and Social Research*, 57, April 1973:356–366.

Venkatesh, Vasanthi and Melanie Randall, "Normative and International Human Rights Law Imperatives for Criminalizing Intimate Partner Sexual Violence: The Marital Rape Impunity in Comparative and Historical Perspective." In *The Right to Say No: Marital Rape and Law Reform in Canada, Ghana, Kenya and Malawi*, Melanie Randall, Jennifer Koshan, and Patricia Nyaundi, eds. New York: Hart Publishing, 2018.

Vidal, David. "Bilingual Education Is Thriving but Criticized." *New York Times*, January 30, 1977.

Vigen, Tyler. Spurious Correlations, New York, NY, Hachette Books, 2015.

"Violence and Socioeconomic Status." American Psychological Association, 2018.

Voeks, Robert A. *The Ethnobotany of Eden: Rethinking the Jungle, Medicine Narrative.* Chicago: University of Chicago Press, 2018.

Volkow, Nora D, Ruben D. Baler, Wilson M. Compton, and Susan R. B. Weiss. "Adverse Health Effects of Marijuana Use." *New England Journal of Medicine,* June 5, 2014:2217–2227.

Wade, Matt. "Australia's Population Hits 24 Million Faster Than Expected." *Sydney Morning Herald,* February 12, 2016.

Wagley, Charles, and Marvin Harris. *Minorities in the New World.* New York: Columbia University Press, 1958.

Wagman, Robert. "Is Japanese Mafia Threat to U.S.?" Syndicated column, November 27, 1981.

Wain, Barry. "Cambodia: What Remains of the Killing Ground." *Wall Street Journal,* January 29, 1981: 24.

Waitzkin, Howard, and Barbara Waterman. *The Exploitation of Illness in Capitalist Society.* New York: Bobbs-Merrill, 1974.

Walker, Alice, and Pratibha Parmar. *Warrior Marks: Female Genital Mutilation and the Sexual Binding of Women.* New York: Harcourt Brace, 1993.

Walsh, Edward, and Amy Goldstein. "Supreme Court Upholds Two Key Abortion Rights." *Washington Post,* June 29, 2000.

Walsh, Mark. "Supreme Court Refuses to Weigh Race-Based College Admissions." *Education Week on the WEB,* July 1, 1996.

Wang, Haibin, Sudhansu K. Dey, and Mauro Maccarrone. "Jekyll and Hyde: Two Faces of Cannabinoid Signaling in Male and Female Fertility." *Endocrine Reviews* 27 (5), 2006:427–448.

Wang, Ya-Nan, Dwight Figueiredo, Xiang-Dong Sun, et al. "Controlling of Glutamate Release by Neuregulin3 via Inhibiting the Assembly of the SNARE Complex." *Proceedings of the National Academy of Sciences of the United States of America,* February 20, 2018.

Warrick, Joby, and Walter Pincus. "Missteps in the Bunker." *Washington Post,* September 23, 2007.

Waugh, David. *Geography: An Integrated Approach,* 4th ed. New York: Oxford University Press, 2014.

Wax, Murray L. *Indian Americans: Unity and Diversity.* Englewood Cliffs, NJ: Prentice Hall, 1971.

Wax, Murray L., and Rosalie H. Wax. "Cultural Deprivation as an Educational Ideology." *Journal of American Indian Education, 3,* January 15–18, 1964.

Wax, Murray L., and Rosalie H. Wax. "Indian Education for What?" *Midcontinent American Studies Journal, 6,* Fall 1965:164–170.

Wax, Rosalie H. "The Warrior Dropouts." *Trans-Action, 4,* May 1967:40–46.

Weber, M. *Theory of Social and Economic Organization.* London: Free Press, 1964. (Originally published 1921)

Wechsler, Henry, and Toben F. Nelson. "What We Have Learned From the Harvard School of Public Health College Alcohol Study: Focusing Attention on College Student Alcohol Consumption and the Environmental Conditions That Promote It." *Journal of Studies on Alcohol and Drugs, 69* (4), 2008:481–490.

Weinberg, George. *Society and the Healthy Homosexual.* New York: Doubleday, 1972.

Weiss, C., E. Murphy-Graham, and A. G. Gandhi. "The Fairy Godmother and Her Warts: Making the Dream of Evidence-Based Policy Come True." *American Journal of Evaluation, 29,* 2008:29–47.

Weitzer, Ronald. "Prostitution: Facts and Fictions." *Contexts, 6* (4), Fall 2007:28–33.

Weitzer, Ronald. "Sociology of Sex Work." *Annual Review of Sociology, 35,* 2009:213–234.

Wells, Ken, and Charles McCoy. "Exxon Says Fast Containment of Oil Spill in Alaska Could Have Caused Explosion." *Wall Street Journal,* April 5, 1989:A3.

Welsh, Jennifer, and Kevin Loria. "23 Health Benefits of Marijuana." *Business Insider,* April 20, 2014.

Wengrow, David. *What Makes Civilization? The Ancient Near East and the Future of the West.* New York: Oxford University Press, 2010.

West, Loraine A., Samantha Cole, Daniel Goodkind, and Wan He. "65+ in the United States: 2010." *Current Population Reports,* June 2014.

West, Richard W., and Gary Steiger. *The Effects of the Seattle and Denver Income Management Experiments on Alternative Measures of Labor Supply.* Menlo Park, CA: SRI International Research Memorandum, 72, May 1980.

Whalen, Jeanne, and Brian Spegele. "China's Role in U.S. Opioid Crisis." *Wall Street Journal,* June 23, 2016.

Wheeler, Madeline. "Gender-Selective Abortion in India Is on the Rise." *Christian Science Monitor,* October 14, 2009.

Whitaker, Mark. "'It Was Like Breathing Fire…'" *Newsweek,* December 17, 1984:26–32.

Whitehead, Tom. "Warning of New Era of Surveillance State." *The Telegraph,* November 12, 2010.

Whitehurst, Carol A. *Women in America: The Oppressed Majority.* Santa Monica, CA: Goodyear, 1977.

Whittier, Nancy. "Rethinking Coalitions: Anti-Pornography Feminists, Conservatives, and Relationships between Collaborative Adversarial Movements." *Social Problems, 61* (2), May 2014.

WHO (World Health Organization). *The Health and Social Effects of Nonmedical Cannabis Use,* 2016.

WHO (World Health Organization). "Female Genital Mutilation." New York: United Nations, February 2018a.

WHO (World Health Organization). "World Health Statistics," Data Tables, Country Data, April 5, 2018.

Whyte, William Foote. "Street Corner Society." In *Down-to-Earth Sociology: Introductory Readings,* 8th ed., James M. Henslin, ed. New York: Free Press, 1995:59–67.

Whyte, William Foote. *Street Corner Society.* Chicago: University of Chicago Press, 1943.

Wilkinson, Emma. "Searching for New Medicines to Treat Alcohol Addiction." *The Pharmaceutical Journal,* March 9, 2017.

Williams, Robert C. "Three Mile Island as History." *Washington University Magazine, 50,* October 1980:56, 58–59, 61–63.

Williams, Timothy. "Old Sound in Harlem Draws New Neighbors' Ire." *New York Times,* July 6, 2008.

Wilson, Fernando. "Fatal Crashes from Drivers Testing Positive for Drugs in the U.S., 1993–2010." *Public Health Reports, 129,* June 23, 2014:342–350.

Wilson, James Q. "Lock Em Up and Other Thoughts on Crime." *New York Times Magazine,* March 9, 1975:11, 44–48.

Wilson, William Julius. "Jobless Poverty: A New Form of Social Dislocation in the Inner-City Ghetto." In *The Inequality Reader: Contemporary and Foundational Readings in Race, Class and Gender,* David B. Grusky and Szonja Szelenyi, eds. Boulder, CO: Westview Press, 2007:142–152.

Wilson, William Julius. *The Bridge over the Racial Divide: Rising Inequality and Coalition Politics.* Berkeley: University of California Press, 2000.

Wilson, William Julius. *The Declining Significance of Race: Blacks and Changing American Institutions.* Chicago: University of Chicago Press, 1978.

Wilson, William Julius. *More Than Just Race: Being Black and Poor in the Inner City.* New York: W.W. Norton, 2009.

Wilson, William Julius. *More Than Just Race: Being Black and Poor in the Inner City.* New York: W.W. Norton, 2010.

Wilson, William Julius. Scholar in Residence Lecture at Southern Illinois University, Edwardsville, June 14, 1992.

Wilson, William Julius. *The Truly Disadvantaged: The Inner City, the Underclass, and Public Policy.* Chicago: University of Chicago Press, 1987.

Wilson, William Julius. *When Work Disappears: The World of the New Urban Poor.* Chicago: University of Chicago Press, 1996.

Wiltz, Teresa. "Indian Tribes Find Opposition to Gambling a Barrier to Recognition." *Pew Stateline,* February 28, 2016.

Windle, James, John F. Morrison, Aaron Winter, and Andrew Silke. *Historical Perspectives on Organized Crime and Terrorism.* London: Routledge, 2018.

Wingfield, Nick, and Justin Scheck. "Push for Looser Pot Laws Gains Momentum." *Wall Street Journal,* January 16, 2010.

Winick, Charles. "Physician Narcotic Addicts." *Social Problems, 9,* Fall 1961:174–186.

Wirth, Louis. "The Problem of Minority Groups." In *The Science of Man in the World Crisis*, Ralph Linton, ed. New York: Columbia University Press, 1945.

Wirth, Louis. "Urbanism as a Way of Life." *American Journal of Sociology*, 44, July 1938:1–24.

Wolfensohn, James D., and Kathryn S. Fuller. "Making Common Cause: Seeing the Forest for the Trees." *International Herald Tribune*, May 27, 1998:11.

Wolfgang, Marvin E. *Patterns in Criminal Homicide*. Philadelphia: University of Pennsylvania Press, 1958.

Wolfgang, Marvin, E., and Marc Reidel. "Rape, Race, and the Death Penalty." *American Journal of Orthopsychiatry*, 45, July 1975:658–668.

Wolfinger, Nicholas H. *Understanding the Divorce Cycle: The Children of Divorce in Their Own Marriages*. New York: University of Cambridge Press, 2005.

Wong, Alia. "The Real Legacy of Crazy Horse." *The Atlantic*. August 2, 2017.

Wong, Jennifer S., and Samantha Balemba. "The Effect of Victim Resistance on Rape Completion." *Trauma, Violence, and Abuse*, August 12, 2016.

Woody, Christopher. "Mexico Had Its Most Homicides in Decades in 2017—and 2018 Is Off to a Gruesome Start." *Business Insider*, January 22, 2018.

Woody, Christopher. "US Agents Nearly Caught $194 Million Worth of Cocaine in a Narco Submarine." *Business Insider*, March 27, 2016.

Woolf, Steven H., Resa M. Jones, Robert E. Johnson, et al. "Avertable Deaths Associated with Household Income in Virginia." *American Journal of Public Health*, 100 (4), April 2010:750–755.

Work, Mike. "Creating Constitutional Procedure: Frye, Laffler, and Plea Bargaining Reform." *Journal of Criminal Law and Criminology*, 104 (2), Spring 204:457–487.

World Bank. "Poverty: Overview," 2015.

World Bank. "Poverty: Overview," 2018.

World Health Organization (WHO). "Female Genital Mutilation." New York: United Nations, February 2016a.

World Health Organization (WHO). "Global Status Report on Alcohol and Health." New York: United Nations, 2015.

World Health Organization (WHO). "Suicide Rates, Data by Country." New York: United Nations, 2016b.

World Health Organization (WHO). "UNITAID and the Clinton HIV/AIDS Initiative Announce New Price Reductions for Key Drugs." 2016c.

World Health Organization (WHO). "UNITAID: HIV and Drug Resistance." 2016d.

World Health Organization (WHO). "1986–2016: Chernobyl at 30." 2016e.

World Population Profile. Washington, DC: Bureau of the Census, U.S. Department of Commerce, various years.

Worm, Boris, et al. "Impacts of Biodiversity Loss on Ocean Ecosystem Services. *Science, 314* (5800), November 3, 2006:787–790.

Wright, Quincy. *A Study of War*, 2 vols. Chicago: University of Chicago Press, 1942.

Wright, Katie. *The Rise of the Therapeutic Society: Psychological Knowledge and the Contradictions of Cultural Change*. Washington, DC: New Academia Publishing, 2011.

"Wrong-Site, Wrong-Procedure, and Wrong-Patient Surgery." *PSNet (Patient Safety Network)*, June 2017.

Wurmbrand, Richard. *Torturado Por Cristo: La Iglesia Martir de Hoy*. Cuernavaca, Mexico: 1970.

Xu, Jiaquan, Sherry L. Murphy, Kenneth D. Kochanek, and Brigham A. Bastian. "Deaths: Final Data for 2013." *National Vital Statistics Reports, 64* (2), February 16, 2016.

Xu, Man K., Darya Gaysina, Roula Tsonaka, et al. "Monoamine Oxidase A (MAOA) Gene and Personality Traits from Late Adolescence through Early Adulthood: A Latent Variable Investigation." *Frontiers of Psychology*, October 11, 2017.

Yablonsky, Judy. "Survey Finds World Trend Toward More Liberal Abortion Laws." Associated Press, May 20, 1981.

Yang, W.W., A.M. Brandon, D.F. Xing, et al. "Progress in Polystyrene Biodegradation and Prospects for Solutions to Plastic Waste Pollution." *IOP Conference Series: Earth and Environmental Science, 150*, 2018.

Yardley, Jim. "In India, Castes, Honor and Killings Intertwine." *New York Times*, July 9, 2010.

Yeoman, Ian, and Michelle Mars. "Robots, Men and Sex Tourism." *Science Direct, 4*, May 2012.

Yllo, Kersti, and Gabriela Torres. *Marital Rape: Consent, Marriage, and Social Change in Global Context*. Oxford University Press, June 2016.

Yonack, Lyn. "Sexual Assault Is about Power." *Psychology Today*, November 24, 2017.

Yuan, D. Y. "Voluntary Segregation: A Study of New York Chinatown." *Phylon, 24*, Fall 1963:255–265.

Zaitseva, Lyudmila, and Kevin Hand. "Nuclear Smuggling Chains: Suppliers, Intermediaries, and End-Users." *American Behavioral Scientist, 46* (6), February 2003:822–844.

Zaman, Sarah. "The Stigma of Reporting a Rape in Pakistan." *Frontline*, PBS, May 28, 2013.

Zaretsky, Natasha. *Radiation Nation: Three Mile Island and the Political Transformation of the 1970s*. New York: Columbia University Press, 2018.

Zhou, Y. Carson. "The Incest Horrible: Delimiting the *Lawrence v. Texas* Right to Sexual Autonomy." *Gender and Law, 187*, 2016.

Zimbardo, Philip G. "The Pathology of Imprisonment." *Society, 9* (6), April 1972:4–8.

Zimbardo, Philip G. "The Pathology of Imprisonment." In *Down-to-Earth Sociology: Introductory Readings*, 15th ed., James M. Henslin, ed. New York: Free Press, 2014. (Originally published in *Society, 9* (6), 1972:4–8)

Zorn, Eric. "'Bubble' Laws Protect Patients and Protesters Alike." *Chicago Tribune*, August 25, 2016.

Name Index

Subject Index

Note: Page number followed by *f* or *t* indicates that the reference is within a figure (*f*) or table (*t*).